W9-BHS-677

Take the Next Step in Your IT Career

Save 10%
on Exam Vouchers*

(up to a $35 value)

CompTIA.

Get details at
sybex.com/go/comptiavoucher

*Some restrictions apply. See web page for details.

 SYBEX®

CompTIA®
A+® Complete Review Guide
Fourth Edition

CompTIA®
A+® Complete Review Guide
Exam 220-1001 and Exam 220-1002
Fourth Edition

Troy McMillan

A Wiley Brand

Senior Acquisitions Editor: Kenyon Brown
Development Editor: Jim Compton
Technical Editor: Robin Abernathy
Senior Production Editor: Christine O'Connor
Copy Editor: Kim Wimpsett
Content Enablement and Operations Manager: Pete Gaughan
Production Manager: Kathleen Wisor
Executive Editor: Jim Minatel
Book Designers: Judy Fung and Bill Gibson
Proofreader: Nancy Carrasco
Indexer: Ted Laux
Project Coordinator, Cover: Brent Savage
Cover Designer: Wiley
Cover Image: Getty Images Inc. / Jeremy Woodhouse

Copyright © 2019 by John Wiley & Sons, Inc., Indianapolis, Indiana

Published simultaneously in Canada

ISBN: 978-1-119-51695-8
ISBN: 978-1-119-51686-6 (ebk.)
ISBN: 978-1-119-51696-5 (ebk.)

Manufactured in the United States of America

No part of this publication may be reproduced, stored in a retrieval system or transmitted in any form or by any means, electronic, mechanical, photocopying, recording, scanning or otherwise, except as permitted under Sections 107 or 108 of the 1976 United States Copyright Act, without either the prior written permission of the Publisher, or authorization through payment of the appropriate per-copy fee to the Copyright Clearance Center, 222 Rosewood Drive, Danvers, MA 01923, (978) 750-8400, fax (978) 646-8600. Requests to the Publisher for permission should be addressed to the Permissions Department, John Wiley & Sons, Inc., 111 River Street, Hoboken, NJ 07030, (201) 748-6011, fax (201) 748-6008, or online at http://www.wiley.com/go/permissions.

Limit of Liability/Disclaimer of Warranty: The publisher and the author make no representations or warranties with respect to the accuracy or completeness of the contents of this work and specifically disclaim all warranties, including without limitation warranties of fitness for a particular purpose. No warranty may be created or extended by sales or promotional materials. The advice and strategies contained herein may not be suitable for every situation. This work is sold with the understanding that the publisher is not engaged in rendering legal, accounting, or other professional services. If professional assistance is required, the services of a competent professional person should be sought. Neither the publisher nor the author shall be liable for damages arising herefrom. The fact that an organization or Web site is referred to in this work as a citation and/or a potential source of further information does not mean that the author or the publisher endorses the information the organization or Web site may provide or recommendations it may make. Further, readers should be aware that Internet Web sites listed in this work may have changed or disappeared between when this work was written and when it is read.

For general information on our other products and services or to obtain technical support, please contact our Customer Care Department within the U.S. at (877) 762-2974, outside the U.S. at (317) 572-3993 or fax (317) 572-4002.

Wiley publishes in a variety of print and electronic formats and by print-on-demand. Some material included with standard print versions of this book may not be included in e-books or in print-on-demand. If this book refers to media such as a CD or DVD that is not included in the version you purchased, you may download this material at http://booksupport.wiley.com. For more information about Wiley products, visit www.wiley.com.

Library of Congress Control Number: 2019936188

TRADEMARKS: Wiley, the Wiley logo, and the Sybex logo are trademarks or registered trademarks of John Wiley & Sons, Inc. and/or its affiliates, in the United States and other countries, and may not be used without written permission. CompTIA and A+ are registered trademarks of CompTIA, Inc. All other trademarks are the property of their respective owners. John Wiley & Sons, Inc. is not associated with any product or vendor mentioned in this book.

C10008887_031819

This book is dedicated to my sweet wife, Heike, who shepherded our family through the horrors of Hurricane Irma.

Acknowledgments

I would like to thank Jim Compton for helping to keep me on track, Ken Brown for continuing to publish my work, and Robin Abernathy for her work in making sure I'm technically correct.

About the Author

Troy McMillan   writes practice tests, study guides, and online course materials for Kaplan IT Cert Prep, while also running his own consulting and training business. He holds more than 30 industry certifications and also appears in training videos for Oncourse Learning and Pearson Press. Troy can be reached at mcmillantroy@hotmail.com.

Contents at a Glance

Introduction		*xxxi*
Part I	**CompTIA A+ Core 1 Exam 220-1001**	**1**
Chapter 1	Mobile Devices	3
Chapter 2	Networking	57
Chapter 3	Hardware	111
Chapter 4	Virtualization and Cloud Computing	235
Chapter 5	Hardware and Network Troubleshooting	249
Part II	**CompTIA A+ Core 2 Exam 220-1002**	**309**
Chapter 6	Operating Systems	311
Chapter 7	Security	463
Chapter 8	Software Troubleshooting	541
Chapter 9	Operational Procedures	577
Appendix	Answers to Review Questions	631
Index		*651*

Contents

Introduction   *xxxi*

Part I   **CompTIA A+ Core 1 Exam 220-1001**   **1**

Chapter 1   **Mobile Devices**   **3**

1.1 Given a scenario, install and configure laptop hardware
and components.   8
    Hardware/device replacement   8
    Exam essential   15
1.2 Given a scenario, install components within the display
of a laptop.   15
    Types   16
    WiFi antenna connector/placement   17
    Webcam   18
    Microphone   18
    Inverter   18
    Digitizer/touchscreen   18
    Exam essentials   19
1.3 Given a scenario, use appropriate laptop features.   19
    Special function keys   19
    Docking station   24
    Port replicator   25
    Physical laptop lock and cable lock   25
    Rotating/removable screens   26
    Exam essentials   26
1.4 Compare and contrast characteristics of various types
of other mobile devices.   26
    Tablets   27
    Smartphones   27
    Wearable technology devices   27
    E-readers   30
    GPS   31
    Exam essentials   31
1.5 Given a scenario, connect, and configure accessories
and ports of other mobile devices.   31
    Connection types   31
    Accessories   36
    Exam essentials   39
1.6 Given a scenario, configure basic mobile device network
connectivity and application support.   39
    Wireless/cellular data network (enable/disable)   39
    Bluetooth   40

Corporate and ISP email configuration 42
Integrated commercial provider email configuration 45
PRI updates/PRL updates/baseband updates 47
Radio firmware 48
IMEI vs. IMSI 49
VPN 49
Exam essentials 49
1.7 Given a scenario, use methods to perform mobile device synchronization. 50
Synchronization methods 50
Types of data to synchronize 51
Mutual authentication for multiple services (SSO) 53
Software requirements to install the application on the PC 53
Connection types to enable synchronization 53
Exam essentials 53
Review Questions 54

Chapter 2   **Networking**   **57**

2.1 Compare and contrast TCP and UDP ports, protocols, and their purposes. 62
Ports and protocols 62
TCP vs. UDP 65
Exam essentials 65
2.2 Compare and contrast common networking hardware devices. 65
Routers 66
Switches 66
Access points 67
Cloud-based network controller 67
Firewall 67
Network interface card 67
Repeater 68
Hub 68
Cable/DSL modem 68
Bridge 69
Patch panel 69
Power over Ethernet (PoE) 70
Ethernet over Power 70
Exam essentials 71
2.3 Given a scenario, install and configure a basic wired/wireless SOHO network. 71
Router/switch functionality 72
Access point settings 72
IP addressing 73

NIC configuration   73
End-user device configuration   74
IoT device configuration   75
Cable/DSL modem configuration   76
Firewall settings   77
QoS   79
Wireless settings   80
Exam essentials   81
2.4 Compare and contrast wireless networking protocols.   82
802.11a   82
802.11b   83
802.11g   83
802.11n   83
802.11ac   83
Frequencies: 2.4, 5.0   84
Channels (1–11)   84
Bluetooth   84
NFC   84
RFID   84
Zigbee   85
Z-Wave   85
3G   85
4G   85
LTE   85
5G   86
Exam essentials   86
2.5 Summarize the properties and purposes of services
  provided by networked hosts.   86
Server roles   86
Internet appliances   88
Legacy/embedded systems   90
Exam essentials   90
2.6 Explain common network configuration concepts.   90
IP addressing   90
DNS   93
DHCP   93
IPv4 vs. IPv6   94
Subnet mask   95
Gateway   96
VPN   96
VLAN   97
NAT   97
Exam essentials   98

2.7 Compare and contrast Internet connection types,
    network types, and their features.   99
    Internet connection types   99
    Network types   101
    Exam essentials   102
2.8 Given a scenario, use appropriate networking tools.   102
    Crimper   103
    Cable stripper   103
    Multimeter   103
    Tone generator and probe   103
    Cable tester   104
    Loopback plug   104
    Punchdown tool   104
    WiFi analyzer   104
    Exam essentials   105
Review Questions   106

Chapter   3   Hardware   111

3.1 Explain basic cable types, features, and their purposes. 120
    Network cables   120
    Video cables   124
    Multipurpose cables   127
    Peripheral cables   130
    Hard drive cables   131
    Adapters   134
    Exam essentials   136
3.2 Identify common connector types.   136
    RJ-11   137
    RJ-45   137
    RS-232   138
    BNC   138
    RG-59   139
    RG-6   139
    USB   139
    Micro-USB/Mini-USB   139
    USB-C   139
    DB-9   139
    Lightning   139
    SCSI   140
    eSATA   140
    Molex   140
    Exam essentials   141
3.3 Given a scenario, install RAM types.   141
    RAM types   142
    Single channel/dual channel/triple channel   144

Error correcting   145
Installation/RAM slots   145
Exam essentials   147
3.4 Given a scenario, select, install, and configure storage
devices.   147
Optical drives   147
Solid-state drives   149
Magnetic hard drives   149
Hybrid drives   151
Flash   152
Configurations   155
Exam essentials   159
3.5 Given a scenario, install and configure motherboards,
CPUs, and add-on cards.   159
Motherboard form factor   160
Motherboard connectors types   162
BIOS/UEFI settings   167
CMOS battery   171
CPU features   172
Compatibility   174
Cooling mechanism   178
Expansion cards   179
Exam essentials   182
3.6 Explain the purposes and uses of various peripheral types.   183
Printer   184
ADF/flatbed scanner   184
Barcode scanner/QR scanner   184
Monitors   184
VR headset   184
Optical   185
DVD drive   185
Mouse   185
Keyboard   185
Touchpad   185
Signature pad   186
Game controllers   186
Camera/webcam   187
Microphone   187
Speakers   187
Headset   187
Projector   187
External storage drives   188
KVM   188
Magnetic reader/chip reader   188
NFC/tap pay device   188

Smart card reader   188
Exam essentials   189
3.7 Summarize power supply types and features.   189
Input 115V vs. 220V   189
Output 5.5V vs. 12V   190
24-pin motherboard adapter   190
Wattage rating   191
Number of devices/types of devices to be powered   191
Exam essentials   194
3.8 Given a scenario, select and configure appropriate
components for a custom PC configuration to meet
customer specifications or needs.   194
Graphic/CAD/CAM design workstation   194
Audio/video editing workstation   195
Virtualization workstation   196
Gaming PC   196
Standard thick client   198
Thin client   198
Network-attached storage device   199
Exam essentials   200
3.9 Given a scenario, install and configure common devices.   200
Desktop   200
Laptop/common mobile devices   201
Exam essentials   202
3.10 Given a scenario, configure SOHO multifunction
devices/printers and settings.   202
Use appropriate drivers for a given operating system.   202
Device sharing   203
Public/shared devices   205
Exam essentials   208
3.11 Given a scenario, install and maintain various print
technologies.   208
Laser   210
Inkjet   220
Thermal   223
Impact   224
Virtual   226
3D printers   227
Exam essentials   227
Review Questions   228

Chapter   4   Virtualization and Cloud Computing   235

4.1 Compare and contrast cloud computing concepts.   237
Common cloud models   237
Shared resources   238

Rapid elasticity	239
On-demand	239
Resource pooling	239
Measured service	239
Metered	240
Off-site email applications	240
Cloud file storage services	240
Virtual application streaming/cloud-based applications	240
Virtual desktop	241
Exam essentials	242
4.2 Given a scenario, set up and configure client-side virtualization.	242
Purpose of virtual machines	242
Resource requirements	243
Emulator requirements	243
Security requirements	243
Network requirements	244
Hypervisor	244
Exam essentials	245
Review Questions	246
Chapter 5 Hardware and Network Troubleshooting	**249**
5.1 Given a scenario, use the best practice methodology to resolve problems.	254
Always consider corporate policies, procedures, and impacts before implementing changes	254
1. Identify the problem.	255
2. Establish a theory of probable cause (question the obvious).	256
3. Test the theory to determine cause.	256
4. Establish a plan of action to resolve the problem and implement the solution.	257
5. Verify full system functionality and, if applicable, implement preventive measures.	257
6. Document findings, actions, and outcomes.	257
Exam Essentials	257
5.2 Given a scenario, troubleshoot problems related to motherboards, RAM, CPUs, and power.	258
Common symptoms	258
Exam Essentials	268
5.3 Given a scenario, troubleshoot hard drives and RAID arrays.	268
Common symptoms	269
Exam Essentials	272

5.4 Given a scenario, troubleshoot video, projector, and
display issues.   272
    Common symptoms   273
    Exam essentials   278
5.5 Given a scenario, troubleshoot common mobile device
issues while adhering to the appropriate procedures.   278
    Common symptoms   279
    Disassembling processes for proper reassembly   288
    Exam essentials   289
5.6 Given a scenario, troubleshoot printers.   289
    Common symptoms   290
    Exam Essentials   296
5.7 Given a scenario, troubleshoot common wired and
wireless network problems.   297
    Common symptoms   297
    Exam essentials   304
Review Questions   305

Part II   **CompTIA A+ Core 2 Exam 220-1002**   **309**

Chapter 6   **Operating Systems**   **311**

1.1 Compare and contrast common operating system types
and their purposes.   321
    32-bit vs. 64-bit   321
    Workstation operating systems   322
    Cell phone/tablet operating systems   323
    Vendor-specific limitations   323
    Compatibility concerns between operating systems   324
    Exam essentials   324
1.2 Compare and contrast features of Microsoft Windows
versions.   324
    Windows 7   325
    Windows 8   325
    Windows 8.1   326
    Windows 10   326
    Corporate vs. personal needs   327
    Desktop styles/user interface   328
    Exam essentials   332
1.3 Summarize general OS installation considerations and
upgrade methods.   332
    Upgrade paths   332
    Boot methods   339
    Types of installations   340
    Partitioning   344
    File system types/formatting   346

Load alternate third-party drivers when necessary	348
Workgroup vs. domain setup	349
Time/date/region/language settings	349
Driver installation, software, and Windows updates	349
Factory recovery partition	350
Properly formatted boot drive with the correct partitions/format	350
Prerequisites/hardware compatibility	350
Application compatibility	350
OS compatibility/upgrade path	350
Exam essentials	350
1.4 Given a scenario, use appropriate Microsoft command-line tools.	351
Navigation	352
ipconfig	354
ping	355
tracert	356
netstat	358
nslookup	359
shutdown	361
dism	361
sfc	361
chkdsk	362
diskpart	363
taskkill	363
gpupdate	364
gpresult	364
format	365
copy	366
xcopy	367
robocopy	368
net use	369
net user	370
[command name] /?	371
Commands available with standard privileges vs. administrative privileges	371
Exam essentials	372
1.5 Given a scenario, use Microsoft operating system features and tools.	372
Administrative	373
MSConfig	378
Task Manager	382
Disk Management	390
System utilities	398
Exam essentials	400

1.6 Given a scenario, use Microsoft Windows Control
Panel utilities.   400
  Internet Options   400
  Display/Display Settings   406
  User Accounts   408
  Folder Options   408
  System   411
  Windows Firewall   414
  Power Options   415
  Credential Manager   416
  Programs and features   417
  HomeGroup   418
  Devices and Printers   418
  Sound   419
  Troubleshooting   420
  Network and Sharing Center   421
  Device Manager   422
  Bitlocker   423
  Sync Center   424
  Exam essentials   424
1.7 Summarize application installation and configuration
concepts.   424
  System requirements   425
  OS requirements   425
  Methods of installation and deployment   425
  Local user permissions   425
  Security considerations   426
  Exam essentials   426
1.8 Given a scenario, configure Microsoft Windows
networking on a client/desktop.   426
  HomeGroup vs. Workgroup   427
  Domain setup   427
  Network shares/administrative shares/mapping drives   429
  Printer sharing vs. network printer mapping   429
  Establish networking connections   431
  Proxy settings   432
  Remote Desktop Connection   433
  Remote Assistance   434
  Home vs. Work vs. Public network settings   435
  Firewall settings   436
  Configuring an alternative IP address in Windows   437
  Network card properties   439
  Exam essentials   440

1.9 Given a scenario, use features and tools of the MacOS
and Linux client/desktop operating systems.   440
    Best practices   441
    Tools   445
    Features   450
    Basic Linux commands   454
    Exam essentials   459
Review Questions   460

Chapter 7   **Security**   **463**

2.1 Summarize the importance of physical security measures.   470
    Mantrap   470
    Badge reader   471
    Smart card   471
    Security guard   472
    Door lock   472
    Biometric locks   472
    Hardware tokens   473
    Cable locks   473
    Server locks   473
    USB locks   473
    Privacy screen   474
    Key fobs   474
    Entry control roster   474
    Exam essentials   474
2.2 Explain logical security concepts.   474
    Active Directory   475
    Software tokens   476
    MDM policies   476
    Port security   476
    MAC address filtering   477
    Certificates   477
    Antivirus/Anti-malware   478
    Firewalls   478
    User authentication/strong passwords   481
    Multifactor authentication   482
    Directory permissions   482
    VPN   484
    DLP   484
    Access control lists   484
    Smart card   484
    Email filtering   484
    Trusted/untrusted software sources   485
    Principle of least privilege   485
    Exam essentials   485

2.3 Compare and contrast wireless security protocols and
   authentication methods.   486
   Protocols and encryption   486
   Authentication   487
   Exam essentials   489
2.4 Given a scenario, detect, remove, and prevent malware
   using appropriate tools and methods.   489
   Malware   489
   Tools and methods   496
   Exam essentials   499
2.5 Compare and contrast social engineering, threats, and
   vulnerabilities.   500
   Social engineering   500
   DDoS   502
   DoS   503
   Zero-day   503
   Man-in-the-middle   503
   Brute force   503
   Dictionary   503
   Rainbow table   504
   Spoofing   504
   Non-compliant systems   504
   Zombie/botnet   504
   Exam essentials   504
2.6 Compare and contrast the differences of basic Microsoft
   Windows OS security settings.   505
   User and groups   505
   NTFS vs. share permissions   506
   Shared files and folders   510
   System files and folders   512
   User authentication   512
   Run as administrator vs. standard user   512
   BitLocker/BitLocker To Go   513
   EFS   513
   Exam essentials   514
2.7 Given a scenario, implement security best practices to
   secure a workstation.   514
   Password best practices   514
   Account management   516
   Disable autorun   519
   Data encryption   519
   Patch/update management   520
   Exam essentials   520

2.8 Given a scenario, implement methods for securing mobile
   devices.   520
   Screen locks   521
   Remote wipes   522
   Locator applications   522
   Remote backup applications   522
   Failed login attempts restrictions   523
   Antivirus/Anti-malware   523
   Patching/OS updates   523
   Biometric authentication   523
   Full device encryption   524
   Multifactor authentication   524
   Authenticator applications   524
   Trusted sources vs. untrusted sources   524
   Firewalls   525
   Policies and procedures   526
   Exam essentials   526
2.9 Given a scenario, implement appropriate data destruction
   and disposal methods.   527
   Physical destruction   527
   Recycling or repurposing best practices   529
   Exam essentials   530
2.10 Given a scenario, configure security on SOHO wireless
   and wired networks.   530
   Wireless specific   531
   Change default usernames and passwords   532
   Enable MAC filtering   533
   Assign static IP addresses   533
   Firewall settings   533
   Port forwarding/mapping   534
   Disabling ports   534
   Content filtering/parental controls   534
   Update Firmware   534
   Physical security   535
   Exam essentials   535
Review Questions   536

Chapter   8   Software Troubleshooting   541

3.1 Given a scenario, troubleshoot Microsoft Windows OS
   problems.   545
   Common symptoms   546
   Common solutions   551
   Exam essentials   557

3.2 Given a scenario, troubleshoot and resolve PC security
issues.   557
 Common symptoms   558
 Exam essentials   561
3.3 Given a scenario, use best practice procedures for
malware removal.   562
 1. Identify and research malware symptoms.   562
 2. Quarantine the infected systems.   562
 3. Disable System Restore (in Windows).   562
 4. Remediate the infected systems.   562
 5. Schedule scans and run updates.   563
 6. Enable System Restore and create a restore point
 (in Windows).   563
 7. Educate the end user.   563
 Exam essentials   563
3.4 Given a scenario, troubleshoot mobile OS and application
issues.   564
 Common symptoms   564
 Exam essentials   570
3.5 Given a scenario, troubleshoot mobile OS and application
security issues.   571
 Common symptoms   571
 Exam essentials   573
Review Questions   574

Chapter 9 Operational Procedures 577

4.1 Compare and contrast best practices associated with
types of documentation.   582
 Network topology diagrams   582
 Knowledge base/articles   583
 Incident documentation   583
 Regulatory and compliance policy   584
 Acceptable use policy   584
 Password policy   585
 Inventory management   586
 Exam essentials   587
4.2 Given a scenario, implement basic change management
best practices.   587
 Documented business processes   588
 Purpose of the change   588
 Scope the change   588
 Risk analysis   589
 Plan for change   589
 End-user acceptance   589

Change board 589
Backout plan 589
Document changes 589
Exam essentials 590
4.3 Given a scenario, implement basic disaster prevention
and recovery methods. 590
Backup and recovery 590
Backup testing 593
UPS 593
Surge protector 594
Cloud storage vs. local storage backups 595
Account recovery options 595
Exam essentials 596
4.4 Explain common safety procedures. 596
Equipment grounding 596
Proper component handling and storage 597
Toxic waste handling 599
Personal safety 601
Compliance with government regulations 603
Exam essentials 603
4.5 Explain environmental impacts and appropriate controls. 603
MSDS documentation for handling and disposal 604
Temperature, humidity level awareness, and proper
ventilation 604
Power surges, brownouts, and blackouts 605
Protection from airborne particles 605
Dust and debris 606
Compliance to government regulations 607
Exam essentials 608
4.6 Explain the processes for addressing prohibited content/
activity, and privacy, licensing, and policy concepts. 608
Incident response 608
Licensing/DRM/EULA 610
Regulated data 611
Follow all policies and security best practices 612
Exam essentials 612
4.7 Given a scenario, use proper communication techniques
and professionalism. 613
Use proper language and avoid jargon, acronyms, and
slang, when applicable 613
Maintain a positive attitude/project confidence 614
Actively listen (taking notes) and avoid interrupting the
customer 614
Be culturally sensitive 614

Be on time (if late, contact the customer)   615
Avoid distractions   615
Set and meet expectations/timeline and communicate
   status with the customer   617
Deal appropriately with customers' confidential and
   private materials   618
Exam essentials   619
4.8 Identify the basics of scripting.   619
Script file types   619
Environment variables   620
Comment syntax   620
Basic script constructs   620
Basic data types   621
Exam essentials   621
4.9 Given a scenario, use remote access technologies.   622
RDP   622
Telnet   623
SSH   625
Third-party tools   625
Security considerations of each access method   626
Exam essentials   626
Review Questions   627

Appendix   Answers to Review Questions   631

Chapter 1: Mobile Devices   632
Chapter 2: Networking   634
Chapter 3: Hardware   636
Chapter 4: Virtualization and Cloud Computing   640
Chapter 5: Hardware and Network Troubleshooting   641
Chapter 6: Operating Systems   642
Chapter 7: Security   645
Chapter 8: Software Troubleshooting   648
Chapter 9: Operational Procedures   649

Index   *651*

Introduction

The A+certification program was developed by the Computing Technology Industry Association (CompTIA) to provide an industry-wide means of certifying the competency of computer service technicians. The A+certification is granted to those who have attained the level of knowledge and troubleshooting skills that are needed to provide capable support in the field of personal computers. CompTIA is a widely respected industry leader in this area.

CompTIA's A+exam objectives are periodically updated to keep the certification applicable to the most recent hardware and software. This is necessary because a technician must be able to work on the latest equipment. The most recent revisions to the objectives—and to the whole program—were introduced in 2018 and are reflected in this book.

This book and the Sybex *CompTIA A+ Complete Study Guide* (both the Standard and Deluxe Editions) are tools to help you prepare for this certification—and for the new areas of focus of a modern computer technician's job.

What Is A+Certification?

The A+certification program was created to offer a wide-ranging certification, in the sense that it's intended to certify competence with personal computers from many different makers/vendors. Everyone must take and pass two exams: 220-1001 and 220-1002.

You don't have to take the 220-1001 exam and the 220-1002 exam at the same time. The A+certification isn't awarded until you've passed both tests. For the latest pricing on the exams and updates to the registration procedures, call Pearson VUE at (877) 551-7587. You can also go to Pearson VUE for additional information or to register online at www.pearsonvue.com/comptia. If you have further questions about the scope of the exams or related CompTIA programs, refer to the CompTIA website at www.comptia.org.

Who Should Buy This Book?

If you want to acquire a solid foundation in personal-computer basics and your goal is to prepare for the exams by filling in any gaps in your knowledge, this book is for you. You'll find clear explanations of the concepts you need to grasp and plenty of help to achieve the high level of professional competency you need to succeed in your chosen field.

If you want to become certified as an A+holder, this book is definitely what you need. However, if you just want to attempt to pass the exam without really understanding the basics of personal computers, this guide isn't for you. It's written for people who want to acquire skills and knowledge of personal-computer basics.

How to Use This Book

We've included several learning tools in the book. These tools will help you retain vital exam content as well as prepare to sit for the actual exams.

Exam Essentials   Each chapter includes a number of exam essentials. These are the key topics that you should take from the chapter in terms of areas on which you should focus when preparing for the exam.

Chapter Review Questions   To test your knowledge as you progress through the book, there are review questions at the end of each chapter. As you finish each chapter, answer the review questions and then check your answers—the correct answers are in the appendix. You can go back to reread the section that deals with each question you got wrong to ensure that you answer correctly the next time you're tested on the material.

Interactive Online Learning Environment and Test Bank

The interactive online learning environment that accompanies *CompTIA A+ Complete Review Guide: Exams 220-1001 and 220-1002, Fourth Edition*, provides a test bank with study tools to help you prepare for the certification exam—and increase your chances of passing it the first time! The test bank includes the following:

Sample Tests   All the questions in this book are provided, including the review questions at the end of each chapter. In addition, there are four practice exams. Use these questions to test your knowledge of the study guide material. The online test bank runs on multiple devices.

Flashcards   One set of questions is provided in digital flashcard format (a question followed by a single correct answer). You can use the flashcards to reinforce your learning and provide last-minute test prep before the exam.

Other Study Tools   A glossary of key terms from this book and their definitions is available as a fully searchable PDF.

Tips for Taking the A+ Exams

Here are some general tips for taking your exams successfully:

- Bring two forms of ID with you. One must be a photo ID, such as a driver's license. The other can be a major credit card or a passport. Both forms must include a signature.
- Arrive early at the exam center so you can relax and review your study materials, particularly tables and lists of exam-related information.

- Read the questions carefully. Don't be tempted to jump to an early conclusion. Make sure you know exactly what the question is asking.

- Don't leave any unanswered questions. Unanswered questions are scored against you.

- There will be questions with multiple correct responses. When there is more than one correct answer, a message at the bottom of the screen will prompt you to either "Choose two" or "Choose all that apply." Be sure to read the messages displayed to know how many correct answers you must choose.

- When answering multiple-choice questions you're not sure about, use a process of elimination to get rid of the obviously incorrect answers first. Doing so will improve your odds if you need to make an educated guess.

- On form-based tests (nonadaptive), because the hard questions will eat up the most time, save them for last. You can move forward and backward through the exam.

- For the latest pricing on the exams and updates to the registration procedures, visit CompTIA's website at www.comptia.org.

CompTIA A+ 1000 Series Exam Objectives

CompTIA goes to great lengths to ensure that its certification programs accurately reflect the IT industry's best practices. The company does this by establishing Cornerstone Committees for each of its exam programs. Each committee comprises a small group of IT professionals, training providers, and publishers that are responsible for establishing the exam's baseline competency level and that determine the appropriate target audience level.

Once these factors are determined, CompTIA shares this information with a group of hand-selected subject-matter experts (SMEs). These folks are the true brainpower behind the certification program. They review the committee's findings, refine them, and shape them into the objectives you see before you. CompTIA calls this process a *job task analysis* (JTA).

Finally, CompTIA conducts a survey to ensure that the objectives and weightings truly reflect the job requirements. Only then can the SMEs go to work writing the hundreds of questions needed for the exam. And, in many cases, they have to go back to the drawing board for further refinements before the exam is ready to go live in its final state. So, rest assured, the content you're about to learn will serve you long after you take the exam.

Exam objectives are subject to change at any time without prior notice and at CompTIA's sole discretion. Please visit the certification page of CompTIA's website at www.comptia.org for the most current listing of exam objectives.

CompTIA also publishes relative weightings for each of the exam's objectives. The following tables list the objective domains and the extent to which they're represented on each exam:

220-1001 Exam Domains	Percent of Exam
1.0 Mobile Devices	14%
2.0 Networking	20%
3.0 Hardware	27%
4.0 Virtualization and Cloud Computing	12%
5.0 Hardware and Network Troubleshooting	27%
Total	100%

220-1002 Exam Domains	Percent of Exam
1.0 Operating Systems	27%
2.0 Security	24%
3.0 Software Troubleshooting	26%
4.0 Operational Procedures	23%
Total	100%

CompTIA A+ Core 1 Exam 220-1001

PART
I

CHAPTER 1: Mobile Devices

CHAPTER 2: Networking

CHAPTER 3: Hardware

CHAPTER 4: Virtualization and Cloud Computing

CHAPTER 5: Hardware and Network Troubleshooting

Chapter

1

Mobile Devices

COMPTIA A+ CERTIFICATION EXAM CORE 1 (220-1001) OBJECTIVES COVERED IN THIS CHAPTER:

✓ **1.1 Given a scenario, install and configure laptop hardware and components.**

- Hardware/device replacement
  - Keyboard
  - Hard drive
    - SSD vs. hybrid vs. magnetic disk
    - 1.8 in vs. 2.5 in
  - Memory
  - Smart card reader
  - Optical drive
  - Wireless card/Bluetooth module
  - Cellular card
  - Video card
  - Mini PCIe
  - Screen
  - DC jack
  - Battery
  - Touchpad
  - Plastics/frames
  - Speaker
  - System board
  - CPU

✓ **1.2 Given a scenario, install components within the display of a laptop.**

- Types
  - LCD
  - OLED
- WiFi antenna connector/placement
- Webcam
- Microphone
- Inverter
- Digitizer/touchscreen

✓ **1.3 Given a scenario, use appropriate laptop features.**

- Special function keys
  - Dual displays
  - Wireless (on/off)
  - Cellular (on/off)
  - Volume settings
  - Screen brightness
  - Bluetooth (on/off)
  - Keyboard backlight
  - Touchpad (on/off)
  - Screen orientation
  - Media options (fast forward/rewind)
  - GPS (on/off)
  - Airplane mode
- Docking station
- Port replicator
- Physical laptop lock and cable lock
- Rotating/removable screens

✓ **1.4 Compare and contrast characteristics of various types of other mobile devices.**

- Tablets
- Smartphones
- Wearable technology devices
  - Smart watches
  - Fitness monitors
  - VR/AR headsets
- E-readers
- GPS

✓ **1.5 Given a scenario, connect, and configure accessories and ports of other mobile devices.**

- Connection types
- Wired
  - Micro-USB/Mini-USB/USB-C
  - Lightning
  - Tethering
  - Proprietary vendor-specific ports (communication/power)
- Wireless
  - NFC
  - Bluetooth
  - IR
  - Hotspot
- Accessories
- Headsets
- Speakers
- Game pads
- Extra battery packs/battery chargers
- Protective covers/waterproofing
- Credit card readers
- Memory/MicroSD

✓ **1.6 Given a scenario, configure basic mobile device network connectivity and application support.**

- Wireless/cellular data network (enable/disable)
    - Hotspot
    - Tethering
    - Airplane mode
- Bluetooth
    - Enable Bluetooth
    - Enable pairing
    - Find a device for pairing
    - Enter the appropriate pin code
    - Test connectivity
- Corporate and ISP email configuration
    - POP3
    - IMAP
    - Port and SSL settings
    - S/MIME
- Integrated commercial provider email configuration
    - iCloud
    - Google/Inbox
    - Exchange Online
    - Yahoo
- PRI updates/PRL updates/baseband updates
- Radio firmware
- IMEI vs. IMSI
- VPN

✓ **1.7 Given a scenario, use methods to perform mobile device synchronization.**

- Synchronization methods
    - Synchronize to the cloud
    - Synchronize to the desktop
    - Synchronize to the automobile

- Types of data to synchronize
  - Contacts
  - Applications
  - Email
  - Pictures
  - Music
  - Videos
  - Calendar
  - Bookmarks
  - Documents
  - Location data
  - Social media data
  - E-books
  - Passwords
- Mutual authentication for multiple services (SSO)
- Software requirements to install the application on the PC
- Connection types to enable synchronization

This chapter will focus on the exam topics related to mobile devices. It will follow the structure of the CompTIA A+ 220-1001 exam blueprint, objective 1, and cover the seven subobjectives that you will need to master before taking the exam. The Mobile Devices domain represents 14 percent of the total exam.

1.1 Given a scenario, install and configure laptop hardware and components.

Whether you choose to call them laptops, notebooks, tablets, or something different is mostly a matter of semantics. In this section, I'll discuss some of the basic components of laptops and their installation (when possible and called for). In many cases, the components are the same as in a desktop computer.

The following topic is addressed in exam objective 1.1:

- Hardware/device replacement

Hardware/device replacement

Replacing hardware and devices in a laptop can be a challenge because of the size limitations. The best way to determine the proper disassembly method is to consult the documentation from the manufacturer.

Some models of notebook PCs require a special T-8 Torx screwdriver. Most PC toolkits come with a T-8 bit for a screwdriver with interchangeable bits, but you may find that the T-8 screws are countersunk in deep holes so that you can't fit the screwdriver into them. In such cases, you need to buy a separate T-8 screwdriver, available at most hardware stores or auto parts stores.

Many laptop manufacturers will consider a warranty void if an unauthorized person opens a laptop case and attempts to repair it.

Prepare a clean, well-lit, flat work surface; assemble your tools and manuals; and ensure that you have the correct parts. Shut down the PC, unplug it, and detach any external devices such as an external keyboard, mouse, or monitor. In this section, with these general guidelines for opening the laptop in mind, you'll look at replacing various components of a laptop. Always ensure that you have grounded yourself before working with computer components of any kind. Use an antistatic wristband and attach it to the case.

Keyboard

When replacing the keyboard, one of the main things you want to keep in mind is *not* to damage the data cable connector to the system board.

1. With the laptop fully powered off and unplugged from the wall, remove the battery. Examine the screws on the back of the laptop. Ideally, icons indicating which screws are attached to the keyboard will be available. If not, look up the model online and determine which of the screws are attached to the keyboard.

2. Remove the screws with a T-8 or Phillips-head screwdriver. With the laptop turned back over, open it. If the keyboard is tucked under any plastic pieces, determine whether those pieces need to have screws removed to get them out of the way; if so, remove the screws and the plastic pieces. In some cases, there may just be clamps that are easily removed.

3. With any plastic covers out of the way, remove any screws at the top and remove the keyboard itself from top to bottom. There should be a thin, but wide, data cable to the system board at the bottom. This is the piece to be careful with!

4. Take a pick and lift the plastic connectors that hold this data cable in place. Remove the data cable. Take the new keyboard and slip the data cable back in between the plastic connectors on the system board. Ensure it's all the way in.

5. Put the plastic connector back into place and make sure it's holding the data cable in. Position the keyboard into place and refasten the keyboard in place at the top, replacing any screws that were there before.

6. Replace any plastic pieces that were covering the keyboard, turn the laptop over, and replace all of the keyboard screws. When you replace the battery and turn it on, check the functionality. If the keyboard doesn't work, the main component to check is the data connector.

Hard drive

Before changing a hard drive, you should back up the old hard drive if the data is needed. Then, to change the hard drive, follow these steps:

1. Turn the laptop upside down and look for a removable panel or a hard drive release mechanism. Laptop drives are usually accessible from the bottom or side of the chassis. Release the drive by flicking a lock/unlock button and/or removing a screw that holds the drive in place.

2. You may be required to remove the drive from a caddy or detach mounting rails from its sides. Attach the rails or caddy to the new drive using the same screws and washers. If required, remove the connector attached to the old drive's signal pins and attach it to the new drive. Make sure it's right side up and do not force it. Damaging the signal pins may render the drive useless.

3. Reverse your steps to place the drive (and caddy if present) into the case. Replace the screws and start the laptop. The system should recognize the drive. If you or the user created a bootable backup disc or a complete image disc (before the drive failed, by the way), place it in the optical drive and follow the instructions for restoring the data. You may have to update a driver or two, but you should otherwise be ready to go.

SSD vs. hybrid vs. magnetic disk

Although many devices still use a magnetic disk hard drive, most laptop vendors are moving to using either solid-state drives or hybrid drives, which are a combination of magnetic disk and solid-state technology.

The advantage of solid-state drives is that they are not as susceptible to damage if the device is dropped, and they are generally faster because no moving parts are involved. They are, however, more expensive, and when they fail, they don't typically display any advanced warning symptoms like a magnetic drive will do.

Hybrid storage products have a magnetic disk and some solid-state memory. These drives monitor the data being read from the hard drive, and they cache the most frequently accessed bits to the high-speed flash memory. These drives tend to cost slightly more than traditional hard drives (but far less than solid-state drives), but the addition of the SSD memory for cached bits creates a surprising improvement in performance. This improvement will not appear initially because the drive must "learn" the most frequently accessed data on the drive.

1.8 in vs. 2.5 in

The 2.5-inch hard drives are small (which makes them attractive for a laptop, where space is at a minimum), but in comparison to 3.5-inch hard drives, they have less capacity and cache, and they operate at a lower speed.

Moreover, whereas 2.5-inch drives operate from 5,400 to 7,200 rpm, 3.5-inch drives can operate from 7,200 to 10,000 rpm. However, 2.5-inch drives use about half the power (again, good for a laptop) of a 3.5-inch drive (2.5 W rather than 5 W).

The 1.8-inch drive is the smallest of the three I'm discussing here. It was originally used in subnotebooks and audio players. It has the least capacity of the three, with the largest up to 320 GB. It has only two platters, each of which can hold 220 GB maximum.

Memory

There should be a panel used for access to the memory modules. If the panels are not marked (many are not), refer to your laptop instruction manuals to locate the panel on the bottom.

1. Remove any screws holding the panel in place, remove the panel from the laptop, and set it aside. If removing an existing memory module, remove it by undoing the module

clamps, gently lifting the edge of the module to a 45-degree angle, and then pulling the module out of the slot.

2. Align the notch of the new module with that of the memory slot and gently insert the module into the slot at a 45-degree angle. With all pins in the slot, gently rotate the module down flat until the clamps lock the module into place.

3. Replace the memory access panel, replace any screws, and power up the system. When the computer is powered back up, it may be necessary to go into the computer BIOS to let the system properly detect the new RAM that has been installed in the computer. Please refer to the user manual for the computer system for any additional information.

Smart card reader

Smart card readers come in both internal and external versions. External versions will most likely plug into a USB port, and replacing them is easy; all you do is plug them in. It is possible that you may need to install a driver for the device; and if so, you should use the installation utility that came with the device if there is one. There are also external readers that use the ExpressCard slot.

Internal readers will reside in a drive bay as a hard drive or optical drive would. Take the following steps to replace one:

1. Remove the hard drive, optical drive, and keyboard screws first, and then remove the screws that hold the bottom case on the laptop. There will also be some screws marked P or P1 inside the case to remove.

2. Once they are removed, turn the laptop over and remove the keyboard screws, keyboard, and the palm rest cables. Don't forget to unplug both the keyboard and the palm rest cables! Underneath you will now be able to access the smart card reader.

3. Unplug the reader, remove the screw holding it in, and remove it. Place the new reader in the same place and reverse these steps.

Optical drive

Replacing an optical drive is usually easier than replacing a hard drive or memory. Remove the screw that secures the optical drive to the bottom of the notebook. Grasp the edge of the optical drive bezel and slide the optical drive out of the base enclosure. Insert the new optical drive into the base enclosure until the connector is seated and replace the screw that secures the optical drive to the bottom of the notebook.

Wireless card/Bluetooth module

Both 802.11 and Bluetooth wireless cards that are built in can be replaced if they go bad. Sometimes they reside near the memory, so you would open the same panel that holds the memory. In other cases (such as a Dell Inspiron), you have to remove the memory, keyboard, optical drive, and hand rest to get to it. The Bluetooth card may be located in the same place, or it may be located at the edge of the laptop with its own small panel to remove. Consult your documentation.

Once you've found either type of wireless card, disconnect the two antenna contacts from the card. Do *not* pull by the wire; pull by the connector itself. Remove any screws from the wireless card and gently pull out the card from the slot. Insert the replacement card into the slot at a 45-degree angle, replace the screws, and reconnect the antenna to the adapter. Replace the parts you were required to remove to get to the card, reversing your steps carefully.

Cellular card

Changing an external mobile broadband card is as simple as pulling the old USB stick out and plugging in the new one. Because USB is plug and play, you shouldn't have to do anything, but even in the case of an issue the manufacturer usually provides a CD with the drivers or you can obtain them from the vendor website.

Changing an internal card is much like the process of changing an internal 802.11 card; follow the instructions indicated in the previous section.

Video card

When changing a graphics card, you must ensure that the card is supported by the laptop and the operating system. This is the process:

1. Remove the hinges using manufacturer instructions.

2. Detach the keyboard and keep track of your screws and where they go!

3. Remove the display assembly, and unplug the video and Wi-Fi cables.

4. Remove the upper shell, and keep track of your screws.

5. Remove the old card, and install the new.

6. Reverse your steps to reassemble the laptop.

Mini PCIe

Since many of the wireless cards are mini-PCIe, replacing any other card in this format will follow the same procedure, with the exception of removing and reconnecting the antenna cables (present only on the wireless cards). You can find the location of the card in the documentation. Make sure that the new card is firmly inserted into the slot after removing the old card.

Screen

The screen is one of the more involved parts to replace, which is why many people throw a laptop away when the screen gets damaged. It's possible to replace a damaged screen, but you have to remove a lot of parts to do so. Start by removing the battery and then hold the power on for 10 seconds to drain the power out of the capacitors.

Remove all the screws on the back of the unit and then turn the laptop over. Remove the speaker bezel and you will see six wires coming from the old screen to the laptop. Remove the keyboard (see the instructions in the section "Keyboard"). Under the keyboard, locate where these six wires connect, and disconnect them. Make note of what went where so you can replace them correctly when you reconnect the new screen.

Remove the screws that are holding the old screen to the hinges of the laptop. Position the new screen in place and screw it into the hinges. Reroute the six wires coming from the new screen through any holes or spaces that lead them to their connection points. These are usually for the video cable, mic jacks, and wireless antenna. Reconnect the keyboard and reinstall it. Replace all parts that were required to get at the keyboard and replace all screws on the back of the unit.

These are general guidelines for this replacement, and you should always check the documentation for any departures from this general approach.

DC jack

Replacing a bad DC jack usually requires soldering. If this is not a skill you possess, just replace the motherboard. If you want to attempt it, remove all the parts to get to the motherboard. In some cases, the old DC jack can still be used; it just needs to have the old solder removed and replaced. If that is not the case, remove the old DC jack by unsoldering it from the connector. Then put the new jack in place and solder it to the connectors. Replace all the parts and pieces you removed to get to the board. In general, a bad DC jack usually means a new board.

Battery

Replacing the battery in a laptop is simply a matter of removing the battery storage bay, removing the old battery from the bay, inserting the new battery into the bay, and replacing the bay. Determining the battery type for the replacement will probably take longer than the replacement procedure. In fact, many users carry extra batteries for situations where they know they will need to use the laptop for longer than the battery life (such as a long plane trip) and change the battery as needed.

 **WARNING**   If BitLocker encryption is enabled, the laptop will not boot after a battery replacement unless the BitLocker encryption key is provided.

Touchpad

This is another repair where many parts must be removed just to get to the piece to be replaced.

1. Remove all the covers from the back of the system first. This may include those for the hard drive, RAM, and wireless card compartments. Remove the RAM, hard drive, and wireless card. Take the screw holding the CD-ROM in place and remove it as well.

2. Turn the laptop back over, open the lid, and remove any plastic pieces in the way of the keyboard. Remove the keyboard (see the section "Keyboard"). Disconnect the video and antenna cables from the motherboard (see the section "Screen"). Remove the Phillips-head screws from the LCD hinges and then remove the LCD.

3. Disconnect the touchpad cable from the motherboard. Separate the upper casing assembly from the bottom casing and set it aside. Remove the touchpad from the upper casing assembly. Install the new touchpad by reversing the previous steps.

Plastics/frames

Several of the replacement procedures in this section have involved plastic pieces that either hold something in place or cover something. These pieces—which are important enough to be noted specifically as a component of this exam—may be held in place by screws, or they may use snaps. In either case, it is easy to damage these parts (especially the snaps) in the disassembly or assembly process. If this occurs, consult the documentation for the laptop. Even these pieces will have part numbers and can be ordered. It's easier to just take great care not to damage them in the first place. The best way to prevent damage to these pieces is to *never* force a piece in place. If you meet resistance, back out and try to determine what the obstruction is. Restoring the full case is also important. Leaving open spaces can tamper with the air circulation as it was originally designed, resulting in overheating. A mobile device, particularly a laptop, will quickly overheat if the case is compromised in any way.

Speaker

To replace speakers, first follow the earlier instructions to remove the hard drive, the battery pack, and all the screws holding the body together.

1. Lift the screen up and separate it from the body (see the section "Screen"). Do *not* remove the wires connecting the screen to the motherboard.

2. Separate the two pieces of plastic body frame to view the inside of the laptop. Locate the speakers, using the documentation if necessary.

3. Unscrew the speakers, and note where they connect to the motherboard. Disconnect the old speakers, and connect the new ones to the same location as where the old speakers were removed.

4. Replace all the parts in the reverse order you removed them.

System board

Replacing the system board requires removing all parts discussed up to this point since they all are either in the way of or connected to the motherboard. Once that is done, take the following steps:

1. Open the processor access door if there is one on the machine. If the processor is removable and one did not come with the new motherboard, remove it, and set it aside in a safe place.

2. Disconnect any remaining wires that are connected to the motherboard.

3. Unplug any cards, such as the video card, that are not built directly into the motherboard.

4. Locate the mounting screws for the motherboard, and unscrew them. Remove the old motherboard, mount the new unit, and reassemble the parts in reverse order.

CPU

If the CPU is not built into the motherboard, it can be replaced. If it is built in, then you will be replacing the motherboard as well. If you are upgrading the processor and not simply replacing it, make sure your BIOS will support the new processor. It may be that you need to flash the BIOS to support the new CPU. You can determine this at the website of either the CPU maker or the laptop. This is important!

Follow the earlier instructions to remove the case, keyboard, and display. This will allow you to separate the two parts of the case.

1. Remove the graphic card and note where it plugs back in.

2. Remove the heat sink from the top of the CPU by removing the screws holding it in place.

3. Remove the single screw holding the CPU in place and pull it out. Insert the new CPU in place, and replace the screw. (In some cases, it is not a screw but a locking bar.)

4. Place some thermal grease between the CPU and the heat sink. Replace the heat sink and its screws.

5. Reverse your steps to reattach all the other parts and pieces.

In some cases, you may encounter a laptop that allows you to get at this from the bottom without removing the keyboard and display. This is why it is best to follow the specific directions in the documentation to save unnecessary component removal.

Exam essential

List the steps to install or replace laptop components.   This includes but is not limited to keyboards, hard drives, memory, optical drives, wireless cards, mini-PCIe cards, screens, DC jacks, batteries, touchpads, speakers, system boards, and CPUs.

1.2 Given a scenario, install components within the display of a laptop.

The display of a laptop contains more components than you may expect. In this section, I'll discuss these components and, in some cases, cover competing technologies. The following topics are addressed in exam objective 1.2:

- Types
- Wi-Fi antenna connector/placement
- Webcam
- Microphone
- Inverter
- Digitizer/touchscreen

Types

Laptop displays can use any of several technologies: LCD, LED, or OLED. This section provides a quick survey of these display types and their characteristics as they apply to laptops. For more information on all three display types, see objective 3.6 in Chapter 3, "Hardware."

LCD

LCDs have completely replaced CRTs as the default display type for both laptops and desktops. Two major types of LCDs are used today: active matrix screens and passive matrix screens. Their main differences lie in the quality of the image. Both types use some kind of lighting behind the LCD panel to make the screen easier to view. One or more small fluorescent tubes are used to backlight the screen.

Passive Matrix   A passive matrix screen uses a row of transistors across the top of the screen and a column of them down the side. It sends pulses to each pixel at the intersection of each row and column combination, telling it what to display. Passive matrix displays are becoming obsolete because they're less bright and have poorer refresh rates and image quality than active matrix displays. However, they use less power than active matrix displays do.

Active Matrix   An active matrix screen uses a separate transistor for each individual pixel in the display, resulting in higher refresh rates and brighter display quality. These screens use more power, however, because of the increased number of transistors that must be powered. Almost all notebook PCs today use active matrix. A variant called thin-film transistor (TFT) uses multiple transistors per pixel, resulting in even better display quality.

TN vs. IPS

There are two major LCD technologies used in LCDs. This section discusses the pros and cons of each.

Twisted Nematic (TN)   Twisted nematic (TN) is the older of the two major technologies for flat-panel displays. While it provides the shortest response time, has high brightness, and draws less power than competing technologies, it suffers from poor quality when viewed from wide angles. It suffers color distortions when viewed from above or from the sides.

In-Plane Switching (IPS)   This is a newer technology that solves the issue of poor quality at angles other than straight on. It also provides better color quality. However, it has much slower response time and is more expensive. Newer versions like Super-IPS (SIPS) make improvements on the response time.

Fluorescent vs. LED backlighting

LCDs can use two kinds of backlighting: LED-based and fluorescent. Fluorescent is an older technology and consists of a fluorescent tube connected to a voltage inverter board that provides power to the backlight. LED-based is a newer technology and uses a matrix of LEDs for the backlighting. Table 1.1 compares the two technologies.

TABLE 1.1   Fluorescent and LED

Characteristic	Fluorescent	LED
Size	Thicker and heavier	Thinner and lighter
Cost	Cheaper	More expensive
Power	High power consumption and heat generation	Lower power consumption and heat generation
Brightness	Lower	Higher
Lifespan	Shorter	Longer

LED

LED-based monitors are still LCDs (they still use liquid crystals to express images on-screen), but they use a different type of backlight than what is normally used. Several types of backlights are used with LED.

The most common for computers is white LEDs (WLEDs). Using a special diffuser, the light is spread to cover the entire screen. A more expensive type is RGB LED. Instead of using WLEDs on one edge of the screen, with RGB LCD layers, like the previous technology, RGB LEDs are aligned all over the panel matrix. Each LED is capable of red-, green-, or blue-colored light. This gives the display more accurate color than WLEDs. Finally, there is WLED on a flat array, covering the entire screen (like an RGB LED using only WLEDs). Currently, it's used only in LED-backlit HDTVs. As you've seen, however, computer output can be directed to the HDTV screen.

OLED

An organic light-emitting diode (OLED) is another type of LED technology. It uses an emissive electroluminescent layer of organic compounds that emit light in response to an electric current. An interesting characteristic of these displays is their flexibility and transparency. This means they can roll up for storage (like a mat), and you can see through the display to objects behind the display. These displays are now available but quite expensive.

WiFi antenna connector/placement

The wireless antenna is located in the display. You may recall that when replacing a laptop screen, you encountered a number of wires coming from the screen to the laptop body. One of these is the cable that connects the wireless antenna (located in the display) with the wireless card located in the body of the laptop.

The antennas built into the display usually work quite well. In any specific situation you may improve your signal by moving the laptop around. This changes the polarization of the antenna and may cause it to line up better to the incoming signal.

Webcam

Many displays today, especially laptop displays, have a webcam built in. They come ready to go with all drivers preinstalled and nothing to configure or set up. If you need to replace the webcam, you will have to disconnect the laptop lid (which holds the display) from the base, remove the screw covers and screws holding the display bezel in place, and remove the bezel. After removing the screws holding the mounting rails to the hinges, remove the LED screen from the lid assembly. Now you can get at the camera, but first carefully remove the tape that holds the camera cable in place and remove it and the camera. Attach the replacement cable to the new camera, install the new camera, and reverse these steps.

Microphone

While many desktop systems lack a built-in microphone, almost all laptops have one. In some cases this microphone will be located on the laptop bottom, but in many cases it will be in the display next to the webcam or off to the side. If you need to replace it, you will need to take the same steps to get inside the display that you took for the webcam.

When you unhook the lid from the bottom, you will need to unplug several things from the board, and one of those will be the microphone cable. If the microphone is not working (which it probably isn't or you wouldn't be replacing it), take a moment to inspect the cable. Sometimes the cable can be cut by the constant opening and closing of the case (it shouldn't, but sometimes it does happen). You may be able to repair the cable without replacing the microphone.

If that is not the case, remove the microphone and cable and replace both with the new mic and cable. Reverse the steps to get into the display, reconnect the cables to the board, and put the back on the bottom.

Inverter

An inverter is a component that takes DC power and converts it to an AC form that can be used by the LCD screen. It is implemented as a circuit board that is located behind the LCD. If problems with flickering display or dimness occur, the inverter is a prime suspect.

If the inverter needs to be replaced, you should be aware that it may contain stored energy, so it may need to be discharged to be safe.

Digitizer/touchscreen

Digitizers read pressure applied to the surface of the display and are what make touchscreens work. In some cases, they work with a stylus or small pen-like device; in others, you simply touch the screen with your finger. The digitizer is a thin piece of clear material that fits on top of the display. It has its own cable just as the display itself does. If it gets cracked, which often happens, it can be replaced without replacing the display itself. Typically when you perform this replacement, you will have to open the display lid, as I covered earlier, and separate the digitizer from the display. It is usually glued to the display, and you can use a hair dryer to heat the glue to make removing it easier. When you put the new digitizer in, you may need to reheat the glue on the display to stick them back together.

Exam essentials

Differentiate the types of displays available in laptops.   Two major types of LCDs are used today: active matrix screens and passive matrix screens.

Describe the location and operational characteristics of the wireless antenna in a laptop. The wireless antenna is located in the display. Moving the laptop changes the polarity of the antenna and may result in a better signal.

Identify the location and function of the inverter.   An inverter is a component that takes DC power and converts it to a form that can be used by the LCD screen. It is implemented as a circuit board behind the LCD.

1.3 Given a scenario, use appropriate laptop features.

Because of the nature of their physical implementation, laptops have some features not found in desktops and some issues that need to be handled differently than with desktops. In this section, I will discuss some of these features and issues along with the use of some special function keys. The following topics are addressed in exam objective 1.3:

- Special function keys
- Docking station
- Port replicator
- Physical laptop lock and cable lock
- Rotating/removable screens

Special function keys

Special function keys exist in both desktops and laptops, but in older laptops function keys have extra functions that may not be present in desktops. These functions are indicated by icons below the letters (F1, F2, and so on), and in the lower-left corner of the keyboard is a key marked Fn. When this key is held down, a function key will perform the function of its icon instead of its usual function. This section describes some of the most common uses of these keys, although manufacturers sometimes implement these keys differently, and some special functions don't use Fn keys, so you should consult the documentation.

Dual displays

When additional displays are connected to the laptop (for example, a projector or second monitor), holding down the Fn key and pressing the function key with an icon of a monitor (or sometimes a laptop display and second screen) will move the active screen from display to display (or display to a projector) and then to a setting where all monitors have the same output. This is valuable when making a presentation or to direct the image to the projector or the laptop screen. It is also worth noting that various laptop keyboards implement this function on different keys, including F1, F4, and F8.

Wireless (on/off)

There is also a function key that will turn the wireless off and on; this key usually has an antenna icon, or perhaps an airplane for airplane mode, and you may not have to hold the Fn key to use it. If wireless does not work (especially if the system is telling you to turn the wireless on), check this setting. It is easy to hit this key and disable the wireless!

Cellular (on/off)

Just as you can turn off the wireless (802.11) connection, you can also turn off the cellular (WWAN) connection (if one exists on the device). You will probably need to refer to the device's documentation to identify the exact key.

Volume settings

On the top row where the keys labeled F1–F12 are located, there are usually a couple of keys (typically F8 and F9) with icons that look like speakers. These keys can be used to raise and lower the volume of the sound. If the icon is blue, you have to hold down the Fn key. Otherwise, you do not need to use the Fn key to activate them. (As a matter of fact, if you hold down the Fn key and use the F8 key, you may be changing the location of the display output, as described in the section "Dual displays.") If these keys are not present, consult the documentation for the key to use in conjunction with Fn to lower and raise the volume. Most laptops also include a mute button marked as such.

Screen brightness

There are usually a couple of function keys (often F4 and F5) with sun icons with arrows pointing up and down, respectively. They could also be located on the lower right on the keyboard. These keys can be used to increase and decrease the brightness of the display. As with the volume settings described in the previous section, you do not need to use the Fn key to activate them. If these keys are not present, consult the documentation for the key to use in conjunction with Fn to increase and decrease the brightness.

Bluetooth (on/off)

In most cases, the same key that turns 802.11 wireless off and on also does the same for Bluetooth. See the section "Wireless (on/off)."

Keyboard backlight

Some keyboards come with backlighting. These models will usually allow you to turn the backlighting on and off by using the Fn key in combination with another key, such as the Z key on some models. Consult the documentation to determine which key combination will perform this function.

Touchpad (on/off)

While touchpads provide you with a way to operate without a mouse, there are cases when you don't want to use the touchpad, and it gets in your way when typing. In other cases, the touchpad does not work, simply because it has been turned off. So, how do you enable and disable the touchpad? It can be done using either software or hardware.

In some cases, you may find there is a touchpad icon in the notification area. If there is, you can right-click or double-click it, and in the settings you should find an enable/disable feature. If there is no icon, it may be possible to go to the mouse settings in Control Panel and find touchpad settings. Finally, you can always open Device Manager and enable and disable the touchpad from there.

There also is usually a way to physically enable and disable the touchpad. This varies from laptop to laptop. For example, on a Lenovo, you hit a location in the upper-right corner of the touchpad, and it acts as a toggle switch between on and off. Consult the documentation that came with the laptop, or look on the vendor's website.

Screen orientation

The screen orientation refers to the position of the image on the screen. This is changed by "rotating" the screen. For example, if you rotated the screen 180 degrees, the image would be upside down. Rotating the screen can be done either by using the display settings or in some cases by using a special key combination. In most cases, if you right-click the desktop, you will find the option to rotate in various ways in the menu. It may also be under the Graphics Options menu, as shown in Figure 1.1.

Media options (fast forward/rewind)

Many laptops also offer keys that are used with media players. For example, you can fast-forward (or go to the next track), rewind (go to the previous track), and stop the player. These keys may have a special location, or they may be included as function keys at the top of the keyboard. If they are in the function keys, you will need to hold down the Fn key as usual. In Figure 1.2, they are located at the top of the keyboard.

FIGURE 1.1   Screen orientation

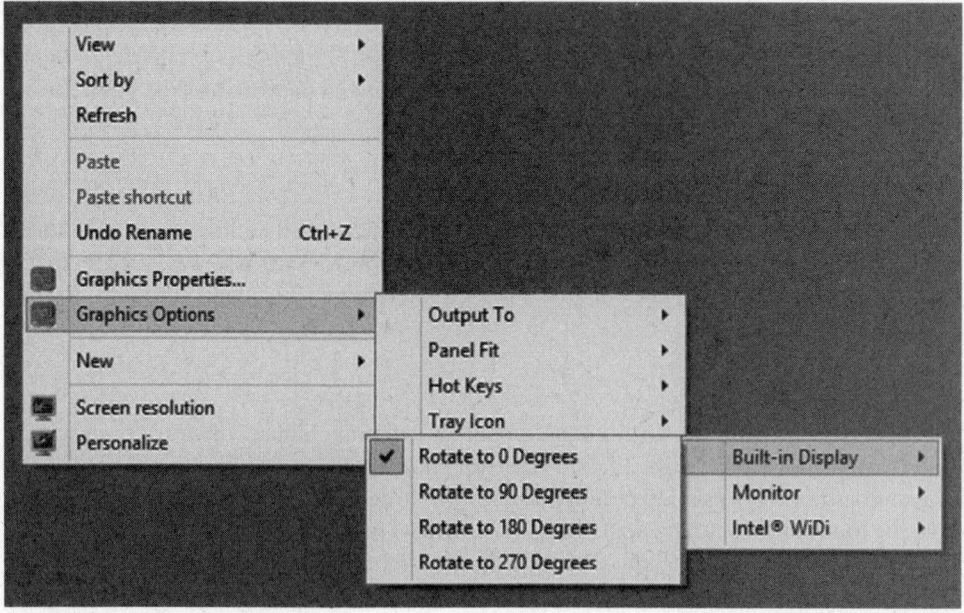

FIGURE 1.2   Media keys

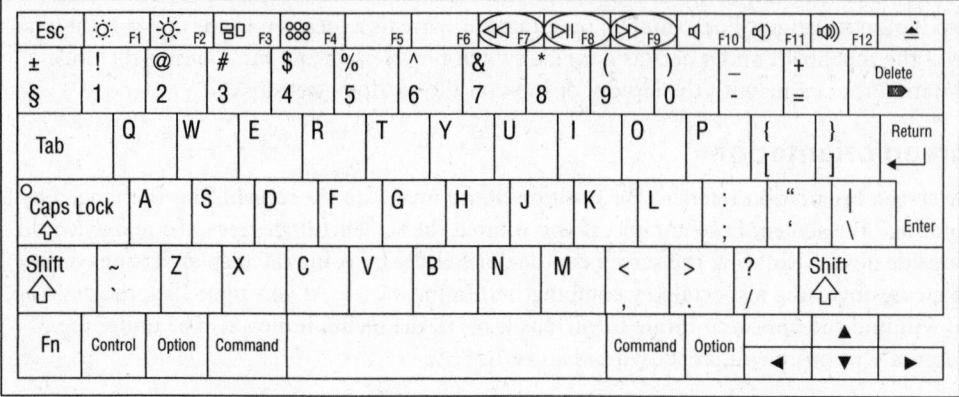

GPS (on/off)

Many devices now come with a built-in GPS feature. You can enable and disable the GPS using the privacy settings in Windows. While you will probably find it is enabled by default, you can disable it in Windows 10 by bringing up the Charms bar. At the bottom, choose the Settings charm. Tap or click the Change PC Settings link and then select Privacy on the left. Choose Location. On this page you can select to either turn it off completely or turn it off for certain applications, as shown Figure 1.3.

FIGURE 1.3   Location tracking

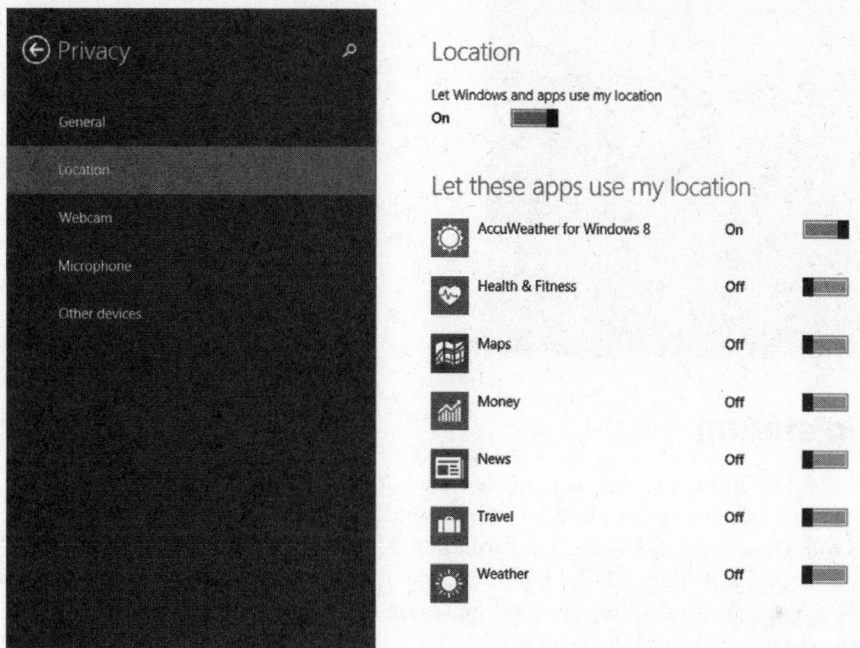

Airplane mode

Airplane mode suspends many of the device's signal-transmitting functions. It's called airplane mode because it disables the transmission of signals that interfere with aircraft signaling (or so they say). Enabling and disabling this mode can be done either in Windows or in some cases by using a special key on the keyboard.

To enable and disable it in Windows 10, navigate to the PC settings, as discussed in the "GPS (on/off)" section. In the PC settings, select Network. Then select Airplane Mode. On the right you will see a button to toggle between on and off, as shown in Figure 1.4. There will be separate controls for Wi-Fi and Bluetooth.

On many laptops this can also be done using one of the function keys. If this feature is present on the laptop, the key will have an airplane icon on it. Use it as you would any function key to toggle between off and on.

FIGURE 1.4 Airplane mode

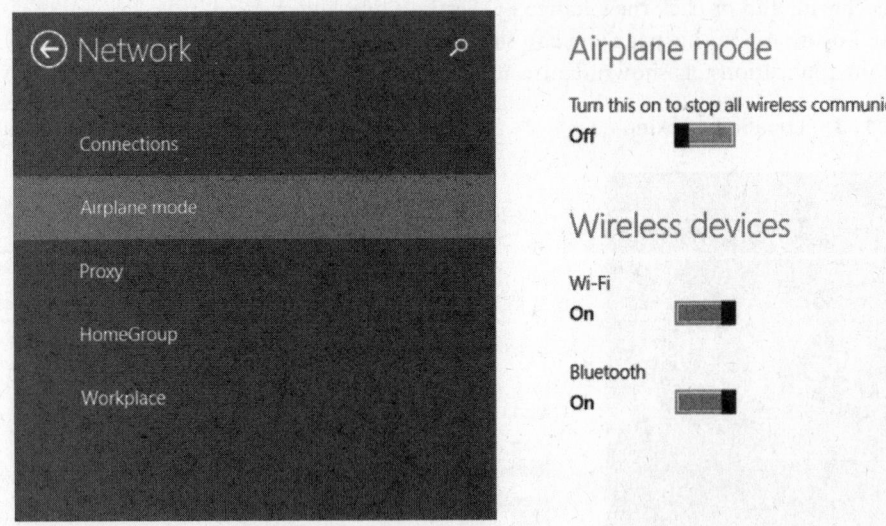

Docking station

Some notebook PCs have optional accessories called *docking stations* or *port replicators*. They let you quickly connect/disconnect with external peripherals and may also provide extra ports that the notebook PC doesn't normally have.

A docking station essentially allows a laptop computer to be converted to a desktop computer. When plugged into a docking station, the laptop has access to things it doesn't have stand-alone—the network, a workgroup printer, and so on. The cheapest form of docking station (if it can be called that) is a port replicator. Typically, you slide a laptop into the port replicator, and the laptop can then use a full-sized monitor, keyboard (rather than the standard 84 keys on a laptop), mouse, and so on. Extended, or enhanced, replicators add other ports not found on the laptop, such as PC slots, sound, and more. The most common difference between port replicators and docking stations is that port replicators duplicate the ports the laptop already has to outside devices, and the docking station expands the laptop to include other ports and devices that the laptop does not natively have.

Laptops can support plug and play at three levels, depending on how dynamically they're able to adapt to changes.

Cold Docking The laptop must be turned off and back on for the change to be recognized.

Warm Docking The laptop must be put in and out of suspended mode for the change to be recognized.

Hot Docking The change can be made and is recognized while running normal operations.

Each docking station works a little differently, but there is usually a button you can press to undock the notebook from the unit. There may also be a manual release lever in case you need to undock when the button is unresponsive. Moreover, the docking station must be purchased from the same vendor you purchased the laptop from because docking stations are vendor-and model-specific.

Port replicator

Port replicators are a form of docking station and were discussed in the previous section.

Physical laptop lock and cable lock

Laptops can be easily stolen. Therefore, they come with a lock slot to which a cable lock can be attached. Figure 1.5 shows the lock slot, and Figure 1.6 shows the connected lock (sometimes called a Kensington lock).

FIGURE 1.5   Lock slot

FIGURE 1.6   Connected lock

Rotating/removable screens

Many mobile devices today have a removable screen. While it appears that the screen is removable, you are actually unhooking the keyboard because the computer is contained in the display. With the keyboard detached, you can use the device as a tablet, and with the keyboard attached, you can interact with the device as you would a laptop.

Many of these same devices also allow for the rotation of the screen when it is attached to the keyboard. This might be a rotation within the frame of the screen, or it could be a rotation in a circle.

Exam essentials

Describe the purpose of special function keys.   In the lower-left corner of the keyboard is a key with blue text that says Fn. When this key is held, other keys with a similar blue marking (such as F1–F12) will perform a different function than their normal function.

Differentiate between docking stations and port replicators.   A docking station essentially allows a laptop computer to be converted to a desktop computer. Extended, or enhanced, replicators add other ports not found on the laptop, such as PC slots, sound, and more. The most common difference between port replicators and docking stations is whether the peripheral provides network access and expands the laptop's capabilities.

Describe approaches to the physical security of a laptop.   Laptops come with a lock slot to which a cable lock can be attached. Also, there is a lock on some models for the lid of the laptop.

1.4 Compare and contrast characteristics of various types of other mobile devices.

At one time, the term *mobile devices* referred only to notebook laptops, tablets, and PDAs. Today this category includes all sort of devices that at one time were only ideas. In this section, you'll look at digital devices that have had their capabilities greatly expanded, such as smart cameras that have become essentially computers with a lens, and smart watches and fitness monitors that almost become part of their owner. The following are the topics covered in exam objective 1.4:

- Tablets
- Smartphones
- Wearable technology devices
- E-readers
- GPS

Tablets

Tablet devices have been in existence in some form or fashion since the early 1990s. Early on they were proprietary devices that didn't have a lot in common with desktop computers, but increasingly the two form factors have gravitated toward one another; now, many new tablets run the same operating systems that are run on desktop systems. Most tablet computers run one of three operating systems: Android, iOS, or Windows 10.

The tablet market was changed significantly with the release of the iPad by Apple. It was the most successful tablet ever at its time of release, and it set the standard for others to meet. Today, typical features of tablets include the following:

- Cameras (in some cases dual)
- GPS
- Handwriting recognition
- Solid-state hard drives
- 3G and 4G mobile support

Tablet devices today use touchscreen displays rather than keyboards, although keyboards can be attached. Some, such as the Microsoft Surface, can be attached and detached at will from a keyboard that also acts as a stand and a cover for the device. In most cases, tablets require applications written for the platform, although the Surface can run the Windows 10 operating system and thus can also run regular desktop applications.

Smartphones

As phones have become smarter and smarter, they more and more resemble computers rather than phones. Today's smartphones are really computers that can make calls. They have touchscreen interfaces, an on-screen keyboard that can be brought up to input data, and sometimes even motion sensors and mobile payment mechanisms.

Moreover, the drive by organizations and individuals to create applications for these devices has exploded. Every week it seems someone has designed and created an application that turns the phone into some new gadget! Because of this phenomenon, the smartphone has become almost part of the body to several younger generations of users.

Most of these devices run either the iOS or Android operating system, although Microsoft continues to release Windows phones that run a special Windows OS for the device. The latest is Windows 10.

Wearable technology devices

Since the days of Dick Tracy's futuristic phone watch, we have waited for wearable technology to arrive, and it has. In this section, I'll survey some of the latest examples of digital devices created to be worn.

Smart watches

Smart watches that are computers on your wrist have arrived! Although the jury is still out on the long-term viability of the smart watch, when Apple introduced one in 2015, most in the industry began to take the devices seriously. These devices run either proprietary operating systems or Android. The Apple model runs an operating system called Watch OS.

These devices are typically paired to a smartphone for the purpose of accessing calls and messages, and they contain GPS features as well. The following are some of the features you may find in these smart watches:

- Anti-lost alert
- Time display
- Call vibration
- Caller ID
- Answer call
- Micro-USB input port

Fitness monitors

While many smart watches can also act as fitness monitors, there is a class of devices that specializes in tracking your movement. Fitness monitors read your body temperature, heart rate, and blood pressure. They do this while also tracking where you are for the purpose of determining the distance you ran or walked and the time it took to do so.

Some of the devices, called *fitness trackers*, are wrist bands that can track the information discussed and communicate wirelessly to an application located on a computer. One of these is shown in Figure 1.7. Other, more sophisticated units combine a strap that goes around the chest with a watch or band that collects the information gathered by the sensors in the band.

FIGURE 1.7   Fitness tracker

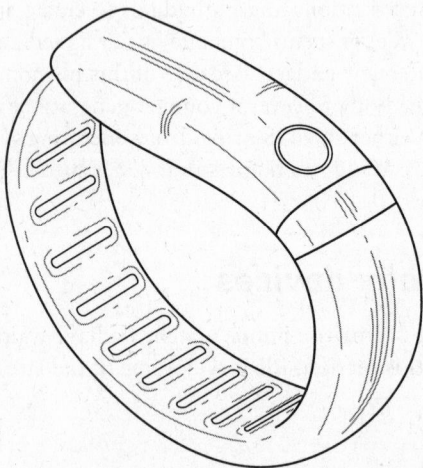

VR/AR headsets

Extended reality is an exciting new field that includes both augmented reality and virtual reality. Both concepts involve wearing special headsets that deliver the visual experience. While reality immerses the user into a virtual environment, much like a four-dimensional game, augmented reality involves glasses that while permitting a clear vison of the real world, can project graphics and text onto this view using a small side screen. A virtual reality headset is shown in Figure 1.8.

FIGURE 1.8   VR headset

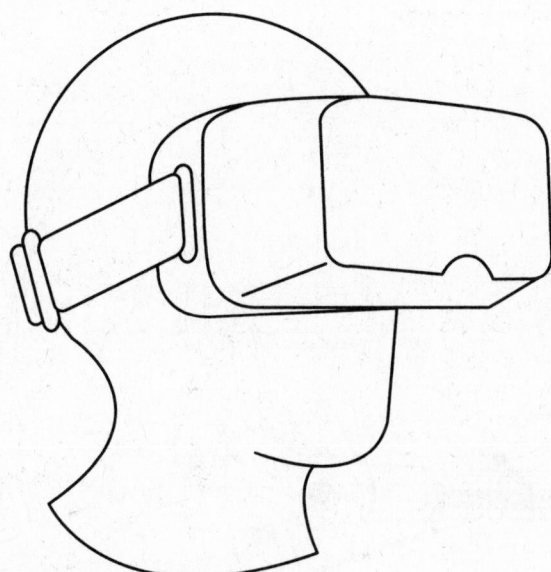

By now, everyone has heard about and probably seen Google Glass, the most well-known and recognizable computing device worn as glasses. Just in case you haven't, Figure 1.9 shows a drawing of the glasses.

FIGURE 1.9   Google Glass

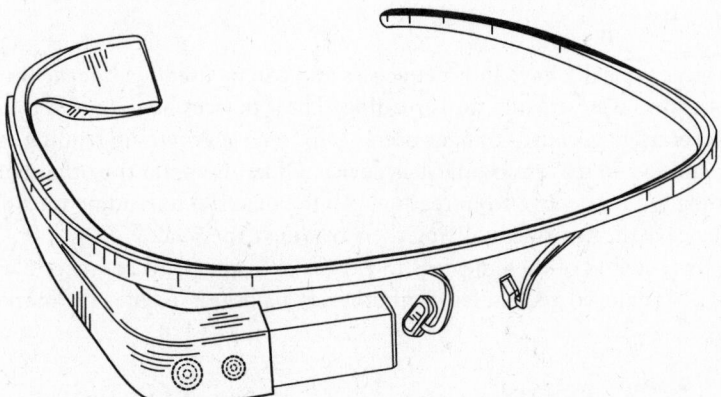

While worn as glasses, they also have a small screen just to the side of one of the eyes that houses the computer screen (think Cyborg). The user can view the screen at any time by just casting a glance at it. Many promising uses have been proposed for the devices, with a number in the healthcare field. Although sale of the devices to individuals was halted, sales to organizations that have or are working to find ways to use the glasses continue.

Another similar device that is not based on glasses but around a headset format is the HC1 headset computer by Zebra. It can respond to voice commands and body movements. One of these is shown in Figure 1.10.

FIGURE 1.10   Headset computer

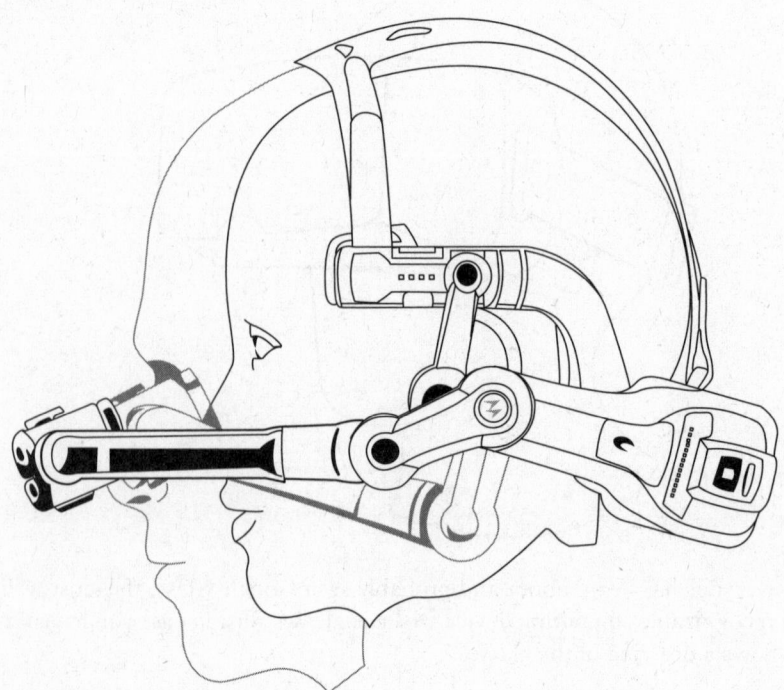

E-readers

While these devices typically have Internet access and can be used for Internet browsing, the main job e-readers were created for is reading. These devices have proven to be more popular with older users because younger users seem to have grown up reading everything on a computer and see no reason for another device. Older users, on the other hand, who are still struggling with the move from reading printed material to reading on a device, like the idea of a device dedicated to enhancing their reading experience.

The Kindle was the first of these devices to garner widespread acceptance. The Nook soon followed. Both enjoyed good sales until other rivals began to enter the market. Sales of these devices are now in decline because of the aging of the main customer base. The following are some of the features found in these devices:

- Touchscreens
- Buttons for turning pages
- Editing tools
- Wireless networking
- Text-to-speech support
- Digital rights management support

GPS

A global positioning system (GPS) uses satellite information to plot the global location of an object and use that information to plot the route to a second location. GPS devices are integrated into many of the mobile devices discussed already and are used for many things, but when I use the term for a stand-alone device, I am usually referring to a navigation aid.

These aids have grown in sophistication over time and now not only can plot your route but also help you locate restaurants, lodging, and other services along the way. Another use for these devices is tracking delivery vehicles and rental cars.

Exam essentials

Describe the common features of tablets.   These features include cameras (in some cases dual), GPS, handwriting recognition, and solid-state hard drives support.

Describe some items that are considered wearable technology.   Wearable technology includes smart watches, fitness monitors, Google Glass, and headset computers.

1.5 Given a scenario, connect, and configure accessories and ports of other mobile devices.

Mobile devices in many cases have the same connection types and ports as laptop and desktop computers, but the accessories can vary somewhat. In this section, you'll look at the types of ports and accessories you will find on mobile devices. Specifically, I will cover the following topics:

- Connection types
- Accessories

Connection types

Mobile devices possess both wireless and wired connection options. In this section, I'll cover both types.

Wired

While mobile devices may not have as many wired options as desktop devices, they still can have a wide range of physical port types.

Micro-USB/Mini-USB/USB-C

The two most common ports found on mobile devices are micro-USB and mini-USB. Both are small–form-factor implementations of the USB standard, the latest of which is USB 3.1. In Figure 1.11, the mini-USB and micro-USB connectors are compared to the regular USB connector.

FIGURE 1.11 USB form factors

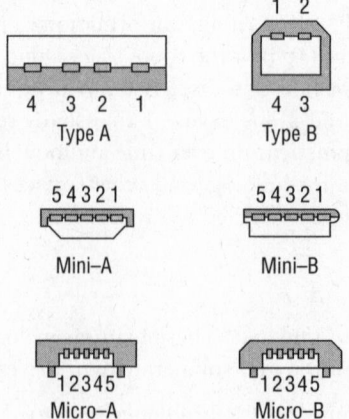

The USB-C is a new port type that can accept either end of its cable, and it doesn't matter if it's upside down! USB-C, also known as USB Type-C, is a 24-pin USB connector system, which is distinguished by its two-fold rotationally symmetrical connector. All Thunderbolt 3 cables will work as USB-C cables as well.

The data rates for various types of USB are in Table 1.2.

TABLE 1.2 USB speeds

Type	Speed
1.0	187.5 KB to 1.5 MB
2.0	60 MB
3.0	625 MB (super speed)
3.1	1.25 GB
3.2	2.5 GB (super speed)

Lightning

The Lightning connector from Apple is an eight-pin connector that while not standard has advantages over USB, according to Apple. The following are some of these advantages:

- It can supply more power.
- It can be inserted either way.
- It is physically more durable than USB.
- It can detect and adapt to connected devices.
- It operates at USB 3.0 speeds.

Figure 1.12 shows a Lightning connector next to a USB cable.

FIGURE 1.12   Lightning connector and USB

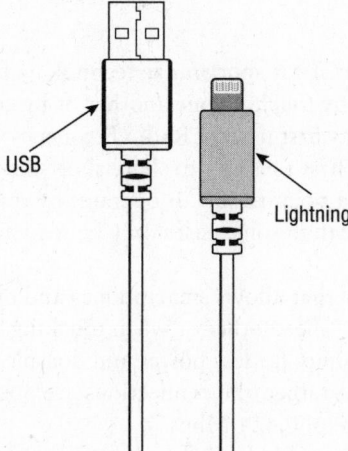

USB

Lightning

Tethering

When one device is connected to another device for the purpose of using the Internet connection, it is said to be *tethered* to the device providing the access. While use of this connection can be done by using 802.11, it can also be done connecting through Bluetooth or a USB cable between the devices. Even with unlimited data programs, the tethering (or mobile hotspot as it is also called) has a limited amount of data, and then the hotspot function only is throttled (max speed reduced).

Proprietary vendor-specific ports (communication/power)

Many mobile devices have proprietary ports that they use either for power or for communication. While this was widespread at one point, vendors have gradually moved toward using standard physical implementations of both power and communication ports. While I can't cover all of these, the best examples are the ports used by Apple in its devices.

Apple uses what it calls the Lightning connector for power. Although it makes an adapter for this connector to convert it to mini-USB, it doesn't encourage its use, because of the limitations the adapter places on the functionality of the proprietary connector.

The following are other examples of proprietary connectors:

- The Sony-Ericsson power connector looks like USB but is not.

- Nokia and Motorola have used coaxial in some power connectors.

For the most part, you will find that many vendors have chosen to adopt standard connection types for both power and communication.

Wireless

Mobile devices can have several types of wireless connection options. In this section we'll look at those.

NFC

Near Field Communication (NFC) is a short-range technology that allows mobile devices to establish radio communication by touching one another or by coming in close proximity to one another. The technology was first used in Radio Frequency ID (RFID) tagging and was implemented on mobile devices first as a way to share short-range information and later as a method to make payments at a point of sale. It operates by reading tags, which are small microchips with antennas that can in some cases only be read and other cases can be read and written to.

NFC is a wireless technology that allows smartphones and other equipped devices to communicate when very near one another or when touching. NFC operates at slower speeds than Bluetooth but consumes far less power and doesn't require pairing. It also does not create a PAN like Bluetooth; rather, the connections are point to point. NFC can operate up to 20 cm at a transfer rate of 0.424 Mbps.

NFC is also a standard managed by the ISO and uses tags that are embedded in the devices. NFC components include an initiator and a target; the initiator actively generates an RF field that can power a passive target. This enables NFC targets to take simple form factors such as tags, stickers, key fobs, or cards that do not require batteries.

These devices connect either using USB or in some rare cases using a serial connection. Consult the documentation to determine whether you need a special driver installed.

A mobile device must have the support for NFC built in, and many already do. Special applications are available that make it easy to use the technology in various ways.

- Making point-of-sale payments
- Reading information stored in tags in posters and advertisements
- Communication between toys used in gaming
- Communication with peripherals

Bluetooth

Mobile devices also support Bluetooth wireless connections. Bluetooth is an infrared technology that can connect a printer to a computer at a short range; its absolute maximum range is 100 meters (330 feet), and most devices are specified to work within 10 meters (33 feet). When printing with a Bluetooth-enabled device (like a PDA or mobile phone) and a Bluetooth-enabled printer, all you need to do is get within range of the device (that is, move closer), select the print driver from the device, and choose Print. The information is transmitted wirelessly through the air using radio waves and is received by the device. Bluetooth speed depends on version. Table 1.3 shows this for the latest versions.

TABLE 1.3   Bluetooth speeds

Version	Speed
2.0	2.1 MB
2.1	2.1 MB
3.0	24 MB (over Wi-Fi connection)
4.0	2.1 MB over Bluetooth and 24MB over Wi-Fi
4.1	2.1 MB over Bluetooth and 24MB over Wi-Fi
4.2	2.1 MB over Bluetooth and 24MB over Wi-Fi
5.0	2.1 MB over Bluetooth and 24MB over Wi-Fi

IR

While infrared (IR) connectors were once common on mobile devices, they disappeared only to reappear recently. Infrared technology requires direct line of sight and has been used for printers in the past. It can operate at a distance of 5 meters and can offer up to 4 Mbps. It is being replaced with Bluetooth over time.

Hotspot

Another way that many mobile devices can connect to other devices is through a hotspot or when tethered to another device. Many mobile devices have the ability to act as 802.11 hotspots for other wireless devices in the area. There are also devices dedicated solely to performing as mobile hotspots.

Accessories

Mobile devices require a lot of accessories to take advantage of many of the features they provide. While many of these are also commonly used with desktop and laptop devices, some are much more likely to be used with mobile devices. In this section, you'll take a brief look at the types of accessories you may find attached to a mobile device.

Headsets

Headsets provide the ability to take your conversation offline or to listen to your music in private. They can be connected both through a wired connection, usually a 3.55 mm audio connector or USB, and by using Bluetooth to pair the device with the headset.

Speakers

Speakers are used in the same fashion as headsets. They can also be connected using the same options that include using USB, using a 3.55 mm audio plug, or by pairing the speakers with the devices using Bluetooth. This includes the speaker systems in many cars, which can now be paired with the devices using Bluetooth as well.

Game pads

People seem to love to kill time playing games on their smartphones and other mobile devices, but they may find their level of enjoyment increased by connecting the devices to a game controller offering them many more input options. These controllers look like any game controller, which can differ based on the game being played and the type of input required for the game.

These controllers can also be small, some fitting on a keychain. They typically are paired to the mobile device using the Bluetooth connection. Some of the newer game controllers for this purpose can be set on a table and the mobile device plugs physically into a slot or holder on the controller, making a connection with the controller. Figure 1.13 shows the layout of a typical game controller.

FIGURE 1.13   Smartphone game controller

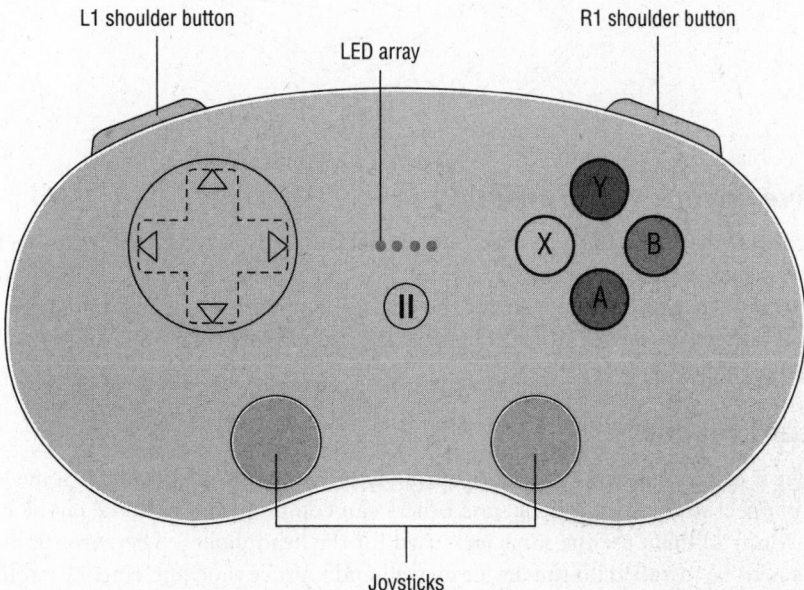

Joysticks

Extra battery packs/battery chargers

Batteries are the lifeline of mobile devices. For a device to stay constantly connected, many users purchase extra battery packs that can be used to power the devices when the battery is dead and no power outlet is available. Some of these packs simply provide power to the device, while others store power used to charge the device's battery. Figure 1.14 shows an example of a battery pack that can be charged while providing power to the device.

FIGURE 1.14 Battery pack

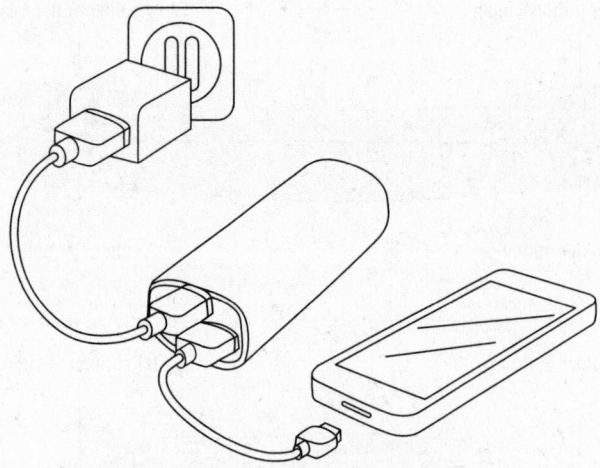

Protective covers/waterproofing

While much work has been done to make mobile devices sturdier and more durable, they are still somewhat delicate pieces of electronics. For this reason, an entire industry has sprung up to provide protective covers for the devices. Some are made of a hard plastic material and protect the device from all but the worst impacts, while others go further and provide waterproofing as well.

Credit card readers

Mobile devices can also accept connections from external credit card readers. Some of these physically connect to the smartphone, and others can communicate with the phone using Bluetooth. Many of them use the same jack used for the headphones. There is usually software that has to be installed on the device as well and a processing agreement established with a provider. Figure 1.15 shows the Square reader.

FIGURE 1.15 Square credit card reader

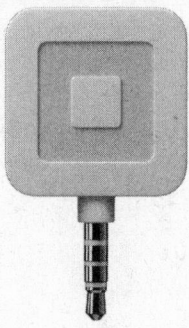

Memory/MicroSD

Secure digital (SD) cards are a type of flash memory. Micro-SD is the smallest of three standards. Many mobile devices have MicroSD slots or ports on them that allow you to connect one to the device. This allows you either to access data on the memory card or to move information to the memory card from the smartphone. For more information on MicroSD, see the section "Solid-state drives" in Chapter 3.

Exam essentials

Describe the most common connection types found on mobile devices.   These include Near Field Communication, proprietary ports, Lightning, Bluetooth, and infrared.

Identify the most common mobile device accessories.   Mobile devices will accept gamepads, headsets, speakers, docking stations, battery packs and chargers, and credit card readers. They can also use protective covers and waterproof containers to protect them.

1.6 Given a scenario, configure basic mobile device network connectivity and application support.

For mobile devices to deliver the functionality that most expect, they must be connected to a network. To use email (one of the most important functions to many users), the device must be set up properly. The subobjectives covered in this section include the following:

- Wireless/cellular data network (enable/disable)
- Bluetooth
- Corporate and ISP email configuration
- Integrated commercial provider email configuration
- PRI updates/PRL updates/baseband updates
- Radio firmware
- IMEI vs. IMSI
- VPN

Wireless/cellular data network (enable/disable)

Like most computing devices, mobile devices provide more robust functionality when connected to a network (especially if that network is the Internet). Two types of networks can be used to gain access to the Internet: cell phone networks and Wi-Fi networks.

Cell phone networks have in the past been the second choice because the performance is not as good as an 802.11 Wi-Fi connection. With the introduction of 4G Long Term Evolution (LTE) technologies, however, the performance delivered by the cell network may become more competitive.

In either case, most mobile devices will have the ability to make an 802.11 connection or use the cell network. If you want to disable the automatic connection to the cell phone network or if it was somehow turned off and needs to be turned back on, you can do this through the settings. One example of the steps to access these settings is Settings ➢ Wireless ➢ Mobile ➢ Enable Data (select or deselect this). This is only one navigational example, and you should consult the documentation that came with the device.

Making a Wi-Fi connection is much like doing so with a laptop. In the settings of the device will be a section for Wi-Fi (in iPhone it's called Wi-Fi, and in Android it's called Wireless And Networks). When you access it, you will see all the Wi-Fi networks within range. Just as you would do with a laptop, select one and attempt to connect to the Wi-Fi network. If the connection requires a password, you will have to supply it. You also can preconfigure a wireless profile for commonly used secure wireless networks as well as those where the service set identifier (SSID) has been hidden.

Hotspot

Hotspots are publicly provided points of access to an 802.11 wireless network connected to the Internet. They typically have little or no security configured to make it as easy as possible for users to connect. Vendors have also created devices that allow a single device to act as a hotspot for other devices in the area. Sometimes these are called *mobile hotspots*. Some mobile devices can be turned into mobile hotspots with a software upgrade or an addition to the service plan.

Tethering

Tethering is the process of sharing the Internet connection of one device with another device. Connection of the phone or tablet with other devices can be done over wireless LAN (Wi-Fi), over Bluetooth, or with a physical connection using a cable, for example through USB. It also may be done by using a mobile hotspot or by using a similar feature on a mobile device.

Airplane mode

Since airlines do not permit enabling the wireless connection on mobile devices during takeoff and landing, vendors created a mode called Airplane mode in which this function is turned off but all other functionality (games and other applications not requiring Internet access) is still fully functional.

Bluetooth

Bluetooth is a short-range wireless technology that is used to create a wireless connection between digital devices. One of its applications is to create connections between mobile devices and items such as speakers, headphones, external GPS units, and keyboards. Before you can take advantage of this technology, the devices must be configured to connect to one another. This section will discuss how to configure a Bluetooth connection.

Enable Bluetooth

On Android mobile devices, follow these steps:

1. From the Home screen, select the Menu button. From the menu, choose Settings ➤ Connections ➤ Bluetooth.
2. Once Bluetooth is selected, wait until a check mark appears next to Bluetooth. Bluetooth is now enabled.

On iOS mobile devices, follow these steps:

1. On the main page, choose Settings ➤ Bluetooth.
2. Tap the slider to enable Bluetooth.

Enable pairing

Pairing a mobile device with an external device (speaker, headphone, and so forth) will enable the two devices to communicate. The first step is to enable pairing. This is much simpler than it sounds. For either mobile operating system, simply turn the external device on and you are ready for the next step. In some cases, you may need to make the external device discoverable. Check the documentation for the external device to see whether this is the case and how you do this.

Find a device for pairing

Now that the external device is on and transmitting a signal, the mobile device is ready for pairing.

On an Android mobile device, follow these steps:

1. Swipe up on an empty spot on the Home screen to open the Apps tray.
2. Select Settings and then Connections.
3. Turn on the Bluetooth switch by tapping it.
4. If the mobile device stops scanning before the Bluetooth device is ready, tap scan again.
5. In the list of Available devices, tap the Bluetooth device to pair it with the phone.
6. Follow any on-screen instructions.
7. If a password is required, consult the documentation or try either 0000 or 1234 (common passcodes).

On an iOS mobile device, when Bluetooth is enabled, it automatically starts scanning for Bluetooth devices. When your device appears in the list, select it. If a PIN is required, move on to the next step.

Enter the appropriate pin code

Many external devices will ask for a PIN when you select the external device from the list of discovered devices. In many cases, the PIN is 0000, but you should check the manual of the external device.

Test connectivity

Once the previous steps are complete, test communication between the two devices. If you're using a headset, turn on some sound and see whether you can hear it in the headphones.

Corporate and ISP email configuration

Email is one of the most important functions that people access on their mobile devices. This section will discuss how to configure email on the device. The following procedures are common examples, and your specific device may differ slightly. Please consult the documentation for your device.

Before you can access email on your mobile device, you must know the settings for the email server of your email provider. There are two protocols that can be used to access email accounts: POP3 and IMAP. If your account offers the use of IMAP, you should select it in the following steps because IMAP accounts have more functionality.

You will need the following information to complete this setup:

- The FQDN of your POP3 server or IMAP server (This server receives the emails sent to you, so it's sometimes called *incoming*.)
- The FQDN of your SMTP server (This server sends your email to the recipient's email server, so it's sometimes called *outgoing*.)
- The port numbers used for both server types
- The security type used (if any)

POP3

On an Android mobile device, follow these steps:

1. In Settings, select Clouds And Accounts and then Accounts.
2. In Accounts, select Add An Account and select Email as the type.
3. Enter the email address and password and select Sign In.
4. After your account is recognized and set up, select Pop3 as the account type.
5. Enter the name of the incoming POP3 server, and if desired, select to enable encryption.
6. Enter **110** as the incoming port, and if desired, select Delete Email Off The Server.
7. Enter the name of the outgoing PO3 server and enter port number **25**.
8. Finally, if desired, turn on SMTP authentication.

On an iOS mobile device, follow these steps:

1. Select Settings ➤ Accounts And Passwords ➤ Add Account.

2. Select Other.

3. Select Add Mail Account. Fill in your name, your email address, your password, and a description. Click Next.

4. Select POP. Verify that the name, address, and description carried over from the last page.

5. Under Incoming Email Server, enter the FQDN of the POP3 server, your email address, and your password.

6. Under Outgoing Mail Server, enter the FQDN of the SMTP server and your email address.

7. Click Next. Click Save in the upper-right corner.

IMAP

On an Android mobile device, follow these steps:

1. In Settings, select Accounts then Add an account.

2. Click the appropriate account type.

3. If prompted for an account subtype, select the type.

4. After entering the email address, tap Next.

5. After entering the password, tap Next.

6. If prompted, enter either the username, password, or server.

7. After configuring any account options desired (Sync Frequency, Inbox Download Size, and so on), click Next.

8. Complete any account options based on the account type chosen.

9. Enter the account name and, if prompted, the name for outgoing messages.

On an iOS mobile device, follow these steps:

1. Select Settings ➤ Accounts And Passwords ➤ Add Account.

2. Select Other.

3. Select Add Mail Account. Fill in your name, your email address, your password, and a description. Click Next.

4. Select IMAP. Verify that the name, address, and description are carried over from the last page.

5. Under Incoming Email Server, enter the FQDN of the IMAP server, your email address, and your password.

6. Under Outgoing Mail Server, enter the FQDN of the SMTP server and your email address.

7. Click Next. Click Save in the upper-right corner.

Port and SSL settings

With either operating system, you can (and should) select to use security if your email server supports it. This will encrypt all traffic between the mobile device and the email server. The choices offered are usually SSL or TLS, so you will need to know which of these is in use.

S/MIME

With respect to the S/MIME configuration, you need the following:

- A digital encryption certificate for yourself as the sender
- A copy of the digital public key from your intended recipient
- An email program capable of handling S/MIME email

Exchange supports S/MIME, so that part is taken care of. Once you have obtained your certificate, you must import it into your device and make it available to the email program. Your certificate must be obtained from a certificate authority company such as VeriSign. The steps to this process will vary from organization to organization. Once you have downloaded the certificate, place it at a location on the device where you can find it during the import process.

Typically, the certificate will come to you in an email that you should open on the Android device. When you click the enrollment link in the email, you will be required to enter the password you set when you requested the certificate. Then you will create another password (called a PKCS#12 passphrase) that you will need during the certificate installation.

When the certificate downloads to the device, it will go into the Downloads folder. Now you have to add it to your credentials. Follow these steps:

1. Navigate to Settings ➤ Security and select Install From Storage.
2. Locate your downloaded certificate file (it's a .pfx file).
3. Enter your PKCS#12 passphrase (this is the one you created just before the downloads, not the one you created during enrollment).
4. Set the certificate name and its use (email).

The certificate is now available to use to encrypt email.

For iOS, follow the organizational steps to request a certificate. When the email arrives, open it on the iOS device as you did in Android. Then follow these steps:

1. Open the Mail app and find the message that contains the .p12 file. Tap the file icon to load it.
2. An Install Profile pop-up will appear for the identity certificate. Tap Install.
3. A warning that this is an unsigned profile may appear. If that happens, tap Install Now to acknowledge it.
4. You will be prompted for your passcode. Enter the passcode you use to unlock your iPad or iPhone when it's at the lock screen.

5. You'll then be asked for the password for the certificate. Enter the passphrase you came up with when you created the .p12 file on your Mac.

6. You may see a note that the certificate is Not Trusted. That's OK.

7. Push the Home button. Find the Settings app and start it.

8. In Settings, find Accounts And Passwords.

9. In the list of accounts, find the account for this email address and tap it.

10. Tap the Account line.

11. Scroll down until you see Advanced. Tap it.

12. Scroll down until you see the S/MIME section.

13. Make sure S/MIME is turned on.

14. Tap Sign. Make sure that the certificate for this account is selected and that Sign is turned on. (If you tap the *i* icon, you should see that the certificate is Trusted.)

15. Tap Advanced or Back to go back to the Advanced screen.

16. Tap Encrypt By Default. Again, select the correct certificate, and make sure Encrypt By Default is turned on.

17. Back out until you're at the Account screen and then tap Done to accept the changes.

Integrated commercial provider email configuration

You probably also want to set up your personal email on a device from a commercial provider. This section will look at some of the major email systems you may encounter.

iCloud

To set up iCloud email on an Android device, follow these instructions:

1. Swipe up or done in the Home screen to access the Apps screen.

2. In Settings, select Accounts then Add an account.

3. Click the account type.

4. If prompted, select the account subtype.

5. After entering the email address, select Next.

6. After entering the password, select Next.

7. If promoted for the username, password, or server name, enter them and select Next.

8. Enter the SMTP server, port number, and outgoing server, and select Next.

9. After configuring any account options desired (Sync frequency, Inbox download size, and so on), click Next.

10. Address any additional options you encounter and select Next.

11. Enter an account name for outgoing messages.

As you can imagine, setting up iCloud email on an iOS device is simple because the applications all reside in the Apple ecosystem. First set up an iCloud email account. If you have an email address that ends with @mac.com or @me.com, you already have an equivalent address that's the same except it ends with @icloud.com. On your IOS device, go to Settings, tap your name, and then select iCloud. Choose the apps—such as Photos, Contacts, Calendars, and third-party apps—that you want to use with iCloud.

Google/Inbox

On an Android mobile device, follow these steps:

1. Select the Gmail icon.
2. Select Already Have A Google account.
3. In the Sign In With Your Google Account field, enter your username and password and select Sign In.

On an iOS mobile device, follow these steps:

1. Select Settings ➤ Accounts & Passwords ➤ Add Account.
2. Select Gmail.
3. Fill in your name, address, password, and description if desired. Click Next.
4. Verify that the address carried over from the last page. Click Next.
5. Select the items you want to sync automatically with the email server and click Done.

Exchange Online

To set up Outlook on Android, first, if required, install Outlook for Android. Follow these steps:

1. On the Android device, select Email icon.
2. After entering the email address and password, select Manually Setting.
3. Complete the Domain\username field.
4. After entering the password for the Exchange server, select Use Secure Connection (SSL) and then Next.
5. In the Account Options interface, select a frequency for checking email and click Next.
6. Finally, if desired, enter a name for the account in the Give This Account A Name field and select Done.

On iOS, follow these steps:

1. Add your Exchange account by tapping Settings ➤ Passwords & Accounts ➤ Add Account ➤ Exchange.
2. Enter your address.
3. Choose either Configure Manually or Sign In to connect to your Exchange Server.

If you select Configure Manually, you can set up an Exchange account with Basic authentication. Enter your email password. You might also be prompted to enter additional server information.

If you select Sign In, your email address is sent to Microsoft to discover your Exchange account information. If your account uses multifactor authentication, you'll be guided through a custom authentication workflow.

Yahoo

Because Yahoo recommends using IMAP as an email client, these are the instructions for setting up IMAP on Android systems:

1. Swipe up or done on the Home screen to access the Apps screen.
2. In Settings, select accounts and then add an account.
3. After selecting the account type, select the subtype if required.
4. Enter the email address and then select Next.
5. After entering the password, select Next.
6. If prompted, enter the username, password, or server and click Next.
7. Configure the SMTP server, port number, and outgoing server and click Next.
8. Select any account options desired, such as Sync Frequency, Inbox Download Size, and so on, and select Next.
9. If prompted, enter an account name and an account for outgoing messages.

    On an iOS device, use these instructions:

1. Tap Select Settings ➤ Accounts & Passwords.
2. Tap Add Account.
3. Tap Yahoo.
4. Enter your name, your email address, your email password, and a description; then tap Next.
5. Optionally, disable aspects of Yahoo Mail from syncing.
6. Tap Save.

PRI updates/PRL updates/baseband updates

The product release information (PRI) is the connection between the mobile device and the radio. From time to time this may need updating, which may add features or increase data speed.

The preferred roaming list (PRL) is a list of radio frequencies residing in the memory of some kinds of digital phones. It lists frequencies the phone can use in various geographic areas. Each area is ordered by the bands the phone should try to use first. Therefore, it's a priority list for which towers the phone should use.

When roaming, the PRL may instruct the phone to use the network with the best roaming rate for the carrier, rather than the one with the strongest signal at the moment. As carrier networks change, an updated PRL may be required.

The baseband is the chip that controls all the GSM and 3G phone RF waves. An update makes the code in the chip current.

All mobile devices may require one or more of these updates at some point. In many cases, these updates will happen automatically, or "over the air." In other cases, you may be required to disable Wi-Fi and enable data for these to occur.

PRL

In Android phones, the location of the PRI update option will differ, but you'll generally find it in one of a few places in the Settings menu.

- Settings ➤ System Updates ➤ Update PRL
- Settings ➤ Sprint System Updates ➤ Update PRL
- Settings ➤ About Phone ➤ Update PRL

In iOS, there is no separate PRL update command on iOS devices, but running a software update will force an update of the PRL.

PRI

A PRI update is a flash process. This usually occurs in over-the-air updates. When done manually, it involves acquiring the file and then performing a flash process with the bootloader, which in many cases also updates the radio (see the next section). The flash process can result in a useless device (bricked), so follow the vendor instructions.

Radio firmware

The radios in mobile devices are equipped with firmware that, like all firmware, may need an update from time to time. In Android, follow these steps:

1. Download the Radio zip file.
2. Rename it to update.zip.
3. Copy it to the root of your phone's SD card.
4. Turn off your phone.
5. Start up in Recovery mode by holding Home and pressing Power.
6. Press Alt+S to apply the update.
7. Once the update is applied, press Home+Back to reboot the phone. The phone will start to boot up and then continue applying the update. Once this is completed, the Recovery menu will ask you for the second time to reboot the phone via Home+Back.
8. Double-check the baseband has been updated properly via choosing Menu ➤ Settings ➤ About Phone. Scroll down until you see the baseband version. You should see the radio version on this row. If not, you will need to update the radio again.

In iOS, follow these steps:

1. After downloading the desired firmware, connect the device to your computer and select it in iTunes. Mac users hold down the Option key, while Windows users hold down the Shift key.

2. Click the Update or Restore button, select the IPSW file you recently downloaded, and click Choose. Your device should now begin to update. Take note that certain browsers may change the `.ipsw` file into a `.zip` file. If this should occur, just rename it to end in `.ipsw`, and iTunes will recognize it.

IMEI vs. IMSI

International Mobile Equipment Identification (IMEI) is used to identify a physical phone device, while International Mobile Subscriber Identification (IMSI) is used to identify a Subscriber Identification Module (SIM) card.

VPN

Many users need to use the mobile devices to connect to the corporate network. This should be done using a VPN connection. To set up a VPN connection in Android, follow these steps:

1. Swipe up or down on the Home screen to select the Apps screen.

2. In Settings, select Connections and then More Connection Settings.

3. After tapping VPN, select the plus icon.

4. If desired, set up a lock screen PIN.

5. In the Name field, enter the name, and in the Type field, select the VPN type.

6. Complete the information in the fields provided for the selected VPN type and click Save.

7. Select any advanced options by selecting Show Advanced Options and complete the provided fields.

Exam essentials

Enable Bluetooth and pair a Bluetooth device with a mobile network.   Describe the process for both the iOS and Android operating systems.

Configure email on a mobile device.   Describe the process of configuring email, including both Exchange and Gmail for both the iOS and Android operating systems.

1.7 Given a scenario, use methods to perform mobile device synchronization.

Keeping information in sync between your desktop or laptop and your mobile device is one of the features that many users want to take advantage of. There are many types of information that can be synced, applications that can be installed to perform the synchronization, and connection methods that can be used to do this. This section discusses mobile device synchronization. The topics addressed in this section include the following:

- Synchronization methods
- Types of data to synchronize
- Mutual authentication for multiple services
- Software requirements to install the application on the PC
- Connection types to enable synchronization

Synchronization methods

When synchronizing the various data types we will discuss shortly, there are three basic ways to make this happen: You can synchronize to the cloud, a desktop, or an automobile's computer system. In this section, you'll look at all three approaches.

Synchronize to the cloud

One synchronization method that is gaining in popularity (along with all things "cloud") is synchronizing all your devices to a cloud server. This provides a central location for your data, settings, and all other items listed in the "Types of data to synchronize" section next. This can be set up such that all devices update with the cloud as soon as they attain Internet access.

Synchronize to the desktop

Another approach is to set up a sync process directly between two devices such as a smartphone and a desktop computer. In this case, the two devices will sync with one another at any time they find themselves on the same network such as a home wireless network.

Synchronize to the automobile

Yes, cars now have computing systems and as such can be synced to the mobile device either by using Bluetooth or by using cables designed by the vendors to connect to the car system.

Types of data to synchronize

Users may be interested in maintaining a consistency between the state of data that exists on the laptop or desktop and the state of the same data on a mobile device. This section discusses common types of data.

Contacts

No one wants to enter a long list of contacts into a mobile device when that same list already exists in your email account. Using push synchronization (*push* means it's automatic and requires no effort on the part of the user), you ensure that any changes made to the contact list either on the mobile device or on the desktop will be updated on the other device the next time you make a connection to the email account from the other device. It will also update if the mobile device makes a direct connection to the desktop (covered later in "Connection types to enable synchronization").

Applications

Program data from applications such as databases can also be synchronized between servers and mobile devices. A good example is the synchronization of the data entered into handheld devices used by the wait staff in restaurants and the server in the back room of the restaurant. Another example is the synchronization of data from handheld scanners in a warehouse with a server that may or may not be on-site. This seamless automatic updating makes the entire operation more productive.

Email

Even more important to users than their contacts is the state of their email. The mobile device will synchronize the contacts, calendar items, and email each time the mobile device makes contact with the email account. This results in a consistent state between what is seen on the desktop and what is seen on the mobile device. Push synchronization will usually allow you to configure the push schedule, such as every 30 minutes. To preserve battery life, push sync should take place less frequently.

Pictures

Pictures are another item that users frequently want to view from their mobile device without going through the process of manually downloading them to the device. Synchronization allows the pictures stored on the desktop (or even a share on a server) to be available on the mobile device, even the one you just added an hour ago.

Music

Music files can also be included in the sync process. This helps to keep your library available on the mobile device. When you start talking about music and video files (see the next section), a word of caution is in order. These large files can quickly add up and fill the hard drive and also add significantly to your data usage if the sync is happening over a wireless cell phone connection using a data plan. They can also be hard on the battery.

Videos

Video libraries can be kept consistent across devices using synchronization. Be aware of the effect of these large files on your drive space, battery level, and data usage if you are syncing wirelessly through a cell phone network.

Calendar

The calendar is a critical application for both work and play. All mobile devices support syncing the calendar between devices. In some cases, it may require a small application, especially when the email system of which the calendar is part of is in a different ecosystem (for example, Google Mail and an iPhone).

Bookmarks

Bookmarks of frequently visited websites make everyone's day easier, and when the same ones are available in the browser of all your devices, including your mobile devices, it doubles the benefit. Bookmarks are another item that can be configured to sync automatically.

Documents

Technology to sync documents located in multiple locations has been around for some time now. Users have come to expect this functionality, and it is present in modern mobile devices as well. Users want to be able to work anywhere on any device and this facilitates that.

Location data

In some cases, users may decide to allow an application to track their location for the purpose of tailoring search results. When this is done, it can be a onetime thing or the users can give the application ongoing permission to do so. Most device browsers will indicate this with some sort of icon or indicator on that page. These settings can also be synchronized between devices as well.

Social media data

While social media was once a guilty distraction, today even businesses and organizations use social media. When users have multiple accounts, many mobile platforms such as Google and Apple offer applications that can allow them to track and post to multiple accounts at once, reducing the time required to "check and update" the accounts.

E-books

Many users have accounts that give them access to books in digital format, or e-books. Naturally, they want to have access to these books (and other content types) on all their devices. Not only can this be done, but the sync process can keep their various devices up-to-date with the latest position of a bookmark in the book or of new items that have been highlighted or notes that have been made.

Passwords

Finally, passwords can also be synchronized across devices. For example, when you change your Gmail password on one device it automatically updates it on all other devices.

Mutual authentication for multiple services (SSO)

Mutual authentication is a process whereby not only does the server verify the credential of the client but the client also verifies the credential of the server. It adds additional security to the process. Both Android and iOS devices support this type of authentication, typically using SSL. One of the challenges presented to performing this type of authentication in mobile devices is their relative lack of processing power when compared with desktop and laptop systems.

Software requirements to install the application on the PC

Some devices come with a sync feature installed, but for the most robust functionality (for example, syncing between devices with different operating systems such as iPhone to Android and Android), synchronization applications that will do a much better job than the built-in applications can be purchased either at the Apple Store site or in other app marketplaces.

When obtaining one of these, ensure that your device meets all the requirements of the application. These applications will call for certain minimum requirements on the mobile device to operate correctly, so observe these guidelines to ensure a successful installation and operation.

Connection types to enable synchronization

The synchronization process can be carried out over several methods of connection between the devices. In some cases, you can connect the mobile device to the laptop or desktop using a USB connector. In other cases, you can establish a Bluetooth connection from the mobile device and the desktop. Finally, an 802.11 WLAN can also be used to establish this connection. In some instances, the synchronization application will allow you to introduce a shared folder into the scenario (like Dropbox, for example), which then allows you to use the Internet to sync from the laptop to the Dropbox and then from the Dropbox to the mobile device.

Exam essentials

Identify synchronization methods.   These include synchronizing to the cloud, synchronizing to the desktop, and synchronizing to the automobile.

Identify type of data to sync.   These include contacts, applications, email, pictures, music, videos, calendars, bookmarks, documents, location data, social media data, e-books, and passwords.

Review Questions

You can find the answers in the Appendix.

1. What is the maximum transmission speed of an ExpressCard in PCIe2 mode?
   A. 280 Mbps
   B. 512 Mbps
   C. 1.6 Gbps
   D. 3.2 Gbps

2. Which interface is natively found only in Apple devices?
   A. USB
   B. Serial
   C. Thunderbolt
   D. PS/2

3. What special screwdriver is typically required to work on a notebook?
   A. Phillips head
   B. T-8 Torx
   C. Hex
   D. Metric

4. What is the easiest thing to damage when removing a laptop keyboard?
   A. The keys
   B. The data cable
   C. The plastic cover
   D. The plastic screws

5. Which component if damaged can render the hard drive useless?
   A. The caddy
   B. The rails
   C. The signal pins
   D. The chassis

6. What size hard drive goes in a laptop?
   A. 1.5 inch
   B. 2.0 inch
   C. 2.5 inch
   D. 3.5 inch

7. Which is *not* an advantage of solid-state drives?

   A. Cheaper

   B. Not as susceptible to damage

   C. Faster

   D. No moving parts

8. Which display uses a row of transistors across the top of the screen and a column of them down the side?

   A. Passive matrix

   B. Active matrix

   C. Twisted nematic

   D. In -plane switching

9. Which display is a newer technology that solves the issue of poor quality at angles other than straight on?

   A. Passive matrix

   B. Active matrix

   C. Twisted nematic

   D. In-plane switching

10. Which of the following lets you quickly connect/disconnect with external peripherals and may also provide extra ports that the notebook PC doesn't normally have?

   A. Docking station

   B. Laptop lock

   C. Table lock

   D. Hot dock

11. In what mode of plug and play must the laptop be turned off and back on for the change to be recognized?

   A. Hot docking

   B. Warm docking

   C. Cold docking

   D. Open docking

12. Which of the following is a class of devices that specializes in tracking your movement?

   A. Fitness monitor

   B. Extended reality

   C. Smartphones

   D. Tablets

13. Which of the following uses satellite information to plot the global location of an object and uses that information to plot the route to a second location?

    A. GPS

    B. Geofencing

    C. Remote wipe

    D. Local wipe

14. Which interface is the most common port found on mobile devices?

    A. USB

    B. Serial

    C. Thunderbolt

    D. PS/2

15. Which is the most common pin code when selecting discovered Bluetooth devices?

    A. 0000

    B. 5555

    C. 1111

    D. 0135

16. Which of the following is the connection between the mobile device and the radio?

    A. PRI

    B. PRL

    C. IEMI

    D. IMSI

17. Which of the following is a process whereby not only does the server verify the credential of the client but the client also verifies the credential of the server?

    A. Mutual authentication

    B. SSO

    C. Multifactor authentication

    D. Biometrics

18. Which of the following is the use of physical factors of authentication?

    A. Mutual authentication

    B. SSO

    C. Multifactor authentication

    D. Biometrics

Chapter

2

Networking

COMPTIA A+ CERTIFICATION EXAM CORE 1 (220-1001) OBJECTIVES COVERED IN THIS CHAPTER:

✓ **2.1 Compare and contrast TCP and UDP ports, protocols, and their purposes.**

- Ports and protocols
  - 21 – FTP
  - 22 – SSH
  - 23 – Telnet
  - 25 – SMTP
  - 53 – DNS
  - 80 – HTTP
  - 110 – POP3
  - 143 – IMAP
  - 443 – HTTPS
  - 3389 – RDP
  - 137-139 – NetBIOS/NetBT
  - 445 – SMB/CIFS
  - 427 – SLP
  - 548 – AFP
  - 67/68 – DHCP
  - 389 – LDAP
  - 161/162 – SNMP
- TCP vs. UDP

✓ **2.2 Compare and contrast common networking hardware devices.**

- Routers
- Switches

- Managed
- Unmanaged
- Access points
- Cloud-based network controller
- Firewall
- Network interface card
- Repeater
- Hub
- Cable/DSL modem
- Bridge
- Patch panel
- Power over Ethernet (PoE)
  - Injectors
  - Switch
- Ethernet over Power

✓ **2.3 Given a scenario, install and configure a basic wired/wireless SOHO network.**

- Router/switch functionality
- Access point settings
- IP addressing
- NIC configuration
  - Wired
  - Wireless
- End-user device configuration
- IoT device configuration
  - Thermostat
  - Light switches
  - Security cameras
  - Door locks
  - Voice-enabled, smart speaker/digital assistant
- Cable/DSL modem configuration
- Firewall settings

- DMZ
- Port forwarding
- NAT
- UPnP
- Whitelist/blacklist
- MAC filtering
- QoS
- Wireless settings
  - Encryption
  - Channels
- QoS

✓ **2.4 Compare and contrast wireless networking protocols.**

- 802.11a
- 802.11b
- 802.11g
- 802.11n
- 802.11ac
- Frequencies
  - 2.4Ghz
  - 5Ghz
- Channels
  - 1–11
- Bluetooth
- NFC
- RFID
- Zigbee
- Z-Wave
- 3G
- 4G
- 5G
- LTE

✓ **2.5 Summarize the properties and purposes of services provided by networked hosts.**

- Server roles
  - Web server
  - File server
  - Print server
  - DHCP server
  - DNS server
  - Proxy server
  - Mail server
  - Authentication server
  - syslog
- Internet appliance
  - UTM
  - IDS
  - IPS
  - End-point management server
- Legacy/embedded systems

✓ **2.6 Explain common network configuration concepts.**

- IP addressing
  - Static
  - Dynamic
  - APIPA
  - Link local
- DNS
- DHCP
  - Reservations
- IPv4 vs. IPv6
- Subnet mask
- Gateway
- VPN
- VLAN
- NAT

✓ **2.7 Compare and contrast Internet connection types, network types, and their features.**

- Internet connection types
  - Cable
  - DSL
  - Dial-up
  - Fiber
  - Satellite
  - ISDN
  - Cellular
    - Tethering
    - Mobile hotspot
  - Line-of-sight wireless Internet service
- Network types
  - LAN
  - WAN
  - PAN
  - MAN
  - WMN

✓ **2.8 Given a scenario, use appropriate networking tools.**

- Crimper
- Cable stripper
- Multimeter
- Tone generator and probe
- Cable tester
- Loopback plug
- Punchdown tool
- WiFi analyzer

CompTIA offers a number of other exams and certifications on networking (Network+, Server+, and so on), but to become A+ certified, you must have good knowledge of basic networking skills. Not only do you need to know the basics of cabling and connectors, but you also need to know how to install and configure a wireless/wired router, apply appropriate settings, and use some basic tools. There are eight objectives for this domain. The Networking domain represents 20 percent of the total exam.

2.1 Compare and contrast TCP and UDP ports, protocols, and their purposes.

Communication across a TCP/IP-based network takes place using various protocols, such as FTP to transfer files, HTTP to view web pages, and POP3 or IMAP to work with email. Each of these protocols has a default port associated with it, and CompTIA expects you to be familiar with them for this exam.

Both Transport Control Protocol (TCP) and User Diagram Protocol (UDP) use port numbers to listen for and respond to requests for communication using various protocols. There are a number of protocols and their port numbers that you must know for this exam, as well as the differences between TCP and UDP. Topics covered include these:

- Ports and protocols
- TCP vs. UDP

Ports and protocols

There are two transport layer protocols in the TCP/IP stack. TCP provides guaranteed, connection-oriented delivery, while UDP provides nonguaranteed, connectionless delivery. Each protocol or service uses one of the two transport protocols (and in some cases both). There will be additional information later in this chapter on TCP and UDP.

TCP and UDP both use port numbers to listen for and respond to requests for communications. RFC 1060 defines *common ports* for a number of services routinely found in use, and these all have low numbers—up to 1,024. You can, however, reconfigure your service to use another port number (preferably much higher) if you're concerned about security and you don't want your site to be available to anonymous traffic.

21 – FTP

File Transfer Protocol is both a TCP/IP protocol and software that permits the transferring of files between computer systems. Because FTP has been implemented on numerous types of computer systems, files can be transferred between disparate systems (for example, a personal computer and a minicomputer). It uses ports 20 and 21 by default. It can be configured to allow or deny access to specific IP addresses and can be configured to work with exceptions. While the protocol can be run within most browsers, a number of FTP applications are available, with FileZilla (http://filezilla-project.org/) being one of the most popular.

It is valuable to note the FTP is not secure, and if confidentiality is required, you should use either SFTP (FTP encrypted with SSH) or FTPS (encrypted with SSL).

22 – SSH

Secure Shell is a remote administration tool that can serve as a secure alternative to using Telnet to remotely access and configure a device like a router or switch. Although it requires a bit more setup than Telnet, it provides an encrypted command-line session for managing devices remotely.

23 – Telnet

Telnet is a protocol that functions at the application layer of the OSI model, providing terminal-emulation capabilities. Telnet runs on port 23 but has lost favor to SSH because Telnet sends data—including passwords—in plain-text format.

25 – SMTP

Simple Mail Transfer Protocol (SMTP) is a protocol for sending email between SMTP servers. Clients typically use either IMAP or POP to access their email server and use SMTP to send email. SMTP uses port 25 by default.

53 – DNS

DNS is the Domain Name System, and it is used to translate hostnames into IP addresses. DNS is an example of a protocol that uses both UDP and TCP.

80 – HTTP

Hypertext Transfer Protocol (HTTP) is the protocol used for communication between a web server and a web browser. It uses port 80 by default.

110 – POP3

The Post Office Protocol (POP) is a protocol for receiving email from a mail server. It runs on port 110. The current version of the protocol is 3 (POP3), and the alternative to it is Internet Message Access Protocol (IMAP).

143 – IMAP

Internet Message Access Protocol (IMAP) is a protocol with a store-and-forward capability. It can also allow messages to be stored on an email server instead of downloaded to the client. The current version of the protocol is 4 (IMAP4), and the alternative to it is Post Office Protocol (POP). IMAP runs on port 143.

443 – HTTPS

Hypertext Transfer Protocol over Secure Sockets Layer (HTTPS) is a protocol used to make a secure connection. It uses port 443 by default.

3389 – RDP

Remote Desktop Protocol (RDP) is used in a Windows environment to make remote desktop communications possible.

137-139 – NetBIOS/NetBT

NetBIOS/NetBT is an early networking protocol that used a flat namespace, unlike the hierarchal one found in DNS. Computers register their services with the other devices and locate one another using NetBIOS names. It uses ports 137–139.

445 – SMB/CIFS

Server Message Block (SMB) is an application layer protocol used to provide shared access to resources. The Common Internet File System (CIFS) protocol is a dialect of SMB. It is primarily used in Windows systems. The latest version is 3.1.1, which was released to support Windows 10 and Windows Server 2016. It operates as a client-server application. It uses port 445.

427 – SLP

Service Location Protocol (SLP) is a service discovery protocol that allows computers and other devices to find services in a local area network. It has been defined in RFC 2608 and RFC 3224 as standards-track documents. All devices are required to listen on port 427 for UDP packets.

548 – AFP

Apple Filing Protocol (AFP) is a proprietary resource-sharing protocol by Apple, one of several it supports. It uses port 548 for communication. The latest version, 3.4, was introduced with the OS Mountain Lion system.

67/68 – DHCP

Dynamic Host Configuration Protocol (DHCP) serves a useful purpose of issuing IP addresses and other network-related configuration values to clients to allow them to operate on the network. It uses ports 67 and 68.

389 – LDAP

Lightweight Directory Access Protocol (LDAP) is a protocol that provides a mechanism to access and query directory services systems. These systems are most likely to be Microsoft's Active Directory but could also be Novell Directory Services (NDS). Although LDAP supports command-line queries executed directly against the directory database, most LDAP interactions are via utilities such as an authentication program (network logon) or a search engine that locates a resource in the directory. LDAP uses port 389.

161/162 – SNMP

Simple Network Management Protocol (SNMP) is a protocol that facilitates network management functionality. It is not, in itself, a network management system (NMS); it is simply the protocol that makes NMS possible. It uses ports 161 and 162.

TCP vs. UDP

Operating at the transport layer of the TCP/IP stack are two key protocols: Transmission Control Protocol and User Datagram Protocol. The biggest difference between these two is that one is connection based (TCP) and the other works in the absence of a dedicated connection (UDP). Both are needed and serve key roles.

If you are sending credit card information to a website, you need a dedicated connection between your host and the server, so TCP handles that task. An example of UDP is DHCP. When a client sends a request for any DHCP server listening to give it an address, it is not requiring a dedicated communication.

Exam essentials

Know the default ports.   There are a number of protocols whose default ports you need to know: FTP (20/21), Telnet (23), SMTP (25), DNS (53), HTTP (80), POP3 (110), IMAP (143), HTTPS (443), and RDP (3389).

Know what the protocols do.   In addition to the protocols for which ports are given, know DHCP, DNS, LDAP, SNMP, SMB, CIFS, SSH, and AFP.

2.2 Compare and contrast common networking hardware devices.

To make a network, you need a number of devices. The most common of those devices are tested on the A+ exam and discussed in this section. Networks are built using multiple devices. For those covered in this section, you should know enough to be able to answer questions about their functions and features on the exam. Topics covered include these:

- Routers
- Switches
- Access points
- Cloud-based network controller
- Firewall
- Network interface card
- Repeater
- Hub
- Cable/DSL modem
- Bridge
- Patch panel
- Power over Ethernet (PoE)
- Ethernet over Power

Routers

A router is used to connect LANs; you can even use a router to connect dissimilar topologies that use the same protocol, because physical specifications don't apply. A router can be a dedicated hardware device or a computer system with more than one network interface and the appropriate routing software. All modern network operating systems include the functionality to act as a router.

Switches

Like routers, switches are the connectivity points of an Ethernet network. Devices connect to switches via twisted-pair cabling, one cable for each device. The difference between hubs and switches is in how the devices deal with the data they receive. Whereas a hub forwards the data it receives to all the ports on the device, a switch forwards it to only the port that connects to the destination device. It does this by learning the Media Access Control (MAC) address of the devices attached to it and then matching the destination MAC address in the data it receives.

Managed

Managed switches are those used in an enterprise network. These switches can be configured with advanced features such as virtual LANs (VLANs), discussed under objective 2.6

later in this chapter, and EtherChannel links. They are managed remotely, using either a command-line interface or in some cases a GUI management interface.

Unmanaged

Unmanaged switches are those that cannot be managed remotely; and while they can provide basic switching services (full duplex service and the like), they cannot be configured with the more advanced services of a managed switch.

Access points

Access points (APs) are transmitter and receiver (transceiver) devices used to create a wireless LAN (WLAN). An AP is typically a separate network device with a built-in antenna, transmitter, and adapter. APs use the wireless infrastructure network mode to provide a connection point between WLANs and a wired Ethernet LAN. APs also typically have several ports, giving you a way to expand the network to support additional clients.

Depending on the size of the network, one or more APs might be required. Additional APs are used to allow access to more wireless clients and to expand the range of the wireless network. Each AP is limited by a transmission range—the distance a client can be from an AP and still obtain a usable signal. The actual distance depends on the wireless standard being used and the obstructions and environmental conditions between the client and the AP.

Cloud-based network controller

The new paradigm in networking is to move the intelligence from the routers, switches, and access points to a cloud-based network controller. Software-defined networking uses a controller to manage all the routing switching and wireless control while the devices simply handle data forwarding.

Firewall

A firewall is a server that sits between the internal network and the rest of the world (or between a public and private network) and filters what goes between the two. While the filtering can be done on programs, most firewalls are created on ports since applications and protocols use ports that are recognized. *Open* ports are those that allow traffic, whereas *closed* ports are those that block traffic. The firewall can be software- or hardware-based, and most incorporate both. The firewall may incorporate a proxy, a gateway, and a filter.

Network interface card

Network interface cards (NICs) are expansion cards that are installed into slots in a desktop computer. These cards connect the computer to a network. In most cases today, devices large and small have integrated or built-in network interfaces.

Repeater

A repeater or extender is a device that regenerates any signal that goes through it. It can be used to extend a cable run that exceeds the maximum allowable distance. For example, if you needed to run a cable with a maximum allowable length of 100 meters for 150 meters, you could put a repeater between two 75-meter lengths of cable, and the problem would be solved. Figure 2.1 illustrates the use of a repeater.

FIGURE 2.1 Repeater

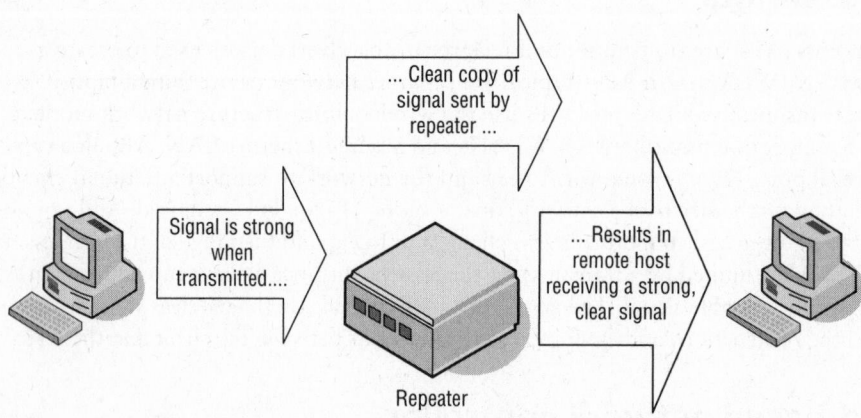

Hub

Hubs are used in networks that use twisted-pair cabling to connect devices, and they can be used to join segments into larger networks. A hub directs data packets to all devices connected to it, regardless of whether the data package is destined for the device. This makes them inefficient by nature and can create a performance bottleneck on busy networks. In its most basic form, a hub does nothing except provide a pathway for the electrical signals to travel along. Such a device is called a *passive* hub. Far more common nowadays is an *active* hub, which, as well as providing a path for the data signals, regenerates the signal before it forwards it to all the connected devices. In addition, an active hub can buffer data before forwarding it. However, a hub does not perform any processing on the data it forwards, nor does it perform any error checking.

Cable/DSL modem

A modem, short for "modulator/demodulator," is a device that converts the digital signals generated by a computer into analog signals that can travel over conventional phone lines.

The modem at the receiving end converts the signal back into a format that the computer can understand. Modems can be used to connect to an ISP or as a mechanism for dialing up a LAN.

Cable and DSL modems, however, are not true modems in that they do not convert between analog and digital. These devices are really systems that take the information and place it on either the cable or DSL network so the ISP can transfer it to the Internet and back.

Bridge

Bridges are used to divide larger networks into smaller sections. Bridges accomplish this by sitting between two physical network segments and managing the flow of data between the two. By looking at the MAC address of the devices connected to each segment, bridges can elect to forward the data (if they believe that the destination address is on another interface) or block it from crossing (if they can verify that it is on the interface from which it came).

Patch panel

A *patch panel* is a device to which the cables running through the walls from the hosts are connected. Then shorter cables called *patch cables* run from the patch panel to the switch or hub. Figure 2.2 shows three types of patch panels.

FIGURE 2.2   Patch panels

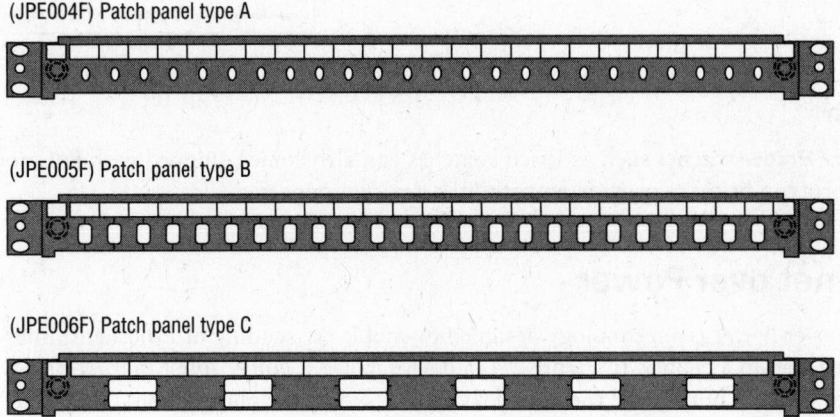

(JPE004F) Patch panel type A

(JPE005F) Patch panel type B

(JPE006F) Patch panel type C

Power over Ethernet (PoE)

Many times when installing devices, the device needs to be located far from an available power outlet. On switches that support Power over Ethernet (PoE), the switch can supply power on the same data cable used to connect to the device. So if you get the device within 100 meters of a switch, you can eliminate the need to install costly power outlets.

Injectors

A PoE injector is a device that can be used to provide PoE to a device when the switch does not support PoE. It plugs into the wall; then a line providing data and PoE is run to the device, and another cable runs to the switch, as shown in Figure 2.3.

FIGURE 2.3 Power over Ethernet

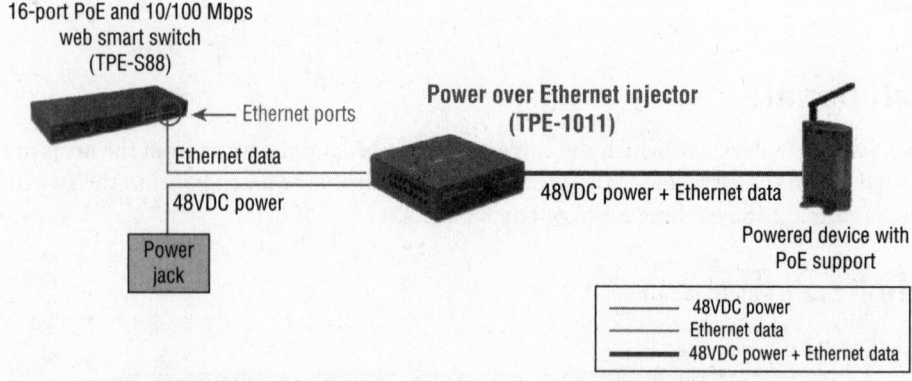

Switch

Enterprise-grade switches such as Cisco switches can also come equipped with PoE ports. These ports can be set to provide power to the devices connected.

Ethernet over Power

Ethernet over Power is a technology designed to enable the sending of Ethernet frames over the power lines in a facility. In Figure 2.4, a device called a *power line Ethernet bridge* plugs into the wall outlet, and then the devices or a switch are plugged into the bridge. This eliminates the need to install costly power outlets and leverages the existing power lines in the building.

FIGURE 2.4   Ethernet over Power

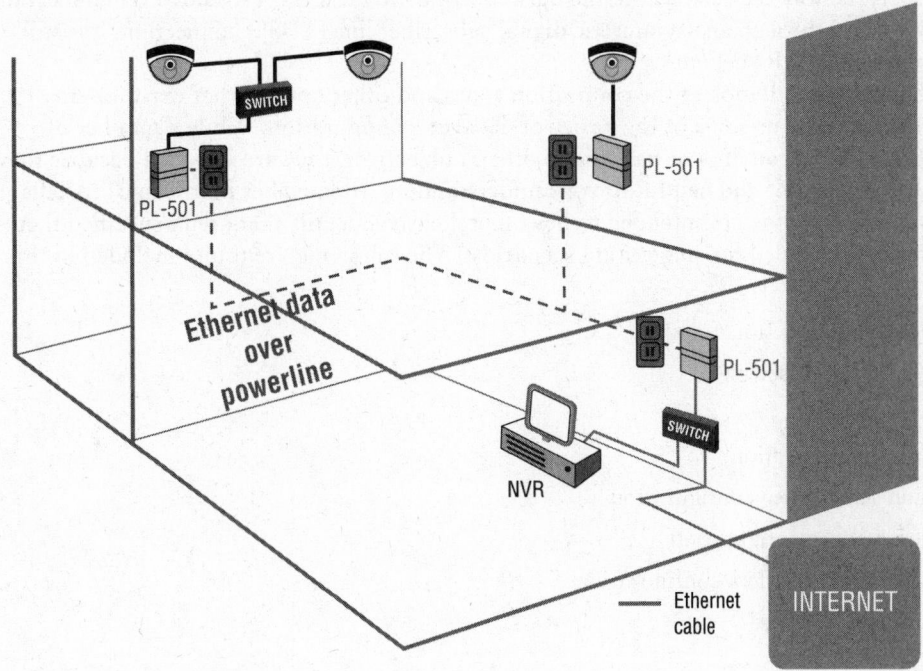

Exam essentials

Know the two types of hubs.   Hubs can be passive or active. If the hub does nothing except provide a pathway for the electrical signals to travel along, it is passive. It if regenerates the signal, it is considered active.

Be able to recognize a firewall.   A firewall is a server that sits between the internal network and the rest of the world and filters what goes between the two.

2.3 Given a scenario, install and configure a basic wired/wireless SOHO network.

Small office and home office (SOHO) networks can be created easily today and relatively inexpensively. You can choose to do so with or without wires. While there isn't a hard-and-fast rule on what the limit is for a SOHO network, the term is generally used for networks of 10 or fewer workstations.

One of the biggest differences between SOHO networks and larger local area networks (LANs) is the way they connect to the outside world. While a LAN would never connect in today's world through an asymmetric digital subscriber line (ADSL) connection, it is still common in a SOHO network.

This section will look at the connection types and other options that exist for small networks, as well as some of the basics of network configuration. While a number of topics in this section are not part of the official objectives, they are included because they are both important and helpful to your understanding. (Remember that CompTIA tells us its objective list is not intended to be comprehensive; details that aren't specified there might still be needed for some exam scenarios.) The following are topics included in this section:

- Router/switch functionality
- Access point settings
- IP addressing
- NIC configuration
- End-user device configuration
- IoT device configuration
- Cable/DSL modem configuration
- Firewall settings
- QoS
- Wireless settings

Router/switch functionality

First, let's consider the physical layout. In a SOHO it is quite likely that the router and the switch are one device and will also have wireless capability. The router/switch will have two IP addresses: one public, received from the ISP, and a private address used to connect to the internal network. The router/switch will also have a DHCP server that supplies IP configurations to the computers. Finally, the router/switch will perform network address translation so that Internet access is possible. When the router/switch is provided by the ISP, the SOHO admin may not have to configure any of this.

Access point settings

The router/switch will also contain a built-in WLAN access point. You as admin may or may not have to configure this. If you do, you must select a Service Set Identifier (SSID), which is a name for the WLAN. You also must ensure that DHCP is functional on the wireless side, as connecting devices will need an IP address. If you choose to broadcast the SSID (which is the default), users will need no wireless profile created. They will simply select the SSID when available networks appear. If, however, you choose to hide the SSID, each user will require the creation manually of a wireless profile that specifies the SSID.

IP addressing

If you're not using DHCP on the router/switch, you'll have to configure the IP addresses of the computers manually. When you do this, ensure the following:

- Each wired interface needs to have an IP address in the same network with the address of the router Ethernet address. Also, the default gateway needs to be set to the address of the router. Finally configure the IP address of the DNS server so name resolution can occur.

- Each wireless interface needs to have an IP address in the same network with the address of the router/switch wireless interface. Also, the default gateway needs to be set to that same address. Finally, configure the IP address of the DNS server so that name resolution can occur.

Note that the requirements are the same for wired and wireless interfaces.

NIC configuration

The end user device will need to have the network interface, either wired or wireless, configured to operate on the network. The most common configuration dialog box is that in Windows 10, shown in Figure 2.5. Other operating systems are quite similar.

FIGURE 2.5   The Windows 10 dialog for configuring a NIC

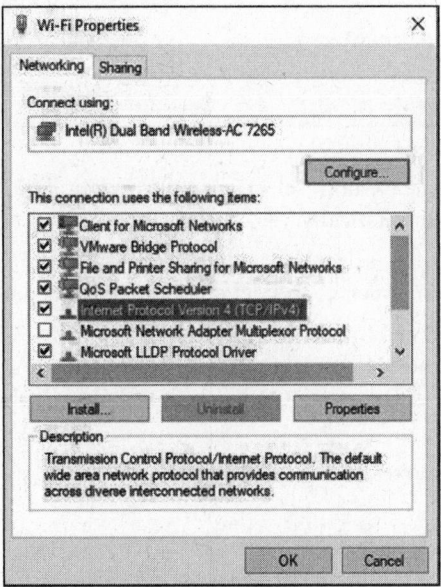

Wired

As a representative procedure, you would take the following steps to configure a NIC in Windows 10:

1. Start by navigating to Control Panel ➤ Network And Internet ➤ Network And Sharing Center ➤ Change Adapter Settings.

2. Right-click the interface you would like to configure and select Properties. You will see the dialog box in Figure 2.5.

3. Highlight Internet protocol version 4 and select Properties. You will see the dialog box in Figure 2.6.

FIGURE 2.6   TCP/IP Properties dialog box

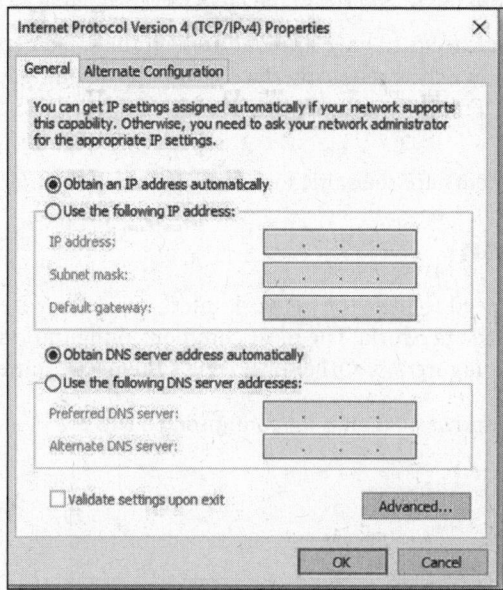

4. If using a DHCP server, leave both selections as shown in Figure 2.6 to obtain IP and DNS server addresses automatically.

5. If using static IP addressing, select the radio button Use The Following IP Address and enter the IP address, subnet mask, and default gateway. The gateway address should be the IP address of the router.

6. In the bottom section, select Use The Following DNS Server Address and enter the IP address of the DNS server. In a SOHO, this will probably be the address of the router/ switch.

7. Click OK on all dialog boxes as you close them.

Wireless

Configuring the IP configuration on the wireless NIC will be the same as just described for the wired NIC.

End-user device configuration

In most cases, you will be using a DHCP server, the one provided by the router/switch. Once the devices are set to operate on the network, some additional setup may be required.

Installation of antivirus software

Follow the documentation that came with the antivirus software and ensure not only that is it installed but that you check for one of two types of updates, either AV engine updates or virus signature updates. Finally, ensure that all systems are set for automatic updates.

Enable the Windows firewall

If your antivirus has a firewall, you can use that, but you also use the Windows Firewall. Go to Control Panel ➤ All Control Panel Items ➤ Security And Maintenance. Select the drop-down arrow next to Security to expand that section. Under Network Firewall, ensure that Windows Firewall is ON.

Install applications

Typically, there will be a set of applications that need to be installed. Follow the directions to install them, always ensuring that you have a software license for each installation. Make sure you use the application's update feature to check whether the application needs any updates. Often the installation file you have is for an older version. Patching applications prior to use is important!

IoT device configuration

If you don't already have an Internet of Things (IoT) device in your home or office, you probably will soon. These are any devices that can be connected to the SOHO network and managed from a smartphone or desktop application.

Thermostat

When IoT-enabled thermostats are installed, they connect to the local wireless network. At some point during their configuration, you will enter the SSID of the network and the password or key. For example, Nest, one of the most popular systems, will display a home screen after the first time you power the system on after wiring it up. (Be sure to follow the manufacturer's directions.) The system will prompt you for language, wireless information, and other settings covering how high and how low you want the temperature to range and whether you want heat, air conditioning, or auto. When the installation is complete, install the app on your phone and follow the directions there for connecting to your thermostat.

Light switches

Lighting systems can also be IoT-enabled. Many of today's systems can be controlled by your personal assistant (Alexa, Cortana, and similar devices). Kasa is a company that makes plugs you introduce between the light and the power outlet that communicate wirelessly with your wireless network. You install a smartphone app and use that to control the light from anywhere you have the Internet!

Security cameras

Security camera systems that can be managed over the Internet are also available and use a smartphone app much like the light switch and thermostat. These systems come with a video recorder to record video for later viewing. After the wireless cameras are physically placed and installed, they typically link up with the video system upon startup. After installing the smart phone app, you can manage and view the cameras from anywhere you have Internet. Follow the specific directions from your system.

Door locks

Smart door locks replace the manual lock system in doors and can be managed remotely. They communicate wirelessly with your network and in some cases may be part of a total package that includes security system and lights. After physical installation of the lock assembly in the doors, follow the directions in the system to install the smartphone app, connect to the doors, and manage the locks.

Voice-enabled, smart speaker/digital assistant

Smart speakers that fulfill your commands are an extension of the digital assistants found in many operating systems today. Alexa, Cortana, and other digital assistants are installed in the speaker. Installing one of these is usually just a matter of turning it on and going through some prompts to enter the wireless network's SSID and password. Then you're up and running.

Cable/DSL modem configuration

Cable and DSL modems typically come from the ISP with the configuration ready. Once you plug them into the wall they will make the connection to the central office. While the device may have a small number of ports, you may need to connect a switch to the device if more ports are needed. In most cases the device will also act as your WLAN AP as well. Let's look at a bit more about these two technologies.

Cable

Two of the most popular methods of connecting to the Internet today are using DSL and cable. Instead of the service coming from a telephone company as with DSL, cable service is provided by the cable provider, and a *cable modem* is used. While speeds vary based on the number of users the cable company is servicing, as a general rule cable-based broadband service is faster than DSL.

DSL

Digital Subscriber Line (DSL) uses existing phone lines with a DSL modem and a network card. A standard RJ-45 connector is used to connect the network card to the DSL modem, and a phone cord with RJ-11 connectors is used to connect the DSL modem to the phone jack. Multiple types of DSL exist; the most popular are *high bit-rate DSL* (HDSL), *symmetric DSL* (SDSL), *very high bit-rate DSL* (VHDSL), *rate-adaptive DSL* (RADSL), and *asymmetric DSL* (ADSL). The latter provides slower upload than download speed and is the most common for home use. While speeds may vary depending on the quality of the connection and the equipment used, Table 2.1 shows the most common upload and download speeds for the various flavors of DSL.

TABLE 2.1   DSL speeds

Type	Upload	Download
ADSL	1 Mbps	8 Mbps
ADSL2	1.3 Mbps	12 Mbps
ADSL2+	1.3 Mbps	24 Mbps
SDSL	4.5 Mbps	4.5 Mbps
VHDSL	3 Mbps ·	55 Mbps

Firewall settings

When configuring a firewall for a SOHO, there are a number of features of which you can take advantage. In this section we'll look at these techniques.

DMZ

The networking equivalent of a security zone is a network security zone. It performs the same function. If you divide a network into smaller sections, each zone can have its own security considerations and measures—just like a physical security zone. This arrangement allows layers of security to be built around sensitive information. The division of the network is accomplished by implementing virtual LANs (VLANs) or instituting demilitarized zones (DMZs).

A *demilitarized zone* is an area where you can place a public server for access by people you might not trust otherwise. By isolating a server in a DMZ, you can hide or remove access to other areas of your network. You can still access the server using your network, but others aren't able to access network resources outside the DMZ. This can be accomplished using firewalls to isolate your network.

When establishing a DMZ, you assume that the person accessing the resource isn't necessarily someone you would trust with other information. By keeping the rest of the network hidden from external users, this lowers the threat of intrusion in the internal network.

Any time you want to separate public information from private information, a DMZ is an acceptable option.

The easiest way to create a DMZ is to use a firewall that can transmit in three directions.

- To the internal network

- To the external world (Internet)

- To the public information you're sharing (the DMZ)

From there, you can decide what traffic goes where; for example, HTTP traffic would be sent to the DMZ, and email would go to the internal network.

Port forwarding

A firewall can be hardware- or software-based. At its simplest, firewall configuration is accomplished by configuring ports and rules. A *port* is an interface that is used to connect to a device and is identified by number. Throughout this book, many well-known ports are discussed by their number (SMTP on port 25, for example).

When you use a service, the default port is implied, but you can always change the *port assignment* if you want to increase security. For example, when you attempt to connect to a website, you'll use port 80 by default. (A socket is the combination of the IP address and the port number. If you were accessing a website at 192.168.0.100, the combination of these two elements would give you a socket; the full address and port description would then be 192.168.0.100:80.)

The assignment can be changed so that a server offers the web service at a port other than the default, such as 8080. If that is done, the client can access the service by specifying the socket: `http://192.168.0.100:8080`.

Port forwarding (also known as port mapping) is the act of mapping one port to another. This is essentially the same as what NAT does, and it allows external users to access the private LAN. This is useful when you want to allow only some external users (partners, for example) to be able to access the network resources remotely. These ports can be left open all the time or turned on only when needed. If the latter is the case, this is known as *port triggering*. With triggering, an inbound attempt at connection triggers the opening of an outbound port, and communication is now possible. Obviously, the trigger is activated only after all authentication measures have been successfully met.

Another aspect of firewall configuration is the establishment of rules. The *rules* are criteria given for what is allowed to pass through or connect to the network. These rules are typically accept- or deny-based (but can be configured to include exceptions). For example, you may choose to deny all connections except those specifically allowed; this is much better than the alternative of allowing all except those specifically denied, which creates a security nightmare.

Rules can typically be created based on the following:

- Direction, which can be inbound or outbound

- Protocol source, which can be either TCP (connection-based) or UDP (connectionless)

- Address source

- Port

- Destination address
- Destination port

If you want to limit all of any one criterion—for example, all destination ports—most firewalls allow you to use the value any for this purpose.

NAT

Network address translation (NAT) creates a unique opportunity to assist in the security of a network. Originally, NAT extended the number of usable Internet addresses. Now it allows an organization to present a single address to the Internet for all computer connections. The NAT server provides IP addresses to the hosts or systems in the network and tracks inbound and outbound traffic. NAT is covered more completely later in this chapter.

UPnP

Universal Plug and Play (UPnP) is a protocol that lets computers, printers, and other devices make themselves easily discoverable to a network router. Promoted by the UPnP Forum, a computer industry initiative, it is available on many wireless APs and routers. While it makes it easier to connect devices, it does have security issues.

In several studies it has been shown that more than 6,900 network-aware products from 1,500 companies at 81 million IP addresses responded to their discovery requests on the Internet. Depending on the security posture of the device, many of those devices can be accessed or manipulated. For this reason, many have called for disabling this feature on wireless routers or APs.

Whitelist/blacklist

In whitelisting, a list of acceptable email addresses, Internet addresses, websites, applications, or some other identifier is configured as good senders or as allowed. Blacklisting identifies bad senders. Graylisting is somewhere in between the two, listing entities that cannot be identified as whitelist or blacklist items. The new entity must then pass through a series of tests to determine whether it will be whitelisted or blacklisted.

Whitelisting, blacklisting, and graylisting are techniques commonly implemented with spam-filtering tools.

MAC filtering

Many security devices allow you to create and enforce a MAC address filter. While this is a security mechanism technically, you should not rely on this solely because it is possible to use a sniffer to derive an allowed address and adopt that address, defeating the MAC filter.

QoS

Quality of Service (QoS) describes the strategies used to manage the flow of network traffic. A network administrator can use QoS to manage the amount of bandwidth provided to applications that are latency-sensitive (those that don't function well with lags—voice and video, for example).

One way QoS accomplishes this is by prioritizing latency-sensitive applications over latency-insensitive ones and then doing priority queuing. Traffic is placed in order based on its importance on delivery time. All data is given access, but the more important and latency-sensitive data is given higher priority.

Wireless settings

SOHO networks can be created easily today and relatively inexpensively. You can choose to do so with or without wires. While there isn't a hard-and-fast rule on what the limit is for a SOHO network, the term is generally used for networks of 10 or fewer workstations.

One of the biggest differences between SOHO networks and larger LANs is the way they connect to the outside world. While a LAN would never connect in today's world through an ADSL connection, it is still common in a SOHO network.

This section will look at the connection types and possibilities that exist for small networks, as well as some of the basics of network configuration.

Encryption

There are a number of wireless encryption mechanisms you need to know for the A+ exam. These are WEP, WPA, WPA2, TKIP, and AES.

Let's take a closer look at each.

WEP   *Wired Equivalent Privacy* (WEP) is a standard that was created as a first stab at security for wireless devices. Using WEP-encrypted data to provide data security has always been under scrutiny for not being as secure as initially intended. WEP is vulnerable because of weaknesses in the way the encryption algorithms are employed. These weaknesses allow the algorithm to potentially be cracked in as few as five minutes using available PC software. This makes WEP one of the most vulnerable protocols available for security.

WPA   The *WiFi Protected Access* (WPA) and *WiFi Protected Access 2* (WPA2) technologies were designed to address the core problems with WEP. These technologies implement the 802.11i standard. The difference between WPA and WPA2 is that the former implements most—but not all—of 802.11i in order to be able to communicate with older wireless cards (which might still need an update through their firmware to be compliant), while WPA2 implements the full standard and is not compatible with older cards.

WPA2   WPA2 implements the full 802.11i standard for security and is not compatible with older wireless cards.

Personal and Enterprise

Both WPA and WPA2 come in an Enterprise version and a personal version. The Enterprise versions use RADIUS for authentication, while the personal versions can use passwords or preshared keys.

TKIP WPA was able to increase security by using a *Temporal Key Integrity Protocol* (TKIP) to scramble encryption keys using a hashing algorithm. The keys are issued an integrity check to verify they have not been modified or tampered with during transit. While a good solution, it was far from perfect. Corporate security today favors WPA2 since it replaces TKIP with Counter Mode with Cipher Block Chaining Message Authentication Code Protocol (CCMP).

AES CCMP uses 128-bit Advanced Encryption Security (AES) with a 48-bit initialization vector, making it much more difficult to crack and minimizing the risk of a replay attack.

> Never assume that a wireless connection is secure. The emissions from a wireless portal may be detectable through walls and for several blocks from the portal. Interception is easy to accomplish, given that RF is the medium used for communication. Newer wireless devices offer data security, and you should use it. You can set newer WAPs and wireless routers to nonbroadcast. This is also sometimes called *disabling the broadcast* of the SSID. Given the choice, you should choose to use WPA2, WPA, or WEP at its highest encryption level in that order.

Channels

Wireless routers can be set to use different channels, which are numbered 1 through 11 (1, 6, and 11 are those commonly used in the United States) for the 2.4 GHz band. Each channel represents a different frequency. You can change the channel to avoid interference—either from another network nearby or from devices also using that frequency.

The channel change is made only on the router because each client should automatically detect and change to the new channel. If you locate APs close to one another they should be on different channels to prevent them interfering with one another.

QoS

Quality of Service (QoS), as described earlier, may be possible to configure on the wireless router. Refer to documentation with the router.

Exam essentials

Know the difference between port forwarding and port triggering. Port forwarding is the act of mapping one port to another (essentially the same as what NAT does). Port triggering involves turning on ports only when they are needed.

Understand MAC filtering. When MAC filtering is implemented, you identify each host by this number and determine specifically which addresses are allowed to access the network.

2.4 Compare and contrast wireless networking protocols.

More and more, networks are using wireless as the medium of choice. It is much easier to implement, reconfigure, upgrade, and use than wired networks. Unfortunately, there can be downsides, with security being one of the largest.

The 802.11 standard applies to wireless networking, and there have been many versions/types of it released; the main ones are a, b, g, and n. Encryption has gone from very weak (WEP) to much stronger with increments along the way, including WPA, WPA2, and implementations of TKIP and AES.

The IEEE 802.11x family of protocols provides for wireless communications using radio frequency transmissions. The frequencies in use for 802.11 standards are the 2.4 GHz and 5 GHz frequency spectrums. Several standards and bandwidths have been defined for use in wireless environments, and they aren't extremely compatible with each other. Topics included in this section are as follows:

- 802.11a
- 802.11b
- 802.11g
- 802.11n
- 802.11ac
- Frequencies
- Channels
- Bluetooth
- NFC
- RFID
- Zigbee
- Z-Wave
- 3G
- 4G
- 5G
- LTE

802.11a

The 802.11a standard provides wireless LAN bandwidth of up to 54 Mbps in the 5 GHz frequency spectrum. The 802.11a standard also uses orthogonal frequency division multiplexing (OFDM) for encoding rather than Frequency Hopping Spread Spectrum (FHSS) or Direct Sequence Spread Spectrum (DSSS).

802.11b

The 802.11b standard provides for bandwidths of up to 11 Mbps (with fallback rates of 5.5, 2, and 1 Mbps) in the 2.4 GHz frequency spectrum. This standard is also called WiFi or 802.11 high rate. The 802.11b standard uses only DSSS for data encoding.

802.11g

The 802.11g standard operates in the 2.4 GHz frequency spectrum. This offers a maximum rate of 54 Mbps and is backward compatible with 802.11b.

802.11n

The goal of the 802.11n standard is to significantly increase throughput in both the 2.4 GHz and 5 GHz frequency ranges. The baseline goal of the standard was to reach speeds of 100 Mbps, but given the right conditions, it is estimated that the 802.11n speeds might be able to reach 600 Mbps. In practical operation, 802.11n speeds will be much slower.

802.11n achieves some of the higher speeds by using multiple antennas on the AP and station, a feature called Multiple In /Multiple Out (MIMO).

802.11ac

The 802.11ac standard builds upon the features of 802.11n and improves on them in the following ways:

- Wider channels (40 MHz, 80 MHz, and 160 MHz)
- New modulation (256 Quadrature amplitude modulation [QAM], which has the potential to provide a 30 percent increase in speed)
- More spatial streams (up to eight spatial streams)
- Improved MIMO and beamforming with the use of multiuser MIMO, allowing an AP to transmit a signal to multiple client stations on the same channel simultaneously if the client stations are in different physical areas

With 802.11ac, which operates only in the 5 GHz frequency range, it is possible to achieve a data rate of almost 2 Gbps if the AP and the station have enough antennas.

Frequencies: 2.4, 5.0

Table 2.2 compares the speed, distance, and frequency of each of the 802.11 standards.

TABLE 2.2   Comparison of 802.11 standards

Standard	Speed	Distance (indoors)	Frequency
802.11a	Up to 54 Mbps	Up to 115 feet	5 GHz
802.11b	Up to 11 Mbps	Up to 115 feet	2.4 GHz
802.11g	Up to 54 Mbps	Up to 125 feet	2.4 GHz
802.11n	Up to 600 Mbps	Up to 380 feet	2.4 GHz/5 GHz
802.11ac	Up to 6.9 Gbps	Up to 115 feet	5 GHz

Channels (1–11)

The use of wireless router channels was discussed in the earlier section "Channels," under objective 2.3.

Bluetooth

Bluetooth is a short-range wireless protocol that uses FHSS. Bluetooth is covered in the section "Bluetooth" in Chapter 1, "Mobile Devices."

NFC

Near field communications (NFC) is a wireless technology that allows smartphones and other equipped devices to communicate when very near one another or when touching. NFC is covered in Chapter 1 in the section "NFC."

RFID

Radio frequency identification (RFID) is a wireless, no-contact technology that makes use of NFC technology. RFID uses radio frequency chips and readers to manage inventory. The chips are placed on individual pieces or pallets of inventory. RFID readers are placed throughout the location to communicate with the chips. Identification and location information are collected as part of the RFID communication. Organizations can customize the information that is stored on an RFID chip to suit their needs.

Two types of RFID systems can be deployed: active reader/passive tag (ARPT) and active reader/active tag (ARAT). In an ARPT system, the active reader transmits signals and receives replies from passive tags. In an ARAT system, active tags are awoken with signals from the active reader.

RFID chips can be read only if they are within a certain proximity of the RFID reader. Different RFID systems are available for different wireless frequencies. If your organization decides to implement RFID, it is important that you fully research the advantages and disadvantages of different frequencies.

Zigbee

IEEE 802.15.4 is a standard for a wireless technology called Zigbee. It is intended to be a simpler approach to personal area networks (PANs) such as those that Bluetooth technology addresses. It provides a wireless ad hoc network that uses only low power, although it provides only a low data rate and requires close proximity (personal area).

Zigbee is designed for wireless light switches, home energy monitors, traffic management systems, and other consumer and industrial devices that require short-range low-rate wireless data transfer. Zigbee has a defined rate of 250 kbps, best suited for intermittent data transmissions from a sensor or input device.

Z-Wave

Operating in the 800–900 MHz frequency range, Z-Wave is a wireless communications protocol used primarily for home automation. Its wireless mesh networking technology enables any node to talk to adjacent nodes directly or indirectly, controlling any additional nodes. Z-Wave has an open-air operating range at 300 feet (outdoor) and 80+ feet (indoor).

3G

Third generation, or 3G, is a cellular phone technology. It introduced web browsing, email, video downloading, picture sharing, and other smartphone technologies. 3G should be capable of handling around 2 Mbps.

4G

Fourth generation, or 4G, is a later cellular technology that specifies 100 Mbps and up to 1 Gbps to pass as 4G. Outside of the covered areas, 4G phones regress to the 3G standards.

LTE

Long-Term Evolution (LTE) is based on the Global System for Mobile Communications/ Enhanced Data rates for GSM Evolution (GSM/EDGE) and Universal Mobile

Telecommunications System/High Speed Packet Access (UMTS/HSPA) technologies. It does not meet the technical criteria of a 4G wireless service, as specified in the 3GPP Release 8 and 9 document series for LTE Advanced. The ITU later decided that LTE, together with certain technologies, can be called 4G technologies. The theoretical greatest speed is up to 150 Mbps.

5G

With speeds of up to 100 gigabits per second, 5G will be as much as 1,000 times faster than 4G, the latest iteration of mobile data technology. It will provide greater network stability to ensure that business-critical mobile functions do not go offline and have the speed necessary to give employees a fully equipped virtual office almost anywhere. Verizon currently offers 5G broadband Internet in the Houston, Sacramento, Indianapolis, and Los Angeles areas.

Exam essentials

Understand wired and wireless connectivity.   Networks work the same whether there is a physical wire between the hosts or that wire has been replaced by a wireless signal. The same order of operations and steps are carried out regardless of the medium employed.

Know the capabilities and limitations of the 802.11x network standards.   The current standards for wireless protocols are 802.11, 802.11a, 802.11b, 802.11g, 802.11n, and 802.11ac.

2.5 Summarize the properties and purposes of services provided by networked hosts.

To configure and provide service to a network, you must be versed in the various roles that servers may play in the network. Armed with this knowledge, you can better ensure the proper function of these servers. There will also be a number of other network devices and appliances. This section will look at both topics. The subobjectives covered in this section include the following:

- Server roles
- Internet appliances
- Legacy/embedded systems

Server roles

Servers are computers that provide some type of shared service to the hosts on the network. There are many roles that servers can play, but this section will discuss some of the more common server roles, focusing on those you are most likely to find in your network.

Web server

Web servers are used to provide access to information for users connecting to the server using a web browser, which is the client part of the application. The browser uses HTTP as its transfer mechanism. These servers can be either contained within a network and are available only within the network (called an *intranet server*) or connected to the Internet where they can be reached from anywhere. To provide security, a web server can be configured to require and use HTTPS, which uses SSL to encrypt the connection with no effort on the part of the user.

File server

File servers are used to store files that can be accessed by the users in the network. Typically, users are encouraged or even required to store any important data on these servers rather than on their local hard drives because these servers are typically backed up on a regular basis, whereas the user machines typically are not. These servers will have significant amounts of storage space and may even have multiple hard drives configured in a RAID (redundant array of independent disks) system to provide quicker recovery from a drive crash than could be provided by recovering with the backup.

Print server

Print servers are used to manage printers, and in cases where that is their only role, they will manage multiple printers. This type of server provides the spooler service to the printers that it manages, and when you view the print queue, you are viewing it on the print server. Many enterprise printers come with a built-in print server, which makes using a dedicated machine for the role unnecessary.

DHCP server

As discussed throughout this chapter, DHCP servers are used to automate the process of providing an IP configuration to devices in the network. These servers respond to broadcast-based requests for a configuration by offering an IP address, subnet mask, and default gateway to the DHCP client. While these options provide basic network connectivity, many other options can also be provided, such as the IP address of a TFTP server that IP phones can contact to download a configuration file.

DNS server

DNS servers resolve device and domain names (website names) to IP addresses, and vice versa. They make it possible to connect to either without knowing the IP address of the device or of the server hosting the website. Clients are configured with the IP address of a DNS server (usually through DHCP) and make requests of the server using what are called *queries*. The organization's DNS server will be configured to perform the lookup of IP addresses for which it has no entry in its database by making requests of the DNS servers on the Internet, which are organized in a hierarchy that allows these servers to more efficiently provide the answer. When they have completed their lookup, they return the IP address to the client so the client can make a direct connection using the IP address.

Proxy server

A proxy server is one that makes Internet connections on behalf of users in a network. In doing so, it prevents them from making direct connections to the Internet and provides a point of exit at which you can control their access in a variety of ways. For example, you may allow certain users to have complete access to the Internet with no restrictions, while other groups of users may be restricted in the sites they can visit and the activities in which they may participate.

An additional feature of these servers is their role in web caching. Web caching is the process of retrieving a web page for a user and then caching that web page so that another request for the page by the same users or other users can be served locally without returning to the Internet to retrieve the page. It results in faster page retrievals in cases where the page has been cached.

Mail server

Mail servers run email server software and use SMTP to send and receive email on behalf of users who possess mailboxes on the server. Those users will use a client email protocol to retrieve their email from the server. Two of the most common are POP3, which is a retrieve-only protocol, and IMAP4, which has more functionality and can be used to manage the email on the server.

Authentication server

An authentication server is one that accepts and verifies the credentials of users. Typically, it not only authenticates them but also provides them with access to resources using single sign-on. Single sign-on allows a user to authenticate once and *not* be required to authenticate again to access the resources to which they have been given access. One of the best examples of this is a domain controller in a Windows Active Directory domain. These servers are the point to which all users are directed when they need to log in to the network.

Syslog

All infrastructure devices such as firewalls, routers, and switches have logs where events of various types are recorded. These logs can contain information valuable for troubleshooting both security and performance of systems. You can direct these event messages to a central server, called a *syslog server*. By doing so, you create a single system for access to all event logs. A syslog server also makes it easier to correlate events on various devices by combining the events into a single log. To ensure proper sequencing of events, all devices should have their time synchronized from a single source using a Network Time Protocol (NTP) server.

Internet appliances

Beyond the roles that you can assign to servers by installing server software, there are network appliances that are dedicated to performing particular functions. In many cases, they perform better than a similar product that is software-based. This section will look at several of the most common ones.

UTM

Unified threat management (UTM) is an approach that involves performing multiple security functions within the same device or appliance. The functions may include the following:

- Network firewalling
- Network intrusion prevention
- Gateway antivirus
- Gateway antispam
- VPN
- Content filtering
- Load balancing
- Data leak prevention
- On-appliance reporting

UTM makes administering multiple systems unnecessary. However, some feel that UTM creates a single point of failure and instead favor creating multiple layers of devices as a more secure approach.

IDS

An intrusion detection system (IDS) is a system responsible for detecting unauthorized access or attacks. It can verify, itemize, and characterize threats from outside and inside the network. Most IDSs are programmed to react in certain ways in specific situations. Event notification and alerts are crucial to IDSs. These notifications and alerts inform administrators and security professionals when and where attacks are detected. The most common way to classify an IDS is based on its information source: network-based or host-based.

The most common IDS, a network-based IDS (NIDS), monitors network traffic on a local network segment. To monitor traffic on the network segment, the network interface card (NIC) must be operating in promiscuous mode. An NIDS can monitor only the network traffic. It cannot monitor any internal activity that occurs within a system, such as an attack against a system that is carried out by logging on to the system's local terminal. An NIDS is affected by a switched network because generally an NIDS monitors only a single network segment.

IPS

An intrusion prevention system (IPS) scans traffic on a network for signs of malicious activity and then takes some action to prevent it. An IPS monitors the entire network. You need to be careful to set an IPS's filters in such a way that false positives and false negatives are kept to a minimum. False positives indicate an unwarranted alarm, and false negatives indicate troubling traffic that does not generate an alarm.

End-point management server

End-point security management is a process of using special software and collections of polices to manage endpoints. The server or appliance that directs this process is called an *end-point management server*. This process is also referred to as *Network Access Control*, as the health of the device is continuously checked. Required elements may include an approved operating system, a VPN client, and antivirus software with current updates. Devices that do not comply with policy are given limited access or quarantined.

Legacy/embedded systems

An *embedded system* is a computer system with a specific function within a larger device. Embedded systems are present in many Internet-connected devices, such as VoIP phones and routers, but they are also increasingly found in devices such as home appliances and automobiles. Legacy embedded systems are those that have been handed down from one version of a system to another with no major revision.

Exam essentials

Identify the major server roles in a network.   These roles include DNS, DHCP, web, proxy, and authentication servers.

Differentiate various network appliances.   Describe the features and use of UTM, IPS, and IDS.

2.6 Explain common network configuration concepts.

The protocol of the Internet is TCP/IP, and because of this, TCP/IP has become the de facto protocol of most networks as well. Far from the only networking protocol available, TCP/IP meets the needs of most organizations and is becoming more and more the one protocol suite that administrators must understand in order to do their jobs. In this section, we'll cover the common configurations and settings required to get TCP/IP up and running.

IP addressing

A host is any machine or interface that participates in a TCP/IP network—whether as a client or a server. Every interface on a TCP/IP network that must be issued an IP address is considered a host. Those addresses can be manually entered or provided dynamically to the host by a DHCP server. (If IPv4 is in use, the addresses fall into three classes—A, B, and C.) The other values needed, besides the IP address, are the subnet mask (identifying the scope of the network on which the host resides) and the default gateway (the router interfacing with the outside world). A default gateway is the address of the local router and serves as the gateway to other networks. Since memorizing complex numerical addresses can be difficult to do, DNS is used to translate hostnames into IP addresses as needed.

Although there is no official IP class objective, it is helpful to understand IP classes in the real world, and knowing about them also enriches your understanding of various CompTIA objectives.

IPv4 addresses (IPv6 is discussed later) are 32-bit binary numbers. Because numbers of such magnitude are difficult to work with, they're divided into four octets (8 bits) and converted to decimal. Thus, 01010101 becomes 85. This is important because the limits on the size of the decimal number exist because they are representations of binary numbers. The range must be from 0 (00000000) to 255 (11111111) per octet, making the lowest possible IP address 0.0.0.0 and the highest 255.255.255.255. Many IP addresses aren't available because they're reserved for diagnostic purposes, private addressing, or some other function.

Three classes of IP addresses are available for assignment to hosts; they're identified by the first octet. Table 2.3 shows the class and the range the first octet must fall into to be within that class. The entire 127.0.0.0 network is missing because that network has been set aside or reserved for diagnostics.

TABLE 2.3   IP address classes

Class	Range
A	1–126
B	128–191
C	192–223

Five classes exist. Class D (multicast) and Class E (experimental) are not assigned to hosts.

Class A   If you're given a Class A address, then you're assigned a number such as 125. With a few exceptions, this means you can use any number between 0 and 255 in the second field, any number between 0 and 255 in the third field, and any number between 0 and 255 in the fourth field. This gives you a total number of hosts that you can have on your network in excess of 16 million. The default subnet mask is 255.0.0.0.

Class B   If you're given a Class B address, then you're assigned a number such as 152.119. With a few exceptions, this means you can use any number between 0 and 255 in the third field and any number between 0 and 255 in the fourth field. This gives you a total number of hosts that you can have on your network in excess of 65,000. The default subnet mask is 255.255.0.0.

Class C   If you're given a Class C address, then you're assigned a number such as 205.19.15. You can use any number between 1 and 254 in the fourth field, for a total of 254 possible hosts (0 and 255 are reserved). The default subnet mask is 255.255.255.0.

The class, therefore, makes a tremendous difference in the number of hosts your network can have. In most cases, the odds of having all hosts at one location are small. Assuming you have a Class B address, will there be 65,000 hosts in one room, or will they be in several locations? Most often, it's the latter.

Static vs. Dynamic

The two methods of entering address information for a host are static and dynamic. Static means that you manually enter the information for the host and it does not change. Dynamic means that DHCP is used for the host to lease information from.

APIPA

Within each of the three major classes of IP addresses, there is a range set aside for *private addresses*. These are addresses that do not communicate directly with the Internet (often using a proxy server or network address translation to do so), so each host's address needs to be unique only within the realm of that network. Table 2.4 lists the private address ranges for Class A, B, and C addresses.

TABLE 2.4   Private address ranges

Class	Range
A	10.0.0.0 to 10.255.255.255
B	172.16.0.0 to 172.31.255.255
C	192.168.0.0 to 192.168.255.255

Automatic Private IP Addressing (APIPA) is a TCP/IP feature Microsoft added to its operating systems. If a DHCP server cannot be found and the clients are configured to obtain IP addresses automatically, the clients automatically assign themselves an IP address, somewhat randomly, in the 169.254.x.x range with a subnet mask of 255.255.0.0. This allows them to communicate with other hosts that have similarly configured themselves, but they are unable to connect to the Internet. If a computer is using an APIPA address, it will have trouble communicating with other clients if those clients do not use APIPA addresses.

Link local

In IPv6, there is a type of address called a *link local address* that in many ways is like an APIPA address in that the device will generate one of these addresses for each interface with no intervention from a human, as is done with APIPA. The scope of the address is also the same, in that it is not routable and is good only on the segment the device is located on.

However, as is the case with APIPA addresses, if two devices connected to the same segment generate these addresses, they will be in the same network, and the two devices will be able to communicate. This is because the devices always generate the address using the same IPv6 prefix (the equivalent of a network ID in IPv4), which is FE80::/64. The remainder of the address is created by spreading the 48-bit MAC address across the last 64 bits, yielding an IPv6 address that looks like the example shown here:

FE80::2237:06FF:FECF:67E4/64

DNS

As stated earlier, every computer, interface, or device on a TCP/IP network is issued a unique identifier known as an *IP address* that resembles 192.168.12.123. Because of the Internet, TCP/IP is the most commonly used networking protocol today. You can easily see that it's difficult for most users to memorize these numbers, so hostnames are used in their place. *Hostnames* are alphanumeric values assigned to a host; any host may have more than one hostname.

For example, the host 192.168.12.123 may be known to all users as Gemini, or it may be known to the sales department as Gemini and to the marketing department as Apollo9. All that is needed is a means by which the alphanumeric name can be translated into its IP address. There are a number of methods of doing so, but for this exam, you need to know only one: the Domain Name System. On a large network, you can add a server to be referenced by all hosts for the name resolution. The server runs DNS and resolves a fully qualified domain name (FQDN) like www.entrepreneurshipcamp.com into its IP address. Multiple DNS servers can serve an area and provide fault tolerance for one another. In all cases, the DNS servers divide their area into zones; every zone has a primary server and any number of secondary servers. DNS works with any operating system and any version.

DHCP

DHCP falls into a different category. Whereas DNS resolves names to IP addresses, DHCP issues IP configuration data.

Rather than an administrator having to configure a unique IP address for every host added on a network (and default gateway and subnet mask), they can use a DHCP server to issue these values. That server is given a number of addresses in a range that it can supply to clients.

For example, the server may be given the IP range (or *scope*) 192.168.12.1 to 192.168.12.200. When a client boots, it sends out a request for the server to issue it an address (and any other configuration data) from that scope. The server takes one of the numbers it has available and leases it to the client for a length of time. If the client is still using the configuration data when 50 percent of the lease has expired, it requests a renewal of the lease from the server; under normal operating conditions, the request is granted. When the client is no longer using the address, the address goes back in the scope and can be issued to another client.

DHCP is built on the older Bootstrap Protocol (BOOTP) that was used to allow diskless workstations to boot and connect to a server that provided them with an operating system and applications. The client uses broadcasts to request the data and thus—normally—can't communicate with DHCP servers beyond their own subnet (broadcasts don't route). A DHCP Relay Agent, usually installed on the router, however, can be employed to allow DHCP broadcasts to go from one network to another.

While the primary purpose of DHCP is to lease IP addresses to hosts, when it gives the IP address, it also often includes the additional configuration information as well: DNS server, router information, and so on.

Reservations

While by default DHCP randomly assigns IP addresses, it is possible to reserve a dynamic IP address for a device. This is advisable when you want the device to keep the same IP address all the time but you still want the device to participate in DHCP so you can keep the device abreast of any changes in the address of the DNS server or the default gateway address.

IPv4 vs. IPv6

IPv4 uses a 32-bit addressing scheme that provides for more than 4 billion unique addresses. Unfortunately, there are a lot of IP-enabled devices added to the Internet every day—not to mention, not all of the addresses that can be created are used by public networks (many are reserved, in classes D and above and are unavailable for public use). This reduces the number of addresses that can be allocated as public Internet addresses.

IPv6 offers a number of improvements, the most notable of which is its ability to handle growth in public networks. IPv6 uses a 128-bit addressing scheme, allowing a huge number of possible addresses: 340,282,366,920,938,463,463,374,607,431,768,211,456. Table 2.5 compares IPv4 to IPv6.

TABLE 2.5 IPv4 vs. IPv6

Feature	IPv4	IPv6
Loopback address	127.0.0.1	0:0:0:0:0:0:0:1 (::1)
Private ranges	10.0.0.0 172.16.0.0 to 172.31.0.0 192.168.0.0	FEC0:: (proposed)
Autoconfigured addresses	169.254.0.0	FE80::

 In IPv6 addresses, repeating zeros can be left out so that colons next to each other in the address indicate one or more sets of zeros for that section.

Subnet mask

Subnetting your network is the process of taking the total number of hosts available to you and dividing it into smaller networks. When you configure TCP/IP on a host, you typically need give only three values: a unique IP address, a default gateway (router) address, and a subnet mask. Table 2.6 shows the default subnet mask for each class of network.

TABLE 2.6 Default subnet values

Class	Default subnet mask
A	255.0.0.0
B	255.255.0.0
C	255.255.255.0

 Purists may argue that you don't need a default gateway. Technically this is true if your network is small and you don't communicate beyond it. For all practical purposes, though, most networks need a default gateway.

When you use the default subnet mask, you're allowing for all hosts to be at one site and not subdividing your network. This is called *classful* subnetting. Any deviation from the default signifies that you're dividing the network into multiple subnetworks, which is called *classless* subnetting.

The problem with classful subnetting is that it allows for only three sizes of networks: Class A (16,777,216 hosts), Class B (65,536 hosts), and Class C (254 hosts). Two of these are too large to operate efficiently in the real world, and when enterprises were issued public network IDs that were larger than they needed, many public IP addresses were wasted. For this reason and simply to allow for the creation of smaller networks that operate better, the concept of classless routing, or Classless Interdomain Routing (CIDR), was born.

Using CIDR, administrators can create smaller networks called *subnets*, by manipulating the subnet mask of a larger classless or major network ID. This allows you to create a subnet that is much closer in size to what you need, thus wasting fewer IP addresses and improving performance in each subnet, as a result of the reduced broadcast traffic generated in each subnet.

CIDR notation is another way to represent the IP address and the subnet mask. The number of bits in the mask is shown after the address and preceded by a slash. For example, the address 192.168.5.5 with a mask of 255.255.255.0 can be written 192.168.5.5/24.

Gateway

A *gateway* can have two meanings. In TCP/IP, a gateway is the address of the machine to send data to that is not intended for a host on the network (in other words, a default gateway). A gateway is also a physical device operating between the Transport and Application layers of the OSI model that can send data between dissimilar systems. The best example of the latter is a mail gateway—it doesn't matter which two networks are communicating; the gateway allows them to exchange email.

A gateway, as it is tested on the exam, is the server (router) that allows traffic beyond the internal network. Hosts are configured with the address of a gateway (called the default gateway), and if they need to correspond with a host outside the internal network, the data is sent to the gateway to facilitate this. When you configure TCP/IP on a host, one of the fields that should be provided is a gateway field, which specifies where data not intended for this network is sent in order to be able to communicate with the rest of the world.

VPN

Virtual private network (VPN) connections use an untrusted carrier network but provide protection of the information through strong authentication protocols and encryption mechanisms. While we typically use the most untrusted network—the Internet—as the classic example, and most VPNs do travel through the Internet, a VPN can be used with interior networks as well whenever traffic needs to be protected from prying eyes.

In VPN operations, entire protocols wrap around other protocols when this process occurs. They include the following:

- A LAN protocol (required)
- A remote access or line protocol (required)
- An authentication protocol (optional)
- An encryption protocol (optional)

A device that terminates multiple VPN connections is called a VPN concentrator. VPN concentrators incorporate the most advanced encryption and authentication techniques available.

VPN connections can be used to provide remote access to teleworkers or traveling users (called remote access VPNs) and can also be used to securely connect two locations (called site-to-site VPNs). The implementation process is conceptually different for these two. In the former, the tunnel that is created has as its endpoints the user's computer and the VPN concentrator. In this case, only traffic traveling from the user computer to the VPN concentrator uses this tunnel.

In the case of two office locations, the tunnel endpoints are the two VPN routers, one in each office. With this configuration, all traffic that goes between the offices will use the tunnel, regardless of the source or destination. The endpoints are defined during the creation of the VPN connection and thus must be set correctly according to the type of remote access link being used.

VLAN

Virtual local area networks (VLANs) are logical subdivisions of a switch that segregate ports from one another as if they were in different LANs. VLANs offer another way to add a layer of separation between sensitive devices and the rest of the network. For example, if only one device should be able to connect to the finance server, the device and the finance server could be placed in a VLAN separate from the other VLANs. As traffic between VLANs can occur only through a router, access control lists (ACLs) can be used to control the traffic allowed between VLANs.

These VLANs can also span multiple switches, meaning that devices connected to switches in different parts of a network can be placed in the same VLAN regardless of physical location.

VLANs have many advantages and few disadvantages. These are listed in Table 2.7.

TABLE 2.7 Advantages of VLANs

Advantages	Disadvantages
Cost: Switched networks with VLANs are less costly than routed networks, as routers cost more than switches.	Managerial overhead securing VLANs
Performance: By creating smaller broadcast domains (each VLAN is a broadcast domain), performance improves.	
Flexibility: Removes the requirement that devices in the same LAN (or in this case VLAN) be in the same location	
Security: Provides one more layer of separation at layer 2 and 3	

NAT

A company that uses network address translation presents a single connection to the external network. This connection may be through a router or a NAT server. The only information that an intruder will be able to get is that the connection has a single address.

NAT effectively hides your internal network devices from the world, making it much harder to determine what systems exist on the other side of the router. The NAT server effectively operates as a firewall for the network. Most new routers support NAT; it provides a simple, inexpensive firewall for small networks.

 It's important to understand that NAT acts as a proxy between the local area network (which can be using private IP addresses) and the Internet. Not only can NAT save IP addresses, it can also act as a firewall.

Most NAT implementations assign internal hosts private IP address numbers and use public addresses only for the NAT to translate to and communicate with the outside world. The private address ranges, all of which are addresses that are nonroutable, are as follows:

- 10.0.0.0–10.255.255.255
- 172.16.0.0–172.31.255.255
- 192.168.0.0–192.168.255.255

 In addition to NAT, port address translation (PAT) is possible. Whereas NAT can use multiple public IP addresses, PAT uses a single one and shares the port with the network. Because it is using only a single port, PAT is much more limited and typically used only on small and home-based networks. Microsoft's Internet Connection Sharing is an example of a PAT implementation.

Destination network address translation (DNAT) is a technique for transparently changing the *destination* IP address of an end route packet and performing the inverse function for any replies.

Also known as *transparent traffic forwarding*, DNAT provides a facility to send HTTP user traffic to another destination, such as a centralized content filter, authentication server, or some other external location, based on defined criteria; it accomplishes a similar goal as port forwarding.

Exam essentials

Understand the purpose and use of NAT.   NAT implementations assign internal hosts private IP address numbers and use public addresses only for the NAT to translate to and communicate with the outside world.

Know the capabilities and limitations of VLANs.   Virtual local area networks (VLANs) are logical subdivisions of a switch that segregate ports from one another as if they were in different LANs. VLANs offer another way to add a layer of separation between sensitive devices and the rest of the network.

2.7 Compare and contrast Internet connection types, network types, and their features.

Your network can connect to the Internet in a number of ways. These can range from the slow dial-up connection that is established only when you need it to be established to a high-speed fiber connection that is always on. This section looks at many of the options available and all that you need to know for this objective on the A+ exam.

Internet connection types

When discussing ways to connect to the Internet, most of the focus is on broadband network techniques. It is imperative that you understand the various types of networks, including broadband. The sections that follow will focus on the key issues associated with connecting to the Internet.

Cable

Two of the most popular methods of connecting to the Internet today are using DSL and cable. Cable deployment is covered in the earlier section "Cable/DSL modem configuration."

DSL

DSL deployment is covered in the earlier section "Cable/DSL modem configuration."

Dial-up

Whereas broadband holds great promise for high-speed connections, there are many people (particularly in rural areas) who cannot take advantage of this. Thankfully, one of the first methods of remote access, dial-up networking, is still in existence. With dial-up, you add a modem to your computer and connect to an Internet service provider (ISP) over the existing phone lines, also known as the *Plain Old Telephone System* (POTS). With a good connection, you can transmit and receive at 56 Kbps.

Fiber

Also introduced earlier in the chapter, fiber-optic cabling provides excellent speed and bandwidth but is expensive. Not only are the cables that you use costly, but the light-emitting/receiving hardware costs also make this an expensive undertaking. Because of the cost involved, fiber is often an option for businesses only when it comes to broadband access.

Fiber to the Home (FTTH) is an attempt some communities are undertaking to offer high-speed connectivity to residential dwellings as well. Verizon's FiOS, a similar implementation, runs single-mode optical fiber to homes and includes phone and television service along with Internet access.

Satellite

Whereas the other broadband technologies discussed require the use of physical wiring, with satellite broadband the service provider sends a microwave signal from a dish to an orbiting satellite and back. One satellite can service many receivers, so this is commonly known as *point-to-multipoint* technology. As a general rule, satellite connections are slower than the other broadband technologies you need to know for the exam, and they are adversely affected by weather and atmospheric conditions.

   With satellite, download speed is much faster than upload speed.

ISDN

Integrated Services Digital Network (ISDN) is a WAN technology that performs link management and signaling by virtue of packet switching. The original idea behind it was to let existing phone lines carry digital communications by using multiplexing to support multiple channels.

Cellular

Mobile devices have made cellular networking popular, though they are not the only devices capable of using networking; for example, a cellular modem can also be quickly added to a laptop. Cellular networks use a central access point (a cell tower) in a mesh network design. For a long time, two competing standards were the *Global System for Mobile Communications* (GSM) and the *Code Division Multiple Access* (CDMA); the latest technology is Long Term Evolution (LTE), which is used in 4G networks.

   Most cellular phone companies now have specialized wireless routers that are used to create mobile hotspots. These cards act as stand-alone routers to the Internet using the cellular phone network.

Tethering

Tethering is the process of connecting a device to a smartphone or tablet with a cellular connection for the purpose of using the Internet connection on the cellular device. Connecting to the phone or tablet with the other device can be done using 802.11, Bluetooth, or a physical connection using a cable, for example through USB.

Mobile hotspot

When the devices using the Internet connection on the cellular device are connected wirelessly using 802.11, it is sometimes called a *mobile hotspot*. This is also the term used for devices that are capable of acting as a hotspot for surrounding WiFi devices. The mobile hotspot device may get its Internet access through either cellular or 802.11.

Line-of-sight wireless Internet service

Line-of-sight wireless, as the name implies, requires you to have a direct line of vision between your location and the ISP transmitter. Because this uninterrupted path must be maintained, distances are quite short, and this method is not widely used.

Network types

You should know the terminology used for networking as well as the major topologies that are available. Networks consist of servers and clients. A *server* is a dedicated machine offering services such as file and print sharing. A *client* is any individual workstation accessing the network. A *workstation* is a client machine that accesses services elsewhere (normally from a server).

Networks differ in size and scope. The size of the network on which servers and clients operate can range significantly.

LAN

A *local area network* is a network that is geographically confined within a small space—a room, a building, and so on. Because it's confined and does not have to span a great distance, it can normally offer higher speeds.

With Ethernet, you can often use the network type to compute the required length and speed of your cabling. For example, 100BaseT tells you three things.

- **100:** The speed of the network, 100 Mbps.
- **Base:** The technology used (either baseband or broadband).
- **T:** Twisted-pair cabling. In the case of 10BaseT, it's generally UTP.

When you configure a network, one of the first places to turn your attention is the routers and access points—they are the hardware components on which network access can rely. Because it must always be possible to find these devices, I suggest that you not use DHCP to issue them addresses but configure their addresses statically.

To increase security, devices should be behind a firewall, and you should always change the administrative username and password that comes preconfigured with these devices to ones that adhere to stringent password policies (a mixture of uppercase and lowercase alphabet, numbers, and special characters), and you should keep the firmware updated.

With wireless access points, you should change the SSID from its default value (if one is preconfigured) and disable broadcasts. MAC filtering can be used on a wireless network, for example, to prevent certain clients from accessing the Internet. You can choose to deny service to a set list of MAC addresses (and allow all others) or allow service only to a set of MAC addresses (and deny all others).

WAN

A *wide area network* (WAN) is a collection of two or more LANs, typically connected by routers and dedicated leased lines (not to mention complicated implementations). The geographic limitation is removed, but WAN speeds are traditionally less than LAN speeds.

PAN

A *personal area network* (PAN) is a LAN created by personal devices. Often, personal devices include networking capabilities and can communicate directly with one another. Wireless technologies have introduced a new term: *wireless personal area network* (WPAN). This refers to the technologies involved in connecting devices in close proximity to exchange data or resources. An example is connecting a laptop with a PDA to synchronize an address book. Because of their small size and the nature of the data exchange, WPAN devices lend themselves well to ad hoc wireless networking. Ad hoc wireless networks are those that have devices connect to each other directly, not through a wireless access point.

MAN

Occasionally, a WAN will be described as a *metropolitan area network* (MAN) when it is confined to a certain geographic area, such as a university campus or city. No formal guidelines dictate the differences between a MAN and a WAN; technically, a MAN *is* a WAN. Perhaps for this reason, the term *MAN* is used less frequently than *WAN*. If any distinction exists, it's that a MAN is smaller than a WAN. A MAN is almost always bigger than a LAN and usually is smaller than or equal to a WAN. MANs utilize an ISP or telecommunications (telco) provider.

WMN

Wireless mesh networks (WMN) are a form of ad hoc WLAN that often consist of mesh clients, mesh routers, and gateways. Each device has multiple wireless connections to other devices forming a rich mesh network with lots of fault tolerance. Mesh routers forward traffic to and from the gateways which may, but need not, be connected to the Internet.

Exam essentials

Identify network types.   These include LAN, WAN, MAN, PAN, and wireless mesh networks.

Describe Internet connection methods.   These include cable, DSL, dial-up, satellite, ISDN, fiber, and cellular.

2.8 Given a scenario, use appropriate networking tools.

To create a network and solve problems with it, you need a toolbox. While some of the tools you use will be in the form of software, many others are hardware, and those are the focus of this objective.

No networking administrators worth their pay would try to troubleshoot a problem without a set of tools. The tools that should be readily on hand include a crimper for fixing connectors, a multimeter for checking signals, a toner probe to find breaks in a cable, a cable tester, a loopback plug, and a punchdown tool, among others.

Crimper

Wire *crimpers* look like pliers but are used to attach media connectors to the ends of cables. For instance, you use one type of wire crimper to attach RJ-45 connectors on an unshielded twisted-pair (UTP) cable. You use a different type of wire crimper to attach Bayonet Neill-Concelman (BNCs) to coaxial cabling.

Cable stripper

A *cable stripper* is used to remove the outer covering of the cable to get to the wire pairs within. You place the end of the cable in the mouth of the device, close the mouth, and then circle the cable, cutting away the outer sheath without damaging the wire pairs within. Figure 2.7 shows a cable stripper.

FIGURE 2.7   Cable stripper

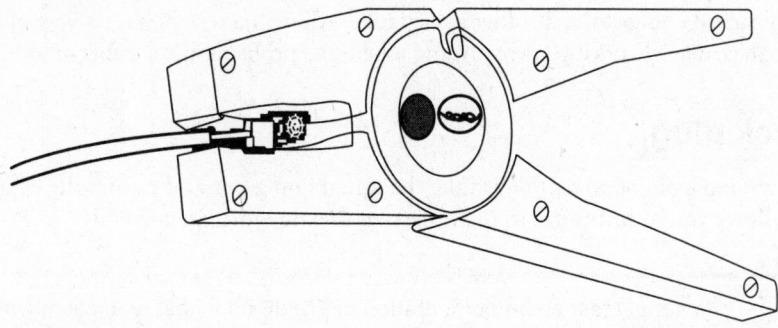

Multimeter

A *multimeter* combines a number of tools into one. There can be slight variations, but a multimeter always includes a voltmeter, an ohmmeter, and an ammeter (and is sometimes called VOM as an acronym). With one basic multimeter, you can measure voltage, current, and resistance (some will even measure temperature).

A multimeter has a display, terminals, probes, and a dial to select various measurement ranges. A digital multimeter has a numeric digital display, and an analog has a dial display. Inside a multimeter, the terminals are connected to different resistors, depending on the range selected.

Tone generator and probe

A *toner probe* has two parts: the tone generator (called the *toner*) and the tone locator (called the *probe*). The toner sends the tone, and at the other end of the cable, the probe receives the toner's signal. This tool makes it easier to find the beginning and end of a cable.

The purpose of the toner probe is to generate a signal that is transmitted on the wire you are attempting to locate. At the other end, you press the probe against individual wires. When it makes contact with the wire that has the signal on it, the locator emits an audible signal or tone.

> A toner probe can be used to find breaks in a cable.

Cable tester

Cable testers (sometimes called *media testers*) are used to verify that the cable you are using is good. Commonly used with network cabling, they enable you to perform many of the same tests as a multimeter. Any tool that facilitates the testing of a cable can be deemed a cable tester, but a media tester allows administrators to test a segment of cable, looking for shorts, improperly attached connectors, or other cable faults. All media testers have a way of telling you whether the cable is working correctly and where the problem in the cable might be.

Loopback plug

Also called wrap plugs, *loopback plugs* take the signal going out and essentially echo it back. This allows you to test ports to make certain they're working correctly.

> To simply test an implementation of TCP/IP on a host, you can always use the loopback address of 127.0.0.1. This is often used with ping (discussed in Chapter 6, "Operating Systems").

Punchdown tool

Punchdown tools are used to attach twisted-pair network cables to connectors within a patch panel. Specifically, they connect twisted-pair wires to the insulation displacement connector (IDC).

WiFi analyzer

A *WiFi analyzer* is a tool that gathers information of all sorts about the RF medium in the area. These may be handheld hardware devices or software that is installed on a laptop that uses the wireless card in the laptop to gather information. These analyzers vary widely in what type of information they are capable of generating and the price point.

The following are among the functions that these analyzers offer:

▪ Noise and inference detection and location

▪ Channel information

- Signal strength
- List of APs in the area

Exam essentials

Know the tools for working with networks.   A good administrator's toolbox will include wire crimpers, a multimeter, a toner probe, cable tester, loopback plugs, and a punchdown tool.

Know the two parts of a toner probe.   A toner probe has two parts: the tone generator (the toner) and the tone locator (the probe).

Review Questions

You can find the answers in the Appendix.

1. Which the following uses port 110?
   A. FTP
   B. SSH
   C. Telnet
   D. POP3

2. Which of the following uses two ports?
   A. FTP
   B. SSH
   C. Telnet
   D. POP3

3. Which the following uses port 22?
   A. FTP
   B. SSH
   C. Telnet
   D. POP3

4. Which device operates at layer 2?
   A. Router
   B. Switch
   C. Repeater
   D. Hub

5. Which device operates at layer 1?
   A. Router
   B. Switch
   C. Bridge
   D. Hub

6. Which device operates at layer 2?
   A. Router
   B. Switch
   C. Repeater
   D. Hub

7. Which of the following is *not* a private IP address range?

   A. 10.0.0.0–10.255.255.255

   B. 172.16.0.0–172.16.255.255

   C. 192.168.0.0–192.168.255.255

   D. 192.168.5.5–192.168.255.255

8. Which of the following delivers an upload speed equal to the download speed?

   A. SDSL

   B. VDSL

   C. VHDSL

   D. RADSL

9. Which of the following is an area where you can place a public server for access by people you might not trust otherwise?

   A. NAT

   B. DMZ

   C. Intranet

   D. Internet

10. Which of the following operates in the 5.0 GHz range?

   A. 802.11a

   B. 802.11b

   C. 802.11g

   D. 802.11

11. Which of the following operates at a maximum of 2 MB?

   A. 802.11a

   B. 802.11b

   C. 802.11g

   D. 802.11

12. Which of the following has the largest cell size?

   A. 802.11a

   B. 802.11b

   C. 802.11g

   D. 802.11

13. Which type of server resolves IP addresses to hostnames?

   A. HTTP

   B. DNS

   C. DHCP

   D. SQL

14. Which type of server provides automatic IP configurations?

   A. HTTP

   B. DNS

   C. DHCP

   D. SQL

15. Which type of server is a database server?

   A. HTTP

   B. DNS

   C. DHCP

   D. SQL

16. Which of the following is a Class B address?

   A. 192.168.5.5

   B. 10.6.6.3

   C. 172.6.8.9

   D. 201.69.3.2

17. Which of the following is a Class A address?

   A. 192.168.5.5

   B. 10.6.6.3

   C. 172.6.8.9

   D. 201.69.3.2

18. Which of the following is a Class C address?

   A. 192.168.5.5

   B. 10.6.6.3

   C. 172.6.8.9

   D. 224.69.3.2

19. When personal devices include networking capabilities and can communicate directly with one another, they create which type of network?

   A. WAN

   B. MAN

   C. PAN

   D. WMN

20. Which of the following is a collection of two or more LANs, typically connected by routers and dedicated leased lines?

   A. WAN

   B. MAN

   C. PAN

   D. WMN

21. Which of the following is a form of ad hoc WLAN?

    A. WAN

    B. MAN

    C. PAN

    D. WMN

22. Which of the following is used to attach media connectors to the ends of cables?

    A. Crimper

    B. Cable stripper

    C. Multimeter

    D. Tone generator

23. Which of the following includes a voltmeter, an ohmmeter, and an ammeter?

    A. Crimper

    B. Cable stripper

    C. Multimeter

    D. Tone generator

24. Which of the following makes it easier to find the beginning and end of a cable?

    A. Crimper

    B. Cable stripper

    C. Multimeter

    D. Tone generator

Chapter

3

Hardware

COMPTIA A+ CERTIFICATION EXAM CORE 1 (220-1001) OBJECTIVES COVERED IN THIS CHAPTER:

✓ **3.1 Explain basic cable types, features, and their purposes.**

- Network cables
  - Ethernet
    - Cat 5
    - Cat 5e
    - Cat 6
    - Plenum
    - Shielded twisted pair
    - Unshielded twisted pair
    - 568A/B
  - Fiber
  - Coaxial
  - Speed and transmission limitations
- Video cables
  - VGA
  - HDMI
  - Mini-HDMI
  - DisplayPort
  - DVI
  - DVI-D
  - DVI-I
- Multipurpose cables
  - Lightning
  - Thunderbolt
  - USB
  - USB-C

- USB 2.0
- USB 3.0
- Peripheral cables
  - Serial
- Hard drive cables
  - SATA
  - IDE
  - SCSI
- Adapters
  - DVI to HDMI
  - USB to Ethernet
  - DVI to VGA

✓ **3.2   Identify common connector types.**

- RJ-11
- RJ-45
- RS-232
- BNC
- RG-59
- RG-6
- USB
- Micro-USB
- Mini-USB
- USB-C
- DB-9
- Lightning
- SCSI
- eSATA
- Molex

✓ **3.3   Given a scenario, install RAM types.**

- RAM types
  - SODIMM
  - DDR2

- DDR3
- DDR4
- Single channel
- Dual channel
- Triple channel
- Error correcting
- Parity vs. non-parity

✓ **3.4   Given a scenario, select, install, and configure storage devices.**

- Optical drives
  - CD-ROM/CD-RW
  - DVD-ROM/DVD-RW/DVD-RW DL
  - Blu-ray
  - BD-R
  - BD-RE
- Solid-state drives
  - M2 drives
  - NVME
  - SATA 2.5
- Magnetic hard drives
  - 5,400rpm
  - 7,200rpm
  - 10,000rpm
  - 15,000rpm
  - Sizes:
- -2.5
- -3.5
- Hybrid drives
- Flash
  - SD card
  - CompactFlash
  - Micro-SD card

- Mini-SD card
- xD
- Configurations
  - RAID 0, 1, 5, 10
  - Hot swappable

✓ **3.5 Given a scenario, install and configure motherboards, CPUs, and add-on cards.**

- Motherboard form factor
  - ATX
  - mATX
  - ITX
  - mITX
- Motherboard connectors types
  - PCI
  - PCIe
  - Riser card
  - Socket types
  - SATA
  - IDE
  - Front panel connector
  - Internal USB connector
- BIOS/UEFI settings
  - Boot options
  - Firmware updates
- Security settings
- Interface configurations
- Security
  - Passwords
  - Drive encryption
    - TPM
    - LoJack
    - Secure boot

- CMOS battery
- CPU features
  - Single-core
  - Multicore
  - Virtual technology
  - Hyperthreading
  - Speeds
  - Overclocking
  - Integrated GPU
- Compatibility
  - AMD
  - Intel
- Cooling mechanism
  - Fans
  - Heat sink
  - Liquid
  - Thermal paste
- Expansion cards
  - Video cards
  - Onboard
  - Add-on card
  - Sound cards
  - Network interface card
  - USB expansion card
  - eSATA card

✓ **3.6 Explain the purposes and uses of various peripheral types.**

- Printer
- ADF/flatbed scanner
- Barcode scanner/QR scanner
- Monitors
- VR headset

- Optical
- DVD drive
- Mouse
- Keyboard
- Touchpad
- Signature pad
- Game controllers
- Camera/webcam
- Microphone
- Speakers
- Headset
- Projector
  - Lumens/brightness
- External storage drives
- KVM
- Magnetic reader/chip reader
- NFC/tap pay device
- Smart card reader

✓ **3.7 Summarize power supply types and features**

- Input 115V vs. 220V
- Output 5.5V vs. 12V
- 24-pin motherboard adapter
- Wattage rating
- Number of devices/types of devices to be powered

✓ **3.8 Given a scenario, select and configure appropriate components for a custom PC configuration to meet customer specifications or needs.**

- Graphic/CAD/CAM design workstation
  - Multicore processor
  - High-end video
  - Maximum RAM

- Audio/video editing workstation
    - Specialized audio and video card
    - Large, fast hard drive
    - Dual monitors
- Virtualization workstation
    - Maximum RAM and CPU cores
- Gaming PC
    - Multicore processor
    - High-end video/specialized GPU
    - High-definition sound card
    - High-end cooling
- Standard thick client
    - Desktop applications
    - Meets recommended requirements for selected OS
- Thin client
    - Basic applications
    - Meets minimum requirements for selected OS
    - Network connectivity
- Network attached storage device
    - Media streaming
    - File sharing
    - Gigabit NIC
    - RAID array

✓ **3.9 Given a scenario, install and configure common devices.**

- Desktop
    - Thin client
    - Thick client
    - Account setup/settings
- Laptop/common mobile devices
    - Touchpad configuration
    - Touchscreen configuration

- Application installations/configurations
- Synchronization settings
- Account setup/settings
- Wireless settings

✓ **3.10 Given a scenario, configure SOHO multifunction devices/printers and settings.**

- Use appropriate drivers for a given operating system
  - Configuration settings
    - Duplex
    - Collate
    - Orientation
    - Quality
  - Device sharing
  - Wired
    - USB
    - Serial
    - Ethernet
  - Wireless
    - Bluetooth
    - 802.11(a, b, g, n, ac)
    - Infrastructure vs. ad hoc
  - Integrated print server (hardware)
  - Cloud printing/remote printing
- Public/shared devices
  - Sharing local/networked device via operating system settings
    - TCP/Bonjour/AirPrint
  - Data privacy
    - User authentication on the device
    - Hard drive caching

✓ **3.11 Given a scenario, install and maintain various print technologies.**

- Laser
  - Imaging drum, fuser assembly, transfer belt, transfer roller, pickup rollers, separate pads, duplexing assembly
  - Imaging process: processing, charging, exposing, developing, transferring, fusing, and cleaning
  - Maintenance: Replace toner, apply maintenance kit, calibrate, clean
- Inkjet
  - Ink cartridge, print head, roller, feeder, duplexing assembly, carriage, and belt
  - Calibrate
  - Maintenance: Clean heads, replace cartridges, calibrate, clear jams
- Thermal
  - Feed assembly, heating element
  - Special thermal paper
  - Maintenance: Replace paper, clean heating element, remove debris
- Impact
  - Print head, ribbon, tractor feed
  - Impact paper
  - Maintenance: Replace ribbon, replace print head, replace paper
- Virtual
  - Print to file
  - Print to PDF
  - Print to XPS
  - Print to image
- 3D printers
  - Plastic filament

This chapter will focus on the exam topics related to PC hardware. It will follow the structure of the CompTIA A+ 220-1001 exam blueprint, objective 3, and it will explore the 11 subobjectives that you will need to master before taking the exam.

3.1 Explain basic cable types, features, and their purposes.

You're expected to know the basic concepts of networking as well as the different types of cabling that can be used. For the latter, you should be able to identify connectors and cables from figures even if those figures are crude line art (think shadows) appearing in pop-up boxes. Objective 3.1 covers the following topics:

- Network cables
- Video cables
- Multipurpose cables
- Peripheral cables
- Hard drive cables
- Adapters

Network cables

For this exam you must know the three specific types of network cables (fiber, twisted pair, and coaxial) and the connectors associated with each. Fiber is the most expensive of the three and can run the longest distance. A number of types of connectors can work with fiber, but three you must know are the subscriber connector (SC), straight tip (ST), and Lucent connector (LC).

Twisted-pair is commonly used in office settings to connect workstations to hubs or switches. It comes in two varieties: unshielded (UTP) and shielded (STP). The two types of connectors commonly used are RJ-11 (four wires and popular with telephones) and RJ-45 (eight wires and used with xBaseT networks—100BaseT, 1000BaseT, and so forth). Two common wiring standards are T568A and T568B.

Coaxial cabling is not as popular as it once was, but it's still used with cable television and some legacy networks. The two most regularly used connectors are F-connectors (television cabling) and BNC (10Base2 and so on).

Ethernet

Ethernet is one of the most common forms of network cable used on wired networks. It is used in a variety of scenarios, such as connecting patch panels to switches in the form of patch cables, connecting a wall outlet to a desktop, and connecting infrastructure devices such as routers and switches. In this section we'll look at its various implementations.

Cat 5

Cat 5 transmits data at speeds up to 100 Mbps and was used with Fast Ethernet (operating at 100 Mbps) with a transmission range of 100 meters. It contains four twisted pairs of copper wire to give the most protection. Although it had its share of popularity (it's used primarily for 10/100 Ethernet networking), it is now an outdated standard. Newer implementations use the 5e standard.

Cat 5e

Cat 5e transmits data at speeds up to 1 Gbps (1000 Mbps). Category 5e cabling can be used up to 100 meters, depending on the implementation and standard used and provides a minimum of 100 MHz of bandwidth. It also contains four twisted pairs of copper wire, but they're physically separated and contain more twists per foot than Category 5 to provide maximum interference protection.

Cat 6

Cat 6 transmits data at speed up to 10 Gbps, has a minimum of 250 MHz of bandwidth, and specifies cable lengths up to 100 meters (using Cat 6a). It contains four twisted pairs of copper wire and is used in 10GBaseT networks. Category 6 cable typically is made up of four twisted pairs of copper wire, but its capabilities far exceed those of other cable types. Category 6 twisted pair uses a longitudinal separator, which separates each of the four pairs of wires from each other and reduces the amount of crosstalk possible.

Plenum

Plenum cable is a specific type of cable that is rated for use in plenum spaces—those spaces in a building used for heating and air-conditioning systems. Most cable cannot be used in the plenum because of the danger of fire (or the fumes the cables give off as they burn). While it is more expensive, plenum cable is fire-rated and meets the necessary standards, which makes it acceptable to use in these locations. It replaces PVC with a Teflon-like material.

Shielded twisted pair

Shielded twisted pair (STP) differs from unshielded twisted pair (UTP) only in the presence of the shielding, which resembles aluminum foil directly beneath the outer insulation. The shielding adds to the cost of the cable, eliminates interference from outside the cable and as a rule of thumb based on current prices is that STP is 30 percent more expensive than UTP for the same length of cable.

Unshielded twisted pair

Unshielded twisted pair (UTP) is the most popular twisted-pair cabling in use and should be used in any scenario where external interference is not an issue.

568A/B

Two wiring standards are commonly used with twisted-pair cabling: T568A and T568B (sometimes referred to simply as 568A and 568B). These are telecommunications standards from TIA and EIA that specify the pin arrangements for the RJ-45 connectors on UTP or STP cables. The number 568 refers to the order in which the wires within the Cat 5 cable are terminated and attached to the connector. The signal is identical for both.

T568A was the first standard, released in 1991. Ten years later, in 2001, T568B was released. Figure 3.1 shows the pin number assignments for the 568A and 568B standards. Pin numbers are read left to right, with the connector tab facing down. Notice that the pin-outs stay the same, and the only difference is in the color coding of the wiring.

FIGURE 3.1 Pin assignments for T568A and T568B

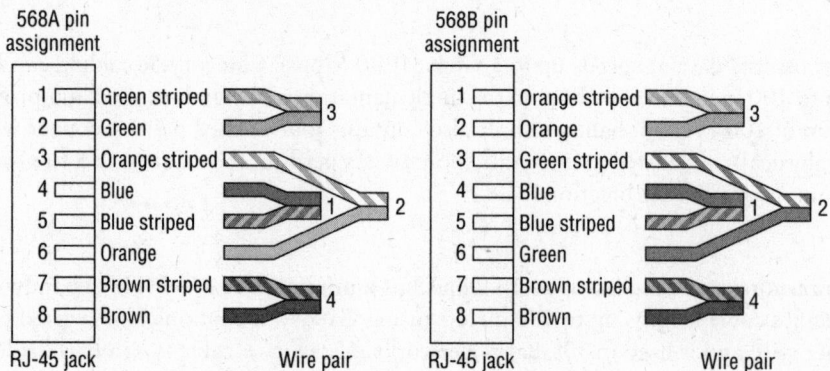

The bottom line here is that if the same standard is used on each end, the cable will be a crossover cable, and if a different standard is used on either end, it will be a straight-through cable. Crossover cables are used to connect like systems such as two computers or two switches or two routers.

Mixing cable types can cause communication problems on the network. Before installing a network or adding a new component to it, make sure the cable being used is in the correct wiring standard.

Fiber

Fiber-optic cabling is the most expensive type of those discussed for this exam. Although it's an excellent medium, it's often not used because of the cost of implementing it. It has a glass core within a rubber outer coating and uses beams of light rather than electrical signals to relay data (see Figure 3.2). Because light doesn't diminish over distance the way electrical signals do, this cabling can run for distances measured in kilometers with transmission speeds from 1 Gbps up to 100 Gbps or higher.

FIGURE 3.2   Fiber-optic cable

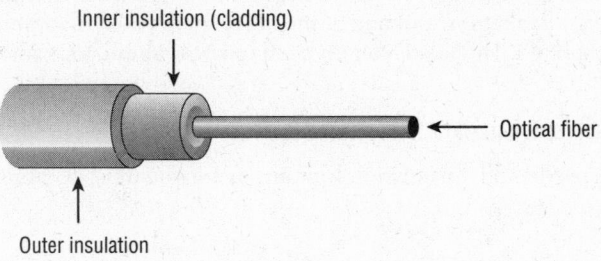

Coaxial

Coaxial cable, or *coax*, is one of the oldest media used in networks. Coax is built around a center conductor or core that is used to carry data from point to point. The center conductor has an insulator wrapped around it, a shield over the insulator, and a nonconductive sheath around the shielding. This construction, depicted in Figure 3.3, allows the conducting core to be relatively free from outside interference. The shielding also prevents the conducting core from emanating signals externally from the cable.

FIGURE 3.3   Coaxial cable construction

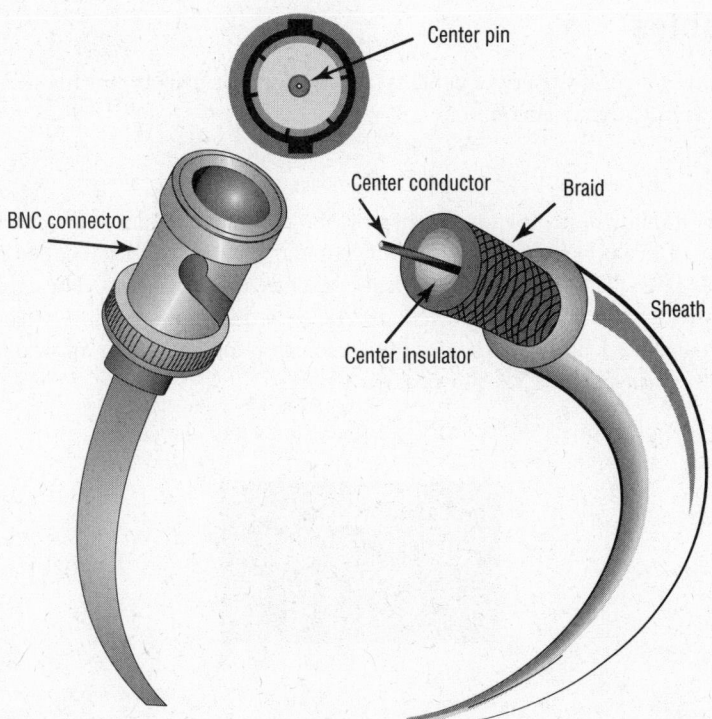

Before you read any further, accept the fact that the odds are incredibly slim that you will ever need to know about coax for a new installation in the real world (with the possible exception of RG-6, which is used from the wall to a cable modem). If you do come across it, it will be in an existing installation, and one of the first things you'll recommend is that it be changed. That said, you do need to know about coax for this exam.

Speed and transmission limitations

Table 3.1 lists the speed and transmission limitations for the most common fiber-optic implementations.

TABLE 3.1   Fiber speeds and limitations

Characteristic	100BaseFX	1000BaseSX	1000BaseLX	10GBaseER
Speed	100 Mbps	1,000 Mbps	1,000 Mbps	10,000 Mbps
Distance (multi-mode)	412 meters	220 to 550 meters	550 meters	(not used)
Distance (single-mode)	10,000 meters	(not used)	5 km	40 km

Video cables

You may require one of a variety of cable types for video or display. In this section we'll survey these types you may encounter.

VGA

This is the traditional connector for the display of a computer, and it is shaped like a *D*. It has three rows of five pins each, for a total of 15 pins. This is also often called the HD-15 (also known as DB-15) connector. A VGA cable carries analog signals. The cable length utilized will affect the resolution achieved: 1024×768 would operate more effectively with 30 feet or less of cable length. As the need for resolution increases, the allowable maximum cable length decreases. Figure 3.4 shows a VGA port.

FIGURE 3.4   VGA port

HDMI

High-Definition Multimedia Interface (HDMI) connectors are used to connect compatible digital items (DVD players and conference room projectors, for example). The Type A connector has 19 pins and is backward-compatible with DVI (discussed later in this chapter). Type B connectors have 29 pins and aren't backward compatible with DVI, but they support greater resolutions. Type C connectors are a smaller version of Type A for portable devices. Type D is an even smaller micro version that resembles a micro-USB connector. Type E is planned for use in automotive applications. HDMI has a theoretical cable length limit of 45 feet or 15 meters. Figure 3.5 shows all HDMI types.

FIGURE 3.5   HDMI connectors

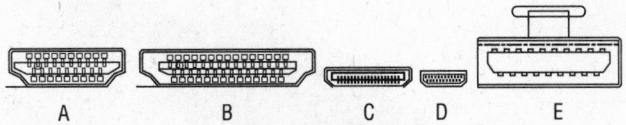

There are several versions of HDMI, as described in Table 3.2.

TABLE 3.2   HDMI versions

Version	1.0	1.1	1.2	1.3	1.4	2.0
Maximum throughput (Gbps)	3.96	3.96	3.96	10.2	10.2	6
Maximum color depth (bit/px)	24	24	24	48	48	48
Maximum audio throughput (Mbps)	36.86	36.86	36.86	36.86	36.86	49.152

Mini-HDMI

A Mini HDMI port is used on DSLR cameras and standard sized tablets. It differs only in the physical size of the connector. Both are shown in Figure 3.6.

FIGURE 3.6   Mini and regular HDMI

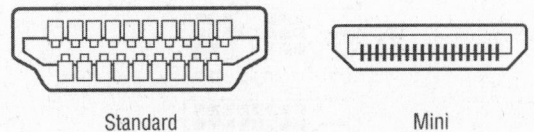

DisplayPort

DisplayPort is a digital interface standard produced by the Video Electronics Standards Association (VESA), used for audio and video. The interface is primarily used to connect a video source to a display device such as a computer monitor or television set. It resembles a

USB connector (see Figure 3.7). Its supports a 1.62, 2.7, 5.4, or 8.1 Gbps data rate per lane; 1, 2, or 4 lanes; (effective total 5.184, 8.64, 17.28, or 25.92 Gbps for 4-lane link); 1 Mbps or 720 Mbps for the auxiliary channel.

FIGURE 3.7   DisplayPort

DVI

There are several types of Digital Video Interface (DVI) pin configurations, but all connectors are D-shaped. The wiring differs based on whether the connector is single-linked or dual-linked (extra pins are used for the dual link). DVI differs from everything else in that it includes both digital and analog signals at the same time, which makes it popular for LCD and plasma TVs. Maximum cable length is 16 feet (5 meters).

DVI connectors can come in several forms, known as DVI-D, DVI-I, and DVI-A. DVI can sometimes do analog and digital at the same time. Figure 3.8 shows the various types of DVI plugs discussed in this section.

FIGURE 3.8   DVI connectors

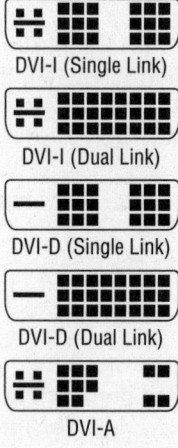

The single link maximum data rate including 8b/10b overhead is 4.95 Gbps at 165 MHz. With the 8b/10b overhead subtracted, the maximum data rate is 3.96 Gbps.

Dual link maximum data rate is twice that of single link. Including 8b/10b overhead, the maximum data rate is 9.90 Gbps at 165 MHz. With the 8b/10b overhead subtracted, the maximum data rate is 7.92 Gbps.

DVI-D

DVI-D (the *D* stands for digital) connectors supply digital signals only. These can also come in a single- or dual-link format. A dual-link format allows for a second data link.

DVI-I

A DVI-I connector (the *I* stands for integrated) has pins that can provide analog and digital. These can also come in a single- or dual-link format.

DVI-A

A DVI-A connector (the *A* stands for analog) has pins that can provide analog and digital. This type comes in a single-link format only.

Multipurpose cables

The following cable types all serve multiple purposes. They are used to connect various peripherals to a system.

Many mobile devices have proprietary ports either for power or for communication. While this approach was widespread at one point, vendors have gradually moved toward using standard physical implementations of both power and communication ports. While I can't cover all of these, I can present the best examples, which are the ports used by Apple in its devices. This section also looks at USB connection types.

Lightning

Apple uses what it calls the Lightning connector for power. Although it makes an adapter to convert this connector to mini-USB (see the next section), Apple doesn't encourage its use because of the limitations the adapter places on the functionality of the proprietary connector.

This is an eight-pin connector that while not standard has advantages over USB, according to Apple. It operates at USB 3.0 speeds of 640 MB. The following are some of these advantages:

- It can supply more power.
- It can be inserted either way.
- It is physically more durable than USB.
- It can detect and adapt to connected devices.

Figure 3.9 shows a Lightning connector next to a USB cable.

FIGURE 3.9   Lightning connector and USB

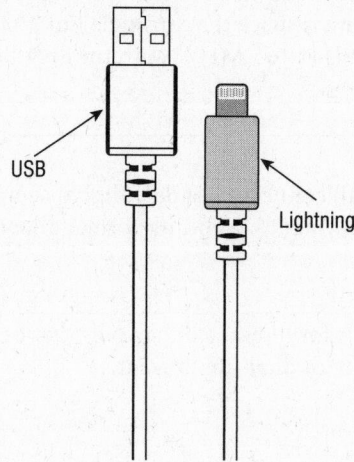

Thunderbolt

Thunderbolt ports are most likely to be found on Apple laptops, but they are now show-ing up on others as well. Figure 3.10 shows a Thunderbolt port on an HP laptop. Notice the "thunderbolt" icon next to the port. Thunderbolt has a maximum speed of 10 Gbps, Thunderbolt 2 has a maximum speed of 20 Gbps, and Thunderbolt 3 has a maximum speed of of 40 Gbps, compared to 800 Mbps for Firewire 800, 5 Gbps for USB 3.0, and 10 Gbps for USB 3.1.

FIGURE 3.10   Thunderbolt port

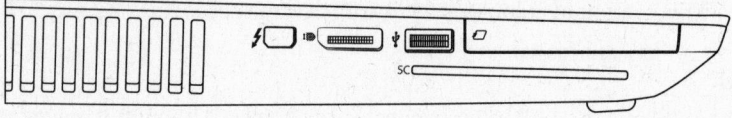

The Thunderbolt cable is shown in Figure 3.11.

FIGURE 3.11   Thunderbolt cable

USB

USB is an expansion bus type that is used almost exclusively for external devices. All motherboards today have at least two USB ports. Some of the advantages of USB include hot-plugging and the capability for up to 127 USB devices to share a single set of system resources. A USB port requires only one IRQ for all USB devices that are connected to it, regardless of the type or number of devices.

Connector types: A, B, mini, micro

USB connectors come in two types and two form factors or sizes. The type A connector is what is found on USB hubs, on host controllers (cards that are plugged into slots to provide USB connections), and on the front and back panels of computers. Type B is the type of USB connector found on the end of the cable that plugs into the devices.

The connectors also come in a mini version and a micro version. The micro version is used on mobile devices, such as mobile phones, GPS units, PDAs, and digital cameras, whereas the mini is found in applications described in the previous paragraph. The choice between a standard A and B and a mini A and B will be dictated by what is present on the device. The cables used cannot exceed 5 meters in length. Figure 3.12 shows, from left to right, a standard Type A, a mini Type A, a standard Type B, and a mini Type B. Some manufacturers have chosen to implement a mini connector that is proprietary, choosing not to follow the standard.

FIGURE 3.12   USB connectors

USB-C

The USB-C connectors connect to both hosts and devices, replacing various USB-B and USB-A connectors and cables with a standard. This type is distinguished by its two-fold rotationally symmetrical connector. The cable is shown in Figure 3.13 next to USB 3.0 cable.

FIGURE 3.13   USB C and USB

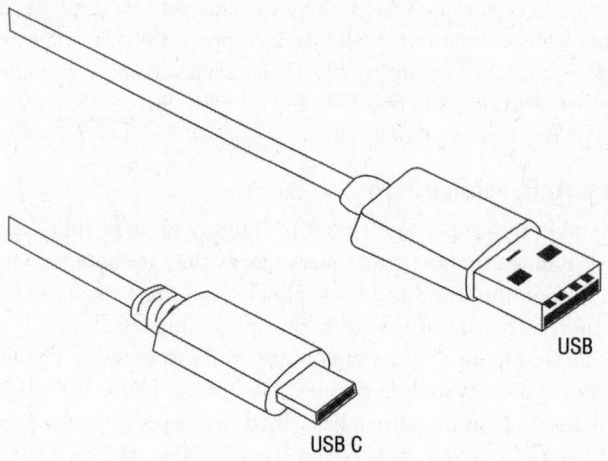

USB

USB C

USB 2.0/3.0

USB 1.1 runs at 12 Mbps and USB 2.0 runs at 480 Mbps.

USB 3.0 has transmission speeds of up to 5 Gbps, significantly reduces the time required for data transmission, reduces power consumption, and is backward-compatible with USB 2.0. Because USB is a serial interface, its width is 1 bit. It is useful to note, however, that a USB 2.0 device will perform at 2.0 speeds even when connected to a 3.0 port.

By utilizing USB hubs in conjunction with the USB ports available on the local machine, you can connect up to 127 of these devices to the computer. You can daisy-chain up to four external USB hubs to a USB port. *Daisy chaining* means that hubs are attached to each other in a line. A USB hub will not function if it is more than four hubs away from the root port.

Peripheral cables

The following cable is used specifically for peripherals.

Serial

Although an older cable type, a serial connector may be found connecting some peripherals to the serial connection on the system. This cable is shown in Figure 3.14. The maximum speed is 115200 bps.

FIGURE 3.14   Serial cable

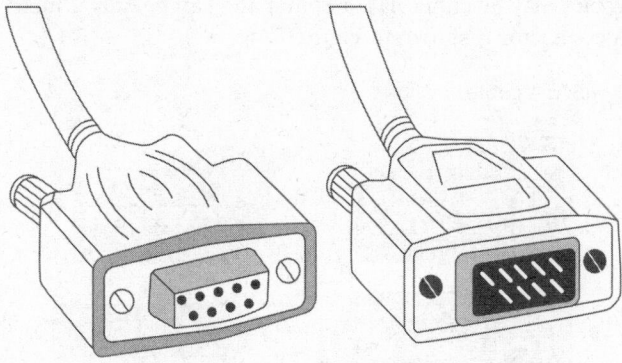

Hard drive cables

When drives are connected internally, there are several options, and the options available on your PC will be a function of how old it is and, in the case of SCSI, whether it is a computer designed to operate as a server.

SATA

Serial AT Attachment (SATA) drives are AT Attachment (ATA) drives that use serial transmission as opposed to parallel. They use a different cable because of this. It is not a ribbon cable but a smaller cable. Both implementations can operate up to 16 GB. Figure 3.15 shows the data cable and its connector.

FIGURE 3.15   Serial ATA data cable and connector

SATA Internal SATA storage devices have 7-pin data cables and a 15-pin power cable.

eSATA eSATA cables may be either flat or round and can be only 2 meters (6 feet) in length. An eSATA connector is shown in Figure 3.16.

FIGURE 3.16 eSATA cable

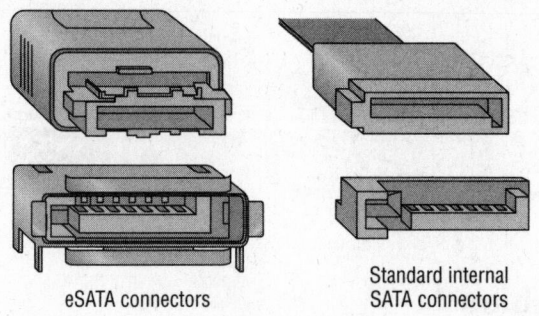

eSATA connectors

Standard internal SATA connectors

IDE

IDE drives are the most common type of hard drive found in computers. But IDE is much more than a hard drive interface; it's also a popular interface for many other drive types, including CD-ROM, DVD, and Zip drives. IDE drives are easy to install and configure, and they provide acceptable performance for most applications. Their ease of use relates to their most identifiable feature—the controller is located on the drive itself. The IDE drive along with its data and power cables is shown in Figure 3.17.

FIGURE 3.17 IDE drive

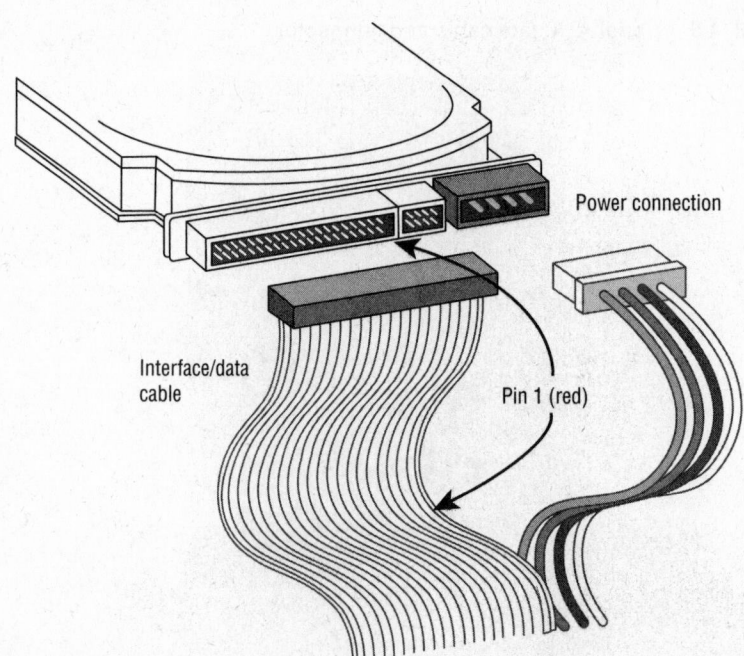

Power connection

Interface/data cable

Pin 1 (red)

The design of the IDE is simple: Build the controller right on the drive and use a relatively short ribbon cable to connect the drive/controller to the IDE interface. This offers the benefits of decreasing signal loss (thus increasing reliability) and making the drive easier to install. The IDE interface can be an expansion board, or it can be built into the motherboard, as is the case on almost all systems today.

IDE generically refers to any drive that has a built-in controller. The IDE you know today is more properly called AT IDE; two previous types of IDE (MCA IDE and XT IDE) are obsolete and incompatible with it.

There have been many revisions of the IDE standard over the years, and each one is designated with a certain AT attachment (ATA) number—ATA-1 through ATA-8. Drives that support ATA-2 and higher are generically referred to as enhanced IDE (EIDE). Here are some of the highlights: With ATA-3, a technology called ATA Packet Interface (ATAPI) was introduced to help deal with IDE devices other than hard disks. ATAPI enables the BIOS to recognize an IDE CD-ROM drive, for example, or a tape backup or Zip drive. Starting with ATA-4, a new technology was introduced called UltraDMA, supporting transfer modes of up to 33 Mbps. ATA-5 supports UltraDMA/66, with transfer modes of up to 66 Mbps. To achieve this high rate, the drive must have a special 80-wire ribbon cable. The drive in Figure 3.17 shows the 40-pin cable, and the motherboard or IDE controller card must support ATA-5. ATA-6 supports UltraDMA/100, with transfer modes of up to 100 Mbps.

 If an ATA-5 or ATA-6 drive is used with a normal 40-wire cable or is used on a system that doesn't support the higher modes, it reverts to the ATA-4 performance level.

ATA-7 supports UltraDMA/133, with transfer modes of up to 150 Mbps and SATA.

ATA-8 made only minor revisions to ATA-7 and also supports UltraDMA/133, with transfer modes of up to 600 Mbps and SATA.

Table 3.3 lists the ATA standards and their details.

TABLE 3.3   ATA standards

Standard	Speed	Cable Type	New Feature
ATA 1	8.3 Mbps	40 wire	Multiword DMA
ATA 2	16.6 Mbps	40 wire	PIO mode
ATA 3	16.6 Mbps	40 wire	ATAPI
ATA 4	33 Mbps	40 or 80 wire	UltraDMA
ATA 5	66 Mbps	40 or 80 wire	UltraDMA 66
ATA 6	100 Mbps	40 or 80 wire	UltraDMA 100
ATA 7	150 Mbps	40 or 80 wire	UltraDMA 133
ATA 8	600 Mbps	40 or 80 wire	Hybrid drive capability

SCSI

Small Computer System Interface (SCSI) is most commonly used for hard disks and tape drives, but it can connect a wide range of other devices, including scanners and CD drives. These devices reside on a single bus, which must be terminated on either end. Eight or sixteen devices can be attached to a single bus (with number one taken by the host bus controller), depending on whether the SCSI bus is wide (0–15) or narrow (0–7) bus. There also is a host bus controller, which is usually plugged into a slot in the computer or can be integrated into the motherboard. Figure 3.18 shows an internal SCSI connector.

FIGURE 3.18 Internal SCSI connector

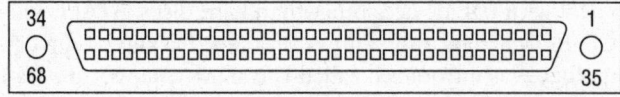

SCSI IDs (0–15)

The devices are identified by a unique SCSI ID. The SCSI ID of a device in a drive enclosure that has a backplane is set either by jumpers or by the slot in the enclosure the device is installed into, depending on the model of the enclosure. In the latter case, each slot on the enclosure's backplane delivers control signals to the drive to select a unique SCSI ID. It is important that all devices have unique IDs. The bootable hard disk should be set with an ID of 0, and the host controller should be set at 7 or 15 in the case of a 16-bit SCSI (it will be the highest number possible based on the SCSI width). Each end of the chain must be terminated.

In some cases, a single SCSI *target* (as they are called) may contain multiple drives within the unit. In these cases, the drives are differentiated with a second number called a *logical unit number* (LUN).

Adapters

In many cases, you will need to attach a device to a computer on which the correct connectors are not present. In these cases, there are adapters (converters) and connectors that can be used to connect the device to a connector type for which it was not designed. In this section, you'll look at some of the more common of these.

DVI to HDMI

These adapters connect from HDMI to DVI and come in a number of gender combinations (male DVI to female HDMI, male DVI to male HDMI, female DVI to male HDMI, and so on) and as either a cable or simply an inline connector. Figure 3.19 shows an inline connector.

FIGURE 3.19   HDMI to DVI

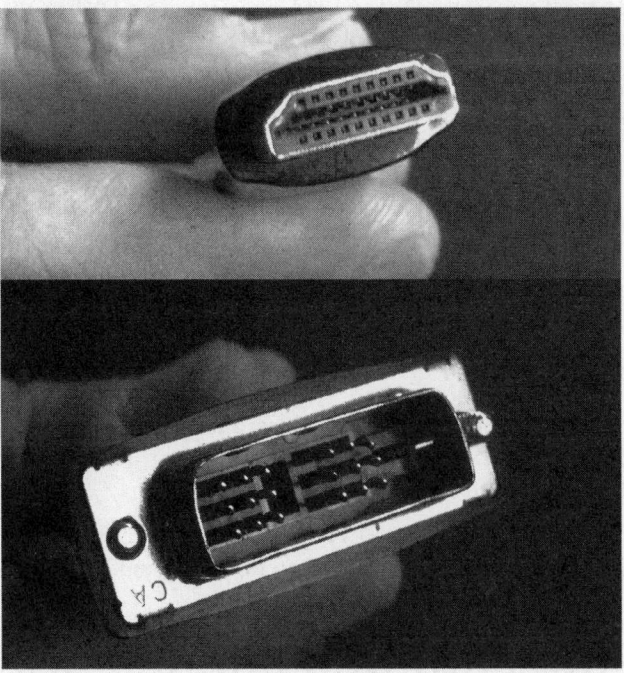

USB to Ethernet

These converters allow you to use a USB port as a network interface. They come both as cables and as inline connectors. Figure 3.20 shows an example of a USB-to-Ethernet adapter.

FIGURE 3.20   USB to Ethernet

DVI to VGA

In cases where you need to convert DVI to VGA, you can use a DVI-to-VGA adapter. These come as a cable or inline connectors and also come in a variety of gender combinations. Figure 3.21 shows an example of the ends of this adapter.

FIGURE 3.21   DVI to VGA

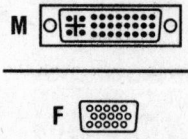

Exam essentials

Identify display connectors, their associated cables, and the maximum cable lengths.   This includes but is not limited to DVI in all variants, DisplayPort, RCA, HD-15 (or DB-15), BNC, miniHDMI, and miniDIN-6.

Identify hard drive cables and adapters.   These include SATA, eSATA, IDE, and SCSI. It also includes adapters like DVI to HDMI, USB to Ethernet, and DVI to VGA.

3.2 Identify common connector types.

A computer's peripheral ports are the physical connectors outside the computer. Cables of various types are designed to plug into these ports and create a connection between the PC and the external devices that may be attached to it. A successful IT technician should have an in-depth knowledge of ports and cables.

Because the peripheral components need to be upgraded frequently, either to keep pace with technological change or to replace broken devices, a well-rounded familiarity with the ports and their associated cabling is required. The topics covered in this objective include the following connector types:

- RJ-11
- RJ-45
- RS-232
- BNC
- RG-59
- RG-6
- USB
- Micro-USB

- Mini-USB
- USB-C
- DB-9
- Lightning
- SCSI
- eSATA
- Molex

RJ-11

An RJ-11, as just described and shown in Figure 3.22, is a standard connector for a telephone line and is used to connect a computer modem to a phone line. It looks much like an RJ-45 but is noticeably smaller.

RJ-45

A registered jack (RJ) is a plastic plug with small metal tabs, like a telephone cord plug. Numbering is used in the naming: RJ-11 has two metal tabs, and RJ-14 has four. RJ-45 has eight tabs and is used for Ethernet 10 BaseT/100 BaseT, 1000Base, and 10GBase networking. The maximum cable length is 100 meters but can vary slightly based on the category of cabling used. Figure 3.22 shows RJ-11 (left) and RJ-45 (right) connectors.

FIGURE 3.22   RJ-11 and RJ-45

RS-232

The RS-232 standard had been commonly used in computer serial ports. A serial cable (and port) uses only one wire to carry data in each direction; all the rest are wires for signaling and traffic control.

Common bit rates include 1,200; 2,400; 4,800; 9,600; 14,400; 19,200; 38,400; 57,600; and 115,200 bits per second. The connector used for serial is a D-shaped connector with a metal ring around a set of pins. These are named for the number of pins/holes used: DB-25, DB-9, HD-15 (also known as DB-15), and so on. Figure 3.23 shows DB-25, DB-15, and DB-9. HD-15 is covered in the section "VGA."

FIGURE 3.23 DB-25, DB-15, and DB-9 ports

BNC

Bayonet Neill–Concelman (BNC) connectors are sometimes used in the place of RCA connectors for video electronics, so you may encounter this connector type, especially when video equipment connects to a PC. Their normal use is with coaxial cabling, however. In many cases, you may be required to purchase an adapter to convert this to another form of connection because it is rare to find one on the PC. Figure 3.24 shows male and female BNC connectors.

FIGURE 3.24 BNC

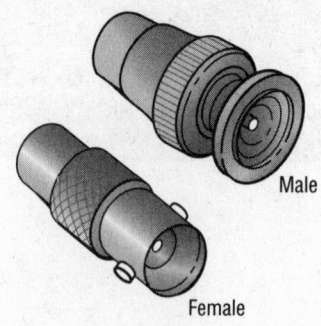

Male

Female

RG-59

The RG-59 connector, which is also normally used for coaxial cabling, is used to generate low-power video connections. This cable cannot be used over long distances because of its high-frequency power losses. In such cases, RG-6 cables are used instead.

RG-6

RG-6 is another connector normally used with coaxial cabling. It is often used for cable TV and cable modems. It can run longer distances than RG-59 and support digital signals.

USB

USB connectors come in two types and two form factors or sizes. The type A connector is what is found on USB hubs, on host controllers (cards that are plugged into slots to provide USB connections), and on the front and back panels of computers. Type B is the type of USB connector found on the end of the cable that plugs into the devices. For more information, see the "USB" section under objective 3.1 earlier in the chapter.

Micro-USB/Mini-USB

USB connectors also come in a mini version and a micro version. The micro version is used on mobile devices, such as mobile phones, GPS units, PDAs, and digital cameras; whereas the mini is found in applications described in the previous paragraph. The choice between a standard A and B and a mini A and B will be dictated by what is present on the device. The cables used cannot exceed 5 meters in length. Figure 3.12 earlier in the chapter shows, from left to right, a standard Type A, a mini Type A, a standard Type B, and a mini Type B. Some manufacturers have chosen to implement a mini connector that is proprietary, choosing not to follow the standard.

USB-C

The USB-C connectors connect to both hosts and devices, replacing various USB-B and USB-A connectors and cables with a standard connection. This connector type was discussed and illustrated earlier in this chapter, in the section "USB-C."

DB-9

The DB-9 is a 9-pin serial connector and was discussed earlier in this chapter in the section "RS-232."

Lightning

Apple uses what it calls the Lightning connector for power. This connector was discussed earlier in this chapter in the section "Lightning" under objective 3.1.

SCSI

Small Computer System Interface (SCSI) is most commonly used for hard disks and tape drives, but it can connect a wide range of other devices, including scanners and CD drives. SCSI was discussed earlier in this chapter in the section "SCSI" under objective 3.1.

eSATA

As introduced and illustrated earlier in the chapter, connections for storage devices can be either SATA or IDE. IDE was the only option early on, and then SATA came on the scene. SATA came out as a standard and was first adopted in desktops and then laptops. Whereas ATA had always been an interface that sends 16 bits at a time, SATA sends only one bit at a time. The benefit is that the cable used can be much smaller, and faster cycling can actually increase performance. SATA uses a seven-wire cable that can be up to 1 meter in length. eSATA cables can be up to 2 meters. Figure 3.15 earlier shows the SATA connector, and Figure 3.16 shows the eSATA connector.

Table 3.4 lists the speeds of the options.

TABLE 3.4   SATA speeds

Standard	Transfer Speed
SATA 1.0	150 MBps
SATA 2.0	300 MBps
SATA 3.0	600 MBps
SATA 3.2	1,969 MBps
eSATA	6 GBps

Molex

Connectors usually used for computer fans are called Molex connectors, and there can be several types. The following are some examples:

- A three-pin Molex connector is used when connecting a fan to the motherboard or other circuit board. Figure 3.25 shows the three-pin Molex.

- A four-pin Molex connector includes an additional pin used for a pulse-width modulation signal to provide variable speed control. These connectors can be plugged into three-pin headers but will lose their fan speed control. Figure 3.26 shows the four-pin Molex connector.

FIGURE 3.25   Three-pin Molex

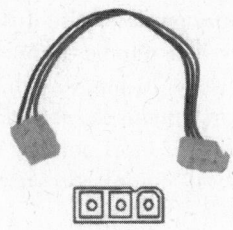

FIGURE 3.26   Four-pin Molex

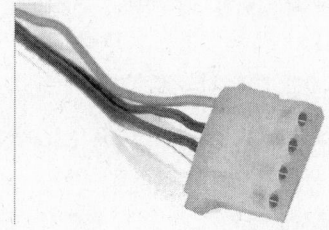

Exam essentials

Identify device connectors.   This includes but is not limited to SATA, eSATA, USB, IEEE 1394, PS/2, and audio.

3.3 Given a scenario, install RAM types.

RAM slots contain the memory chips. There are many and varied types of memory for PCs today, which I'll outline in this section. Objective 3.3 includes the following topics:

- RAM types
- Single channel
- Dual channel
- Triple channel
- Error correcting
- Parity versus nonparity

   PCs use memory chips arranged on a small circuit board. These circuit boards are called *single inline memory modules* (SIMMs) or *dual inline memory modules* (DIMMs). DIMMs utilize connectors on both sides of the board, whereas SIMMS utilize single connectors that are mirrored on both sides. DIMM is 64-bit and SIMM is 32-bit. There is also

a high-speed type of RAM called *Rambus dynamic RAM* (RDRAM), which comes on circuit boards called *Rambus inline memory modules* (RIMMs).

Along with chip placement, memory modules also differ in the number of conductors, or
pins, that the particular module uses. The number of pins used directly affects the overall
size of the memory slot. Slot sizes include 30-pin, 72-pin, 168-pin, and 184-pin. Laptop
memory comes in smaller form factors known as *small outline DIMMs* (SODIMMs).
Figure 3.27 shows the form factors for the most popular memory chips. Notice that they
basically look the same, but the memory module sizes are different.

FIGURE 3.27   Various memory module form factors

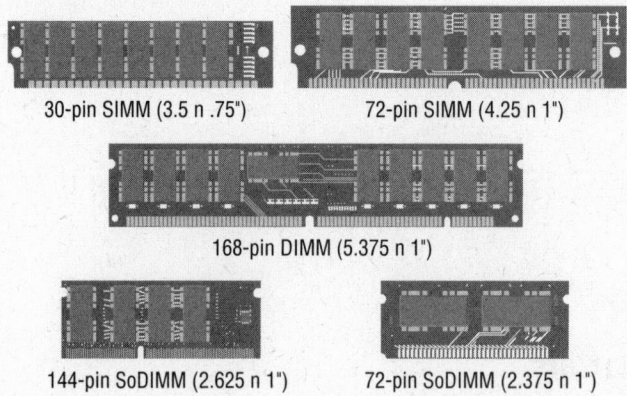

30-pin SIMM (3.5 n .75")   72-pin SIMM (4.25 n 1")

168-pin DIMM (5.375 n 1")

144-pin SoDIMM (2.625 n 1")   72-pin SoDIMM (2.375 n 1")

Installing RAM is simply a matter of sliding the RAM into its slot and pressing down
until it clicks. The more difficult part is making sure you have the correct RAM type and
the RAM type matches in all slots.

RAM types

Physically, RAM is a collection of integrated circuits that store data and program information as patterns of 1s and 0s (on and off states) in the chip. Most memory chips require
constant power (also called a *constant refresh*) to maintain those patterns of 1s and 0s. If
power is lost, all those tiny switches revert to the off position, effectively erasing the data
from memory. Some memory types, however, don't require a refresh.

This section discusses those RAM types and features.

SODIMM

Portable computers (notebooks and subnotebooks) require smaller sticks of RAM because
of their smaller size. One of the two types used is small outline DIMM (SODIMM), which
can have 72, 144, or 200 pins, while desktops use a full-size DIMM. Figure 3.27 earlier
shows the form factors for 72- and 144-pin SODIMMs.

DDR

Double Data Rate (DDR) is clock-doubled SDRAM. The memory chip can perform reads and writes on both sides of any clock cycle (the up, or start, and the down, or ending), thus doubling the effective memory executions per second. So, if you're using DDR SDRAM with a 100 MHz memory bus, the memory will execute reads and writes at 200 MHz and transfer the data to the processor at 100 MHz. The advantage of DDR over regular SDRAM is increased throughput and thus increased overall system speed.

DDR2

DDR SDRAM is Double Data Rate 2 (DDR2). This allows for two memory accesses for each rising and falling clock and effectively doubles the speed of DDR. DDR2-667 chips work with speeds at 667 MHz and are also referred to as PC2-5300 modules.

DDR3

The primary benefit of DDR3 over DDR2 is that it transfers data at twice the rate of DDR2 (eight times the speed of its internal memory arrays), enabling higher bandwidth or peak data rates. By performing two transfers per cycle of a quadrupled clock, a 64-bit-wide DDR3 module may achieve a transfer rate of up to 64 times the memory clock speed in megabytes per second. In addition, the DDR3 standard permits chip capacities of up to 8 GB.

DDR4

DDR4 SDRAM is an abbreviation for double data rate fourth-generation synchronous dynamic random-access memory. DDR4 is not compatible with any earlier type of random-access memory (RAM). The DDR4 standard allows for DIMMs of up to 64 GB in capacity, compared to DDR3's maximum of 8 GB per DIMM. Higher bandwidths are achieved by sending more read/write commands per second. To allow this, the standard divides the DRAM banks into two or four selectable bank groups so that transfers to different bank groups may be done more rapidly. Table 3.5 lists the selected memory standards, speeds, and formats.

TABLE 3.5   Selected memory details

Module Standard	Speed	Format
DDR500	4,000 MBps	PC4000
DDR533	4,266 MBps	PC4200
DDR2-667	5,333 MBps	PC2-5300
DDR2-750	6,000 MBps	PC2-6000

TABLE 3.5   Selected memory details *(continued)*

Module Standard	Speed	Format
DDR2-800	6,400 MBps	PC2-6400
DDR3-800	6,400 MBps	PC3-6400
DDR3-1600	12,800 MBps	PC3-12800
DDR4-1866M	14,933 MBps	PC4-14900
DDR4-2133P	17,066.67 MBps	PC4-17000
DDR4-2400R	19,200 MBps	PC4-19200
DDR4-2666U	21,333 MBps	PC4-21333
DDR4-2933W	23,466 MBps	PC4-23466
DDR4-3200W	25,600 MBps	PC4-25600

Single channel/dual channel/triple channel

Utilizing multiple channels between the RAM and the memory controller increases the transfer speed between these two components. Single-channel RAM does not take advantage of this concept, but dual-channel memory does and creates two 64-bit data channels. Do *not* confuse this with DDR or double data rate. DDR doubles the rate by accessing the memory module twice per clock cycle.

This strategy requires a motherboard that supports it and two or more memory modules. The modules go in separate color-coded banks, as shown in Figure 3.28.

FIGURE 3.28   Dual-channel memory slots

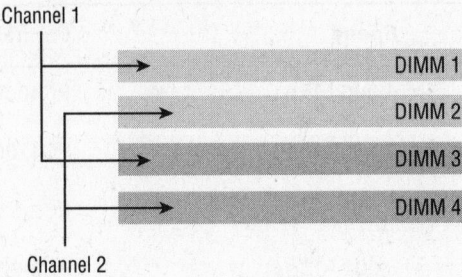

Triple-channel architecture adds a third memory module and reduces memory latency by interleaving or accessing each module sequentially with smaller bits of data rather than completely filling up one module before accessing the next one. Data is spread among the modules alternatingly with the potential to triple bandwidth as opposed to storing the data all on one module.

Error correcting

There are two error checking methods used in memory: testing for a parity bit or its absence and using Error Correction Code. This section looks at both methods.

Parity vs. Nonparity

RAM is supplied either with no parity (8 data bits per byte) or with parity (8 data bits and 1 parity bit per byte, for a total of 9 bits per byte). If present, parity bits are used to determine whether data moving to and from memory has been corrupted or damaged (thus changed) in the transmission. You can identify parity SIMMs by counting the number of chips on the stick. If there are nine, it's parity RAM. If there are eight, it's nonparity.

When do you choose parity RAM? Usually, the motherboard requires either parity or nonparity RAM; a few motherboards will accept either. Nowadays, parity RAM is needed only in highly critical computing tasks because advances in RAM technology have created reliable RAM that seldom makes errors.

ECC vs. Non-ECC

Another type of RAM error correction is Error Correction Code (ECC). RAM with ECC can detect and correct errors. As with parity RAM, additional information needs to be stored, and more processing needs to be done, making ECC RAM more expensive and a little slower than nonparity and parity RAM. Both ECC and parity memory work in ECC mode. However, ECC memory does not work in plain parity checking mode because the extra bits cannot be individually accessed when ECC memory is used. This type of parity RAM is now obsolete. Most RAM today is non-ECC.

Installation/RAM slots

RAM slots contain the memory chips. There are many and varied types of memory for PCs today, as discussed under "RAM types" earlier in this chapter. As mentioned, PCs use memory chips arranged on a small circuit board. These circuit boards are called *single inline memory modules* (SIMMs) or *dual inline memory modules* (DIMMs). Figure 3.29 illustrates SIMMs, and Figure 3.30 illustrates DIMMs. DIMMs utilize connectors on both sides of the board, whereas SIMMS utilize single connectors that are mirrored on both sides. DIMM is a 64-bit format, and SIMM is 32-bit. There is also a high-speed type of RAM called *Rambus dynamic RAM* (RDRAM), which comes on circuit boards called *Rambus inline memory modules* (RIMMs).

FIGURE 3.29 SIMMs

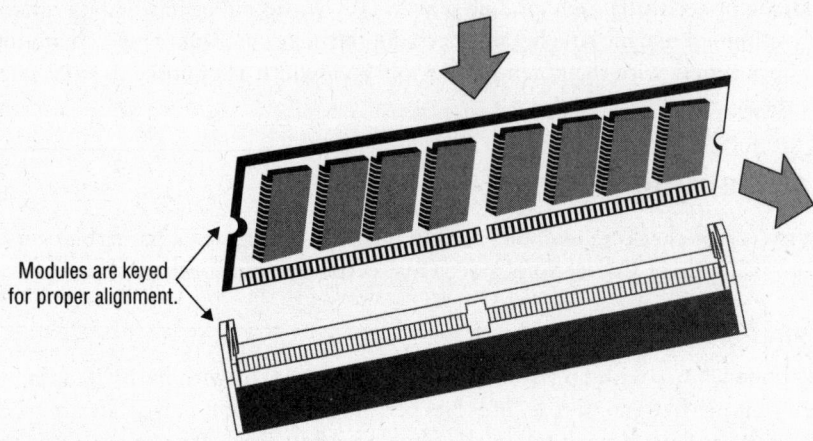

Modules are keyed
for proper alignment.

FIGURE 3.30 DIMMs

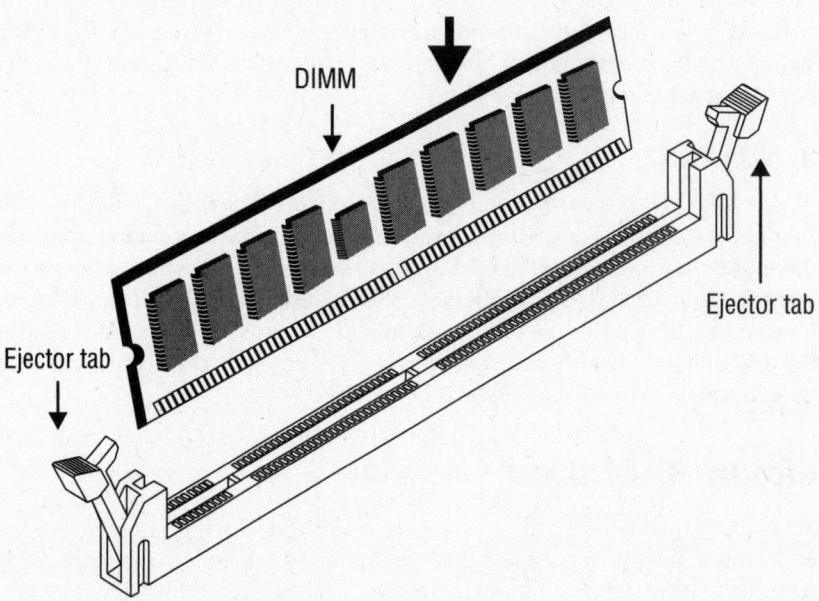

DIMM

Ejector tab

Ejector tab

   Along with chip placement, memory modules also differ in the number of conductors, or pins, that the particular module uses. The number of pins used directly affects the overall size of the memory slot. Slot sizes include 30-pin, 72-pin, 168-pin, and 184-pin. Laptop memory comes in smaller form factors known as *small outline DIMMs* (SODIMMs), shown in Figure 3.27 earlier.

Memory slots are easy to identify on a motherboard. They're usually white and placed close together. The number of memory slots varies from motherboard to motherboard, but the appearance of the different slots is similar. Metal pins in the bottom make contact with the soldered tabs on each memory module. Small metal or plastic tabs on each side of the slot keep the memory module securely in its slot.

Exam essentials

Identify the types of memory. Types of memory include single data rate (SDRAM), double data rate (DDR), DDR2, and DDR3. These types differ in their data rate. Memory can also differ in packaging. There are SIMMS (single module) and DIMMs (double modules). They also can use either parity or ECC for error checking and can be single, dual, or triple channel, with multiple channels widening the path between the memory and the memory controller.

Follow RAM speed and compatibility guidelines. Faster memory can be added to a PC with slower memory installed, but the system will operate only at the speed of the slowest module present. RAM types cannot be mixed.

3.4 Given a scenario, select, install, and configure storage devices.

Storage media hold the data being accessed, as well as the files the system needs to operate and the data that needs to be saved. The various types of storage differ in terms of capacity, the access time, and the physical media being used. This section covers the installation and configuration of various storage devices. The topics addressed in objective 3.4 include the following:

- Optical drives
- Solid-state/flash drives
- Magnetic hard drives
- Hybrid drives
- Flash
- Configurations

Optical drives

Optical drives work by using a laser rather than magnetism to change the characteristics of the storage medium. This is true for CD-ROM drives, DVD drives, and Blu-ray, all of which are discussed in the following sections.

CD-ROM/CD-RW

CD-ROM stands for Compact Disc Read-Only Memory. The CD-ROM media is used for long-term storage of data. CD-ROM media is read-only, meaning that once information is written to a CD, it can't be erased or changed. Access time for CD-ROM drives is considerably slower than for a hard drive. Standard CDs normally hold 650 MB to 700 MB of data and use the ISO 9660 standard, which allows them to be used on multiple platforms.

Compact Disc-ReWritable (CD-RW) media is a rewritable optical disc. A CD-RW drive requires more sensitive laser optics. It can write data to the disc but also has the ability to erase that data and write more data to the disc. It does this by liquefying the layer where the data resides (removing the reflectivity placed there by the writing process used to create the old data) and then creating new reflectivity in the same layer upon writing again that represents the new data. Two states of reflectivity are used to represent the 0s and 1s for the data. CD-RWs cannot be read in some CD-ROM drives built prior to 1997.

DVD-ROM/DVD-RW/DVD-RW DL

Because DVD-ROM drives use slightly different technology than CD-ROM drives, they can store up to 4.7 GB of data in a single-layer configuration. This makes DVDs a better choice than CDs for distributing large software bundles. Many software packages today are so huge that they require multiple CDs to hold all the installation and reference files. A single DVD, in a double-sided, double-layered configuration, can hold as much as 17 GB (as much as 26 regular CDs).

As you might expect, the primary advantage of DVD-RW drives over DVD-R drives is the ability to erase and rewrite to a DVD-RW disc. In these drives, a layer of metal alloy on the disk is manipulated to erase and write the data, rather than burning into the disc itself, similar to the operation of CD-RW.

A dual-layer DVD-RW disc employs a second physical layer within the disc itself. The drive with dual-layer capability accesses the second layer by shining the laser through the first semitransparent layer.

Blu-ray

Blu-ray recorders have been available since 2003, and they have the ability to record more information than a standard DVD using similar optical technology. In recent years, Blu-ray has been more synonymous with recording television and movie files than data, but the Blu-ray specification (1.0) includes two data formats: BD-R for write-once and BD-RE for rewritable media (more later in this section). BD-J is capable of more sophisticated bonus features than provided by standard DVD, including network access, picture-in-picture, and access to expanded local storage. With the exception of the Internet access component, these features are called Bonus View. The addition of Internet access is called BD Live.

In the official specification, as noted on the Blu-ray Disc Association website (http://us.blu-raydisc.com/), the *r* is lowercase. CompTIA favors the uppercase *R*.

The current capacity of a Blu-ray is 100 GB. As a final note, there was a long-running (but finally complete) battle between Blu-ray and HD DVD to be the format of the future, and Blu-ray won.

BD-R

Blu-ray players have two data formats: BD-R for recording computer data and BD-RE for rewritable media. BD-R can be written to only one time.

BD-RE

Blu-ray Disc Recordable Erasable (BD-RE) can be erased and written to multiple times. Disc capacities are 25 GB for single-layer discs, 50 GB for double-layer discs, 100 GB for triple-layer discs, and 128 GB for quad-layer discs.

Solid-state drives

Solid-state drives (SSDs) retain data in nonvolatile memory chips and contain no moving parts. Compared to electromechanical hard disk drives (HDDs), SSDs are typically less susceptible to physical shock, are silent, have lower access time and latency, use less power, but are more expensive per gigabyte.

M2 drives

M.2, formerly known as the Next Generation Form Factor (NGFF), is a specification for internally mounted computer expansion cards and associated connectors. It replaces the mSATA standard. M.2 modules are rectangular, with an edge connector on one side and a semicircular mounting hole at the center of the opposite edge. They can use PCI-Express, Serial ATA, and USB 3 connectors The M.2 standard allows module widths of 12, 16, 22, and 30 mm, and lengths of 16, 26, 30, 38, 42, 60, 80, and 110 mm.

NVME

NVM Express (NVMe) or Non-Volatile Memory Host Controller Interface Specification (NVMHCIS) is an open logical device interface specification for accessing nonvolatile storage media attached via a PCI Express (PCIe) bus. It allows host hardware and software to fully exploit the levels of parallelism possible in modern SSDs. The latest version is 1.3c.

SATA 2.5

SATA revision 2.5 consolidated the specification to a single document.

Magnetic hard drives

Before the development and use of SSDs, magnetic drives were—and are still as of this writing—the main type of hard drive used. The drive itself is a mechanical device that spins a number of disks or platters and uses a magnetic head to read and write data to the surface of the disks. One of the advantages of SSDs (discussed in the next section) is the absence of mechanical parts that can malfunction. Figure 3.31 shows the parts of a magnetic hard drive.

FIGURE 3.31   Magnetic hard drive

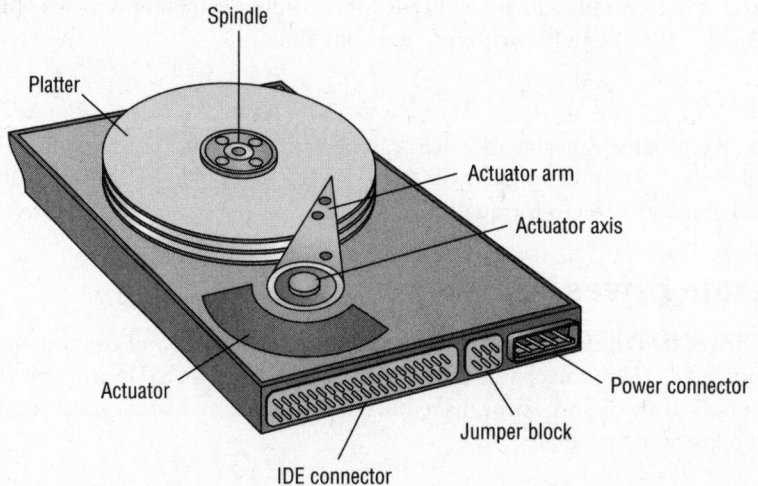

The basic hard disk geometry consists of three components: the number of sectors that each track contains, the number of read/write heads in the disk assembly, and the number of cylinders in the assembly. This set of values is known as CHS (for cylinders/heads/sectors). A *cylinder* is the set of tracks of the same number on all the writeable surfaces of the assembly. It is called a cylinder because the collection of all same-number tracks on all writable surfaces of the hard disk assembly looks like a geometric cylinder when connected vertically. Therefore, cylinder 1, for instance, on an assembly that contains three platters comprises six tracks (one on each side of each platter), each labeled track 1 on its respective surface. Figure 3.32 illustrates the key terms presented in this discussion.

FIGURE 3.32   Cylinders, heads, and sections

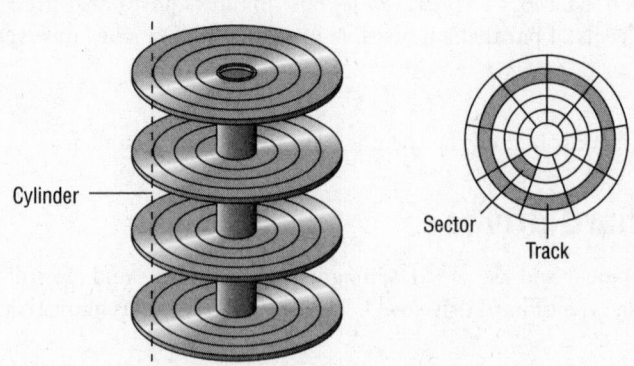

5,400 rpm

The rotational speed of the disk or platter has a direct influence on how quickly the drive can locate any specific disk sector on the drive. This locational delay is called *latency* and is measured in milliseconds (ms). The faster the rotation, the smaller the delay will be. A drive operating at 5,400 rpms will experience about 5.5 ms of this delay.

7,200 rpm

Drives that operate at 7,200 rpm will experience about 4.16 ms of latency. A typical 7,200 rpm desktop hard drive has a sustained data transfer rate up to 1,030 Mbps. This rate depends on the track location, so it will be higher for data on the outer tracks and lower toward the inner tracks.

10,000 rpm

At 10,000 rpm, the latency will decrease to about 3 ms. Data transfer rates also generally go up with a higher rotational speed but are influenced by the density of the disk (the number of tracks and sectors present in a given area).

15,000 rpm

Drives that operate at 15,000 rpm are higher-end drives and suffer only 2 ms of latency. These drives also generate more heat, requiring more cooling to the case. They also offer faster data transfer rates for the same areal density.

Sizes: 2.5/3.5

Magnetic hard drives come in two sizes, 2.5 inch and 3.5 inch. Smaller drives are for laptops, while the larger size is for desktop computers.

Hybrid drives

A hybrid drive is one in which both traditional mechanical and SSD technologies are combined. This is done to take advantage of the speed of SSDs while maintaining the cost effectiveness of mechanical drives.

There are two main approaches to this: dual-drive hybrid and solid-state hybrid. Dual-drive systems contain both types of drives in the same machine, and performance is optimized by the user placing more frequently used information on the SSD and less frequently accessed data on the mechanical drive. In some cases, the operating system can create hybrid volumes using space in both drives.

An SSD, on the other hand, is a single storage device that includes solid-state flash memory in a traditional hard drive. Data that is most related to the performance of the machine is stored in the flash memory, resulting in improved performance. Figure 3.33 shows the two approaches to hybrid drives.

FIGURE 3.33 Hybrid drive approaches

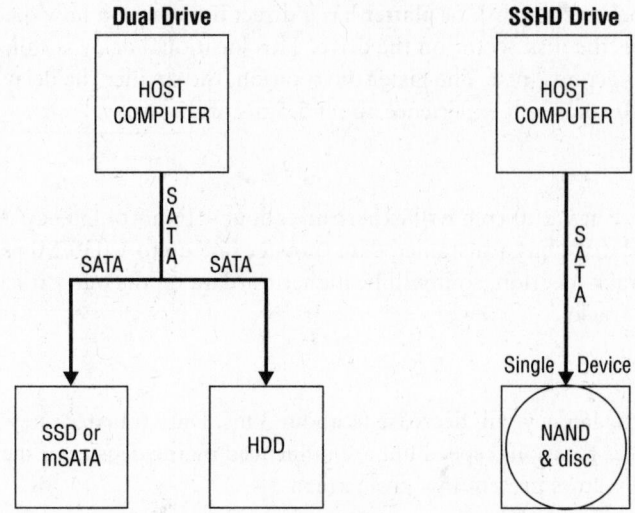

Flash

Thumb drives are USB flash drives that have become extremely popular for transporting files. Figure 3.34 shows three thumb drives (also known as keychain drives) next to a pack of gum for size comparison.

FIGURE 3.34 USB flash

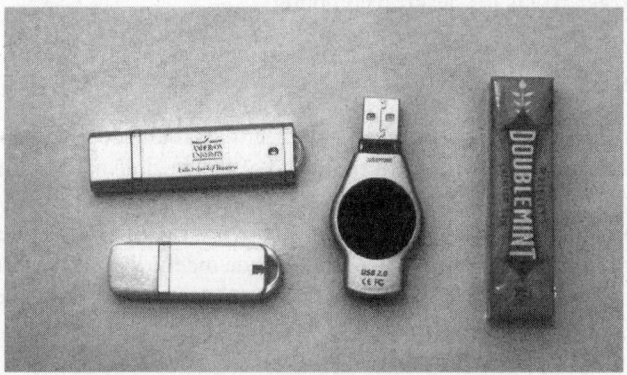

Like other flash drives, thumb drives can be found in a number of different size capacities. Many models include a write-protect switch to keep you from accidentally overwriting files stored on the drive. Most include an LED to show when they're connected to the USB port. Other names for thumb drives include travel drives, flash drives, and jump drives.

Flash drives (which are solid-state) have been growing in popularity for years and completely replaced floppy disks because of their capacity and small size. Flash technology is ideally suited for use not only with computers but also with many other things—digital cameras, MP3 players, and so on. This section discusses the various forms of these drives.

SD card

Secure Digital (SD) cards are just one type of flash; there are many others. The maximum capacity of a standard SD card is 512 GB, and there are two other standards that go beyond this: Secure Digital High Capacity (SDHC) can go to 32 GB and Secure Digital Extra Capacity (SDXC) to 2 TB. Figure 3.35 shows a Compact Flash card (the larger of the two) and an SD card along with an eight-in-one card reader/writer. The reader shown connects to the USB port and then interacts with Compact Flash, Compact Flash II, Memory Stick, Memory Stick PRO, SmartMedia, xD-Picture cards, SD, and MultiMediaCards. The SD card specification defines three physical sizes, discussed in the following sections.

FIGURE 3.35   SD and Compact Flash

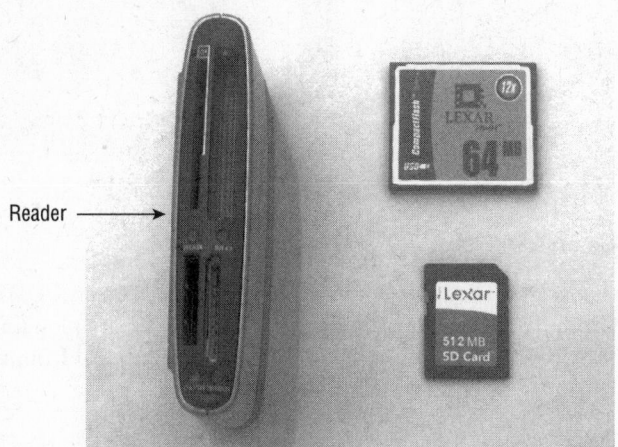

Reader

CompactFlash

Compact Flash (CF) cards are a widely used form of solid-state storage. There are two main subdivisions of CF cards: Type I (3.3-mm thick) and the thicker Type II (CF2) cards (5-mm thick). CF cards can be used directly in a PC card slot with a plug adapter, used as an ATA (IDE) or PCMCIA storage device with a passive adapter or with a reader, or attached to other types of ports such as USB or FireWire. Figure 3.35 shows a CF card.

Micro-SD card

Micro-SD is the smallest of the three. It is 11 mm × 15 mm × 1 mm.

Mini-SD card

Mini-SD is the middle child of the three SD form factors shown in Figure 3.36. It is
20 mm × 21.5 mm × 1.4 mm.

FIGURE 3.36   SD, micro, and mini SD

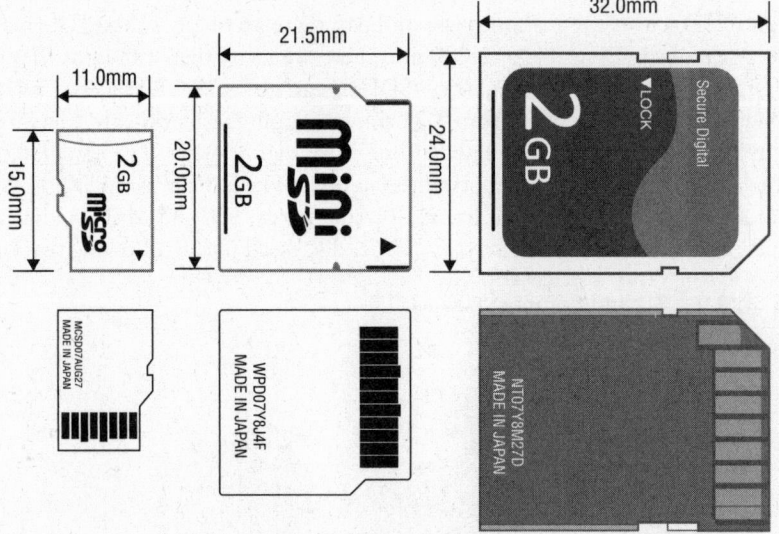

xD

xD-Picture card is a flash memory card format, used mainly in older digital cameras. xD
stands for Extreme Digital. xD cards are available in capacities from 16 MB up to 2 GB.
Pictures are transferred from a digital camera's xD card to a PC by plugging the camera
into the USB or IEEE 1394 (FireWire) cable or by removing the card from the camera and
inserting it into a card reader. Figure 3.37 shows an xD card.

FIGURE 3.37   xD card

Configurations

There are some special configuration scenarios that you should also understand. These include IDE and SCSI configurations, RAID levels, and hot swappable drives.

IDE configuration and setup (master, slave, cable select)

The primary benefit of IDE is that it's nearly universally supported. Almost every motherboard has IDE connectors.

A typical motherboard has two IDE connectors, and each connector can support up to two drives on the same cable. That means you're limited to four IDE devices per system unless you add an expansion board containing another IDE interface. In contrast, with SCSI (covered in the next section), you can have up to seven drives per interface (or even more on some types of SCSI).

Performance also may suffer when IDE devices share an interface. When you're burning CDs, for example, if the hard drive you are reading from is on the same cable as the CD drive you are writing to, errors may occur. SCSI drives are much more efficient with this type of transfer.

To install an IDE drive, do the following:

1. Set the master/slave jumper on the drive.

2. Install the drive in the drive bay.

3. Connect the power-supply cable.

4. Connect the ribbon cable to the drive and to the motherboard or IDE expansion board. Ensure that the master device is closest to the connection to the motherboard.

5. Configure the drive in BIOS Setup if it isn't automatically detected.

6. Partition and format the drive using the operating system.

Each IDE interface can have only one master drive on it. If there are two drives on a single cable, one of them must be the slave drive. This setting is accomplished via a jumper on the drive. Some drives have a separate setting for Single (that is, master with no slave) and Master (that is, master with a slave); others use the Master setting generically to refer to either case. The Cable Select setting will assume you have the primary drive first and secondary drive second on the cable. Figure 3.38 shows a typical master/slave jumper scenario, but different drives may have different jumper positions to represent each state. Today, the need for jumper settings has decreased because many drives can autodetect the master/slave relationship.

Most BIOS Setup programs today support plug and play, so they detect the new drive automatically at startup. If this doesn't work, the drive may not be installed correctly, the jumper settings may be wrong, or the BIOS Setup may have the IDE interface set to None rather than Auto. Enter BIOS Setup and find out. All you usually have to do is set the IDE interface to Auto and allow the BIOS to detect the drive.

FIGURE 3.38   Master/slave jumpers

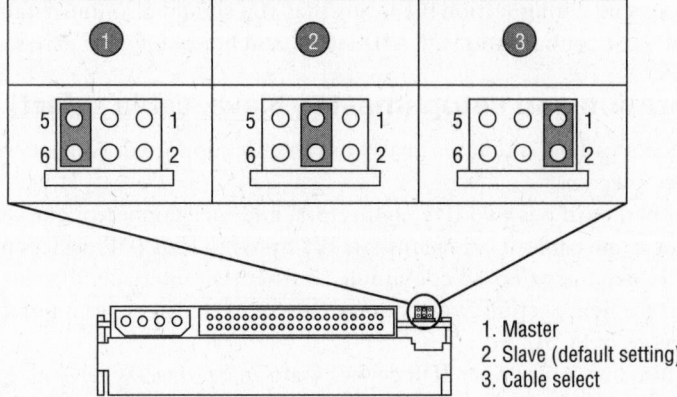

1. Master
2. Slave (default setting)
3. Cable select

In BIOS Setup for the drive, you might have the option of selecting a Direct Memory Access (DMA) channel or Programmed Input/Output (PIO) setting for the drive. Both are methods for improving drive performance by allowing the drive to write directly to RAM, bypassing the CPU when possible. For modern drives that support Ultra Direct Memory Access (UltraDMA), neither of these settings is necessary or desirable. The Ultra DMA interface is the fastest method used to transfer data through the ATA controller, usually between the computer and an ATA device.

When the drive is installed, you can proceed to partition and format it for the operating system you've chosen. Then, you can install your operating system of choice.

For a Windows 10 system, allow the Windows Setup program to partition and format the drive (when installing the operating system), or use the Disk Management utility in Windows to perform those tasks. To access Disk Management, from the Control Panel choose Administrative Tools and then Computer Management.

RAID 0, 1, 5, 10

RAID stands for Redundant Array of Independent (or Inexpensive) Disks. It's a way of combining the storage power of more than one hard disk for a special purpose such as increased performance or fault tolerance. RAID is more commonly done with SCSI drives, but it can be done with IDE or SATA drives. This section outlines the most common types of RAID. Because of the methods used to provide fault tolerance, the total amount of usable space in the array will vary, as discussed for each type.

RAID 0   RAID 0 is also known as *disk striping*. This is technically not RAID because it doesn't provide fault tolerance. Data is written across multiple drives, so one drive can be reading or writing while the next drive's read/write head is moving. This makes for faster data access. However, if any one of the drives fails, all content is lost. In RAID 0, since there is no fault tolerance, the usable space in the drive is equal to the total space on all the drives. So if the two drives in an array have 250 GB each of space, 500 GB will be the available drive space. RAID 0 is shown in Figure 3.39.

FIGURE 3.39   RAID 0

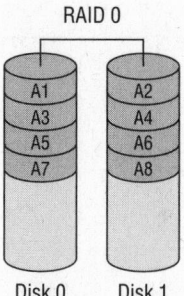

RAID 1   RAID 1 is also known as *disk mirroring*. This is a method of producing fault tolerance by writing all data simultaneously to two separate drives. If one drive fails, the other drive contains all the data and may also be used as a source of the data. However, disk mirroring doesn't help access speed, and the cost is double that of a single drive. Since RAID 1 repeats the data on two drives, only one half of the total drive space is available for data. So if two 250 GB drives are used in the array, 250 GB will be the available drive space. RAID 1 is shown in Figure 3.40.

FIGURE 3.40   RAID 1

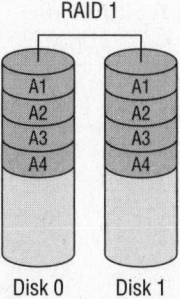

RAID 5   RAID 5 combines the benefits of RAID 0 and RAID 1 and is also known as *striping with parity*. It uses a parity block distributed across all the drives in the array, in addition to striping the data across them. That way, if one drive fails, the parity information can be used to recover what was on the failed drive. A minimum of three drives is required. RAID 5 uses $1/n$ (n = the number of drives in the array) for parity information

(for example, one-third of the space in a three-drive array), and only 1 ($1/n$) is available for data. So if three 250 GB drives are used in the array (for a total of 750 GB), 500 GB will be the available drive space. RAID 5 is shown in Figure 3.41.

FIGURE 3.41   RAID 5

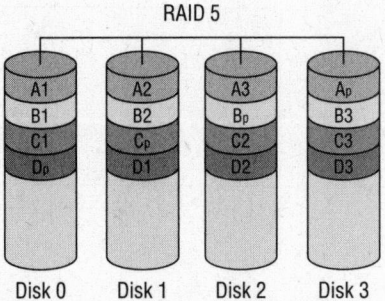

RAID 10   RAID 10 is also known as RAID 1+0. Striped sets are mirrored (a minimum of four drives, and the number of drives must be even). It provides fault tolerance and improved performance but increases complexity. Since this is effectively a mirrored stripe set and a stripe set gets 100 percent use of the drive without mirroring, this array will provide half of the total drive space in the array as available drive space. For example, if there are four 250 GB drives in a RAID 10 array (for a total of 1 TB), the available drive space will be 500 GB. RAID 10 is shown in Figure 3.42.

FIGURE 3.42   RAID 10

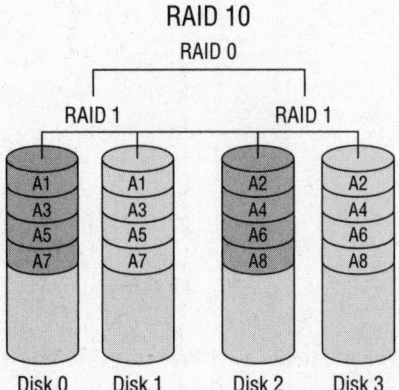

Hot swappable

If a drive can be attached to the PC without shutting down the PC, it is described as a hot-swappable drive. Drive types that are hot-swappable include USB, FireWire, SATA, and those that connect through Ethernet. You should always check the documentation to ensure that your drive supports this feature.

Exam essentials

Identify and differentiate the optical drive options for the long-term storage of data. Those options include CD-ROM, DVD-ROM, and Blu-Ray. When the ability to erase and rewrite to the disk is required, the options include CD-RW, DVD-RW, dual-layer (DL) DVD-RW, and Blu-ray Disc Recordable Erasable (BD-RE).

Describe the types of interfaces to connect a drive to the system.   Drives can be connected externally using USB, FireWire (IEEE 1394), eSATA, and Ethernet. Internally the connection types are SATA, IDE, and SCSI.

Appreciate the importance of the Master/Slave settings for IDE.   Each IDE interface can have only one master drive on it. If there are two drives on a single cable, one of them must be the slave drive. This setting is accomplished via a jumper on the drive.

Describe the operations of the SCSI bus.   SCSI devices reside on a single bus, which must be terminated on either end. Up to 8 or 16 devices can be attached to a single bus, depending on whether the SCSI bus is wide (0–15) or narrow (0–7). There also is a host bus controller, which is usually plugged into a slot in the computer or integrated into the motherboard.

Identify the advantages and disadvantages to both magnetic and solid-state drive operations. SSDs retain data in nonvolatile memory chips and contain no moving parts. Compared to electromechanical HDDs, SSDs are typically less susceptible to physical shock, are silent, and have lower access time and latency, but they are more expensive per gigabyte.

List the capacities of various storage systems.   These range from 650 MB for a CD-ROM up to 17 GB for a double-sided DL DVD.

Identify the pros and cons of various RAID options.   RAID 0 provides only performance enhancement, whereas RAID 1 and RAID 5 provide fault tolerance. RAID 10 provides both performance enhancement and fault tolerance. The cost for these options is the use of multiple hard drives in various arrangements.

3.5 Given a scenario, install and configure motherboards, CPUs, and add-on cards.

When working with motherboards, CPUs, and add-on cards, you are working with the basic components of a PC. In this section we'll look at the following topics from objective 3.5:

- Motherboard form factor
- Motherboard connectors types
- BIOS/UEFI settings
- CMOS battery
- CPU features

- Compatibility
- Cooling mechanism
- Expansion cards

Motherboard form factor

The motherboard is the physical platform through which all the connected components communicate. The motherboard provides basic services needed for the machine to operate and provides communication channels through which connected devices such as the processor, memory, disk drives, and expansion devices communicate.

 The figures in this section are representative of what can be expected. Minor variations depend on the motherboard manufacturer. Consult the documentation for your motherboard.

The spine of the computer is the *system board*, or *motherboard*. This component is made of green or brown fiberglass and is placed in the bottom or side of the case. It's the most important component in the computer because it connects all the other components of a PC together. On the system board you'll find the central processing unit (CPU), underlying circuitry, expansion slots, video components, RAM slots, and a variety of other chips. There are a number of different sizes or *form factors* of motherboards, which will be discussed in this section.

ATX

An older but still used form factor, Advanced Technology Extended (ATX), provided many design improvements over the previous version, the AT. These improvements include I/O ports built directly into the side of the motherboard, the CPU positioned so that the power-supply fan helps cool it, and the ability for the PC to be turned on and off via software. It uses a PS/2-style connector for the keyboard and mouse, which is rarely used today because USB keyboards are used. Newer ATX models have removed PS/2 connectors. The expansion slots are parallel to the narrow edge of the board. See Figure 3.43.

FIGURE 3.43   An ATX-style motherboard

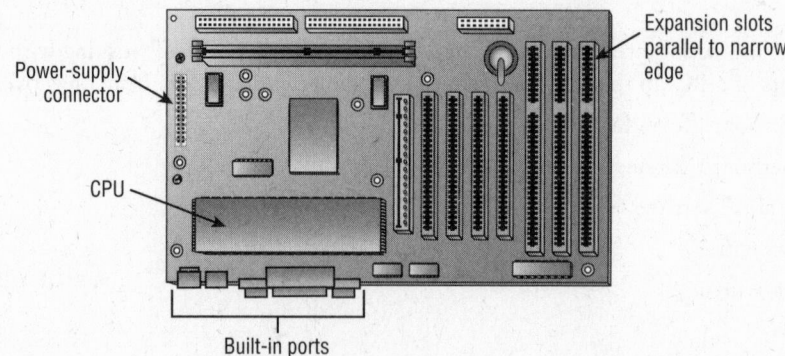

mATX

The mini-ATX has dimensions of 15 cm × 15 cm (5.9 in × 5.9 in) and is slightly smaller than the mini-ITX (discussed in the next section). It was originally part of the ATX specification but was removed after the introduction of micro-ATX. It uses less power, generates less heat, and fits into a single DIN space.

ITX

The Information Technology eXtended (ITX) motherboards—the mini-ITX, nano-ITX, and pico-ITX—were proposed by VIA Technologies. The mini-ITX fits in the same case as the micro-ATX; uses low power, which means it can be passively cooled (no fan); and has one expansion slot. The nano-ITX is even smaller; it is used for set-top boxes, media centers, and car computers. The pico-ITX is even smaller again, half the size of the nano-ITX. It uses daughter cards (extensions of the motherboard) to supply additional functionality.

Figure 3.44 compares common motherboard types and their sizes.

FIGURE 3.44   Motherboard sizes

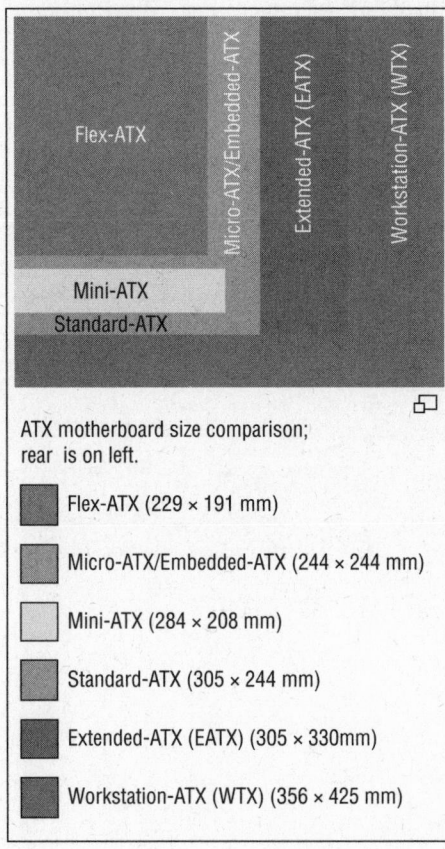

mITX

Mini-ITX is a 17 cm × 17 cm (6.7 in × 6.7 in) motherboard. It is commonly used in small-configured computer systems.

Motherboard connectors types

Expansion slots exist on a motherboard to allow for the addition of new interfaces to new technologies without replacing the motherboard. If expansion slots did not exist, you would have to buy a new motherboard every time you wanted to add a new device that uses an interface to the board that does not currently exist on the board. This section reviews various types of expansion slots as well as connecters on the board for components such as drives, panel lights, and the USB connector.

PCI

The Peripheral Component Interconnect (PCI) bus is a fast (33 MHz), wide (32-bit or 64-bit) expansion bus that was a modern standard in motherboards for general-purpose expansion devices. Its slots are typically white. PCI devices can share interrupt requests (IRQs) and other system resources with one another in some cases. You may see two PCI slots, but most motherboards have gone to newer standards. Figure 3.45 shows some PCI slots.

FIGURE 3.45 PCI bus connectors

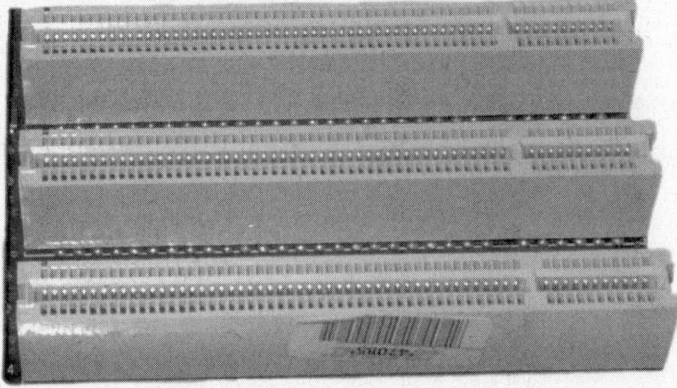

PCI cards that are 32-bit with 33 MHz operate up to 133 MBps, whereas 32-bit cards with 64 MHz operate up to 264 MBps. PCI cards that are 64-bit with 33 MHz operate up to 266 MBps, whereas 64-bit cards with 66 MHz operate up to 538 MBps.

PCIe

PCI Express (PCIE, PCI-E, or PCIe) uses a network of serial interconnects that operate at high speed. It's based on the PCI system; you can convert a PCIe slot to PCI using an adapter plug-in card, but you cannot convert a PCI slot to PCIe. Intended as a replacement for AGP and PCI, PCIe has the capability of being faster than AGP while maintaining the flexibility of PCI. There are five versions of PCIe: Version 1 is up to 8 GBps, version 2 is up to 16 GBps, version 3 is up to 32 GBps, version four is up to 64 GBps, and version five up to 128 GBps. Figure 3.46 shows the slots discussed so far in this section.

FIGURE 3.46 PCI slots

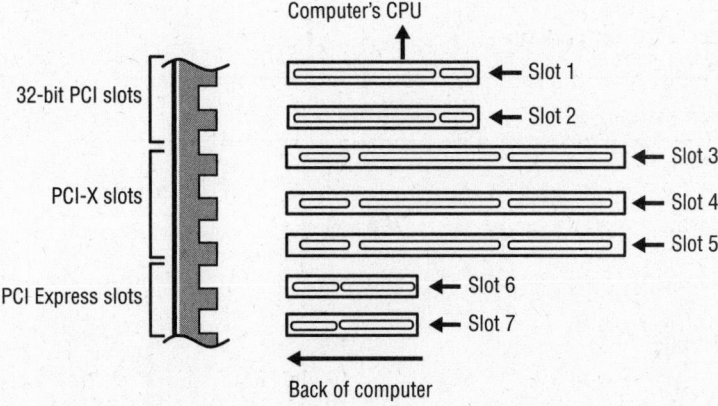

miniPCI

Laptops and other portable devices utilize an expansion card called the miniPCI. It has the same functionality as the PCI but has a much smaller form factor. Unlike portable PCM-CIA cards, which are inserted externally into a slot, these are installed inside the case. Figure 3.47 shows a miniPCI card alongside a miniPCI Express card. Table 3.6 lists the specifications of all the slot types discussed in this section.

FIGURE 3.47   miniPCI

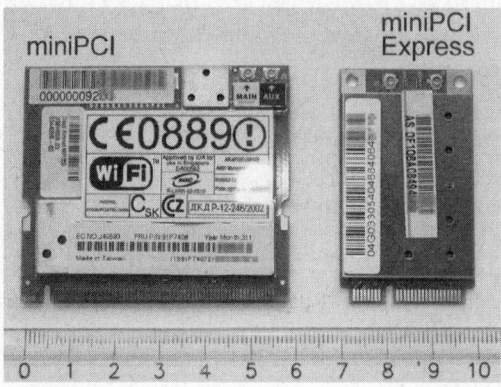

TABLE 3.6   PCI comparison

Type	Speeds
PCI 33 MHz 32-bit	133 MBps
PCI 33 MHz 64-bit	266 MBps
PCI 66 MHz 32-bit	264 MBps
PCI 66 MHz 64-bit	538 MBps
PCI-X version 1	1.06 GBps
PCI-X version 2	4.26 GBps

Riser card

Although it isn't common, you may occasionally encounter a slim-line case, which is a desktop-oriented case that is shorter and thinner than a normal one—so short that normal expansion boards won't fit perpendicular to the motherboard. In such cases a riser card is installed, which sits perpendicular to the motherboard and contains expansion slots. The expansion cards can then be oriented parallel to the motherboard when installed. So, it's a card that hosts other cards. Figure 3.48 shows a riser card from two angles.

FIGURE 3.48   Riser card

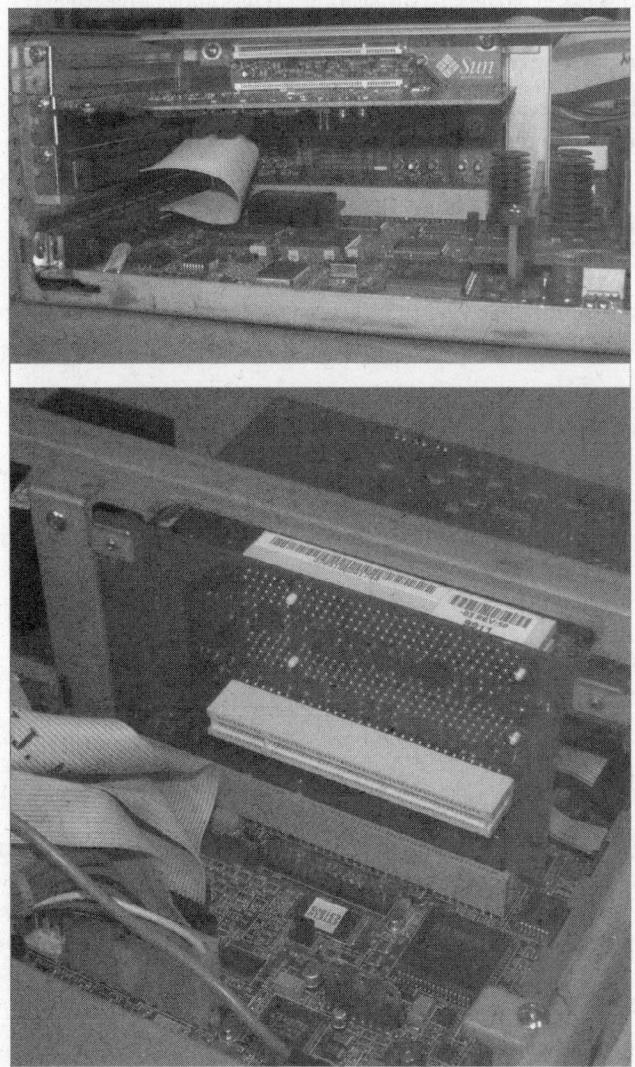

Socket types

To review, there are two basic socket types now on the board, Serial ATA and IDE.

SATA

SATA and eSATA were discussed earlier, in the section "eSATA" under objective 3.2.

IDE

IDE drives were discussed earlier, in the section "IDE" under objective 3.2.

Front panel connector

There are a number of interfaces, buttons, lights, and audio jacks in the front panel of the computer that must be connected to the board for power and functionality. This section discusses each of these and their respective methods of connection to the motherboard.

Internal USB connector

When USB ports exist on the front panel (as they almost always do these days), they must be connected to the motherboard so that the connected USB device can communicate with the computer. This is done with a 10-pin connector located on the board, as shown in Figure 3.49.

FIGURE 3.49 Front-panel power connectors

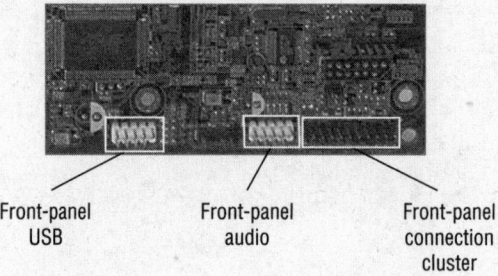

Front-panel
USB

Front-panel
audio

Front-panel
connection
cluster

Audio

When audio plugs or jacks exist in the front panel, as they do in most computers now, they must be connected to the motherboard if you are using the integrated sound card. (Otherwise, they may connect directly to the sound card.) Figure 3.49 shows an example of the audio plug on the board.

Power button

The power button located in the front panel must also be connected to the motherboard to communicate on/off information to the computer. This connector is located along with the remaining connectors discussed in this section, clustered in a group on the motherboard in the section labeled "Front-panel connection cluster" in Figure 3.49.

Power light

The power indicator light must also be provided with power and a connection to the board. It is also located in the section labeled "Front-panel connection cluster" in Figure 3.49.

Drive activity lights

The drive activity light, which indicates when a hard drive is being either read or written to, must have a connection to the motherboard both for power and to transmit the drive activity information. It is also located in the section labeled "Front-panel connection cluster" in Figure 3.49.

Reset button

The reset button, like all the other front-panel components, has a connection to the motherboard and is located in the section labeled "Front-panel connection cluster" in Figure 3.49.

BIOS/UEFI settings

PCs and other devices that use an operating system usually also contain firmware that provides low-level instructions to the device even in the absence of an operating system. This firmware, called either the Basic Input/Output System (BIOS) or the Unified Extensible Firmware Interface (UEFI), contains settings that can be manipulated as well as diagnostic utilities that can be used to monitor the device. This section discusses those settings and utilities.

Boot options

Each system has a default boot order, which is the order in which it checks the drives for a valid operating system to which it can boot. Usually, this order is set for the hard disk and then CD-ROM, but these components can be placed in any boot order. For example, you might set CD-ROM first to boot from a disk that already contains an operating system. If you receive an error message when booting, always check the CD-ROM, and if a nonsystem disk is present, remove it and reboot.

Firmware updates

Computer BIOSs don't go bad; they just become out-of-date or contain bugs. In the case of a bug, an upgrade will correct the problem. An upgrade may also be necessary when the BIOS doesn't support some component that you would like to install—a larger hard drive or a different type of processor, for instance.

Most of today's BIOSs are written to an electrically erasable programmable read-only memory (EEPROM) chip and can be updated through the use of software. Each manufacturer has its own method for accomplishing this. Check out the documentation for complete details. Regardless of the exact procedure, the process is referred to as *flashing* the BIOS. It means the old instructions are erased from the EEPROM chip and the new instructions are written to the chip.

UEFI is a standard firmware interface for PCs, designed to replace BIOS. Some advantages of UEFI include the following:

- Better security, which protects the preboot process
- Faster startup times and resuming from hibernation
- Support for drives larger than 2.2 TB
- Support for 64-bit firmware device drivers
- Capability to use BIOS with UEFI hardware

UEFI can also be updated by using an update utility from the motherboard vendor. In many cases, the steps are as follows:

1. Download the update file to a flash drive.
2. Insert the flash drive and reboot the machine.
3. Use the specified key sequence to enter the BIOS settings.
4. If necessary, disable secure boot.
5. Save the changes and reboot.
6. Reenter the BIOS settings.
7. Choose boot options, and boot from the flash drive.
8. Follow the specific directions with the update to locate the upgrade file on the flash drive.
9. Execute the file (usually by typing **flash**).
10. While the update is completing, ensure that you maintain power to the device.

Security settings

A number of security features are built into most BIOSs. They include BIOS passwords, drive encryption, Trusted Platform Module (TPM), and LoJack. These items are discussed in this section.

BIOS Passwords   In most CMOS Setup programs, you can set a supervisor password. Doing so requires a password to be entered in order to use the CMOS Setup program, effectively locking out users from making changes to it. You may also be able to set a user password, which restricts the PC from booting unless the password is entered.

To reset a forgotten password, you can remove the CMOS battery to reset everything. There also may be a Reset jumper on the motherboard. The CMOS battery is shown in Figure 3.53 later in the chapter.

Drive Encryption   Many operating systems provide the ability to encrypt an entire volume or drive, protecting a mobile device's data in the event of theft. A good example of this is BitLocker, which is available in Windows 10. The drives are encrypted with encryption keys, and the proper keys are required to boot the device and access the data.

BitLocker can be used with a TPM chip (discussed in the next paragraph), but it is not required. When this feature is in effect with no TPM chip, the keys are stored on a USB drive that must be presented during startup to allow access to the drives. Without the USB drive holding the key, the device will not boot.

TPM Chips   When the device has a TPM chip present on the motherboard, additional security and options become available. First the chip contains the keys that unlock the drives. When the computer boots, the TPM chip unlocks the drive only after it compares hashes of the drive to snapshots of the drive taken earlier. If any changes have been made or tampering has been done to the Windows installation, the TPM chip will not unlock the drives.

Moreover, you can (and should) combine this with a PIN entered at startup or a key located in a USB drive. In this scenario, the computer will not start unless the hashes pass the test and the PIN or key is provided.

LoJack   LoJack is a product made by Absolute Software that allows you to remotely locate, lock, and delete the data on a mobile device when it is stolen. It is a small piece of software that embeds itself on the computer and is difficult to detect. Once activated, it stays in contact with a monitoring center, allowing you to send the commands to lock and delete data via the center. Not only can you protect the data in this fashion, but it will also gather forensic data that can help to locate the device and aid in its recovery.

Secure Boot   Secure Boot is a standard adopted by many vendors that requires the operating system to check the integrity of all system files before allowing the boot process to proceed. By doing so, it protects against the alteration or corruption of these system files. As with any emerging technology, issues have already been discovered that can enable a hacker to not only bypass Secure Boot but to also change a key value in the settings that will "brick" the device (render it useless).

Interface configurations

There are settings in the BIOS that can affect several components including the voltage, clock, and bus speed. At startup, the BIOS will attempt to detect the devices and components at its disposal. The information that it gathers, along with the current state of the components, will be available for review in the BIOS settings. Some of the components and the types of information available with respect to these devices and components are covered in this section.

You can view and adjust a computer's base-level settings through the CMOS Setup program, which you access by pressing a certain key at startup, such as F1 or Delete (depending on the system). The most common settings to adjust in CMOS include port settings (parallel, serial, USB), drive types, boot sequence, date and time, and virus/security protections. The variable settings that are made through the CMOS Setup program are stored in nonvolatile random-access memory (NVRAM), while the base instructions that cannot be changed (the BIOS) are stored on an EEPROM chip. NVRAM is memory that does not lose its content when power is lost to the machine. Figure 3.50 shows an example of NVRAM on a motherboard.

FIGURE 3.50 NVRAM

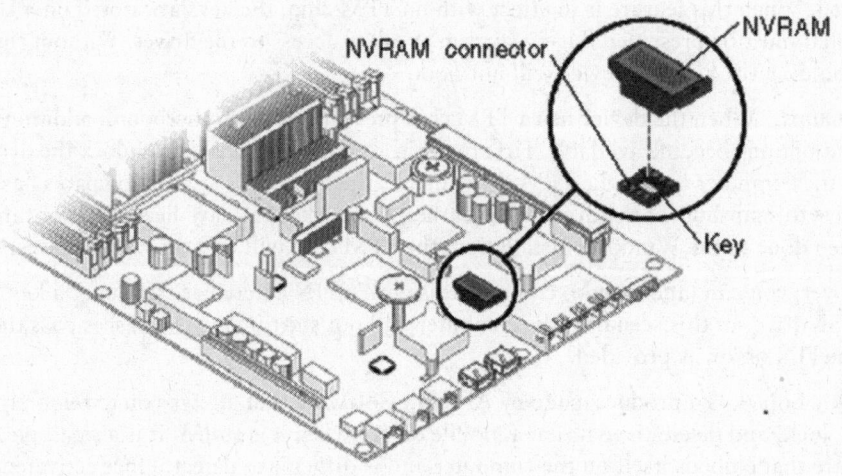

Voltage

You can also monitor and change the voltage settings in the BIOS. Be cautious in changing these settings, because improper settings can damage the system or shorten the life of the CPU. Possible settings include the following:

- CPU voltage

- Memory voltage, which will typically be 1.5 volts

- Motherboard voltage

- Voltage of the graphics card

These are just a few examples. Figure 3.51 shows an example of these and many more voltage settings.

FIGURE 3.51 Voltage settings in the BIOS

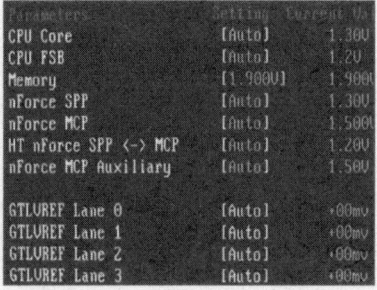

Clock

The CMOS clock is located on the computer's motherboard and keeps time when the computer is off. The operating system gets its time from the BIOS clock at boot time. This clock can be set using the BIOS if it is not correct. Figure 3.52 shows the time setting.

FIGURE 3.52   Setting the CMOS clock in the BIOS

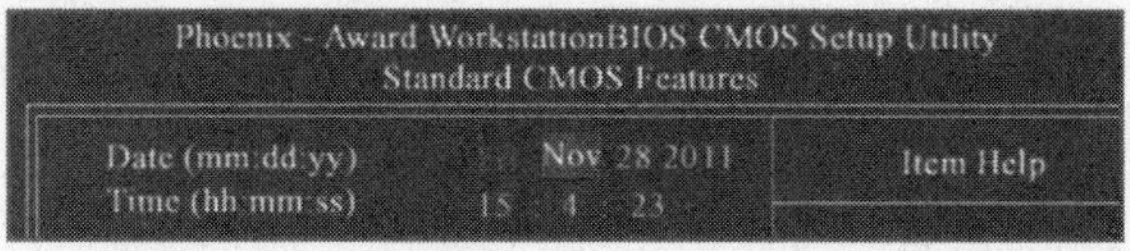

Bus Speed

The processor's ability to communicate with the rest of the system's components relies on the supporting circuitry. Part of the system board's underlying circuitry is called the *bus*. The computer's bus moves information into and out of the processor and other devices. A bus allows all devices to communicate with one another. The motherboard has several buses. The *external data bus* carries information to and from the CPU and is the fastest bus on the system. The *address bus* typically runs at the same speed as the external data bus and carries data to and from RAM. The address bus gives the address to which the data should go. The data bus uses the address supplied by the address bus and carries the data to the specified location. The PCI, AGP, and ISA interfaces also have their own buses with their own widths and speeds. With newer architectures, the system or front-side bus (FSB) connects the CPU to the north bridge (or memory) hub. The back-side bus (BSB) connects the CPU with the Level 2 (L2) cache, also called the *secondary* or *external* cache. The memory bus connects the north bridge (or memory) hub to RAM.

The bus speed, like the CPU speed, can also be set. (See the discussion of the relationship between the bus speed, the CPU speed, and the multiplier in the section "Speeds" later in this chapter.) Usually, this should be left alone because it is normally set to a setting proper for the memory, but it can be changed. In many systems, this must be done with jumpers on the motherboard.

CMOS battery

The CMOS chip must have a constant source of power to keep its settings. To prevent the loss of data, motherboard manufacturers include a small battery to power the CMOS memory. On modern systems, this is a coin-style battery, about the diameter of a U.S. dime and about as thick. Figure 3.53 shows the location of the CMOS battery.

FIGURE 3.53   CMOS battery

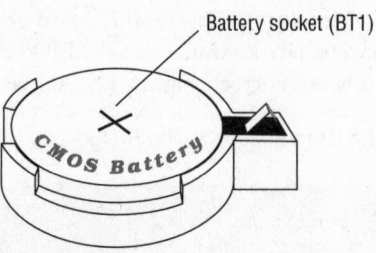

Battery socket (BT1)

CMOS Battery

CPU features

CPUs have a number of features that bear discussion. In the following sections we'll look at some of these.

Single-Core/ Multicore

CPUs can have a single core, or they can be dual-core, quad-core, or even dual-quad-core (eight CPUs total). When multiple cores exist, they operate as individual processors, so the more the better. The largest boost in performance will likely be noticed in improved response time while running CPU-intensive processes, such as virus scans, ripping/burning media (requiring file conversion), or file searching.

The addition of more cores does not have a linear effect on performance. The potential impact of multiple cores also depends on the amount of cache or memory present to serve the CPU. When a computer is designed for the processor, this will have been taken into consideration, but when adding a multicore processor to a PC, it is an issue to consider.

Dual-Core Processors

Dual-core processors, available from Intel as well as AMD, essentially combine two processors into one chip. Instead of adding two processors to a machine (making it a multiprocessor system), you have one chip splitting operations and essentially performing as if it is two processors in order to get better performance. A *multicore* architecture simply has multiple, completely separate processor dies in the same package, whether it's dual core, triple core, or quad core. The operating system and applications see multicore processors in the same way that they see multiple processors in separate sockets. Both dual-core and quad-core processors are common cases for the multicore technology. Most multicore processors from Intel come in even numbers, whereas AMD's Phenom series can contain odd numbers (such as the triple-core processor).

Virtual technology

When using virtualization technology, a fuller realization of its benefits can be achieved when the processor supports this concept.

The benefit derived from this support is to allow the virtualization product (also called a *hypervisor*) to use hardware-assisted virtualization. This allows the hypervisor to dynamically allocate CPU to the virtual machines (VMs) as required. Both AMD and Intel offer CPUs that support hardware virtualization.

Hyperthreading

One feature available since the Pentium 4 is *hyperthreading* technology. This feature enables the computer to multitask more efficiently between CPU-demanding applications. An advantage of hyperthreading is improved support for multithreaded code, allowing multiple threads to run simultaneously and thus improving reaction and response time.

Speeds

Clock speed is a measurement of the rate at which the clock signal oscillates; it is expressed in millions of cycles per second or megahertz. The motherboard must be set to utilize the proper clock settings for the CPU installed in the computer. The BIOS usually detects the type of CPU and automatically sets the proper timings. In some older systems, you may have to use jumpers to set the correct clock speed and CPU.

External Speed (Clock Speed)   The *clock speed*, or *external speed*, which is usually expressed in megahertz or gigahertz, is the speed at which the motherboard communicates with the CPU. It's determined by the motherboard, and its cadence is set by a quartz crystal (the system crystal) that generates regular electrical pulses.

Internal Speed   The *internal speed* is the maximum speed at which the CPU can perform its internal operations. This may be the same as the motherboard's speed (the external speed), but it's more likely to be a multiple of it. For example, a CPU may have an internal speed of 1.3 GHz but an external speed of 133 MHz. That means for every tick of the system crystal's clock, the CPU has 10 internal ticks of its own clock.

When the proper CPU speed is known, you must make sure the relationship between the speed of the CPU and that of the motherboard bus is correct. This is done with a value called the *multiplier*. Although the bus speed can also be manipulated, usually it is set to accommodate the required speed of the memory to be used, and so it is more likely you will be using the multiplier to achieve the proper relationship between the CPU speed and the bus speed.

For example, if you have a processor that has a CPU speed of 1.82 GHz, the proper settings for the BIOS would be a bus speed of 166 MHz and a multiplier of 11 (166 MHz × 11 = 1.826 GHz). So if the bus needed to be 166 MHz, you would set the multiplier for 11. On the other hand, if you changed the bus speed to 332 MHz (just a random example), the closest multiplier would be 5.5 to maintain 1.826 GHz (332 MHz × 5.5 = 1.826 GHz). When setting the speed of either is required, refer to the documentation from the CPU and motherboard.

Overclocking

Overclocking is when you set the bus speed using a multiplier that is higher than recommended or is specified in the documentation. An overclocked device may be unreliable or fail completely if the additional heat load is not removed or power delivery components cannot meet increased power demands. Many device warranties state that overclocking and/or over-specification voids any warranty.

Integrated GPU

A graphics processing unit (GPU) is a specialized circuit designed to rapidly manipulate and alter memory to accelerate the building of images in a frame buffer intended for output to a display. It improves the graphic abilities of the PC when this feature is present in the CPU.

Some visual features provided by operating systems such as Windows 10 are unavailable unless the CPU has dedicated graphics memory or a GPU. For example, the Aero view in Windows 10 requires a card capable of DirectX, which is a technology that requires the DirectCompute API, which in turn requires a GPU.

Compatibility

Processors must be compatible with the sockets in which you install them. Let's take a closer look at sockets, compatibility, and the two major CPU types.

AMD

Advanced Micro Devices (AMD) is one of two major processor vendors in the world. Athlon models are AMD processors. See Table 3.7 for models and socket compatibility.

TABLE 3.7   Socket types and the processors they support

Connector Type	Processor
Socket 1	486 SX/SX2, 486 DX/DX2, 486 DX4 Overdrive
Socket 2	486 SX/SX2, 486 DX/DX2, 486 DX4 Overdrive, 486 Pentium Overdrive
Socket 3	486 SX/SX2, 486 DX/DX2, 486 DX4 486 Pentium Overdrive
Socket 4	Pentium 60/66, Pentium 60/66 Overdrive
Socket 5	Pentium 75-133, Pentium 75+ Overdrive
Socket 6	DX4, 486 Pentium Overdrive
Socket 7	Pentium 75-200, Pentium 75+ Overdrive

Connector Type	Processor
Socket 8	Pentium Pro
Socket 370	Pentium III
Socket 423	Pentium 4
Socket 478	Pentium 4 and Celeron 4
SECC (Type I), Slot 1	Pentium II
SECC2 (Type II), Slot 2	Pentium III
Slot A	Athlon
Socket 603	Xeon
Socket 754	AMD Athlon 64
Socket 939	Some versions of Athlon 64
Socket 940	Some versions of Athlon 64 and Opteron
Socket LGA 775	Core 2 Duo/Quad
Socket AM2	Athlon 64 family (replacing earlier socket usage)
Socket F	Opteron
Socket AM2+	AMD Athlon64, X2, Phenom, and Phenom II
Socket P	Intel Core2
Socket 441	Intel Atom
Socket LGA 1366/B	Intel Core i7, Xeon (35xx, 36xx, 55xx, 56xx series)
G1/G2/rPGA 988A/B	Intel Core i7, i5, i3, P6000, P4000
Socket AM3	AMD Phenom, Athlon II, Sempron
Socket H/LGA 1156	Intel Core i7, i5, Xeon, Penitium G5000, G1000
Socket G34	AMD Opteron 6000 series
Socket C32	AMD Opteron 4000 series

TABLE 3.7 Socket types and the processors they support *(continued)*

Connector Type	Processor
LGA 1150	Intel Haswell, Haswell Refresh, and Broadwell
Socket AM3+	AMD FX Vishera, AMD FX Zambezi, AMD Phenom II, AMD Athlon II, AMD Sempron
Socket FM2	AMD Trinity Processors
Socket FM2+	AMD Kaveri
LGA 1248	Intel Titanium 9300 series
LGA 1567	Intel Xeon 6500/7500 series
Socket H2/LGA 1155	Intel Sandy Bridge-DT
Socket R/LGA 2011	Intel Sandy Bridge B2 (also referred to as Xeon E5)
Socket FM1	AMD Llano (also referred to as A-series)

Intel

The market leader in chip manufacturing is Intel Corporation, with Advanced Micro Devices (AMD) gaining a market share in the home PC market. Here's a quick list of socket types from both manufacturers you may encounter:

Intel: LGA 775, 1155, 1156, 1366, 1150, 2011   Earlier in this chapter, Table 3.7 lists the various Intel CPU slots and sockets you may find in a motherboard and explains which CPUs will fit into them.

AMD: AM3, AM3+, FM1, FM2, FM2+   Table 3.7 also lists the various AMD CPU slots and sockets you may find in a motherboard and which CPUs will fit into them. These later-generation AMD sockets were launched as the successor to Socket AM2+. In 2009, AMD3 was released alongside the initial grouping of Phenom II processors designed for it. The principal change from AM2+ to AM3 is support for DDR3 SDRAM. The AM3+ socket has been designed for the AMD FX series Zambezi processors based on the Bulldozer architecture. Socket FM2 is a CPU socket launched in September 2012. Motherboards using the FM2 utilize AMD's new A85X chipset. The FM2+ uses three PCI Express cores: one 2×16 core and two 5×8 cores, for a total of 64 lanes.

CPU Sockets

The CPU slot permits the attachment of the CPU to the motherboard, allowing the CPU to use the other components of the system. There are many different types of processors, meaning there are many types of CPU connectors.

The CPU slot can take on several different forms. In the past, the CPU slot was a rectangular box called a *pin grid array* (PGA) socket, with many small holes to accommodate the pins on the bottom of the chip. With the release of new and more powerful chips, additional holes were added, changing the configuration of the slot and its designator or number. Figure 3.54 shows a typical PGA-type CPU socket.

FIGURE 3.54 A PGA CPU socket

With the release of the Pentium II, the architecture of the slot went from a rectangle to more of an expansion-slot style of interface called a *single-edge contact cartridge* (SECC). This style of CPU slot includes Slot 1 and Slot 2 for Intel CPUs and Slot A for Athlon (AMD) CPUs. This type of slot looks much like an expansion slot, but it's located in a different place on the motherboard from the other expansion slots. Figure 3.55 shows an SECC.

FIGURE 3.55 SECC

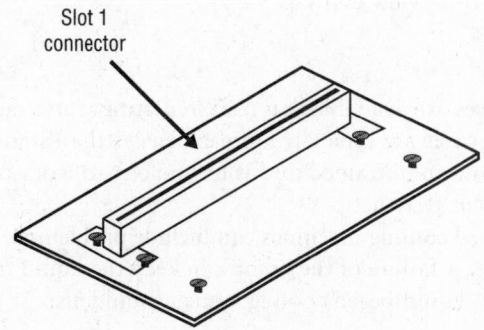

To see which socket type is used for which processors, examine Table 3.7. This list is not exhaustive. Some of the slots may fit processors that are not specifically listed.

Sockets are the interface with which CPUs are plugged into the motherboard. These sockets have evolved over the years along with the changes in CPU architecture and design. There are three form factors for CPU chips: pin grid array (PGA), single-edge contact cartridge (SECC), and land grid array (LGA). The PGA style is a flat square or rectangular ceramic chip with an array of pins in the bottom. The actual CPU is a silicon wafer embedded inside that ceramic chip. The SECC style is a circuit board with the silicon wafer mounted on it. The circuit board is then surrounded by a plastic cartridge for protection; the circuit board sticks out of the cartridge along one edge. This edge fits into a slot in the motherboard.

Cooling mechanism

CPUs produce heat, and the more powerful the CPU, the more heat it produces. Heat is an enemy to the PC in general because it causes problems such as random reboots. Methods of cooling the CPU and in turn the overall interior of the case have evolved with the increasing need to remove this heat. This section covers options that are used.

Among methods of cooling, technology that transfers heat away from components uses thermoelectric cooling, and components that perform this function are called Peltier components. Heat sinks, cooling fans, and cooling fins are Peltier components. Liquid cooling, on the other hand, cools not by transferring heat away from components but by circulating a cool liquid around them.

Fans

Active heat sinks have a fan that sits atop the heat sink. It pulls the heat out of the heat sink and away from it. Then the case fan shunts the heat out the back or side of the case.

Heat Sink

The cooling can be either active or passive. A *passive heat sink* is a block of heat-conductive material that sits close to the CPU and wicks away the heat into the air. An *active heat sink* contains a fan that pulls the hot air away from the CPU. The heat sink sits atop the CPU, in many cases obscuring it from view entirely.

Liquid

Liquid-based cooling cases are available that use circulating water rather than fans to keep components cool. These cases are typically more expensive than standard ones and may be more difficult for a technician untrained in this technology to work on, but they result in an almost completely silent system.

Issues with liquid-based cooling machines can include problems with hoses or fittings, the pump, or the coolant. A failure of the pump can keep the liquid from flowing and cause the system to overheat. A liquid-based cooling system should also be checked every so often for leaks or corrosion on the hoses and fittings, and the reservoir should be examined to make sure it is full and does not contain contaminants. Liquid-based cooling is more expensive, less noisy, and more efficient than Peltier components.

Thermal paste

Most *passive heat sinks* are attached to the CPU using a glue-like thermal compound (called *thermal glue*, *thermal compound*, or *thermal paste*). This makes the connection between the heat sink and the CPU more seamless and direct. Thermal compound can be used on active heat sinks, too, but generally it isn't because of the possibility that the fan may stop working and need to be replaced. Thermal compound improves thermal transfer by eliminating tiny air pockets between the heat sink and CPU (or other device like a north bridge or video chipset). Thermal compound provides both improved thermal transfer and adds bonding for heat sinks when there are no mounting holes to clamp the heat sink to the device to be cooled.

Expansion cards

Expansion cards allow you to add functionality to the PC. In this section, I'll discuss the types of cards and the functionality they provide. I'll also talk about installing them and configuring them properly.

Newer cards will install in the PCI or PCIe slots and will probably be detected by the operating system. If the operating system already contains the driver for the device in its preinstalled driver library, the process will be done as soon as you restart the PC. If it is not present in the driver cache, you will have to install the driver that came with it.

Video cards

PCs today also contain internal video cards, but as with sound cards, you can achieve better video quality with more expensive video cards. This is especially true when the video card has its own dedicated memory.

Onboard

In earlier times, most internal cards were vastly inferior to the cards you could buy, but that is much less the case today when users have learned to expect better video quality.

Newer operating systems, like Windows 10, have helped raise the bar for internal cards as well in that they require a card with a minimum set of features and a minimum amount of dedicated RAM to appreciate the visual capabilities of the operating system.

Just a Word

If you decide to install an add-on card in a system that has an onboard card, the technician will need to disable the onboard card (using the UEFI).

Add-on card

Video cards can be installed in the AGP, PCI, and PCIe slots. At one point, the best choice was clear, and that was the AGP slot. However, the newer PCIe slots provide more bandwidth. AGP provides a wider data path because it's parallel, whereas PCIe is serial. But PCIe now goes up to 16,000 MBps as compared to AGP, which is 2,000 MBps. Figure 3.56 shows the AGP slot next to some slots you have already learned about.

FIGURE 3.56   AGP and PCI slots

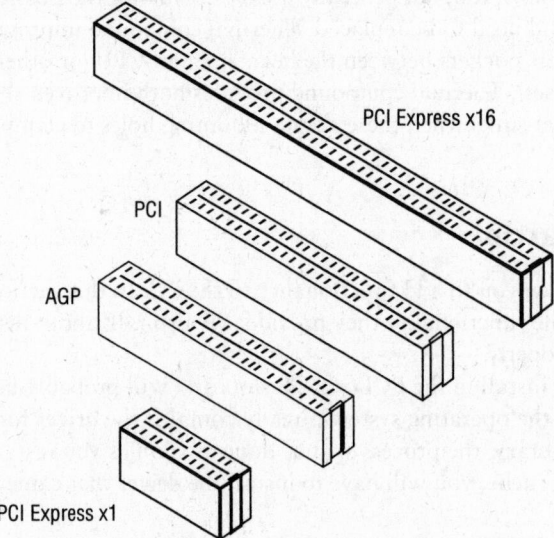

Some of the special functions you may get with a more expensive video card are 3D imaging, MPEG decoding (decoding simply means it can interpret this file type), and TV output. The ability to use multiple monitors is also built into many cards.

Sound cards

Most computers these days come with an integrated sound card, but for more robust sound or advanced features, you may need to install a sound card. Sound cards can be either internal or external. Internal cards require opening the case and installing the card in a slot. External cards plug into the USB socket.

In some cases, an audio cable will be connected from the card to the CD-ROM. This is rarely required these days. Figure 3.57 shows the connectors present on most sound cards today.

FIGURE 3.57   Sound card connectors

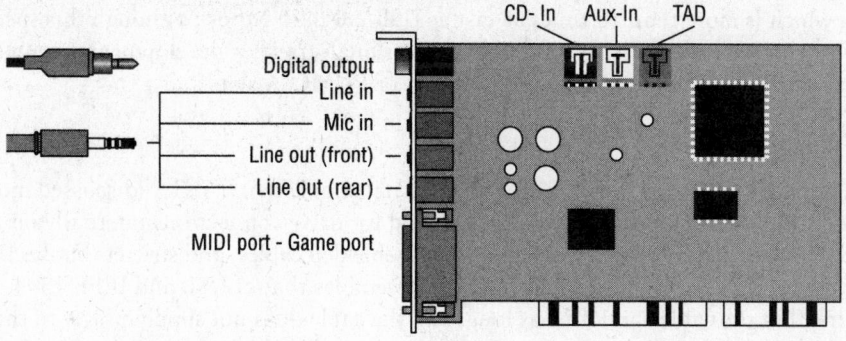

Network interface card

Network cards do exactly what you would think; they provide a connection for the PC to a network. In general, network interface cards (NICs) are added to a PC via an expansion slot or they are integrated into the motherboard, but they may also be added through a USB or PCMCIA slot (also known as PC card). The most common issue that prevents network connectivity is a bad or unplugged patch cable.

Network cards are made for Ethernet, fiber-optic, token ring (rarely used now), and 802.11 (wireless) connections. The Ethernet, token ring, and fiber-optic cards accept the appropriate cable, and the wireless cards have radio transmitters and antennas.

The most obvious difference between network cards is the speed of which they are capable. Most networks today operate at 100 MBps or 1 GBps. Regardless of other components, the PC will operate at the speed of the slowest component, so if the card is capable of 1 GBps but the cable is capable of only 100 MBps, the PC will transmit only at 100 MBps.

Another significant feature to be aware of is the card's ability to perform autosensing. This feature allows the card to sense whether the connection is capable of full duplex and to operate in that manner with no action required.

There is another type of autosensing, in which the card is capable of detecting what type of device is on the other end and changing the use of the wire pairs accordingly. For example, normally a PC connected to another PC requires a crossover cable, but if both ends can perform this sensing, that is not required. These types of cards are called auto-MDIX.

USB expansion card

Universal Serial Bus (USB) expansion cards are used to provide a USB connection (or an additional connection) to a PC that has none (pretty rare today). All modern motherboards today have at least two USB slots. Some of the advantages of USB include hot-plugging and the capability for up to 127 USB devices to share a single set of system resources.

USB 1.1 runs at 12 Mbps, and USB 2.0 runs at 480 Mbps. Because USB is a serial interface, its width is 1 bit. USB 3.0 specifies a maximum transmission speed of up to 5 Gbps (625 MBps), which is more than 10 times as fast as USB 2.0 (480 Mbps), although this speed is typically achieved only by using powerful, professional-grade or developmental equipment.

These cards are made to plug into PCI, PCIe, or PCMCIA slots.

eSATA card

eSATA provides a form of SATA meant for external connectivity. SATA (discussed more completely earlier in the section "eSATA") is used for drive connections internally on many PCs. eSATA uses a more robust connector, longer shielded cables, and stricter (but backward-compatible) electrical standards. The interface resembles that of USB and IEEE 1394 (FireWire), but the cable cannot be as long, and the cable does not supply power to the device. The advantage it has over the other technologies is speed—it is approximately three times as fast as either FireWire or USB 2.0 (although USB 3.0 is faster).

An eSATA card is shown in Figure 3.58. This card offers two eSATA slots on the part of the card that extends out the back of the system.

FIGURE 3.58   eSATA card

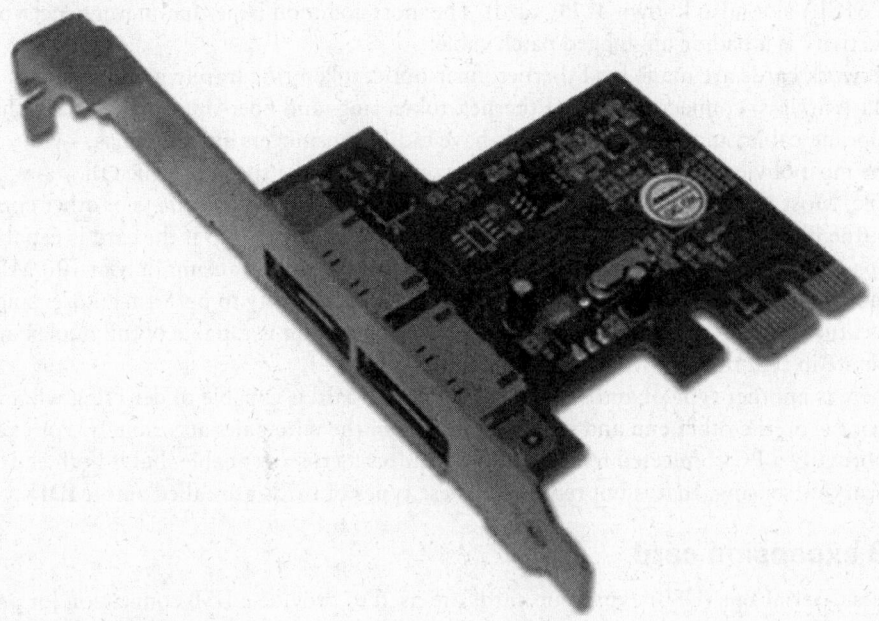

Exam essentials

Differentiate the motherboard form factors.   The ATX is the oldest and largest of the mother-board sizes still being manufactured. The micro-ATX is for smaller and cheaper systems. The smaller ITX motherboards come in three sizes: the mini-ITX, the nano-ITX, and the pico-ITX.

Identify expansion slot types.   PCI slots are the standard for general-purpose cards. The PCI-X provides higher bandwidth for servers. PCIe is a newer high-speed slot based on the PCI system. MiniPCI slots are used in laptops.

Locate the CPU socket on the motherboard.   The CPU socket can take on several different forms. In the past, the CPU socket was a rectangular box called a PGA socket, with many small holes to accommodate the pins on the bottom of the chip. With the release of the Pentium II, the architecture of the socket went from a rectangle to more of an expansion-slot style of interface called an SECC.

Identify front connections.   While the USB and audio jacks will be connected with 10-pin connectors, the remaining front-panel components will connect with much smaller plugs in a cluster in one area on the board.

3.6 Explain the purposes and uses of various peripheral types.

Installing devices is much easier today than it was at one time. In most cases, the device is detected and set up for you by the operating system as soon as you plug it in. This section discusses any deviations from that along with any special issues related to a particular device type. The topics addressed in objective 3.6 include the following:

- Printer
- ADF/flatbed scanner
- Barcode scanner/QR scanner
- Monitors
- VR headset
- Optical
- DVD drive
- Mouse
- Keyboard
- Touchpad
- Signature pad
- Game controllers
- Camera/webcam
- Microphone
- Speakers
- Headset

- Projector
- External storage drives
- KVM
- Magnetic reader/chip reader
- NFC/tap pay device
- Smart card reader

Printer

One of the most common peripherals is the printer. Printers are covered in detail under objective 3.10. They are also the focus of objective 3.11, discussed later in the chapter.

ADF/flatbed scanner

Scanners are used to convert paper documents or photographs to digital files so they can be stored on a PC and transmitted as files across the network. The installation process is much like a print device. Because so many of these now are USB, plugging them in will install the driver. In cases where that does not work (usually when it is a new model and the operating system is older), use the installation disc to install the driver.

Barcode scanner/QR scanner

Barcode readers read and input codes used to identify products. They are used in warehouses and at retail checkouts. Once you plug the device into either the serial or the USB connector, you need to install the software that comes with the reader. Use the installation disc that comes with the reader.

Monitors

Before connecting or disconnecting a monitor, ensure that the power to both the PC and the monitor is off. Then, connect a VGA (DB-15) cable or a USB cable as the situation calls for from the monitor to the PC's video card, and connect the monitor's power cord to an AC outlet. If a better connection is available (DVI, for example), use it.

VR headset

VR headsets are widely used with computer games, but they are also used in other applications, including simulators and trainers. They are worn on the head and cover the eyes with stereo sound, and head motion tracking sensors. Most connect to either the USB or HDMI connector, although some are wireless. Several types are shown in Figure 3.59.

FIGURE 3.59   VR headsets

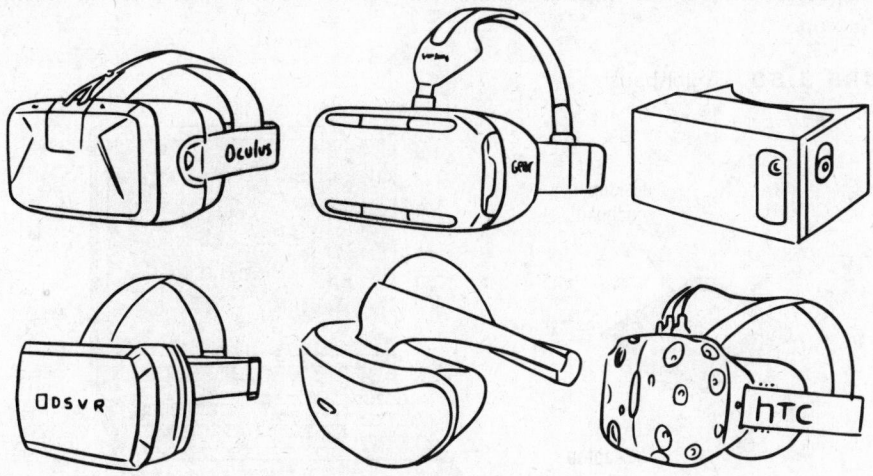

Optical

The installation and use of optical devices was covered in the section "Optical Drives" under objective 3.4.

DVD drive

The installation and use of DVD devices was covered in the section "Optical Drives" under objective 3.4.

Mouse

Mice are typically USB devices these days and require you only to plug them in; in moments they are functional. In some rare cases (especially for a mouse with special capabilities), you may need to install a driver for the mouse. These types typically have a CD you can access that will install those drivers for you.

Keyboard

Keyboards can be treated the same as mice. Follow the guidelines in the section on mice.

Touchpad

While touchpads come on laptops, you can also buy add-on touchpads. These allow you to perform basic mouse functions on the device. In most cases, they use a USB connector. To install them, you simply connect them, and if the operating system does not have the drivers, you provide these drivers during installation. Figure 3.60 shows an external touchpad and a laptop.

FIGURE 3.60   Touchpads

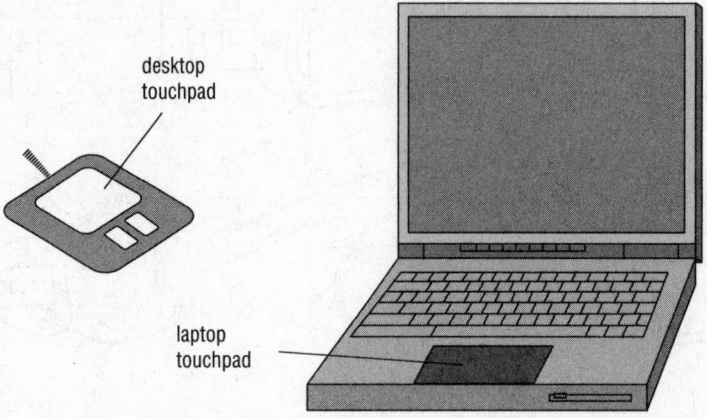

desktop
touchpad

laptop
touchpad

Signature pad

Signature pads are really touchpads that are designed specifically to record signatures for credit cards and the like. They are installed in a similar manner to touchpads.

Game controllers

You may begin to notice a pattern. Game pads are also usually USB and install in the same way as biometric devices and barcode readers. Install the software and connect the device when instructed. One additional thing you may need to do with the game pad is to calibrate it. Once it's installed, locate the device in Control Panel in the correct section (usually Game Controllers), open the properties of the device, and click the option Calibrate. Follow the instructions. This will make it operate correctly. Some game pads require a DB-15 serial port, as shown in Figure 3.61.

FIGURE 3.61   DB-15 game port

GAME

Camera/webcam

Digital cameras usually connect to the PC with a USB cable. In many cases, the operating system comes with software that may detect the camera and assist you in accessing the pictures and moving them to the computer. In other instances, you may want to install software that came with the camera. Doing so will often allow you to take fuller advantage of the features the camera offers. SD cards can be used to transfer images from the camera if a cable is not available.

Microphone

Microphones are simple to install. Typically, all you do is plug them into the mini-TRS connector. There are usually two of these: one for headphones (or speakers) and the other for a microphone (or line in). In some systems, you may be prompted to specify the mic or line in when you plug in a headset. Others connect by a USB cord.

Speakers

Installing speakers is more a matter of connecting them properly than installing them. Usually, one of the speakers will connect to a power source, and the other will connect to the powered speaker. Once they are connected to a power source, connect the speaker cable to the proper plug in the PC. These plugs will be marked with icons that indicate which is for a microphone and which is for speakers.

Headset

Headsets that are not VR are probably for audio and may have a microphone as well. They plug either into the USB port and/or into the small microphone plug.

Projector

In the business world, it is frequently necessary to share the desktop with others in a meeting. This is easily accomplished by directing the output of the PC to a projector. The projector can be plugged into the same connector as the monitor, and in most cases both can be used at the same time. Some projectors require an HDMI connector.

Lumens/brightness

When discussing bulbs for projectors, brightness is a description of light output, which is measured in lumens (not watts). Ensure that you are purchasing the correct bulb for the projector and maximize the life of the bulb by turning the projector off when not in use.

External storage drives

External storage drives were covered earlier, under objective 3.4.

KVM

A keyboard, video, and mouse (KVM) device allows you to plug multiple PCs (usually servers) into the device and to switch easily back and forth from system to system using the same mouse, monitor, and keyboard. The KVM is actually a switch that all the systems plug into. There is usually no software to install. Just turn off all the systems, plug them all into the switch, and turn them back on; then you can switch from one to another using the same keyboard, monitor, and mouse device connected to the KVM switch. In some cases a key combination is used to switch from one PC to another.

Magnetic reader/chip reader

Credit and debit card readers typically read both magnetic stripes on cards as well as the chips that are present in many of today's cards. These devices connect either using USB or in some rare cases a serial connection. Consult the documentation to determine whether you need a special driver installed.

NFC/tap pay device

You may have noticed these small devices in retail outlets. They communicate wirelessly with NFC cards and smartphones. In some cases, it requires tapping the phone on the device, and in others cases that is not required.

Near field communications (NFC) is a wireless technology that allows smartphones and other equipped devices to communicate when very near one another or when touching. NFC operates at slower speeds than Bluetooth but consumes far less power and doesn't require pairing. It also does not create a PAN like Bluetooth; rather, the connections are point-to-point. NFC can operate up to 20 cm at a transfer rate of 0.424 Mbps.

NFC is also a standard managed by the ISO and uses tags that are embedded in the devices. NFC components include an initiator and a target; the initiator actively generates an RF field that can power a passive target. This enables NFC targets to take simple form factors such as tags, stickers, key fobs, or cards that do not require batteries.

These devices connect either using USB or in some rare cases a serial connection. Consult the documentation to determine whether you need a special driver installed.

Smart card reader

Smart card readers are used to accept input from a smart card, which is a credit card–sized piece of plastic that can be used to input credentials securely. They are small and usually USB based, as shown in Figure 3.62. To install them, you simply connect them, and if the operating system does not have the drivers, you provide these drivers during installation.

FIGURE 3.62   Smart card reader

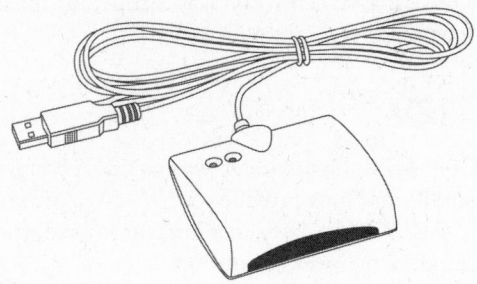

Exam essentials

Install input devices.   These include the mouse, keyboard, scanner, barcode reader, biometric devices, game pads, joysticks, digitizer, motion sensor, touchpads, smart card readers, digital cameras, microphone, webcam, camcorder, and MIDI-enabled devices.

Install devices that are both input and output.   These include but are not limited to touch-screen devices, KVMs, smart TVs, and set-top boxes.

3.7 Summarize power supply types and features.

The power supply provides a number of connectors for various devices as well as a plug for the motherboard. It is important to understand these connector types and to appreciate the power drawn by various devices. Knowledge of the power needs of the devices can allow the technician to choose a power supply that provides the total power needs of the PC. The topics addressed in objective 3.7 include the following:

- Input 115V versus 220V
- Output 5.5V versus 12V
- 24-pin motherboard adapter
- Wattage rating
- Number of devices/types of devices to be powered

Input 115V vs. 220V

Most power supplies have a recessed, two-position slider switch (often a red one) on the rear that is exposed through the case. Selections read 110 and 220, 115 and 230, or 120 and 240. This voltage selector switch is used to select the voltage level used in the country where the computer is in service. For example, in the United States, the power grid supplies anywhere from 110 VAC to 120 VAC. However, in Europe, for instance, the voltage supplied is double, ranging from 220 VAC to 240 VAC.

Output 5.5V vs. 12V

In 2004, the ATX 12V 2.0 (now 2.03) standard was passed, changing the main connector from 20 pins to 24. The additional pins provide +3.3V, +5V, and +12V (the fourth pin is a ground) for use by PCIe cards. When a 24-pin connector is used, there is no need for the optional four- or six-pin auxiliary power connectors.

24-pin motherboard adapter

A power connector allows the motherboard to be connected to the power supply. On an ATX, there is a single power connector consisting of a block of 20 holes (in two rows). On an AT, there is a block consisting of 12 pins sticking up; these pins are covered by two connectors with six holes each.

Figure 3.63 shows a versatile motherboard that has both kinds so you can compare them. The upper connector is for ATX, and the lower one is for AT.

FIGURE 3.63   Power connectors on a motherboard

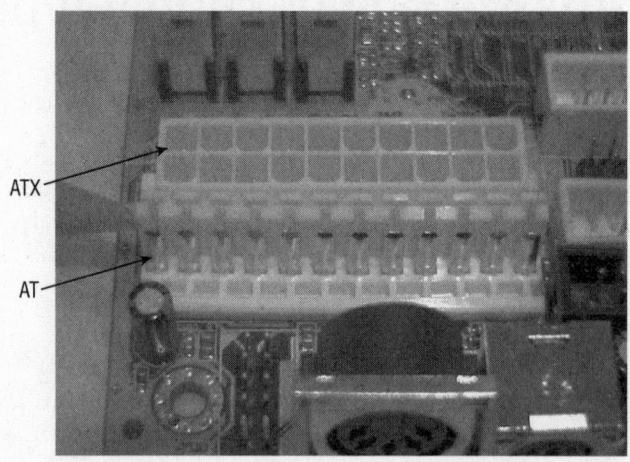

When using the AT power connector, the power cable coming from the power supply will have two separate connectors, labeled P8 and P9. When you are attaching the two parts to the motherboard, the black wires on one should be next to the black wires on the other for proper function.

Wattage rating

When the wattage needs of each device and of the motherboard and CPU are totaled, you will know the wattage that the power supply must provide. A power supply has a rated output capacity in watts, and when you fill a system with power-hungry devices, you must make sure that maximum capacity isn't exceeded. Otherwise, problems with power can occur, creating lockups or spontaneous reboots. Most power supplies provide between 250 watts and 1,200 watts. It's always a good idea to have more than the minimum required for the devices that are present so that additional devices can be added in the future.

Number of devices/types of devices to be powered

To determine the wattage a device draws, multiply voltage by current. For example, if a device uses 5 amps of +3.3 V and 0.7 amps of +12 V, a total of 25 watts is consumed. Do this calculation for every device installed. Most devices have labels that state their power requirements.

When selecting a power supply, two issues become important. You need to supply the total wattage required by all the devices and the motherboard of the PC, and you must ensure that it has the connector types required by your devices. This section discusses the voltage requirements of various connector types.

SATA

The SATA power connector has 15 pins, with 3 pins designated for 3.3 V, 5 V, and 12 V and with each pin carrying 1.5 amps. This results in a total draw of 4.95 watts + 7.5 watts + 18 watts, or about 30 watts. Figure 3.64 shows the SATA power connector.

FIGURE 3.64   SATA power connector

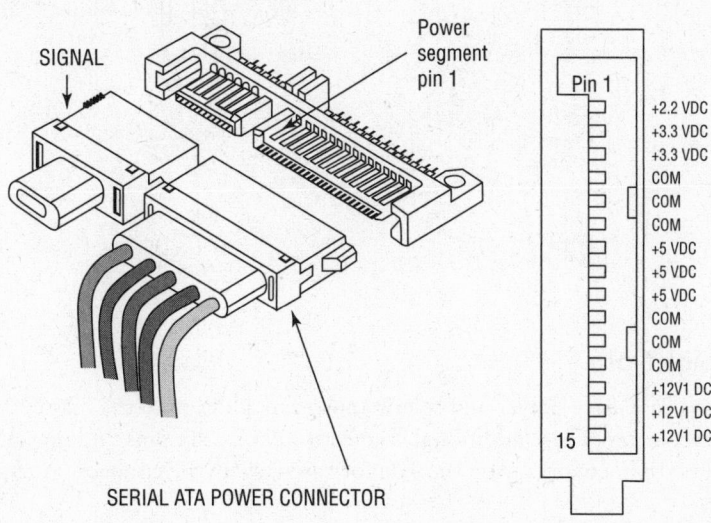

Molex

A Molex connector is used to provide power to drives of various types. It has four pins, two of which have power (one 12 V and the other 5 V). These are standard for IDE (PATA) or older SCSI drives. The total power demands are from 5 to 15 watts for IDE and 10 to 40 watts for SCSI. The four-pin Molex connector was shown in Figure 3.26 earlier.

Four/eight-pin 12 V

With the introduction of the Pentium 4, motherboards began to require more power. Supplemental power connections were provided to the motherboard in 4-, 6- (discussed later in this section), or 8-pin formats. These were in addition to the 20-pin connector (also discussed later) that was already provided.

There is a four-pin square mini version of the ATX connector, which supplies two pins with 12V, and an eight-pin version (two rows) that has four 12V leads. These connect to other items, such as the processor, or to other components, such as a network card that may need power that exceeds what can be provided with the ATX connection to the board. Figure 3.65 shows the eight-pin version and the four-pin square mini version.

FIGURE 3.65   Eight-pin and four-pin 12V

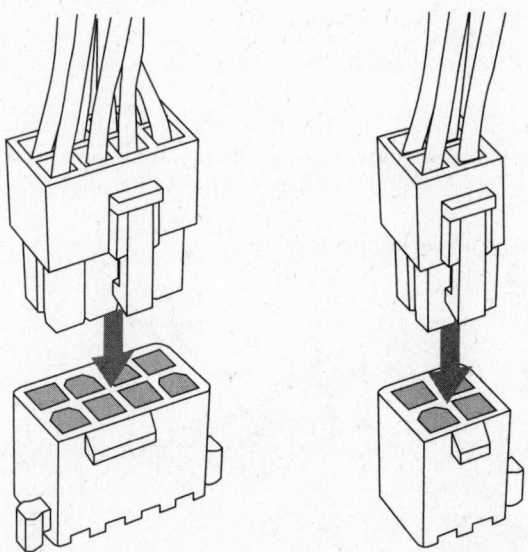

PCIe six/eight-pin

PCIe slots also draw more power and require power in addition to the main 20-pin connector (discussed next). These additional connectors can be six pins and may also contain an additional two-pin connector on the side for cases where the connection required is eight-pin.

20-pin

The main ATX connector, referenced earlier, is a 20-pin connector. The four pins carrying power are 3.3V, 3.3V, 5V, and 5V. This allows the motherboard to pull about 20 to 30 watts. Figure 3.66 shows the 20-pin ATX.

FIGURE 3.66   20-pin ATX

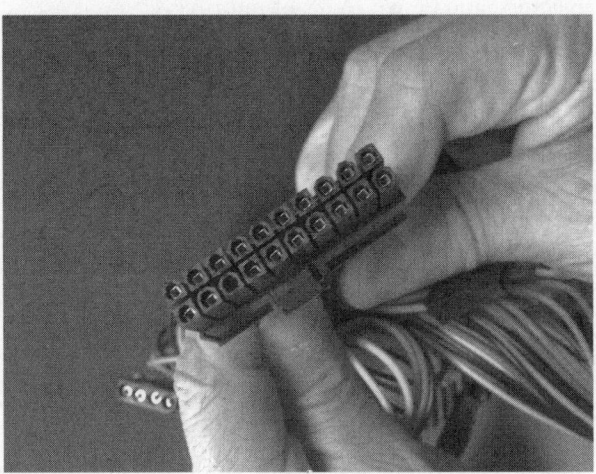

24-pin

The 24-pin ATX connector is simply the 20-pin connector discussed earlier along with the extra 4-pin connector on the side. This provides the four pins carrying power as discussed earlier plus an additional four pins with 5V standby, 12V,12V, and 3.3. Figure 3.67 shows the 24-pin ATX.

FIGURE 3.67   24-pin ATX

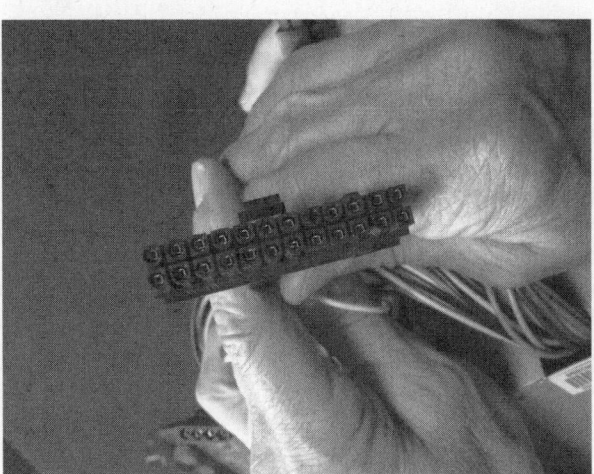

Exam essentials

Identify common power connector types and their voltages.   These include but are not limited to SATA, Molex, 4- to 8-pin 12V, PCIe 6- to 8-pin, 20-pin, 24-pin, and floppy connectors.

Understand the specifications of power supplies.   Differentiate power supplies by wattage, size, number of connectors, and design (ATX or mini-ATX).

Describe a dual-wattage power supply.   This is a supply that can be set to accept either 110 volts or 220 volts.

3.8 Given a scenario, select and configure appropriate components for a custom PC configuration to meet customer specifications or needs.

In many cases, an off-the-shelf computer does not fill the needs of a customer. In these cases, a unit must be custom built to accommodate their specific needs. This section describes some common custom configurations and options to meet specific needs. The topics addressed in objective 3.8 include the following:

- Graphic/CAD/CAM design workstation
- Audio/video-editing workstation
- Virtualization workstation
- Gaming PC
- Standard thick client
- Thin client
- Network-attached storage device

Graphic/CAD/CAM design workstation

Computers used for graphic design, computer-aided design (CAD) applications, and computer-aided manufacturing (CAM) require much more horsepower than the standard PC. Specifically, they require multiple or more powerful processors, more robust video cards, and significantly more memory. In this section, these needs are discussed.

Multicore processor

The resource-intensive applications used with graphics, CAD, and CAM require high-end multicore processors. For example, to run a 64-bit version of Autodesk AutoCAD software, you need a 64-bit 1 GHz processor. Keep in mind this is only the minimum. For good performance, this minimum should be exceeded.

High-end video

As you can imagine, the video demands of graphics such as 3D are much higher than those of common office applications. Continuing with the example of AutoCAD 2012, this requires a 1360 × 768 true-color video display adapter. Note that the graphics card should have a minimum of 128 MB of VRAM for its operations.

Maximum RAM

There can never be enough RAM, and in the case of CAD/CAM and graphics, the minimum (using the same example) is 4 GB of RAM. When the minimum to run the software is 2 GB, you need much more than that for good performance.

Audio/video editing workstation

Looking at the requirements of these specialty solutions, you may notice a recurring theme: RAM, CPU, and graphics. It's no different with an audio- or video-editing machine. These are the components that are saddled with the workload and will be the ones that require boosting above what would be used on a standard workstation.

With audio and video editing, however, additional components can make the workstation more productive to the user. This section discusses those items.

Specialized audio and video card

Many video- and audio-editing software packages come with a special capture card that works in concert with the accompanying software to provide ease of use. For example, it might be an internal PCI card that captures video from any analog or DV source. You can also output video to a VCR or an analog or DV camcorder from this card. They still require (you guessed it) a high-end audio and video card as well and plenty of memory and a processor that may not have quite the requirements of CAD/CAM but still should be 2.4 GHz or higher.

Large, fast hard drive

Your hard drive should be at least 7,200 rpm. You will also want at least two drives if not three. When doing audio, use one for the operating system and programs and a second drive for audio files. When doing video, consider a third drive used exclusively for video files.

Even better, consider a RAID setup. Many motherboards include a SATA RAID controller built in. Use RAID 0 to enhance performance (see the section "RAID 0, 1, 5, and 10" under objective 3.4).

Dual monitors

Especially when doing video editing, a second monitor is well worth the money and the desk real estate. You may need to read or refer to something on one screen while using the other for the editing software. The material could be tutorials or source material.

It also may be that you should move your tools (for example, Photoshop controls) to one screen so they don't clutter the image you are working on.

Virtualization workstation

A virtualization workstation is also called a *virtualization host*. The VMs that reside on this operating system are called *guest* operating systems. The host operating system and the guest must all share the total amount of RAM and CPU that the host machine possesses. This section discusses these issues.

Maximum RAM and CPU cores

The amount of RAM that is required depends on the number of VMs that you anticipate operating at the same time, not on how many exist on the desktop. Total the memory requirements of each VM that will be open at the same time, in addition to the requirements of the host operating system. That should be the minimum. Then add more for overhead to ensure performance.

The memory issue is not something you can fudge. If there is not enough memory, the VM will not start, and you will be notified with an error message that there is insufficient memory.

With regard to CPU, it should be dual- if not quad-core, and multiple CPUs would be even better.

Gaming PC

Gaming PCs may place the highest demands on the system of any specialty PC discussed here because the machines are in competition with other machines. The skill of the player is certainly a big factor in success, but at some point the user with the more powerful PC is going to be able to raise the level of the game through hardware.

Multicore processor

When it comes to the processor, the question becomes "How much do you want to spend?" Just as a comparison (prices change daily!), for almost $10,000 you can get the 878151-L21 HPE Xeon Platinum 8160M 24 Core 2.10GHz LGA. Also keep in mind that multiple processors or multicore processors will always improve the gaming experience.

High-end video/specialized GPU

When playing a game, it is critical that the action you are seeing (and reacting to) is rendered to the screen as quickly as possible. With gaming machines, dual GPU cards are often used. The higher-end cards also require water cooling of GPUs. In fact, the faster cards all need water cooling (covered later in this section).

High-definition sound card

When you're considering the features of a sound card, you want those features to be performed in hardware. Anytime these functions are performed in software, it simply means the main CPU is going to get the workload. Also, you want to go with a high-definition card. The following are things to consider:

- Using the PCI Express slot (better bandwidth) is better than using the PCI slot.
- Make sure the card has its own onboard memory (less work for the main CPU).
- If you are using a Mac, a Thunderbolt card is the way to go.

High-end cooling

With all the heat being generated by the CPUs and GPUs, fans may not be sufficient to remove the heat. Water-cooling systems will cool the system better and will be quieter as well. Cooling kits circulate water through the case in tubes that enter and exit the box to a unit where the water is cooled again (think of the cooling system in your car). Figure 3.68 shows a cooling system.

FIGURE 3.68   Water-cooling system

Standard thick client

When discussing thin and thick clients, you should understand that a thick client is a PC that has all the capabilities of a standard PC. It runs all applications locally from its own hard drive. A thin client (discussed in the next section) is one that has minimal capabilities and runs the applications (and perhaps even the operating system itself) from a remote server.

Desktop applications

A thick client has the applications installed locally and will need to have sufficient resources to support the applications. Applications state these requirements in the documentation. With a thick client, since all application support will come from the local machine, these requirements must be met to use the software.

Meets recommended requirements for selected OS

A standard thick client will need to provide all the hardware requirements of the installed operating system. This is because unlike the thin client (discussed in the next section) none of the processing will be offloaded to a server. It all must be supplied by the thick client. Requirements for various operating systems are covered in Chapter 6, "Operating Systems."

Thin client

A thin client is a PC with minimal resources. Such a system is responsible only for receiving the processed output of an operating system and application running on a server and rendering the output in the screen.

The latest example of this is a computer running the Windows Thin PC (WinTPC) operating system, which is designed to run on older hardware.

Basic applications

Some applications are created to function in a client-server architecture. When these are used in a thin client, the client side of the application operates on the thin client but requires minimal system resources. The server side of the application performs all the processing, and the client side simply renders the output to the display and transmits keystrokes to the server.

Meets minimum requirements for selected OS

Even thin client operating systems have minimum requirements. Follow the documented requirements to ensure good performance. In many cases, older computers that would be of no use as thick clients are suitable candidates to be thin clients.

Network connectivity

Most traditional thin clients come with a NIC built in. They require the same settings that any networked device does, including IP address, subnet mask, and default gateway. These can be static configuration, or the device can receive these through Dynamic Host Configuration Protocol (DHCP).

Network-attached storage device

Many homes and small offices have a network of computers to rival a small enterprise. In these cases, sometimes it makes sense to centralize the location of resources for both ease of use and security of information. This section discusses some common roles of a network-attached storage device or home server.

Media streaming

The home server can act as a streaming media server to other computers in the home network if the operating system provides this capability. An example of such an operating system is Windows Home Server. Once the streaming feature is enabled, other systems can use their Windows Media Players to connect to any shared content and stream that content to the other PC. One of the benefits of this is centralized storage of content and reduced duplication of the content on other machines in the network. This type of server should have plenty of disk space and memory.

File sharing

For the same reasons that centralized storage of media content reduces content duplication in the network, so can file sharing from a home server. Another great benefit of this is a central location to perform regular backups of the files so that this does not need to be done on all the other machines in the network. This server should have plenty of disk space.

Gigabit NIC

When a machine is acting as the home server for all these functions, the network card will be busy. For that reason, it is probably a good idea to ensure that it is a Gigabit NIC, which allows it to operate 10 times faster than the standard 100 MB NIC. Make sure that the cabling supports 1 GB, or you will be wasting your time and money.

RAID array

To speed the access to data or to provide fault tolerance to any data stored on the home server, consider using multiple hard drives and implementing a RAID 0, RAID 1, or RAID 5 hard disk system. See the section "RAID 0, 1, 5, and 10" under objective 3.4.

Exam essentials

Describe the specific requirements of specialty workstations.   These include but are not limited to graphics, CAD/CAM, audio/video editing, virtualization, gaming, home theater, and home server systems.

Identify the difference between a thick and a thin client.   A thick client runs the operating system and applications from the local hard drive, whereas a thin client runs these components from a remote server.

3.9 Given a scenario, install and configure common devices.

Installing a laptop or desktop system is not all that involved once the operating system is installed (covered in Chapter 6, "Operating Systems"). Some settings may need to be made to certain components, and user accounts must be prepared to support the users. The topics in this objective include the following:

- Desktop
- Laptop/common mobile devices

Desktop

Both thin and thick clients will need network configurations to operate on the network and user accounts must be created and secured.

Thin client

The thin client must have a network configuration. In most cases you should use DHCP for this. If you have a wireless router, it can issue these configurations. For better performance, however, plug the thin client into the Ethernet ports that typically come with ISP-provided routers. If DHCP is not in use, ensure that the thin client has an IP configuration that will enable it to connect to the server and to other required resources including the Internet.

Thick client

Treat the installation of the thick client in the same way you would the thin client. If you have a wireless router, it can issue these configurations. For better performance, however, plug the thick client into the Ethernet ports that typically come with ISP-provided routers. If DHCP is not in use, ensure that the thick client has an IP configuration that will enable it to connect to required resources including the Internet.

Account setup/settings

On both thin and thick clients you must create user accounts and passwords for those who will be using the device. Ensure accountability by using no shared accounts. Each user should have a unique username/password combination.

Laptop/common mobile devices

Laptops have many components that do not appear in a desktop, and the A+ exam covers their details in objective 1.0. However, the current objective also touches on some of these components. Let's look at those.

Touchpad configuration

Touchpads do not typically need configuration and were covered in detail in Chapter 1, "Mobile Devices."

Touchscreen configuration

Touchscreens sometimes need calibration. Calibration is a process that varies by vendor but is usually requires touching the screen in certain places when it tells you to. See the documentation on the exact method.

Application installations/configurations

It is likely that the system will not have all required applications installed. Just as you must ensure that the system has sufficient resources (memory, CPU, storage space) for the operating system, you must do the same for the applications. Also, be mindful of how the applications will be used. If multiple applications will be in use simultaneously, ensure that resources are sufficient to run all of them effectively at the same time.

Synchronization settings

Some data types may need to be synchronized across the various locations where they may be stored. Synchronization is covered in Chapter 1.

Account setup/settings

Treat the setup of accounts and their security the same with a laptop as you would with the desktop. Ensure accountability by using no shared accounts. Each user should have a unique username/password combination.

Wireless settings

Laptops often are moved around and use WLAN connections. To support this, the wireless card should be set for DHCP, as each wireless AP you encounter will provide an IP configuration that works on that WLAN.

Also ensure that you have a WLAN profile created for any WLAN you will connect to that has a hidden SSID. Enter any required credentials and save them in the profile to save the user the aggravation of entering this each time they are connected.

Exam essentials

Install input devices.   These include the mouse, keyboard, scanner, barcode reader, biometric devices, game pads, joysticks, digitizer, motion sensor, touchpads, smart card readers, digital cameras, microphone, webcam, camcorder, and MIDI-enabled devices.

Install output devices.   These include printers, speakers, and display devices. Take appropriate precautions if encountering an LCD.

Install devices that are both input and output.   These include but are not limited to touchscreen devices, KVMs, smart TVs, and set-top boxes.

3.10 Given a scenario, configure SOHO multifunction devices/printers and settings.

Printers are one of the most common elements in any computing environment, from home to office. The range they cover is phenomenal—everything from a free printer included by a vendor with the purchase of a PC up to a monolith in a large office churning out hundreds of pages a minute. Regardless of where a printer falls in that spectrum, they are all the same in that they must be installed and properly configured to be of use. Moreover, most printing devices today are multifunction devices. They print, scan, and fax in various combinations.

The topics addressed in objective 3.10 include the following:

- Using appropriate drivers for a given operating system
- Device sharing
- Public/shared devices

Use appropriate drivers for a given operating system.

Besides understanding the printer's operation, for the exam you need to understand how these devices talk to a computer. The driver software controls how the printer processes the print job. When you install a printer driver for the printer you are using, it allows the computer to print to that printer correctly (assuming you have the correct interface configured between the computer and printer). Also keep in mind that drivers are specific to the operating system, so you need to select the one that is both for the correct printer and for the correct operating system.

An interface is the collection of hardware and software that allows the device to communicate with a computer. Each printer, for example, has at least one interface, but some printers have several to make them more flexible in a multiplatform environment. If a printer has several interfaces, it can usually switch between them on the fly so that several computers can print at the same time.

Configuration settings

You need to be familiar with the various settings that are available and what these settings do. This section covers the more common settings, features, and characteristics of printers.

Duplex   An optional component that can be added to printers (usually laser but also inkjet) is a duplexer. This can be an optional assembly added to the printer, or built into it, but the sole purpose of duplexing is to turn the printed sheet over so it can be run back through the printer and allow printing on both sides.

Collate   Collating is the process of arranging the output of a print job so that multiple individual sets of the output are in proper order. A collator is a unit that if present on the printer will allow the printer to collate.

Orientation   The orientation of a document refers to how the printed matter is laid out on the page. In the landscape orientation, the printing is written across the paper turned on its long side, while in portrait the paper is turned up vertically and printed top to bottom.

Quality   Print quality is a description of the look of the printing, its sharpness, and its color depth. It is impacted by the quality of the paper, the speed of the printing process, and the resolution settings. It can also be affected by the DPI setting. This setting controls the size of objects on the page and therefore their sharpness. As you increase the size of an object, its quality will usually decrease a bit.

Device sharing

Printer sharing covers the hardware technologies involved in getting the information to and from the computer. There are several types, which can be broken into two broad categories: wired and wireless.

Wired

The wired forms of connection this exam tests on are USB, parallel, serial, and Ethernet. Each is addressed in the sections that follow.

USB

The most popular type of printer interface as this book is being written is USB. It's the most popular interface for just about every peripheral. The benefits for printers are that it has a higher transfer rate than either serial or parallel, and it automatically recognizes new devices. USB is also fully plug and play, and it allows several printers to be connected at once without adding ports or using up additional system resources.

Serial

This is the traditional RS-232 serial port found on most PCs. Because it is the original printer interface on the earliest computers, it has fallen out of favor and is seldom used anymore for printing because it's so slow.

Ethernet

Most large-environment printers (primarily laser and LED printers) have a special interface that allows them to be hooked directly to a network. These printers have a NIC and ROM-based software that let them communicate with networks, servers, and workstations.

Wireless

The wireless forms of connection included on this exam are Bluetooth, 802.11x, and Infrared (IR). Each is addressed in the sections that follow.

Bluetooth

Bluetooth is an infrared technology that can connect a printer to a computer at a short range; its absolute maximum range is 100 meters (330 feet), and most devices are specified to work within 10 meters (33 feet). When printing with a Bluetooth-enabled device (like a PDA or mobile phone) and a Bluetooth-enabled printer, all you need to do is get within range of the device (that is, move closer), select the print driver from the device, and choose Print. The information is transmitted wirelessly through the air using radio waves and is received by the device.

802.11(a, b, g, n, ac)

A network-enabled printer that has a wireless adapter can participate in a wireless Ethernet (IEEE 802.11b, a, g, n, or ac) network, just as it would as a wired network client.

Infrastructure vs. ad hoc

The architecture of the wireless network may affect the way you set up a wireless printer. In ad hoc mode, all devices communicate directly in a peer-to-peer fashion. This means that each user who accesses the wireless printer will establish their own connection to the wireless printer, and they need to ensure they are in the same IP network with the printer as well as the same WLAN. In infrastructure mode, the wireless network is using an access point (AP), and all communication goes through the AP. In this case, the printer must be set up to automatically connect to the AP so it is on the same network as the wireless clients that need to use the printer.

Integrated print server (hardware)

A print server is a popular option for adding a printer to the network and not adding a host computer. To be a print server, the NIC in the printer differs from a NIC in a computer in that it has a processor on it to perform the management of the NIC interface, and it is made by the same manufacturer as the printer.

For a printer to qualify as a print server, when someone on the network prints, the print job must go directly to the printer and not through any third-party device. This tends to make printing to that printer faster and more efficient—that NIC is dedicated to receiving print jobs and sending printer status to clients.

Cloud printing/remote printing

While printing remotely to a printer over the Internet has been available for a number of years, cloud printing is a new service being offered by cloud vendors. In a cloud arrangement, you connect your printer to the vendor's cloud, and then the printer is available to you anywhere you can get Internet access, just as cloud-based resources are available anywhere you can get Internet access.

While cloud-ready printers are not required, cloud vendors encourage their use in this arrangement. These are printers that need no PC to connect to the Internet, which makes the process of connecting to the cloud print server much simpler.

Another option is to create a VPN connection to your home network. Once connected to the home network over the VPN, you should be able to connect to and print to the printer as if you were sitting in your home office.

Public/shared devices

All operating systems allow you to share a local printer or connect over the network to one that has been shared. To connect to a printer in Windows 10, choose Start ➤ Control Panel ➤ Hardware and Sound ➤ Devices and Printers, and it will show the currently recognized printers (see Figure 3.69) and allow you to add new ones.

FIGURE 3.69   The Devices And Printers window in Windows 10

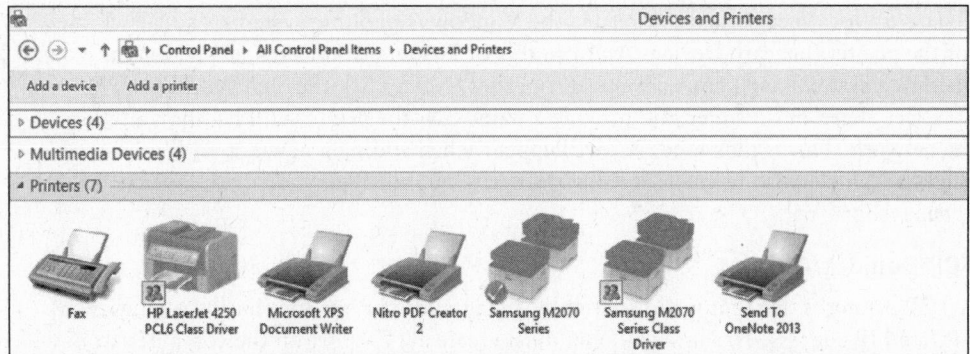

The image of a check box on the first instance of the Samsung M 2070 shows that it is the current default printer, and the image of two people on the second instance of the device means that it is shared. Clicking Add A Printer (at the top of the dialog box) starts the wizard shown in Figure 3.70.

FIGURE 3.70   Adding a printer

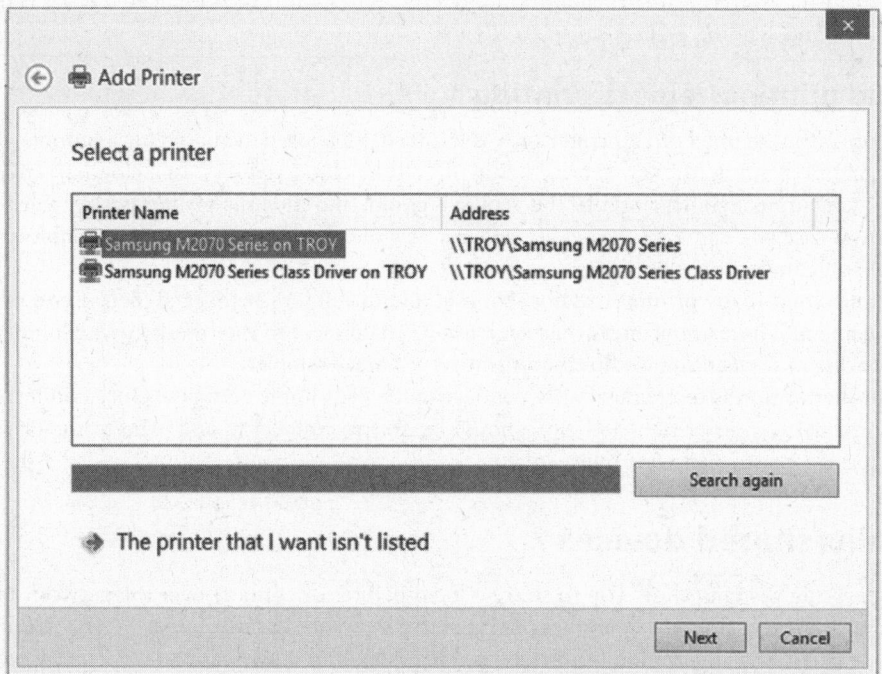

Sharing local/networked device via operating system settings

To share a local/networked printer via the Windows operating systems, right-click the icon for the printer (beneath Devices And Printers or Printers And Faxes, depending on your operating system) and choose Printer Properties. Next, click the Sharing tab.

Select Share This Printer and provide a name that the printer will be known by on the network. This is the name that will appear when adding a new network printer on a client, and it can also be referenced by the entire qualified name using the syntax \\host\share_name.

TCP/Bonjour/AirPrint

A TCP printer is one that is not shared by a computer but one that has its own network card and IP address. To share one, you must create a TCP port on the computer from which you would like to print, pointing to the IP address of the printer. Then, when adding the printer, select the TCP port you created instead of selecting a local port (USB, and so on) as you would do if setting up a printer that is connected locally.

Bonjour is an Apple technology that discovers devices on a network. It can also be used to facilitate the sharing of a printer in the network. While it can work with Windows, the steps for using it on a Mac are as follows:

1. Click the System Preferences icon in the Dock to open the System Preferences window.

2. Click Print And Scan in the Hardware section to open the Print And Scan window.

3. Click the + button under the Printers list box to open the Add window.

4. Click the Default tab to display the list of available printers. Choose the name of the network printer from the list of printers. The system automatically searches for and installs the appropriate driver for the printer.

5. If the system cannot find a printer driver, click the Use box and manually select it from the pop-up menu. Click Add to automatically make the printer available in the printer queue.

AirPrint is the Apple technology for printing wirelessly to a printer in the network. Many printers come ready to support AirPrint. One important thing to note is that AirPrint does not support printing directly to the wireless printer; it must be done through an access point. This means that you can use this technology only in a WLAN where an access point is present.

Data privacy

In any scenario where users are sharing a device, data privacy is an issue. There are several things that can be done to protect the privacy of data sent to the printer.

- Ensure that all users are authenticated to the device (discussed next).

- Ensure that users are given only the rights to the device they need to perform their job.

- Consider the use of data loss prevention (DLP). These services can be used to control the printing, emailing, sharing, or deleting of documents.

Make use of the auditing features to maintain an awareness of who does what and when they do it.

User authentication on the device

While nearly all enterprise-grade multifunction devices support user authentication, it may be easier and make more sense in a large network to perform this on the print server and use domain credentials to take advantage of single sign-on. In any case, user authentication forms the bedrock for auditing.

Hard drive caching

It is also important to realize that most enterprise-grade multifunction devices have hard drives and cache information on those hard drives. You must take steps to protect that data; it can be stolen from the hard drive, either by remote access or by extracting the data once the drive has been removed.

Options for securing the data on the device include the following:

Encryption   Encodes the data stored on the hard drive so that it cannot be retrieved even if the hard drive is removed from the machine.

Overwriting   Changes the values of the bits on the disk that make up a file by overwriting existing data with random characters. By overwriting the disk space that the file occupied, its traces are removed, and the file can't be reconstructed as easily.

Exam essentials

Be familiar with the possible interfaces that can be used for printing.   The types generally fall into two categories: wired (USB, parallel, Ethernet) and wireless (Bluetooth and 802.11x).

Know how to install printers.   The manufacturer is the best source of information about installing printers. You should, however, know about the wizards available in Windows as well.

Know how to share printers.   This includes how to share in Windows and by using AirPrint and Bonjour.

3.11 Given a scenario, install and maintain various print technologies.

This objective tests your knowledge of five types of printers: laser, inkjet (sometimes called *ink dispersion*), thermal, impact, and virtual. Make certain you understand the imaging process associated with each of these printer types and—in particular—can name the steps in the laser imaging process. The A+ certification exams have traditionally focused heavily on laser printers, but you can expect to also see questions about other printer types. The topics covered in objective 3.11 include the following:

- Laser
- Inkjet
- Thermal
- Impact
- Virtual
- 3D printers

Printer Introduction

Before moving on to the specific topics for objective 3.11, it will be helpful to review some of the basics of printer technologies, particularly the different ways of classifying printers and general maintenance issues.

Printer categories

As you review the following descriptions of printer types, keep in mind that printers may be differentiated from one another in several ways, including the following:

Impact vs. Nonimpact   Impact printers physically strike an inked ribbon and therefore can print multipart forms; nonimpact printers deliver ink onto the page without striking it. Dot matrix is impact; all the other printers you need to know for the exam are nonimpact.

Continuous Feed vs. Sheet Fed   Continuous-feed paper feeds through the printer using a system of sprockets and tractors. Sheet-fed printers accept plain paper in a paper tray. Dot matrix is continuous feed; everything else is sheet fed.

Line vs. Page   Line printers print one line at a time; page printers compose the entire page in memory and then place it all on the paper at once. Dot matrix and inkjet are line printers; lasers are page printers.

General maintenance

Beyond what is covered in objective 3.11, it is important to know good principles of general printer maintenance. To keep your printers working efficiently and extend their life as much as possible, you should start by creating a log of scheduled maintenance as outlined by the vendor's guidelines and then make certain this maintenance log is adhered to. For many printers, the scheduled maintenance includes installing maintenance kits. Maintenance kits typically include a fuser, transfer roller, pickup rollers (for the trays), separation rollers, and feed rollers. (Note that after installing the maintenance kit, you need to reset the maintenance counter as explained in the vendor's documentation.)

Pay a great deal of attention to the ambient surroundings of the printers as well. High temperature, high humidity, and high levels of dust and debris can negatively affect the life of the printer and the quality of print jobs. Always make certain you use recommended supplies. It may be cheaper to buy off-brand supplies that aren't intended for your equipment, but you're taking a gamble with shortening the life of your printer and decreasing the quality of your output.

Some general preventive maintenance includes the following:

- Never reuse paper in a laser printer that has been through the printer once. Although it may look blank, you're repeating the charging and fusing process on a piece of paper that most likely has *something* already on it.

- Change the toner when needed. You should recycle; most toner manufacturers participate in a recycling program of some type. The toner cartridge should never be exposed to light for longer than a few minutes; it usually comes sealed in a black plastic light-resistant bag.

- Clean any toner that accidentally spills into the printer with a dry, lint-free cloth. Bear in mind that spilled toner in the paper path should clear after you run a few blank pages through. If toner gets on your clothes, wipe them with a dry cloth and wash them with cold water (hot water works like the fusing process to set them into the material).

- Clean any paper shreds, dust, or dander that gets deposited in the printer. Pressurized air is the most effective method of removal.

- Keep the drum in good working order. If it develops lines, replace it.

- Install the maintenance kit when needed and reset the page count. The maintenance kit (sometimes called a *fuser kit*) typically includes a fusing assembly, rollers, and separation pads. A message such as "Perform Printer Maintenance" indicates the printer has reached its maintenance interval and a maintenance kit needs to be installed.

- Don't be afraid to cycle the power for an unresponsive printer. Turning it off, leaving it off for one minute to clear, and then turning it back on can solve a great many problems.

- For inkjet and impact printers, you should periodically clean the print head.

While the previous list offers good rules of thumb, for this objective CompTIA wants you to be familiar with maintenance for four types of printers: laser, thermal, impact, and virtual. The following sections will look at each of those.

Laser

Laser printers are referred to as *page printers* because they receive their print job instructions one page at a time. They're sheet-fed, nonimpact printers. Another name for a laser printer is an *electrophotographic* (EP) printer.

 LED printers are much like laser printers except they use light-emitting diodes (LEDs) instead of lasers. Their process is similar to that of laser printers.

Imaging drum, fuser assembly, transfer belt, transfer roller, pickup rollers, separate pads, duplexing assembly

First let's discuss the major components used in the laser printing process and then discuss the process steps. An EP (laser) printer consists of the following major components:

Printer Controller   This is a large circuit board that acts as the motherboard for the printer. It contains the processor and RAM to convert data coming in from the computer into a picture of a page to be printed.

Imaging Drum   The toner cartridge and drum are typically packaged together as a consumable product that contains the toner. Toner is a powdery mixture of plastic resin and iron oxide. The plastic allows it to be melted and fused to the paper, and the iron oxide allows it to be moved around via positive or negative charge. Toner comes in a cartridge, like the one shown in Figure 3.71.

FIGURE 3.71   An EP toner cartridge

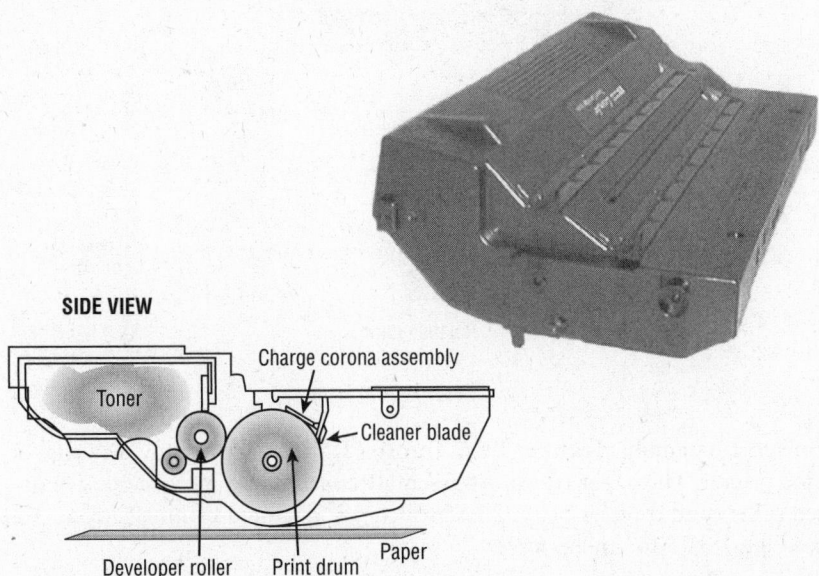

The drum is light sensitive; it can be written to with the laser scanning assembly. The toner cartridge in Figure 3.71 contains the print drum, so every time you change the toner cartridge, you get a new drum. In some laser printers, the drum is a separate part that lasts longer, so you don't have to change it every time you change the toner.

Primary Corona (Charge Corona)   This applies a uniform negative charge (around –600V) to the drum at the beginning of the printing cycle.

Laser Scanning Assembly   This uses a laser beam to neutralize the strong negative charge on the drum in certain areas, so toner will stick to the drum in those areas. The laser scanning assembly uses a set of rotating and fixed mirrors to direct the beam, as shown in Figure 3.72.

FIGURE 3.72   The EP laser scanning assembly (side view and simplified top view)

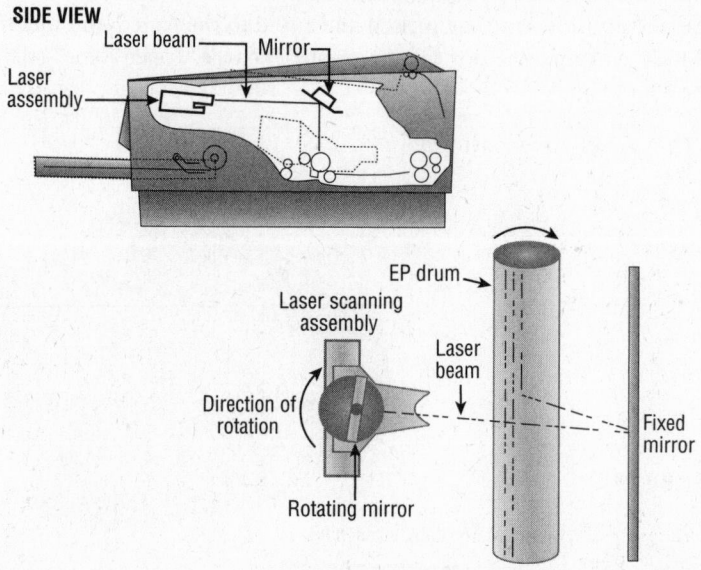

Paper Transport Assembly (Transfer Belt, Transfer Rollers)   This moves the paper through the printer. The paper transport assembly consists of a motor and several rubberized rollers and transfer belts. These rollers are operated by an electronic stepper motor. See Figure 3.73 for an example.

FIGURE 3.73   Paper transport rollers

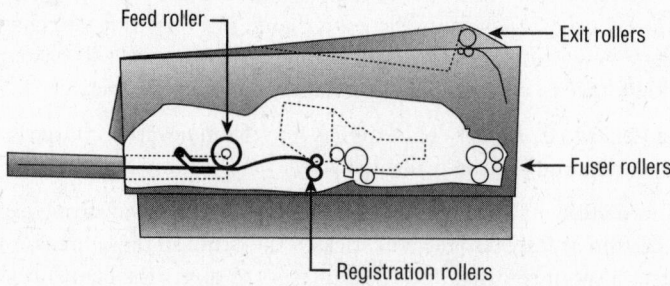

Pickup Rollers   Pickup rollers are rubber wheels that grab the paper and feed it in. When these parts get old, they lose their ability to grip the paper, so they should be checked and changed regularly.

Separate Pads   These pads are used to separate sheets in a stack of printing paper. It does this as the paper passes over them by creating friction that separates the paper. These pads are usually 2 to 3 inches wide, and when they start to wear out, they lose their ability to create friction, and you start getting two and three sheets at a time pulled through.

Transfer Corona   This applies a uniform positive charge (about +600V) to the paper. When the paper rotates past the drum, the toner is pulled off the drum and onto the paper. Then the paper passes through a static eliminator that removes the positive charge from it (see Figure 3.74). Some printers use a transfer corona wire; others use a transfer corona roller.

FIGURE 3.74   The transfer corona assembly

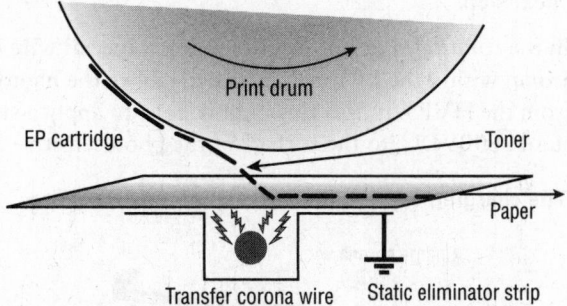

High-Voltage Power Supply (HVPS)   This delivers the high voltages needed to make the printing process happen. It converts ordinary 120V household AC current into high-DC voltages used to energize the primary and transfer corona wires (discussed later).

DC Power Supply   This delivers lower voltages to components in the printer that need much lower voltages than the corona wires do (such as circuit boards, memory, and motors).

Fusing Assembly   This melts the plastic resin in the toner so that it adheres to the paper. The fusing assembly contains a halogen heating lamp, a fusing roller made of Teflon-coated aluminum, and a rubberized pressure roller. The lamp heats the fusing roller, and as the paper passes between the two rollers, the pressure roller pushes the paper against the hot fusing roller, melting the toner into the paper (see Figure 3.75).

FIGURE 3.75   The fusing assembly

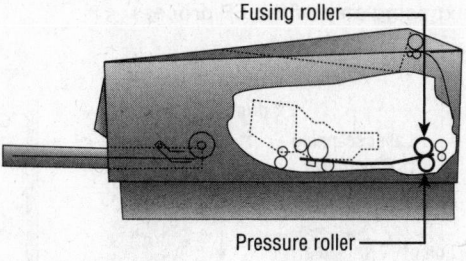

Duplex Assembly   Duplex assemblies were discussed in the section "Duplex" under objective 3.10 earlier in this chapter.

Imaging process: processing, charging, exposing, developing, transferring, fusing, and cleaning

The laser (EP) print process consists of seven steps. Here are the steps in the order you'll see them on the exam:

Step 1: Processing   In this step the data is received by the printer software and the images are rendered for the next step.

Step 2: Charging   In the *conditioning* step (Figure 3.76), a special wire (called a *primary corona* or *charge corona*) within the EP toner cartridge (above the photosensitive drum) gets a high voltage from the HVPS. It uses this high voltage to apply a strong, uniform negative charge (around −600VDC) to the surface of the photosensitive drum.

FIGURE 3.76   The charging or conditioning step of the EP process

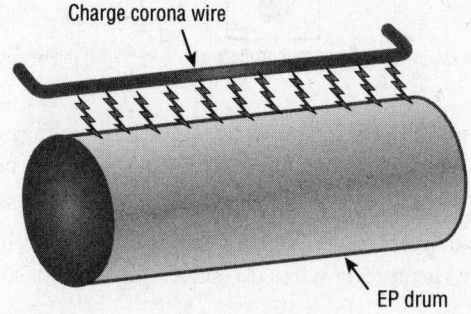

Step 3: Exposing   In the *writing* step of the EP process, the laser is turned on and scans the drum from side to side, flashing on and off according to the bits of information the printer controller sends it as it communicates the individual bits of the image. In each area where the laser touches the photosensitive drum, the drum's charge is severely reduced from −600VDC to a slight negative charge (around −100VDC). As the drum rotates, a pattern of exposed areas is formed, representing the image to be printed. Figure 3.77 shows this process.

FIGURE 3.77   The exposing step of the EP process

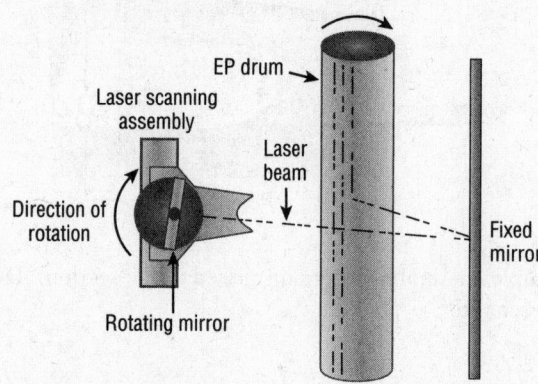

At this point, the controller sends a signal to the pickup roller to feed a piece of paper into the printer, where it stops at the registration rollers.

Step 4: Developing   Now that the surface of the drum holds an electrical representation of the image being printed, its discrete electrical charges need to be converted into something that can be transferred to a piece of paper. The EP process's *developing* step accomplishes this (Figure 3.78). In this step, toner is transferred to the areas that were exposed in the writing step.

FIGURE 3.78   The developing step of the EP process

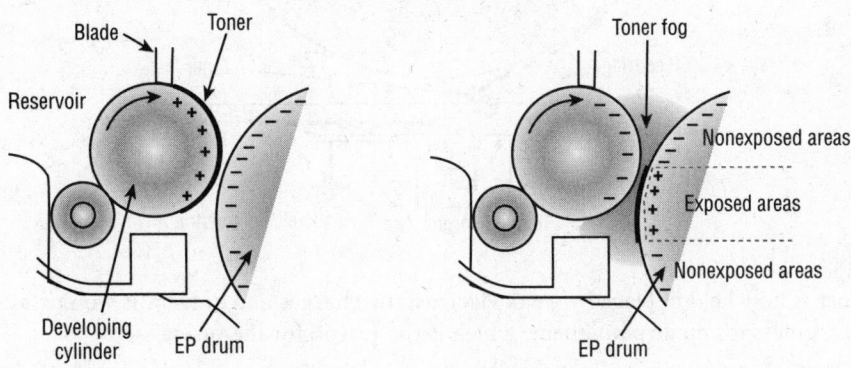

A metallic *developing roller* or *cylinder* inside an EP cartridge acquires a –600VDC charge (called a *bias voltage*) from the HVPS. The toner sticks to this roller because there is a magnet located inside the roller and because of the electrostatic charges between the toner and the developing roller. While the developing roller rotates toward the photosensitive drum, the toner acquires the charge of the roller (–600VDC). When the toner comes between the developing roller and the photosensitive drum, the toner is attracted to the areas that have been exposed by the laser (because these areas have a lesser charge of –100VDC). The toner also is repelled from the unexposed areas (because they're at the same –600VDC charge and like charges repel). This toner transfer creates a fog of toner between the EP drum and the developing roller.

The photosensitive drum now has toner stuck to it where the laser has written. The photosensitive drum continues to rotate until the developed image is ready to be transferred to paper in the next step.

Step 5: Transferring   At this point in the EP process, the developed image is rotating into position. The controller notifies the registration rollers that the paper should be fed through. The registration rollers move the paper underneath the photosensitive drum, and the process of transferring the image can begin with the *transferring* step.

The controller sends a signal to the corona wire or corona roller (depending on which one the printer has) and tells it to turn on. The corona wire/roller then acquires a strong *positive* charge (+600VDC) and applies that charge to the paper. The paper, thus charged, pulls the toner from the photosensitive drum at the line of contact between the roller and the paper because the paper and toner have opposite charges. Once the registration rollers move the paper past the corona wire, the static-eliminator strip removes all charge from that line of the paper. Figure 3.79 details this step. If the strip didn't bleed this charge away, the paper would attract itself to the toner cartridge and cause a paper jam.

FIGURE 3.79 The transferring step of the EP process

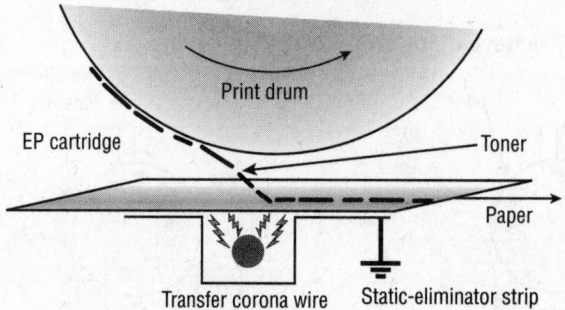

The toner is now held in place by weak electrostatic charges and gravity. It won't stay there, however, unless it's made permanent, which is the reason for the fusing step.

Step 6: Fusing In the next step, *fusing*, the toner image is made permanent. The registration rollers push the paper toward the fuser rollers. Once the fuser grabs the paper, the registration rollers push for only a short time more. The fuser is now in control of moving the paper.

As the paper passes through the fuser, the fuser roller melts the polyester resin of the toner, and the rubberized pressure roller presses it permanently into the paper (Figure 3.80). The paper continues on through the fuser and eventually exits the printer.

FIGURE 3.80 The fusing step of the EP process

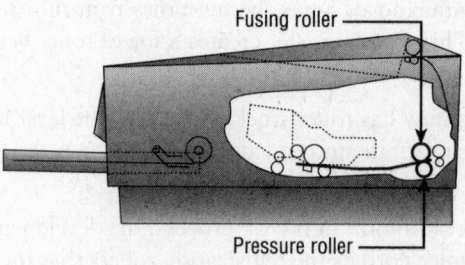

Step 7: Cleaning In the last part of the laser print process, a rubber blade inside the EP cartridge scrapes any toner left on the drum into a used-toner receptacle inside the EP cartridge, and a fluorescent lamp discharges any remaining charge on the photosensitive drum (remember that the drum, being photosensitive, loses its charge when exposed to light). See Figure 3.81.

FIGURE 3.81   The cleaning step of the EP process

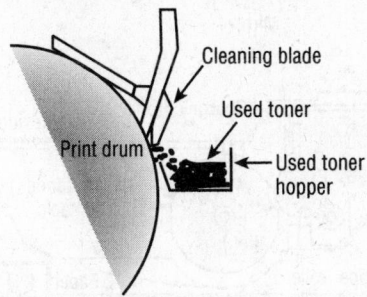

 A color laser is much like a regular laser printer except that multiple passes over the page are made, one for each ink color. Consequently, the printing speed is rather low.

The EP cartridge is constantly cleaning the drum. It may take more than one rotation of the photosensitive drum to make an image on the paper. The cleaning step keeps the drum fresh for each use. If you didn't clean the drum, you would see ghosts of previous pages printed along with your image.

 The actual amount of toner removed in the cleaning process is quite small. The cartridge will run out of toner before the used toner receptacle fills up.

Putting it all together

Figure 3.82 summarizes all the EP process printing steps. First, the printer uses a rubber scraper to clean the photosensitive drum. Then the printer places a uniform –600VDC charge on the photosensitive drum by means of a charge corona. The laser paints an image onto the photosensitive drum, discharging the image areas to a much lower voltage (–100VDC). The developing roller in the toner cartridge has charged (–600VDC) toner stuck to it. As it rolls the toner toward the photosensitive drum, the toner is attracted to (and sticks to) the areas of the photosensitive drum that the laser has discharged. The image is then transferred from the drum to the paper at its line of contact by means of the corona wire (or corona roller) with a +600VDC charge. The static-eliminator strip removes the high, positive charge from the paper, and the paper, now holding the image, moves on. The paper then enters the fuser, where the fuser roller and the pressure roller make the image permanent. The paper exits the printer, and the printer starts printing the next page or returns to its ready state.

FIGURE 3.82 The EP print process

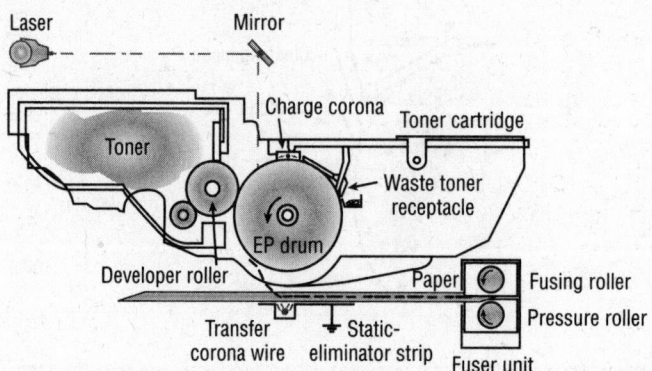

 An optional component that can be added to printers (usually laser but also inkjet) is a duplexer. This can be an optional assembly added to the printer, or built into it, but the sole purpose of *duplexing* is to turn the printed sheet over so it can be run back through the printer and allow printing on both sides.

Maintenance: Replace toner, apply maintenance kit, calibrate, clean

Just as laser printers are the most complicated of the types (and offer the most capabilities), they also have the most things that can go awry. A thermal fuse is included to keep the system from overheating, and if it becomes faulty, it can prevent the printer from printing. Many high-capacity laser printers also include an ozone filter to prevent the corona's ozone output from reaching too high a level. On these printers, the filter should be changed as part of regular maintenance.

Other common problems and solutions are as follows:

Paper Jams While paper jams can be caused by numerous problems, two common ones are the paper not feeding correctly and moisture. To correct improper feeds, make sure you set the alignment guides for the paper you are using and verify that the paper is feeding in straight. Keep the paper from getting any moisture before feeding into the printer because moisture often causes pages to stick together and bind. Paper jams can also be caused by using paper that is not approved for the printer—particularly thick cardstock.

 One employee routinely had problems with a printer each time he went to print on high-quality paper—a problem experienced by no one else. Upon close examination, it turned out that each time he chose to print to the expensive paper, he counted the number of sheets he loaded into the printer—counting that involved licking his finger and then touching each page. A simple directive to stop doing this solved the problem.

Regardless of the cause of a paper jam, you need to always fully clear the printer of any traces of paper (torn or whole) before attempting to print again.

Error Codes   Many laser printers include LCDs for interaction with the printer. When error codes appear, refer to the manufacturer's manuals or website for information on how to interpret the codes and solve the problem causing them.

Out-of-Memory Error   While PCs now may need a minimum of 1 GB of RAM to run at a base level, it is not uncommon to find printers that still have only 4 MB or 8 MB of memory. If you are routinely running out of memory on a printer, add more memory if possible, and replace the printer when it is no longer possible to do so.

Lines and Smearing   Lines and smearing can be caused by the toner cartridge or the fuser. Try replacing the toner first (and cleaning any that may have spilled). If this does not fix the problem, replace the fuser.

Blank Pages Print   Verify that there is toner in the cartridge. If it's an old cartridge, you can often shake it slightly to free up toner once before replacing. If it's a new cartridge, make sure the sealing tape has been removed from the cartridge prior to placing it in the printer.

 Be careful when doing this operation. Someone who has asthma or who is sensitive to microfine particles could be adversely affected by the toner.

Dark Spots Print   The most likely culprit is too much toner. Run blank pages through the printer to clean it.

Garbled Pages Print   Make sure you're using the right printer driver in your application.

Ghosted Images Print   Ghosting—repeating text or images on the page—is usually caused by a bad cartridge. There can be damage to the drum or charging roller, and if there is, replacing the cartridge will help with the problem.

No Connectivity   If a network printer is not able to receive jobs, the issue may be with the IP address that it has (or, more correctly, does not have). Often the printer will need to be manually assigned an IP address to make sure that it has the same one each time. Read the manufacturer's documentation for assigning an IP address to the printer and walk through the steps to do so.

 Never overlook the obvious. Connectivity problems also occur when the printer is turned off.

Print-Quality Problems   See whether your printer has the ability to turn Resolution Enhancement Technology (RET) on and off. This is what allows the printer to use partial-sized dots for images that are rounded. If it's turned off, turn it back on. If there are small marks or defects in the same spot on every page printed, the most likely culprit is a scratch on the drum.

Replacing Toner   Toner represents the consumable within the laser printer. Toner cartridges are used by laser printers to store toner. Use toner that is recommended for your printer. Using bad supplies could ruin your printer and void your warranty. Remove the toner before moving or shipping a printer to avoid spills.

Applying a Maintenance Kit   Maintenance kits are marketed by the manufacturer. Each kit varies in contents based on the printer in question but typically consists of a fuser, transfer roller, and feed/separation rollers. A counter on the laser printer often identifies when the maintenance kit is needed, and you can reset the counter after applying the new kit.

Calibration   With laser printers and inkjets, there is often a need to calibrate. Calibration is the process by which the result produced matches what was created. All the hardware, including the monitor, scanner, and printer, need to match on color, margins, and so forth.

The calibration process is different for each manufacturer but is usually similar to the following:

1.   During installation of the software, you are asked (by the installation wizard) if you want to calibrate now (say Yes).

2.   The printer prints multiple sets of numbered lines. Each set of lines represents an alignment instance, and you are asked which set looks the best.

3.   You enter the set number and click OK. In some cases, the alignment ends here. In other cases, the alignment page is reprinted to verify that the settings are correct, and you are given a chance to change.

4.   You exit the alignment routine.

Cleaning   It is important to keep the printer and the area around it clean. Each time you replace the toner or perform any maintenance, be sure to clean the debris.

Inkjet

Inkjet printers are one of the most popular types in use today. This type of printer sprays ink on the page to print text or graphics. It's a nonimpact, sheet-fed printer. Figure 3.83 shows an ink cartridge.

FIGURE 3.83   A typical ink cartridge

There are two kinds of inkjet printers: *thermal* and *piezoelectric*. These terms refer to the way the ink is sprayed onto the paper. A thermal inkjet printer heats the ink to about 400 degrees Fahrenheit, creating vapor bubbles that force the ink out of the cartridge. Thermal inkjets are also sometimes called *bubble jets*. A piezoelectric printer does the same thing but with electricity instead of heat.

Inkjet printers are popular because they can print in color and are inexpensive. However, their speed isn't quite as good as that of a laser printer, and the per-page cost of ink can be higher than for a laser printer. Therefore, most businesses prefer laser printers for their main printing needs, perhaps keeping one or two inkjet printers around for situations requiring color printing.

Ink cartridge, print head, roller, feeder, duplexing assembly, carriage, and belt

Components of an inkjet printer are covered in the following sections.

Ink cartridge

These cartridges contain the ink. Some cartridges contain the print head for that color of ink; you get a new print head each time you replace the cartridge. On other printer models, the ink cartridge is just an ink reservoir, and the heads don't need replacing.

Print head

The print head has a series of nozzles from which the ink is sprayed onto the paper. They may be attached to the ink cartridge, or those two components may be separate. In cases where they are one piece, you will be getting a new print head each time you get a new ink cartridge.

Roller

Just as on a laser printer, rollers are used to pull the paper in from the tray or feeder and advance the paper when the print head assembly is ready for another pass. As is the case with any rollers, they will need to be replaced when they lose their ability to "grab" the paper.

Feeder

The feeder looks like a tray and is where you load paper. It is from here that it is pulled into the printer when a new sheet is required. These feeders do not usually hold as much paper as a tray in a printer will.

Duplexing assembly

A duplexing assembly performs the same function on an inkjet printer that it does on a laser printer, which is to flip a sheet over to print on the back side.

Carriage and belt

The carriage holds the ink cartridges, and it uses a belt to move the entire piece across the paper as it is printing. As it prints, it uses ink from the various cartridges in whatever proportion is necessary to create the desired colors.

Calibrate

Calibrating an inkjet printer is the process of ensuring that there is proper alignment of the cartridges to one another and to the paper so that high quality is maintained. When a printer gets out of calibration, the print quality will decline. When a new cartridge is loaded, the printer will usually perform a calibration, but you may need to do this manually from time to time, especially on printers that are not used often enough to require a cartridge change as often as a calibration may be required.

On an inkjet printer, calibration is more commonly known as *head alignment*. The printer will automatically try to align ink cartridges each time they are replaced (or installed). If you want to make sure they are in the right place, most printers allow you to print an alignment page from the maintenance menu.

If characters are not properly formed or are appearing as straight lines along the margin (usually the left), you can use the maintenance menu settings to align the ink cartridges.

Maintenance: Clean heads, replace cartridges, calibrate, clear jams

While inkjet printers use a different technology to print, they require many of the same maintenance procedures. These are discussed briefly in this section.

Clean Heads   Two maintenance tasks apply to the print heads. If your colors don't look the same or your blacks are getting a bronze look, you need to clean the nozzles. This can be done with the head cleaning cycle, which will clear out the nozzles. The second task is head alignment. If you see white repeating lines or a grid-like pattern in the printing, the head is misaligned. While some newer printers have an automatic alignment and cleaning function, you may need to do this manually using the printer documentation.

Replace Cartridges   When ink runs low (and most printers will alert you before you run out), you must remove the old cartridge and replace it with a new one. The procedure is as follows:

1. Open the printer cover and locate the button that is used to place the cartridge in the replacement position.

2. Open the cover that may be over the cartridge.

3. Grasp and remove the empty cartridge.

4. Take the new cartridge out of its packaging.

5. Place the new cartridge in the empty position left by the old cartridge. It should click into place.

6. Replace the cartridge cover.

7. Use the same button you used to place the cartridge into the replacement positon to move it back to the home position.

Calibration   Calibration is a task usually performed by accessing the properties of the printer and looking for the calibration function either on the General tab or on the

Advanced tab. Just select it, and the printer will perform a calibration. It is also useful to know that in most cases a calibration is done whenever you replace one of the cartridges.

Clear Jams   While keeping in mind that many paper jams are a result of using poor-quality paper, there will be times you suffer jams with good paper. To clear a jam, do the following:

1. Check the paper tray. If you see a piece protruding from where the paper is picked up, pull it out gently.

2. If there is still a jam, remove the rear access door and look into the printer. If you see any paper stuck inside, pull it out, making sure you get all the pieces out.

3. Check the front door of the printer and see whether any pieces are stuck in that section; if so, gently pull them out.

4. At any point in this process you can select the Resume button, and if you have cleared the jam, the print process will resume.

Thermal

Thermal printers can be found in many older fax machines (most newer ones use either inkjet or laser printing) that print on a waxy paper that comes on a roll; the paper turns black when heat passes over it. These are also found on many handheld package tracking and point-of-sale (POS) devices such as credit card terminals. These printers should not be used for documents that need long-term storage as the printed image quickly degrades (disappears) so you are just left with a blank sheet of paper. This is especially true of receipts that need to be retained for tax purposes.

Feed assembly, heating element

Thermal printers work by using a print head the width of the paper. When it needs to print, the print head heats and cools spots on the print head. The paper below the heated print head turns black in those spots. As the paper moves through the printer, the pattern of blackened spots forms an image on the page of what is being printed.

Another type of thermal printer uses a heat-sensitive ribbon instead of heat-sensitive paper. A thermal print head melts wax-based ink from the ribbon onto the paper. These are called *thermal transfer* or *thermal wax-transfer* printers.

Thermal direct printers typically have long lives because they have few moving parts. However, the paper is somewhat expensive, doesn't last long, and produces poorer-quality images (that tend to fade over time) than most of the other printing technologies.

There are some variations of thermal printing that exist. They're all high-end color graphics printers designed for specialty professional usage. Here are four popular ones:

Thermal Wax Transfer   This is a color, nonimpact printer that uses a solid wax. A heater melts the wax and then sprays it onto the page, somewhat like an inkjet. The quality is very high, but so is the price.

Dye Sublimation   This is another color, nonimpact line printer. This one converts a solid ink into a gas that is then applied to the paper. Color is applied in a continuous tone, rather than individual dots, and the colors are applied one at a time. The ink comes on film rolls. The paper is expensive, as is the ink. Print speeds are low. The quality is extremely high.

Feed Assembly   Feed assemblies, commonly called *feeders*, are available to allow you to feed in the media you are printing on (paper, cards, and so on). Some feeders allow you to switch between multiple feeds, which is helpful if you need to alternate printing on different types of stock.

Heating Element   The heating element for a thermal printer is what generates the heat and does the actual printing. It is often the most expensive component.

Special thermal paper

To print with a thermal printer, you need to use heat-sensitive paper designed for the thermal printer as opposed to paper for any other type of printer. Rolls of thermal paper are available in a variety of sizes and colors.

Maintenance: Replace paper, clean heating element, remove debris

The amount of maintenance required on a thermal printer pales in comparison to laser since there are no moving parts to speak of. The following sections look at the key items to be aware of related to thermal printers as you study for the exam.

Replace Paper   Replace the thermal paper as it is needed; be sure to keep the feed area clean of paper slivers and other debris.

Clean Heating Element   Before even looking at a heating element, always unplug the printer and make certain it is cool. Thermal printer cleaning cards, cleaning pens, and kits are available and recommended for cleaning.

Remove Debris   Keep the printer free of dust and debris. Any particulates that get into the printer can interfere with the paper feeding properly or can affect the print quality. Use compressed air or a computer vacuum to remove any debris.

Impact

A dot-matrix printer is an impact printer; it prints by physically striking an inked ribbon, much like a typewriter. It's an impact, continuous-feed printer.

The print head on a dot-matrix printer consists of a block of metal pins that extend and retract. These pins are triggered to extend in patterns that form letters and numbers as the print head moves across the paper. Early models, known as near letter-quality (NLQ), printed using only nine pins. Later models used 24 pins and produced much better letter-quality (LQ) output.

The main advantage of dot matrix is its impact (physical striking of the paper). Because it strikes the paper, you can use it to print on multipart forms. Nonimpact printers can't do that. Dot-matrix printers aren't commonly found in most offices these days because of their disadvantages, including noise, slow speed, and poor print quality.

 Dot-matrix printers are still found in many warehouses, and other businesses, where multipart forms are used or where continuous feed is required.

Print head, ribbon, tractor feed

Key elements of an impact printer are discussed in the sections that follow.

Print Head   The pins in the print head are wrapped with coils of wire to create a solenoid and are held in the rest position by a combination of a small magnet and a spring. To trigger a particular pin, the printer controller sends a signal to the print head, which energizes the wires around the appropriate print wire. This turns the print wire into an electromagnet, which repels the print pin, forcing it against the ink ribbon and making a dot on the paper.

Ribbon   The ribbon is like that on an old typewriter. Most impact printers have an option to adjust how close the print head rests from the ribbon. So if your printing is too light, you may be able to adjust the print head closer to the ribbon. If it's too dark or you get smeared printing, you may be able to move the print head back.

Tractor Feed   The tractor feed unit feeds in the continuous feed paper. This paper has holes running down both edges.

Impact paper

An impact printer uses continuous feed paper fed to it by the tractor feed unit.

Maintenance: Replace ribbon, replace print head, replace paper

A dot-matrix print head reaches high temperatures, and care must be taken to avoid a user or technician touching it and getting burned. Most dot-matrix printers include a temperature sensor to tell whether the print head is getting too hot. The sensor interrupts printing to let the print head cool down and then allows printing to start again. If this sensor becomes faulty, it can cause the printer to print a few lines, stop for a while, print more, stop, and so on. The following sections look at the key items to be aware of related to impact printers as you study for the exam.

Replace ribbon.   A common culprit with poor printing is the ribbon. A tight ribbon, or one that isn't advancing properly, will cause smudges or overly light printout. To solve this problem, replace the ribbon.

Replace print head.   The print head should never be lubricated, but you can clean off debris with a cotton swab and denatured alcohol. Print pins missing from the print head will cause incomplete images or characters or white lines running through the text. This can be remedied by replacing the print head.

If the print head isn't at fault, make certain it's close enough to the platen to make the right image. The print head can be moved closer and farther from the platen (the surface on which typing occurs) depending on the thickness of the paper and other considerations.

Replace paper.   Preventive maintenance includes not only keeping the print head dry and clean but also vacuuming paper shreds from inside the machine. This should be done more often if needed but always when you replace the paper.

Virtual

There is also virtual printing, which is not really printing at all but a way to convert a document to a particular format. There are a number of ways this conversion can take place.

Print to file

Print to file is quite an old concept by now but still available as an option when printing. When you do this, the information that would normally be sent to the printer is saved, usually as a ·prn file. It is a way to avoid the printing process from within an application (which may be time-consuming or inconvenient) and print it (convert it) once and then save the file so that whenever you need a copy, you can simply send that to the printer.

Print to PDF

If you can print to file, you can print to PDF. In applications that support this feature, it will be an option presented when you select to print. When you select this option, it produces an Adobe PDF instead of a printout. It is a convenient format because you can still print the document later, search it, and send it; and when you do send it, you can be certain that the way the document appears to you will be the way it does to the recipient, regardless of the device type on which they are viewing it.

Print to XPS

An XPS document is a standardized open format and is Microsoft's answer to the PDF. It is always offered as a printer type in Windows. It will be called a Microsoft XPS Document Writer and will appear with other printers in the printer's folder, as shown in Figure 3.69 earlier. When your file is converted, it will appear with an ·opxs file extension (Open XPS). While Microsoft encourages the use of these documents and of the default XPS device and offers more support for it then for PDF, the document type is not as widely supported elsewhere as the PDF.

Print to image

Finally, printing to an image is somewhat like scanning because it creates an image of the document. This typically requires a third-party application. Many of the applications that will create a PDF, such as Nitro PDF Writer, will also allow for you to convert those formats to a ·jpg file.

3D printers

3D printers create objects or parts by joining or solidifying materials under computer control to create a three-dimensional object. Some versions use a data source such as an Additive Manufacturing File (AMF) file (usually in sequential layers).

Plastic filament

3D printers use rolls of special plastic filament as the material source. This filament comes in various colors and is shown in Figure 3.84 with objects created from the filament.

FIGURE 3.84　3D filament

Exam essentials

Identify the components of laser printers.　These include the imaging drum, fuser assembly, transfer belt, transfer roller, pickup rollers, separate pads, and duplexing assembly.

Describe the function of the components of an inkjet printer.　These include the ink cartridge, print head, roller, feeder, duplexing assembly, carriage, and belt.

Identify examples of using a virtual printer.　These include print to file, print to PDF, print to XPS, and print to image.

Review Questions

You can find the answers in the Appendix.

1. Which cable type comes in two varieties: unshielded and shielded?

    A. Fiber optic

    B. Coaxial

    C. Twisted pair

    D. Serial

2. Which cable type transmits data at speeds up to 100 Mbps and was used with Fast Ethernet (operating at 100 Mbps) with a transmission range of 100 meters?

    A. Cat 4

    B. Cat 5

    C. Cat 5e

    D. Cat 6

3. Which cable type has a glass core within a rubber outer coating?

    A. Fiber optic

    B. Coaxial

    C. Twisted pair

    D. Serial

4. Which connector is used for telephone cord?

    A. RJ-11

    B. RJ-45

    C. RS-232

    D. BNC

5. Which standard has been commonly used in computer serial ports?

    A. RJ-11

    B. RJ-45

    C. RS-232

    D. BNC

6. Which connectors are sometimes used in the place of RCA connectors for video electronics?

    A. RJ-11

    B. RJ-45

    C. RS-232

    D. BNC

7. Which RAM type is used in laptops?

  A. DIMM

  B. SODIMM

  C. Rambus

  D. BNC

8. Which RAM type allows for two memory accesses for each rising and falling clock?

  A. DIMM

  B. SODIMM

  C. DDR3

  D. DDR2

9. Which RAM type is not compatible with any earlier type of random-access memory?

  A. DDR5

  B. DDR4

  C. DDR3

  D. DDR2

10. Which of the following is a rewritable optical disc?

  A. CD

  B. CD-RW

  C. DVD

  D. CD-ROM

11. Which of the following is a specification for internally mounted computer expansion cards and associated connectors that replaces the mSATA?

  A. M2

  B. NVME

  C. SATA

  D. SATA 2.5

12. At what speed will latency on a magnetic drive decrease to about 3 ms?

  A. 5400 rpm

  B. 7200 rpm

  C. 10,000 rpm

  D. 15,000 rpm

13. Laptops and other portable devices utilize which expansion card?

    A. MiniPCI

    B. PCIe

    C. PCI

    D. SATA

14. Which of the following is a standard firmware interface for PCs, designed to replace BIOS?

    A. UEFI

    B. NVRAM

    C. CMOS

    D. CHS

15. Which of the following is memory that does not lose its content when power is lost to the machine?

    A. UEFI

    B. NVRAM

    C. CMOS

    D. CHS

16. Which of the following devices allows you to plug multiple PCs (usually servers) into the device and to switch easily back and forth from system to system using the same mouse, monitor, and keyboard?

    A. KVM

    B. NVRAM

    C. CMOS

    D. CHS

17. Which of the following is a description of light output?

    A. KVM

    B. Lumens

    C. Contrast

    D. CHS

18. Which of the following is a standard managed by the ISO and uses tags that are embedded in the devices?

    A. KVM

    B. Lumens

    C. NFC

    D. CHS

19. In 2004, the ATX 12V 2.0 (now 2.03) standard was passed, changing the main connector from 20 pins to how many?

   A. 16

   B. 22

   C. 24

   D. 28

20. When using the AT power connector, the power cable coming from the power supply will have two separate connectors, labeled what?

   A. P8 and P9

   B. P1 and P2

   C. P9 and P10

   D. P2 and P3

21. The SATA power connector has how many pins?

   A. 8

   B. 12

   C. 15

   D. 18

22. Which of the following is a desktop computer system?

   A. Thin client

   B. Thick client

   C. NAS

   D. SAN

23. Which of the following is a PC that has all the capabilities of a standard PC?

   A. Thin client

   B. Standard client

   C. Thick client

   D. Thin host

24. The amount of RAM that is required in a virtualization workstation depends on which of the following?

   A. Number of processors

   B. Number of drives

   C. Number of VMs

   D. Speed of NIC

25. Which IP setting is optional for network connectivity on a thin client?
    A. IP address
    B. Subnet mask
    C. Default gateway
    D. Proxy server

26. Which of the following needs the most resources?
    A. Thin client
    B. Thick client
    C. Medium client
    D. Stationary client

27. How is accountability ensured?
    A. Dual accounts
    B. Shared accounts
    C. No shared accounts
    D. No audit trails

28. What software controls how the printer processes the print job?
    A. Driver
    B. Interface
    C. Network
    D. Line

29. What printer component turns the printed sheet over so it can be run back through the printer and allow printing on both sides?
    A. Driver
    B. Duplexer
    C. Orientation
    D. Collator

30. Which of the following refers to how the printed matter is laid out on the page?
    A. Driver
    B. Duplex
    C. Orientation
    D. Collate

31. Which of the following feeds through the printer using a system of sprockets and tractors?

   A. Continuous feed

   B. Sheet fed

   C. Impact

   D. Thermal

32. Which of the following should not be used more than once?

   A. Toner

   B. Paper

   C. Cable

   D. Inkjets

33. Which of the following is a large circuit board that acts as the motherboard for the printer?

   A. Printer controller

   B. Imaging drum

   C. Toner cartridge

   D. Maintenance kit

Chapter 4

Virtualization and Cloud Computing

**COMPTIA A+ CERTIFICATION EXAM
CORE 1 (220-1001) OBJECTIVES COVERED
IN THIS CHAPTER:**

✓ **4.1 Compare and contrast cloud computing concepts.**

- Common cloud models
  - IaaS
  - SaaS
  - PaaS
  - Public vs. private vs. hybrid vs. community
- Shared resources
  - Internal vs. external
- Rapid elasticity
- On-demand
- Resource pooling
- Measured service
- Metered
- Off-site email applications
- Cloud file storage services
  - Synchronization apps
- Virtual application streaming/cloud-based applications
  - Applications for cell phones/tablets
  - Applications for laptops/desktops
- Virtual desktop
  - Virtual NIC

✓ **4.2 Given a scenario, set up and configure client-side virtualization.**

- Purpose of virtual machines
- Resource requirements
- Emulator requirements
- Security requirements
- Network requirements
- Hypervisor

This chapter will focus on the exam topics related to virtualization. It will follow the structure of the CompTIA A+ 220-1001 exam blueprint, objective 4, and it will explore the two subobjectives that you will need to master before taking the exam.

4.1 Compare and contrast cloud computing concepts.

Cloud computing and its underlying technology, virtualization, have moved beyond the "new" stage and are now becoming ubiquitous. In this section we'll look at some of the techniques that make the cloud possible and some of the features it provides. The topics in this section include the following:

- Common cloud models
- Shared resources
- Rapid elasticity
- On-demand
- Resource pooling
- Measured service
- Metered
- Off-site email applications
- Cloud file storage services
- Virtual application streaming/cloud-based applications
- Virtual desktop

Common cloud models

Increasingly, organizations are utilizing cloud-based storage instead of storing data in local data centers. The advantages to this approach include the ability to access the data from anywhere, the ability to scale computing resources to meet demand, and robust fault tolerance options. This section will look at various cloud models and some of the concepts that make it a viable option for the enterprise.

IaaS

Infrastructure as a service (IaaS) involves the vendor providing the hardware platform or data center, and the company installs and manages its own operating systems and application systems. The vendor simply provides access to the data center and maintains that access.

SaaS

When an enterprise contracts with a third party to provide cloud services, there is a range of options, differing mostly in the division of responsibilities between the vendor and the client. Software as a service (SaaS) involves the vendor providing the entire solution. This includes the operating system, the infrastructure software, and the application. The company may provide you with an email system, for example, whereby it hosts and manages everything for you.

PaaS

Platform as a service (PaaS) involves the vendor providing the hardware platform or data center and the software running on the platform. This includes the operating systems and infrastructure software. The company is still involved in managing the system.

Public vs. private vs. hybrid vs. community

When a company pays another company to host and manage this environment, it is called a *public* cloud solution. If the company hosts this environment itself, it is a *private* cloud solution.

There is trade-off when a decision must be made between the two architectures. The private solution provides the most control over the safety of your data but also requires the staff and the knowledge to deploy, manage, and secure the solution. A public cloud puts your data's safety in the hands of a third party, but that party is often more capable and knowledgeable about protecting data in this environment and managing the cloud environment.

When the solution is partly private and partly public, the solution is called a *hybrid solution*. It may be that the organization keeps some data in the public cloud but may keep more sensitive data in a private cloud, or the organization may have a private cloud that when overtaxed may utilize a public cloud for additional storage space or additional compute resources.

Finally, a *community* cloud is one that is shared by multiple organizations for some common purpose. This could be to share data for a joint project, for example.

Shared resources

Devices in a cloud data center are virtual machines (VMs) that share the resources of the underlying host. Virtual machines represent virtual instances of an operating system that exist as files on the physical host. Technicians can appropriate these resources in whichever relative percentages they are comfortable. One of the benefits of hypervisor-driven virtualization is the ability of the hypervisor to recognize momentary needs for more resources by one of the VMs and react by shifting some percentage of the resource in contention to the overloaded VM.

Internal vs. external

Regardless of whether the solution is public or private , the shared resources might be located either externally or internally. In an internal solution, all the resources are located in an organization's data center and are owned by the organization. In an external solution, all the resources are located at the service provider's data center and are owned by the service provider.

Rapid elasticity

One of the advantages of a cloud environment is the ability to add resources as needed on the fly and release those resources when they are no longer required. This makes for more efficient use of resources, allocating them where needed at any particular point in time. These include CPU and memory resources. This is called *rapid elasticity* because it occurs automatically according to the rules for resource sharing that have been deployed.

On-demand

In a cloud environment, it is typically possible for customers to add additional compute resources at any time to their cloud solution without involving the cloud provider. This is called *on-demand resource utilization* and results in the customer paying for what is used, rather than paying for unused resources.

Resource pooling

Resource pooling is a cloud concept whereby collections of resources (CPU and memory) are stored in containers called *pools*. These pools can be configured to be shared by certain virtual systems. The relative priority to the usages of the resources is controlled by the configuration of what are called *resource shares*. It is also possible to use another concept in combination with resource shares called *resource guarantees*. These settings are used to ensure that certain systems always have required resources. Finally, resource limits can be used to prevent a system from monopolizing the resources in the pool.

Measured service

Measured service is a term used to describe the process of tracking resource utilization by the customer for the purpose of charging for those resources. This works much in the same way that a utility company charges the organization only for the power used in a period. In this case, the customer is charged for the compute resources utilized in a period. Measured services are recommended for customers who are *not* able to predict their required usage.

Metered

Metered service is an agreed upon and committed level of service that does not change and is paid in advance. So even if you don't use it all, you pay for it all. For instance, you can select the number of Oracle compute processor units (OCPUs) or the amount of memory. Customers can change their service capacity as needed, which will increase/decrease their bill. Metered services are recommended for customers who can predict their required usage.

Off-site email applications

An example of SaaS is off-site email such as Gmail for the Enterprise, in which customers pay for the entire solution and support by the month. SaaS is particularly well suited for small businesses. Instead of investing in additional in-house server capacity and software licenses, companies simply can adjust their SaaS subscription on a monthly basis, scaling consumption requirements up and down based on project demands and other variables.

Cloud file storage services

Cloud file storage services, such as Box, Dropbox, and Drive, offer a way to save money on storage capacity and the management of said capacity though a storage as a service offering. Again, SaaS is particularly well suited for small businesses. Rather than spending money on hardware that will perhaps be obsolete in five years, smaller organizations can treat this as an expense rather than a capital expenditure.

Synchronization apps

Most cloud storage services come with an application that can be used to keep the files in the cloud synchronized with the files as they exist in local storage. These apps can automate the synchronization process for you. Moreover, they typically provide versioning services as well, allowing you to recover from any accidental edits or deletions.

Virtual application streaming/cloud-based applications

Cloud-based applications differ from web applications in that they are not always exclusively dependent on web browsers to work. They can be custom-built apps installed on Internet-connected devices, such as desktops and mobile phones, and can be used to access a wider range of services, such as on-demand computing cycle, storage, application development platforms, and even application streaming.

Applications for cell phones/tablets

Some examples of cloud-based applications for cell phone/tablets include Mozy, Evernote, Sugar Sync, Salesforce, Dropbox, NetSuite, and Zoho.com. Most of these services also offer the same application functionality in a laptop and desktop configuration.

Applications for laptops/desktops

The same applications offered for cell phones/tablets come in a version compatible with laptops/desktops, and as shown in Figure 4.1, the proper app is sent based on the connecting device platform.

FIGURE 4.1   Cloud app delivery

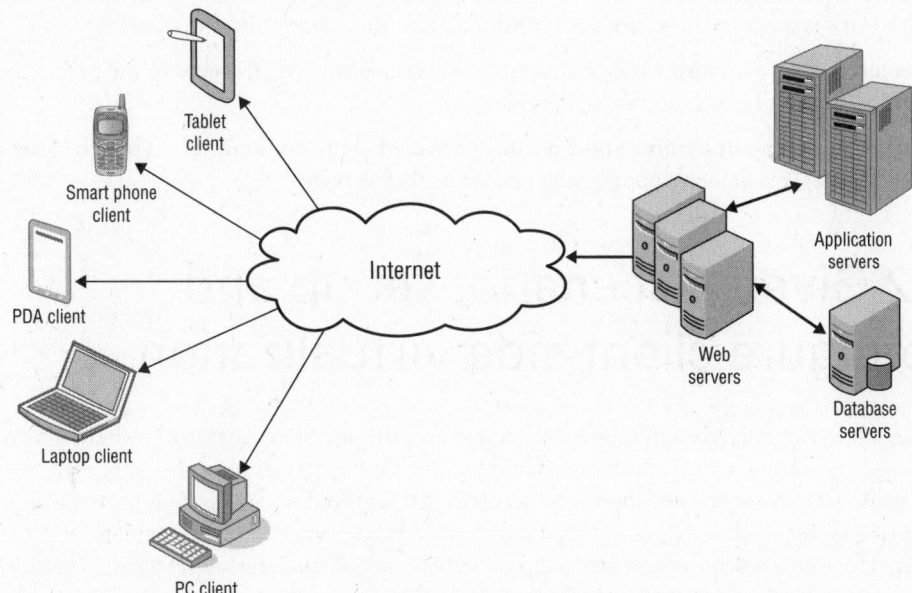

Virtual desktop

Virtual desktop infrastructures (VDIs) host desktop operating systems within a virtual environment in a centralized server. Users access the desktops and run them from the server. There are three models for implementing VDI.

Centralized   All desktop instances are stored in a single server, requiring significant processing power on the server.

Hosted   Desktops are maintained by a service provider. This model eliminates capital cost and is instead subject to operation cost.

Remote Virtual Desktops   An image is copied to the local machine, making a constant network connection unnecessary.

Virtual NIC

Virtual network interface cards (VNICs) are software packages that act in the place of a physical network interface card (NIC) for a VM. Virtual NICs and virtual switches alone can form a virtual network for only virtual machines and the host physical machine, but if any communicating is required between the virtual network and the physical network, the virtual NIC must be configured to communicate with the physical NIC of the underlying host.

Exam essentials

Describe the cloud service models.   These include SaaS, PaaS, and IaaS. Differentiate the models with respect to the various responsibilities of the vendor and the customer.

Differentiate cloud architectures.   Describe the architectural differences in the private, public, hybrid, and community cloud models.

Identify basic terms describing some of the benefits of cloud computing.   These include rapid elasticity, on-demand computing, and measured service.

4.2 Given a scenario, set up and configure client-side virtualization.

A client-side virtualized computer is one that is an instance of an operating system that is managed centrally on a server and executed locally. One key feature of this approach is that while a constant connection to the server is not required for the system to function, the operating system disk image is updated and backed up by synchronizing regularly with a server. This section will look at the setup of a client-side virtualization scenario. The sub-objectives covered in this section include the following:

- Purpose of virtual machines
- Resource requirements
- Emulator requirements
- Security requirements
- Network requirements
- Hypervisor

Purpose of virtual machines

Traditionally, workstations can have multiple operating systems installed on them but run only one at a time. By running virtualization software, the same workstation can be running Window 10 along with Windows Server 2016 and Red Hat Enterprise Linux (or almost any other operating system) at the same time, allowing a developer to test code in various environments as well as cut and paste between VMs.

From a networking standpoint, each of the VMs will typically need full network access, and configuring the permissions for each can sometimes be tricky.

Resource requirements

The resource requirements for virtualization are largely based on what environments you are creating. The hardware on the machine must have enough memory, hard drive space, and processor capability to support the virtualization. You also need the software to make virtualization possible (discussed in the next section).

Emulator requirements

XP Mode is a free emulator from Microsoft that you can download and use as a virtual emulator. A number of others are also available. In most cases, the motherboard and associated BIOS settings need no alteration to provide services to these VMs. Some of the virtualization products, however (such as Microsoft's Hyper-V, Windows 7 Virtual PC, and Windows 10 Client Hyper-V), require that the motherboard support hardware-assisted virtualization. The benefit derived from using hardware-assisted virtualization is that it reduces overhead and improves performance.

VMware Player allows you to work in multiple environments on one system. For more information, go to www.vmware.com/products/player.

Security requirements

Tales of security woes that can occur with attackers jumping out of one VM and accessing another have been exaggerated. Although such threats are possible, most software solutions include sufficient protection to reduce the possibility to a small one.

Most virtualization-specific threats focus on the hypervisor (the software that allows the VMs to exist). If the hypervisor can be successfully attacked, the attacker can gain root-level access to all virtual systems. While this is a legitimate issue—and one that has been demonstrated to be possible in most systems (including VMware, Xen, and Microsoft Virtual Machine)—it is one that has been patched each time it has appeared. The solution to most virtualization threats is to always apply the most recent patches and keep the systems up-to-date.

It is much easier to attack a virtual machine than a hypervisor because admins do not think about the security of each individual VM. It is also important to ensure that all VMs are updated with patches for both the OS and all applications. If VMs are allowed to run with outdated OS or software, known vulnerabilities will exist that attackers will take advantage of.

Keep in mind that in any virtual environment, each virtual server that is hosted on the physical server must be configured with its own security mechanisms. These mechanisms include antivirus and anti-malware software and all the latest service packs and security updates for all the software hosted on the virtual machine.

Network requirements

Network access is not a requirement in every virtual environment (for example, if you were decoding an application that would run only locally) but is often needed in most. During implementation of the virtualization, you can configure the network functionality for the machine (known as *internal*) or combine elements of the network together to provide network virtualization (known as *external*). The difference between internal and external implementations is usually based on which software package you are using.

Hypervisor

The hypervisor is the software that allows the VMs to exist. Figure 4.2 shows the relationship between the host machine, its physical resources, the resident VMs, and the virtual resources assigned to them. Also, remember that all the virtual servers share the resources of the physical device.

FIGURE 4.2   Virtualization

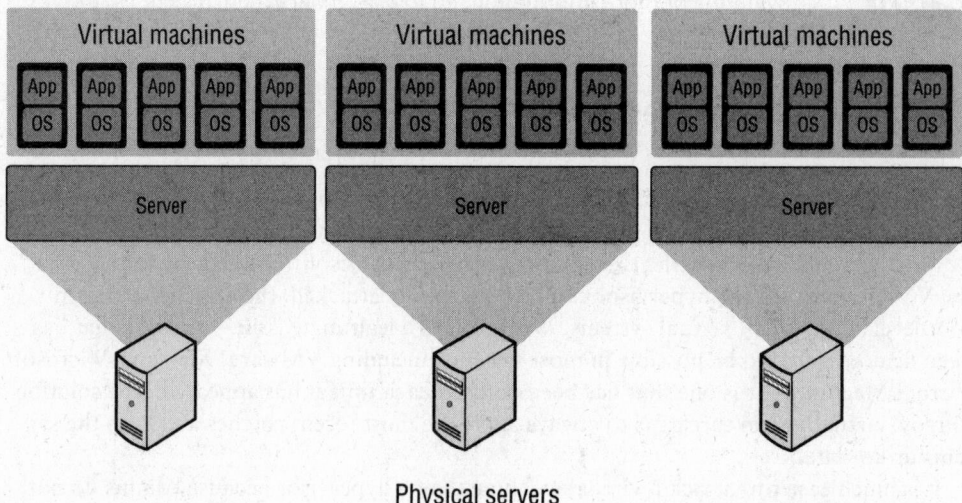

Physical servers

Type I Hypervisor

The hypervisor that manages the distribution of the physical server's resources can be either Type I or Type II. A Type I hypervisor (or native, bare metal) runs directly on the host's hardware to control the hardware and to manage guest operating systems. A guest operating system runs on another level above the hypervisor. Examples of these are VMware Workstation and Oracle VirtualBox.

Type II Hypervisor

A Type II hypervisor runs within a conventional operating system environment. With the hypervisor layer as a distinct second software level, guest operating systems run at the third level above the hardware. VMware Workstation and VirtualBox exemplify Type II hypervisors. Figure 4.3 compares the two approaches.

FIGURE 4.3   Type I and Type II hypervisors

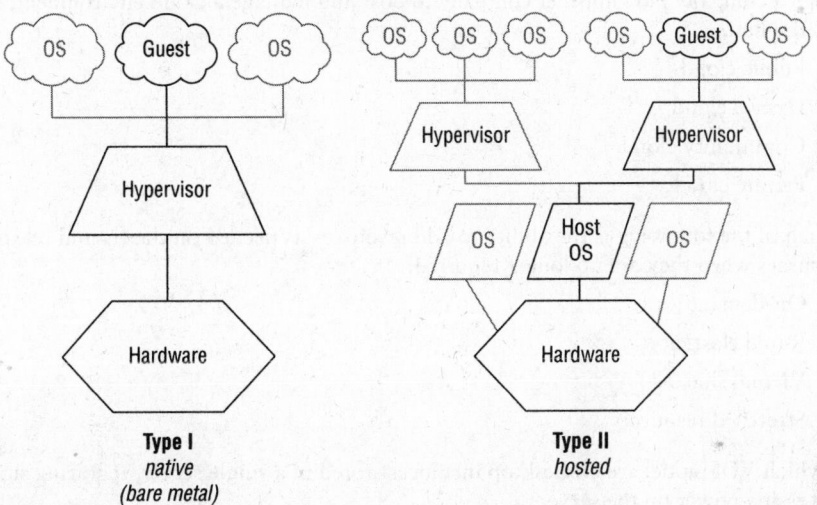

Exam essentials

Be familiar with virtualization terminology.   The hypervisor is the software that allows the VMs to exist. VMs are separate instances of an operating system, and they function independently of one another on a host physical machine.

Know security concerns related to virtualization.   Most virtualization-specific threats focus on the hypervisor. If the hypervisor can be successfully attacked, the attacker can gain root-level access to all virtual systems.

Review Questions

You can find the answers in the Appendix.

1. Which of the following involves the vendor providing the entire solution?
   A. IaaS
   B. SaaS
   C. PaaS
   D. SIEM

2. When a company pays another company to host and manage a cloud environment, it is called what?
   A. Public cloud
   B. Hybrid cloud
   C. Community cloud
   D. Private cloud

3. Which of the following is the ability to add resources as needed on the fly and release those resources when they are no longer required?
   A. On-demand
   B. Rapid elasticity
   C. Virtual sharing
   D. Stretched resources

4. In which VDI model are all desktop instances stored in a single server, requiring significant processing power on the server?
   A. Centralized
   B. Hosted
   C. Remote
   D. Local

5. Which of the following involves the vendor providing the hardware platform or data center and the software running on the platform?
   A. IaaS
   B. SaaS
   C. PaaS
   D. DaaS

6. What is the benefit derived from using hardware-assisted virtualization?

    A. Better performance

    B. Better security

    C. Less power consumption

    D. Easier troubleshooting

7. Which of the following is the software that allows the VMs to exist?

    A. DIMM

    B. Hypervisor

    C. Azureware

    D. NAT

8. Which hypervisor type runs directly on the host's hardware?

    A. Type I

    B. Type II

    C. Hybrid

    D. Core

9. Which of the following is an example of a Type II hypervisor?

    A. Oracle VirtualBox

    B. VMware NSX

    C. Hyper-V

    D. Citrix Xen Server

10. Which of the following hypervisors runs within a conventional operating system?

    A. Type I

    B. Type II

    C. Type III

    D. Container-based

Chapter 5

Hardware and Network Troubleshooting

COMPTIA A+ CERTIFICATION EXAM CORE 1 (220-1001) OBJECTIVES COVERED IN THIS CHAPTER:

✓ **5.1 Given a scenario, use the best practice methodology to resolve problems.**

- Always consider corporate policies, procedures, and impacts before implementing changes

- 1. Identify the problem

  - Question the user and identify user changes to computer and perform backups before making changes

  - Inquire regarding environmental or infrastructure changes

  - Review system and application logs

- 2. Establish a theory of probable cause (question the obvious)

  - If necessary, conduct external or internal research based on symptoms

- 3. Test the theory to determine cause

  - Once the theory is confirmed, determine the next steps to resolve problem

  - If theory is not confirmed, reestablish new theory or escalate

- 4. Establish a plan of action to resolve the problem and implement the solution

- 5. Verify full system functionality and, if applicable, implement preventive measures

- 6. Document findings, actions, and outcomes

✓ **5.2 Given a scenario, troubleshoot problems related to motherboards, RAM, CPUs, and power.**

- Common symptoms
  - Unexpected shutdowns
  - System lockups
  - POST code beeps
  - Blank screen on bootup
  - BIOS time and setting resets
  - Attempts to boot to incorrect device
  - Continuous reboots
  - No power
  - Overheating
  - Loud noise
  - Intermittent device failure
  - Fans spin—no power to other devices
  - Indicator lights
  - Smoke
  - Burning smell
  - Proprietary crash screens (BSOD/pinwheel)
  - Distended capacitors
  - Log entries and error messages

✓ **5.3 Given a scenario, troubleshoot hard drives and RAID arrays.**

- Common symptoms
  - Read/write failure
  - Slow performance
  - Loud clicking noise
  - Failure to boot
  - Drive not recognized
  - OS not found
  - RAID not found

- RAID stops working
- Proprietary crash screens (BSOD/pinwheel)
- S.M.A.R.T. errors

✓ **5.4 Given a scenario, troubleshoot video, projector, and display issues.**

- Common symptoms
  - VGA mode
  - No image on screen
  - Overheat shutdown
  - Dead pixels
  - Artifacts
  - Incorrect color patterns
  - Dim image
  - Flickering image
  - Distorted image
  - Distorted geometry
  - Burn-in
  - Oversized images and icons
  - Multiple failed jobs in logs

✓ **5.5 Given a scenario, troubleshoot common mobile device issues while adhering to the appropriate procedures.**

- Common symptoms
  - No display
  - Dim display
  - Flickering display
  - Sticking keys
  - Intermittent wireless
  - Battery not charging
  - Ghost cursor/pointer drift
  - No power

- Num lock indicator lights
- No wireless connectivity
- No Bluetooth connectivity
- Cannot display to external monitor
- Touchscreen non-responsive
- Apps not loading
- Slow performance
- Unable to decrypt email
- Extremely short battery life
- Overheating
- Frozen system
- No sound from speakers
- GPS not functioning
- Swollen battery
- Disassembling processes for proper reassembly
  - Document and label cable and screw locations
  - Organize parts
  - Refer to manufacturer resources
  - Use appropriate hand tools

✓ **5.6   Given a scenario, troubleshoot printers.**

- Common symptoms
  - Streaks
  - Faded prints
  - Ghost images
  - Toner not fused to the paper
  - Creased paper
  - Paper not feeding
  - Paper jam
  - No connectivity
  - Garbled characters on paper

- Vertical lines on page

- Backed-up print queue

- Low memory errors

- Access denied

- Printer will not print

- Color prints in wrong print color

- Unable to install printer

- Error codes

- Printing blank pages

- No image on printer display

✓ **5.7 Given a scenario, troubleshoot common wired and wireless network problems.**

- Common symptoms

- Limited connectivity

- Unavailable resources

  - Internet

  - Local resources

    - Shares

    - Printers

    - Email

- No connectivity

- APIPA/link local address

- Intermittent connectivity

- IP conflict

- Slow transfer speeds

- Low RF signal

- SSID not found

This chapter will focus on the exam topics related to hardware and network troubleshooting. It will follow the structure of the CompTIA A+ 220-1001 exam blueprint, objective 5, and it will explore the seven subobjectives that you will need to master before taking the exam.

5.1 Given a scenario, use the best practice methodology to resolve problems.

Most of those employed in the IT field who will be seeking CompTIA's A+ certification are regularly in positions where they need to know how to troubleshoot, repair, and maintain computer systems. The following subobjective is covered in this section.

- Always consider corporate policies, procedures, and impacts before implementing changes.

    1. Identify the problem.
    2. Establish a theory of probable cause (question the obvious).
    3. Test the theory to determine cause.
    4. Establish a plan of action to resolve the problem and implement the solution.
    5. Verify full system functionality and, if applicable, implement preventive measures.
    6. Document findings, actions, and outcomes.

Always consider corporate policies, procedures, and impacts before implementing changes

When implementing the steps in the troubleshooting theory discussed in this section, always keep in mind that before you make any changes or take any actions, you should ensure the changes are consistent with your corporate policies. You should also determine whether a particular change you are considering has an established procedure defined in the corporate guidelines. Finally, have a clear understanding of the potential impact of any change you make, and always ensure that a rollback plan has been established in advance. Whenever you determine that a change has the potential to cause widespread issues, try to make the change in a test environment or on a small, low-impact section of the network. Technicians should check to see whether there is already a defined solution for the stated problem. Often the help desk documentation will include notes of a previous instance of a problem. Going to that documentation first should be a standard practice.

1. Identify the problem.

Although it may sound obvious, you can't troubleshoot a problem without knowing what the problem is. In some cases, the problem will be obvious. But in others, especially when relying on the description of the problem by the user, it will appear to be one thing on the surface when in actuality the issue the user is experiencing is a symptom of a different, possibly larger problem. In this section, processes that can help bring clarity to the situation are discussed, and a cautionary note about this step is covered as well.

Question the user and identify user changes to computer and perform backups before making changes

Identify the problem by questioning the user and identifying user changes to the computer. Before you do anything else, ask the user the following:

- What the problem is
- When the last time was that the problem didn't exist
- What has changed since

Be sure that you do a backup before you make any changes so that all your actions can be undone, if necessary.

When performing this step, be wary of accepting the user's diagnosis of the problem at face value. For example, a user may start the conversation with the statement "The email server is down." At this point, ask the question, "Is there anything else you cannot do besides open your email?" Ask them to try accessing a shared folder or the Internet. If either of those tasks fails, the problem is probably not the email server but basic network connectivity of their computer. At this point, determine the scope of the issue, that is, how many users are experiencing the issue.

Inquire regarding environmental or infrastructure changes

Make note of everything that has or may have changed recently in the immediate environment of the system. Question the user about what recent changes have been made to the device, and also question the team about recent infrastructure changes. Has construction/ maintenance been performed to the building/facilities/utilities that could have caused this? Has there been HVAC issues recently? Storms? Power go out?

Review system and application logs

The system and application logs can tell you many things the user is either unwilling or unable to share with you. It can tell you what was going on in the software and hardware at the moment of the failure or issue.

2. Establish a theory of probable cause (question the obvious).

As you get answers to your initial questions, theories will begin to evolve as to the root of the problem. Analyze the problem, including potential causes, and make an initial determination of whether it's a software or hardware problem. As you narrow down the problem, determine whether it is hardware or software related so you can act accordingly.

Once you have developed a list of possible causes, develop a list of tests you can perform to test each possibility to narrow the list by eliminating each theory one by one. Don't forget to consider the obvious and make no assumptions. Just because the cable has worked every day for the last five years doesn't mean the person cleaning the office may not have caught the vacuum cleaner on the cable and damaged its connector last night.

If necessary, conduct external or internal research based on symptoms

You are not expected to immediately know the solution to every issue the user may have. You are, however, expected to perform whatever research is required to solve the issue. That can include using the Internet, calling trusted fellow technicians, and contacting vendors for assistance. Later in this section you will learn that when a resolution is found, you should always documents these lessons learned in a form that you can use later to solve the same or similar issues.

3. Test the theory to determine cause.

Test related components, including connections and hardware and software configurations. Also use Device Manager and consult vendor documentation. Whatever the problem may be, the odds are good that someone else has experienced it before. Use the tools at your disposal—including manuals and websites—to try to zero in on the problem as expeditiously as possible.

Once the theory is confirmed, determine the next steps to resolve problem

If your theory is confirmed, then determine the next steps you need to take to resolve the problem. In cases where you have determined the device where the problem lies but you have no expertise in that area, escalate the problem to someone as needed. For example, if you have narrowed down the problem to the router and you don't understand or manage the router, escalate the problem to the router administrator.

If theory is not confirmed, reestablish new theory or escalate

If your theory is not confirmed, then come up with a new theory or bring in someone with more expertise (escalate the problem). If you make changes to test one theory, make sure you reverse those changes before you test another theory. Making multiple changes can cause new problems and make the diagnostic process even more difficult.

4. Establish a plan of action to resolve the problem and implement the solution.

Evaluate the results and develop an action plan of steps to fully resolve the problem. Keep in mind that it's possible that more than one thing is causing the problem. If that is the case, you may need to solve one problem and then turn your attention to the next.

Once you have planned your work, work your plan. Methodically make the required changes while always having a back-out plan if your changes cause a larger problem.

5. Verify full system functionality and, if applicable, implement preventive measures.

When the problem is believed to be resolved, verify that the system is fully functional. If there are preventive measures that can be put in place to keep this situation from recurring, take those measures on this machine and all others where the problem may exist. Also keep in mind that times like this are great learning moments to teach users what role they may have played and what actions they may be able to take on their own in the future to prevent the problem, if that is appropriate.

6. Document findings, actions, and outcomes.

Document your activities and outcomes. Experience is a wonderful teacher, but only if you can remember what you've done. Documenting your actions and outcomes will help you (or a fellow administrator) troubleshoot a similar problem when it crops up in the future.

In some cases, you may think you have solved a problem only to find it occurs again later because you only treated the symptom of a larger problem. When this type of thing occurs, documentation of what has occurred in the past can be helpful in seeing patterns that otherwise would remain hidden.

Exam Essentials

Know the six main steps in the troubleshooting process. The six steps are as follows: identify the problem; establish a theory of probable cause; test the theory to determine the cause; establish a plan of action to resolve the problem and implement the solution; verify full system functionality and, if applicable, implement preventive measures; and document findings, actions, and outcomes.

5.2 Given a scenario, troubleshoot problems related to motherboards, RAM, CPUs, and power.

While problems can occur with the operating system with little or no physical warning, that is rarely the case when it comes to hardware problems. Your senses will often alert you that something is wrong based on what you hear, smell, or see. This section discusses common issues with the main players. The following topic is addressed in exam objective 5.2:

- Common symptoms
  - Unexpected shutdowns
  - System lockups
  - POST code beeps
  - Blank screen on bootup
  - BIOS time and setting resets
  - Attempts to boot to incorrect device
  - Continuous reboots
  - No power
  - Overheating
  - Loud noise
  - Intermittent device failure
  - Fans spin—no power to other devices
  - Indicator lights
  - Smoke
  - Burning smell
  - Proprietary crash screens (BSOD/pinwheel)
  - Distended capacitors
  - Log entries and error messages

Common symptoms

Once you have performed troubleshooting for some time, you will notice a pattern. With some exceptions, the same issues occur over and over and usually give you the same warnings each time. This section covers common symptoms or warning signs. When you learn what these symptoms are trying to tell you, it makes your job easier.

Unexpected shutdowns

It doesn't get any more obvious that something is wrong than when the computer just shuts down on its own. In some cases, a blue screen on the display with a lot of text precedes this shutdown. If that occurs, the problem is related to the operating system and may not involve a hardware issue. Operating system issues related to the Blue Screen of Death are covered in the section "Proprietary crash screens (BSOD/pinwheel)" later in this chapter.

One common reason for shutdowns is overheating. Often when that is the case, however, the system reboots itself rather than just shutting down. Reboots are covered later in this section.

Always check the obvious, such as the power cable and the source of power. Check to see whether a breaker flipped in the power box as well. Checking these items is an example of starting the process at the physical layer. If the computer is plugged into a power strip or UPS that has a fuse or breaker, check to see whether the fuse blew or the breaker flipped because of a power surge.

System lockups

Sometimes the system just freezes up and will not respond to any keyboard input or mouse clicks. The difference between a blue screen and a system lockup is whether the dump message that accompanies a blue screen is present. With a regular lockup, things just stop working. As with blue screens, lockups have been greatly reduced in more recent versions of the Microsoft and Mac operating systems (a notable exception may occur with laptops, which go to hibernate and then occasionally do not want to exit this mode). If lockups occur, you can examine the log files to discover what was happening (such as a driver loading) and take steps to correct it.

From a hardware standpoint, freezes or lockups can be caused by the following:

Memory Problems   Memory problems include a bad or failing memory chip, using memory that's too slow for the system, or using applications that require more memory than is present in the computer. Replace and upgrade the memory as required. Too little memory can also be an issue when more is required for an application.

Virus or Malware   If the system freezes and there is still significant hard drive activity occurring, a virus could be present. Scan the system, preferably from an external source such as a flash drive or CD.

Video Driver   Bad video drivers can sometimes cause a lockup. Update the video driver. In the case of a driver you just updated, you can roll back the driver to the old driver until you can obtain a new version of the driver that does not cause issues.

POST code beeps

During the bootup of the system, a power-on self-test (POST) occurs, and each device is checked for functionality. If the system boots to the point where the video driver is loaded and the display is operational, any problems will be reported with a numeric error code.

If the system cannot boot to that point, problems will be reported with a beep code. Although each motherboard manufacturer's set of beep codes and their interpretation can be found in the documentation for the system or on the website of the BIOS/UEFI manufacturer, one short beep always means everything is OK. Some examples of items tested during this process include the following:

▪ RAM

▪ Video card

▪ Motherboard

To interpret the beep codes in the case where you cannot read the error codes on the screen, use the chart provided at www.computerhope.com/beep.htm.

During startup, problems with devices that fail to be recognized properly, services that fail to start, and so on, are written to the system log and can also be viewed with Event Viewer in Microsoft or in the Console in Mac. If no POST error code prevents a successful boot, this utility provides information about what's been going on system-wise to help you troubleshoot problems. Event Viewer shows warnings, error messages, and records of things happening successfully. You can access it through Computer Management, or you can access it directly from the Administrative Tools in Control Panel.

Blank screen on bootup

When the screen is blank after bootup and there are signs that the system has power and some functionality (perhaps you can hear the fan or see lights on the system), the problem could lie in several areas. Consider these possibilities:

▪ Make sure the monitor is on. It has a power switch, so check it.

▪ If you hear the fan but the system doesn't boot, it could be the power to the motherboard. Check and reseat the power cable to the motherboard.

▪ Make sure the cable from the monitor to the system is connected properly and try changing it out with a known good cable.

▪ Try a known good video card to rule out a bad card.

▪ Ensure that the brightness setting is set high enough.

▪ In cases where a laptop has been used to direct output to a second display, ensure that the image is being sent to the main display and not just to the external monitor.

▪ As a last solution, try replacing the monitor.

BIOS time and setting resets

If you find that you are continually resetting the system time, it could be that the CMOS battery is dying. Sometimes a symptom of this is that the hard drive and other settings stored in the BIOS are lost. In the absence of an external time source, the time in the BIOS is where the system gets its cue for the date and time. Change the CMOS battery and the problem should be solved.

Attempts to boot to incorrect device

When multiple volumes or partitions exist on the computer or there are multiple hard drives and maybe CD/DVD and flash drives as well, there are multiple potential sources for the boot files. If the system delivers an "operating system not found" message, it could be that the system is looking in the wrong location for the boot files.

The boot order is set in the BIOS/UEFI. Check the boot order and ensure that it is set to boot to the partition, volume, and hard drive where the boot files are located. If there is an external flag drive connected, it may also attempt to boot to it. When the system is running down the list of potential sources of boot files, in all other cases if it looks in a location and finds no boot files, it will move on to the next location in the list. However, if a floppy is in the floppy drive and it checks the floppy drive and no boot files are present, it does not proceed but stops and issues the nonsystem disk message.

Boot problems can also occur with corruption of the boot files or missing components (such as the NTLDR file being "accidentally" deleted by an overzealous user). Luckily, during the installation of the OS, log files are created in the %SystemRoot% or %SystemRoot%\Debug folder or C:\Windows and C:\Windows\Debug, depending on the operating system. If you have a puzzling problem, look at these logs to see whether you can find error entries there. These are primarily helpful during installation. For routine troubleshooting, you can activate boot logging by selecting Enable Boot Logging from the Windows ➤ Advanced Options menu to create an ntbtlog.txt log file in the %systemroot% folder.

Continuous reboots

If the system reboots on its own, consider the following possibilities:

- Electrical problems such as brownouts (not a total loss of power but a sag in the power level) or blackouts can cause reboots.

- Power supply problems can cause reboots as well. The power supply continually sends a Power_Good signal to the motherboard, and if this signal is interrupted, the system will reset.

- Overheating is also a big cause of reboots. When CPUs get overheated, a cycle of reboots can ensue. Make sure the fan is working on the heat sink and the system fan is also working. If required, vacuum the dust from around the vents.

Because overheating plays a large role in reboots, ensure that a laptop is sitting on a flat surface that allows for proper cooling (not on a bed, pillow, or other soft surface).

No power

Power problems usually involve the following issues and scenarios:

- Check the power cord, and if it's plugged into a power strip or UPS, ensure that the strip is plugged in (and if it has a breaker, check to see whether it was tripped by a surge or whether the switch that turns off the entire strip has been inadvertently turned to the off position). In the case of a UPS, check whether the UPS battery is dead. If the cord and UPS are OK, also try a second wall outlet.

- Try replacing the power supply with a known good unit to see whether the power supply failed.

Overheating

Under normal conditions, the PC cools itself by pulling in air. That air is used to dissipate the heat created by the processor (and absorbed by the heat sink). When airflow is restricted by clogged ports, a bad fan, and so forth, heat can build up inside the unit and cause problems. Chip creep—the unseating of components—is one of the more common byproducts of a cycle of overheating and cooling of the inside of the system.

Since the air is being pulled into the machine, excessive heat can originate from outside the PC as well because of a hot working environment. The heat can be pulled in and cause the same problems. Take care to keep the ambient air within normal ranges (approximately 60–90 degrees Fahrenheit) and at a constant temperature.

Replacing slot covers is vital. Computers are designed to circulate air with slot covers in place or cards plugged into the ports. Leaving slots on the back of the computer open alters the air circulation and causes more dust to be pulled into the system.

Finally, note whether the fan is working; if it stops, that is a major cause of overheating.

Loud noise

When it comes right down to it, there are not a lot of moving parts within a PC. When you hear noise, you can begin to readily narrow down the possible culprits. The most common are the fan and the hard drive (except for solid-state drives, which make no such noises). No matter what is responsible, you will want to take immediate steps to shut down the machine and start the replacement process. When you remove the cover, see whether you can tell which component the noise is coming from. Change each component you suspect with a known good replacement until the noise stops.

Intermittent device failure

Among the most vexing issues to troubleshoot is any that comes and goes. When presented with this type of behavior, consider the following possibilities:

- Try replacing the problem component with a known good one.

- A bad motherboard can cause these types of problems when there are issues with its circuitry. Try replacing the motherboard with a known good motherboard.

Fans spin—no power to other devices

This issue can be caused by an external device requiring more than the available power being supplied. Ensure that you are not requiring more power than the power supply can provide.

Indicator lights

Many of the components in the system have an indicator light that should be in a specific state during normal operation. Status lights are often found on the network interface card (NIC) as well as on the front of a desktop model and in the display area of a laptop.

On the NIC, a display other than a green light can indicate that there are problems with the network; more important, though, the lack of any light can indicate that the card itself has gone bad.

The hard drive, CD-ROM, and tape or DVD drive lights will be on when activity is occurring and will blink accordingly. The power light should be a steady green.

Smoke

Smoke is never a good thing. Shut the system down immediately to prevent further damage. This is usually a burning or overheating component, usually the CPU.

Burning smell

A burning smell usually accompanies smoke but could be present after the smoke has ended because the burning component is now dead. Try to identify the damaged component through a visual inspection; if that is not possible, try to determine the damaged component by replacing parts one by one until functionality returns.

Proprietary crash screens (BSOD/pinwheel)

Some operating systems have a proprietary method of notifying the user that the worst may have just happened. In this section you'll look at two of the most widely known methods.

BSOD

Once a regular occurrence when working with Windows, blue screens (also known as the Blue Screen of Death) have become much less frequent since Windows 2000. Occasionally, systems will lock up, and you can usually examine the log files to discover what was happening when this occurred and then take the necessary steps to correct it. For example, if you see that a driver or application was loading before the crash, you can begin to isolate it as a possible problem. The details included in the BSOD error that comes up can help in troubleshooting the problem. It is often easy to query Microsoft's Knowledge Base with the first part of the BSOD error to discover the component causing the problem. Often, the Knowledge Base article gives a detailed explanation of how to fix the problem as well.

In more recent versions of Windows, such as Windows 10, information from such crashes is written to XML files by the operating system. When the system becomes stable, a prompt usually appears asking for approval to send this information to Microsoft. The goal that Microsoft has in collecting this data is to be able to identify drivers that cause such problems and work with vendors to correct these issues.

Better-known error messages include the following:

Data_Bus_Error   This error is described on the Microsoft website: "The most common cause of this error message is a hardware problem. It usually occurs after the installation of faulty hardware, or when existing hardware fails. The problem is frequently related to defective RAM, L2 RAM cache, or video RAM. If hardware has recently been added to the system, remove it and test to see if the error still occurs."

Unexpected_Kernel_Mode_Trap   This error is described on the Microsoft website: "If hardware was recently added to the system, remove it to see if the error recurs. If existing hardware has failed, remove or replace the faulty component. Run hardware diagnostics supplied by the system manufacturer, especially the memory scanner, to determine which hardware component has failed. For details on these procedures, see the owner's manual for your computer. Setting the CPU to run at speeds above the rated specification (known as overclocking the CPU) can also cause this error."

Page_Fault_in_nonpaged_area   This error is described on the Microsoft website: "This Stop message usually occurs after the installation of faulty hardware or in the event of failure of installed hardware (usually related to defective RAM, either main memory, L2 RAM cache, or video RAM). If hardware has been added to the system recently, remove it to see if the error recurs. If existing hardware has failed, remove or replace the faulty component. Run hardware diagnostics supplied by the system manufacturer. For details on these procedures, see the owner's manual for your computer."

irq1_not_less_or_equal   This error is described on the Microsoft website: "This Stop message indicates that a kernel-mode process or driver attempted to access a memory address to which it did not have permission to access. The most common cause of this error is an incorrect or corrupted pointer that references an incorrect location in memory. A pointer is a variable used by a program to refer to a block of memory. If the variable has an incorrect value in it, the program tries to access memory that it should not. When this occurs in a user-mode application, it generates an access violation. When it occurs in kernel mode, it generates a STOP 0x0000000A message. If you encounter this error while upgrading to a newer version of Windows, it might be caused by a device driver, a system service, a virus scanner, or a backup tool that is incompatible with the new version."

Pinwheel

While Microsoft users have the BSOD to deal with, Apple users have similarly come to have the same negative feelings about the Pinwheel of Death (PWOD). This is a multicolored pinwheel mouse pointer (shown in Figure 5.1) that signifies a temporary delay while the system "thinks." In the death scenario, waiting until doomsday will yield no relief to the user.

FIGURE 5.1   The Apple PWOD

In many cases, the situation may not be as dire as it appears. It can be that a single application is holding the device captive. If this is the case, either clicking the desktop or bringing another application to the front will return control to the user. While that will solve the issue for the moment, there was some reason why that application caused the lockup, and it will probably occur again. Two things can be done to prevent a problem from recurring.

First, it could be that the system permissions associated with the application and the files it uses have gotten corrupted. You can use Disk Utility to perform a "permissions repair," which restores file or folder permissions to the state the OS and applications expect them to be in.

Second, it may help to clear the dynamic link editor cache. This is a cache of recently used entry points to the dynamic link library. If this cache gets corrupted, it can cause the PWOD. To clear the cache, follow these steps:

1. Launch Terminal, located at `/Applications/Utilities/`.

2. At the Terminal prompt, enter the following command. Please note this is a single line; some browsers may show this command spanning multiple lines.

   `sudo update_dyld_shared_cache -force`

3. Press Enter or Return.

4. Enter the administrator account password.

5. Terminal may display warnings about mismatches in the `dlyd` cache. These are normal, and you can proceed.

On the other hand, if you are experiencing this spinning wheel at startup, the problem is more severe. It means that the system is corrupted. The recovery options will be found by booting to the recovery hard drive, which is a partition created for this purpose in OS X 10.13.4. To do this, start the device, and after the chime, press and hold Command+R until a menu appears. Then select to boot to the recovery partition. Figure 5.2 shows the menu that will appear. You have four options.

- Restore the system from a Time Machine backup by selecting Restore From Time Machine Backup. Then use a backup to restore the system.

- Boot to the Apple servers, which can be done only on newer systems. To do this, select Reinstall OS X. Of course, this will require an Internet connection to be working.

- Get Help Online, which will allow you to use Safari to browse to the Apple support site. This will require an Internet connection to be working as well. To do this, select Get Help Online.

- Repair the hard drive and permissions, in which you select Disk Utility from the menu. Click the First Aid tab and select Repair.

FIGURE 5.2 OS X Utilities

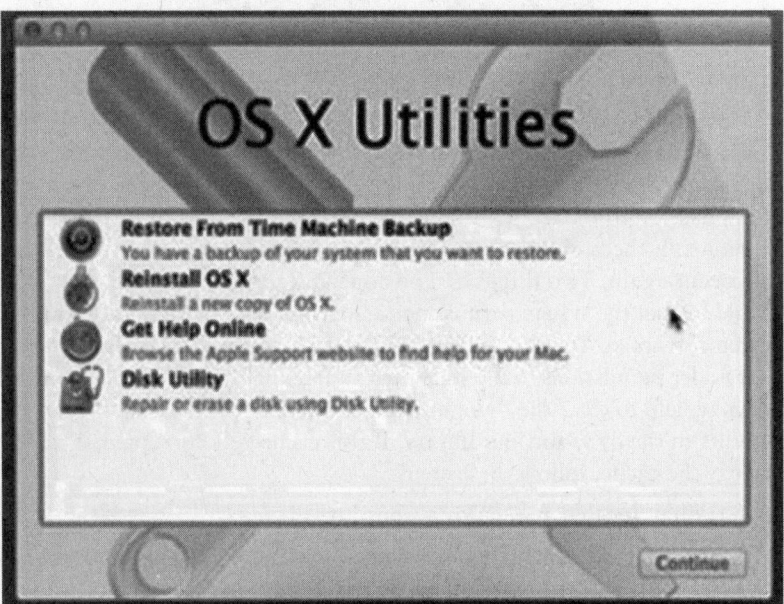

If none of the options discussed so far works, you may need to delete the recovery partition. Take the following steps to do that:

1. Confirm the presence of the recovery partition. Open Terminal.app and enter **diskutil list** to do that.

2. Assuming you see a recovery partition listed on the screen that appears, go back to Terminal.app and enter the following:

   `defaults write com.apple.DiskUtility  DUDebugMenuEnabled 1`

3. Open the Disk Utility app. Now, in the menu bar at the top, select Debug ➤ Show Every Partition.

4. Select Recovery HD and click the Mount icon to make it active.

5. Once the option Recovery HD is no longer grayed out, you can right-click to delete it or use Control+click and select Erase.

6. There is still an empty partition, so select the Partition tab and click the Recovery HD partition to select it. Then click the minus sign to remove it.

Distended capacitors

A swollen or distended capacitor on the motherboard does not always indicate a failed or failing capacitor, but at the least it indicates one that is in poor health and should be replaced. A distended capacitor will look normal on the side, but the top of it will be swollen a bit, and there may be brown residue coming out of the top of the capacitor. This is caused by gassing of the electrolyte, meaning the electrolyte has been broken down into gas and no longer contributes to the capacitance of the capacitor. The symptoms of this are a system that reboots intermittently and will start only intermittently or not at all.

While replacing a failed capacitor is not easy and in some cases not worth the time and effort compared with replacing the motherboard, to replace a failed capacitor, follow these steps:

1. Locate the failed capacitor. Look for those that exhibit any of the physical symptoms shown in Figure 5.3.

FIGURE 5.3 Failed capacitors

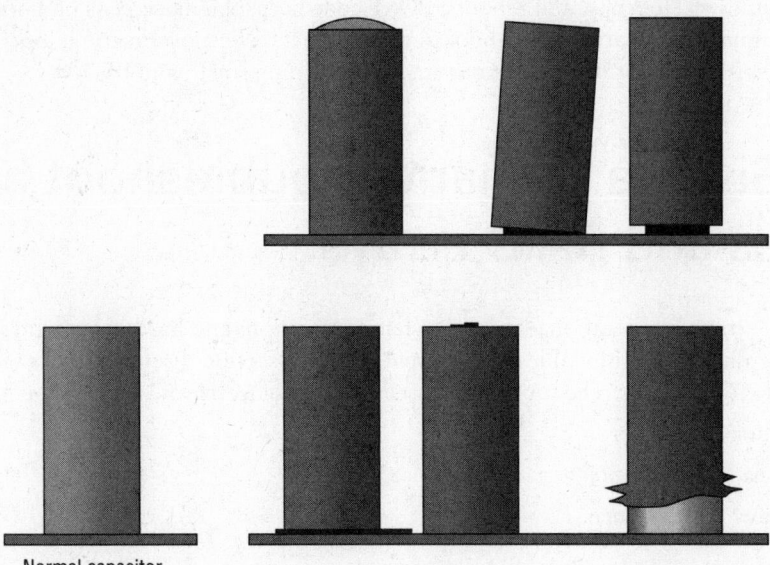

Normal capacitor

2. Procure a replacement capacitor. It should have the following:

   ▪ The same voltage

   ▪ The same or larger capacity

   ▪ The same external size

   While you can use a capacitor that has a higher voltage or a larger capacity, it is best to use one that matches the one you are replacing.

3. Remove the battery from the board.

4. Use a soldering iron to heat the connection to the board until you can remove the old capacitor. Be careful not to heat the board so much that you damage the connections of other components.

5. Clean the remaining hole, and if necessary, use a pin to enlarge the hole for the new capacitor.

6. Insert the new capacitor. Heat some solder and allow it to flow into the hole to seal. Try to keep the remaining drop on the outside as small as possible. This should be performed only by an experienced technician. Soldering incorrectly can ruin the motherboard.

Log entries and error messages

The final place where clues may be found is in the system log or from error messages that are generated. When an error message is generated, there is usually a matching entry in the log with more details.

Exam Essentials

Describe the common symptoms of hardware problems.   These symptoms include unexpected shutdowns, lockups, and reboots; POST code beeps; blank screens on bootup; loss of system timekeeping; attempts to boot to an incorrect device; overheating; loss of power; loud noises; intermittent device failures; smoke; a burning smell; and BSODs.

5.3 Given a scenario, troubleshoot hard drives and RAID arrays.

Hard drives must be operational for the system to function, and hard drive arrays such as RAID introduce an additional level of complexity. This section discusses issues with hard drives and RAID arrays. The topics addressed in exam objective 5.3 include the following:

▪ Common symptoms

   ▪ Read/write failure

   ▪ Slow performance

- Loud clicking noise
- Failure to boot
- Drive not recognized
- OS not found
- RAID not found
- RAID stops working
- Proprietary crash screens (BSOD/pinwheel)
- S.M.A.R.T. errors

Common symptoms

Hard drives and RAID arrays typically exhibit symptoms before they fail. Learning to read these clues is critical to troubleshooting. The following are the most common of these clues and symptoms.

Read/write failure

Read/write failures occur when areas of the hard drive require repeated attempts before successful reads or writes occur. This is because these areas are at least partially damaged, although perhaps not enough to be marked as bad sectors. You should perform a hard drive scan using an OS utility to determine whether there are lots of bad sectors. If over time the bad sectors increase, it is an indication that drive failure is imminent and the drive should be replaced. Make sure to back up.

Slow performance

Another symptom of hard drive issues is slow access to the drive. Oddly, one of the potential causes of this is insufficient memory. When this is the case, it causes excessive paging. Another cause can be a drive that needs to be defragmented. When a drive is fragmented, it takes much longer for all the parts of a file to be located before the file will open. Other issues that cause slow performance are controller cards that need updating, improper data cables, and slower devices sharing the same cable with the hard drive. Finally, insufficient drive space alone will slow performance.

Loud clicking noise

A loud clicking noise, sometimes referred to as the *click of death*, is caused by the read/write heads making contact with the platters. After that happens, both the heads and the platters become damaged, and the system becomes unable to establish a successful starting point to read the drive. This is serious damage and cannot be repaired. Back up all the data if that's still possible. If the drive is no longer readable, the only option to recover the data is with the help of a professional data recovery service. At that point, you must balance the cost of the recovery with the value of the data. This is a case where performing regular backups saves the day!

Failure to boot

A failure of the system to boot can be caused by a number of issues:

- Failure of the system to locate the boot files. See the section "Attempts to boot to incorrect device."

- If you are presented with an "IDE drive not ready" message at startup, the drive may not be spinning fast enough to be read. Enable or increase the hard disk predelay time.

- If you receive the message "Immediately back up all your data and replace your hard drive. A fault may be imminent," take it seriously. This means the drive is using Self-Monitoring, Analysis, and Reporting Technology to predict a failure.

- The hard drive data cable or power cable may have become unseated. Sometimes even if the cable appears to be seated fine, reseating it can have a positive effect. Also ensure that the data cable has not been reversed.

Drive not recognized

If the system does not recognize the drive, the problem could be one of the following:

- The hard drive data cable or power cable may have become unseated. See the "Failure to boot" section.

- If you just added a drive, ensure that both drives have not been set to master or slave and that the boot drive is set as master on the first channel.

- If the system uses SATA and you just added a drive, ensure that all the onboard SATA ports are enabled.

- If you just added a drive, ensure that there is no conflict between the new drive and another device.

- If you receive the "No boot device available, strike F1 to retry boot, F2 for setup utility" message, the cause could be incorrect drive geometry (probably not the case if this drive has been functioning properly before), bad CMOS battery, or inability to locate the active partition or master boot record.

OS not found

When you receive the "operating system not found" message, it's usually a software error rather than a hardware error. It could be that the master boot record cannot be located or the active partition cannot be located. These issues can be corrected in Windows by rebooting the computer into Recovery mode and executing one of several commands at the command line of the Recovery environment.

RAID not found

RAID can be either software- or hardware-based. When hardware-based RAID is implemented, a RAID controller card is installed into a slot, and the RAID drives connect to that controller card. When the RAID array cannot be located, usually it's a problem with the controller card.

One item to check after you first install the RAID controller card is that RAID is set in the BIOS. It is also possible that the computer has a built-in RAID controller. If that is the case, there will be ports for the drives in the motherboard. Ensure that the two hard drives (or three) are connected to the same port group.

If the RAID system has been operational, check all the cables connecting the drives to the motherboard, reseating them to ensure a good connection. Also ensure that the BIOS/UEFI is still set to RAID.

If there is no integrated RAID controller and the controller card is installed in a slot, ensure that the card is seated properly (maybe even try reseating it). Also ensure that all the drives are securely connected to the ribbon cable coming from the controller card.

RAID stops working

In some cases, one of the drives in the RAID array will cease to function and, depending on the type of RAID, can cause the entire array to be unavailable.

If this is a RAID 1 or a mirrored set, you should still be able to access the other drive. To determine which drive is bad, remove each drive one by one and reboot until you have identified the bad drive. Replace the bad drive and use the RAID software to rebuild the array.

If this is a RAID 5 array, follow the same procedure. The bad news is that if more than one drive has failed, you will not be able to rebuild the array. You will need to create the array again after replacing the bad drives and then restore the data from backup.

Once the bad drives have been replaced, the system may rearrange the drives such that the system cannot locate the drive with the operating system. Use the RAID setup program that you access during bootup to set the boot order of the drives in the array with the drive with the operating system first in the list.

Proprietary crash screens (BSOD/pinwheel)

Earlier in this chapter I discussed the Blue Screen of Death and the Pinwheel of Death. When presented with either of these, it's often difficult to interpret the problem. Always try rebooting, which in many cases causes it to go away. When dealing with the ambiguity of the crash screen, it is often useful to ask yourself these questions:

- Did I just make any changes?
- Is there any component that has been exhibiting symptoms of a problem?

If you just changed a hard drive, made a hard drive configuration change, installed a new driver, or have been dealing with hard drive issues, you have reason to suspect these actions as the source of the crash. Try reversing the change you made and rebooting; if that helps, it indicates something faulty or detrimental about your change.

If you have multiple drives, try removing them one by one and observe the effect on the crash. Once you have located the drive causing the crash, begin to consider what the problem with the drive is or simply replace it, if no possible remedy comes to mind.

S.M.A.R.T. errors

SMART (Self-Monitoring, Analysis, and Reporting Technology; often written as S.M.A.R.T.) is a system included in hard drives and solid-state drives that detects and reports on drive reliability, with a goal of anticipating hardware failures. It requires software on the computer to read the data from the drives and performs its analysis during startup.

Errors reported by SMART should be accepted as predictions that the drive will soon fail, and you should back up all the data as soon as possible, even if the drive appears to be performing normally and passes other disk checks you may run. One error that you may be able to mitigate is overheating. If you can increase ventilation such that the error disappears, you are probably safe to continue using the drive.

Exam Essentials

Identify the most common symptoms of hard drive issues.   These include but are not limited to read/write failures, slow performance, loud clicking noises, boot failures, unrecognizable drives, missing operating systems, and Blue Screens of Death.

List symptoms of RAID array issues.   These include missing arrays and RAID arrays that stop functioning.

5.4 Given a scenario, troubleshoot video, projector, and display issues.

Video, projector, and display problems may not rate at the top of the priority list for technicians (unless the display is not functioning at all), but to a user, problems with their display may seem like a huge issue. This section discusses common video- and display-related symptoms and their possible sources. The topics addressed in exam objective 5.4 include the following:

- Common symptoms
  - VGA mode
  - No image on screen
  - Overheat shutdown
  - Dead pixels
  - Artifacts
  - Incorrect color patterns
  - Dim image
  - Flickering image
  - Distorted image
  - Distorted geometry

- Burn-in
- Oversized images and icons
- Multiple failed jobs in logs

Common symptoms

Display monitors and projectors can exhibit a wide range of symptoms when video-related problems arise. Some are as obvious as no signal whatsoever, whereas other symptoms can be so slight as to almost defy detection. This section discusses common symptoms and some approaches to dealing with these issues.

VGA mode

When a display ceases to function at the resolution level supported by the video card and reverts to 16-bit VGA mode (low resolution in Windows 7, 10, and Vista), the problem is almost always video drivers. If the issue arises during the installation of a new video card, then the driver was not found in the cache of drivers provided with the operating system.

Even if the video card is plug and play, the driver must be present. If it is not, the computer will not be able to use the card and will revert to using VGA mode (low resolution). Another common problem associated with drivers is not having the current version—as problems are fixed, the drivers are updated, and you can often save a great deal of time by downloading the latest drivers from the vendor's site early in the troubleshooting process.

The easiest way to see or change drivers in Windows 7 or 10 is to click the Driver tab in the Properties dialog box for the device. For example, to see the driver associated with the hard drive, double-click the hard drive in Device Manager (Start ➤ Control Panel ➤ Hardware And Sound ➤ Devices And Printers, and then click Device Manager in the Task list) and choose the Driver tab. Among other things, this shows the provider, date, version, and signer for the driver. You can choose to view details about it, update it, roll it back to a previous driver, or uninstall it. If the installation of the device resulted in VGA mode (low resolution in Windows 7 or 10), then you need to select Update Driver and point the system to the CD or local folder where the correct driver is located.

No image on screen

When there is no image on the screen, the display is either dead or not receiving the signal from the computer. Check the cable from the back of the PC to the monitor, ensure it is tightly screwed in place, and reseat the cables if required. Also ensure that the monitor is plugged into a functional power outlet and that the brightness settings are high enough. Finally, for a laptop, you should use the appropriate Fn key to ensure that the signal isn't being sent to an external monitor.

To eliminate the video card as the problem, connect a known good display to the computer and see whether the same problem exists. If so, then the problem is not the display. If it works fine, the problem is the display. Displays do die and usually are not cost-effective to repair. The usual solution is to replace the display.

If the card is the problem, try reseating it. If that provides no relief, insert a known good card. Operating in the same fashion as you did with the display, you can determine whether the video card is the problem.

Overheat shutdown

When the video card is overheating, it can cause display problems and shutdowns. Overheating video cards usually exhibit symptoms like garbled output on the display or artifacts (covered later in this section). They also can result in flickers and flashes. In some cases, the display will cease functioning after being on a few seconds. After you restart the computer, the display again works for a few seconds and then fails.

When overheating is the problem, you must find the reason for the overheating. Clean all the dust out of the inside of the case and inspect all fans to ensure they are functioning—especially the fan on the video card if one is present. If the problem has been happening for some time, the card may have become damaged. Try using a different card and see whether the problem goes away. You may need to replace the video card.

Projectors

When projector bulbs are overheating, they may shut down to cool down. Simply waiting until the bulb has cooled and then restarting the projector will usually solve the problem. It may also be helpful to inform the users that many projectors will not allow the bulb to be restarted soon after you turn it off, so they may want to consider that if they intend to restart the projector soon after shutting it down.

Dead pixels

Pixels are the small dots on the screen that are filled with a color; as a group they present the image you see on the screen. Two conditions can occur with the pixels: stuck pixels and bad or dead pixels.

Stuck pixels have been filled with a color and are not changing as required to display changes in the image. Dead pixels are simply black with no color in them.

When there are few of these and they are not clustered in the same spot, you may not even be able to notice them. When they build to the point where they are noticeable, they cannot be fixed, and the monitor must be replaced. You may be able to get some satisfaction from the manufacturer depending on how old the monitor is and the policy of the vendor.

Artifacts

Artifacts are visual anomalies that appear on the screen. They might be pieces of images left over from a previous image or a "tear in the image" (it looks like the image is divided into two parts and the parts don't line up).

Artifacts can be generated whenever hardware components such as the processor, memory chip, or cabling malfunction, causing data corruption. This may be caused by physical damage, but the first thing to check is the overheating of the graphics processor or video card. Use the same techniques described in the section "Overheat shutdown."

Incorrect color patterns

When the image displayed uses incorrect color patterns or is garbled, the root of the problem could depend on when the condition presents itself. If the screen looks fine during the POST but then goes bad when Windows starts to load, it is probably because of an incorrect setting of the video card. For example, it may be set to do something the card is incapable of doing. Restart in safe mode (which will cause the system to use the VGA driver) and check all the settings of the card while ensuring that it is not set for a resolution level for which the card or the monitor is not capable. You may also try updating the driver if a new one is available.

If this problem occurs from the moment you turn the system on, the problem is hardware, and you should check the monitor, cable, and card, replacing each with a known good piece until you isolate the bad component.

Dim image

If the image is fine but dim, first check the brightness setting, usually found in the front of the monitor. If this is a laptop, remember there are function keys that when hit inadvertently will dim the screen as well. Check that.

If the display is an LCD, the backlight may be going bad. You learned earlier that these are pencil-sized lights that go behind the screen. They can be replaced on a laptop by following the procedure for opening the laptop lid (where the display resides) and replacing the backlight. Keep in mind that opening the case voids the warranty, so if you still have warranty left, make use of that option.

If it is the backlight on a desktop LCD, the backlight can be replaced for about $20, so it makes a repair worth doing if you want to open the monitor. Use the documentation or the vendor website for details on opening the case.

Projectors

When projectors have a dim image, it can be that the bulb is going bad. All bulbs have a stated lifetime that can be found in the documentation of the projector. The hours of lifetime that you find in the documentation have usually been stretched a bit, meaning that toward the end of the lifetime the bulb will start to fade in brightness.

Flickering image

When the image is flickering, check the cables and ensure they are seated properly. If that doesn't help, try different cables because it could be a problem with the cable itself.

Another possible reason is a mismatch between the resolution settings and the refresh rate. If this is the problem, it will occur only when using the higher resolutions. You should increase the refresh rate to support the higher resolutions.

While you won't see many CRT monitors, flickering on those can indicate a source of electromagnetic interference (EMI) or radio frequency interference (RFI) near the display, such as a radio. Degaussing CRT monitors can help.

Distorted image

This behavior can be caused by problems with power. Try replacing the power cable, and if that doesn't help, try plugging the monitor into a different wall outlet. Sometimes other devices on the same line (air conditioner, refrigerator, and so forth) can cause problems for the supply of power to the monitor.

Distorted geometry

Distorted geometry can occur in projectors. It's simpler to show the symptoms than it is to explain what causes it, but it is a defect in the optical lens system. Figure 5.4 shows the most common forms.

FIGURE 5.4   Geometric distortion

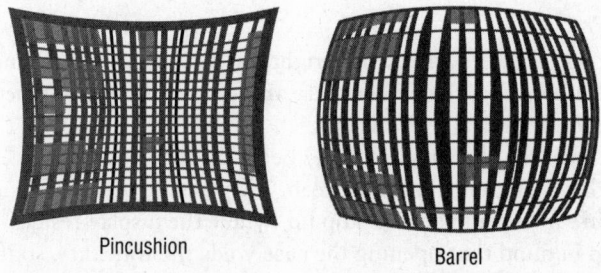

Pincushion   Barrel

There is usually a Keystone setting that can be used to compensate and correct the distortion. You simply move the slider in this setting until the image is corrected. Figure 5.5 shows a sample of the correction buttons you may find on a projector remote.

FIGURE 5.5   Correction buttons on a projector remote

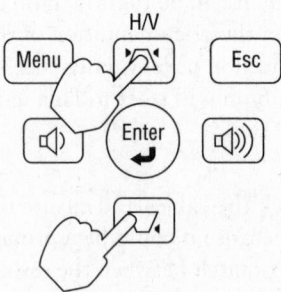

Burn-in

Burn-in is a condition that affected CRT monitors and still affects plasma and OLED displays. LCDs are generally not affected. The condition occurs when images are left for extended periods of time on the screen. The early screen savers were designed to prevent this in unattended displays by displaying a constantly changing image.

Software and utilities can be used to remedy burn-in but will have little effect if the burn-in is severe. It is also useful to know that the display will be most susceptible to this when it is new in the first few hours of operation. DVDs can be purchased that will "break in" a screen, and in some cases they can even eliminate existing burn-in if it is not severe.

Oversized images and icons

When a user is experiencing oversized images and icons, it is typically caused by a misconfigured setting. In the iOS operating system it could be that the zoom is on. In Windows 7 and 8.1 there is a slider on the Display settings page, as shown in Figure 5.6, that can be used to enlarge all items on the screen. This setting is called Change The Size Of All Items. Check this setting and adjust as required.

FIGURE 5.6   Changing the size of all items

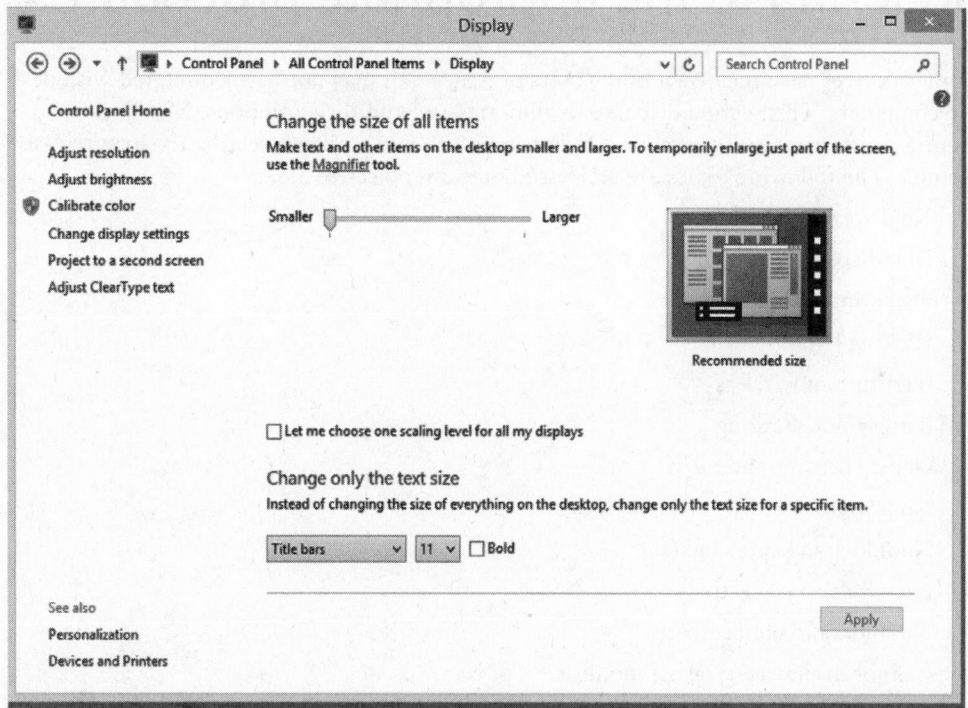

Multiple failed jobs in logs

Finally, in almost all cases where display issues are present, there will probably be an event in the system or application log. These messages are sometimes cryptic, requiring some research to determine the meaning of an error number, but they can contain valuable clues about the root cause of the issue.

Exam essentials

List the common symptoms of display problems and the appropriate troubleshooting technique for each. These include but are not limited to reversion to VGA mode; no image; overheating; dead pixels; artifacts; incorrect color patterns; dim, flickering, or distorted image; discoloration (degaussing); and BSOD. Resolution techniques include updating drivers, degaussing, changing resolution settings, and replacing the monitor.

5.5 Given a scenario, troubleshoot common mobile device issues while adhering to the appropriate procedures.

Mobile devices have their own unique sets of issues that may not be encountered with desktop computers. This section discusses common issues and their solutions. Mobile devices require a different set of procedures for opening the case while protecting the integrity of the unit. The following topics are addressed in exam objective 5.5:

- No display
- Dim display
- Flickering display
- Sticking keys
- Intermittent wireless
- Battery not charging
- Ghost cursor/pointer drift
- No power
- Num lock indicator lights
- No wireless connectivity
- No Bluetooth connectivity
- Cannot display to external monitor
- Touchscreen non-responsive
- Apps not loading
- Slow performance
- Unable to decrypt email
- Extremely short battery life
- Overheating

- Frozen system
- No sound from speakers
- GPS not functioning
- Swollen battery
- Disassembling processes for proper reassembly

Common symptoms

Not all mobile device issues are unique to mobile devices. They suffer from many of the same issues as desktop machines. However, some problems are unique to laptops and mobile devices or at least are more prone to occur with laptops, as you will learn in this section.

No display

The backlight is the light in the device that powers the LCD screen. It can go bad over time and need to be replaced, and it can also be held captive (locked up) by the inverter. The inverter takes the DC power the laptop is providing and boosts it up to AC to run the backlight. If the inverter goes bad, you can replace it on most models (it's cheaper than the backlight).

Before going to the trouble of opening the case, however, ensure that the screen has not been inadvertently dimmed to the off position with the Fn keys or that the system has not been set to direct the output to an external monitor.

Dim display

As with a blank display, the backlight and inverter can cause dimming problems, but in most cases the screen has been dimmed inadvertently with the Fn keys. It is also possible that the switch on the laptop that tells the system the lid is closed may be held down by some obstruction. Check that as well.

Flickering display

Flickering screens can be caused by video drivers. The first thing to try is updating the driver. Another cause can be a low screen-refresh rate. Make sure the rate is set according to the documentation. Keep in mind that if you set it incorrectly, another symptom that may appear is more than one image displaying with the top image appearing transparent.

Flickering can also be caused by a loose connection. You may remember that a cable connects the laptop display to the motherboard. Open the lid as described in Chapter 1, "Mobile Devices," and reseat the cable.

Sticking keys

Problems with keyboards can range from collecting dust (in which case you need to blow it out) to their springs wearing out. In the latter case, you can replace the keyboard (they cost about 10 times more than desktop keyboards) or choose to use an external one (provided the user isn't traveling and having to lug another hardware element with them). As you can imagine, spilled liquids are often the cause of sticking keys.

Intermittent wireless

Most laptops today include an internal wireless card. This is convenient, but it can be susceptible to interference (resulting in low signal strength) between the laptop and the access point (AP). Do what you can to reduce the number of items blocking the signal between the two devices, and you'll increase the strength of the signal. It is also possible that the cable that connects the antenna to the laptop needs to be reseated. Open the lid as described in Chapter 1.

Battery not charging

Most NiCad batteries build up memory, and that memory can prevent a battery from offering a full charge. The biggest issue with DC power problems is a battery's inability to power the laptop as long as it should. If a feature is available to fully drain the battery, you should use it to eliminate the memory (letting the laptop run on battery on a regular basis greatly helps). If you can't drain the battery and eliminate the memory effect, you should replace the battery.

Ghost cursor/pointer drift

A second, or ghost, cursor can be caused when the laptop has a track pad that is too sensitive. Some laptops and tablets also vent warm air through the keyboard, and when the lid is left down, it heats up the track pad and causes this type of cursor behavior. Updating the driver for the touchpad has been known to help this problem. Another approach is to disable the touchpad completely and use an external mouse.

Pointer drift occurs when the mouse cursor slowly drifts across the screen with no assistance from the user. In some cases, it occurs only on a second or third monitor and not the main monitor. If that is the case, there is a setting in the display properties that may solve the issue. In Windows 10, navigate to the display properties by right-clicking the display and select Preferences. Then in the menu at the bottom left of the resulting screen, choose Display. On the Display Settings page shown in Figure 5.6 earlier, select the check box next to the selection Let Me Choose One Scaling Level For All My Displays.

In other cases, the problem is not related to multiple monitors at all. If you find that it is occurring only with certain applications, it may be neither a pointer nor a device problem at all but rather an application issue. Finally, on some laptops and other small devices that use trackpads, you or the user may be leaving your hand resting on a part of the device very close to the trackpad and it is picking that up and causing the pointer to move.

No power

In the absence of AC power, the device will attempt to run off its battery. This solution is good for a time, but AC power must be available to keep the battery charged and the laptop running. Most laptops have an indicator light showing whether AC power is being received, and the AC cord typically has an indicator light on it as well to show that it's receiving power. If no lights are lit on the cord or the laptop indicating that AC power is being received, try a different outlet or a different cord. Also try reseating the cord in the power adapter. The cord between the wall and the adapter is removable (to interchange for different countries' outlet types), and sometimes it comes loose from the brick.

The presence of AC can affect the action of the NIC. To conserve power, the NIC is often configured not to be active when running on DC power (see Figure 5.7). In some laptop models, you can access this dialog box through Start ➤ Control Panel ➤ Internal NIC Configuration. If power problems arise, ensure that this setting is enabled.

FIGURE 5.7   NIC settings

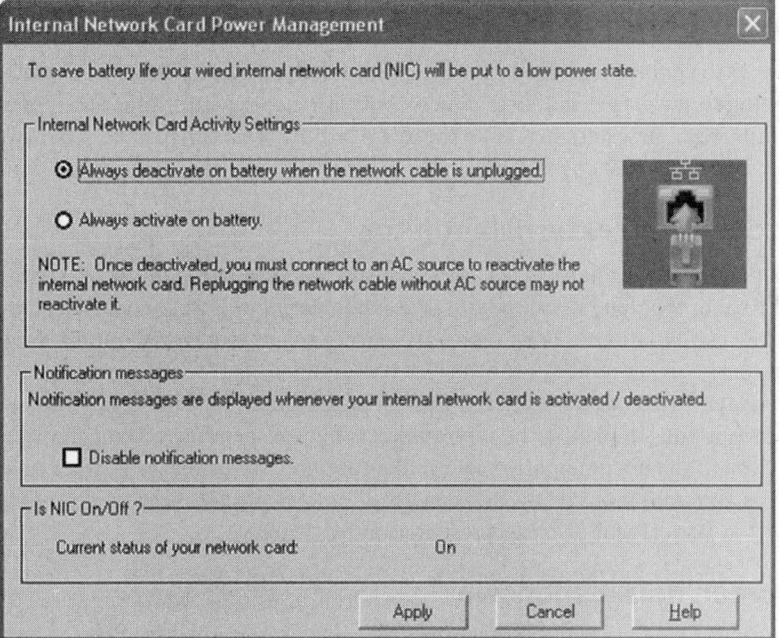

In Windows 10, use Device Manager to set Allow The Computer To Turn Off This Device To Save Power in the Properties ➤ Power Management tab. Then use the Power Options to set the NIC to Maximum Power Saving.

Num lock indicator lights

Sometimes the Num Lock indicator light does not function. This can be a hardware issue, but many times it is a case of the user not understanding the process for enabling and disabling Num Lock. In many laptops you simply hit the key once to turn it on and again to turn it off. However, on some devices, you must also use the Fn key simultaneously. Spilling liquids on the laptop can also cause these problems and usually requires taking the laptop in for service to clean the internal parts.

No wireless connectivity

When there is no wireless connectivity, the cause is usually one of two things.

- The wireless capability is disabled (enabling and disabling this function is usually done with a key combination or Fn key) because this is easy to disable inadvertently. This can also be a hardware switch on the side, front, or back of the case.
- The wireless antenna is bad or the cable needs to be reseated.

No Bluetooth connectivity

Bluetooth is also enabled and disabled with a key combination and can be disabled easily. The first thing to try is to reenable it. The second thing to try is to reseat the antenna cable. If all else fails, try a new antenna. Like the WLAN NIC, this can also be a hardware switch on the side, front, or back of the case.

Cannot display to external monitor

It's always possible that a hardware issue is causing an external monitor to not work when connected to a laptop; but, again, in most cases the problem is an incomplete understanding of the key combination to use to send the output to the external monitor. It can also be that the resolution is set too high for the external monitor.

On some laptops you need to use the Fn key in combination with keys on the top row; on other laptops you simply use the top row keys. Before spending too much time troubleshooting, consult the documentation and make sure you are using the correct procedure. In some models, external monitor display can also be controlled from the video control panel or from within PowerPoint or other presentation software.

Touchscreen non-responsive

Tablets, phablets, and smartphones use a touchscreen interface that eliminates the need for a keyboard. Touchscreen monitors use two technologies: touch flow and multitouch. Before we dive into solving a nonresponsive touchscreen, let's review these technologies.

Touch flow

Touch flow, or TouchFLO, is a user interface feature designed by HTC. It is used by dragging your finger up and down or left and right to access common tasks on the screen. This movement is akin to scrolling the screen up and down or scrolling the screen left and right.

Multitouch

Multitouch allows the screen to recognize multiple simultaneous screen touches. This allows for movements such as those used for expanding or enlarging pictures with two fingers and then reducing them back again with the reverse movement.

The first thing that all documentation will tell you to try is to restart the device, and in many cases the documentation is not blowing smoke at you; this does actually solve the issue. Unfortunately, if the screen is broken or the wires are cut, this will not help, but you should always try this first.

Devices with the Android operating system have a Device Diagnostics tool, which can test the touchscreen, among other things. To access this tool, use a special key sequence (see the documentation) on the same keypad where you dial phone numbers. When you hit the proper sequence, the menu for the tool will appear; Figure 5.8 shows the menu for the Device Diagnostic tool for the Samsung S4. There are two tests found here that apply to the touchscreen, the TSP Dot Mode and the TSP Grid Mode.

FIGURE 5.8   Samsung Device Diagnostics menu

TSP Dot mode allows you to verify that the screen is reading your touch. It will place a dot on the screen everywhere you touch it where it is reading the input. The TSP Grid mode allows you to test each section or grid of the screen. You can drag your finger across the screen and identify any dead spots that may be present.

If the device passes both of these tests, you have no problem with the screen; you have an issue with software, not hardware. Try removing the battery while the device is on (a soft reset). If the device doesn't allow this, it will typically have an operation you can execute called a *simulated battery pull*. If neither of these steps helps, the next step is to reboot the device to safe mode.

If booting to safe mode solves the issue, the issue lies in your application. It may be outdated or corrupt, so try reinstalling the latest version. But if none of the techniques so far works, you are ready to get more extreme and perform a hard reset, which returns the device to the factory settings. Don't do this until you have backed up all the data on the device. Also, do not do this if the device exhibited any hardware issues when you ran the diagnostics test. You will need it to work properly when you finish the reset so you can set up the phone again.

If the device fails the diagnostic test, you have a hardware issue. If the damage is from liquids, submerge the phone in 99 percent isopropyl alcohol. Dry the phone completely and turn it on. This has actually fixed some phones with water damage. Unfortunately, in most cases, when the diagnostic test fails, you have to replace the screen.

These same options are also available with touchscreens on devices like the Microsoft Surface. The same general approach applies with some variation (clean screen, restart, recalibrate the screen, install the latest updates, restore from backup, refresh, reset). The terms *refresh* and *reset* mean the same here as when dealing with laptops and desktops.

Apps not loading

Many times after a user purchases an app or accesses a free application, the app does not appear to load and function. The following are some possible solutions:

- Close the problematic application and all other applications and start the process of opening the application anew. This process will be unique to the device. If you find the application to be missing when you attempt to restart it, download the app again.

- Restart the device. When the device has started, if you find the application to be missing, download the app again.

- Reauthorize the device. This means to unauthorize the device to use the app and then authorize it again. This process will be unique to the device.

- Uninstall the app and then reinstall it.

Slow performance

Many of the causes of slow performance in mobile devices are the same as the causes of slow performance in desktop machines. For the purposes of this discussion, I will focus on performance that deteriorates after being acceptable as opposed to system performance that is poor from the outset (which could be a matter of insufficient resources such as RAM). Here is a list of possibilities:

- The first thing to check is the presence of a virus. If the system seems to have an over-abundance of disk activity, scan it for viruses, using a virus program that resides externally on a CD/DVD or memory stick.

- Defragment the hard drive or, in the case of a smartphone, the memory. The more fragmented the storage is, the slower the access will be.

- Check the space on the hard drive or memory. When the partition or volume where the operating system is located becomes full, performance will suffer. This is why it is a good idea to store data and applications on a different partition from that holding the system files.

- Ensure that the latest updates are installed. In many cases, updates help to solve performance problems, so make sure they are current.

Some specific tips for smartphones are as follows:

- Kill background apps that may be running.

- Keep all apps up-to-date.

- Turn off background data services such as Facebook, Twitter, and WeatherBug.

- On an Android device, turn off Google Services.

- Delete any apps no longer in use.

Unable to decrypt email

Some mobile devices have trouble decrypting encrypted emails either because the selected encryption mechanism does not work using the device's browser or because the device cannot locate the certificate and corresponding key required to decrypt the message. Some vendors, such as Trend Micro, have simply chosen to not support any mobile browsers because of the large number in existence. In such cases, you will receive a message like the following:

> Forward this email to m@zd.trendmicro.com and receive URLs to view the message on mobile devices.

Then an intermediate device will decrypt the email and send you a link, which is valid for a short time for you to view the email.

In other cases, the issue is the inability to locate the required certificate and key. The solution could be as simple as inserting a smart card containing the key. In other cases, you may need to install or reinstall the certificate and corresponding private key required to decrypt the messages. In other cases, it is an issue that can be solved by applying an operating system patch. Just one more reason for keeping all operating systems fully updated!

Finally, sometimes S/MIME is not enabled in the device. Many systems, such as BlackBerry, use S/MIME for encryption, and the receiving device must have this enabled.

Extremely short battery life

When battery life is not what it should be in a mobile device, there are a number of possible reasons. The following are some things that can drain a good battery:

- Leaving display brightness too high
- Constantly enabled wireless connections
- Constantly enabled location services
- Constantly enabled background data services

You may detect a trend in this list, and that is leaving things on! All of those services eat the battery. Setting the device to Airplane mode stops all of that battery sucking. Yes, you may have to manually turn it on to check email, but the convenience is eating the battery.

In other cases, the battery is nearing the end of its life. If using Airplane mode doesn't help, it's probably time for a new battery. All batteries have a limited number of recharges in them. Check the documentation of the device for guidance on this. If the battery does suddenly die shortly after a charge, it's a red flag.

Overheating

When a mobile device is getting hot (and I'm talking very hot here, not just warm), the cause can be the battery. If you find that is the source of the heat, replace the battery. Beyond that, some issues that can cause or contribute to overheating are as follows:

- Excessive gaming
- Excessive browsing
- Using the device while charging the device

On a laptop, excessive heat can indicate that the vents are blocked. It also can be a case of running too many things at once. Clean vents often and ensure they are not blocked when the device is on. Laptops need a hard, even surface so the vents can expel heat. This is why running a device on your lap produces so much heat.

Frozen system

Mobile devices can lock and become unresponsive just like desktop systems can and may do so for some of the same reasons. But they have their own special set of issues that can cause this. The following are some things that you can try to prevent and/or undo a system freezing:

- Clear the application memory cache, which can be overloaded. Closing all applications or restarting the device can solve this issue.

- If the lockup occurred during texting, enable Airplane mode and then disable Airplane mode to force the device to reestablish the connection.

Many of the same issues that cause slow performance also cause lockups. Think of lockups as the next step after slowness. Therefore, some of the same tactics discussed in the section "Slow performance" apply here as well.

No sound from speakers

When no sound is coming from the speakers of a device, start by checking the obvious.

- Is the volume on the device turned down?

- Is the device set on vibrate or to "no sound"?

If the obvious has been checked, then consider when this issue arises. If it arises only when accessing certain sites or when using certain apps, it's an issue with either site compatibility or with the application. In some cases, only taking out the battery and putting it back in (or using a function on the device that does the same) will solve an issue with an application.

If it occurs at all times, then try the following approaches:

- Refresh the device (saves your data but not your apps).

- Reset the device to factory defaults (back up all data!).

- Check for any updates you may have missed.

GPS not functioning

When location services do not appear to be working (these are the services that make the GPS feature work), keep the following principles in mind:

- Make sure GPS is turned on!

- Keep in mind it always works best outdoors rather than indoors.

- Check for Internet access. If you don't have that, you won't have GPS services.

- The first time you use the GPS service, it will take longer because it must find the GPS location.

- As always, the first thing to try is restarting the device.

The GPS performance on some mobile devices can also be affected by the position of your hand on the device. If your hand covers the antenna used for GPS, performance can be negatively affected. It also has been reported that certain UV-protected windshields can block GPS.

Swollen battery

Just as swollen capacitors are a bad thing, so are swollen batteries. A swollen battery occurs when the battery's cells are overcharged because lithium-ion batteries react unfavorably to overcharging. When you encounter a swollen battery, the only solution is to replace it. But you should practice the following safe battery handling procedures when dealing with swollen batteries:

- Be careful not to puncture a swollen battery. The casing is under stress from the built-up gasses within.

- If the swollen state makes the battery difficult to remove, take the device to an expert for removal.

- If you are able to safely remove the swollen battery, store it in a safe cool container and take it to an authorized acceptance center. Do not throw it in the trash!

To avoid a swollen battery altogether, follow the guidelines in the section "Extremely short battery life" to extend the life of batteries.

Disassembling processes for proper reassembly

Disassembling a laptop in such a way that you end up with no leftover parts after the reassembly can be more of a challenge than with desktop machines. This section discusses best practices for this process.

Document and label cable and screw locations

With a desktop computer there is often plenty of empty space in the case. In a laptop, space is at a premium, and because of that, every screw is crucial! To avoid playing a guessing game about which screw goes where, you should create a map that tells you not only where each screw goes (and organize the screws by whatever naming convention you choose) but also where each cable plugs in. You should create this map as you disassemble the laptop and follow it carefully when reassembling it. Taking photos with your phone as you work can also suffice.

Organize parts

As you disassemble the device, organize the parts in such a way that you can reverse your steps when it comes time to reassemble the laptop. Keep screws of the same type together and be careful about making assumptions about screws that appear to be the same kind. Keep all screws that hold a particular component in place together in the same place, perhaps in a cup or on a paper plate.

Another helpful idea is to maintain the parts in the same sequence in which they were taken off the laptop. This will help you remember which part must go back on before another, which may not be as obvious as you think when the time comes to put the laptop back together.

Refer to manufacturer resources

There is no better source of information about the idiosyncrasies of disassembling and reassembling a particular laptop model than the manufacturer documentation. No, it's not cheating to look at that! Each model's documentation has certain small tips that can save much time and grief.

Use appropriate hand tools

Mobile device tools were discussed earlier in this chapter. The important message beyond what is provided there is to use the correct tools. If you render a screw useless by trying to take it out with the wrong kind of screwdriver, you will be wishing you had just bought the correct tool.

Exam essentials

Identify common symptoms of mobile device issues.   Some of the symptoms include a dim, flickering, or blank display; sticking keys; intermittent or nonexistent wireless or Bluetooth connectivity; battery and power issues; ghost cursors; problems with Num Lock indicator lights; and an inability to use an external monitor.

Describe proper disassembly and reassembly procedures.   Use the following guidelines:

- Document and label cable and screw locations.
- Organize parts.
- Refer to manufacturer resources.
- Use appropriate hand tools.

5.6 Given a scenario, troubleshoot printers.

In the real world, you'll find that a large portion of all service calls relate to printing problems. This section will give you some general guidelines and common printing solutions to resolve printing problems. The topics addressed in exam objective 5.6 include the following:

- Common symptoms
    - Streaks
    - Faded prints
    - Ghost images
    - Toner not fused to the paper
    - Creased paper
    - Paper not feeding
    - Paper jam
    - No connectivity
    - Garbled characters on paper
    - Vertical lines on page
    - Backed-up print queue
    - Low memory errors
    - Access denied

- Printer will not print
- Color prints in wrong print color
- Unable to install printer
- Error codes
- Printing blank pages
- No image on printer display
- Multiple failed jobs in logs

Common symptoms

There is no single shared device in the network that more users come in contact with and use every day than the printer. You may have to troubleshoot the common symptoms in this section on a daily basis, depending on your environment. Your ability to get a down printer working will make you more valuable to your employer.

Streaks

With laser printers, streaks usually indicate that the fuser is not fusing the toner properly on the paper. It could also be that the incorrect paper is being used. In laser printers, you can sometimes tell the printer that you are using a heavier paper. For dot-matrix, you can adjust the platen for thicker paper.

If you can pick up a sheet from a laser printer, run your thumb across it, and have the image come off on your thumb, you have a fuser problem. The fuser isn't heating the toner and fusing it onto the paper. This could be caused by a number of things—but all of them can be taken care of with a fuser replacement. For example, if the halogen light inside the heating roller has burned out, that will cause the problem. The solution is to replace the fuser. The fuser can be replaced with a rebuilt unit, if you prefer. Rebuilt fusers are almost as good as new fusers, and some even come with guarantees. Plus, they cost less.

The whole fuser may not need to be replaced. You can order fuser components from parts suppliers and then rebuild them. For example, if the fuser has a bad lamp, you can order a lamp and replace it in the fuser.

Another, similar problem happens when small areas of smudging repeat themselves down the page. Dents or cold spots in the fuser heat roller cause this problem. The only solution is to replace either the fuser assembly or the heat roller.

If an ink cartridge becomes damaged or develops a hole, it can put too much ink on the page, and the letters will smear. In this case, the solution is to replace the ink cartridge. (However, a small amount of smearing is normal if the pages are laid on top of each other immediately after printing.) Because damage is possible in the process, you need to be careful when refilling cartridges, and many manufacturers do not suggest using refilled cartridges at all.

With inkjet or dot-matrix printers, streaks can mean the print head needs cleaning. If cleaning doesn't help, try replacing the cartridge (inkjet) or the ribbon (dot-matrix).

Faded prints

In laser printers, faded output usually indicates that the toner cartridge is just about empty. You can usually remove it, shake it, and replace it and then get a bit more life out of it before it is completely empty, but this is a signal that you are near the end.

Another possibility is that the ink cartridge has dried out from lack of use. That's why the manufacturers include a small suction pump inside the printer that primes the ink cartridge before each print cycle. If this priming pump is broken or malfunctioning, this problem will manifest itself, and the pump will need to be replaced.

For dot-matrix printers, faded printing means you need to replace the ribbon, which is the source of ink in that printer type.

Ghost images

A problem unique to laser printers, *ghosting*, occurs when you can see light images of previously printed pages on the current page. This is caused by one of two things: bad erasure lamps or a broken cleaning blade. If the erasure lamps are bad, the previous electrostatic discharges aren't completely wiped away. When the electrophotographic (EP) drum rotates toward the developing roller, some toner sticks to the slightly discharged areas. A broken cleaning blade, on the other hand, causes old toner to build up on the EP drum and consequently present itself in the next printed image.

Replacing the toner cartridge solves the second problem. Solving the first problem involves replacing the erasure lamps in the printer. Because the toner cartridge is the least expensive cure, you should try that first. Usually, replacing the toner cartridge will solve the problem. If it doesn't, you'll then have to replace the erasure lamps.

Toner not fused to the paper

In laser printers, when the toner does not fuse properly to the paper, it will streak and smudge. See the section "Streaks" for more information.

Creased paper

Creased paper is a sign of a paper jam inside the printer that, although not grinding the entire operation to halt (see the "Paper Jam" section later in this section), is mangling your paper. Approach this problem with the same techniques described in the section "Paper jam." You may also be using paper that is too thick.

Paper not feeding

When the paper is not feeding into the printer, it means the pickup rollers have hardened and lost their ability to pick up the paper. Replacing these rollers usually fixes the problem.

In some cases, it's not the rollers but the paper-feed sensor. It is designed to tell the printer when it is out of paper. Always try cleaning the sensor first before replacing it. High humidity can also cause the paper to not feed properly.

Paper jam

Laser printers today run at copier speeds. As a result, their most common problem is paper jams. Paper can get jammed in a printer for several reasons. First, feed jams happen when the paper-feed rollers get worn. The solution to this problem is easy: replace the worn rollers.

 If your paper-feed jams are caused by worn pickup rollers, there is something you can do to get your printer working while you're waiting for the replacement pickup rollers. Scuff the feed rollers with a pot scrubber pad (or something similar) to roughen up the surfaces. This trick works only once. After that, the rollers aren't thick enough to touch the paper.

Another cause of feed jams is related to the drive of the pickup roller. The drive gear (or clutch) may be broken or have teeth missing. Again, the solution is to replace it. To determine whether the problem is a broken gear or worn rollers, print a test page, but leave the paper tray out. Look into the paper-feed opening with a flashlight, and see whether the paper pickup rollers are turning evenly and don't skip. If they turn evenly, the problem is more than likely worn rollers.

Worn exit rollers can also cause paper jams. These rollers guide the paper out of the printer into the paper-receiving tray. If they're worn or damaged, the paper may catch on its way out of the printer. These types of jams are characterized by a paper jam that occurs just as the paper is getting to the exit rollers. If the paper jams, open the rear door and see where the paper is. If the paper is close to the exit roller, the exit rollers are probably the problem.

The solution is to replace all the exit rollers. You must replace all of them at the same time, because even one worn exit roller can cause the paper to jam. Besides, they're inexpensive. Don't be cheap and skimp on these parts if you need to have them replaced.

Paper jams can be the fault of the paper. If your printer consistently tries to feed multiple pages into the printer, the paper isn't dry enough. If you live in an area with high humidity, this could be a problem. Some solutions are pretty far-out but may work (such as keeping the paper in a Tupperware-type airtight container or microwaving it to remove moisture). The best all-around solution, however, is humidity control and keeping the paper wrapped until it's needed. Keep the humidity around 50 percent or lower (but greater than 25 percent if you can in order to avoid problems with electrostatic discharge). Poor paper quality can also cause this problem.

Finally, a metal, grounded strip called the *static eliminator strip* inside the printer drains the corona charge away from the paper after it has been used to transfer toner from the EP cartridge. If that strip is missing, broken, or damaged, the charge will remain on the paper and may cause it to stick to the EP cartridge, causing a jam. If the paper jams after reaching the corona assembly, this may be the cause.

No connectivity

A number of software issues can cause printer problems. Sometimes it's difficult to tell exactly where in the process the communication between the computer and the printer is breaking down. It could be that you are not establishing a connection with the printer, or an incorrect setting or driver could be preventing successful printing.

To determine whether it is a connectivity problem, ping the IP address of the printer. If you cannot ping the printer by IP address, that problem must be solved or all other trouble-shooting of settings and drivers will be wasted effort. Use this simple test to rule out a network connectivity problem.

If the printer is connected directly to the computer (locally connected), then check the cables. If they check out, ensure that the printer port is enabled and that the correct driver for the printer is installed.

Garbled characters on paper

Many problems with a printer that won't work with the operating system or that prints the wrong characters can be traced to problems with its software. Computers and printers can't talk to each other by themselves. They need interface software known as drivers to translate software commands into commands the printer can understand.

For a printer to work with a particular operating system, a driver must be installed for it. This driver specifies the page description language (PDL) the printer understands, as well as information about the printer's characteristics (paper trays, maximum resolution, and so on). For laser printers, there are two popular PDLs: Adobe PostScript (PS) and Hewlett-Packard Printer Control Language (PCL). Almost all laser printers use one or both of these.

If the wrong printer driver is selected, the computer will send commands in the wrong language. If that occurs, the printer will print several pages of garbage (even if only one page of information was sent). This "garbage" isn't garbage at all, but the printer PDL commands printed literally as text instead of being interpreted as control commands.

Vertical lines on page

Vertical lines can appear in either of two forms.

Vertical black lines on the page

With laser printers, a groove or scratch in the EP drum can cause the problem of vertical black lines running down all or part of the page. Because a scratch is lower than the surface, it doesn't receive as much (if any) of a charge as the other areas. The result is that toner sticks to it as though it were discharged. Because the groove may go around the circumference of the drum, the line may go all the way down the page.

Another possible cause of vertical black lines is a dirty charge corona wire, which prevents a sufficient charge from being placed on the EP drum. Because the EP drum has almost zero charge, toner sticks to the areas that correspond to the dirty areas on the charge corona wire.

The solution to the first problem is, as always, to replace the toner cartridge (or EP drum, if your printer uses a separate EP drum and toner). You can also solve the second problem with a new toner cartridge, but in this case that would be an extreme solution. It's easier to clean the charge corona with the brush supplied with the cartridge.

When dealing with inkjet printers, vertical black lines on the page can mean the print head needs cleaning or that the print cartridge needs to be replaced.

Vertical white lines on the page

With laser printers, vertical white lines running down all or part of the page are a relatively common problem on older printers, especially ones that see little maintenance. They're caused by foreign matter (more than likely toner) caught on the transfer corona wire. The dirty spots keep the toner from being transmitted to the paper at those locations, with the result that streaks form as the paper progresses past the transfer corona wire.

The solution is to clean the corona wires. Some printers come with a small corona-wire brush to help in this procedure. To use it, remove the toner cartridge and run the brush in the charge corona groove on top of the toner cartridge. Replace the cartridge and use the brush to brush away any foreign deposits on the transfer corona. Be sure to put it back in its holder when you're finished.

For inkjet printers, clean the print head first (or run the built-in cleaning cycle) and then try replacing the cartridge. This behavior is usually caused by dust or debris.

Backed-up print queue

Sometimes the printer will not print, and all attempts to delete print jobs or clear the print queue fail. It's almost as if the printer is just frozen. When this occurs, the best thing to do is restart the print spooler service on the computer that is acting as the print server. Unfortunately, all users will have to resend their print jobs after this, but at least the printer will be functional again.

Low memory errors

A printer can have several types of memory errors. The most common is insufficient memory to print the page. Sometimes you can circumvent this problem by doing any of the following:

- Turn off the printer to flush out its RAM and then turn it back on and try again.
- Print at a lower resolution. (Adjust this setting in the printer's properties in Windows.)
- Change the page being printed so it's less complex.
- Try a different printer driver if your printer supports more than one PDL. (For example, try switching from PostScript to PCL or vice versa.) Doing so involves installing another printer driver.
- Upgrade the memory, if the printer allows.

Access denied

Printers are considered network resources just like files and folders and as such can have permissions attached to them. When a user receives an "Access Denied" message, it means they lack the print permission. Typically, a printer that has been shared will automatically give all users the print permission, but when permissions have been employed to control which users can print to a particular printer, that default has been altered.

When checking permissions, keep in mind that in Windows, users may have permissions derived from their personal account and from groups of which they are a member. You must ensure that users have not been explicitly denied print permission through their accounts or through any groups of which they are members. A single Deny will prevent them from printing, regardless of what other permissions they may have to the printer.

Also, *print availability* or *print priority* can affect access to the printer. Print availability is used to permit certain users to print only during certain times. With print priority, print jobs from certain users or groups are assigned a higher priority than other users or groups. These settings, usually set by an administrator, can prevent or delay successful printing.

Printer will not print

If your printer isn't spitting out print jobs, it may be a good idea to print a test page and see whether that works. The test page information is stored in the printer's memory, so there's no formatting or translating of jobs required. It's simply a test to make sure your printer hears your computer. In addition to the Windows ➤ Print Test Page button, try the built-in test function on the printer if your printer has one. While the Windows test verifies driver and connectivity, testing or printing at the print device tests the device itself.

When you install a printer, one of the last questions it asks you is whether to print a test page. If there's any question, go ahead and do it. If the printer is already installed, you can print a test page from the printer Properties window. Just click the Print Test Page button and it should work. If nothing happens, double-check your connections and stop and restart the print spooler. If garbage prints, there is likely a problem with the printer's memory or the print driver.

In many cases, a printer will fail to print because it is not turned on, it doesn't have power, or the print queue is stopped or paused. Printing a test page will identify these issues before they affect users.

Color prints in wrong print color

Incorrect colors or colors that are faint or washed out are often the result of a dirty print head, although this effect can also mean that one of the colors is running out. Head cleaning (for inkjet or dot-matrix printers) is a crucial operation that should be carried out at least once a month under normal usage. This is a procedure carried out in the properties or preferences of the printer (which may vary by printer).

You should not perform this procedure if the ink or toner cartridges are low because it takes ink to do this. Check them first and, if they are low, replace any cartridges that need it and then run the head-cleaning procedure.

Unable to install printer

Installing a printer and attaching to a shared printer are two different operations in the Windows environment. Users with no administrative rights can attach to an existing shared printer, but installing a printer on the machine (which means that machine will function as the print server for that device) requires administrative permissions in the local machine. When an inability to install occurs, verify that you are logged into the computer with an administrator account.

Error codes

Many laser printers include LCDs for interaction with the printer. When error codes appear, refer to the manufacturer's manuals or website for information on how to interpret the codes and solve the problem causing them.

Printing blank pages

When an inkjet printer prints blank pages, the issue is usually a clogged print head. When printers of this type sit for an extended period without use, the ink that may be in the print head dries out, clogging the head. Consequently, when you print, everything else in the process occurs correctly, but the ink cannot get through the clogged head and you get no ink on the paper. The solution is to clean the head and replace any cartridges that may be low.

Another reason for this can be an incorrect print driver. This is not a typical symptom of a bad driver, but changing it can still be the solution in some printers. Try updating and/or downloading the driver if clogged ink cartridges are not the issue.

If it is a laser printer, check the following items:

- Empty toner cartridge
- Malfunctioning laser shutter (prevents creation of image in the drum)
- No voltage to the transfer roller (prevents transfer of toner from the drum to the paper)
- No bias charge on the drum (prevents transfer of toner to the drum)
- Defective laser scanner cable (prevents image creation on the drum)

No image on printer display

When the display located on the physical printer is blank, it may be a formatter failure. While the failure of a formatter is not common, the solution, replacing the formatter, is not difficult. The formatter assembly is a self-contained unit that can be purchased and installed in the place of the bad formatter.

In some cases, the display may go into a sleep mode when not in use. If this is the case, touching the screen (if it is touchscreen) may wake it up. Make sure there is power to the unit, and if there is not, check the power supply. Finally, some screens have a brightness setting that may be set so low you can't read it, so consider that possibility as well.

Exam Essentials

Identify the most common symptoms of printing problems.   These include streaks, faded prints, ghost images, incompletely fused toner, creased paper, paper jams and feeding issues, no connectivity, garbled characters, vertical lines, print queue issues, low memory errors, permission issues, total print failure, and incorrect print colors.

5.7 Given a scenario, troubleshoot common wired and wireless network problems.

At one time, wireless networks were considered an extravagant and insecure addition to the enterprise network, but now users expect wireless access. No longer is it a business advantage; it is now a business requirement. This section discusses troubleshooting both wired and wireless networks. The topics addressed in exam objective 5.7 include the following:

- Common symptoms
  - Limited connectivity
  - Unavailable resources
  - No connectivity
  - APIPA/link local address
  - Intermittent connectivity
  - IP conflict
  - Slow transfer speeds
  - Low RF signal
  - SSID not found

Common symptoms

Network problems, usually manifesting themselves as an inability to connect to resources, can arise from many different sources. This section discusses some common symptoms of networking issues.

Limited connectivity

In some cases, the computer has connectivity to some but not all resources. When this is the case, issues that may reside on other layers of the OSI model should come under consideration. These include the following:

Authentication Issues   Does the user have the permission to access the resource?

DNS Issues   You may be able to ping the entire network using IP addresses, but most access is done by name, not IP address. If you can't ping resources by name, DNS is not functional, meaning either the DNS server is down or the local machine is not configured with the correct IP address of the DNS server. If recent changes have occurred in the DNS mappings or if your connection to the destination device has recently failed because of a temporary network issue that has been solved, you may need to clear the local DNS cache using the `ipconfig /flushdns` command.

Remote Problem   Don't forget that establishing a connection is a two-way street, and if the remote device has an issue, communication cannot occur. Always check the remote device as well. Any interconnecting device between the computer and resource, such as a switch or router, should also be checked for functionality.

Unavailable resources

When resources are unavailable, keep in mind that the issue could lie either in the source device or in the destination device that is holding the resource. It also might be a router or switch between the devices as well. Start your troubleshooting at one end or the other and using the method described in the section "No connectivity" check the connections between each pair of intermediate devices until your locate the problem devices.

Internet

When all other access is fine but there is no Internet access, the issue is frequently DNS. See the tips in the section "DNS issues."

Local resources

When a computer can communicate only on its local network or subnet, the problem is usually one of the following:

Incorrect Subnet Mask   Sometimes an incorrect mask will prevent all communication, but in some cases it results in successful connections locally but not remotely (outside the local subnet). The subnet mask value should be the same mask used on the router interface connecting to the local network.

Incorrect Default Gateway Address   If the computer cannot connect to the default gateway, it will be confined to communicating with devices on the local network. This IP address should be that of the router interface connecting to the local network.

Router Problem   If all users on the network are having connectivity problems, you likely have a routing issue that should be escalated to the proper administrators.

SHARES

When troubleshooting issues regarding shares, keep in mind that the issue could be a network connectivity problem, in which case you would use the methods described in the sections "Limited connectivity" and "No connectivity" to isolate and resolve the issue.

However, the issue could be permissions. It could be that either the user lacks the proper permissions or the permissions are misconfigured. You should check first with the data owner (typically a department head but not always) to verify the proper permissions that should be in place and, if required, configure them correctly. You may have to inform the user that they currently lack said permission and direct them to the data owner for the permission needed. Never take it on yourself to make that decision.

PRINTERS

Printer connectivity issues are covered in detail in this chapter in the previous section "No connectivity" in the printer section.

EMAIL

Email connectivity issues follow the same troubleshooting approach covered in the previous section "Limited connectivity." As discussed in that section, email issues typically revolve around DNS issues, network connectivity, or a failure in authentication. One issue to check is the setup of the account. For example if the client is set to use POP3 and the server is using IMAP, there will be a connectivity issue.

No connectivity

When no connectivity can be established with the network, your troubleshooting approach should begin at the physical layer and then proceed up the OSI model. As components at each layer are eliminated as the source of the problem, proceed to the next higher layer. A simple yet effective set of steps might be as follows:

1. Check the network cable to ensure it is the correct cable type (crossover or straight through) and that it is functional. If in doubt, try a different cable.

2. Ensure that the NIC is functional and TCP/IP is installed and functional by pinging the loopback address 127.0.0.1. If required, install or reinstall TCP/IP and/or replace or repair the NIC.

3. Check the local IP configuration and ensure that the IP address, subnet mask, and gateway are correct. If the default gateway can be pinged, the computer is configured correctly for its local network, and the problem lies beyond the router or with the destination device. If pings to the gateway are unsuccessful, ensure that the IP configurations of the router interface and the computer are compatible and in the same subnet.

   When dealing with a wireless network, ensure that the wireless card is functional. The wireless card is easily disabled with a keystroke on a laptop and should be the first thing to check. If the network uses a hidden SSID, ensure that the station in question is configured with the correct SSID.

APIPA/link local address

Automatic Private IP Addressing (APIPA) is a TCP/IP feature Microsoft added to its operating systems. If a Dynamic Host Configuration Protocol (DHCP) server cannot be found, the clients automatically assign themselves an IP address, somewhat randomly, in the 169.254.x.x range with a subnet mask of 255.255.0.0. This allows them to communicate with other hosts that have similarly configured themselves, but they will be unable to connect to the Internet or to any machines or resources that have DHCP-issued IP addresses.

If the network uses DHCP for IP configuration and the computer with the connectivity issue has an APIPA address, the problem is one of these three things:

- The DHCP server is out of IP addresses.

- The DHCP server is on the other side of a router and there is no functional DHCP relay present or no IP helper address configured on the router—all of which is to say the DHCP request is not reaching the DHCP server.

- The computer has a basic connectivity issue preventing it from connecting to the network (see the section "No connectivity").

In Chapter 2 "Networking," you learned about a type of IPv6 address called a *link local address* that in many ways is like an APIPA address in that the device will generate one of these addresses for each interface with no intervention from a human, as is done with APIPA. The scope of the address is also the same, in that it is not routable and is good only on the segment where the device is located.

However, as is the case with APIPA addresses, if two devices that are connected to the same segment generate these addresses, they will be in the same network, and the two devices will be able to communicate. This is because the devices always generate the address using the same IPv6 prefix (the equivalent of a network ID in IPv4), which is fe80::/64. The remainder of the address is created by spreading the 48-bit MAC address across the last 64 bits, yielding an IPv6 address that looks like the following one:

```
FE80::2237:06FF:FECF:67E4/64
```

Intermittent connectivity

When a connectivity issue comes and goes, it can be a hardware issue or a software issue. The following hardware components should be checked for functionality:

Network Cable   A damaged cable can cause intermittent connectivity.

Network Interface Card   If the NIC is not properly seated or has worked its way partially out of its slot, it can cause connections that come and go.

Interference   On a wireless network, cordless phones, microwave ovens, and other wireless networks can interfere with transmissions. Also, users who stray too far from the AP can experience a signal that comes and goes.

The following are software issues that can cause intermittent connectivity:

DHCP Issues   When the DHCP server is down or out of IP addresses, the problem will not manifest itself to those users who already have an IP address until their lease expires and they need a new address. In this case, some users will be fine and others will not, and then users who were fine earlier in the day may have problems later when their IP address lease expires.

DNS Problems   If the DNS server is down or malfunctioning, it will cause problems for DNS clients who need name resolution requests answered. For users who have already connected to resources in the last hour before the outage, connectivity to those resources will still be possible until the name to IP address mapping is removed from the client DNS resolver cache.

IP conflict

IP address conflicts are somewhat rare when DHCP is in use, but they can still happen. DHCP servers and clients both check for IP duplication when the DHCP client receives an IP address, but the process doesn't always work. Moreover, if someone with a statically configured IP address connects to the network with the same address as another machine, a conflict will exist. Using the `ipconfig/release` and `ipconfig/renew` commands will usually solve the issue.

Regardless of how the conflict occurs, it must be resolved because until it is, one or possibly both computers with the same address will not be able to operate on the network. You can determine the MAC address of the computer with which you are experiencing the conflict by using the `ping` command followed by the `arp -d` command.

Slow transfer speeds

Slow transmission on the network can be caused by hardware and software issues. Some of the physical issues that can cause slow performance are as follows:

Interference   Both wireless and wired networks can be affected by electromagnetic interference (EMI) and radio frequency interference (RFI). EMI will degrade network performance. This can be identified by the poor operation you may experience. Be sure to run cables around (not over) ballasts and other items that can cause EMI. RFI is a similar issue introduced by radio waves. Wireless networks suffer even more from both of these issues.

Incorrect Cabling   The network can go only as fast as its weakest link. Using CAT3 cabling, for example, will only allow the network to operate at 10 Mbps even if all the network cards are capable of 10 Gbps.

Malfunctioning NIC   NICs can malfunction and cause a broadcast storm. These broadcast packets fill the network with traffic that slows performance for all users. Use a protocol analyzer to determine the MAC address of the offending computer.

From a software standpoint, the following issues can result in less than ideal performance:

Router Misconfiguration   If the router is not configured correctly, it can cause slow performance because of less than optimal routing paths. Escalate the issue to the appropriate administrators.

Switch Misconfiguration   An improperly implemented redundant switch network can result in switching loops that cause slow performance. Escalate the issue to the appropriate administrators.

Low RF signal

In a wireless network, the signal coming from the AP has a distance limit. With some variation by standard, this is about 100 meters. However, this distance is impacted by obstructions and interference in the area. The WLAN design should include a site survey that identifies these issues and locates APs and antenna types in such a way as to mitigate these effects.

It is also useful to know that APs and some client radios have a setting to control signal strength. It is not a normal practice to change the setting in a laptop wireless card, but it may be necessary to change the transmit level on an AP. In many cases, it is actually beneficial to reduce the transmit level of an AP in situations where it is interfering with other APs in your network or you want to limit the range of the signal to prevent it from leaving the building. This is especially true in high-density areas where several APs are co-located in the same area for increased throughput.

SSID not found

In an 802.11 WLAN, the service set identifier (SSID) is used as both a network name and in some cases the magic word that allows access to the network. One of the ways you can increase the security of a WLAN (not sufficient in and of itself but a good addition to a layered approach to WLAN security) is to "hide" the SSID. This is also referred to as disabling SSID broadcast. It is accomplished by setting the AP to *not* list the SSID in the beacon frames. These frames contain the information that is used to populate the list of available wireless networks when you "scan" for wireless networks on your wireless device.

When the SSID is hidden, the *only* way a device can connect to the WLAN is to be configured with a profile that includes the SSID of the WLAN. While every operating system is slightly different, to do this in Windows 10, you follow these steps:

1. Open the Network And Sharing Center, as shown in Figure 5.9.

FIGURE 5.9   Network And Sharing Center

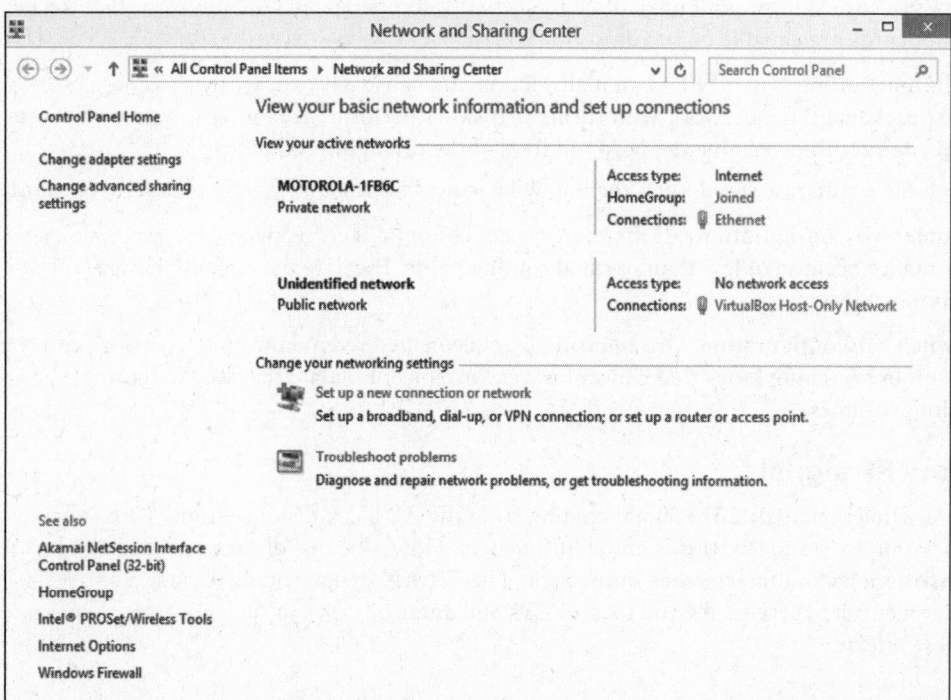

2. Select Set Up A New Connection Or Network, opening the dialog shown in Figure 5.10.

FIGURE 5.10   Set Up A New Connection Or Network.

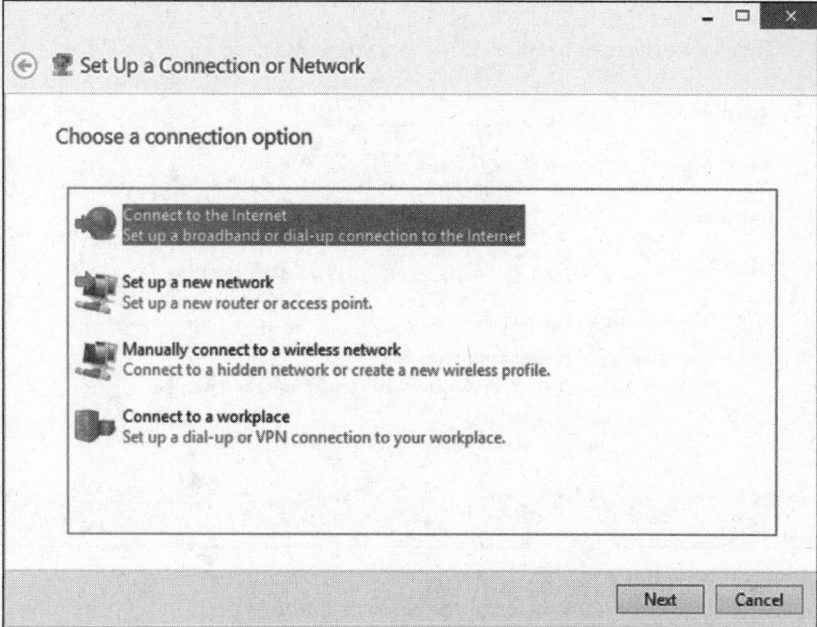

3. Select the option Manually Connect To A Wireless Network and click Next, opening the dialog shown in Figure 5.11.

FIGURE 5.11 Manually Connect To A Wireless Network.

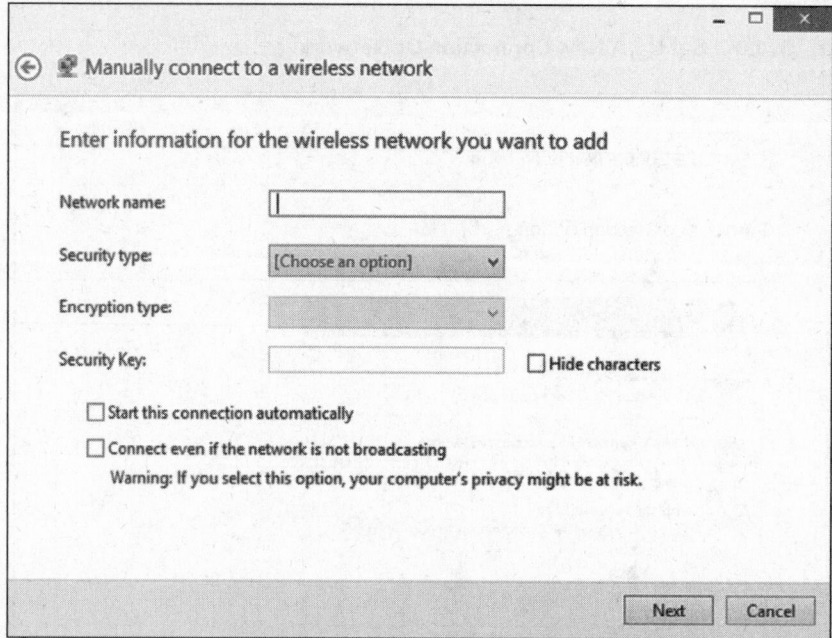

4. Complete the network name, security type, encryption type, and security key; check the box Connect Even If The Network Is Not Broadcasting; and click Next. Now the profile is complete and you should be able to connect to the "hidden" network. To make it easier for the user, you may also want to check the box Start This Connection Automatically.

Exam essentials

Identify common symptoms of network issues and their potential causes. Examples include limited, intermittent, local-only, or no connectivity, APIPA addresses, IP conflict, slow transfer speeds, and low RF signal.

Review Questions

You can find the answers in the Appendix.

1. Which of the following is the final step in the CompTIA troubleshooting method?
   A. Establish a plan of action to resolve the problem and implement the solution.
   B. Document findings, actions, and outcomes.
   C. Establish a theory of probable cause (question the obvious).
   D. Identify the problem.

2. Which of the following is the first step in the CompTIA troubleshooting method?
   A. Establish a plan of action to resolve the problem and implement the solution.
   B. Document findings, actions, and outcomes.
   C. Establish a theory of probable cause (question the obvious).
   D. Identify the problem.

3. What is the most common reason for an unexpected reboot?
   A. Overheating
   B. ESD damage
   C. RFI
   D. Memory leak

4. Which of the following is typically not a cause of system lockups?
   A. Memory issues
   B. Virus
   C. Video driver
   D. Bad NIC driver

5. What are proprietary screen crashes called in Windows?
   A. Pin wheel
   B. BSOD
   C. Bomb screen
   D. PSOID

6. Which operating system uses the Pinwheel of Death as a proprietary screen crash?
   A. Apple
   B. LINUX
   C. Windows
   D. UNIX

7. What are the small dots on the screen that are filled with a color?

    A. Pixels

    B. Hypervisors

    C. Cells

    D. Capacitors

8. What are visual anomalies that appear on the screen called?

    A. Pixels

    B. Artifacts

    C. Cells

    D. Dead spots

9. What is the light in the device that powers the LCD screen?

    A. Backlight

    B. Inverter

    C. Charger

    D. Reflector

10. Which of the following is a user interface feature designed by HTC?

    A. Type I

    B. TouchFLO

    C. Type II

    D. Container-based

11. Which of the following indicates that the fuser is not fusing the toner properly on the paper?

    A. Black spots

    B. Streaks

    C. Blank spots

    D. Garbled output

12. Which of the following indicates that the toner cartridge is just about empty?

    A. Black spots

    B. Streaks

    C. Faded prints

    D. Garbled output

13. If you can ping resources by IP address but not by name, _____ is not functional.

  A. HTTP

  B. DNS

  C. DHCP

  D. ARP

14. Which of the following should be set to the IP address of the router interface connecting to the local network?

  A. IP address

  B. Subnet mask

  C. Default gateway

  D. DHCP server

CompTIA A+ Core 2 Exam 220-1002

PART II

CHAPTER 6: Operating Systems

CHAPTER 7: Security

CHAPTER 8: Software Troubleshooting

CHAPTER 9: Operational Procedures

Chapter

6

Operating Systems

COMPTIA A+ CERTIFICATION EXAM CORE 2 (220-1002) OBJECTIVES COVERED IN THIS CHAPTER:

✓ **1.1 Compare and contrast common operating system types and their purposes.**

- 32-bit vs. 64-bit
  - RAM limitations
  - Software compatibility
- Workstation operating systems
  - Microsoft Windows
  - Apple Macintosh OS
  - Linux
- Cell phone/tablet operating systems
  - Microsoft Windows
  - Android
  - iOS
  - Chrome OS
- Vendor-specific limitations
  - End-of-life
  - Update limitations
- Compatibility concerns between operating systems

✓ **1.2 Compare and contrast features of Microsoft Windows versions.**

- Windows 7
- Windows 8
- Windows 8.1
- Windows 10

- Corporate vs. personal needs
  - Domain access
  - Bitlocker
  - Media center
  - Branchcache
  - EFS
- Desktop styles/user interface

✓ **1.3   Summarize general OS installation considerations and upgrade methods.**

- Boot methods
  - USB
  - CD-ROM
  - DVD
  - PXE
  - Solid state/flash drives
  - Netboot
  - External/hot-swappable drive
  - Internal hard drive (partition)
- Types of installations
  - Unattended installation
  - In-place upgrade
  - Clean install
  - Repair installation
  - Multiboot
  - Remote network installation
  - Image deployment
  - Recovery partition
  - Refresh/restore
- Partitioning
  - Dynamic
  - Basic

- Primary
- Extended
- Logical
- GPT
- File system types/formatting
  - ExFAT
  - FAT32
  - NTFS
  - CDFS
  - NFS
  - ext3, ext4
  - HFS
  - Swap partition
  - Quick format vs. full format
- Load alternate third-party drivers when necessary
- Workgroup vs. Domain setup
- Time/date/region/language settings
- Driver installation, software, and Windows updates
- Factory recovery partition
- Properly formatted boot drive with the correct partitions/format
- Prerequisites/hardware compatibility
- Application compatibility
- OS compatibility/upgrade path

✓ **1.4 Given a scenario, use appropriate Microsoft command line tools.**

- Navigation
  - dir
  - cd
  - ..
- ipconfig

- ping

- tracert

- netstat

- nslookup

- shutdown

- dism

- sfc

- chkdsk

- diskpart

- taskkill

- gpupdate

- gpresult

- format

- copy

- xcopy

- robocopy

- net use

- net user

- [command name] /?

- Commands available with standard privileges vs. administrative privileges

✓ **1.5 Given a scenario, use Microsoft operating system features and tools.**

- Administrative

  - Computer Management

  - Device Manager

  - Local Users and Groups

  - Local Security Policy

  - Performance Monitor

  - Services

  - System Configuration

- Task Scheduler
- Component Services
- Data Sources
- Print Management
- Windows Memory Diagnostics
- Windows Firewall
- Advanced Security
- Event Viewer
- User Account Management
- MSConfig
  - General
  - Boot
  - Services
  - Startup
  - Tools
- Task Manager
  - Applications
  - Processes
  - Performance
  - Networking
  - Users
- Disk Management
  - Drive status
  - Mounting
  - Initializing
  - Extending partitions
  - Splitting partitions
  - Shrink partitions
  - Assigning/changing drive letters
  - Adding drives
  - Adding arrays

- Storage spaces
- System utilities
  - Regedit
  - Command
  - Services.msc
  - MMC
  - MSTSC
  - Notepad
  - Explorer
  - Msinfo32
  - DxDiag
  - Disk Defragmenter
  - System Restore
  - Windows Update

✓ **1.6 Given a scenario, use Microsoft Windows Control Panel utilities.**

- Internet Options
  - Connections
  - Security
  - General
  - Privacy
  - Programs
  - Advanced
- Display/Display Settings
  - Resolution
  - Color depth
  - Refresh rate
- User Accounts
- Folder Options
  - View hidden files
  - Hide extensions

- General options
- View options
- System
  - Performance (virtual memory)
  - Remote settings
  - System protection
- Windows Firewall
- Power Options
  - Hibernate
  - Power plans
  - Sleep/suspend
  - Standby
- Credential Manager
- Programs and features
- HomeGroup
- Devices and Printers
- Sound
- Troubleshooting
- Network and Sharing Center
- Device Manager
- Bitlocker
- Sync Center

✓ **1.7 Summarize application installation and configuration concepts.**

- System requirements
  - Drive space
  - RAM
- OS requirements
  - Compatibility
- Methods of installation and deployment
  - Local (CD/USB)

- Network-based
  - Local user permissions
    - Folder/file access for installation
  - Security considerations
    - Impact to device
    - Impact to network

✓ **1.8 Given a scenario, configure Microsoft Windows networking on a client/desktop.**

- HomeGroup vs. Workgroup
- Domain setup
- Network shares/administrative shares/mapping drives
- Printer sharing vs. network printer mapping
- Establish networking connections
  - VPN
  - Dial-ups
  - Wireless
  - Wired
  - WWAN (Cellular)
- Proxy settings
- Remote Desktop Connection
- Remote Assistance
- Home vs. Work vs. Public network settings
- Firewall settings
  - Exceptions
  - Configuration
  - Enabling/disabling Windows Firewall
- Configuring an alternative IP address in Windows
  - IP addressing
  - Subnet mask
  - DNS
  - Gateway

- Network card properties
  - Half duplex/full duplex/auto
  - Speed
  - Wake-on-LAN
  - QoS
  - BIOS (on-board NIC)

✓ **1.9 Given a scenario, use features and tools of the MacOS and Linux client/desktop operating systems.**

- Best practices
  - Scheduled backups
  - Scheduled disk maintenance
  - System updates/App Store
  - Patch management
  - Driver/firmware updates
  - Antivirus/Anti-malware updates
- Tools
  - Backup/Time Machine
  - Restore/Snapshot
  - Image recovery
  - Disk maintenance utilities
  - Shell/Terminal
  - Screen sharing
  - Force Quit
- Features
  - Multiple desktops/Mission Control
  - Key Chain
  - Spot Light
  - iCloud
  - Gestures
  - Finder
  - Remote Disc

- Dock
- Boot Camp
- Basic Linux commands
  - ls
  - grep
  - cd
  - shutdown
  - pwd vs. passwd
  - mv
  - cp
  - rm
  - chmod
  - chown
  - iwconfig/ifconfig
  - ps
  - su/sudo
  - apt-get
  - vi
  - dd
  - kill

This chapter focuses on the exam topics related to operating systems. It follows the structure of the CompTIA A+ 220-1002 exam blueprint, objective 1, and it explores the nine subobjectives that you need to master before taking the exam. The Operating Systems domain represents 27 percent of the total exam.

1.1 Compare and contrast common operating system types and their purposes.

While the overwhelming percentage of devices you will come into contact with will be Windows devices, you will also encounter other operating systems. The Linux operating system and the macOS are increasingly found in enterprise networks in situations where their strengths can be leveraged. There are also many other technologies that you may not be directly managing, but you should still be familiar with them and understand their purpose. This chapter will focus on these areas, as well as other operating systems such as those found on smartphones. It covers the following topics:

- 32-bit vs. 64-bit
- Workstation operating systems
- Cell phone/tablet operating systems
- Vendor-specific limitations
- Compatibility concerns between operating systems

32-bit vs. 64-bit

The primary difference between 32-bit and 64-bit computing is the amount of data the processor (CPU) is able to process effectively. To run a 64-bit version of the operating system, you must have a 64-bit processor. To find out whether you are running the 32-bit or 64-bit version of Windows, you can look at the information shown in the System applet in the Control Panel in any of the Windows versions you need to know for this exam.

Other differences between 64-bit and 32-bit systems are their hardware requirements and the types of applications you can run on them. You can run a 32-bit application on either a 64-bit or 32-bit operating system, but you can only run 64-bit applications on a 64-bit system.

RAM limitations

All operating systems have a minimum amount of RAM required to operate. It's not just a matter of functioning well; if you don't have that minimum memory, it won't install! Always consult the documentation to ensure that you meet this requirement.

There is also a maximum amount of memory that an operating system can use, which is also useful to know. There is no use wasting memory in a device in which the operating system simply ignores it. The documentation that comes with the operating system will tell how much memory the system can support.

Software compatibility

Software is written to operate on a specific operating system or systems. For example, if it's written for Windows, it may not work on MacOS. If you intend to use an application, always check to see the operating system(s) it supports, which will be in the documentation. This may even influence the operating system you install.

Workstation operating systems

Workstations are the most common types of devices in our networks. These are the user machines, both laptop and desktops. There are three main operating systems used on workstations, Windows, Apple (MacOS), and Linux.

Microsoft Windows

While there are many Windows operating systems available, this exam asks that you know the intricacies of only four that run on the personal computer: Windows 7, Windows 8, Windows 8.1, and Windows 10. Each will be covered in its own section in this chapter.

Apple Macintosh OS

In your career, you are almost certain to come in contact with the MacOS operating systems (since 2001 the MacOS system has been called OS X, so you may consider those terms interchangeable). Even though these systems constitute only a small percentage of the total number of devices found in enterprise environments, there are certain environments where they dominate and excel such as music and graphics.

Linux

Linux is probably used more often than MacOS in enterprise networks, in part because many proprietary operating systems that reside on devices such as access points, switches, routers, and firewalls are Linux-based. Linux systems also predominate in the software development area.

In this section of the chapter, you will be introduced to some of the common features and functions in these operating systems.

Cell phone/tablet operating systems

Computer operating systems are not the only type of operating system with which you will come into contact. Many tablets, smartphones, and other small devices will have operating systems that are designed to run on devices that have different resource capabilities and therefore require different systems. This section will look at operating systems for such mobile devices.

Microsoft Windows

The Windows operating system, which is the most widely used for desktops and laptops, may also be found on some mobile devices such as smartphones and tablets, but it is not used as widely for these device types as iOS and Android. This is one of the best examples of closed source software.

Android

The Android operating system from Google is built on a Linux kernel with a core set of libraries that are written in Java. It is an open source operating system, which means that developers have full access to the same framework application programming interfaces (APIs) used by the core applications.

iOS

Apple iOS is a vendor-specific system made by Mac for mobile devices. Developers must use the software development kit (SDK) from Apple and register as Apple developers.

Chrome OS

Chrome is another operating system by Google that runs on its Chrome laptop. Based on the Linux kernel, it uses the Chrome browser as an interface. Originally it ran Chrome apps, but now Android apps have been made to run on it.

Vendor-specific limitations

Vendors of operating systems impose certain restrictions and limitations on the support provided to their systems. Two of the more important of these are covered in this section.

End-of-life

Whenever a vendor sets an end-of-life date, it means that after that date they will no longer offer help and support for that product. After that you are on your own regarding errors and troubleshooting.

Update limitations

When Microsoft and possibly other vendors release operating system updates, they sometimes make the update package available only to those who purchased a full copy of the previous version. For example, you can install Windows 10 as an update only if you have a full installation of Windows 8.1; going from Windows 7 to 10, you would pay for a full install. In cases like this, the update package will be cheaper than the full operating system, the idea being to give the customer credit for the purchase of the previous system. Those without the previous system must pay full price for a new installation of the updated operating system.

Compatibility concerns between operating systems

While using a mix of desktop operating systems in an organization is not recommended, you may find yourself in that scenario. If that is the case, you may also find yourself supporting many more applications, as they are specific to the OS, and sometimes even to an OS version such as Windows 7 or Windows 10. Be aware that you may encounter compatibility issues between the systems and between the documents produced by the applications. Always research online about these issues, as someone has probably already solved the issue!

Exam essentials

Describe the major differences between the Android and iOS operating systems.   Android is an open source operating system, and iOS is a vendor-specific system made by Apple. Apps for Android systems can be obtained from Google Play or many other sites, whereas iOS apps are available only on the Apple Store site.

1.2 Compare and contrast features of Microsoft Windows versions.

This section contains numerous tables because of the nature of the information that it covers. It is imperative that you be familiar with Windows 7, Windows 8, Windows 8.1, and Windows 10. Make certain you understand the features available in each of these versions of Windows as well as the editions that were made available for each of them. The topics covered in this section of the chapter are as follows:

- Windows 7
- Windows 8
- Windows 8.1
- Windows 10
- Corporate vs. personal needs
- Desktop styles/user interface

Windows 7

Windows 7 was released in 2009, much to the delight of many users who were dissatisfied with Windows Vista. It has had one service pack and is still widely used even though three operating system versions have been released since. It comes in six editions, each of which differs in requirements and capabilities.

Table 6.1 shows the available editions and their hardware requirements.

TABLE 6.1 Windows 7 editions

Features	Starter	Home Basic	Home Premium	Professional	Enterprise	Ultimate
Licensing scheme	OEM licensing	Retail and OEM	Licensing scheme	OEM licensing	Retail and OEM	Licensing scheme
Maximum physical memory (RAM) (32-bit)	2 GB	4 GB	4 GB	4 GB	4 GB	4 GB
Maximum physical memory (RAM) (64-bit)	N/A	8 GB	16 GB	192 GB	192 GB	192 GB
Maximum physical CPUs supported	1	1	1	2	2	2

Windows 8

Windows 8 was released in 2012 and was never fully embraced. Many corporate teams skipped from Windows 7 to Windows 10. Among the chief complaints about Windows 8 were the confusing Start screen and the new Metro desktop. Sometimes it's not good to shake things up too soon.

Table 6.2 shows the editions of Windows 8 and their hardware requirements.

TABLE 6.2   Windows 8 editions

Features	Windows RT	Windows 8 (Core)	Windows 8 Pro	Windows 8 Enterprise
Availability	Pre-installed on devices	Most channels	Most channels	Volume License customers
Architecture	ARM (32-bit)	IA-32 (32-bit) or x64 (64-bit)	IA-32 (32-bit) or x64 (64-bit)	IA-32 (32-bit) or x64 (64-bit)
Maximum physical memory (RAM)	4 GB	128 GB on x64 4 GB on IA-32	512 GB on x64 4 GB on IA-32	512 GB on x64 4 GB on IA-32

Windows 8.1

Released a year after its predecessor, Windows 8.1 expanded functionality available to apps compared to Windows 8, but still was avoided because of the new interface. It did introduce OneDrive integration and added expanded tutorials for the new interface (to no avail).

The following are hardware requirement for Windows 8.1:

- **Processor:** 1 gigahertz (GHz) or faster with support for physical address extension (PAE), NX, and Streaming SIMD Extensions 2 (SSE2)
- **RAM:** 1 gigabyte (GB) (32-bit) or 2 GB (64-bit)
- **Hard disk space:** 16 GB (32-bit) or 20 GB (64-bit)
- **Graphics card:** Microsoft DirectX 9 graphics device with WDDM driver

Windows 10

It seems that Microsoft has fallen into a pattern of succeeding with every other version number as Windows 10 has been a success. In May 2018 it did undergo an update that seems to cause no major issues. Windows 10 supports universal apps, which are those designed to run across multiple platforms. Its interface is friendly to both the mouse and touchscreen navigation. The movement away from the tablet look in Windows 8 has been well received.

The following are hardware requirements for Windows 10:

- **Processor:** 1 GHz or faster processor or SoC
- **RAM:** 1 (GB) for 32-bit or 2 GB for 64-bit
- **Hard disk space:** 16 GB for 32-bit OS 20 GB for 64-bit OS
- **Graphics card:** DirectX 9 or later with WDDM 1.0 driver
- **Display:** 800×600

Corporate vs. personal needs

There are features present in Windows that cater to personal needs, while others are more relevant to the corporate environment. In this section we'll look at a few of these features.

Domain access

Not all editions of Windows can join a domain. Home editions cannot, while Professional and Enterprise editions can. To join a Windows 7/8/10 computer to a domain, do the following:

1. Navigate to Start ➤ Control Panel ➤ System And Security ➤ System ➤ Advanced System Settings. In the Control Panel's Category view, you can simply select System.

2. Click the Computer Name tab and click the Change button.

3. Select the Domain radio button and enter the name of the domain.

4. Click OK, and the join process will start.

Bitlocker

BitLocker allows you to use drive encryption to protect files—including those needed for startup and logon. This is available with the Ultimate and Enterprise editions of Windows 7 and the Pro and Enterprise editions of Windows 8, 8.1, and 10. For removable drives, BitLocker To Go provides the same encryption technology to help prevent unauthorized access to the files stored on them.

Media center

Media Center is one of the features that will probably be used more at home. It is a digital video recorder and media player created by Microsoft. Media Center was first introduced to Windows in 2002. It was discontinued after Windows 7 and available as a paid add-on in Windows 8 and 8.1. It is not available in Windows 10.

Branchcache

BranchCache is a bandwidth-optimization feature that started with Windows 7. Each client has a cache and acts as an alternate source for content requested by devices on its own network. There are two modes, Hosted Cache and Distributed. In Hosted Cache mode, designated servers act as a cache for files requested by clients in its area. In Distributed mode, each client contains a cached version of the BranchCache-enabled files it has requested and received, and it acts as a distributed cache for other clients requesting that same file.

EFS

The Encrypting File System (EFS) is an encryption tool built into Windows 7, and Windows 8 or 8.1 Professional or Enterprise. (EFS is not fully supported on Windows 7 Starter, Windows 7 Home Basic, and Windows 7 Home Premium or Windows 10 editions.) It allows a user to encrypt files that can be decrypted only by the user who encrypted the files. It can be used only on NTFS volumes but is simple to use.

To encrypt a file in Windows 8.1, simply right-click the file, access the file's properties, and on the General tab click the Advanced button. That will open the Advanced Attributes dialog box, as shown in Figure 6.1. On this page, select the Encrypt Contents To Secure Data box.

FIGURE 6.1 Advanced Attributes dialog box

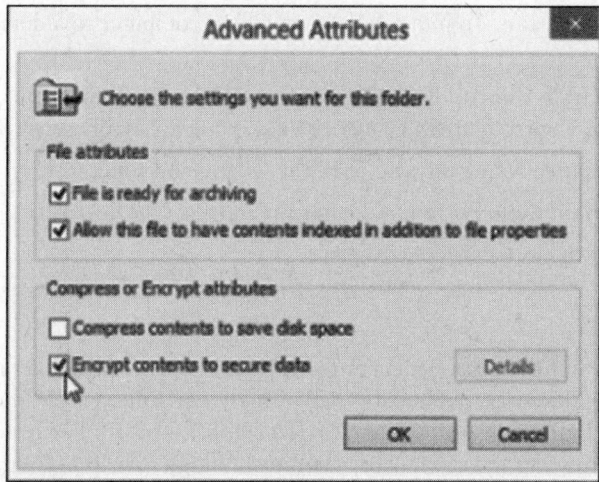

Desktop styles/user interface

Desktop styles or interfaces have changed slightly from Windows 7 to Windows 10. The following are some of the features of the interfaces.

Aero

The Aero interface offers a glass design that includes translucent windows. It was new with Windows Vista. It requires a graphics card with DirectX 9 graphics with 128 MB RAM to functions and can be enabled in Control Panel.

Gadgets

These are mini programs, introduced with Windows Vista, that can be placed on the desktop (Windows 7), allowing them to run quickly and letting you personalize the PC (clock, weather, and so on). Windows 7 renamed these Windows Desktop Gadgets (right-click the desktop and click Gadgets in the context menu; then double-click the one you want to add). In 2011, Microsoft announced it is no longer supporting the development or uploading of new gadgets. No operating system after Windows 7 supports Gadgets.

XP Mode as a VM?

You can also install an XP mode virtual machine using these instructions:

https://www.download3k.com/articles/How-to-add-an-XP-Mode-Virtual-Machine-to-Windows-10-or-8-using-Hyper-V-00770

Side-by-side apps

Windows 8.1 and 10 allow you to run a Metro application (also called at various times Tileworld apps and modern apps; these are apps you get at the Windows Store) and a desktop application at the same time, or up to four Metro apps at the same time, which on other devices such as a smartphone may not be possible.

To do this, you must split the screen into two parts, which can be done in two ways.

- If you have a keyboard, you can press Windows+< or Windows+>. The current app's window is now shoved to the left or right side. When you open a second app (from the Start screen or the app switcher), it fills the newly opened space.

- You can also drag the left edge of an open app and divide the screen.

Metro UI

In Windows 8.1, the user interface is different from earlier versions of Windows. The Start menu was removed, and the desktop replaced with a new look called Metro. This look resembles the interface of a smartphone or tablet and represents the Microsoft vision of a common interface on all devices. Information, settings, and applications are housed in *tiles*. Figure 6.2 shows this look.

FIGURE 6.2   The Windows 8.1 Metro or Start screen

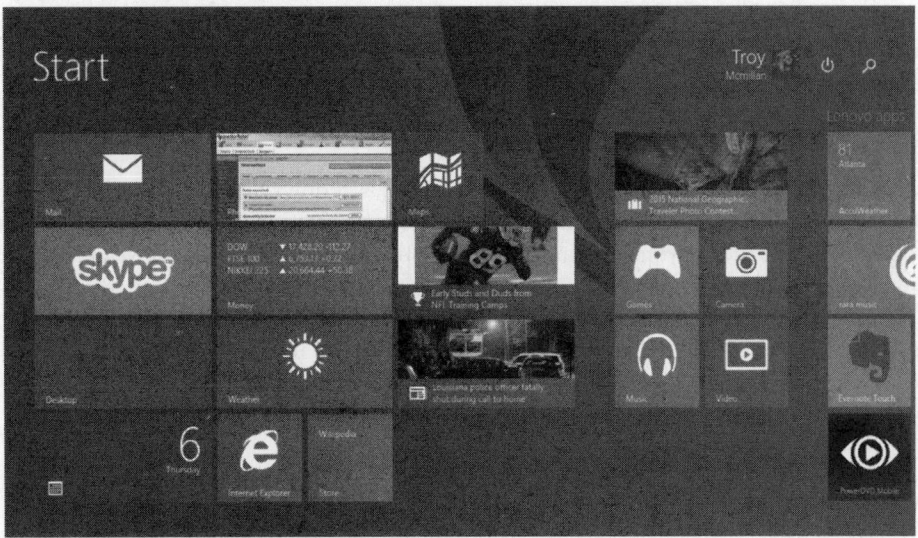

This look received negative reactions from most desktop and laptop users and more positive reactions from those raised on the smartphone interface. Microsoft reacted by changing the name of the look to the Microsoft design language. While there were rumors of a return to the Start menu, Microsoft made the classic Start menu available in Windows 8.1 but by default stuck to its guns and continued to use a Start screen rather than a Start menu. (The Start screen is covered in the "Start screen" section.)

Pinning

Pinning is the process of configuring an icon for a program on the taskbar so that it is easier to locate. It was introduced in Windows 7 and continued in Windows 8, 8.1, and 10, and for frequently used applications, it saves navigating through the Start menu or Start screen to locate the application.

To pin the program to the taskbar in Windows 7, do one of the following:

- If the program is running, right-click the program's button on the taskbar (or drag the button toward the desktop) to open the program's Jump List and then click Pin This Program To Taskbar.

- If the program is not running, click Start, find the program's icon, right-click the icon, and then click Pin To Taskbar.

To pin the program to the taskbar in Windows 8, 8.1, and 10, follow these steps:

1. Point to the lower-right corner of the screen, move the mouse pointer up, and then click Search. On a touchscreen device, swipe in from the right edge of the screen and then tap Search.

2. Enter the name of the program in the search box.

3. In the search results, right-click Internet Explorer and then click Pin To Taskbar.

Prior to Windows 8, if you set up multiple monitors, you could have the taskbar only on the primary monitor, which meant you had to go back to that monitor (which may not be where you are currently engaged) to access the taskbar. In Windows 8 and 8.1, you can now have your taskbar on all monitors by selecting the option in the properties of the taskbar, as shown in Figure 6.3.

Charms

Charms are a bit like icons and were introduced with Windows 8 and the Metro UI. They are organized on a Charms bar that will appear on the right side of the screen when invoked. With the mouse you bring up the bar by moving the cursor into the right corner of the desktop; on a touchscreen, you swipe from the right edge toward the center.

There are five charms there that are like doors to other lists of options. The five charms are Search, Share, Start, Devices, and Settings. The Start charm simply opens the Start screen, which replaces the Start menu. Figure 6.4 shows the Charms bar.

FIGURE 6.3   Enabling the multimonitor taskbar

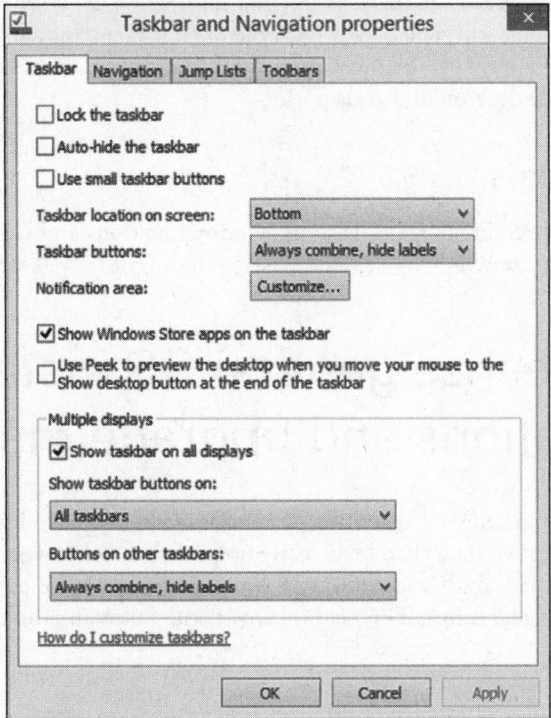

FIGURE 6.4   The Windows 8 Charms bar

Start screen

One of the more controversial changes to the user interface with Windows 8 and 8.1 was removing the Start menu and replacing it with the Start screen. Shown in Figure 6.2 earlier, this is the screen that appears to be the future of all Windows operating systems, despite the resistance of many desktop and laptop users.

Exam essentials

Identify the hardware requirements of various Windows editions and versions.   These include all editions of the Windows 7, Windows 8, Windows 8.1, and Windows 10 versions.

1.3 Summarize general OS installation considerations and upgrade methods.

When installing or upgrading an operating system, it is important to know what is possible and what is not. Not all systems can be directly upgraded to the newest version. Some must be completely reinstalled. In this section, we'll look at some possible upgrade paths and other installation considerations. This section covers the following topics:

- Boot methods
- Types of installations
- Partitioning
- File system types/formatting
- Load alternate third-party drivers when necessary
- Workgroup vs. domain setup
- Time/date/region/language settings
- Driver installation, software, and Windows updates
- Factory recovery partition
- Properly formatted boot drive with the correct partitions/format
- Prerequisites/hardware compatibility
- Application compatibility
- OS compatibility/upgrade path

Upgrade paths

There are several things to be aware of regarding upgrade paths, including the differences between in-place upgrades, the available compatibility tools, and the Windows Upgrade Advisor.

Differences between in-place upgrades

One Windows operating system can often be upgraded to another, if compatible. With the case of Windows 7, it is even possible to upgrade from one edition of the operating system to another. When you are faced with a scenario in which you cannot upgrade, you can always do a clean installation. There's one more thing to consider when evaluating installation methods. Some methods work only if you're performing a clean installation and not an upgrade.

Table 6.3 lists the minimum system requirements, which are the same for the various editions of Windows 7.

TABLE 6.3 Windows 7 minimum hardware

Hardware	Minimum supported for all editions of Windows 7
Processor	1 GHz
Memory	1 GB for 32-bit; 2 GB for 64-bit
Free hard disk space	16 GB free for 32-bit; 20 GB free for 64-bit
CD-ROM or DVD	DVD-ROM
Video	DirectX 9 with WDDM 1.0 (or higher) driver
Mouse	Required (but not listed as a requirement)
Keyboard	Required (but not listed as a requirement)
Internet access	Not listed as a requirement

Table 6.4 lists the minimum system requirements for Windows 8, and Table 6.5 lists the minimum system requirements for Windows 8.1. Table 6.6 lists the minimum system requirements for Windows 10.

TABLE 6.4 Windows 8 minimum hardware

Hardware	Minimum supported for all editions of Windows 8
Processor	1 GHz with support for PAE, NX, and SSE
Memory	1 GB for 32-bit; 2 GB for 64-bit
Free hard disk space	16 GB free for 32-bit; 20 GB free for 64-bit
CD-ROM or DVD	DVD-ROM
Video	DirectX 9 with WDDM 1.0 (or higher) driver

TABLE 6.5   Windows 8.1 minimum hardware

Hardware	Minimum supported for all editions of Windows 8.1
Processor	1 GHz with support for PAE, NX and SSE
Memory	1 GB for 32-bit; 2 GB for 64-bit
Free hard disk space	16 GB free for 32-bit; 20 GB free for 64-bit
CD-ROM or DVD	DVD-ROM
Video	DirectX 9 with WDDM 1.0 (or higher) driver

TABLE 6.6   Windows 10 minimum hardware

Hardware	Minimum supported for all editions of Windows 10
Processor	1 GHz with support for PAE, NX, and SSE
Memory	1 GB for 32-bit; 2 GB for 64-bit
Free hard disk space	16 GB free for 32-bit; 20 GB free for 64-bit
CD-ROM or DVD	DVD-ROM
Video	DirectX 9 with WDDM 1.0 (or higher) driver

If there is one thing to be learned from Tables 6.3 through 6.6, it is that Microsoft is nothing if not optimistic. For your own sanity, though, I strongly suggest you always take the minimum requirements with a grain of salt. They are minimums. Even the recommended requirements should be considered minimums. Bottom line: Make sure you have a good margin between your system's performance and the minimum requirements listed. Always run Windows on more hardware rather than less!

Certain features in Windows 7 have further hardware requirements that are listed here:

http://windows.microsoft.com/en-US/windows7/products/
system-requirements

The easiest way to see whether your current hardware can run Windows 7 is to download and run the Windows 7 Upgrade Advisor available here:

http://windows.microsoft.com/en-us/windows/downloads/upgrade-advisor

You can also always check hardware in the Windows 7 Compatibility Center here:

www.microsoft.com/windows/compatibility/windows-7/en-us/default.aspx

Upgrading to Windows 7

If you want to do an upgrade instead of a clean installation, review the upgrade options in Table 6.7 (it is worth pointing out again that a "No" does not mean you can't buy the Windows 7 upgrade but rather that you can't keep your files, programs, and settings).

TABLE 6.7 Windows 7 upgrade options

Existing operating system	Windows 7 Home Premium 32-bit	Windows 7 Home Premium 64-bit	Windows 7 Professional 32-bit	Windows 7 Professional 64-bit	Windows 7 Ultimate 32-bit	Windows 7 Ultimate 64-bit
Windows XP	No	No	No	No	No	No
Windows Vista Starter 32-bit	No	No	No	No	No	No
Windows Vista Starter 64-bit	No	No	No	No	No	No
Windows Vista Home Basic 32-bit	Yes	No	No	No	Yes	No
Windows Vista Home Basic 64-bit	No	Yes	No	No	No	Yes
Windows Vista Home Premium 32-bit	Yes	No	No	No	Yes	No
Windows Vista Home Premium 64-bit	No	Yes	No	No	No	Yes
Windows Vista Business 32-bit	No	No	Yes	No	Yes	No
Windows Vista Business 64-bit	No	No	No	Yes	No	Yes
Windows Vista Ultimate 32-bit	No	No	No	No	Yes	No
Windows Vista Ultimate 64-bit	No	No	No	No	No	Yes

The Enterprise editions play by different rules since they are licensed directly from Microsoft. In the case of Windows 7, both Windows Vista Business and Windows Vista Enterprise can be upgraded to Windows 7 Enterprise.

Those operating systems not listed in Table 6.7 do not include any upgrade options to Windows 7 and cannot be done with upgrade packages (you must buy the full version of Windows 7). An easy way to remember upgrade options for the exam is that you must have at least Windows Vista to be able to upgrade to Windows 7. In the real world, the Windows Vista machine should be running Service Pack 1 at a minimum, and you can always take an earlier OS and upgrade it to Vista SP1 and then upgrade to Windows 7.

As of this writing, Service Pack 1 is the latest available for Windows 7, the Windows 8.1 upgrade is the latest for Windows 8, and there is no service pack for Windows 8.1. You can find the latest here:

http://windows.microsoft.com/en-US/windows/downloads/
service-packs

In the past, all service packs used to be cumulative—meaning you needed to load only the last one. Starting with XP SP3, however, all Windows service packs released have been incremental, meaning that you must install the previous ones before you can install the new one.

Microsoft created the Windows 7 Upgrade Advisor to help with the upgrade to this operating system. You can download the advisor from http://windows.microsoft.com/upgradeadvisor. It will scan your hardware, devices, and installed programs for any known compatibility issues. Once it is finished, it will give you advice on how to resolve the issues found and recommendations on what to do before you upgrade. The reports are divided into three categories: System Requirements, Devices, and Programs.

Upgrade Advisor

Other versions of Windows also have Upgrade Advisors!

After all incompatibilities have been addressed, the upgrade can be started from an installation disc or from a download (preferably to a USB drive). If the setup routine does not begin immediately on boot, look for the setup.exe file and run it. When the Install Windows page appears, click Install Now.

You'll be asked if you want to get any updates (recommended) and to agree to the license agreement. After you've done so, choose Upgrade for the installation type and follow the steps to walk through the remainder of the installation. I highly recommend that after the installation is complete, you run Windows Update to get the latest drivers.

NOTE

New to Windows 7 was the ability to upgrade at any time from one edition of the operating system to a higher one (for example, from Home Premium to Professional) using the Windows Anytime Upgrade utility in the System And Security section of the Control Panel (it can also be accessed by clicking the Start button and choosing All Programs; scroll down the list and choose Windows Anytime Upgrade).

Upgrading to Windows 8

With Windows 8 you can upgrade based on the operating system that you are coming from. Table 6.8 lists the upgrade paths for each Windows 8 edition based on the operating system you are coming from. Those listed as "No" must be clean installations.

It's worth mentioning that there is a version called RT that has been discontinued. It was for tablets.

TABLE 6.8   Upgrade paths for Windows 8

Existing operating system	Windows 8	Windows 8 Pro	Windows 8 Enterprise
Windows 7 Starter	Yes	Yes	No
Windows 7 Home Basic	Yes	Yes	No
Windows 7 Home Premium	Yes	Yes	No
Windows 7 Professional	No	Yes	No
Windows 7 Ultimate	No	Yes	No
Windows 7 Pro (volume licensed)	No	No	Yes
Windows 7 Enterprise (volume licensed)	No	No	Yes
Windows 8 (volume licensed)	No	No	Yes

Upgrading to Windows 8.1

With Windows 8.1 you can upgrade based on the operating system that you are coming from. Table 6.9 lists the upgrade paths for each Windows 8.1 edition based on the operating system you are coming from. Those listed as "No" must be clean installations.

Although not in the table you can also upgrade Windows 7 to Windows 8.1 as well.

TABLE 6.9 Upgrade paths for Windows 8.1

Existing operating system	Windows 8.1	Windows 8.1 Pro	Windows 8.1 Enterprise
Windows 8	Yes	Yes	No
Windows 8 Pro	No	Yes	Yes
Windows 8 Pro with Media Center	No	Yes	Yes
Windows 8.1	No	Yes	No
Windows 8 Enterprise	No	No	No
Windows 8.1 Pro	No	No	Yes

Upgrading to Windows 10

With Windows 10, the in-place upgrade is now a first-class deployment option and is now the preferred approach for Windows 10 deployment—even in enterprises. It allows Windows 10 installations to be initiated from within the existing Windows 7 or newer OS.

Windows Upgrade OS Advisor

The Windows Upgrade Advisor from Microsoft can be useful in any upgrade process. It will check your system, verify that it can run the desired operating system, and give you a report of any identified compatibility issues. There are versions under various names for Windows 7, Windows 8, Windows 8.1, and Windows 10.

Compatibility tools

Several features are available to enhance the compatibility of the operating system with the applications you are running. First there is the Windows Compatibility Center, a site you can access that will scan your device for compatible device drivers, app updates, and downloads. You just enter the name of the program, and it will tell you whether it is supported; if you need a driver or an update, it will provide it.

Running the application in a compatibility mode that supports it can make the application work. Simply right-click the program file and choose Run In Compatibility Mode and then select an operating system that supports the application.

In some cases, it may not be possible to use an application without creating a *shim*, which is a small piece of software that communicates between the unsupported application and the operating system. This is done with an Application Compatibility toolkit. There are such toolkits for Windows 7, Windows 8, Windows 8.1, and Windows 10. Their use is beyond the scope of this book.

Boot methods

You can begin the installation or upgrade process by booting from a number of sources. There are eight in particular that CompTIA wants you to be familiar with:

- USB
- CD-ROM
- DVD
- PXE
- Solid-state or flash drives
- NetBoot
- External/hot swappable drives
- Internal hard drives

USB

Most systems will allow you to boot from a USB device, but you must often change the BIOS settings to look for USB first. Using a large USB drive, you can store all the necessary installation files on the one device and save the time needed to swap media.

CD-ROM

The option most commonly used for an attended installation is the CD-ROM/DVD boot (they are identical). Since Windows 7 and newer come only on DVD, though, CD-ROM applies to older operating systems and not this one.

DVD

A DVD boot is the most common method of starting an installation.

PXE

Booting the computer from the network without using a local device creates a *Preboot Execution Environment* (PXE). Once it is up, it is common to load the Windows Preinstallation Environment (WinPE) into RAM as a stub operating system and install the operating system image to the hard drive.

WinPE can be installed onto a bootable CD, USB, or network drive using the copype.cmd command. This environment can be used in conjunction with a Windows deployment from a server for unattended installations.

Solid state/flash drives

If boot files and installation files are located on a solid-state drive or flash drive and the device is set to look on those drives for boot files, you can boot from these devices and install the operating system in the same way that you boot from a CD or DVD drive.

Netboot

NetBoot is a method developed by Apple that allows an Apple device to boot from a network location rather than from the hard drive. The device uses Dynamic Host Configuration Protocol (DHCP) to receive a network configuration and to receive the IP address of a Trivial File Transport protocol (TFTP) server from which the device will download an operating system image from a server. This entire process is similar to the way an IP phone learns through DHCP the IP address of the server from which it downloads its configuration file.

External/hot-swappable drive

Just as boot files can be located on a USB drive, CD, DVD, and flash drive, they can also be located on an external hard drive. Most of these drives are also hot-swappable (you can connect and remove them with the devices on). As always, you will probably have to alter the boot order of the device so that it looks on the external drive before the other drives if boot files are also located in these locations.

Internal hard drive (partition)

Finally, the most common location of boot files is on the internal hard drive. These files are placed there during the installation and will be executed as long as the device is set to look for them there. By default most systems are set to look on the internal hard drive first, and even if the device is not set to look there first, it will eventually boot to those files if there are no boot files located on any of the other drives or boot sources.

Types of installations

Operating system installations can be lumped into two generic methods: attended or unattended. During an attended installation, you walk through the installation and answer the questions as prompted. Questions typically ask for the product key, the directory in which you want to install the OS, and relevant network settings.

As simple as attended installations may be, they're time-consuming and administrator-intensive in that they require someone to fill in a fair number of fields to move through the process. Unattended installations allow you to configure the OS with little or no human intervention. Table 6.10 shows you four common unattended installation methods and when they can be used.

TABLE 6.10   Windows unattended installation methods

Method	Clean installation	Upgrade
Unattended Install	Yes	Yes
Bootable media	Yes	No
Sysprep	Yes	No
Remote install	Yes	No

Another decision you must make is which method you are going to use to access the Windows installation files. It is possible to boot to the installation DVD and begin the installation process. However, your system must have a system BIOS that is capable of supporting bootable media.

If you don't have a bootable DVD, you must first boot the computer using some other bootable media, which then loads the disk driver so that you can access the installation program on the DVD.

Unattended installation

Answering the myriad of questions posed by Windows Setup doesn't qualify as exciting work for most people. Fortunately, there is a way to answer the questions automatically: through an unattended installation. In this type of installation, an *answer file* is supplied with all the correct parameters (time zone, regional settings, administrator username, and so on), so no one needs to be there to tell the computer what to choose or to hit Next 500 times.

Unattended installations are great because they can be used to upgrade operating systems. The first step is to create an answer file. This XML file, which must be named unattend.xml, contains configuration settings specific to the computer on which you are installing the OS, which means that for every installation the answer file will be unique. See the following for details on these settings:

https://docs.microsoft.com/en-us/windows-hardware/manufacture/desktop/
update-windows-settings-and-scripts-create-your-own-answer-file-sxs

Generally speaking, you'll want to run a test installation using that answer file first before deploying it on a large scale because you'll probably need to make some tweaks to it. After you create your answer file, place it on a network share that will be accessible from the target computer. (Most people put it in the same place as the Windows installation files for convenience.)

Boot the computer that you want to install on using a boot disk or CD, and establish the network connection. Once you start the setup process, everything should run automatically.

In-place upgrade

An upgrade involves moving from one operating system to another and keeping as many of the settings as possible. An example of an upgrade would be changing the operating system on a laptop computer from Windows Vista to Windows 7 and keeping the user accounts that existed.

It is also possible to upgrade from one edition of an operating system to another— for example, from Windows 7 Professional to Windows 7 Ultimate. This is known as a Windows 7 *Anytime Upgrade*.

To begin the upgrade, insert the DVD, and the Setup program should automatically begin (if it doesn't, run setup.exe from the root folder). From the menu that appears, choose Install Now and then select Upgrade when the Which type Of Installation Do You Want? screen appears. Answer the prompts to walk through the upgrade.

Booting from the DVD is also possible but recommended only if the method just described does not work. When you boot, you will get a message upon startup that says Press Any Key To Boot From CD, and at this point you simply press a key. (Don't worry that it is a DVD and not a CD.)

Clean install

With a clean installation, you delete the volume where the old operating system existed and place a new one there. An example of a clean installation would be changing the operating system on a laptop from Windows 8 to Windows 10. The user accounts and other settings that existed with Windows 8 would be removed in the process and need to be re-created under Windows 10.

Repair installation

A repair installation overwrites system files with a copy of new ones from the same operating system version and edition. For example, a laptop running Windows 7 is hanging on boot, and the cause is traced to a corrupted system file. A repair installation can replace that corrupted file with a new one (from the DVD or other source) without changing the operating system or settings (for configuration, accounts, and so on).

Multiboot

Multiple operating systems can exist on the same machine in one of two popular formats: in a multiboot configuration or in virtual machines. With a multiboot configuration, when you boot the machine, you choose which operating system you want to load of those that are installed. You could, for example, boot into Windows 10, reboot and bring up Windows 7, reboot and bring up Windows 8, and test a software application you've created in each OS. It is possible in this scenario to have multiple editions of the same OS installed (Professional, Ultimate, and so forth) and choose which to boot into in order to test your application. The key to this configuration, however, is that you can have only one operating system running at a time.

Each installation should have its own folder. Make sure you don't install into a folder that already contains an OS or you will overwrite it.

An alternative to multiboot that has become more popular in recent years is to run virtual machines. You could boot into Windows 7, for example, and run a virtual machine of Windows 10 and one of Windows 8 and test your application in the three environments that are all running at the same time.

Remote network installation

Older Windows Server operating systems have a feature called Remote Installation Service (RIS), which allows you to perform several network installations at one time. Beginning with Windows Server 2003 SP2, RIS was replaced by Windows Deployment Service (WDS). This utility offers the same functionality as RIS.

A *network installation* is handy when you have many installs to do and installing by CD is too much work. In a network installation, the installation CD is copied to a shared location on the network. Then individual workstations boot and access the network share. The workstations can boot either through a boot disk or through a built-in network boot device known as a PXE ROM. Boot ROMs essentially download a small file that contains an OS and network drivers and has enough information to boot the computer in a limited fashion. At the least, it can boot the computer so it can access the network share and begin the installation.

Creating an image

Creating an image isn't actually an objective, but it is something important that you'll need to know how to do in the real world. Creating an image involves taking a snapshot of a model system (often called a *reference computer*) and then applying it to other systems (see the section "Image deployment" later). A number of third-party vendors offer packages that can be used to create images, and you can use the system preparation tool, or *Sysprep*. The Sysprep utility works by making an exact image or replica of the reference computer (sometimes also called the *master computer*) to be installed on other computers. Sysprep removes the master computer's security ID (a process sometimes called *generalization*) and will generate new IDs for each computer where the image is used to install.

All Sysprep does is create the system image. You still need a cloning utility to copy the image to other computers.

Perhaps the biggest caveat to using Sysprep is that because you are making an exact image of an installed computer (including drivers and settings), all the computers that you will be installing the image on need to be identical (or close) to the configuration of the master computer. Otherwise, you would have to go through and fix driver problems on every installed computer. Sysprep images can be installed across a network or copied to a CD or DVD for local installation. Sysprep cannot be used to upgrade a system; plan on all data on the system (if there is any) being lost after a format.

Similar to Sysprep, ImageX is the preferred command-line utility for imaging Windows 7 and other version of Windows . You can find more information about it at http://technet.microsoft.com/en-us/library/cc722145(v=ws.10).

Several third-party vendors provide similar services, and you'll often hear the process referred to as *disk imaging* or *drive imaging*. The third-party utility makes the image, and then the image file is transferred to the computer without an OS. You boot the new system with the imaging software and start the image download. The new system's disk drive is made into an exact sector-by-sector copy of the original system.

Imaging has major upsides. The biggest one is speed. In larger networks with multiple new computers, you can configure tens to hundreds of computers by using imaging in just hours, rather than the days it would take to individually install the OS, applications, and drivers.

Image deployment

System images created with Sysprep and other tools can be deployed for installation on hosts across the network. The Windows Automated Installation Kit (AIK) can be useful for this purpose (http://technet.microsoft.com/library/dd349348.aspx).

Recovery partition

In the past, many devices that were purchased with the operating system installed by the OEM came with recovery media that could be used to boot the device and recover or replace the operating system if needed. Now many come with an additional partition on the drive called a *recovery partition*. The users could use a specific key sequence during bootup that would cause the device to boot to the recovery partition and make available tools to either recover the installation or replace it. The downside of this approach is that if the hard drive fails or if the partition is overwritten, the recovery partition is useless. In an effort to address this concern, many OEMs now make available recovery media if requested by the user.

Refresh/restore/reset

Windows 8, 8.1, and 10 offer three methods of dealing with a device that either won't boot, is corrupted, or is simply performing badly. These three options are refresh, restore, and reset; and it is critical that you understand the consequences of each. When a refresh is performed, the user's data is unaffected, while the operating system is returned to the factory default state. Although the data remains intact, any applications or programs that the user installed will be gone. All default applications that come with the system will remain, and any purchased from the Windows Store will remain as well. When a restore is performed, the system is restored to a point in time in the past. It removes no user data, but any configuration changes made or programs and service packs installed since that point in time will be gone. Finally, the third and most drastic option is the reset, which removes all data and programs and reinstalls a fresh copy of the operating system.

Partitioning

For a hard disk to be able to hold files and programs, it has to be partitioned and formatted. Partitioning is the process of creating logical divisions on a hard drive. A hard drive can have one or more partitions. Formatting is the process of creating and configuring a file allocation table (FAT) and creating the root directory. Several file system types are supported by the various versions of Windows, such as FAT16, FAT32, and NTFS (partitions are explored later in the discussion of disk management).

The partition that the operating system boots from must be designated as *active*. Only one partition on a disk may be marked active. Each hard disk can be divided into a total of four partitions, either four primary partitions or three primary and one extended partition. Some of the other possibilities are examined in the following sections.

Dynamic

Partitions can be made dynamic, which—as the name implies—means they can be configured and reconfigured on the fly. The big benefits they offer are that they can increase in size (without reformatting) and can span multiple physical disks. Dynamic partitions can be simple, spanned, or striped.

Dynamic partitions that are simple are similar to primary partitions and logical drives (which exist on basic partitions, discussed next). This is often the route you choose when you have only one dynamic disk and want the ability to change allocated space as needed.

Choosing spanned partitions means that you want space from a number of disks (up to 32) to appear as a single logical volume to users. A minimum of two disks must be used, and no fault tolerance is provided by this option.

Striped partitions are similar to spanned in that multiple disks are used, but the big difference is that data is written (in fixed-size stripes) across the disk set in order to increase I/O performance. Although read operations are faster, a concern is that if one disk fails, none of the data is retrievable (like Spanned, the Striped option provides no fault tolerance).

Basic

With basic storage, Windows drives can be partitioned with *primary* or *logical* partitions. Basic partitions are a fixed size and are always on a single physical disk. This is the simplest storage solution and has been the traditional method of storing data for many years.

You can change the size of primary and logical drives by *extending* them into additional space on the same disk. You can create up to four partitions on a basic disk, either four primary or three primary and one extended.

Primary

A primary partition contains the boot files for an operating system. In older days, the operating system had to also be on that partition, but with the Windows versions you need to know for this exam, the OS files can be elsewhere as long as the boot files are in that primary partition.

Primary partitions cannot be further subdivided.

Extended

Extended partitions differ from primary in that they can be divided into one or more logical drives, each of which can be assigned a drive letter.

Logical

In reality, all partitions are logical in the sense that they don't necessarily correspond to one physical disk. One disk can have several logical divisions (partitions). A logical partition is any partition that has a drive letter.

> Sometimes, you will also hear of a logical partition as one that spans multiple physical disks. For example, a network drive that you know as drive H might actually be located on several physical disks on a server. To the user, all that is seen is one drive, or H.

GPT

Devices that use the Unified Extensible Firmware Interface (UEFI) specification (discussed in the section "BIOS/UEFI settings" in Chapter 3, "Hardware") instead of a BIOS also use a partitioning standard called GUID Partition Table (GPT). Since 2010, most operating systems support this and using a master boot record (MBR), which is the alternative method of booting to a legacy BIOS firmware interface. Today, almost all operating systems support it, and many *only* support booting from a GPT rather than from an MBR.

Moreover, GPT is also used on some BIOS systems because of the limitations of MBR partition tables, which was the original driver for the development of UEFI and GPT. MBR works with disks up to 2 TB in size, but it can't handle larger disks. MBR also supports only up to four primary partitions, so to have more than four, you had to make one of your primary partitions an "extended partition" and create logical partitions inside it. GPT removes both of these limitations. It allows up to 128 partitions on a GPT drive.

File system types/formatting

New Technology File System (NTFS) is available with all the versions of Windows you need to know for the exam, but all versions also recognize and support FAT16 and FAT32. The file table for the NTFS is called the Master File Table (MFT).

This section lists the major file systems and the differences among them.

ExFAT

Extended File Allocation Table (exFAT) is a Microsoft file system optimized for flash drives. It is proprietary and has also been adopted by the SD Card Association as the default file system for SDXC cards larger than 32 GB. The proprietary nature and licensing requirements make this file system difficult to use in any open source or commercial software. This file system is supported in Windows 7, Windows 8, Windows 8.1, and Windows 10.

FAT32

FAT, which stands for File Allocation Table, is an acronym for the file on a file system used to keep track of where files are. It's also the name given to this type of file system, introduced in 1981. The largest FAT disk partition that could be created was approximately 2 GB. FAT32 was introduced along with Windows 95 OEM Service Release 2. As disk sizes grew, so did the need to be able to format a partition larger than 2 GB. FAT32 was based more on VFAT than on FAT16. It allowed for 32-bit cluster addressing, which in turn provided for a maximum partition size of 2 TB (2048 GB). It also included smaller cluster sizes to avoid wasted space. FAT32 support is included in current Windows versions.

NTFS

Introduced along with Windows NT (and available on Windows 7, Windows 8, Windows 8.1, and Windows 10), NT File System (NTFS) is a much more advanced file system in almost every way than all versions of the FAT file system. It includes such features as individual file security and *compression*, RAID support, and support for extremely large file and partition sizes and disk transaction monitoring. It is the file system of choice for higher-performance computing. Finally, it supports both file compression and file encryption.

CDFS

While not a file system that can be used on a hard drive, CD-ROM File System (CDFS) is the file system of choice for CD media and has been used with 32-bit Windows versions since Windows 95. A CD mounted with the CDFS driver appears as a collection.

NFS

Network File System (NFS) is a distributed file system protocol originally developed by Sun Microsystems. While it is supported on some Windows systems, it is primarily used on Unix-based systems; the SMB-based Common Internet File System (CIFS) is more common on Windows systems for access to resources on other devices. To support NFS, Windows systems make available the client for NFS. While the client for NFS is available in Windows 7, the Services for the Network File System (NFS) feature is available only in the Windows 8 Enterprise edition. This feature is not available in Windows 8 and Windows 8 Pro editions. It is available in Windows 10.

ext3, ext4

ext3 and ext4 are Linux file systems. While ext4 has the following advantages, it should be noted that it is not compatible with Windows, while ext3 is. The following are the strengths of ext4:

- It supports individual file sizes up to 16 TB (16 GB for ext3).
- The overall maximum ext4 file system size is 1 EB (exabyte); 1 EB = 1024 PB (petabyte), and 1 PB = 1024 TB (terabyte) (32 TB limit for ext3).
- The directory can contain 64,000 subdirectories as opposed to 32,000 in ext3.
- You can mount an existing ext3 fs as ext4 fs (without having to upgrade it).
- It improves the performance and reliability of the file system when compared to ext3.
- In ext4, you also have the option of turning off the journaling feature. A journaling file system is a file system that keeps track of changes not yet committed to the file system.

HFS

Hierarchical File System (HFS) is a file system developed by Apple for use in computer systems running MacOS. Designed for floppy and hard disks, it can also be found on read-only media such as CD-ROMs. With the introduction of MacOS X 10.6, Apple dropped support for formatting or writing HFS disks and images, which remain supported as read-only volumes.

REFS

Resilient File System (ReFS) was created for Windows 8 and was built on NTFS technology. Its main contribution is the resilience to data corruption and maintenance of integrity.

Swap partition

The swap partition is used by the Linux kernel in order to implement the memory-swap mechanism. Whenever there is a memory shortage, the system moves some information out of memory temporarily to the swap portion of the hard drive. When the memory crunch is over, the information is moved back to memory. Swap files in Linux are the equivalent of page files in Windows.

Quick format vs. full format

When you're installing any Windows OS, you will be asked first to format the drive using one of the disk technologies just discussed. Choose the disk technology based on what the computer will be doing and which OS you are installing. For recent versions of Windows, nearly all users should choose NTFS.

To format a partition, you can use the FORMAT command. FORMAT.EXE is available with all versions of Windows. You can run FORMAT by using the command prompt or by right-clicking a drive in Windows Explorer and selecting Format if Windows is already installed. However, when you install Windows, it performs the process of partitioning and formatting for you if a partitioned and formatted drive does not already exist. You can usually choose between a *quick format* or a *full format*. With both formats, files are removed from the partition; the difference is that a quick format does not then check for bad sectors (a time-consuming process).

WARNING   Be extremely careful with the FORMAT command! When you format a drive, all data on the drive is erased.

Load alternate third-party drivers when necessary

During the installation, it may be necessary to load a third-party driver that you update later. The goal during installation is to get the operating system up and running and in a state where you can interact with it. Some of the drivers included with media are not the latest from the vendor but can be used to complete the installation. Once installation is done, you can access the websites of third-party vendors and download and then install the latest drivers. To add a mass storage driver (which is what you need to access the drive), you hit the F7 key when you are prompted during the installation.

Workgroup vs. domain setup

When installing an operating system, by default the device will be placed in a workgroup. This is a small group of devices that might represent, for example, a home network or a SOHO network. In an organization, however, the devices will more likely reside in a domain. A domain is Windows grouping made possible when using Active Directory, the Windows Directory service. Placing a device in a domain was covered earlier in this chapter in the section "Domain access."

The following versions of Windows support joining a domain:

- Windows 7 Professional
- Windows 7 Ultimate
- Windows 7 Enterprise
- Windows 8 Professional
- Windows 8.21 Professional
- Windows 10 Professional
- Windows 10 Enterprise

Time/date/region/language settings

During installation of the operating system, you are asked to choose the correct settings for the local time, date, and region. As mentioned earlier, the goal during installation is to complete the process as quickly as possible, and you may need to tweak these settings later.

Once the installation is complete, there are a number of ways to change these values, the easiest of which is to right-click the clock in the lower-right corner of the taskbar and choose Adjust Date/Time. In the Control Panel, you can choose the Region And Language applet to configure date and time formats, as well as change language and location settings. Language interface packs (LIPs) are available that can be installed to modify what appears in wizards, dialog boxes, and such (see http://windows.microsoft.com/en-US/windows7/Install-or-change-a-display-language for more information).

Driver installation, software, and Windows updates

During the installation process of Windows 7, Windows 8, Windows 8.1, and Window 10, you will be presented with the option to download any required updates and new driver packages that may have become available since the time the installation DVD was created. If the device will have an active Internet connection, you may want to take advantage of this because it will download the required files and make them part of the installation. If this is not an option, you can always perform this step by visiting Windows Update after the installation.

Factory recovery partition

A recovery partition is one created in Windows that makes returning the device to its factory settings possible. This can also be used to revive the system when it fails. Although it is possible to delete this partition, it is not advisable as it will limit recovery options.

Properly formatted boot drive with the correct partitions/format

Clearly it important to properly create and format the boot drive prior to the installation. Please review the sections "Partitioning," "File system types/formatting," and "Quick format vs. full format."

Prerequisites/hardware compatibility

Prior to installing or upgrading an OS, it is advisable to ensure that the system supports all the hardware prerequisites (these were provided earlier in this chapter). It also is a good idea to check whether any additional hardware is compatible with the system. The upgrade advisors provided with many upgrade programs can assist with this as well. If you don't check ahead of time, the installation or upgrade may fail when you attempt it.

Application compatibility

This is another area where some prior research can be invaluable. Applications are made to work on specific operating systems. While you'll have fewer problems with an upgrade, a new installation, especially when going from one vendor to another (Windows to Apple) may result in application incompatibility. The upgrade advisors mentioned earlier can also assess your application's compatibility.

OS compatibility/upgrade path

Keep in mind that some upgrades are not possible and require new installations. See the tables earlier in this chapter on allowable upgrade paths.

Exam essentials

Identify the versions of Windows that support domain setup.   These include Windows 7 Professional, Windows 7 Ultimate, Windows 7 Enterprise, Windows 8 Professional, Windows 8.1 Professional, Windows 10 Professional, and Windows 10 Enterprise.

1.4 Given a scenario, use appropriate Microsoft command-line tools.

Although the exam is on the Windows operating systems, it tests many concepts that carry over from the earlier Microsoft Disk Operating System (MS-DOS), which was never meant to be extremely friendly. Its roots are in CP/M, which was based on the command line, and so is MS-DOS. In other words, these systems use long strings of commands typed in at the computer keyboard to perform operations. Some people prefer this type of interaction with the computer, including many folks with technical backgrounds (such as yours truly). Although Windows has left the full command-line interface behind, it still contains a bit of DOS, and you get to it through the command prompt.

Although you can't tell from looking at it, the Windows command prompt is actually a Windows program that is intentionally designed to have the look and feel of a DOS command line. Because it is, despite its appearance, a Windows program, the command prompt provides all the stability and configurability you expect from Windows. You can access a command prompt by running CMD.EXE.

A number of diagnostic utilities are often run at the command prompt. Since knowledge of each is required for the exam, they are discussed next in the order given. The commands in this section include the following:

- Navigation commands
- ipconfig
- ping
- tracert
- netstat
- nslookup
- shutdown
- dism
- sfc
- chkdsk
- diskpart
- taskkill
- gpupdate
- gpresult
- format
- copy
- xcopy

- robocopy
- net use
- net user
- [command name] /?
- Commands available with standard privileges vs. administrative privileges

Navigation

Some commands are used to navigate the file system. The three commands in this section are used for that purpose.

dir

The DIR command is simply used to view a listing of the files and folders that exist within a directory, subdirectory, or folder. The following is the syntax:

```
dir [Drive:][Path][FileName] [...] [/p] [/q] [/w] [/d]
[/a[[:]attributes]][/o[[:]SortOrder]] [/t[[:]TimeField]] [/s] [/b]
[/l] [/n] [/x] [/c] [/4]
```

The parameters are as follows:

[*Drive:*] [*Path*]	Specifies the drive and directory for which you want to see a listing
[*FileName*]	Specifies a particular file or group of files for which you want to see a listing
/p	Displays one screen of the listing at a time. To see the next screen, press any key on the keyboard.
/q	Displays file ownership information
/w	Displays the listing in wide format, with as many as five file-names or directory names on each line
d	Same as /w but files are sorted by column.
i	Displays only the names of those directories and files with the attributes you specify
/o [[:]*SortOrder*]	Controls the order in which DIR sorts and displays directory names and filenames
/t [[:]*TimeField*]	Specifies which time field to display or use for sorting
/s	Lists every occurrence, in the specified directory and all subdirectories, of the specified filename

/b	Lists each directory name or filename, one per line, including the filename extension. /b does not display heading information or a summary. /b overrides /w.
/l	Displays unsorted directory names and filenames in lowercase. /l does not convert extended characters to lowercase.
/n	Displays a long list format with filenames on the far right of the screen
/x	Displays the short names generated for files on NTFS and FAT volumes. The display is the same as the display for /n, but short names are displayed after the long name.
/c	Displays the thousand separator in file sizes
/4	Displays four-digit year format

cd and ..

The change directory (cd) command is used to move to another folder or directory. It is used in both UNIX and Windows. Parameters are shown below.

Unix

cd or cd ~	Puts you in your home directory
cd .	Leaves you in the same directory you are currently in
cd ~username	Puts you in username's home directory
cd dir (without a /)	Puts you in a subdirectory
cd –	switches you to the previous directory
cd ..	Moves you up one directory

DOS and Windows

no attributes	Prints the full path of the current directory
-p	Prints the final directory stack
-n	Entries are wrapped before they reach the edge of the screen.
-v	Entries are printed one per line, preceded by their stack positions.
cd\	Returns to the root dir
..	Moves you up one directory

ipconfig

The ipconfig command is used to view the IP configuration of a device and, when combined with certain switches or parameters, can be used to release and renew the lease of an IP address obtained from a DHCP server and to flush the DNS resolver cache. Its most common use is to view the current configuration. Figure 6.5 shows its execution with the / all switch, which results in a display of a wealth of information about the IP configuration.

FIGURE 6.5   Using ipconfig

```
C:\Users\tmcmillan>ipconfig/all

Windows IP Configuration

    Host Name . . . . . . . . . . . . : tmcmillan
    Primary Dns Suffix  . . . . . . . : alpha.kaplaninc.com
    Node Type . . . . . . . . . . . . : Hybrid
    IP Routing Enabled. . . . . . . . : No
    WINS Proxy Enabled. . . . . . . . : No
    DNS Suffix Search List. . . . . . : alpha.kaplaninc.com
                                        kaplaninc.com

Ethernet adapter Local Area Connection:

    Connection-specific DNS Suffix  . : alpha.kaplaninc.com
    Description . . . . . . . . . . . : Broadcom NetXtreme 57xx Gigabit Controlle
r
    Physical Address. . . . . . . . . : 00-1A-A0-E1-95-AB
    DHCP Enabled. . . . . . . . . . . : Yes
    Autoconfiguration Enabled . . . . : Yes
    Link-local IPv6 Address . . . . . : fe80::ada3:8b73:a66e:6bc0%10(Preferred)
    IPv4 Address. . . . . . . . . . . : 10.88.2.103(Preferred)
    Subnet Mask . . . . . . . . . . . : 255.255.254.0
    Lease Obtained. . . . . . . . . . : Monday, January 30, 2012 9:38:37 AM
    Lease Expires . . . . . . . . . . : Tuesday, January 31, 2012 9:38:37 AM
    Default Gateway . . . . . . . . . : 10.88.2.6
    DHCP Server . . . . . . . . . . . : 10.88.10.48
    DHCPv6 IAID . . . . . . . . . . . : 234887840
    DHCPv6 Client DUID. . . . . . . . : 00-01-00-01-14-EE-0F-98-00-1A-A0-E1-95-AB

    DNS Servers . . . . . . . . . . . : 10.88.10.48
                                        10.75.139.18
    NetBIOS over Tcpip. . . . . . . . : Enabled
```

A scenario in which this command would be valuable is when you are dealing with a device you have never touched before that is having communication issues. This command would show a wealth of information with its output.

You can use ipconfig to release and then renew a configuration obtained from a DHCP server by issuing the following commands:

```
ipconfig /release
ipconfig /renew
```

It is also helpful to know that when you have just corrected a configuration error (such as an IP address) on a destination device, you should ensure that the device registers its new IP address with the DNS server by executing the ipconfig /registerdns command.

It may also be necessary to clear incorrect IP addresses to hostname mappings that may still exist on the devices that were attempting to access the destination device. This can be done by executing the ipconfig /flushdns command.

If you are using a Linux or Unix system, the command is not ipconfig but ifconfig. Figure 6.6 shows an example of the command and its output. The ifconfig command with the -a option shows all network interface information, even if the network interface is down.

FIGURE 6.6 Using ifconfig

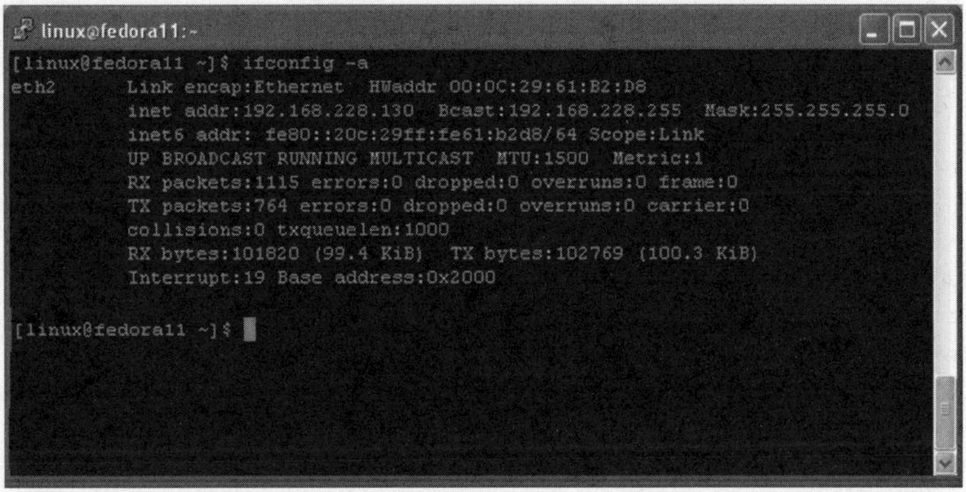

```
[linux@fedora11 ~]$ ifconfig -a
eth2      Link encap:Ethernet  HWaddr 00:0C:29:61:B2:D8
          inet addr:192.168.228.130  Bcast:192.168.228.255  Mask:255.255.255.0
          inet6 addr: fe80::20c:29ff:fe61:b2d8/64 Scope:Link
          UP BROADCAST RUNNING MULTICAST  MTU:1500  Metric:1
          RX packets:1115 errors:0 dropped:0 overruns:0 frame:0
          TX packets:764 errors:0 dropped:0 overruns:0 carrier:0
          collisions:0 txqueuelen:1000
          RX bytes:101820 (99.4 KiB)  TX bytes:102769 (100.3 KiB)
          Interrupt:19 Base address:0x2000

[linux@fedora11 ~]$
```

ping

The ping command makes use of the Internet Control Message Protocol (ICMP) to test connectivity between two devices. ping is one of the most useful commands in the TCP/IP suite. It sends a series of packets to another system, which in turn sends a response. The ping command can be extremely useful for troubleshooting problems with remote hosts.

The ping command indicates whether the host can be reached and how long it took for the host to send a return packet. On a LAN, the time is indicated as less than 10 milliseconds. Across WAN links, however, this value can be much greater. When the -a parameter is included, it will also attempt to resolve the hostname associated with the IP address. Figure 6.7 shows an example of a successful ping.

FIGURE 6.7 The ping command

```
C:\Users\tmcmillan>ping 10.88.2.103

Pinging 10.88.2.103 with 32 bytes of data:
Reply from 10.88.2.103: bytes=32 time<1ms TTL=128
Reply from 10.88.2.103: bytes=32 time<1ms TTL=128
Reply from 10.88.2.103: bytes=32 time<1ms TTL=128
Reply from 10.88.2.103: bytes=32 time<1ms TTL=128

Ping statistics for 10.88.2.103:
    Packets: Sent = 4, Received = 4, Lost = 0 (0% loss),
Approximate round trip times in milli-seconds:
    Minimum = 0ms, Maximum = 0ms, Average = 0ms
```

A common scenario for using ping is when you need to determine whether the network settings are correct. If you can ping another device that is correctly configured, the settings are correct. The syntax is as follows:

ping [-t] [-a] [-n *count*] [-l *size*] [-f] [-i *TTL*] [-v *TOS*] [-r *count*] [-s *count*] [-w *timeout*] [-R] [-S *srcaddr*] [-p] [-4] [-6] target [/?]

Some switches used with ping are in Table 6.11.

TABLE 6.11 ping switches

Switch	Purpose
t	Pings the target until you force it to stop by using Ctrl+C
-a	Resolves, if possible, the hostname of an IP address target
-n *count*	Sets the number of ICMP echo requests to send (4 by default)
-l *size*	Sets the size, in bytes, of the echo request packet (32 by default)
-f	Prevents ICMP echo requests from being fragmented by routers between you and the target
-i *TTL*	Sets the Time to Live (TTL) value, the maximum of which is 255
-r *count*	Specifies the number of hops between your computer and the target computer
-s *count*	Reports the time, in Internet Timestamp format, that each echo request is received and when an echo reply is sent

tracert

The tracert command (called traceroute in Linux and Unix) is used to trace the path of a packet through the network. Its best use is in determining exactly where in the network the packet is being dropped. It will show each hop (router) the packet crosses and how long it takes to do so. Figure 6.8 shows a partial display of a traced route to www.msn.com.

FIGURE 6.8   Using tracert

```
C:\Users\tmcmillan>tracert www.msn.com

Tracing route to us.co1.cb3.glbdns.microsoft.com [70.37.131.153]
over a maximum of 30 hops:

  1     11 ms      1 ms      1 ms   10.88.2.6
  2      2 ms      2 ms      1 ms   208-47-7-130.dia.static.qwest.net [208.47.7.130]

  3      7 ms      7 ms      7 ms   frp-edge-04.inet.qwest.net [205.168.14.213]
  4      7 ms      7 ms      7 ms   frp-core-02.inet.qwest.net [205.171.22.49]
  5     22 ms     22 ms     22 ms   chx-edge-03.inet.qwest.net [67.14.38.1]
  6     22 ms     22 ms     23 ms   63-234-10-14.dia.static.qwest.net [63.234.10.14]

  7     23 ms     23 ms     23 ms   xe-0-1-2-0.ch1-16c-1b.ntwk.msn.net [207.46.43.20
4]
  8     24 ms     24 ms     24 ms   xe-0-1-0-0.ch1-96c-1a.ntwk.msn.net [207.46.46.13
3]
  9     34 ms     34 ms     34 ms   ge-2-1-0-0.ash-64cb-1b.ntwk.msn.net [207.46.45.1
4]
 10     38 ms     38 ms     38 ms   ge-4-0-0-0.nyc-64cb-1b.ntwk.msn.net [207.46.46.5
7]
 11     39 ms     38 ms     38 ms   xe-3-1-0-0.ewr-96cbe-1b.ntwk.msn.net [207.46.47.
2]
 12     39 ms        *       39 ms   xe-3-0-0-0.ewr-96cbe-1a.ntwk.msn.net [207.46.43.
250]
 13
```

A common scenario for using tracert is when there is a slow remote connection and you would like to find out which part of the path is problematic.

The syntax used is as follows:

tracert [-d] [-h *MaxHops*] [-w *TimeOut*] [-4] [-6] *target* [/?]

Table 6.12 shows some selected switches used with tracert.

TABLE 6.12   tracert switches

Switch	Purpose
-d	Prevents tracert from resolving IP addresses to hostnames
-h *MaxHops*	Specifies the maximum number of hops in the search for the target (30 by default)
-w *TimeOut*	Specifies the time, in milliseconds, to allow each reply before timeout using this tracert option
-4	Forces tracert to use IPv4 only
-6	Forces tracert to use IPv6 only
target	Destination, either an IP address or a hostname
/?	Shows detailed help about the command

netstat

The netstat (network status) command is used to see what ports are listening on the TCP/IP-based system. The -a option is used to show all ports, and /? is used to show what other options are available (the options differ based on the operating system you are using). When executed with no switches, the command displays the current connections, as shown in Figure 6.9.

FIGURE 6.9 Using netstat

```
C:\Users\tmcmillan>netstat

Active Connections

  Proto  Local Address          Foreign Address            State
  TCP    10.88.2.103:51273      64.94.18.154:https         ESTABLISHED
  TCP    10.88.2.103:51525      srat1060:microsoft-ds      ESTABLISHED
  TCP    10.88.2.103:51529      gmonsalvatge:microsoft-ds  ESTABLISHED
  TCP    10.88.2.103:51573      sjc-not18:http             ESTABLISHED
  TCP    10.88.2.103:51716      schexv02:2785              ESTABLISHED
  TCP    10.88.2.103:51720      schvoip01:epmap            ESTABLISHED
  TCP    10.88.2.103:51721      schvoip01:1297             ESTABLISHED
  TCP    10.88.2.103:51722      schvoip01:1299             ESTABLISHED
  TCP    10.88.2.103:51824      69.31.116.27:http          CLOSE_WAIT
  TCP    10.88.2.103:51965      dcalpsch2:1026             ESTABLISHED
  TCP    10.88.2.103:53865      cs219p3:5050               ESTABLISHED
  TCP    10.88.2.103:53871      sip109:http                ESTABLISHED
  TCP    10.88.2.103:62522      ord08s08-in-f22:https      ESTABLISHED
  TCP    10.88.2.103:62567      ord08s08-in-f22:https      CLOSE_WAIT
  TCP    10.88.2.103:62682      by2msg3010613:http         ESTABLISHED
  TCP    10.88.2.103:63554      baymsg1020213:msnp         ESTABLISHED
  TCP    10.88.2.103:63770      v-client-2b:https          CLOSE_WAIT
  TCP    10.88.2.103:63771      ec2-174-129-205-197:https  CLOSE_WAIT
  TCP    10.88.2.103:63772      v-client-2b:https          CLOSE_WAIT
  TCP    10.88.2.103:63773      65.55.121.231:http         ESTABLISHED
  TCP    10.88.2.103:63774      168.75.207.20:http         ESTABLISHED
  TCP    10.88.2.103:63777      65.55.17.30:http           ESTABLISHED
  TCP    10.88.2.103:63779      70.37.131.11:http          ESTABLISHED
  TCP    10.88.2.103:63781      65.124.174.56:http         ESTABLISHED
  TCP    10.88.2.103:63788      69.31.76.41:http           ESTABLISHED
  TCP    10.88.2.103:63791      207.46.140.46:http         ESTABLISHED
  TCP    10.88.2.103:63792      64.4.21.39:http            ESTABLISHED
  TCP    127.0.0.1:2002         tmcmillan:51543            ESTABLISHED
  TCP    127.0.0.1:19872        tmcmillan:51571            ESTABLISHED
  TCP    127.0.0.1:51543        tmcmillan:2002             ESTABLISHED
  TCP    127.0.0.1:51549        tmcmillan:51550            ESTABLISHED
  TCP    127.0.0.1:51550        tmcmillan:51549            ESTABLISHED
  TCP    127.0.0.1:51571        tmcmillan:19872            ESTABLISHED
  TCP    127.0.0.1:53869        tmcmillan:53870            ESTABLISHED
  TCP    127.0.0.1:53870        tmcmillan:53869            ESTABLISHED
  TCP    127.0.0.1:63557        tmcmillan:63574            ESTABLISHED
  TCP    127.0.0.1:63574        tmcmillan:63557            ESTABLISHED

C:\Users\tmcmillan>
```

A common scenario for using netstat is when you suspect that a host is "calling home" to a malicious server. If so, the connection would appear in the output.

The syntax is as follows:

```
ping [-t] [-a] [-n count] [-l size] [-f] [-i TTL] [-v TOS] [-r count]
[-s count] [-w timeout] [-R] [-S srcaddr] [-p proto] [-4] [-6] target [/?]
```

Table 6.13 shows some switches used with `netstat`.

TABLE 6.13   netstat switches

Switch	Purpose
-a	Displays all connections and listening ports
-b	Displays the executable involved in creating each connection or listening port
-e	Displays Ethernet statistics
-f	Displays fully qualified domain names for foreign addresses (in Windows Vista/7 only)
-n	Displays addresses and port numbers in numerical form
-o	Displays the owning process ID associated with each connection
-p *proto*	Shows connections for the protocol specified by *proto*
-r	Displays the routing table

nslookup

The `nslookup` command is a command-line administrative tool for testing and troubleshooting DNS servers. It can be run in two modes, interactive and noninteractive. While noninteractive mode is useful when only a single piece of data needs to be returned, interactive allows you to query for either an IP address for a name or a name for an IP address without leaving `nslookup` mode.

A common scenario for using `nslookup` is when a system cannot resolve names and you need to see what DNS server it is using.

The command syntax is as follows:

`nslookup [-option] [hostname] [server]`

Table 6.14 shows selected switches used with `nslookup`.

TABLE 6.14   nslookup switches

Switch	Purpose
all	Prints all options, current server, and host info
[no]debug	Provides debugging info

TABLE 6.14   nslookup switches *(continued)*

Switch	Purpose
[no]d2	Provides exhaustive debugging info
[no]defname	Appends a domain name to each query
[no]recurse	Asks for a recursive answer to the query
[no]search	Uses the domain to search the list
[no]vc	Always uses a virtual circuit
domain=*name*	Sets the default domain name to *name*

To enter interactive mode, simply enter nslookup as shown next. When you do this, by default it will identify the IP address and name of the DNS server that the local machine is configured to use, if any, and then will go to the > prompt. At this prompt you can enter either an IP address or a name, and the system will attempt to resolve the IP address to a name or the name to an IP address.

```
C:\> nslookup
Default Server: nameserver1.domain.com
Address: 10.0.0.1
>
```

The following are other queries that can be run that may prove helpful when trouble-shooting name resolution issues:

- Looking up different data types in the database (such as Microsoft records). For example, the following command will filter for mail server records:

```
C: Nslookup
Set Type=mx
```

- Querying directly from another name server (different from the one the local device is configured to use). The command for the DNS server named some.dns.server in the somewhere.com domain is as follows:

```
nslookup somewhere.com some.dns.server
```

- Performing a zone transfer. This example is from wayne.net to dns.wayne.net:

```
C: nslookup
set Type=any
> ls -d wayne.net > dns.wayne.net
> exit
```

shutdown

The SHUTDOWN.EXE utility can be used to schedule a shutdown (complete or a restart) locally or remotely. A variety of reasons can be specified and announced to users for the shutdown. Three parameters to be aware of are /S (turns the computer off), /R (restarts the computer), and /M (lets you specify a computer other than this one).

dism

Deployment Image Servicing and Management (DISM.exe) is a command-line tool that can be used to service a Windows image or to prepare a Windows Preinstallation Environment (Windows PE) image. The syntax is as follows:

```
DISM.exe {/Image:<path_to_image> | /Online} [dism_global_options]
{servicing_option} [<servicing_argument>]
```

For example, to determine whether any corruption exists in the operating system, execute this command:

DISM /Online /Cleanup-Image /CheckHealth

For more information, see the following:

```
https://docs.microsoft.com/en-us/windows-hardware/manufacture/desktop/
dism-image-management-command-line-options-s14
```

sfc

The System File Checker (SFC) is a command line–based utility that checks and verifies the versions of system files on your computer. If system files are corrupted, the SFC will replace the corrupted files with correct versions.

The syntax for the SFC command is as follows:

```
SFC [switch]
```

While the switches vary a bit between different versions of Windows, Table 6.15 lists the most common ones available for SFC.

TABLE 6.15   SFC switches

Switch	Purpose
/CACHESIZE=X	Sets the Windows File Protection cache size, in megabytes
/PURGECACHE	Purges the Windows File Protection cache and scans all protected system files immediately
/REVERT	Reverts SFC to its default operation

TABLE 6.15   SFC switches *(continued)*

Switch	Purpose
/SCANFILE (Windows 7 and Vista only)	Scans a file that you specify and fixes problems if they are found
/SCANNOW	Immediately scans all protected system files
/SCANONCE	Scans all protected system files once
/SCANBOOT	Scans all protected system files every time the computer is rebooted
/VERIFYONLY	Scans protected system files and does not make any repairs or changes
/VERIFYFILE	Identifies the integrity of the file specified and makes any repairs or changes
/OFFBOOTDIR	Does a repair of an offline boot directory
/OFFFWINDIR	Does a repair of an offline Windows directory

To run the SFC, you must be logged in as an administrator or have administrative privileges. If the System File Checker discovers a corrupted system file, it will automatically overwrite the file by using a copy held in the %systemroot%\system32\dllcache directory. If you believe that the dllcache directory is corrupted, you can use SFC /SCANNOW, SFC /SCANONCE, SFC /SCANBOOT, or SFC /PURGECACHE, depending on your needs, as described in Table 6.15, to repair its contents.

> The C:\Windows\System32 directory is where many of the Windows system files reside.

If you attempt to run SFC, or many other utilities, from a standard command prompt, you will be told that you must be an administrator running a console session in order to continue. Rather than opening a standard command prompt, choose Start ➤ All Programs ➤ Accessories and then right-click Command Prompt and choose Run As Administrator. The User Account Control (UAC) will prompt you to continue, and then you can run SFC without a problem.

chkdsk

You can use the Windows CHKDSK utility to create and display status reports for the hard disk. CHKDSK can also correct file system problems (such as cross-linked files) and scan for and attempt to repair disk errors. CHKDSK can be run from the command line, or you can use a version in Windows Explorer.

To use the Windows Explorer version, right-click the problem disk and select Properties. This will bring up the Properties dialog box for that disk, which shows the current status of the selected disk drive. By clicking the Tools tab at the top of the dialog box and then clicking the Check button in the Error Checking section, you can start CHKDSK.

diskpart

The diskpart command shows the partitions and lets you manage them on the computer's hard drives. A universal tool for working with hard drives from the command line, it allows you to convert between disk types, extend/shrink volumes, and format partitions and volumes, as well as list them, create them, and so on. The diskpart command sets the command prompt at the diskpart prompt as follows:

Diskpart>

Then subcommands like those in Table 6.16 are used.

TABLE 6.16 Diskpart parameters

Parameter	Purpose
ACTIVE	Marks the selected partition as active
ADD	Adds a mirror to a simple volume
ATTRIBUTES	Manipulates volume or disk attributes
ASSIGN	Assigns a drive letter or mount point to the selected volume
ATTACH	Attaches a virtual disk file
AUTOMOUNT	Enables and disables automatic mounting of basic volumes
BREAK	Breaks a mirror set
CLEAN	Clears the configuration information, or all information

And that's only the beginning. You can find a list of all the available commands at http://technet.microsoft.com/en-us/library/bb490893.aspx.

taskkill

The TASKKILL.EXE utility is used to terminate processes. Those processes can be identified by either name or process ID number (PID), and the process can exist on the machine where the administrator is sitting (the default) or on another machine, in which case you signify the other system by using the /S switch.

The /IM parameter is used to specify the image name of a process to kill and can include wildcard (*) characters. If the process ID number is used in place of the name, then the /PID switch is needed. The processes in question are the same that can be killed through the Task Manager.

gpupdate

Configuration settings on Windows devices can be controlled through the use of policies. These policies can be applied on a local basis or on a domain and organizational unit basis when a device is a member of an Active Directory domain. When changes are made by an administrator to these policies, some types of changes will not take effect until the next schedule refresh time.

An administrator can force a device to update its policies after a change by executing the gpupdate command on the device. This is the syntax of the command:

```
gpupdate [/target:{computer|user}] [/force] [/wait:value] [/logoff] [/boot]
```

The parameters are as follows:

/target: { computer | user }	Processes only the *computer* settings or the current *user* settings. By default, both the computer settings and the user settings are processed.
/force	Ignores all processing optimizations and reapplies all settings
/wait: *value*	Number of seconds that policy processing waits to finish. The default is 600 seconds. 0 means "no wait," and -1 means "wait indefinitely."
/logoff	Logs off after the refresh has completed. This is required for those Group Policy client-side extensions that do not process on a background refresh cycle but that do process when the user logs on, such as user Software Installation and Folder Redirection. This option has no effect if there are no extensions called that require the user to log off.
/boot	Restarts the computer after the refresh has completed. This is required for those Group Policy client-side extensions that do not process on a background refresh cycle but do process when the computer starts up, such as computer Software Installation. This option has no effect if there are no extensions called that require the computer to be restarted.

gpresult

Group policies can be applied to Windows devices at the local, organizational unit (OU), and domain levels, and when the policies are applied to the device, the results can be somewhat confusing because of variables that can affect how the policies interact with one another. If you need to determine the policies that are in effect for a particular device, you can execute the gpresult command on the device, and it will list the currently applied and defective policies. This is the command syntax:

```
gpresult [/s <COMPUTER> [/u <USERNAME> [/p [<PASSWORD>]]]] [/user
[<TARGETDOMAIN>\]<TARGETUSER>] [/scope {user | computer}]
{/r | /v | /z | [/x | /h] <FILENAME> [/f] | /?}
```

The parameters are as follows:

/s <COMPUTER>	Specifies the name or IP address of a remote computer. Do not use backslashes. The default is the local computer.
/u <USERNAME>	Uses the credentials of the specified user to run the command. The default user is the user who is logged on to the computer that issues the command.
/p [<Password>]	Specifies the password of the user account that is provided in the /u parameter. If /p is omitted, gpresult prompts for the password. /p cannot be used with /x or /h.
/user [<TARGETDOMAIN>\] <TARGETUSER>	Specifies the remote user whose data is to be displayed
/scope {user	computer}	Displays data for either the user or the computer. If /scope is omitted, gpresult displays data for both the user and the computer.
[/x	/h] <FILENAME>	Saves the report in either XML (/x) or HTML (/h) format at the location and with the filename that is specified by the FILENAME parameter. This cannot be used with /u, /p, /r, /v, or /z.
/f	Forces gpresult to overwrite the filename that is specified in the /x or /h option
/r	Displays summary data
/v	Displays verbose policy information. This includes detailed settings that were applied with a precedence of 1.
/z:	Displays all available information about Group Policy. This includes detailed settings that were applied with a precedence of 1 and higher.

format

The FORMAT command is used to wipe data off disks and prepare them for new use. Before a hard disk can be formatted, it must have partitions created on it. (Partitioning is done in

Windows 7, Windows Vista, Windows 8, Windows 8.1, and Windows 10, using DISKPART, discussed earlier.) The syntax for FORMAT is as follows:

FORMAT [volume] [switches]

The volume parameter describes the drive letter (for example, D:), mount point, or volume name. Table 6.17 lists some common FORMAT switches.

TABLE 6.17   FORMAT switches

Switch	Purpose
/FS:[filesystem]	Specifies the type of file system to use (FAT, FAT32, or NTFS)
/V:[label]	Specifies the new volume label
/Q	Executes a quick format

There are other options as well to specify allocation sizes, the number of sectors per track, and the number of tracks per disk size. However, I don't recommend you use these unless you have a specific need. The defaults are just fine.

So, if you wanted to format your D: drive as NTFS with a name of HDD2, you would enter the following:

FORMAT D: /FS:NTFS /V:HDD2

 WARNING   Before you format anything, be sure you have it backed up or be prepared to lose whatever is on that drive!

copy

The COPY command does what it says: It makes a copy of a file in a second location. (To copy a file and remove it from its original location, use the MOVE command.) Here's the syntax for COPY:

COPY [filename] [destination]

It's pretty straightforward. There are several switches for COPY, but in practice they are rarely used. The three most used ones are /A, which indicates an ASCII text file; /V, which verifies that the files are written correctly after the copy; and /Y, which suppresses the prompt asking whether you're sure you want to overwrite files if they exist in the destination directory.

When any sort of copy operation is performed, the file will take on the permissions of the folder in which you place it.

The COPY command cannot be used to copy directories. Use XCOPY for that function.

One useful tip is to use wildcards. For example, in DOS (or at the command prompt), the asterisk (*) is a wildcard that means *everything*. So, you could enter COPY *.EXE to copy all files that have an .EXE extension, or you could enter COPY *.* to copy all files in your current directory.

xcopy

If you are comfortable with the COPY command, learning XCOPY shouldn't pose too many problems. It's basically an extension of COPY with one notable exception—it's designed to copy directories as well as files. The syntax is as follows:

XCOPY [source] [destination][switches]

There are 26 XCOPY switches; Table 6.18 lists some of the commonly used ones.

TABLE 6.18 XCOPY switches

Switch	Purpose
/A	Copies only files that have the Archive attribute set and does not clear the attribute. This is useful for making a quick backup of files while not disrupting a normal backup routine.
/E	Copies directories and subdirectories, including empty directories
/F	Displays full source and destination filenames when copying
/G	Allows copying of encrypted files to a destination that does not support encryption
/H	Copies hidden and system files as well
/K	Copies attributes (By default, XCOPY resets the Read-Only attribute.)
/O	Copies file ownership and ACL information (NTFS permissions)
/R	Overwrites read-only files
/S	Copies directories and subdirectories but not empty directories
/U	Copies only files that already exist in the destination
/V	Verifies each new file

Perhaps the most important switch is /O. If you use XCOPY to copy files from one location to another, the file system creates a new version of the file in the new location without changing the old file. In NTFS, when a new file is created, it inherits permissions from its new parent directory. This could cause problems if you copy files. (Users who didn't have access to the file before might have access now.) If you want to retain the original permissions, use XCOPY /O.

robocopy

The ROBOCOPY command (Robust File Copy for Windows) is included with Windows 7, 8, 8.1, and 10 and has the big advantage of being able to accept a plethora of specifications and keep NTFS permissions intact in its operations. The /MIR switch, for example, can be used to mirror a complete directory tree.

You can find an excellent TechNet article on how to use Robocopy at http://technet .microsoft.com/en-us/magazine/ec85e01678.aspx.

The syntax is as follows:

```
robocopy <Source> <Destination> [<File>[ ...]] [<Options>]
```

Some of the more common switches when using the copy option are in Table 6.19.

TABLE 6.19 Robocopy switches

Switch	Purpose
/s	Copies subdirectories. Note that this option excludes empty directories.
/e	Copies subdirectories. Note that this option includes empty directories.
/lev:<N>	Copies only the top N levels of the source directory tree
/z	Copies files in restartable mode
/b	Copies files in Backup mode
/efsraw	Copies all encrypted files in EFS RAW mode
/copy:<copyflags>	Specifies the file properties to be copied. The following are the valid values for this option:
D	Data

Switch	Purpose
A	Attributes
T	Time stamps
S	NTFS access control list (ACL)
O	Owner information
U	Auditing information
/dcopy:<copyflags>	Defines what to copy for directories. Default is DA. Options are D = data, A = attributes, and T = timestamps.

net use

Network shares can be mapped to drives to appear as if the resources are local. The NET USE command is used to establish network connections via a command prompt. For example, to connect to a shared network drive and make it your M drive, you would use the syntax net use m: \\server\share. Figure 6.10 shows an example of mapped drives. This can also be done in File Explorer, as shown in Figure 6.11.

FIGURE 6.10　　Mapped network drives

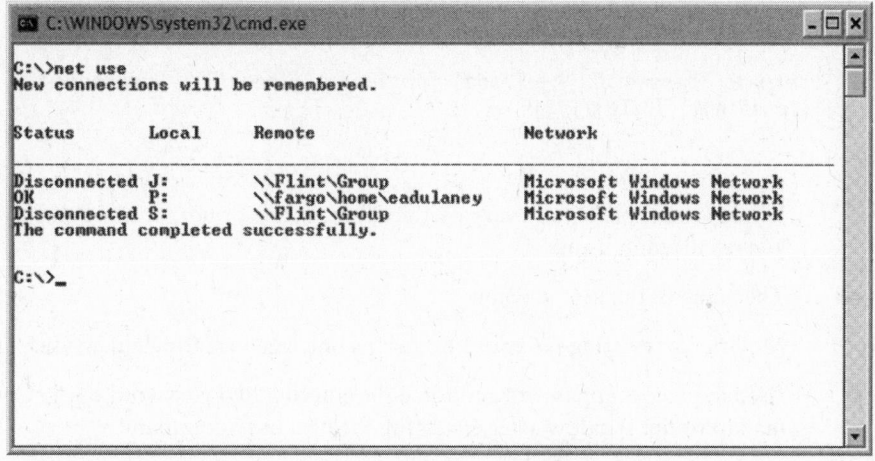

FIGURE 6.11   Mapping a drive

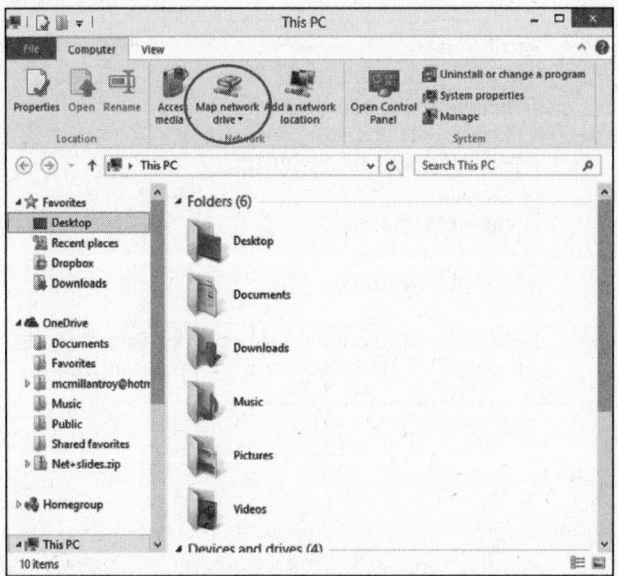

NET USE can also be used to connect to a shared printer: net use lpt1: \\printername.

net user

The net user command is used to add, remove, and make changes to the user accounts on a computer, all from the command prompt. It has the following command syntax:

```
netuser [username [password | *] [/add] [options]] [/domain]] [username
[/delete] [/domain]] [/help] [/?]
```

where:

netuser	Displays a simple list of every user account, active or not, on the computer you're currently using
Username	The name of the user account
Password	Modifies an existing password or assigns one when creating a new username
*	Used in place of a password to force the entering of a password in the Command Prompt window after executing the net user command
/add	Adds a new username on the system
/domain	Forces net user to execute on the current domain controller instead of the local computer
/delete	Removes the specified username from the system
/help	Displays detailed information

[command name] /?

You can also get help information by typing /? after a command.

> The /? switch is slightly faster and provides more information than the HELP command. HELP provides information only for system commands (it does not include network commands). For example, if you enter **help ipconfig** at a command prompt, you get no useful information (except to try /?); however, typing **ipconfig /?** provides the help file for the ipconfig command.

Commands available with standard privileges vs. administrative privileges

In Windows 7, Windows 8, Windows 8.1, and Windows 10 some commands are unavailable to a user logged in with a standard privilege account. This set of commands can be executed only if the user is logged on with an administrator account or possesses an administrative account and references it by using the runas command. When this command is used and references an administrative account, privileges for that command *only* are elevated.

This is the syntax of the runas command:

```
runas [{/profile | /noprofile}] [/env] [{/netonly | /savecred}]
[/smartcard] [/showtrustlevels] [/trustlevel] /user:<UserAccountName>
"<ProgramName> <PathToProgramFile>"
```

The parameters are as follows:

/profile	Loads the user's profile. This is the default. This parameter cannot be used with the /netonly parameter.
/no profile	Specifies that the user's profile is not to be loaded. This allows the application to load more quickly, but it can also cause a malfunction in some applications.
/env	Specifies that the current network environment be used instead of the user's local environment
/netonly	Indicates that the user information specified is for remote access only. This parameter cannot be used with the /profile parameter.
/savecred	Indicates whether the credentials have been previously saved by this user. This parameter is not available and will be ignored on Windows Vista Home or Windows Vista Starter Editions. This parameter cannot be used with the /smartcard parameter.

/smartcard	Indicates whether the credentials are to be supplied from a smartcard. This parameter cannot be used with the /savecred parameter.
/showtrustlevels	Displays the trust levels that can be used as arguments to /trustlevel
/trustlevel	Specifies the level of authorization at which the application is to run. Use /showtrustlevels to see the trust levels available.
/user:*<UserAccountName>* "*<ProgramName>* *<PathToProgramFile>*"	Specifies the name of the user account under which to run the program, the program name, and the path to the program file. The user account name format should be either *<User>*@*<Domain>* or *<Domain>**<UserAccountName>*.

Exam essentials

Use command-line tools and their switches.   These tools include ipconfig, ping, tracert, netstat, lookup, shutdown, dism, sfc, chkdsk, diskpart, taskkill, gpupdate, gpresult, format, copy, xcopy, robocopy, net use, and net user.

1.5 Given a scenario, use Microsoft operating system features and tools.

This objective requires you to know how to work at the command line and run common command-line utilities available with the Windows-based operating systems, as well as use administrative tools. Some of the material here overlaps with other objectives, but you'll want to make certain you know each utility discussed.

Although most of the information presented about Windows utilities and administration should seem like second nature to you (on-the-job experience is expected for A+ certification), you should read these sections thoroughly to make certain you can answer any questions that may appear about them. The topics covered in this section include the following:

- Administrative
- MSConfig
- Task Manager
- Disk Management
- System utilities

Administrative

Table 6.20 lists the administrative tools, and the purpose for each, that you need to know for this objective. The majority of these run in the Microsoft Management Console (MMC).

TABLE 6.20   Windows administrative tools

Tool	Purpose
Computer Management	The Computer Management Console includes the following system tools: Device Manager, Event Viewer, Shared Folders, and Performance/Performance Logs And Alerts (based on the OS you are running, you may also see Local Users And Groups or Task Scheduler). Computer Management also has the Storage area, which lets you manage removable media, defragment your hard drives, and manage partitions through the Disk Management utility. Finally, you can manage system services and applications through Computer Management as well. It also has a Storage section, which includes Disk Management and a Services and Applications section, which includes Services and WMI Control.
Device Manager	Device Manager shows a list of all installed hardware and lets you add items, remove items, update drivers, and more.
Local Users And Groups	If Local Users And Groups is not visible in the left pane of MMC, choose File Add/Remove Snap-in and select Local Users And Groups from the list of possible snap-ins. You can choose to manage the local computer or another computer (requiring you to provide its address). The built-in groups for a domain are a superset of local groups. Local Users And Groups is not available for Windows 7 editions lower than Professional. In all other editions, you must manage user accounts using the User Accounts applet in the Control Panel, and you cannot create or manage groups. The default users created are Administrator, Guest, and the administrative account created during the install.
Local Security Policy	The Local Security Policy (choose Start and then enter `secpol.msc`) allows you to set the default security settings for the system. This feature is available only in Windows 7 Professional, Windows 7 Ultimate, Windows 7 Enterprise, Windows 8.1 Pro, Windows 8 Ultimate, Windows 8 Professional (old Business), and Windows 8 Enterprise editions.
Performance Monitor	Performance Monitor differs a bit between Windows versions but has the same purpose throughout: to display performance counters. Two tools are available—System Monitor and Performance Logs And Alerts. System Monitor will show the performance counters in graphical format. The Performance Logs And Alerts utility collects the counter information and then sends it to a console (such as the one in front of the admin so they can be aware of the problem) or event log.

TABLE 6.20   Windows administrative tools *(continued)*

Tool	Purpose
Services	The Services tab is illustrated and discussed later in this section.
System Configuration	MSConfig, known as the System Configuration utility, helps you trouble-shoot startup problems by allowing you to selectively disable individual items that normally are executed at startup. It works in all versions of Windows, although the interface window is slightly different among versions.
Task Scheduler	Task Scheduler allows you to configure jobs to automatically run unattended. For the run frequency, you can choose any of the following options: Daily, Weekly, Monthly, One Time Only, When The Computer Starts, or When You Log On. You can access a job's advanced properties any time after the job has been created. To do so, double-click the icon for the job in the Scheduled Tasks screen. In the resulting dialog box, you can configure such things as the username and password associated with the job, the actual command line used to start the job (in case you need to add parameters to it), and the working directory. At any time, you can delete a scheduled job by deleting its icon, or you can simply disable a job by removing the check mark from the Enabled box on the Task tab of the task's properties dialog box. For jobs that are scheduled to run, a picture of a clock appears in the bottom-left corner of the icon; jobs not scheduled to run do not have that clock.
Component Services	Component Services is an MMC snap-in that allows you to administer, as well as deploy, component services and to configure behavior such as security (Component Services is located beneath Administrative Tools).
Data Sources	ODBC Data Source Administrator (located beneath Administrative Tools) allows you to interact with database management systems.
Print Management	Available in Windows 7 and Windows Vista, Print Management (located beneath Administrative Tools) allows you to manage multiple printers and print servers from a single interface. Print Management is not available for Windows 7 in any edition lower than Windows 7 Professional. In all later editions of Windows (Vista, 8, 8.1, 10), you must manage individual printers using the Printers applet in the Control Panel.
Windows Memory Diagnostics	The Windows Memory Diagnostic Tool (located beneath Administrative Tools) can be used to check a system for memory problems. For the tool to work, the system must be restarted. The two options that it offers are to restart the computer now and check for problems or wait and check for problems on the next restart. Upon reboot, the test will take several minutes, and the display screen will show which pass number is being run and the overall status of the test (percentage complete). When the memory test concludes, the system will restart again, and nothing related to it is apparent until you log in. If the test is without error, you'll see a message that no errors were found. If anything else is found, the results will be displayed.

Tool	Purpose
Windows Firewall	Windows Firewall (Start ➤ Control Panel ➤ Windows Firewall) is used to block access from the network, and in Windows 7, it is divided into separate settings for private networks and public networks. While host-based firewalls are not as secure as other types of firewalls, this provides much better protection than previously and is turned on by default. It is also included in the Security component of the Action Center and can be tweaked significantly using the Advanced Settings.
Advanced Security	Continuing the discussion of Windows Firewall, once you click Advanced Settings, Windows Firewall with Advanced Security opens. Here, you can configure inbound and outbound rules as well as import and export policies and monitor. Monitoring is not confined only to the firewall; you can also monitor security associations and connection security rules. Not only can this MMC snap-in do simple configuration, but it can also configure remote computers and work with Group Policy.
User Account Management	Used to create, delete, and configure properties of user accounts in Windows 10.

Event Viewer

Windows employs comprehensive error and informational logging routines. Every program and process theoretically could have its own logging utility, but Microsoft has come up with a rather slick utility, Event Viewer, which, through log files, tracks all events on a particular Windows computer. Normally, though, you must be an administrator or a member of the Administrators group to have access to Event Viewer.

The process for starting Event Viewer differs based on the operating system you are running, but always log in as an administrator (or equivalent). With Windows 7, using Small or Large icons view, choose Start Control Panel Administrative Tools Event Viewer; on earlier systems, choose Start Programs Administrative Tools Event Viewer (or you can always right-click the Computer desktop icon and choose Manage Event Viewer). In the resulting window (shown in Figure 6.12), you can view the System, Application, and Security log files. If you are running Windows 7, Windows 8, Windows 8.1, or Windows 10, you will also see log files available for Setup and Forwarded Events.

- The System log file displays alerts that pertain to the general operation of Windows.

- The Application log file logs application errors.

- The Security log file logs security events such as login successes and failures.

- The Setup log will appear on domain controllers and will contain events specific to them.

- The Forwarded Events log contains events that have been forwarded to this log by other computers.

FIGURE 6.12   The opening interface of Event Viewer

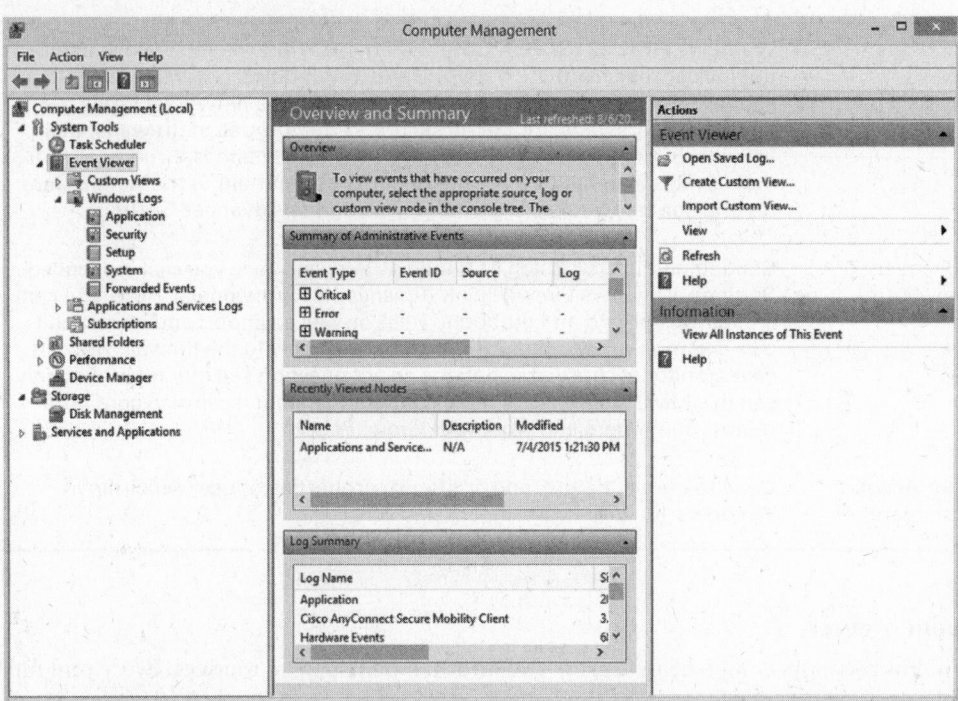

These log files can give a general indication of a Windows computer's health.

To access Event Viewer in Windows 8 and Windows 8.1, just enter **event viewer** in the desktop Search box, and when the option for opening Event Viewer appears, select it.

One situation that does occur with Event Viewer is that the log files get full. Although this isn't really a problem, it can make viewing log files confusing because there are so many entries. Even though each event is time- and date-stamped, you should clear Event Viewer every so often. To do this, open Event Viewer, and in Windows 7, right-click the log, choose Properties, and click the Clear Log button; in earlier OS versions, choose Clear All Events from the Log menu. Doing so erases all events in the current log file, allowing you to see new events more easily when they occur. You can set maximum log size by right-clicking the log and choosing Properties. By default, when a log fills to its maximum size, old entries are deleted in first in, first out (FIFO) order. Clearing the log, setting maximum log size, and setting how the log is handled when full are done in the Log Properties dialog box, as shown in Figure 6.13.

FIGURE 6.13   The Log Properties dialog box

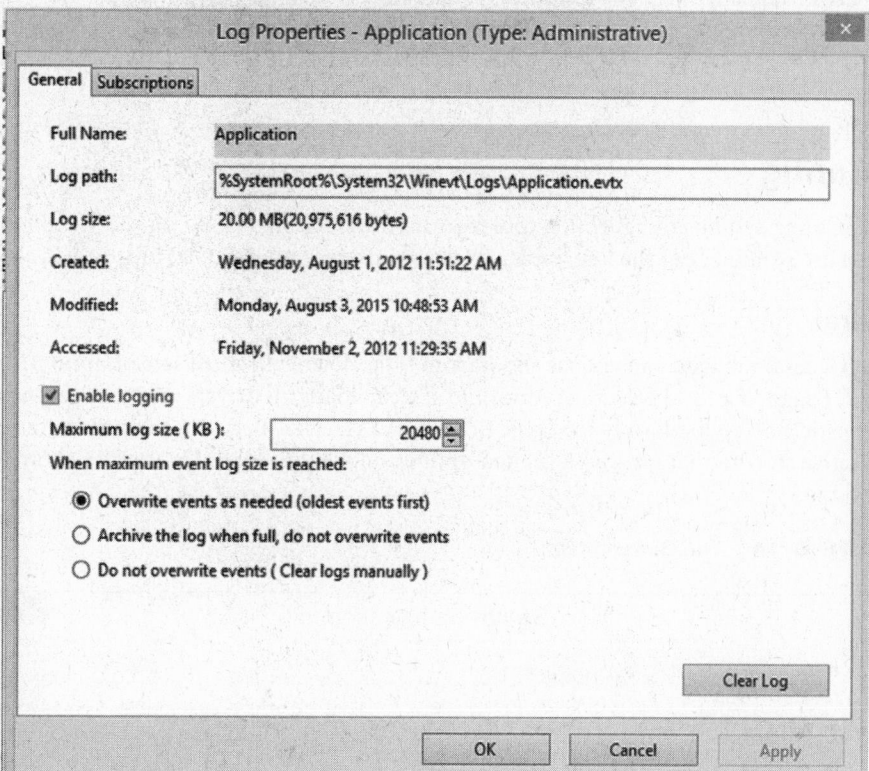

 You can save the log files before erasing them. The saved files can be burned to a CD or DVD for future reference. Often, you are required to save the files to CD or DVD if you are working in a company that adheres to strict regulatory standards.

In addition to just erasing logs, you can configure three different settings for what you want to occur when the file does reach its maximum size. The first option is Overwrite Events As Needed (Oldest Events First), which replaces the older events with the new entries. The second option is Archive The Log When Full, Do Not Overwrite Events, which will create another log file as soon as the current one runs out of space. The third option, Do Not Overwrite Events (Clear Logs Manually), will not record any additional events once the file is full.

A scenario for using Event Viewer would be in the case of an attempted improper login. You could use the log to identity the time, machine, and other information concerning the attempt.

MSConfig

The MSConfig system configuration tool features different tabs based on the Windows version you are running, but the key ones are General, Boot, Services, Startup, and Tools.

General

On the General tab, you can choose the startup type. There are three sets of options: Normal, Diagnostic, and Selective. A normal startup loads all drivers and services, whereas a diagnostic startup loads only the basic drivers and services. Between the two extremes is the selective startup that gives you limited options on what to load. Figure 6.14 shows the General tab.

FIGURE 6.14   The General tab

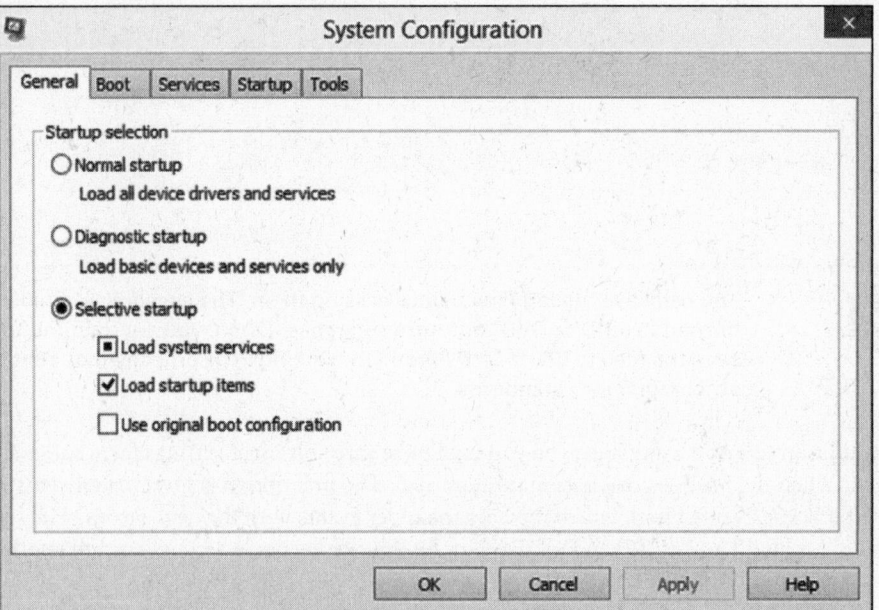

Boot

The Boot tab shows the boot menu and allows you to configure parameters such as the number of seconds the menu should appear before the default option is chosen and whether you want go to safe boot. You can toggle on/off the display of drivers as they load during startup and choose to log the boot, go with basic video settings, and similar options. Figure 6.15 shows the Boot tab.

FIGURE 6.15   The Boot tab

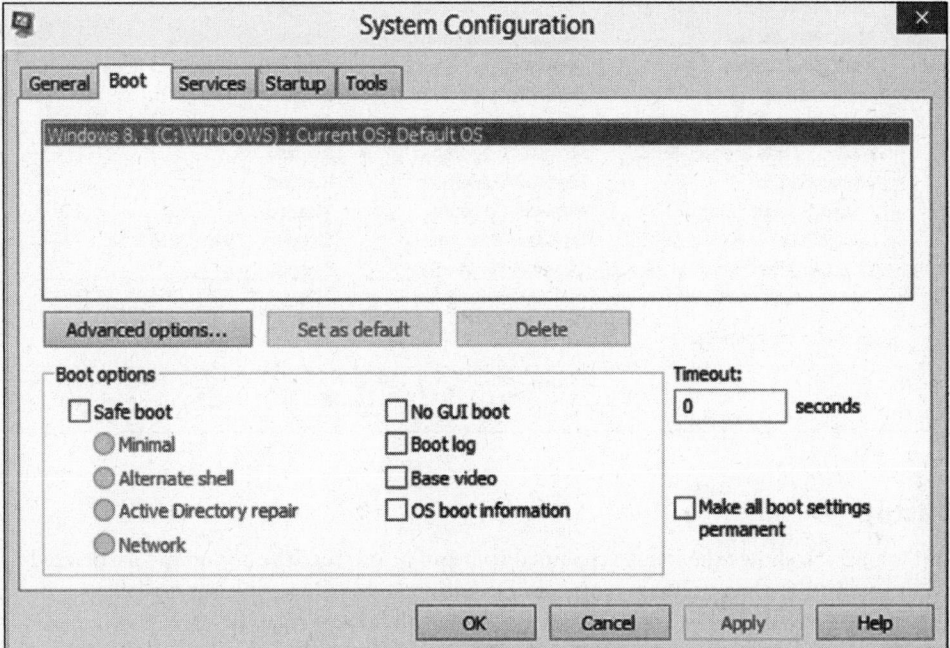

Services

The Services tab shows the services configured and their current status. From here, you can enable or disable all and hide Microsoft services from the display (which greatly reduces the display in most cases). Figure 6.16 shows the Services tab.

FIGURE 6.16   The Services tab

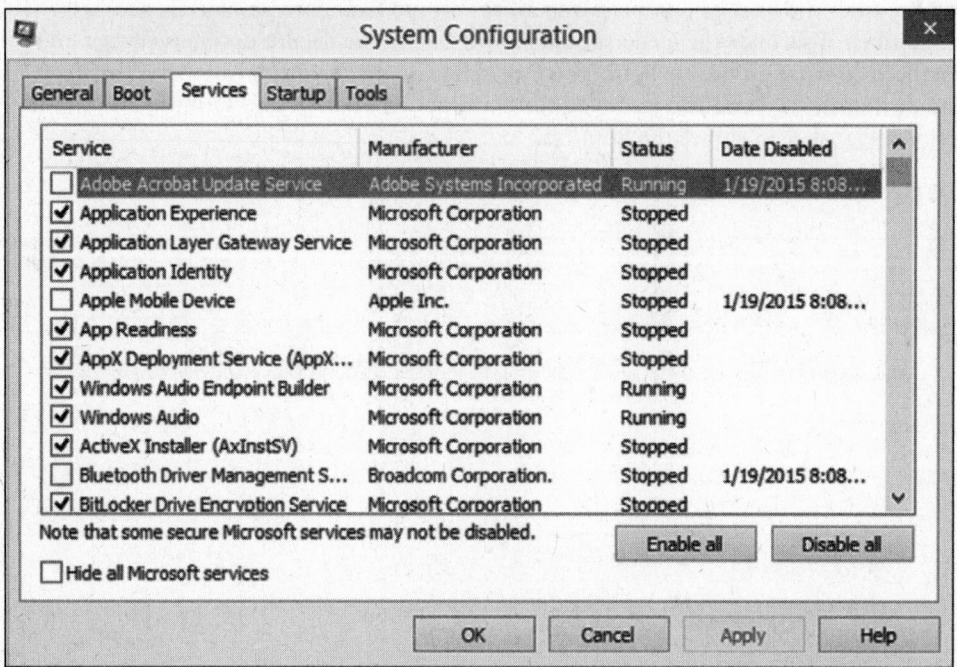

Startup

The Startup tab shows the items scheduled to begin at startup, the command associated with them, and the location where the configuration is done (usually, but not always, in the Registry). From here, you can enable or disable all. If a particular startup item has been disabled in Windows 7, the date and time it was disabled will appear in the display. Figure 6.17 shows the Startup tab for Windows 7 and earlier.

This functionality has been moved to Task Manager in Windows 8, Windows 8.1, and Windows 10; Figure 6.18 shows the Startup tab.

FIGURE 6.17   The Startup tab in Windows 7

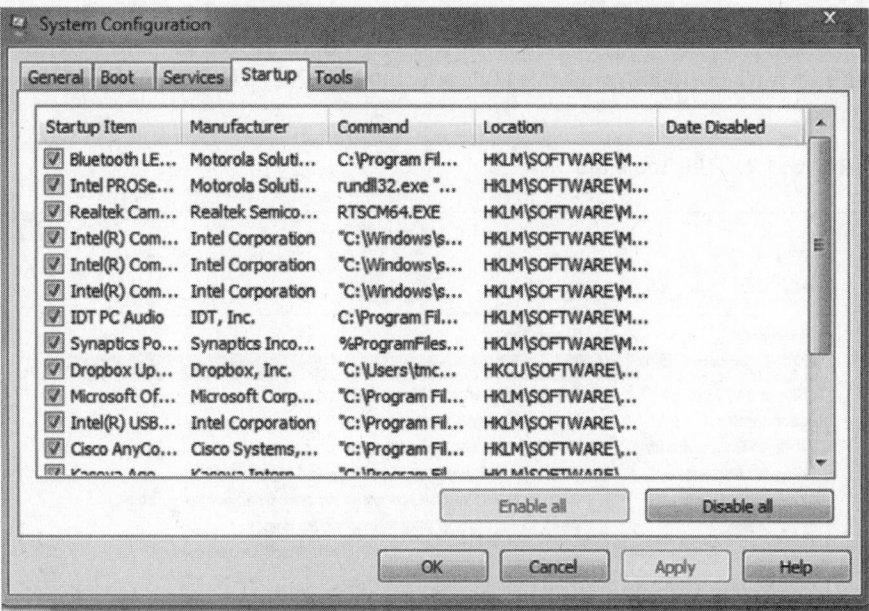

FIGURE 6.18   The Startup tab in Windows 8, 8.1, and 10

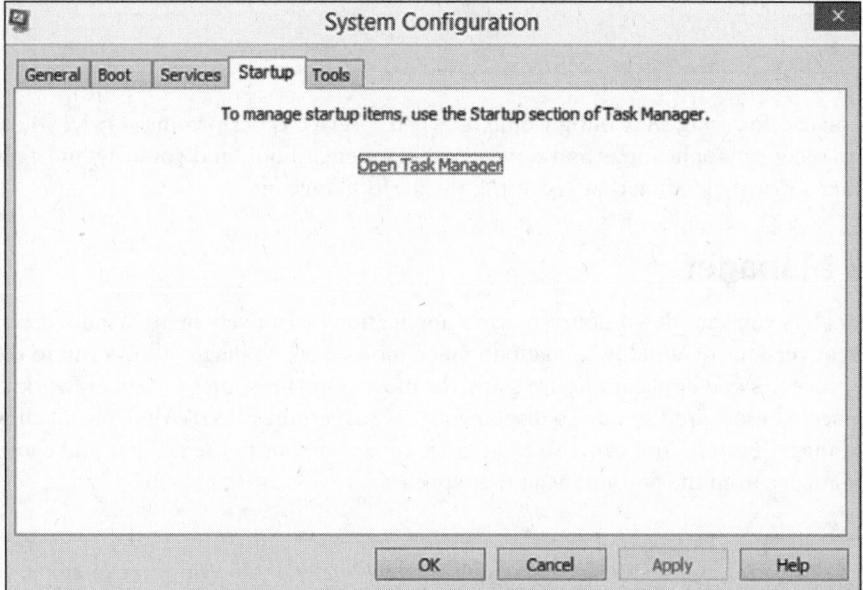

Tools

The Tools tab contains quick access to some of the most useful diagnostic tools in Windows. You can launch such items as the Registry Editor as well as many Control Panel applets, and you can enable or disable User Account Control (UAC). Figure 6.19 shows the Tools tab.

FIGURE 6.19   The Tools tab

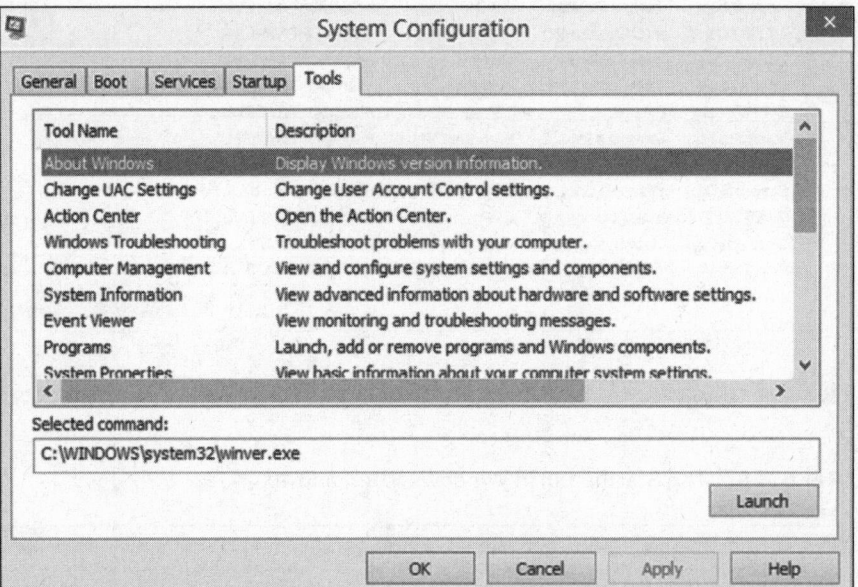

A scenario for using MSConfig would be when a device is performing slowly; you can check to see what applications and services are starting at boot, and you may find spyware and other software loading that is causing the performance hit.

Task Manager

This tool lets you shut down nonresponsive applications selectively in all Windows versions. In current versions of Windows, it can do much more. Task Manager allows you to see which processes and applications are using the most system resources, view network usage, see connected users, and so on. To display Task Manager, press Ctrl+Alt+Del and click the Task Manager button. You can also right-click an empty spot in the taskbar and choose Task Manager from the pop-up menu that appears.

To get to the Task Manager directly in any of the Windows versions, you can press Ctrl+Shift+Esc.

In Windows 7, Task Manager has six tabs: Applications, Processes, Performance, Networking, and Users. The Networking tab is shown only if your system has a network card installed (it is rare to find one that doesn't). The Users tab is displayed only if the computer you are working on is a member of a workgroup or is a stand-alone computer. The Users tab is unavailable on computers that are members of a network domain. In Windows 8, 8.1, and 10, there is an additional tab called Details, and the Applications tab is replaced with the App History tab. Let's look at these tabs, in the order of their appearance, in more detail in Windows 8.1.

Applications

The Applications tab (shown in Figure 6.20) lets you see which tasks are open on the machine. You also see the status of each task, which can be either Running or Not Responding. If a task or application has stopped responding (that is, it's hung), you can select the task in the list and click End Task. Doing so closes the program, and you can try to open it again. Often, although certainly not always, if an application hangs, you have to reboot the computer to prevent the same thing from happening again shortly after you restart the application. You can also use the Applications tab to switch to a different task or create new tasks.

FIGURE 6.20   The Applications tab

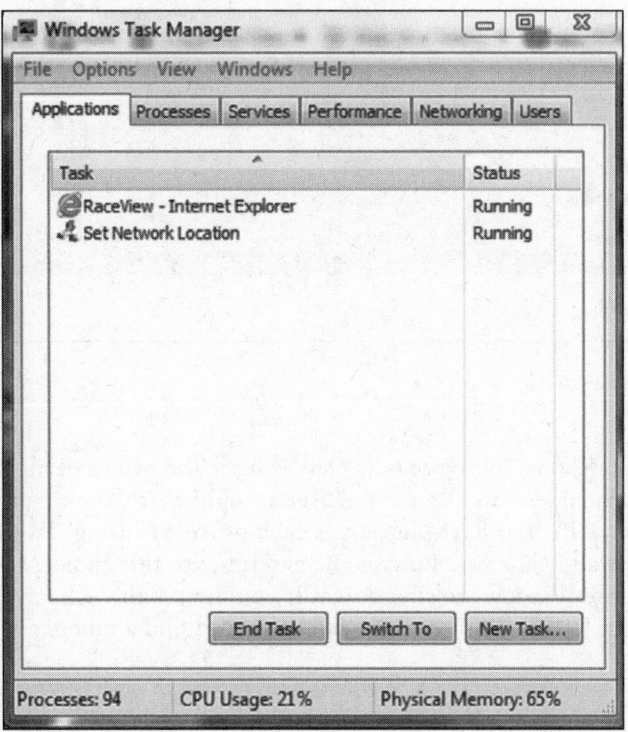

App History (Windows 8, 8.1, and 10 Only)

The App History tab in Windows 8, Windows 8.1, and Windows 10 (shown in Figure 6.21) displays the history of the usage of Metro apps only.

FIGURE 6.21 The App History tab

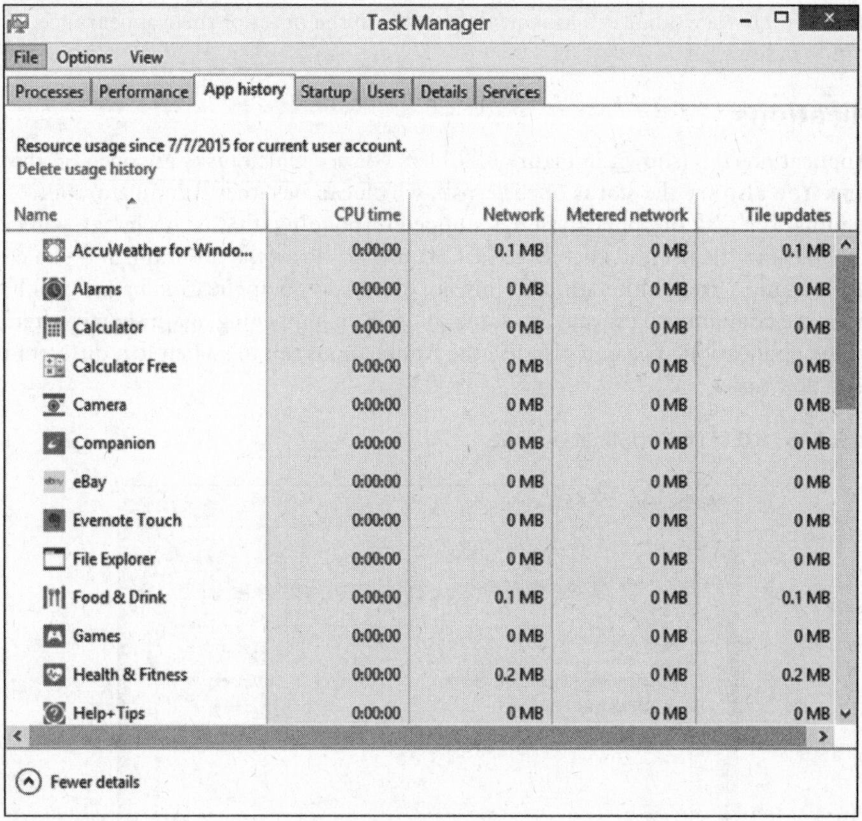

Name	CPU time	Network	Metered network	Tile updates
AccuWeather for Windo...	0:00:00	0.1 MB	0 MB	0.1 MB
Alarms	0:00:00	0 MB	0 MB	0 MB
Calculator	0:00:00	0 MB	0 MB	0 MB
Calculator Free	0:00:00	0 MB	0 MB	0 MB
Camera	0:00:00	0 MB	0 MB	0 MB
Companion	0:00:00	0 MB	0 MB	0 MB
eBay	0:00:00	0 MB	0 MB	0 MB
Evernote Touch	0:00:00	0 MB	0 MB	0 MB
File Explorer	0:00:00	0 MB	0 MB	0 MB
Food & Drink	0:00:00	0.1 MB	0 MB	0.1 MB
Games	0:00:00	0 MB	0 MB	0 MB
Health & Fitness	0:00:00	0.2 MB	0 MB	0.2 MB
Help+Tips	0:00:00	0 MB	0 MB	0 MB

Task Manager — File Options View — Processes | Performance | App history | Startup | Users | Details | Services

Resource usage since 7/7/2015 for current user account.
Delete usage history

Fewer details

Processes

The Processes tab (shown in Figure 6.22) lets you see the names of all the processes running on the machine. You also see the user account that's running the process, as well as how much CPU and RAM resources each process is using. To end a process, select it in the list and click End Process. Be careful with this choice, since ending some processes can cause Windows to shut down. If you don't know what a particular process does, you can look for it in any search engine and find a number of sites that will explain it.

FIGURE 6.22   The Processes tab

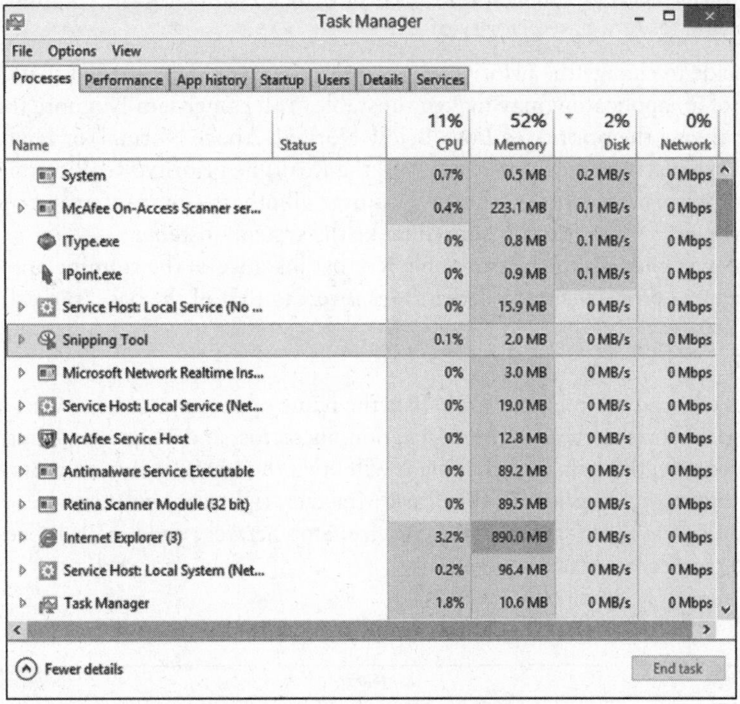

You can also change the priority of a process in Task Manager's Processes display by right-clicking the name of the process and choosing Set Priority.

In Windows 10

In Windows 10, setting the priority is done on the Details tab.

The six priorities, from lowest to highest, are as follows:

Low   For applications that need to complete sometime but that you don't want interfering with other applications. On a numerical scale from 0 to 31, this equates to a base priority of 4.

Below Normal   For applications that don't need to drop all the way down to Low. This equates to a base priority of 6.

Normal   The default priority for most applications. This equates to a base priority of 8.

Above Normal   For applications that don't need to boost all the way to High. This equates to a base priority of 10.

High   For applications that must complete soon, when you don't want other applications to interfere with the application's performance. This equates to a base priority of 13.

Realtime   For applications that must have the processor's attention to handle time-critical tasks. Applications can be run at this priority only by a member of the Administrators group. This equates to a base priority of 24.

If you decide to change the priority of an application, you'll be warned that changing the priority of an application may make it unstable. You can generally ignore this warning when changing the priority to Low, Below Normal, Above Normal, or High, but you should heed it when changing applications to the Realtime priority. Realtime means that the processor gives precedence to this process over all others—over security processes, over spooling, over everything—and is sure to make the system unstable.

Task Manager changes the priority only for that instance of the running application. The next time the process is started, priorities revert to that of the base (typically Normal).

Services

The Services tab (shown in Figure 6.23) lists the name of each running service, as well as the process ID associated with it, its description, its status, and its group. A button labeled Services appears on this tab, and clicking it will open the MMC console for Services, where you can configure each service. Within Task Manager, right-clicking a service will open a context menu listing three choices: Start Service, Stop Service, and Go To Process (which takes you to the Processes tab).

FIGURE 6.23   The Services tab

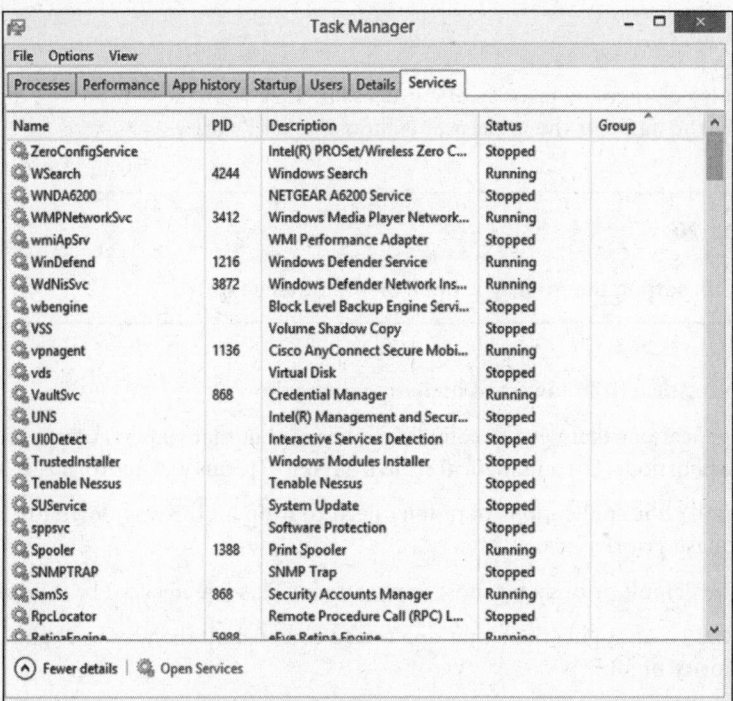

Performance

The Performance tab (shown in Figure 6.24) contains a variety of information, including overall CPU usage percentage, a graphical display of CPU usage history, page-file usage in megabytes, and a graphical display of page-file usage.

FIGURE 6.24 The Performance tab

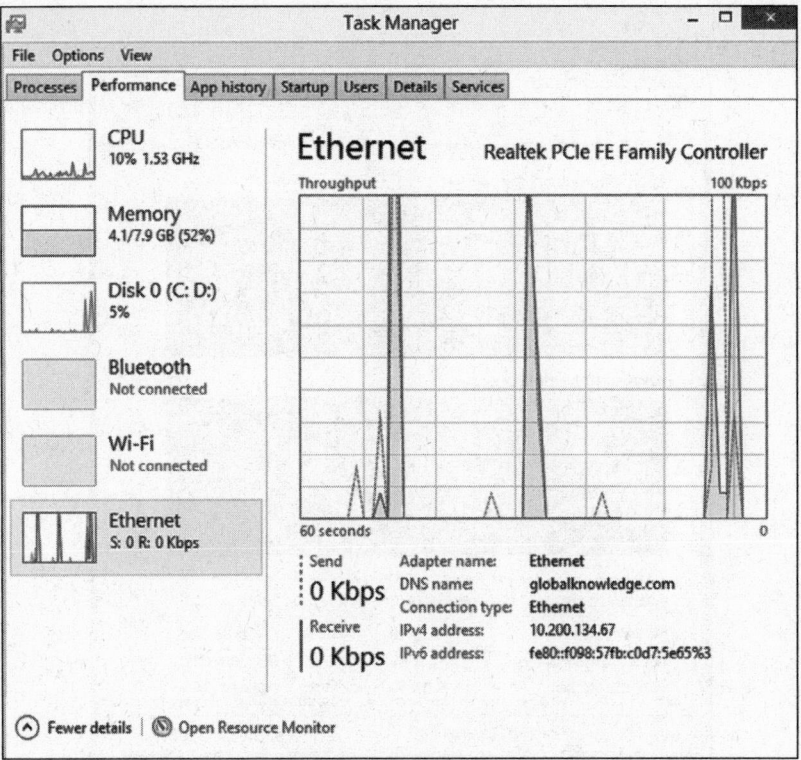

This tab also provides you with additional memory-related information such as physical and kernel memory usage, as well as the total number of handles, threads, and processes. Total, limit, and peak commit-charge information also displays. Some of the items are beyond the scope of this book, but it's good to know that you can use the Performance tab to keep track of system performance. Note that the number of processes, CPU usage percentage, and commit charge always display at the bottom of the Task Manager window, regardless of which tab you have currently selected.

In Windows 7 this pane has a button marked Resource Monitor, which breaks down resource usage on a per-process basis.

Networking

The Networking tab (shown in Figure 6.25) provides you with a graphical display of the performance of your network connection. It also tells you the network adapter name, link speed, and state. If you have more than one network adapter installed in the machine, you can select the appropriate adapter to see graphical usage data for that adapter.

FIGURE 6.25 The Networking tab

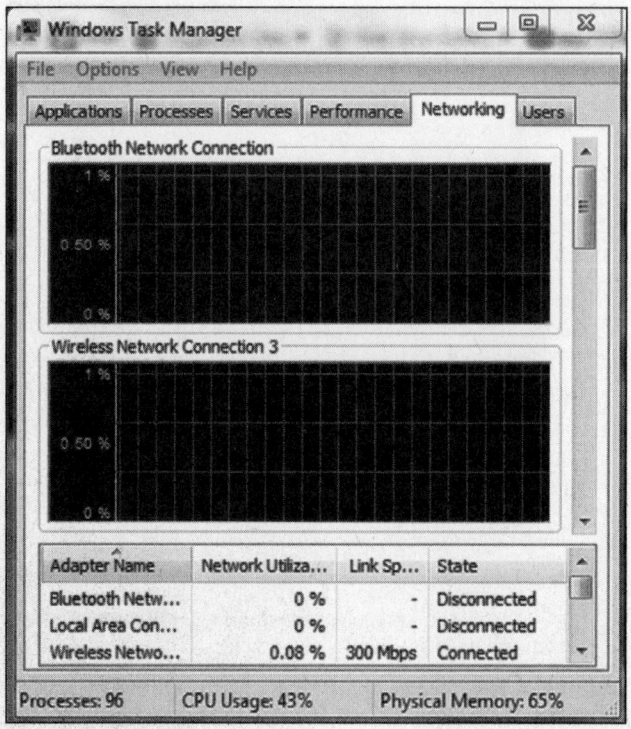

Users

The Users tab (shown in Figure 6.26) provides you with information about the users connected to the local machine. You'll see the username, ID, status, client name, and session type. You can right-click any connected user to perform a variety of functions, including sending the user a message, disconnecting the user, logging off the user, and initiating a remote-control session to the user's machine.

FIGURE 6.26   The Users tab

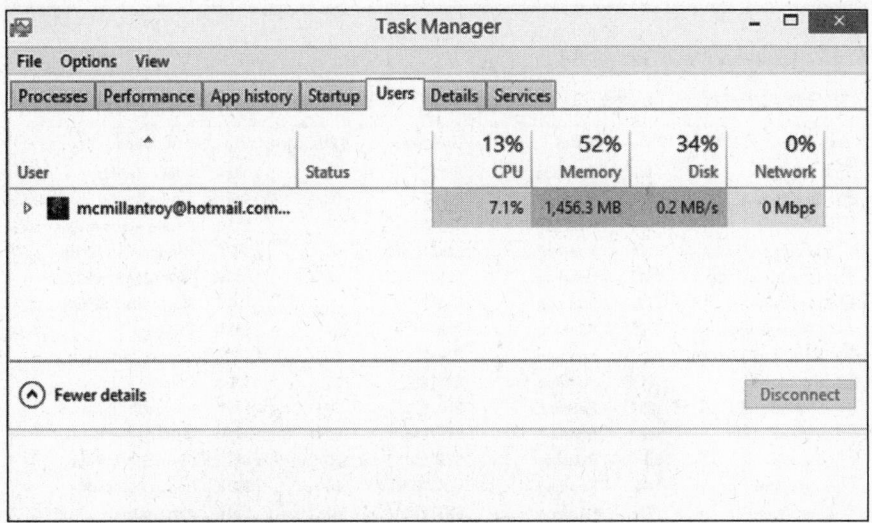

Windows 10

Windows 10 has only the functions Disconnect and Manage User Accounts.

Use Task Manager whenever the system seems bogged down by an unresponsive application.

Details (Windows 8, 8.1, and 10 Only)

The Details tab (shown in Figure 6.27) displays information about the processes that are running on the computer. A process can be an application that you start or subsystems and services that are managed by the operating system.

A scenario for using Task Manager is when you have a performance issue and you want to determine which compute resource (memory, disk, network, CPU) is overtaxed. By observing the percentage of use of each resource, you can first determine which resource is the problem and then locate the process that is using most of that resource.

FIGURE 6.27 The Details tab

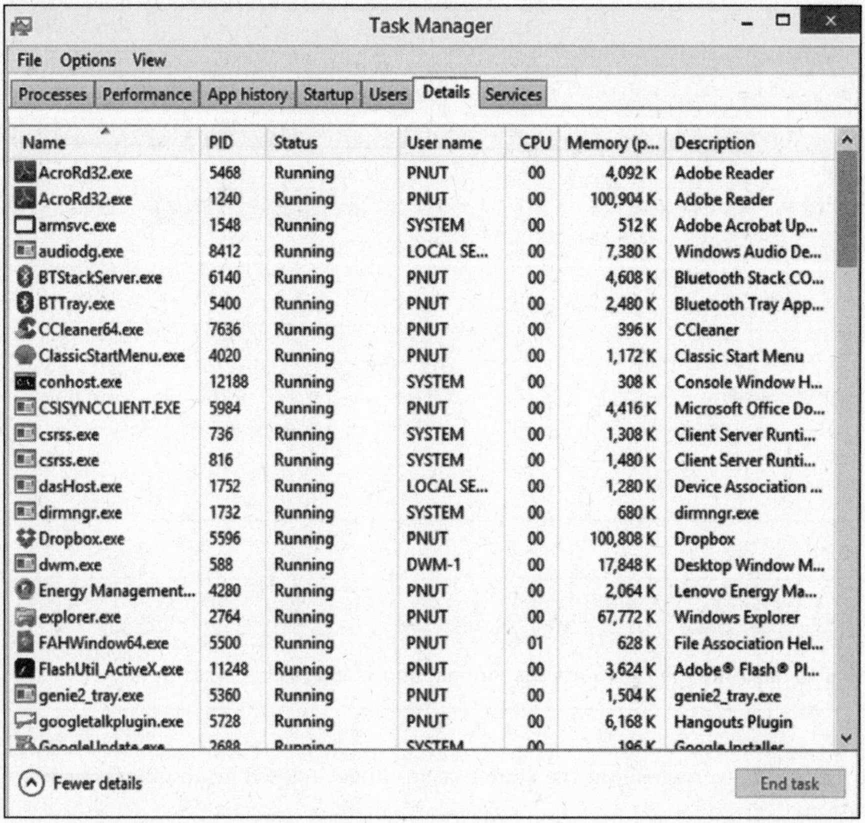

Disk Management

In Windows, you can manage your hard drives using the Disk Management tool. To access Disk Management, access the Control Panel and double-click Administrative Tools. Then double-click Computer Management. Finally, double-click Disk Management.

The Disk Management screen lets you view a host of information regarding all the drives installed in your system, including CD-ROM and DVD drives. The list of devices in the top portion of the screen shows you additional information for each partition on each drive, such as the file system used, status, free space, and so on. If you right-click a partition in either area, you can perform a variety of functions, such as formatting the partition and changing the name and drive letter assignment. For additional options and information, you can also access the properties of a partition by right-clicking it and selecting Properties.

The basic unit of storage is the disk. Disks are partitioned (primary, logical, extended) and then formatted for use. With the Windows operating systems this exam focuses on, you can choose to use either FAT32 or NTFS; the advantage of the latter is that it offers security and many other features that FAT32 can't handle. Both Windows 7 and Windows Vista can be installed only in NTFS, but they will recognize FAT partitions.

> If you're using FAT32 and want to change to NTFS, the convert utility will allow you to do so. For example, to change the E: drive to NTFS, the command is `convert e: /FS:NTFS`.

Once the disk is formatted, the next building block is the directory structure, in which you divide the partition into logical locations for storing data. Whether these storage units are called directories or folders is a matter of semantics—they tend to be called *folders* when viewed in the graphical user interface (GUI) and *directories* when viewed from the command line.

Drive status

The status of a drive can have a number of variables associated with it (System, Boot, and so on), but what really matters is whether it falls into the category of *healthy* or *unhealthy*. As the title implies, if it is healthy, it is properly working, and if it is unhealthy, you need to attend to it and correct problems. In Figure 6.28 you can see in the Status column of Disk Management that all drives are healthy.

FIGURE 6.28   Status in Disk Management

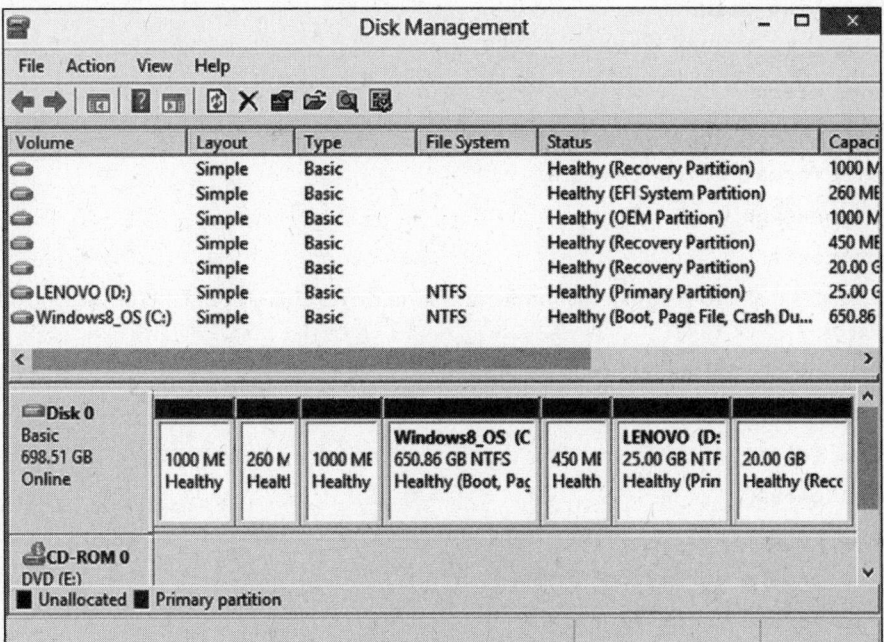

You can find a list of status states that are possible and require action at https://technet.microsoft.com/en-us/library/cc771775.aspx.

Mounting

Drives must be mounted before they can be used. Within Windows, most removable media (flash drives, CDs, and so forth) are recognized when attached and mounted. Volumes on basic disks, however, are not automatically mounted and assigned drive letters by default. To mount them, you must manually assign them drive letters or create mount points in Disk Management.

 You can also mount from the command line using either the Diskpart or Mountvol utility.

Initializing

Initializing a disk makes it available to the disk management system, and in most cases the drive will not show up until you do this. Once the drive has been connected or installed, it should be initialized. Initializing the drive can be done at the command line using diskpart or in the Disk Management tool. You need to know that initialization will wipe out any drive contents! To use diskpart to perform the initialization on 2 TB drives and smaller, follow these steps:

1. Open the Start menu and enter **diskpart**.
2. Enter **list disk**.
3. Enter **select disk** X (where X is the number your drive shows up as).
4. Enter **clean**.
5. Enter **create partition primary**.
6. Enter **format quick fs=ntfs**.
7. Enter **assign**.
8. Enter **exit**.

To use diskpart to perform the initialization on drives that are 2.5 TB or larger, follow these steps:

1. Open the Start menu and enter **diskpart**.
2. Enter **list disk**.
3. Enter **select disk** X (where X is the number your drive shows up as)
4. Enter **clean**.
5. Enter **convert gpt**.
6. Enter **create partition primary**.
7. Enter **format quick fs=ntfs**.

8. Enter **assign**.

9. Enter **exit**.

To use Disk Management, follow this procedure:

1. Install the drive and reboot the device.

2. In the search line, enter **Disk Management**. With the drive connected, you will get the pop-up box shown in Figure 6.29.

3. If you got the pop-up, choose either MBR or GPT and click OK.

FIGURE 6.29   The Initialize Disk pop-up

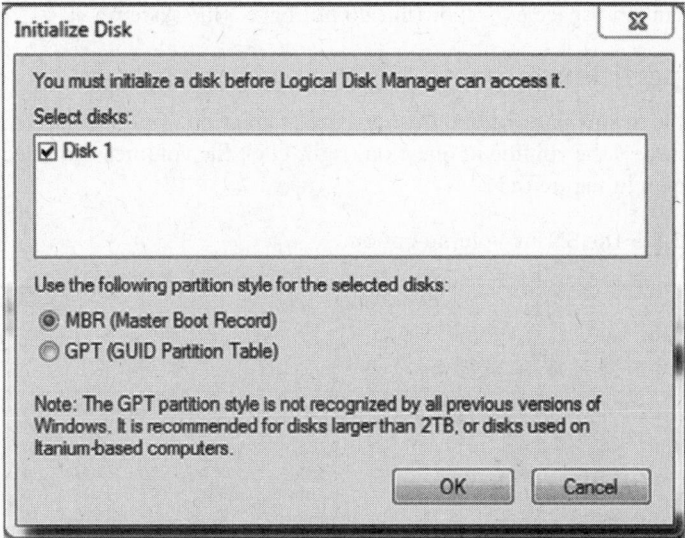

If you didn't get the pop-up, right-click and select to initialize the newly added drive under where it says Disk 1, as shown in Figure 6.30.

FIGURE 6.30   The Initialize Disk option

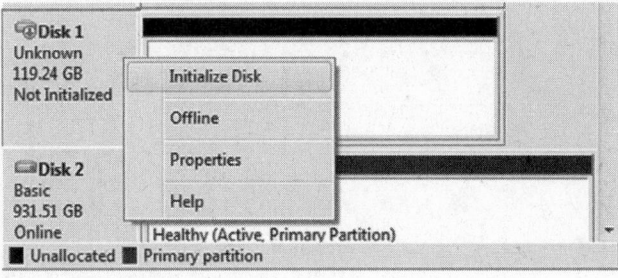

Extending partitions

It is possible to add more space to partitions (and logical drives) by extending them into unallocated space. This is done in Disk Management by right-clicking and choosing Extend or using the Diskpart utility.

Splitting partitions

Just as you can extend a partition, you can also reduce the size of it. While this operation is generically known as *splitting* the partition, the menu option in Disk Management is Shrink. By shrinking an existing partition, you are creating another with unallocated space that can then be used for other purposes. You can shrink only basic volumes that use the NTFS file system (and space exists) or that do not have a file system.

Shrinking partitions

It is also possible to shrink a volume from its size at creation. To do so in Disk Management, access the volume in question, right-click the volume, and select Shrink Volume, as shown in Figure 6.31.

FIGURE 6.31   The Shrink Volume option

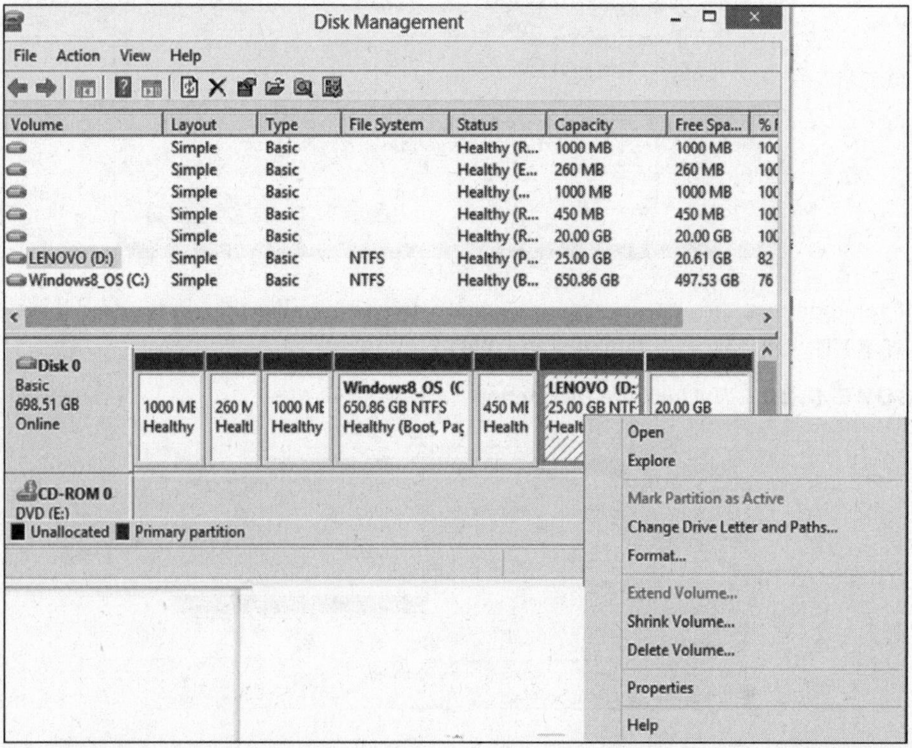

This will open another box that will allow you to control how much you want to shrink the volume, as shown in Figure 6.32.

FIGURE 6.32 Setting the volume size

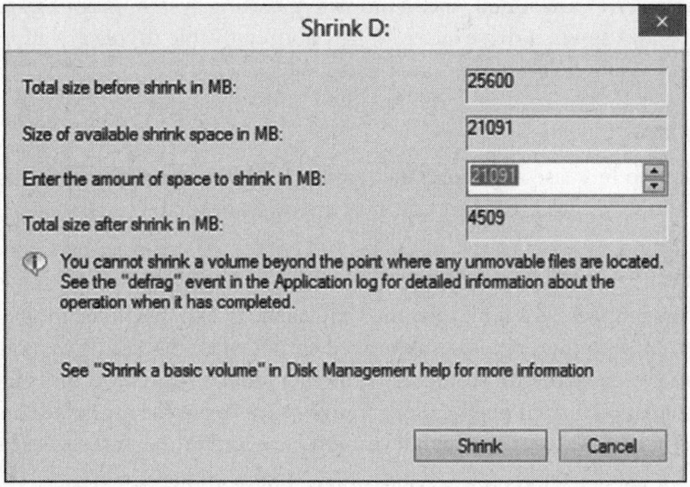

Shrink D:
Total size before shrink in MB:
25600
Size of available shrink space in MB:
21091
Enter the amount of space to shrink in MB:
21091
Total size after shrink in MB:
4509
You cannot shrink a volume beyond the point where any unmovable files are located. See the "defrag" event in the Application log for detailed information about the operation when it has completed.
See "Shrink a basic volume" in Disk Management help for more information
Shrink
Cancel

Assigning/changing drive letters

Mounting drives and assigning drive letters are two tasks that go hand-in-hand. When you mount a drive, you typically assign it a drive letter to be able to access it. Right-clicking a volume in Disk Management gives the option Change Drive Letter And Paths, as shown in Figure 6.33.

FIGURE 6.33 Changing the drive letter

Disk Management
File Action View Help
Volume Layout Type File System Status
Simple Basic Healthy (Recovery Partition) 1000
Simple Basic Healthy (EFI System Partition) 260
Simple Basic Healthy (OEM Partition) 1000
Simple Basic Healthy (Recovery Partition) 450
Simple Basic Healthy (Recovery Partition) 20.00
LENOVO (D:) Simple Basic NTFS Healthy (Primary Partition) 25.00
Windows8_OS (C:) Simple Basic NTFS Healthy (Boot, Page File, Crash Du... 650.86
Disk 0
Basic
698.51 GB
Online
Windows8_OS (C
650.86 GB NTFS
LENOVO (D:
25.00 GB NTF
20.00 GB
CD-ROM 0
DVD (E:)
Unallocated
Primary partition
Open
Explore
Mark Partition as Active
Change Drive Letter and Paths...
Format...
Extend Volume...
Shrink Volume...
Delete Volume...
Properties
Help

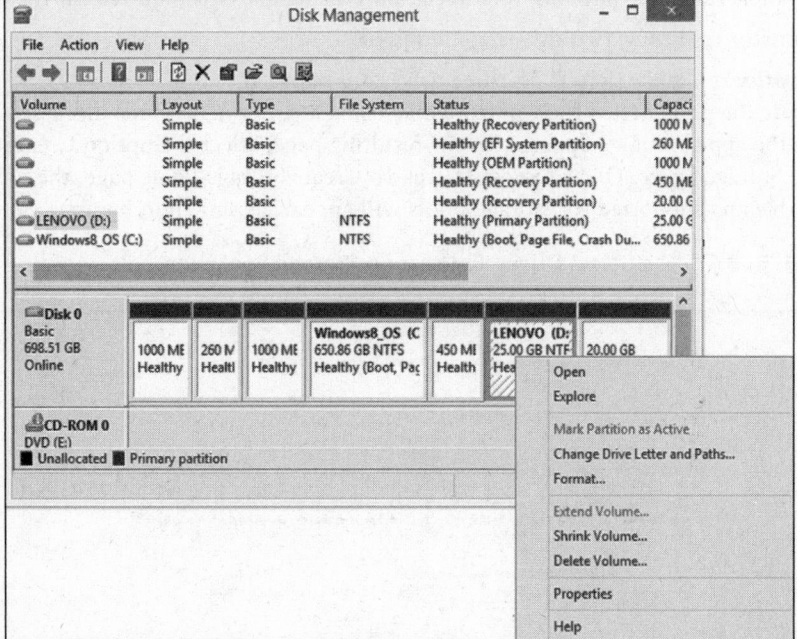

Adding drives

When removable drives are added, the Windows operating system is configured, by default, to identify them and assign a drive letter. When nonremovable drives are added, you must mount them and assign a drive letter, as mentioned earlier.

Adding arrays

Arrays are added to increase fault tolerance (using RAID) or performance (striping). Disk Management allows you to create and modify arrays as needed.

Storage spaces

Configuring storage spaces is a fault tolerance and capacity expansion technique that can be used as an alternative to the techniques described earlier when discussing dynamic volume types. It enables you to virtualize storage by grouping industry-standard disks into storage pools and then creating virtual disks called *storage spaces* from the available capacity in the storage pools. This means that, at a high level, you have to do three tasks to use storage spaces.

1. Create a storage pool, which is a collection of physical disks.

2. From the storage pool, create a storage space, which can also be thought of as a virtual disk.

3. Create one or more volumes on the storage space.

First let's look at creating the pool from several physical disks. Each of the disks must be at least 4 GB in size and should not have any volumes in it. The number of disks required depends on the type of resiliency you want to provide to the resulting storage space. Resiliency refers to the type of fault tolerance desired. Use the following guidelines:

▪ For simple resiliency (no fault tolerance), only a single disk is required for the pool.

▪ For mirror resiliency, two drives are required.

▪ For parity resiliency (RAID 5), three drives are required.

To create the pool, access the Control Panel using any of the methods discussed so far and click the applet Storage Spaces. On the resulting page, select the option Create A New Pool And Storage Space. On the Select Drives To Create Storage Pools page, the drives that are available and supported for storage pools will appear, as shown in Figure 6.34.

FIGURE 6.34   The Select Drives To Create A Storage Pool page

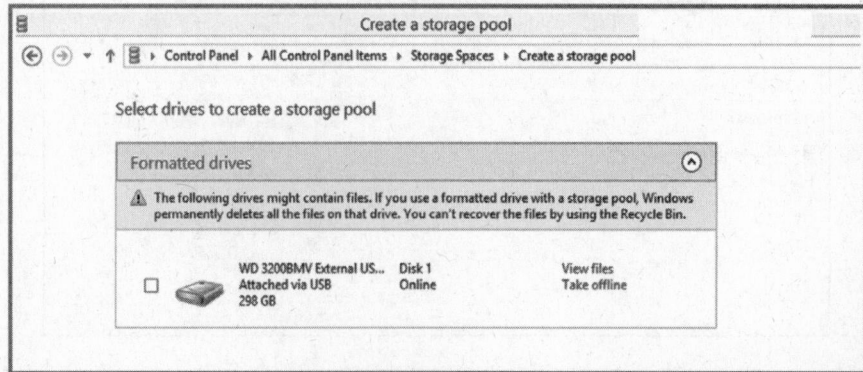

In this case, only one drive is eligible, so you can create only a simple type pool. Check the drive and click the Create Pool button at the bottom of the page. On the next page, give the space a name, select a drive letter, and choose the file system (NTFS or REFS), the resiliency type (in this case you can select only Simple), and the size of the pool. Figure 6.35 shows the pool as Myspace, with a drive letter of F, an NTFS file system, simple resiliency, and a maximum size of 100 GB. When you click Create Storage Space, the space will be created. Be aware that any data on the physical drive will be erased in this process!

FIGURE 6.35   Creating a storage space

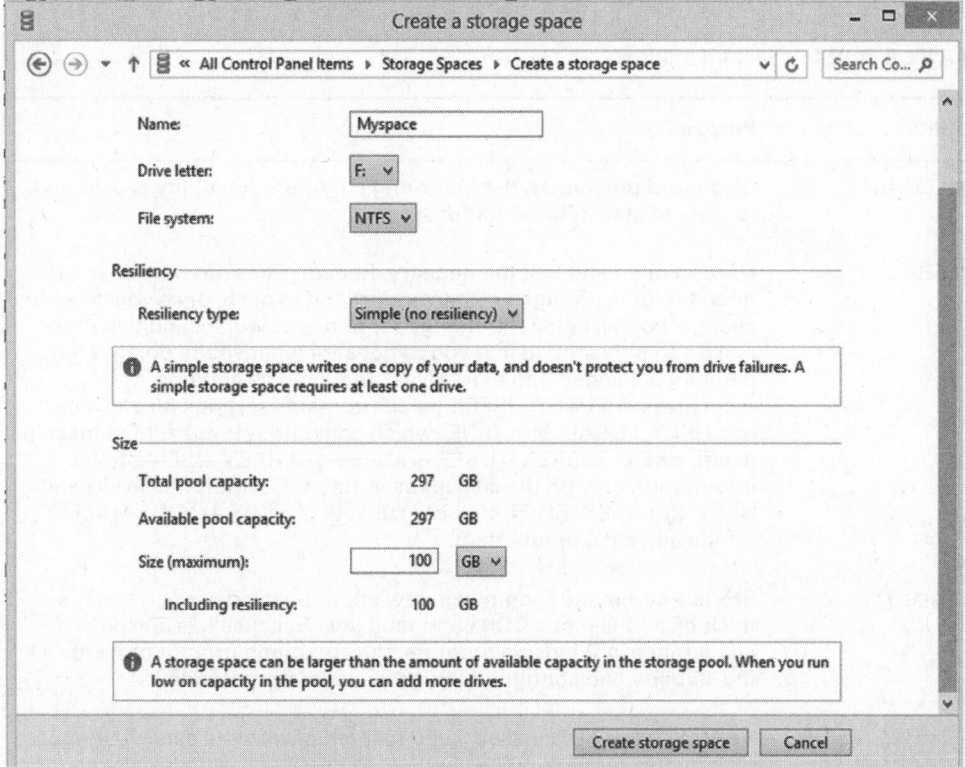

When the process is finished, the new space will appear on the Manage Storage Spaces page. Now you have a pool and a space derived from the pool. The last step is to create a volume in the storage space. If you now access Disk Management, you will see a new virtual disk called Myspace. It will be a basic disk, but you can convert it to dynamic by right-clicking it and selecting Convert To Dynamic Disk. This will allow to you shrink or delete the existing volume if you desire.

A scenario for using `diskpart` is to extend a partition that is getting full.

1.   In the command prompt, enter **diskpart**.

2.   At the Diskpart prompt, enter **list disk**.

3.   Then enter **select disk** *n* where *n* is the partition you want to extend.

4. Enter **list partition**.

5. Select the partition which you want to extend. Enter **partition** *n*, where *n* is the partition you want to extend.

6. Enter **extend size**=*n*, where *n* is the size in megabytes you want to add to the partition.

System utilities

Table 6.21 lists the utilities CompTIA singles out as relevant to know for this section. All of these can be started from Start Run by typing the name and pressing Enter.

TABLE 6.21   System utilities

Utility	Purpose
MSCONFIG	Discussed previously, the MSConfig configuration utility is useful for looking at start-related settings.
REGEDIT	Used to open and edit the Registry. Regedit does not have save or undo features (though you can import and export); once you make a change, you've made the change for better or worse, and this is not a place to play around in if you're not sure what you're doing. The Registry is divided into five "hives" that hold all settings. The two main hives are HKEY_USERS (which contains settings for all users) and HKEY_LOCAL_MACHINE (which contains settings for the machine itself). HKEY_CURRENT_USER is a subset of HKEY_USERS, holding information only on the current user. HKEY_CURRENT_CONFIG and HKEY_CLASSES_ROOT are both subsets of HKEY_LOCAL_MACHINE for the current configuration.
COMMAND	Starts a command prompt window intentionally designed to have the look and feel of a DOS command line. Because it is, despite its appearance, a Windows program, the command prompt provides all the stability and configurability you expect from Windows.
SERVICES.MSC	An MMC snap-in that allows you to interact with the services running on the computer. The status of the services will typically be either started or stopped, and you can right-click and choose Start, Stop, Pause, Resume, or Restart from the context menu. Services can be started automatically or manually, or they can be disabled. If you right-click the service and choose Properties from the context menu, you can choose the startup type as well as see the path to the executable and any dependencies.
MMC	Starts the management console, allowing you to run any snap-in (such as SERVICES.MSC)

Utility	Purpose
MSTSC	Remote Desktop Connection Usage is used to configure remote desktop connections.
NOTEPAD	Starts a simple editor. You can edit a file that already exists or create a new one.
EXPLORER	Starts the Windows interface, allowing you to interact with files and folders
MSINFO32	The System Information dialog box, this tool displays a thorough list of settings on the machine. You cannot change any values from here, but you can search, export, save, and run a number of utilities. It is primarily used during diagnostics because it is an easy way to display settings such as IRQs and DMAs.
DXDIAG	The DirectX Diagnostic tool (which has the executable name dxdiag) allows you to test DirectX functionality, with a focus on display, sound, and input. When started, you can also verify that your drivers have been signed by Microsoft. DirectX is a collection of APIs related to multimedia.
Defrag	Defrag is a tool that can be used to reorganize the data on a drive such that all parts of each file are located in the same place, improving performance.
System Restore	System Restore is a tool that can be used to create restore points, or snapshots of a system at certain points in time that can be returned to when a system gets corrupted. When a restore is performed, it leaves all data unaltered but returns the operating system settings to the state they were in when the restore point was created.
Windows Update	Windows Update is a tool that can be used to automate the process of checking for updates and patches. Once the feature is enabled, the system will check with the Update website for missing patches on a schedule and keep the device up-to-date. You have four choices for the update process: Install Updates Automatically downloads the updates and installs them when they are available; Download Updates And Let Me Choose When To Install downloads the updates and notifies the user; Check For Updates But Let Me Choose Whether To Download And Install Them just notifies the user an update is available; Never Check For Updates stops all update notifications.

Exam essentials

Describe the Administrative tools in Windows.   These tools include Computer Management, Device Manager, Users and Groups, Local Security Policy, Performance Monitor, Services, System Configuration, Task Scheduler, Component Services, Data Sources, Print Management, Windows Memory Diagnostics, Windows Firewall, Advanced Security, and User Account Management.

1.6 Given a scenario, use Microsoft Windows Control Panel utilities.

The Control Panel is often the first place to turn for configuration settings. The applets contained within it allow you to customize the system and personalize it for each user.

Among the applets that every version of Windows has in common, CompTIA specifically singles out a number of them for you to know. The topics covered in this chapter include the following:

- Internet Options
- Display/Display Settings
- User Accounts
- Folder Options
- Windows Firewall
- Power Options
- Credential Manager
- Programs and features
- HomeGroup
- Devices and Printers
- Sound
- Troubleshooting
- Network and Sharing Center
- Device Manager
- Bitlocker
- Sync Center

Internet Options

The configuration settings for Internet Options provide a number of Internet connectivity possibilities. The tabs here include Connections, Security, General, Privacy, Content, Programs, and Advanced.

Connections

As the name implies, from this tab you can configure connections for an Internet connection, a dial-up or VPN connection, and LAN settings, as shown in Figure 6.36.

FIGURE 6.36   The Connections tab

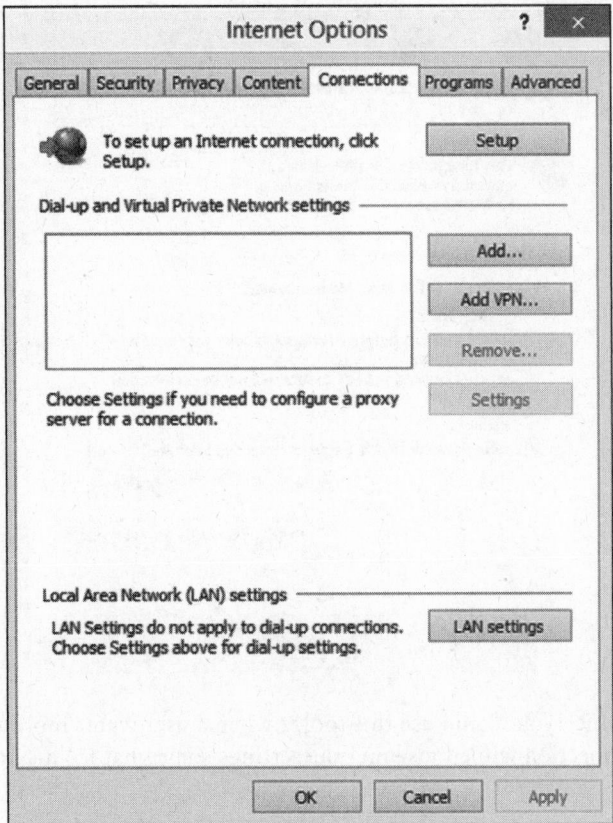

A scenario for using this tool would be when a user needs you to configure his laptop with a VPN connection to the office.

Security

On the Security tab, as shown in Figure 6.37, you can choose both a zone and a security level for the zone. The zones include Internet, Local Intranet, Trusted Sites, and Restricted Sites. The default security level for most of the zones is between High and Medium-High, but you can also select lower levels.

FIGURE 6.37   The Security tab

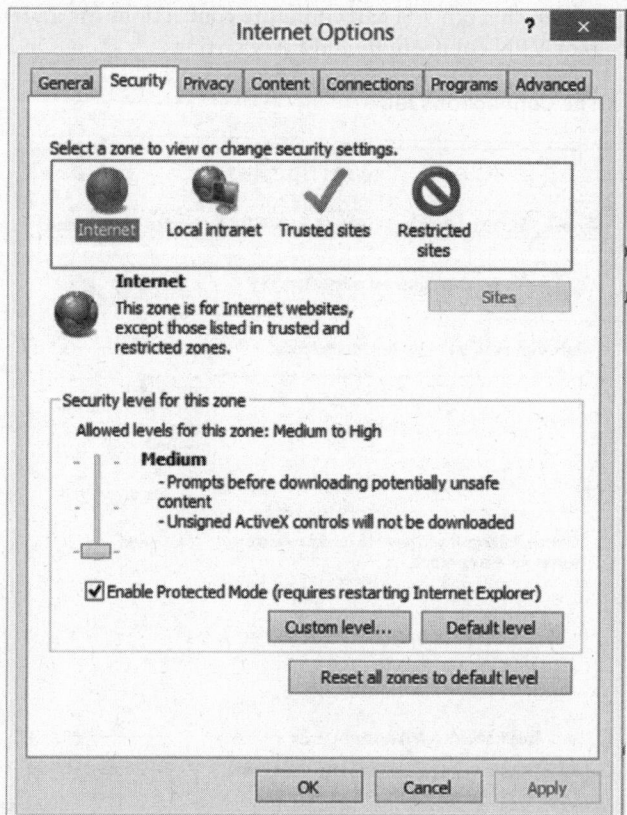

A scenario in which you would use this tool is when a user wants more secure settings on his Internet connection while loosening the settings somewhat for his home network.

General

On the General tab, as shown in Figure 6.38, you can configure the home page that appears when the browser starts or a new tab is opened. You can also configure the history settings, search defaults, what happens by default when new tabs are opened, and the appearance of the browser (colors, languages, fonts, and accessibility).

FIGURE 6.38 The General tab

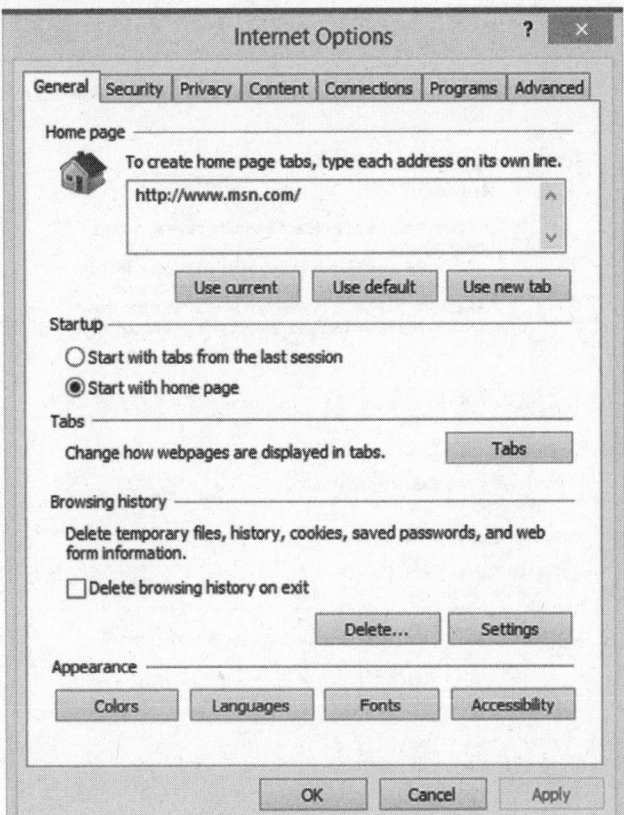

A scenario for using this tool is when a user would like to change his home page to the company intranet site.

Privacy

Privacy settings, as shown in Figure 6.39, allow you to configure the privacy level, choose whether you want to provide location information, use Pop-up Blocker, and disable toolbars (and extensions) when InPrivate Browsing starts.

FIGURE 6.39   The Privacy tab

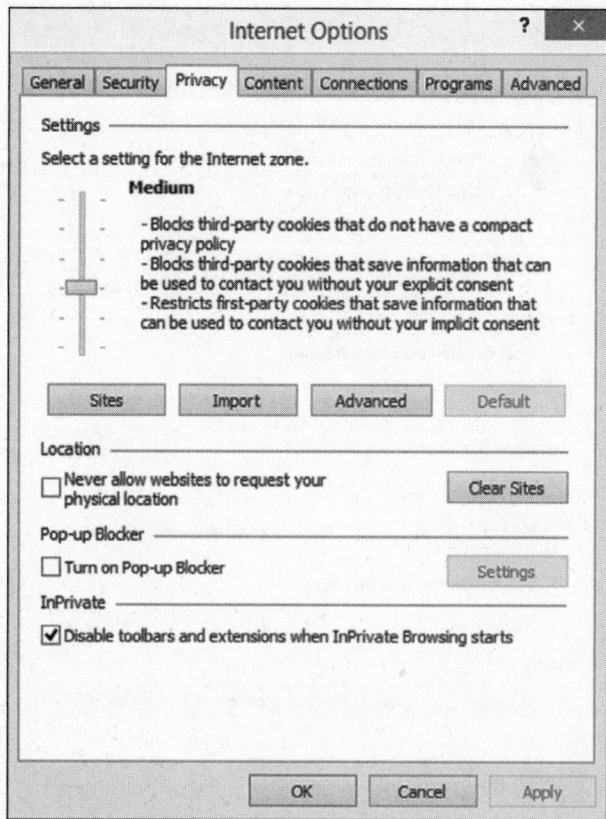

A scenario for using this tool would be when a user needs to disable pop-ups for a site that requires them to function properly.

Programs

On the Programs tab, as shown in Figure 6.40, you specify which browser you want to be the default browser, what editor to use if HTML needs editing, and what programs to associate with various file types. You can also manage add-ons from here.

FIGURE 6.40   The Programs tab

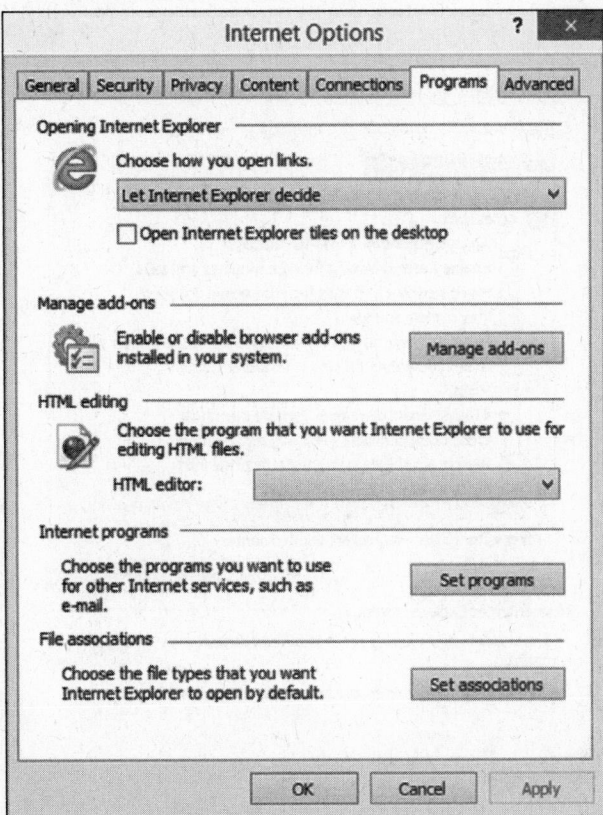

A scenario for using this tool is when a user has an unusual file type that his system doesn't recognize. You could use this tool to associate the file type with the application that opens it.

Advanced

On the Advanced tab, as shown in Figure 6.41, you can reset settings to their default options. You can also toggle configuration settings for granular settings not found on other tabs.

FIGURE 6.41   The Advanced tab

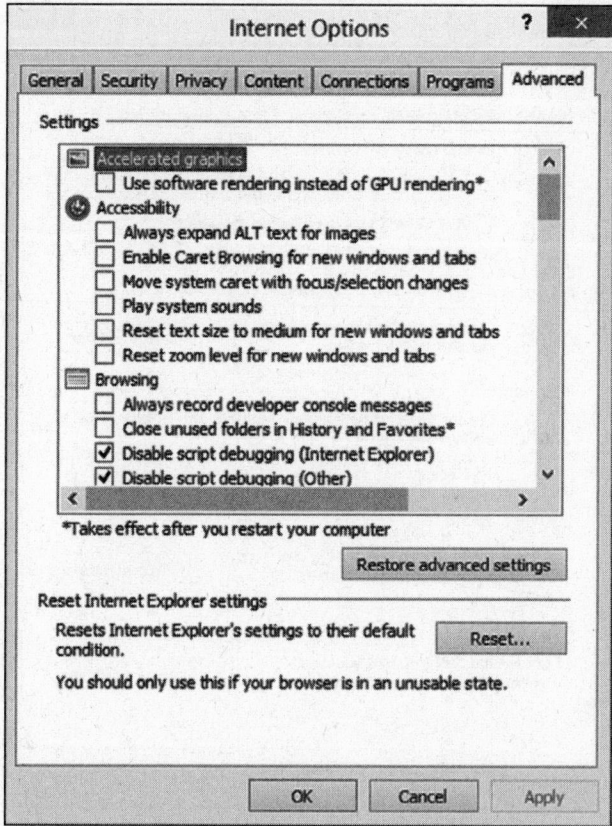

A scenario for using this tab would be when a user has played with the settings and would like to get them back to the default; this tool will do it.

Display/Display Settings

Display or Display Settings can be found by right-clicking the desktop and selecting Display Settings.

Resolution

The resolution settings vary based on the OS, but when you need to set the resolution, this is the place to do it. The documentation that comes with the computer will prescribe a Recommended setting that you should not exceed.

Color depth

Color depth is either the number of bits used to indicate the color of a single pixel, in a bit-mapped image or video frame buffer, or the number of bits used for each color component of a single pixel. In Windows 7, this can be set on the Monitor tab of the properties of the adapter, as shown in Figure 6.42.

FIGURE 6.42   Windows 7 color depth

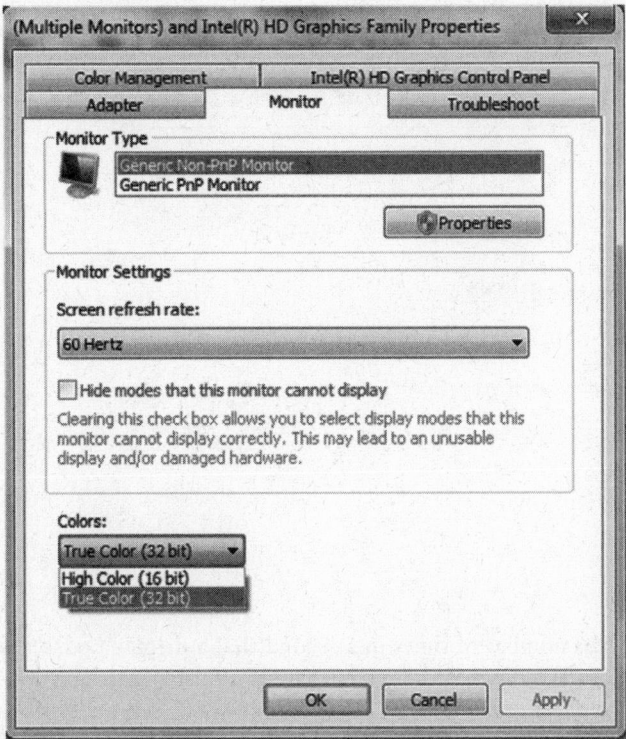

In Windows 8, 8.1 and Windows 10, color depth, resolution, and refresh rate are all the same drop-down box and are found after clicking the List All Modes button on the Adapter tab of the display, as shown in Figure 6.43.

FIGURE 6.43 Windows 8.1 color depth, refresh rate, and resolution

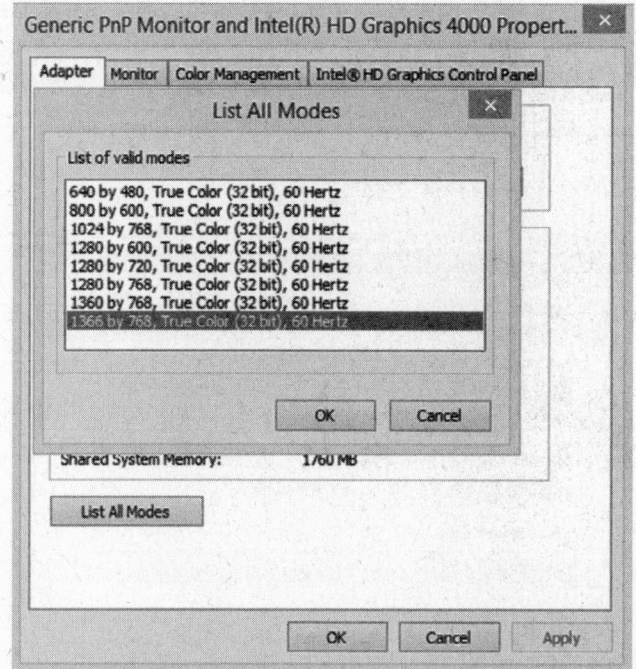

Refresh rate

The refresh rate is the number of times in a second that a display updates its buffer and is expressed in hertz. In Windows 7, the refresh rate is set using a drop-down box just above the setting for color depth (see Figure 6.42). In Windows 8, 8.1, and 10, the setting is located as described in the previous section, "Color depth."

User Accounts

This dialog box lets you create and manage user accounts, parental controls, and related settings. The default users created are Administrator, Guest, and the administrative account created during the install.

Folder Options

This dialog box lets you configure how folders are displayed in Windows Explorer.

View hidden files

On the View tab, shown in Figure 6.44, beneath Advanced Settings, you can choose the option Show Hidden Files, Folders, And Drives, and this will allow you to see those items. The opposite of this—the default setting—is Don't Show Hidden Files, Folders, Or Drives. Radio buttons allow you to choose only one of these options.

FIGURE 6.44   View tab

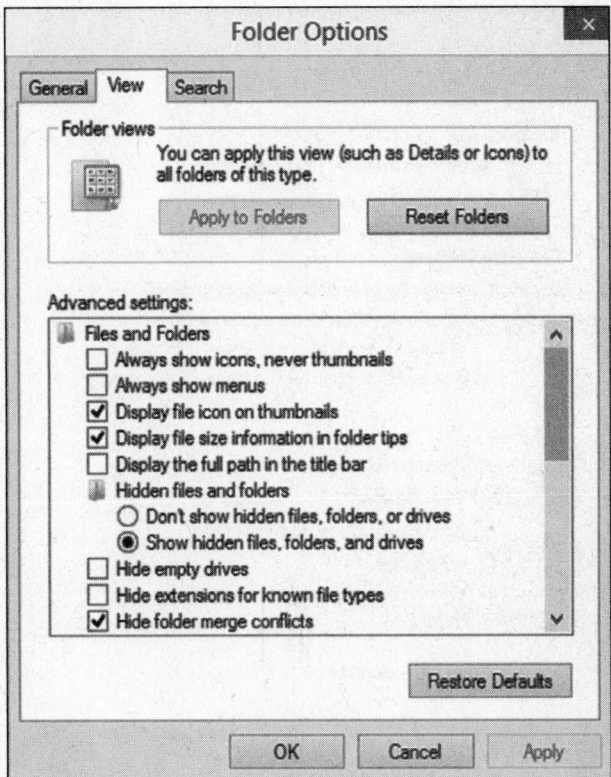

A related check box that you should also clear in order to see all files is Hide Protected Operating System Files (Recommended) (Not shown in Figure 6.44.) When this check box is cleared, those files will also appear in the view you are seeing.

Hiding these files is recommended so that users do not inadvertently delete or change these critical files. Hiding them is the default setting.

Hide extensions

On the View tab, shown in Figure 6.44, you must clear the check box Hide Extensions For Known File Types in order for the extensions to be shown with the files.

General options

You can configure the layout on the General tab of Folder Options (shown in Figure 6.45). Browsing options allow you to choose whether each folder will open in its own folder or the same folder. The Navigation Pane setting allows you to control what items are included in the tree structure that appears to the left when using File Explorer.

FIGURE 6.45   The General tab

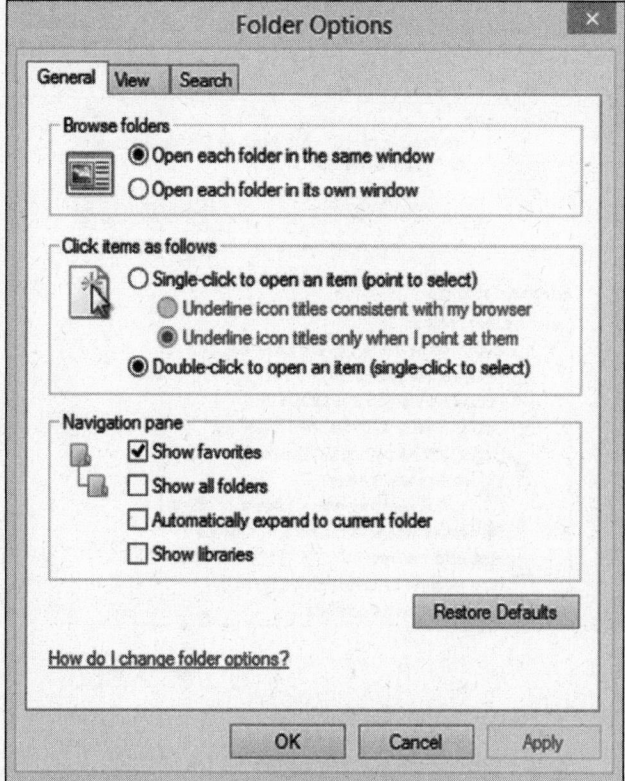

View options

Along with the setting that allows you to hide or show file extensions and to show hidden files are a number of other settings that affect what you see when you use File Explorer (as shown in Figure 6.44 earlier).

Always Show Icons, Never Thumbnails   Always show icons, rather than thumbnail previews of files. Use this setting if thumbnail previews are slowing down your computer.

Always Show Menus   Always show menus above the toolbar. Use this setting if you want access to the classic menus, which are hidden by default.

Display File Icon On Thumbnails   Always shows the icon for a file in addition to the thumbnail (for easier access to the related program).

Display File Size Information In Folder Tips   See the size of a folder in a tip when you point to the folder.

Hide Protected Operating System Files   See all system files that are usually hidden from view.

Hide Empty Drives In The Computer Folder   Show removable media drives (such as card readers) in the Computer folder even if they currently don't have media inserted.

Launch Folder Windows In A Separate Process   Increase the stability of Windows by opening every folder in a separate part of memory.

Restore Previous Folder Windows At Logon   Automatically open the folders that you were using when you last shut down Windows whenever you start your computer.

Show Drive Letters   Hide or show the drive letter of each drive or device in the Computer folder.

Show Encrypted Or Compressed NTFS Files In Color   Display encrypted or compressed NTFS files with unique color coding to identify them.

Show Pop-Up Description For Folder And Desktop Items   Turn off the tips that display file information when you point to files.

Show Preview Handlers In Preview Pane   Never show or always show the contents of files in the preview pane. Use this setting to improve the performance of your computer or if you don't want to use the preview pane.

Use Check Boxes To Select Items   Add check boxes to file views for easier selection of several files at once. This can be useful if it's difficult for you to hold down the Ctrl key while clicking to select multiple files.

When typing into list view, there are two radio buttons.

Automatically Type Into The Search Box   Automatically puts the cursor in the search box when you start typing.

Select The Type Item In The View   Does not automatically put the cursor in the search box when you start typing.

System

This utility allows you to view and configure various system elements. From within this one relatively innocuous panel, you can make a large number of configuration changes to a Windows machine. The different versions of Windows have different options available in this panel, but they will include some of the following: General, Network Identification, Device Manager, Hardware, Hardware Profiles, User Profiles, Environment, Startup/Shutdown, Performance, System Restore, Automatic Updates, Remote, Computer Name, and Advanced. System is found in Control Panel.

The General tab gives you an overview of the system, such as OS version, registration information, basic hardware levels (Processor and RAM), and the service pack level that's installed, if any.

Performance (virtual memory)

Performance settings are configured on the Advanced tab, as shown in Figure 6.46. Clicking the Settings button allows you to change the visual effects used on the system and configure Data Execution Prevention (DEP). Data execution prevention is a security feature that prevents the execution of certain processes in key files. You can also configure virtual memory on the Advanced tab. Virtual memory is the paging file used by Windows as RAM.

FIGURE 6.46   Advanced tab

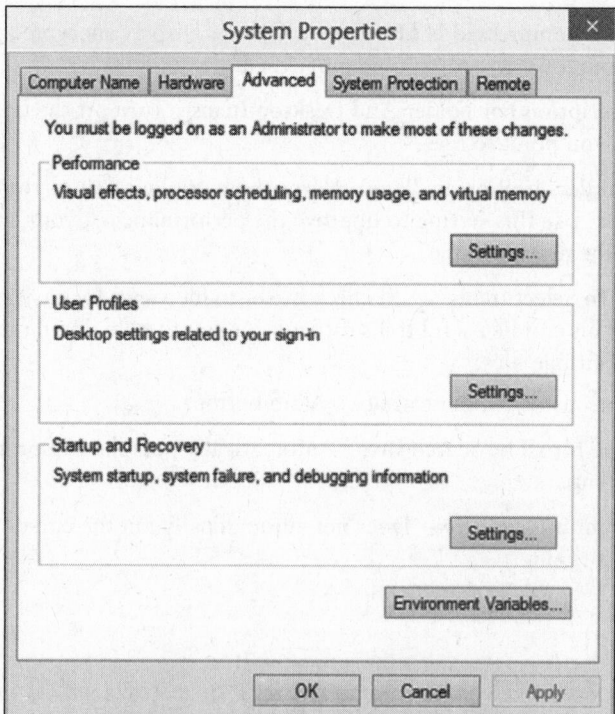

In most cases you should never change the virtual memory section but in cases where performance is lagging you can try to dedicate more disk space for this function.

Remote settings

On the Remote tab, as shown in Figure 6.47, you can choose whether to allow Remote Assistance to be enabled.

FIGURE 6.47   Remote tab

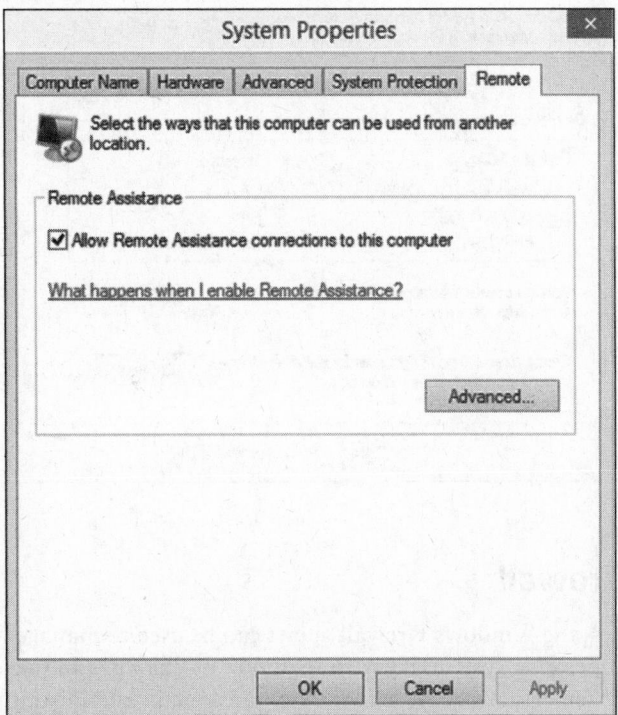

System protection

On the System Protection tab, as shown in Figure 6.48, you can choose to do a system restore as well as create a manual restore point and see the date and time associated with the most recent automatic restore point.

FIGURE 6.48   The System Protection tab

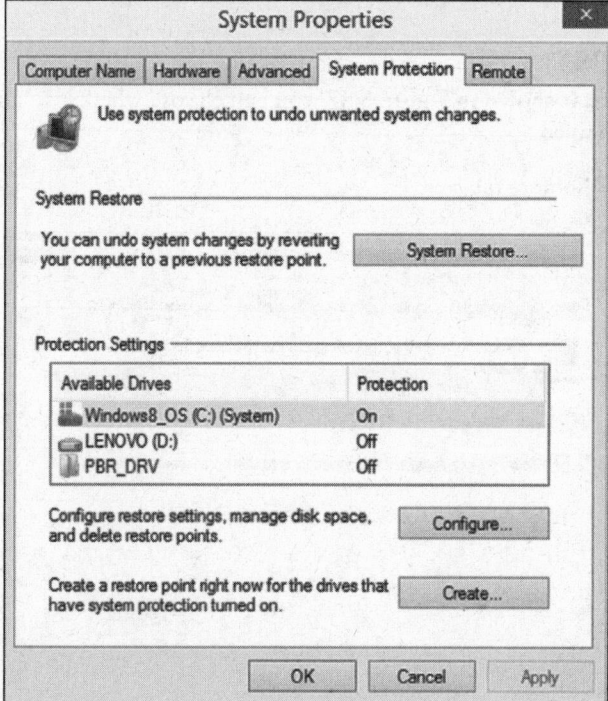

Windows Firewall

As the name implies, the Windows Firewall applet can be used to manage the firewall included with the operating system. Figure 6.49 shows an example. In this case, the computer's firewall settings are being managed by the domain administrator. When the computer is outside of that network, the firewall settings are available to the user of the computer.

FIGURE 6.49   The Windows Firewall

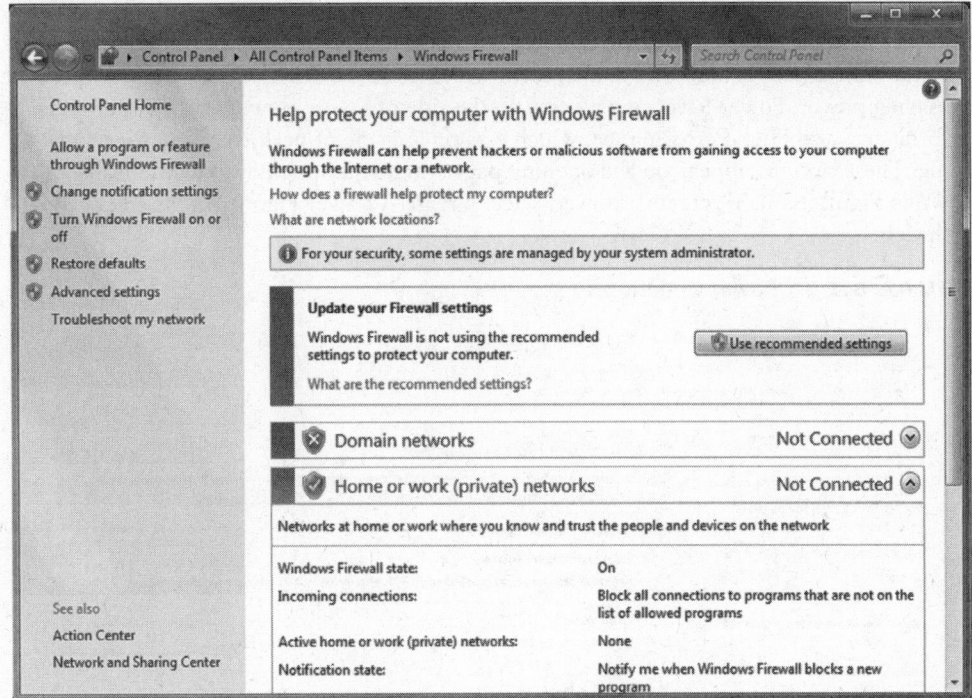

Power Options

Here you can configure different power schemes to adjust power consumption, dictating when devices—the display and the computer—will turn off or be put to sleep. Through the Advanced Settings, you can configure the need to enter a password to revive the devices, as well as configure wireless adapter settings, Internet options (namely, JavaScript), and the system sleep policy. Common choices include the following:

- **Standby** puts your computer into energy-saving mode, where it uses little power.

- **Hibernate** saves your workspace (all your open windows) and then turns the computer off.

- **Sleep/suspend** puts your computer into an even deeper energy-saving mode than Standby, where it uses even less power.

Power plans

Power plans are collections of power settings that determine when various components in the device are shut down. There are some built-in plans available, or you can create your own. There are three default plans: Balanced, which strikes a balance between performance and saving power; Power Saver, which errs on the side of saving power at the expense of performance; and High Performance, which errs on the side of performance over power saving. These options appear on the opening page when you open Power Options, as shown in Figure 6.50. To create a power, select Create A Power Plan from the tree menu on the left.

FIGURE 6.50   Power Options

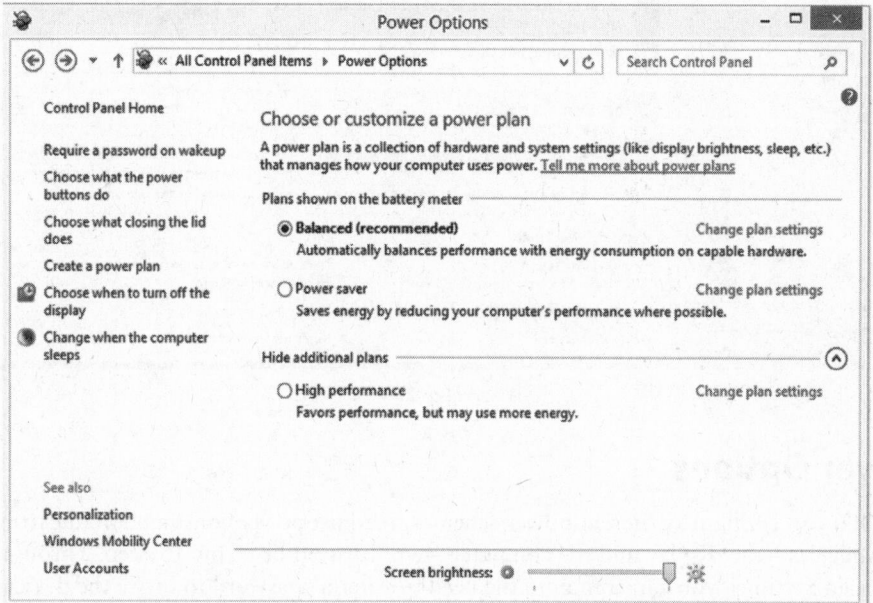

Credential Manager

This applet, shown in Figure 6.51, allows you to manage the credentials you have saved when prompted if you would like to save them for a site. The web passwords (which are cut off for security reasons) appear in a list below the heading "Web passwords." When you select the Windows credentials icon, the same list for Windows credentials appears.

FIGURE 6.51   Credential Manager

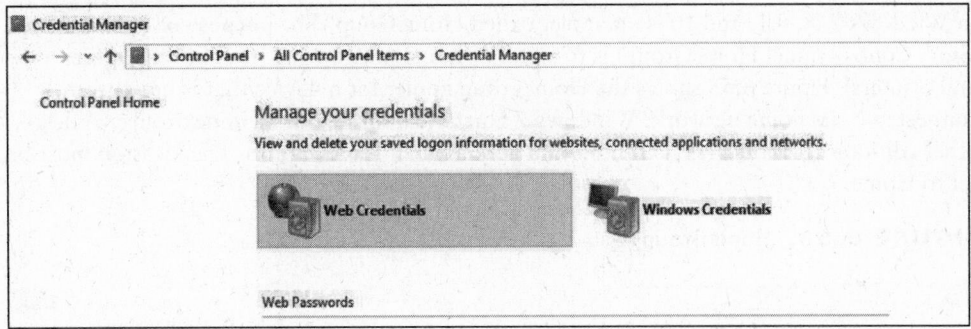

Programs and features

Formerly known as Add/Remove Programs, this tool allows you to manage the programs running on the machine and the Windows features as well. Windows Features are tools and utilities that come with the operating system that may or may not be installed and running. You can uninstall any program you have installed here. When you select Turn Windows Features On Or Off from the menu on the left, you get a box that allows you to enable and disable Windows features, as shown in Figure 6.52.

FIGURE 6.52   Programs and features

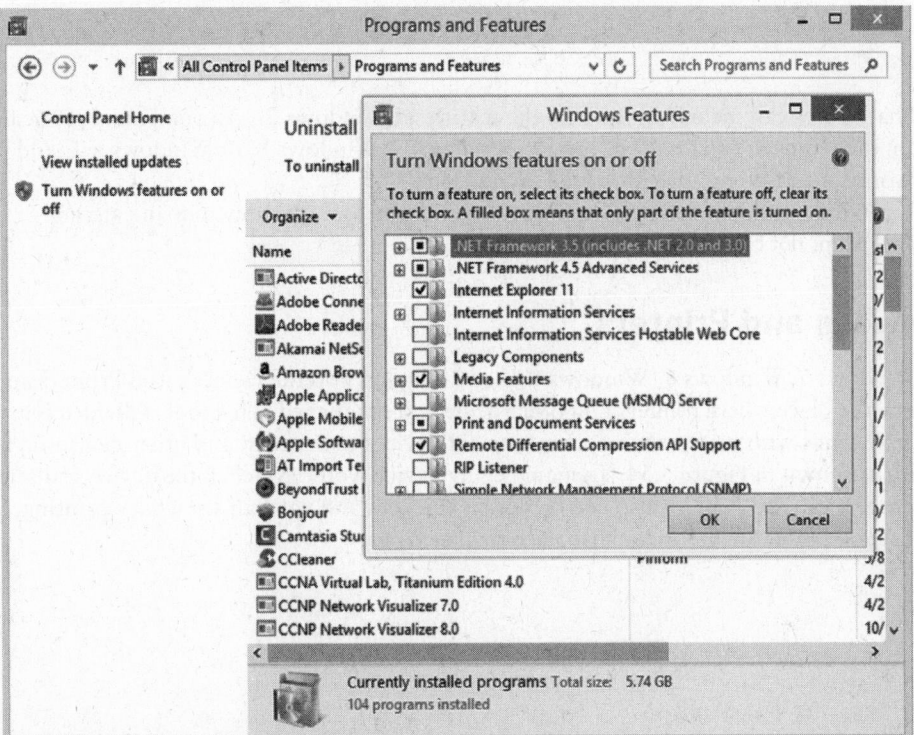

HomeGroup

In Windows 7, 8, 8.1, and 10 is an applet called HomeGoup. The purpose of HomeGroup (Start Control Panel HomeGroup) is to simplify home networking (the sharing of files and printers). Figure 6.53 shows the Homegroup applet for a device that is not currently connected to its home network. Windows 7 Starter can only join a HomeGroup, while all other editions of Windows 7 can both join and create a HomeGroup. The location must be set to Home.

FIGURE 6.53   HomeGroup

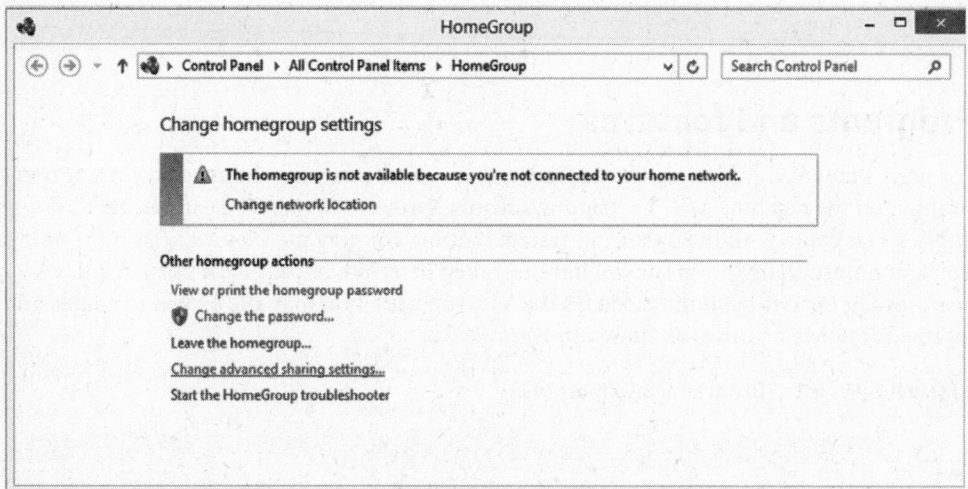

Shared files can include libraries (a big feature of Windows 7). All computers participating in the HomeGroup must be running Windows 7, Windows 8, or Windows 8.1, and the network cannot extend outside of the small group.

If a Windows 10 computer is part of a domain, the user can only join an existing Homegroup, not create one.

Devices and Printers

In Windows 7, Windows 8, Windows 8.1, and Windows 10 the Devices And Printers applet is now the place where printers and other devices are managed. This tool is divided into three sections with printers in one, multimedia devices in another, and other devices in a third, as shown in Figure 6.54. To manage any device, you right-click the device and select its properties. The printers also can be double-clicked, and you can see what's printing, manage the print queue, and adjust additional settings.

FIGURE 6.54   The Devices And Printers applet

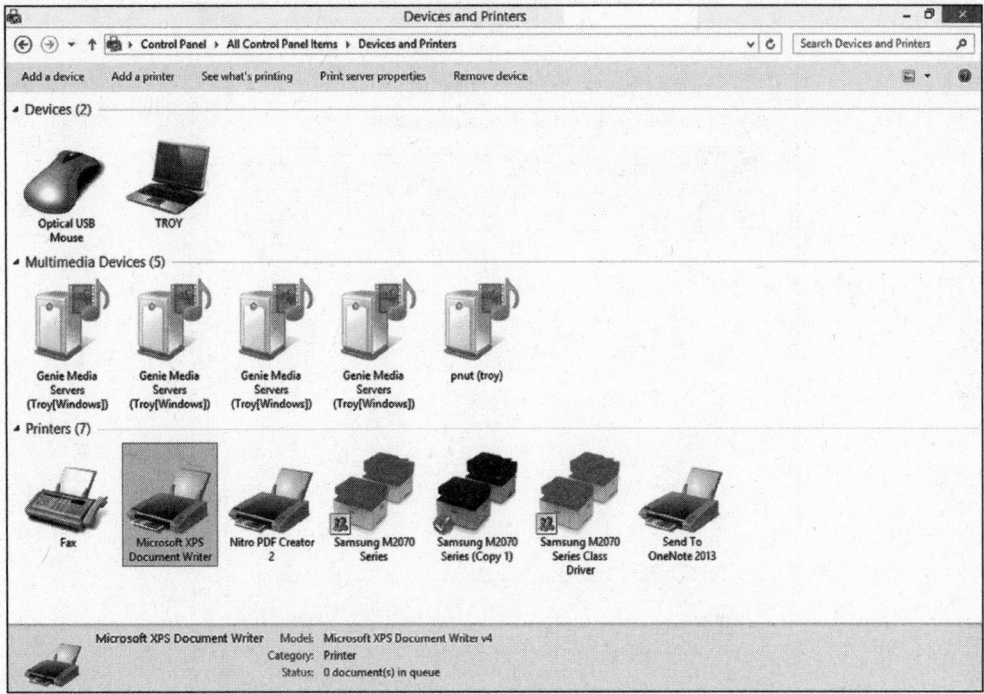

Sound

Windows 7, Windows 8, Windows 8.1, and Windows 10 have a Control Panel item called Sound that is used to manage all sound settings. You can manage the input devices (microphones, lines in) and the output devices (speakers, headphones) in one place. Moreover, you can enable and disable the various Windows sounds that you hear when certain events occur. Figure 6.55 shows the Sound applet.

FIGURE 6.55 Sound applet

Troubleshooting

Available in Windows 7, 8, 8.1, and 10, this applet (Start ➤ Control Panel ➤ Troubleshooting) is used to provide a simple interface to attack many common problems. All links preceded by a shield require administrator permissions to run and are often tied to UAC prompts before continuing. Most of the problems found will be "automatically fixed" without any prompts. For example, clicking the link Improve Power Usage will start the Power Troubleshooter and then fix problems that it identifies. Clicking the link to get help from a friend brings up Remote Assistance, allowing someone to connect to this computer.

You can also offer to be the one helping another. Figure 6.56 shows this applet.

FIGURE 6.56   The Troubleshooting applet

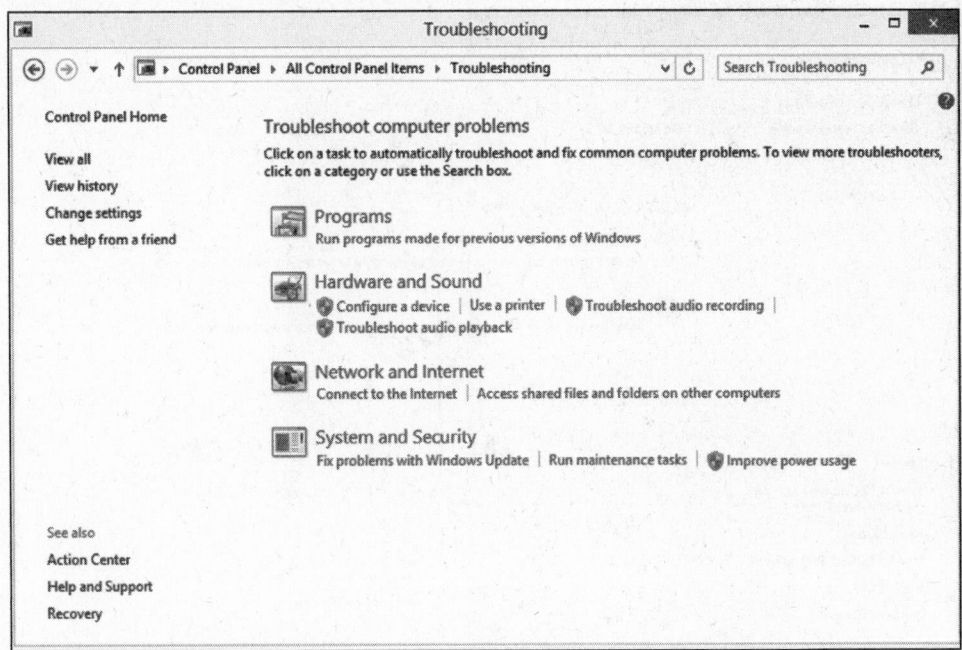

Network and Sharing Center

In Windows 7, 8, 8.1, and 10, all network settings have been combined in an applet called Network And Sharing Center, where many sharing functions have also been relocated. While most of the tools are dedicated to creating and managing both wireless and wired network connections, some Advanced sharing functions are available in this applet. Figure 6.57 shows this applet.

FIGURE 6.57 The Network And Sharing Center applet

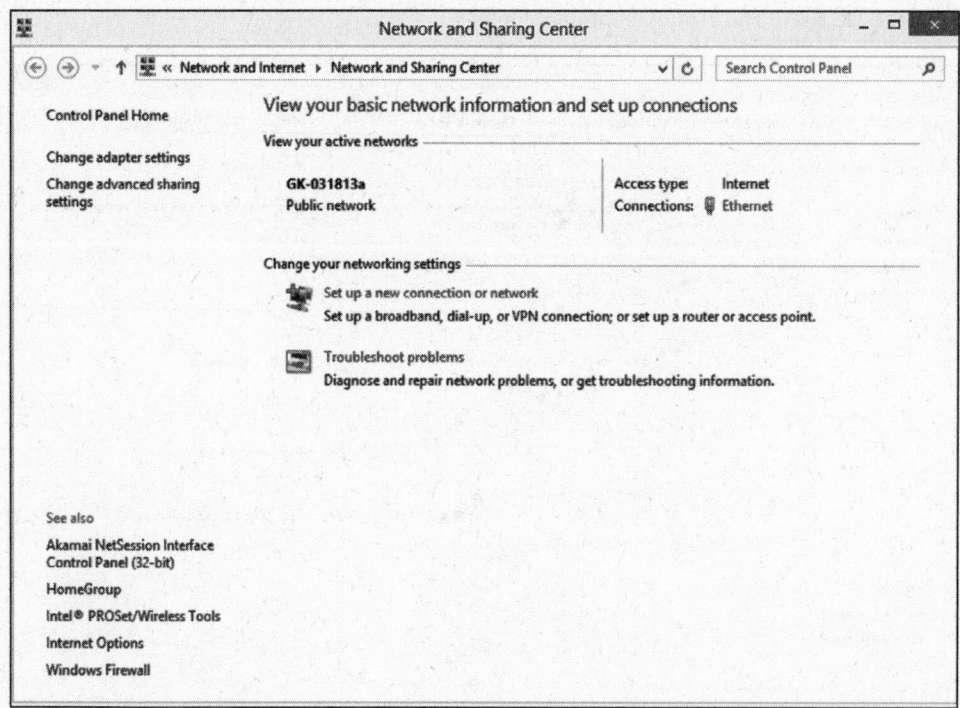

Device Manager

Device Manager has been discussed in several sections so far, including in Table 6.20 and under objective 1.5 earlier in this chapter. Figure 6.58 shows this applet.

FIGURE 6.58   Device Manager

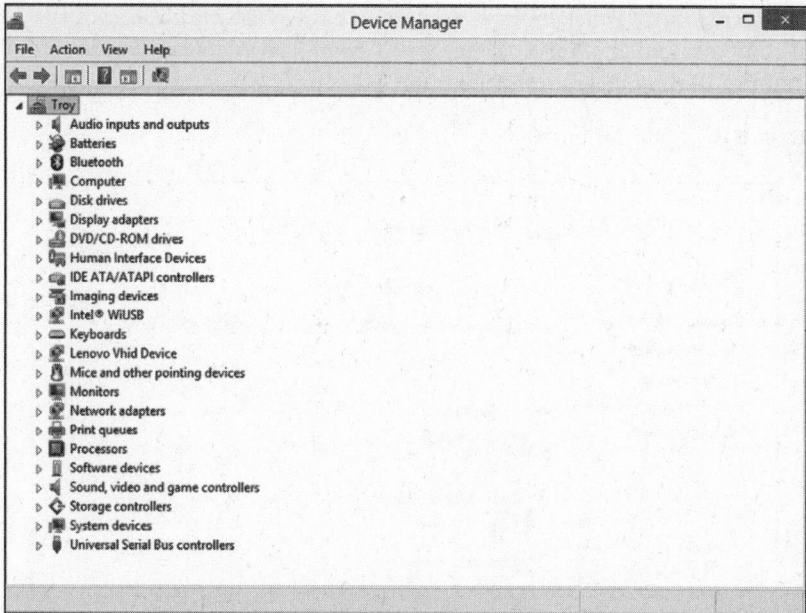

Bitlocker

The BitLocker Drive Encryption Control Panel applet is used to turn on, suspend, or turn off BitLocker whole-drive encryption on your hard drives and flash drives. This applet is not available in Windows 10 but is found in all others. It is shown in Figure 6.59.

FIGURE 6.59   BitLocker Drive Encryption

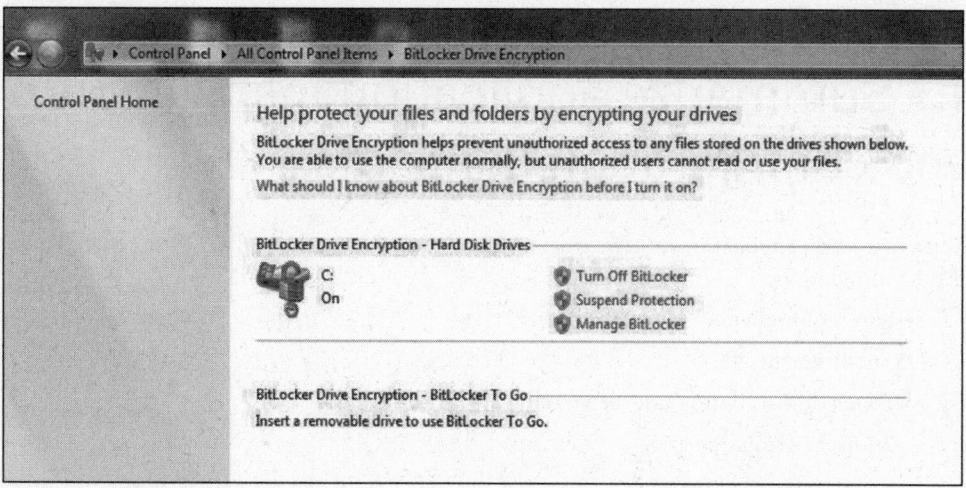

Sync Center

The Sync Center Control Panel applet is used to manage synchronization activity between your local computer and another location. Sync Center is available in Windows 8, Windows 7, and Windows 10. It is shown in Figure 6.60.

FIGURE 6.60   Sync Center

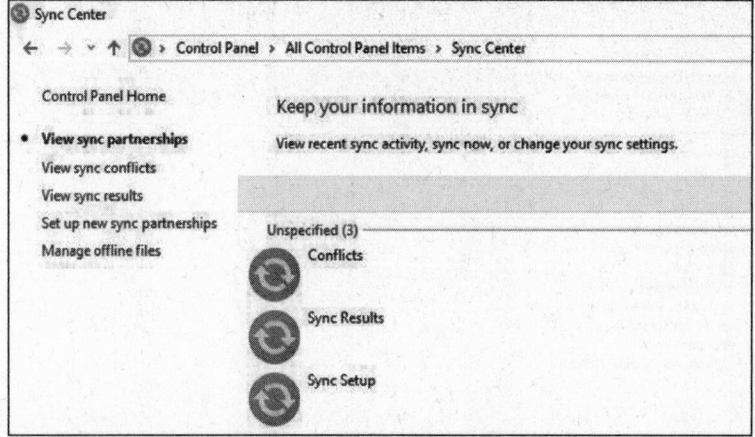

Exam essentials

Identify the purpose of Control Panel utilities.   These tools include Internet Options, Display/Display Settings, User Accounts, Folder Options, Windows Firewall, Power Options, Credential Manager, Programs And Features, HomeGroup, Devices And Printers, Sound, Troubleshooting, Network And Sharing Center, Device Manager, BitLocker, and Sync Center.

1.7 Summarize application installation and configuration concepts.

When installing applications, there are a number of considerations. This objective consists of the following topics:

- System requirements
- OS requirements
- Methods of installation and deployment
- Local user permissions
- Security considerations

System requirements

Every application has minimum system requirements with regard to computing resources. The two most critical to proper operation are covered in this section.

Drive space

Consult the documentation of the software to determine the minimum amount of disk space required to hold the installation. These minimums are not suggestions; the software will simply not install if they are not met.

RAM

The minimum of RAM required should be viewed as just that, a minimum. Make sure you have more than required for satisfactory performance.

OS requirements

Beyond the disk space and RAM, there are operating system considerations as well.

Compatibility

As mentioned earlier, applications are written to be compatible with various operating systems and the compatibility with your system must be ensured.

Methods of installation and deployment

There are a couple of ways the installation files may be introduced to your system. Let's look at the two most common.

Local (CD/USB)

Outside of the enterprise, most installations are done by using the CD that came with the software or by placing these same files on a USB stick and accessing them from the USB drive.

Network-based

In most enterprises, installations are done by placing the installation files in a network location and accessing and running them from the network location. This saves administrative effort involved in visiting each machine manually with the installation CD.

Local user permissions

Keep in mind that administrative privileges will be required to install software. This is typically not an issue in the home since users are typically administrators of their local machine. In the enterprise, however, that may not be the case and should be a consideration when deploying software.

Folder/file access for installation

When a network location has been configured as an installation point, ensure that users that will be accessing the share have the proper permissions to the folder holding the installation files. They must be able to execute the files in the folder.

Security considerations

Applications can serve as a security opening to hackers. Always research and consider the relative security of an application.

Impact to device

Some software can be compromised in such a way as to potentially allow compromise of the entire device. Consider the application's reputation in the industry with regard to such weaknesses.

Impact to network

While it's bad enough that a software compromise can lead to device compromise, it can also lead to a compromise of multiple devices on the network.

Exam essentials

Identify methods of installation and deployment.   These methods include local (CD/USB) and network-based.

Understand critical system requirements   Identify the system resources that must be fulfilled during each installation including RAM, CPU, and disk space.

1.8 Given a scenario, configure Microsoft Windows networking on a client/desktop.

CompTIA offers a number of exams and certifications on networking (Network+, Server+, and so on), but to become A+ certified, you must have good knowledge of basic networking skills as they relate to the Windows operating system.

It's important to know how network addressing works and the features offered in the Windows operating systems to simplify configuration. CompTIA expects you to have a broad range of knowledge in this category, including some obscure features (such as QoS). The topics covered in this chapter include the following:

- HomeGroup vs. Workgroup
- Domain setup
- Network shares/administrative shares/mapping drives

- Printer sharing vs. network printer mapping
- Establish networking connections
- Proxy settings
- Remote Desktop Connection
- Remote Assistance
- Home vs. Work vs. Public network settings
- Firewall settings
- Configuring an alternative IP address in Windows
- Network card properties

HomeGroup vs. Workgroup

As you learned in the previous objective, HomeGroup offers a simplified way to set up a home network. It allows you to share files (including libraries) and prevent changes from being made to those files by those sharing them (unless you give them permission to do so).

All computers participating in the HomeGroup must be running Windows 7, 8, 8.1, or 10, and the network can never grow beyond a limited size. While all editions of Windows 7 can join a HomeGroup, not all can create a HomeGroup. Windows 8 and Windows 8.1 clients can do both.

An alternative to make sharing easier in the home is to add all the computers to a peer-to-peer network. A peer-to-peer network, one of two network types you can create in Windows (also known as a *workgroup*), consists of a number of workstations (two or more) that share resources among themselves. The resources shared are traditionally file and print access, and every computer has the capacity to act as a workstation (by accessing resources from another machine) and as a server (by offering resources to other machines).

The other network type is client-server (or a domain). The primary distinction between workgroups and client-server networks is where security is controlled: locally on each workstation or centrally on a server. A domain is a centrally managed group of computers, and physical proximity does not matter; the computers within a domain may all be on the same LAN or spread across a WAN.

The advantage of a peer-to-peer network is that the cost is lower; you need only add cards and cables to the computers you already have if you're running an operating system that allows such modifications. With a server-based network, you must buy a server—a dedicated machine—and thus the costs are higher. It's never recommended that a peer-to-peer network be used for more than 10 workstations because the administration and management become so significant that a server-based network makes far greater sense.

Domain setup

In a domain (also known as a *client-server network*), users log on to the server by supplying a username and password. They're then authenticated for the duration of their session. Rather than requiring users to give a password for every resource they want to access (which would be share-level), security is based on how they authenticated themselves at the beginning of their session. This is known as *user-level* security, and it's much more powerful than share-level security.

Enterprise networks join servers, workstations, and other devices into security associations called *domains* or *realms*. These associations are made possible through the use of directory services such as Active Directory. These associations are what make the concept of single sign-on possible. This means that any user can log into the network using any device that is a domain member and receive all his assigned rights and privileges by using a single logon.

Joining a computer to the domain can be done during the installation in some cases, but most administrators do this after the successful installation of the operating system. An example of how this is done in Windows 10 is shown in Figure 6.61. This is done on the Computer Name tab of System Properties by clicking the Change button. To navigate to System Properties, open Control Panel and select the System icon (using icon view). Then select Advanced System Settings from the menu on the left side of the page. This opens the System Properties dialog box shown in Figure 6.61.

FIGURE 6.61   Joining the server to the domain

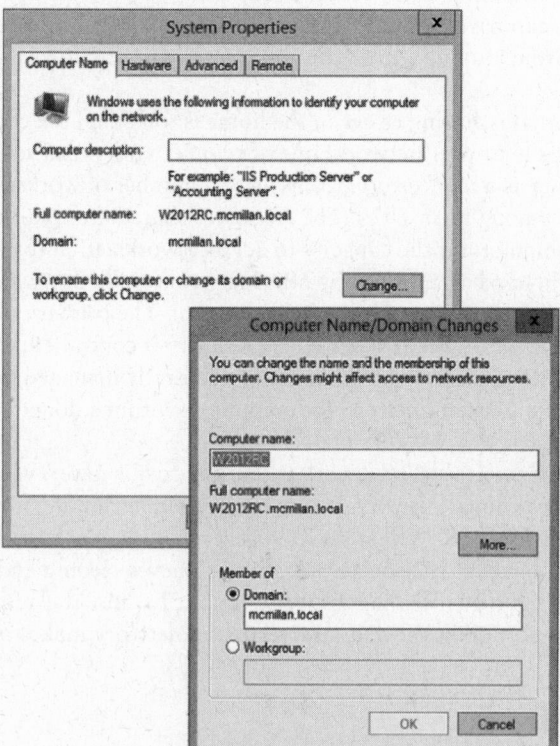

Network shares/administrative shares/mapping drives

Network shares can be mapped to drives to appear as if the resources are local. The NET USE command is used to establish network connections via a command prompt. For example, to connect to a shared network drive and make it your M drive, you would use the syntax net use m: \\server\share. This can also be done in File Explorer, as shown in Figure 6.11 earlier.

NET USE can also be used to connect to a shared printer: net use lpt1: \\printername.

An administrative share is one that is hidden to those file browsing. To connect to these drives, you must reference the name of the drive. While you can create a hidden drive at any time simply by adding a dollar sign at the end of its name, there are some default administrative drives.

Table 6.22 gives information on the default administrative drives.

TABLE 6.22 Default administrative drives

Share name	Location	Purpose
ADMIN$	%SystemRoot%	Remote administration
IPC$	N/A	Remote interprocess communication
print$	%SystemRoot%\System32\spool\drivers	Access to printer drivers
C$, D$, E$ and so on	The root of any drive	Remote administration

Printer sharing vs. network printer mapping

In Chapter 3, "Hardware" in the section "Public/shared devices," you learned how to share a printer that is connected locally to a computer. It is also possible to connect to a network printer that is not tied to a computer but has its own IP address and probably built-in print server. To connect or map a user's device to one of these devices, follow the procedure to add a shared printer, and on the page you normally enter the UNC path to the shared printer, select the option Add A Printer Using A TCP/IP Address Or Hostname, as shown in Figure 6.62, and click Next.

FIGURE 6.62   Adding a printer using a TCP/IP address

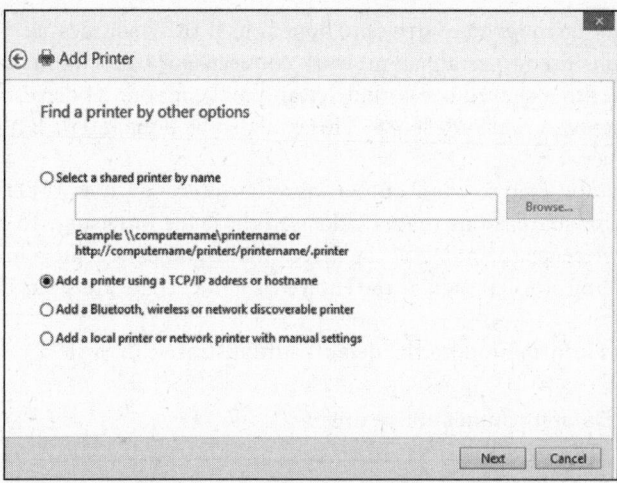

Enter the IP address or the hostname of the printer, as shown in Figure 6.63, and click Next.

FIGURE 6.63   Adding the printer IP address

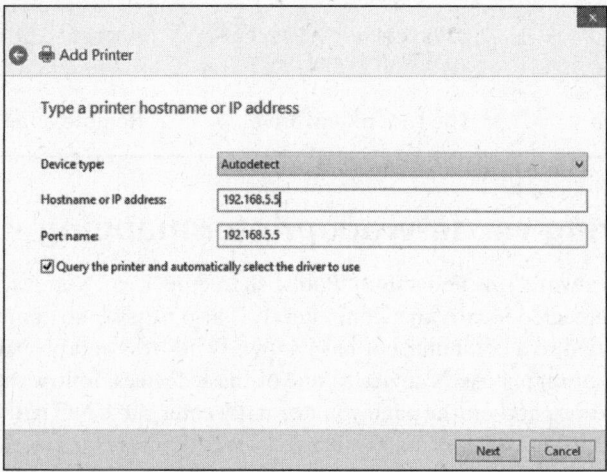

If the IP address is correct and can be reached, the printer driver will download, and the printer will be added to the printer's area of Control Panel.

Establish networking connections

When configuring the connection method for accessing the Internet, the three choices Windows offers are This Computer Connects Directly To The Internet, This Computer Connects Through A Residential Gateway Or Another Computer, and Other. If you choose the first option, you can turn on Internet Connection Sharing (ICS) and allow this machine to serve as a proxy. The network connection you configure can be wireless or wired, dial-up, or a virtual private network (VPN).

VPN   A VPN is used when you want to connect from a remote location (such as home) to the company's network (authenticating the user and encrypting the data).

Dial-ups   Dial-up connections are used when a modem must be used to gain access. Typically, the dial-up connection is to an Internet service provider (ISP) and used in remote locations where faster forms of access are not available.

Wireless   A wireless connection uses one of the 802.11 technologies, along with encryption to connect to the network.

Wired   A wired connection uses a wire to connect the computer to the network. Typically, this is an Ethernet cable, such as 100BaseT, which connects to a hub or switch and offers network access to the host.

WWAN (Cellular)   A wireless wide area network (WWAN) connection is one that uses cellular to connect the host to the network. A wireless service provider (such as AT&T, Sprint, or T-Mobile) will provide a card that is plugged into the host to make the cellular connection possible.

The choices will vary slightly based on the version of Windows you are using, but those commonly available are shown in Table 6.23.

TABLE 6.23   Network connection options

Option	Purpose
Connect To The Internet	Use for connection to a proxy server or other device intended to provide Internet access. This includes wireless, broadband, and dial-up.
Set Up A Wireless Router Or Access Point	If the wireless device will be connected to this machine, this is the option to use.
Manually Connect To A Wireless Network	If you have a wireless network already in place and the device (such as the router) is not directly connected to this machine, use this option.
Set Up A Wireless Ad Hoc (Computer-To-Computer) Network	This is meant for peer-to-peer resource sharing via wireless network cards and is typically a temporary connection.

TABLE 6.23   Network connection options *(continued)*

Option	Purpose
Set Up A Dial-Up Connection	If you live someplace where the only way to access a network is by using a dial-up modem, this is the option to select.
Connect To A Workplace	If you need to dial into a VPN from a remote location, this is the option to use.

Regardless of which option you choose, you will need to fill out the appropriate fields for the device to be able to communicate on the network. With TCP/IP, required values are an IP address for the host, subnet mask, address for the gateway, and DNS information.

Proxy settings

Proxy settings identify the proxy server to be used to gain Internet access. The proxy server is responsible for making the Internet access possible and may utilize Network Address Translation (NAT) to translate between the public network (Internet) and the private network (on which the host sits). These settings are configured by using the LAN Settings button in the Connections tab to open the dialog box shown in Figure 6.64.

FIGURE 6.64   LAN settings

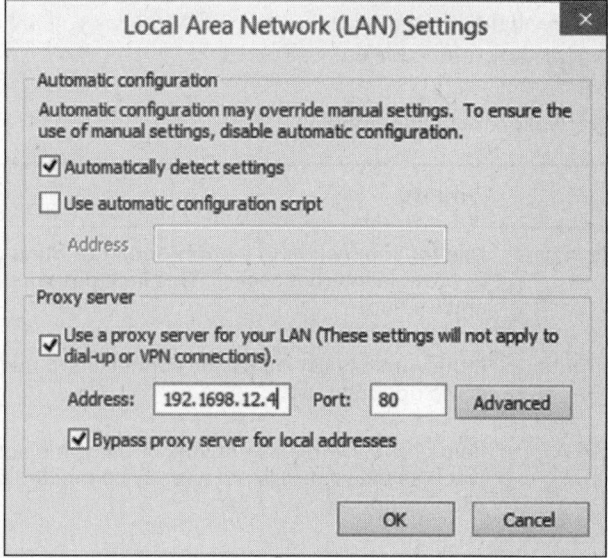

Remote Desktop Connection

Remote Desktop, which is not included in the Home editions of the operating systems, allows members of the Administrators group to gain access to the workstation. (You can specifically allow other users as well.) By default, Remote Desktop is not enabled on Windows 7, but you can enable it from Remote Settings in the Control Panel applet System And Security. To enable Remote Desktop connections in Windows 7, follow these steps:

1. Right-click the Computer icon and choose Properties, or you can enter **system** into the Start menu search box and then find the entry for System.

2. Click the Remote Settings link on the left side.

3. Select one of the two options allowing Remote Desktop connections, as shown in Figure 6.65.

FIGURE 6.65   Enabling Remote Desktop in Windows 7

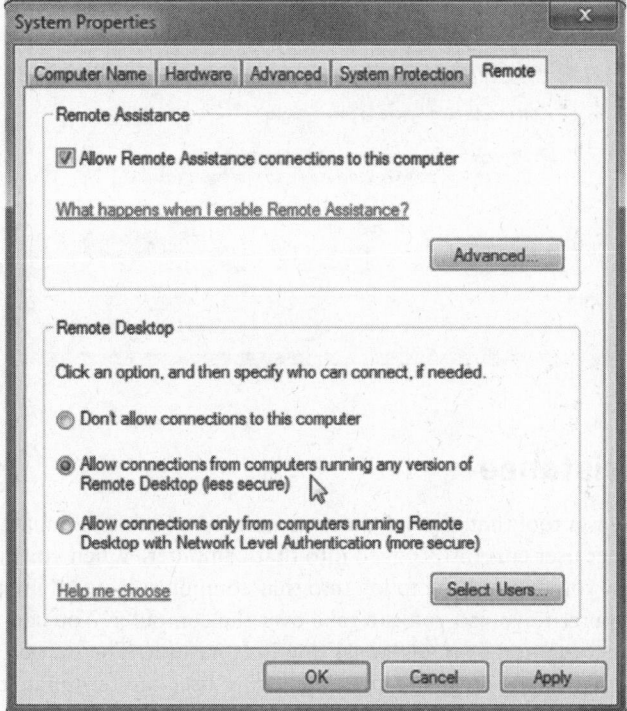

To enable Remote Desktop connections in Windows 8, 8.1, and 10, follow these steps:

1. Open the desktop Control Panel and find the System panel there, or you can search for *Remote Access* in the Start menu or Start screen.

2. Click Allow Remote Access To Your Computer.

3. When the System Properties dialog box appears, as shown in Figure 6.66, change the selection to allow Remote Desktop connections.

FIGURE 6.66   Enabling Remote Desktop in Windows 8 and later

Remote Assistance

Remote Assistance is a tool that allows you to connect to a remote computer to provide assistance to another user currently logged into that computer. When you connect via Remote Assistance, you do not have to log into that computer; instead, invitations are sent from the host computer to you so you can take over the computer. You can use the remote computer (the host computer) as if you are sitting in front of it. The user on the other end can watch your activities on-screen. At any time, either user can terminate the session. To configure this feature, follow these steps:

1. Enter Remote.

2. Click Settings under the Search box.

3. Click Allow Remote Assistance Invitations To Be Sent From This Computer. The System Properties dialog box appears, with the Remote tab showing.

4. Click Allow Remote Assistance Connections To This Computer, as shown in Figure 6.67.

5. Click OK.

FIGURE 6.67   Enabling Remote Assistance in Windows 8, 8.1, and 10

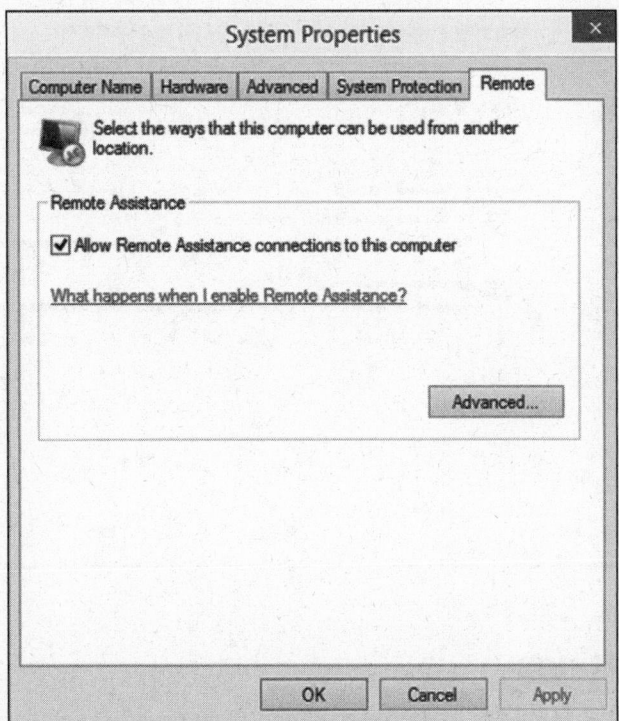

A user on the host computer can now send an invitation to you to allow you to connect to that computer for repair or training purposes.

Home vs. Work vs. Public network settings

In Windows 7, 8, 8.1, and 10 when you make a new connection, you are asked to identify whether it is a home network, work network, or public network. If you choose one of the first two, *network discovery* is on by default, allowing you to see other computers and other computers to see you. If you choose Public, network discovery is turned off.

Network discovery, when enabled, is a security issue, and this function should *not* be used on untrusted networks.

In Figure 6.68, you can see that the device is connected to a public network.

FIGURE 6.68 Public network

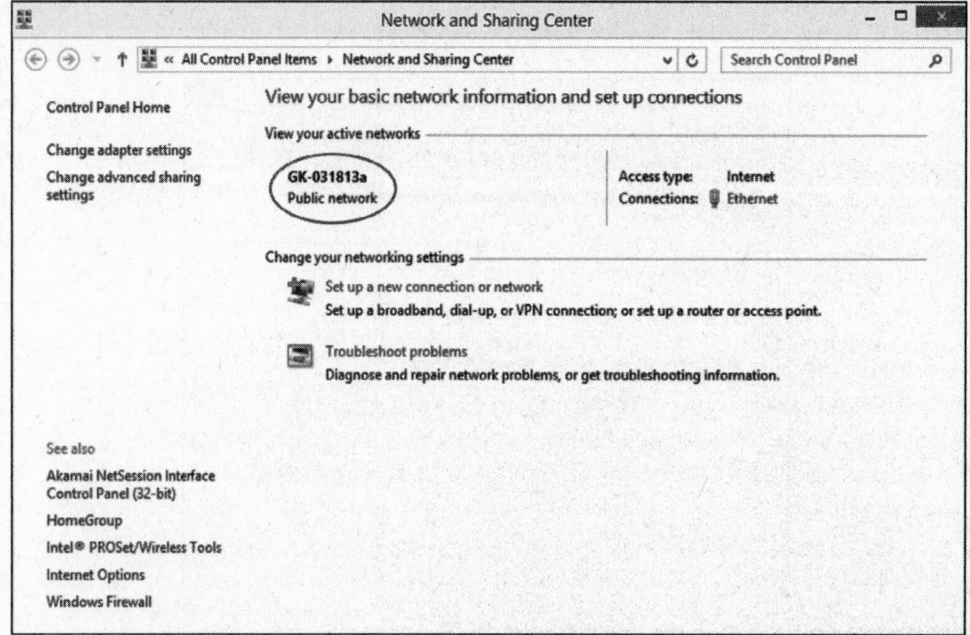

Firewall settings

Windows Firewall (Start ➤ Control Panel ➤ Windows Firewall) is used to block access from the network. In Windows 7, 8, 8.1, and 10, it is divided into separate settings for private networks and public networks.

Exceptions

Exceptions are configured as variations from the rules. Windows Firewall will block incoming network connections except for the programs and services that you choose to allow through. For example, you can make an exception for Remote Assistance to allow communication from other computers when you need help (the scope of the exception can be set to allow any computer, only those on the network, or a custom list of allowed addresses you create). Exceptions can include programs as well as individual ports.

A scenario for using exceptions would be when you want to block all traffic with the exception of *only* required traffic. You define each allowed traffic type as an exception and disallow all others by default.

Configuration

Most of the configuration is done as network connection settings. You can configure both ICMP and Services settings. Examples of ICMP settings include allowing incoming echo requests, allowing incoming router requests, and allowing redirects. Examples of services often configured include an FTP server, Post-Office Protocol Version 3 (POP3), and web server (HTTP).

A scenario for using this setting is to disallow ICMP traffic to prevent ping sweeps. This type of network probing is used to discover the devices in your network.

Enabling/disabling Windows Firewall

On the General tab of Windows Firewall, it is possible to choose the radio button Off (Not Recommended). As the name implies, this turns Windows Firewall completely off. The other radio button option, On (Recommended), enables the firewall. You can also toggle the check box Don't Allow Exceptions. This option should be enabled when you're connecting to a public network in an unsecure location (such as an airport or library), and it will then ignore any exceptions that were configured.

A scenario where you might choose to turn the firewall off is when you are using another firewall product instead. You want to use only one firewall.

Configuring an alternative IP address in Windows

Windows 7, 8, 8.1, and 10 all allow the use of an alternate IP address. This is an address that is configured for the system to use in the event the first choice is not available. The first choice can be either a dynamic or static address, and the alternate is used only if the primary cannot be found or used, such as when the DHCP server is down.

The Properties dialog box for each instance of IPv4—on any of the Windows operating systems this exam focuses on—contains an Alternate Configuration tab. To make changes, you must click it.

A scenario for using this is when your corporate network uses a DHCP server while you use a static address at home. You can set for DHCP and then make the alternate address the static address required at home.

IP Addressing

Two radio buttons appear on the Alternate Configuration tab, as shown in Figure 6.69 Automatic Private IP Address and User Configured. The default is the first, meaning that the alternate address used is one in the APIPA range (169.254.x.x). Selecting User Configured requires you to enter a static IP address to be used in the IP address field. The entry entered must be valid for your network for it to be usable.

FIGURE 6.69   APIPA

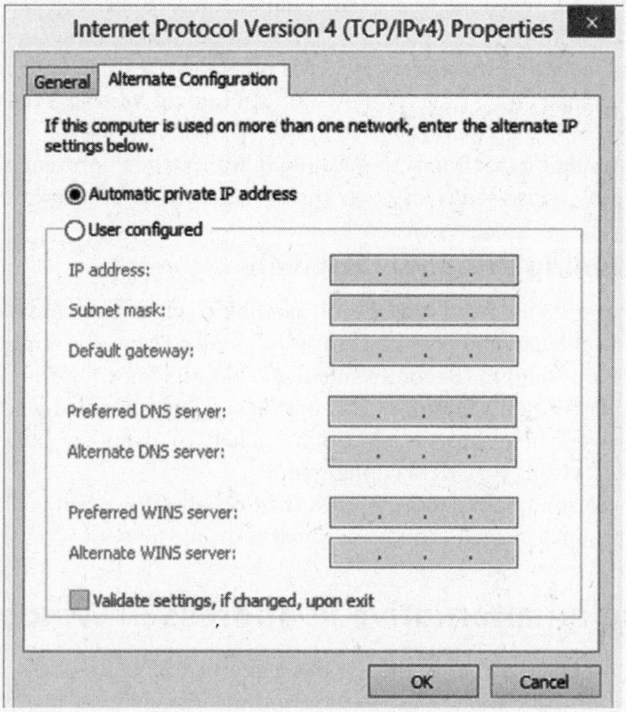

Internet Protocol Version 4 (TCP/IPv4) Properties

General | **Alternate Configuration**

If this computer is used on more than one network, enter the alternate IP settings below.

● Automatic private IP address

○ User configured

IP address:

Subnet mask:

Default gateway:

Preferred DNS server:

Alternate DNS server:

Preferred WINS server:

Alternate WINS server:

☐ Validate settings, if changed, upon exit

OK   Cancel

Subnet Mask

When you select the User Configured radio button on the Alternate Configuration tab, you must enter a value in the Subnet Mask field. This value must correspond with the subnet values in use on your network and work with the IP address you enter in the field above (see Chapter 2, "Networking" for more information on subnet addresses).

DNS

When you select the User Configured radio button on the Alternate Configuration tab, you should also enter values in the fields Preferred DNS Server and Alternate DNS Server. These entries are needed in order to translate domain names into IP addresses (see Chapter 2 for more information on DNS).

Gateway

When you select the User Configured radio button on the Alternate Configuration tab, you must enter a value in the Default Gateway field. This value must correspond with the subnet values and the IP address you enter in the fields above. This address identifies the router to be used to communicate outside the local network (see Chapter 2 for more information on default gateways).

Network card properties

Like other devices, network cards can be configured to optimize performance. Configuration is done through the Properties dialog box for each card.

Half duplex/full duplex/auto

Duplexing is the means by which communication takes place.

- With *full duplexing*, everyone can send and receive at the same time. The main advantage of full-duplex over half-duplex communication is performance. NICs can operate twice as fast in full-duplex mode as they do normally in half-duplex mode.

- With *half duplexing*, communications travel in both directions, but in only one direction at any given time. Think of a road where construction is being done on one lane— traffic can go in both directions but in only one direction at a time at that location.

- With *auto duplexing*, the mode is set to the lowest common denominator. If a card senses another card is manually configured to half duplex, then it also sets itself at that.

Duplexing is set using the Advanced tab on the Properties of the network card, as shown in Figure 6.70.

FIGURE 6.70   Setting speed and duplex

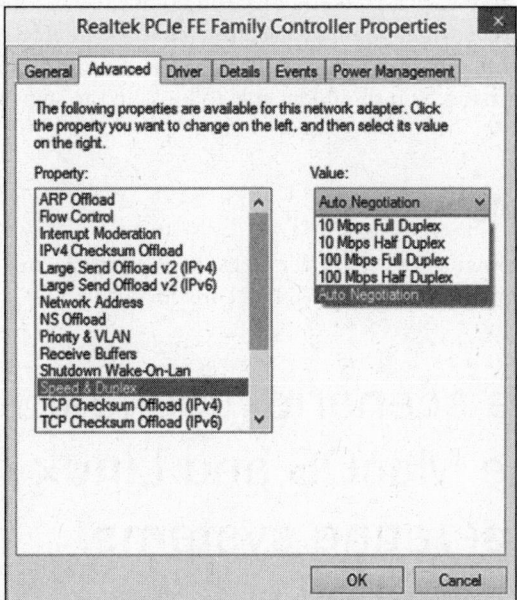

Speed

The speed setting allows you to configure whether the card should run at its highest possible setting. You often need to be compatible with the network on which the host resides. If, for example, you are connecting a workstation with a 10/100BaseT card to a legacy network, you will need to operate at 10 MBps to match the rest of the network. Speed is set along with duplex, as shown in Figure 6.69.

Wake-on-LAN

Wake-on-LAN (WoL) is an Ethernet standard implemented via a card that allows a "sleeping" machine to awaken when it receives a wakeup signal from across the network.

QoS

Quality of Service (QoS) implements packet scheduling to control the flow of traffic and help with network transmission speeds. No properties can be configured for the service itself.

BIOS (Onboard NIC)

While some older devices may have network cards installed in slots, most devices now have integrated or built-in network interfaces on the motherboard. While these interfaces will be recognized and set up automatically, if you find you do not see an integrated interface when you go to Network And Sharing, you may need to enable the interface in the BIOS. The steps to locate this setting are specific to the BIOS on the machine, but if you identify the BIOS vendor and the version, you should be able to look up the steps on the BIOS vendor website.

Exam essentials

Join a computer to a domain.   Describe the steps involved in placing a computer in a domain using a directory service such as Active Directory.

1.9 Given a scenario, use features and tools of the MacOS and Linux client/ desktop operating systems.

In your career, you are almost certain to come in contact with both the Linux and MacOS operating systems (since 2001, the MacOS system has been called OS X, so you may consider those terms interchangeable). Although these systems constitute only a small percentage of the total number of devices found in the enterprise, the proponents of both of these systems are cult-like in their devotion to their operating systems. Linux is probably used more often, in part because many proprietary operating systems that reside on devices such as access points, switches, routers, and firewalls are Linux-based. In this section of the chapter, you will be introduced to some of the common features and functions in these operating systems. The subobjectives covered in this section include the following:

- Best practices
- Tools
- Features
- Basic Linux commands

Best practices

Like any operating system, Linux and MacOS will function better and with more reliability when given the proper care. This section will discuss some of the best practices that have been developed over the years for using these operating systems.

Scheduled backups

In Linux, backups of data can be scheduled using the rsync utility from the command line. While there is another utility, cp, that can be used, rsync prevents unnecessary copying when the destination file has not been changed. It also can operate both locally and remotely. It also encrypts the transfer. The basic syntax is as follows, where the -a switch tells rsync to work in "archive" mode:

```
rsync -a [source dir] [destination dir]
```

As with any command-line utility, you can create batch files and schedule these backups.

In MacOS, you can also use rsync, but another tool is available. With Time Machine, you can back up your entire Mac, including system files, apps, music, photos, emails, and documents. When Time Machine is enabled, it automatically backs up your Mac and performs hourly, daily, and weekly backups of your files.

Scheduled disk maintenance

Because Linux systems manage the disk differently than Windows, they need no defragmentation. There is a maintenance task you may want to schedule in Linux. From time to time you should run a file system checker called fsck. This is a logical file system checker.

The MacOS needs defragmentation in only a small number of cases. If the user creates large numbers of multimedia files and the drive has been filling for quite some time, the system may benefit from defragmentation. However, in most cases, this is not required.

One task that is beneficial to execute from time to time is to check the health of the disk using the Disk Utility's Verify Disk functionality. While many disk operations (including the use of Time Machine) require booting to a different drive to perform the operation on the drive in question, Disk Utility can perform a live verification without doing this.

System updates/App Store

Many of the versions of Linux now make updates much easier than in the past. Both Ubuntu and Fedora offer a GUI tool (shocking!) for this. In Ubuntu, for example, choosing System ➤ Administration and then selecting the Update Manager entry will open Update Manager. When it opens, click the Check button to see whether there are updates available. Figure 6.71 shows a list of available updates.

FIGURE 6.71 Ubuntu Update Manager

Of course, you can still do this from the command line. Follow these steps:

1. Open a terminal window.

2. Issue the command **sudo apt-get upgrade**.

3. Enter your user's password.

4. Look over the list of available updates and decide whether you want to go through with the entire upgrade.

5. When the desired updates have been selected, click the Install Updates button.

6. Watch as the update happens.

In MacOS, updates can come either directly from Apple or from the Apple Store. To make updates automatic, access Software Update preferences, where you can set it to daily, monthly, or weekly, as shown in Figure 6.72.

FIGURE 6.72   Software Update preferences

Patch management

While in the past patch management in Linux and MacOS presented more of a challenge than with Windows, today the same tool used to manage patches with Windows (System Center Configuration Manager) can now be used to patch additional systems such as Linux and Mac. There are also third-party tools such as Spacewalk that can manage updates.

Driver/firmware updates

Updating drivers and firmware in Linux can be done either during the installation or afterward. Some versions, such as Red Hat, recommend installing first and then performing the upgrade. While the upgrade process varies from version to version, in Ubuntu either you can wait until a new version of the OS is released (which is once every six months) and get the update from the Software Update Center, or you can access what is called a *personal package archive* (PPA). These PPAs are repositories containing drivers that can be easily made available to the Ubuntu Update Manager by adding the PPA to the local system. Once added, the drivers will appear as available when you access the local Ubuntu Update Manager, as shown in Figure 6.73.

FIGURE 6.73   Update Manager with PPA

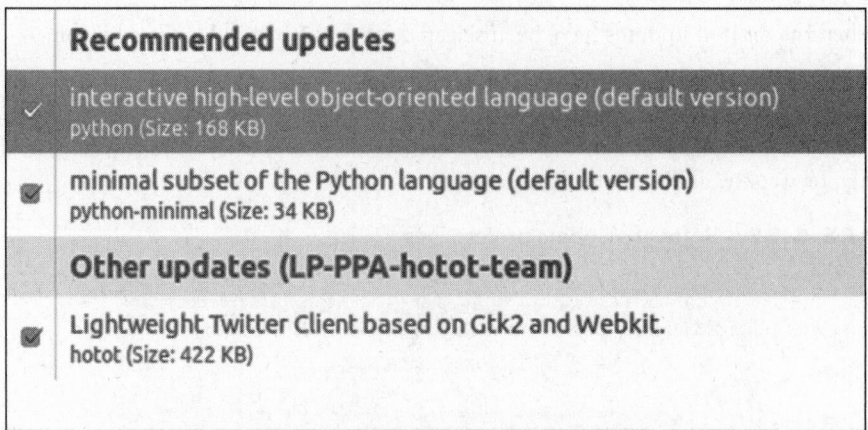

In Red Hat, driver and firmware updates, download the driver update RPM package from the location specified by Red Hat or your hardware vendor. Then locate and double-click the file that you downloaded. The system might prompt you for the root password, after which it will present the Installing packages box, shown in Figure 6.74. Then click Apply.

FIGURE 6.74   Installing packages

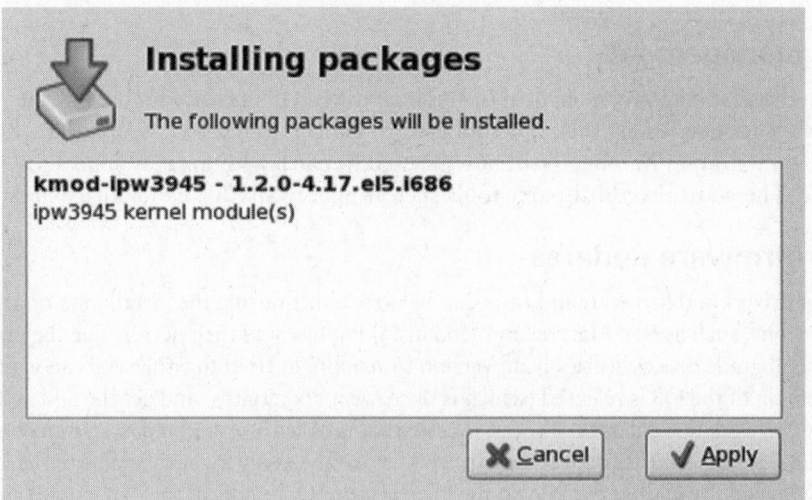

On MacOS, firmware and driver updates are obtained from the Apple Support site. After the update finishes downloading, the system will restart, and while a gray screen appears, the update will be applied.

Antivirus/Anti-malware Updates

All the major antivirus and antimalware vendors create products for both Mac and commercial versions of Linux. Updates to the engines and definitions for these applications are done in a similar fashion to Windows. Checks for updates can be scheduled just as is done in Windows.

Tools

Tools exist to perform maintenance, some of which I have already mentioned. This section will cover some of these utilities and functions.

Backup/Time Machine

For all Linux versions, backup tools are available for free and for a fee. You can also use the tar and cpio command-line utilities to construct full or partial backups of the system. Each utility constructs a large file that contains, or *archives*, other files. In addition to file contents, an archive includes header information for each file it holds. Table 6.24 lists the parameters of the tar command.

TABLE 6.24 tar parameters

Option	Effect
--append (-r)	Appends files to an archive
--catenate (-A)	Adds one or more archives to the end of an existing archive
--create (-c)	Creates a new archive
--delete	Deletes files in an archive, not on tapes
--diff (-d)	Compares files in an archive with disk files
--extract (-x)	Extracts files from an archive
--help	Displays a help list of tar options
--list (-t)	Lists the files in an archive
--update (-u)	Like the -r option, but the file is not appended if a newer version is already in the archive

On MacOS you can use Time Machine, discussed earlier in the section "Scheduled Backups." Figure 6.75 shows this tool and some of its options.

FIGURE 6.75 Time Machine

Restore/Snapshot

In Linux, the snapshot feature provides the ability to create a volume image of a device at a particular instant without causing a service interruption. When a change is made to the original device (the origin) after a snapshot is taken, the snapshot feature makes a copy of the changed data area as it was prior to the change so that it can reconstruct the state of the device. You can use the -s argument of the lvcreate command to create a snapshot volume.

To restore a snapshot, first change the directory to where the snapshots are located. Once there, change to the hidden subdirectory called .snapshot. There you will find directories such as nightly.0, nightly.1, nightly.2, hourly.0, hourly.1, ..., and hourly.10 (use the ls to command to see them). Change to the directory that still contains your file and copy it to its original location.

You can use the Time Machine tool to restore files in Mac. The steps are as follows:

1. Select the Time Machine icon from the menu.

2. Select Enter Time Machine.

3. You'll be taken to the Time Machine window. Here you can navigate to the file or folder you need to retrieve.

4. Locate the file or folder and click the Restore button.

5. Time Machine will copy that file to its original location on your hard disk.

Image Recovery

Recovering an entire image in either system is not different from restoring a single file. In Linux, you can use the `rsync` utility to restore a snapshot. On Mac you use Disk Utility in conjunction with a backup of the system and the OS media. To do this, follow these steps:

1. Connect the external hard drive that contains the backup to the Mac to which you are restoring.

2. Insert the OS X CD and restart it.

3. Hold down the C key while booting to boot to the MacOS X CD and select your language.

4. From the Utilities menu, select Disk Utility.

5. Select the drive the backup is stored on.

6. Select the Restore tab. Select that disk and drag that to the Source window. If you created a `.dmg` image, you'll need to click the drive you saved the image to (do not drag it), click Image, and select the disk image from the drive you stored it on.

7. In the left pane of Disk Utility, click your hard drive and drag it to the Destination window.

8. Check the Erase Destination check box to erase your old hard drive and replace it with the disk image you've selected as the source.

9. Click Restore. Click OK to verify.

Disk maintenance utilities

While I covered the disk maintenance utilities in the various sections earlier, Table 6.25 summarizes the tools discussed.

TABLE 6.25   Disk maintenance utilities

Tool	Function
rsync	Backs up and restores files
Time Machine	Backs up and restores files and images
Fsck	File system checker
Disk utilities	Verifies disk health and restores images
Tar	Backs up files
lvcreate	Creates a snapshot volume

Shell/Terminal

In Linux, a shell is a command-line interface, of which there are several types. A terminal is a window that appears when you press Ctrl+Alt+T. They both accept commands, but they are two separate programs. The following are some differences:

- A terminal window can run different shells depending on what you have configured.

- Certain interactive applications can be run in the terminal emulator, and they will run in the same window.

- Remote logins, using a program like SSH, can be run from inside a terminal window.

MacOS calls the shell Terminal, and you can find it under Applications ➢ Utilities ➢ Terminal, as shown in Figure 6.76.

FIGURE 6.76 The Mac terminal

Screen sharing

In Linux, you can share a screen with others by using third-party tools, but you can also do it using the following procedure as a root user: change permissions to allow users to be added to the session by typing chmod u+s /usr/bin/screen (which allows a user to run an executable file of the specific owner who is launching the screen).

1. Change the access permission of the screen mode by typing **chmod 755 /var/run/ screen**.

2. Log out from SSH as a root user.

3. Enter the command **Screen** to start the new screen.

4. Change the screen mode from single user to multiuser. Press Ctrl+A and then Enter
    ':multiuser on' //.

5. Add the user into the screen, press Ctrl+A, and then enter **':acladd acl *name*' //**.
    For example, use **:acladd jack -**.

6. The user joins the screen so that both can work in the same terminal by typing
    screen -x name_of_screen_session.

In Mac, a screen-sharing tool is built in. In OS X Yosemite, the process is as follows:

1. Open Sharing preferences (choose Apple menu ➤ System Preferences and then click
    Sharing).

2. Select the Screen Sharing check box. If Remote Management is selected, you must
    deselect it before you can select Screen Sharing.

3. To specify who can share your screen, select one of the following:

    -   **All users:** Anyone with a user account on your Mac can share your screen.

    -   **Only these users:** Screen sharing is restricted to specific users.

4. If you selected Only These Users, click Add at the bottom of the users list and then do
    one of the following:

    -   Select a user from Users & Groups, which includes all the users of your Mac.

    -   Select a user from Network Users or Network Groups, which includes everyone on
        your network.

5. To let others share your screen without having a user account on your Mac, click
    Computer Settings, and then select one or both of the following:

    -   **Anyone may request permission to control screen:** Before other computer users
        begin screen sharing your Mac, they can ask for permission instead of entering a
        username and password.

    -   **VNC viewers may control screen with password:** Other users can share your
        screen using a VNC viewer app—on iPad or a Windows PC, for example—by
        entering the password you specify here.

Force Quit

Force Quit can be used on a Mac to stop an unresponsive application. To use this function,
follow these steps:

1. Choose Force Quit from the Apple menu or press Command+Option+Esc.

2. Select the unresponsive app in the Force Quit Applications window, as shown in
    Figure 6.77, and then click Force Quit.

FIGURE 6.77 Force Quit Applications window

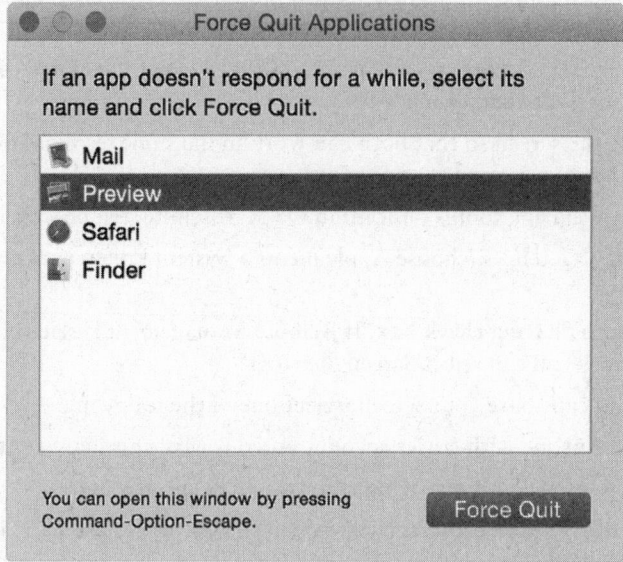

In Linux you can use the xkill feature to kill a program you click. To do this, follow these steps:

1. Press Alt+F2 and enter **gnome-terminal** to open a terminal session.

2. Inside the terminal, enter **sudo xkill**, and then click any window to kill it.

Features

Now that you have looked at maintenance on these systems, let's examine some of the key features you will find in the MacOS and Linux variants. You can find many of these features in Windows with different names and different combinations of functions.

Multiple Desktops/Mission Control

In Apple, Mission Control provides a quick way to see everything that's currently open on your Mac. To use Mission Control, do one of the following:

- Swipe up with three or four fingers on your trackpad.
- Double-tap the surface of your Magic Mouse with two fingers.
- Click the Mission Control icon in the Dock or Launchpad.
- On an Apple keyboard, press the Mission Control key.

Regardless of how you invoke Mission Control, all your open windows and spaces are visible, grouped by app. You can also use the tool to create desktops that are called *spaces* and place certain apps in certain spaces. Moreover, you can switch between the spaces in the same session.

When you enter Mission Control, all your spaces appear along the top of your screen. The desktop you're currently using is shown below the row of spaces. To move an app window to another space, drag it from your current desktop to the space at the top of the screen.

To switch between spaces, do one of the following:

- Enter Mission Control and click the space you want at the top of the Mission Control window.

- Swipe three or four fingers left or right across your trackpad to move to the previous or next space.

- Press Ctrl+Right Arrow or Ctrl+Left Arrow on your keyboard to move through your current spaces. Then click a window to bring it to the front of your view.

In Linux you can do this using what are called *workspace switchers*, which must be activated. For example, Figure 6.78 shows the activation window in Ubuntu Unity. Once it's activated, you can create and populate workspaces and use Workspace Switcher to move from one to another, much like you do in Mac.

FIGURE 6.78   Enabling workspaces

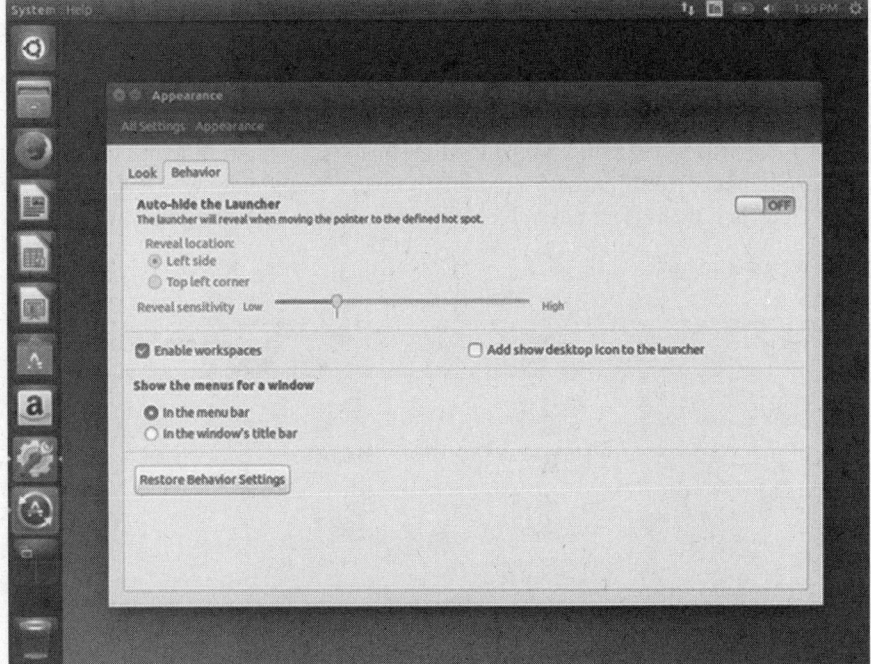

Keychain

Keychain is the password management system in OS X. It can contain private keys, certificates, and secure notes. In MacOS X, keychain files are stored in ~/Library/Keychains/,

/Library/Keychains/, and /Network/Library/Keychains/. Keychain Access is a MacOS X application that allows a user to access the Keychain and configure its contents.

Spot Light

Spot Light is a search tool built into Mac systems. To open Spot Light, click the magnifying glass icon in the upper-right corner of the menu bar, or press Command+spacebar from any app. Spot Light results can include dictionary definitions, currency conversions, and quick calculations. It will search the Web as well, but you can limit its scope to just search the local computer.

iCloud

iCloud is Apple's cloud storage solution, much like OneDrive in Windows. It also allows for the automatic synchronization of information across all devices of the user. In addition, it can be used to locate an iPhone and can be a location to which a backup can be stored. All Mac users are provided with 5 GB of free storage and then can purchase additional storage for a monthly fee.

Gestures

Gestures are used in Mac to interact with a touchscreen. The system is based on using multitouch, which allows you to touch the screen in more than one place and initiate specific subroutines called *gestures* such as when expanding or reducing a photo.

Finder

While Finder can also be used on a Mac to search for files, its main function is a file system navigation tool, much like Windows Explorer. To open a new Finder window, click the Finder icon in the Dock and then select File ➤ New Window. Figure 6.79 shows a Finder window.

FIGURE 6.79 Finder

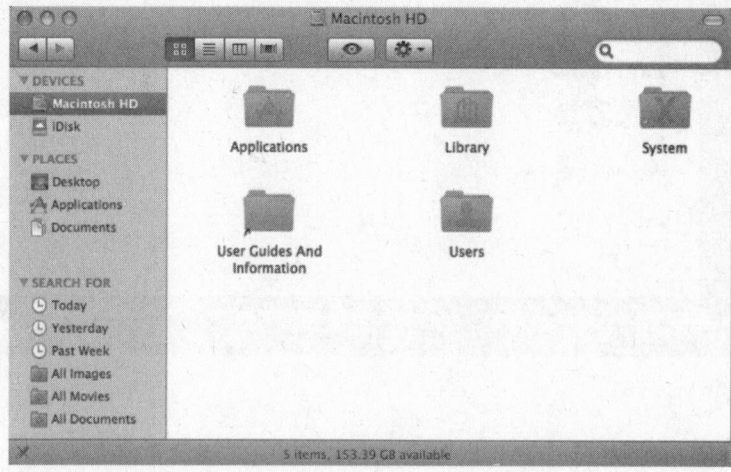

Remote Disk

Remote Disk is an icon that appears under Devices as well as under Computer that allows you to see which computers on the same network have drives available to share with your Mac. When computers on the same network have disk sharing enabled and are online, you can highlight that icon to see a list of them. To share optical discs from a Mac that has a built-in or external optical drive, use these steps:

1. On the Mac that has an optical drive, choose System Preferences from the Apple menu.
2. Click the Sharing icon in the System Preferences window.
3. Enter a name in the Computer Name field.
4. Enable the check box DVD Or CD Sharing.
5. You can also restrict who has access to your optical drive by selecting Ask Me Before Allowing Others To Use My DVD Drive.

Dock

The Dock is the series of icons that appear usually on the bottom of the screen on a Mac. It provides quick access to applications that come with the Mac, and you can add your own items to the Dock as well. In many ways, it is like the taskbar in Windows. It keeps apps on its left side. Folders, documents, and minimized windows are kept on the right side of the Dock. Figure 6.80 shows the Dock.

FIGURE 6.80   The Dock

Boot Camp

Boot Camp is a utility on a Mac that allows you to create a multiboot environment. While Apple only supports using the tool to install a version of Windows, it has been used to also create a bootable version of Linux. The Boot Camp Assistant, shown in Figure 6.81, guides the user through the process of setting up the system.

FIGURE 6.81   Boot Camp

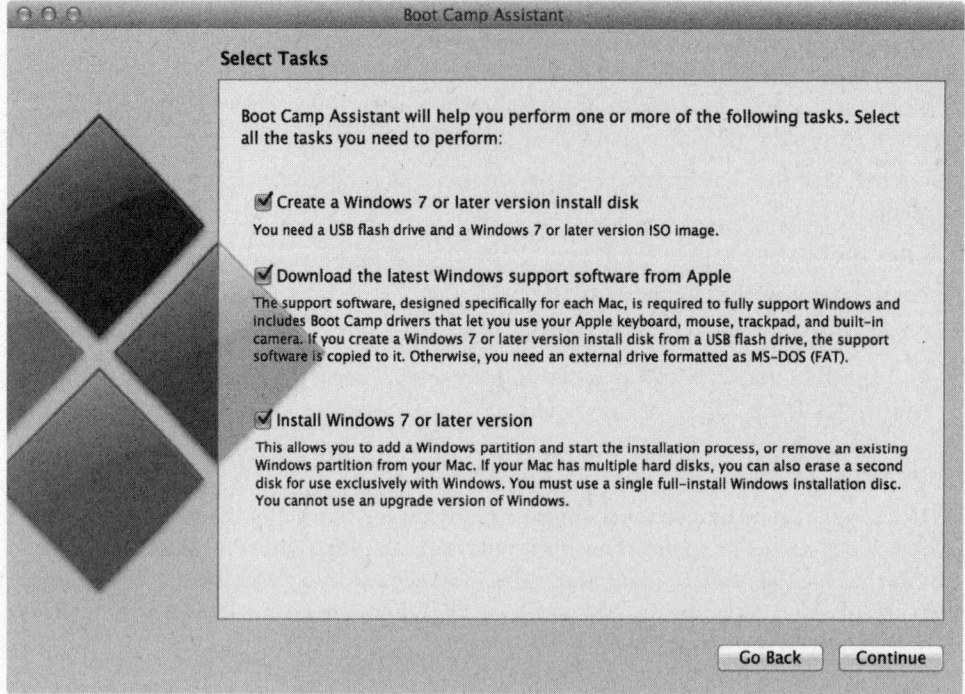

Basic Linux commands

While you may not be expected to be an expert in Linux, you will be responsible for knowing some basic Linux commands. This section will go over the main ones you need to know.

ls

The ls command lists information about the files in the current directory. Its syntax is as follows:

```
ls [OPTION]... [FILE]...
```

While the file options are too numerous to mention here, they mostly specify the format of the output. For a complete listing and their use, see http://linuxcommand.org/man_pages/ls1.html.

grep

The grep command is used to search text or to search the given file for lines containing a match to the given strings or words. Its syntax is as follows, where *PATTERN* is the pattern you are trying to match:

```
grep [OPTIONS] PATTERN [FILE...]
```

It has options that govern the matching process as well as options that specify the output. For more information on the options and their use, see www.computerhope.com/unix/ugrep.htm.

cd

The cd command is used to change the current directory just as it does at the Windows command line. Its syntax is as follows:

cd [option] [directory]

The parameters that can be used with this command are as follows:

-L   This option forces symbolic links to be followed. In other words, if you tell cd to move into a directory that is actually a symbolic link to a directory, it moves into the directory the symbolic link points to.

-P   This option uses the physical directory structure without following symbolic links. In other words, change into the specified directory only if it actually exists as named; symbolic links will not be followed. This is the opposite of the -L option, and if they are both specified, this option will be ignored.

-e   If the -P option is specified and the current working directory cannot be determined, this option tells cd to exit with an error. If -P is not specified along with this option, this option has no function.

shutdown

The shutdown command brings the system down in a secure way. Its syntax is as follows:

shutdown [-akrhPHfFnc] [-t sec] time [message]

There are too many parameters to list here. For more information, see www.computerhope.com/unix/ushutdow.htm.

pwd vs. passwd

While the passwd command changes passwords for user accounts, the pwd command prints the full path name of the current working directory. The syntax for the passwd command is as follows:

passwd [options] [LOGIN]

For information on the numerous options that can be used, see www.computerhope.com/unix/upasswor.htm.

The syntax for the pwd command is as follows:

pwd [OPTION]...

The options that can be used are as follows:

-L, --logical	If the contents of the environment variable PWD provide an absolute name of the current directory with no . or .. components, then output those contents, even if they contain symbolic links. Otherwise, fall back to the default -P handling.
-P, --physical	This prints a fully resolved name for the current directory in which all components of the name are actual directory names and not symbolic links.
--help	This displays a help message and exits.
--version	This displays version information and exits.

mv

While the mv command can be used to move or rename a file in Linux, it's usually used to move a file. In that scenario, the syntax is as follows:

mv [OPTION]... [-T] SOURCE DEST

For information on the parameters that can be used, see www.computerhope.com/unix/umv.htm.

cp

The cp command is used to copy files and directories. Its syntax is as follows:

cp [OPTION]... SOURCE... DIRECTORY

For information on the parameters that can be used, see www.computerhope.com/unix/ucp.htm.

rm

The rm command removes (deletes) files or directories when it is combined with the -r option. The syntax is as follows:

rm [OPTION]... FILE...

For information on using parameters, see www.computerhope.com/unix/urm.htm.

chmod

The chmod command is used to change the permissions of files or directories. Its syntax is as follows:

chmod options permissions filename

For information on using parameters, see www.computerhope.com/unix/uchmod.htm.

cmkdir

The cmkdir command is used to create a Cryptographic File System (CFS) directory. These directories are stored in encrypted format. The command will prompt you for a password that will be used to encrypt the directory. The syntax of the command is as follows:

cmkdir [*option*] *directory*

For information concerning possible options, see www.linuxcertif.com/man/1/cmkdir/.

chown

The chown command is used to change the ownership of a file. The syntax is as follows, where *new_owner* is the username or the numeric user ID (UID) of the new owner and *object* is the name of the target file, directory, or link:

chown [*options*] *new_owner object(s)*

The ownership of any number of objects can be changed simultaneously.
The options are as follows:

- -R operates on file system objects recursively.
- -v (verbose) provides information about every object processed.
- -c reports only when a change is made.

iwconfig/ifconfig

The ifconfig and iwconfig commands are used to configure network interfaces. While the ifconfig command is dedicated to wired connections, the iwconfig command is used on wireless interfaces. Here is the syntax of the two commands:

iwconfig *interface* [*essid* X] [*nwid* N] [*mode* M] [*freq* F] [*channel* C]
[*sens* S] [*ap* A] [*nick* NN] [*rate* R] [*rts* RT] [*frag* FT] [*txpower* T]
[*enc* E] [*key* K] [*power* P] [retry R] [commit]

and

ifconfig *interface* [*aftype*] *options* | *address* ...

For information on the options, see

www.linuxcommand.org/man_pages/iwconfig8.html

and

http://linux.die.net/man/8/ifconfig.

ps

The ps command displays information about a selection of the active processes. Its syntax is as follows:

ps [*options*]

For information on the use of the options, see http://linuxcommand.org/man_pages/ps1.html.

q

The q command is used to quit the Unix full-screen editor called vi. It can be used in two ways:

q   Quits vi without saving, provided no changes have been made since the last save

q!   Quits vi without saving, leaving the file as it was in the last save

su/sudo

The sudo command can be added at the front of a command to execute the command using root privileges. For example, to remove a package with root privileges, the command is as follows:

```
sudo apt-get remove {package-name}
```

The su command is used to change from one user account to another. When the command is executed, you will be prompted for the password of the account to which you are switching, as shown here:

```
$ su mact
password:
mact@sandy:~$
```

apt-get

apt-get is the command-line tool for working with Advanced Packaging Tool (APT) software packages. These tools install packages on your system. The syntax of the command is as follows:

```
apt-get [-asqdyfmubV] [-o=config_string] [-c=config_file]
[-t=target_release][-=architecture] {update | upgrade |
dselect-upgrade | dist-upgrade |install pkg [{=pkg_version_number |
/target_release}]... | remove pkg... | purge pkg... | source pkg
[{=pkg_version_number | /target_release}]... | build-dep pkg
[{=pkg_version_number | /target_release}]... | download pkg
[{=pkg_version_number | /target_release}]... | check | clean |
autoclean | autoremove | {-v | -version} | {-h | -help}}
```

For additional information on its use and the options, see www.computerhope.com/unix/apt-get.htm.

vi

The vi command is used to invoke the vi editor (mentioned in the section about the q command), which is a full-screen editor with two modes of operation: command mode that causes action to be taken on the file and insert mode in which entered text is inserted into the file. To enter vi, you use vi *filename*. If the file named *filename* exists, then the first page (or screen) of the file will be displayed; if the file does not exist, then an empty file and screen are created into which you may enter text. To exit this mode when done, use one of the following commands, based on your intentions:

x   Quits vi, writing out the modified file to the file named in the original invocation

wq   Quits vi, writing out the modified file to the file named in the original invocation

q   Quits (or exits) vi

q!   Quits vi even though the latest changes have not been saved for this vi call

dd

The dd command copies a file, converting the format of the data in the process, according to the operands specified. Its syntax is as follows:

dd [*OPERAND*]...

    or as follows:

dd *OPTION*

Kill

To send any signal to a process from the command line, use kill.

    To list all available signals, use the -l option. Frequently used signals include HUP, INT, KILL, STOP, CONT, and 0. Signals may be specified in three ways.

- By number (for example, -9, where the process ID is 9)
- With the SIG prefix (for example, -SIGKILL)
- Without the SIG prefix (for example, -KILL)

    For information on the available operands and options, see www.computerhope.com/unix/dd.htm.

Exam essentials

Identify basic Linux commands. These command include ls, grep, cd, shutdown, pwd, passwd, mv, cp, rm, chmod, cmkdir, chown, iwconfig, ifconfig, ps, q, su, sudo, apt-get, vi, dd, and kill.

Review Questions

You can find the answers in the Appendix.

1. Which of the following is an interface that offers a glass design that includes translucent windows?
    A. Sidebar
    B. Aero
    C. Metro
    D. Start screen

2. Which of the following are mini programs, introduced with Windows Vista, that can be placed on the desktop (Windows 7) or on the Sidebar (Windows Vista)?
    A. Gadgets
    B. Metro apps
    C. Widgets
    D. Shims

3. Into which tool has the Security Center been rolled in Windows 7?
    A. Action Center
    B. Control Panel
    C. Windows Firewall
    D. Defender

4. What is the name of the user interface in Windows 8 and 8.1?
    A. Aero
    B. Metro
    C. Sidebar
    D. Start

5. What is the minimum RAM required for 64-bit Windows 7?
    A. 512 MB
    B. 750 MB
    C. 1 GB
    D. 2 GB

6. Which version of Windows 7 can be upgraded to Windows 8?
    A. Windows 7 Professional
    B. Windows 7 Ultimate
    C. Windows 7 Pro (volume licensed)
    D. Windows 7 Home Basic

7. Which Windows command is used to view a listing of the files and folders that exist within a directory, subdirectory, or folder?

A. `net use`

B. `dir`

C. `cd`

D. `ipconfig`

8. Which Windows command is used to move to another folder or directory?

A. `net use`

B. `dir`

C. `cd`

D. `ipconfig`

9. Which Windows tool shows a list of all installed hardware and lets you add items, remove items, update drivers, and more?

A. Device Manager

B. Event Viewer

C. Users And Groups

D. Sync Center

10. Which Windows tool tracks all events on a particular Windows computer?

A. Device Manager

B. Event Viewer

C. Users And Groups

D. Sync Center

11. Which of the following is either the number of bits used to indicate the color of a single pixel, in a bitmapped image or video frame buffer, or the number of bits used for each color component of a single pixel?

A. Resolution

B. Refresh rate

C. Color depth

D. Pixel count

12. Which of the following is the number of times in a second that a display updates its buffer and is expressed in hertz?

A. Resolution

B. Refresh rate

C. Color depth

D. Pixel count

13. Which of the following should you exceed for good performance?

    A. Minimum RAM

    B. Resolution

    C. Disk space

    D. Pixel count

14. Which type of installation is most likely to take place in a SOHO?

    A. Network

    B. RIS

    C. CD

    D. Unattended

15. Which of the following offers a simplified way to set up a home network?

    A. Peer-to-peer

    B. Domain

    C. HomeGroup

    D. Workgroup

16. Which of the following can be used to connect to a shared printer?

    A. net use

    B. net user

    C. robocopy

    D. xcopy

17. Which of the following is a command-line interface in Linux?

    A. shell

    B. domain

    C. cmd

    D. DOS

18. Which of the following provides a quick way to see everything that's currently open on your Mac?

    A. Shell

    B. Mission Control

    C. Sandbox

    D. Beeker

Chapter

7

Security

COMPTIA A+ CERTIFICATION EXAM CORE 2 (220-1002) OBJECTIVES COVERED IN THIS CHAPTER:

✓ **2.1 Summarize the importance of physical security measures.**

- Mantrap
- Badge reader
- Smart card
- Security guard
- Door lock
- Biometric locks
- Hardware tokens
- Cable locks
- Server locks
- USB locks
- Privacy screen
- Key fobs
- Entry control roster

✓ **2.2 Explain logical security concepts.**

- Active Directory
  - Login script
  - Domain
  - Group policy/updates
  - Organizational Units
  - Home Folder
  - Folder redirection

- Software tokens
- MDM policies
- Port security
- MAC address filtering
- Certificates
- Antivirus/Anti-malware
- Firewalls
- User authentication/strong passwords
- Multifactor authentication
- Directory permissions
- VPN
- DLP
- Access control lists
- Smart card
- Email filtering
- Trusted/untrusted software sources
- Principle of least privilege

✓ **2.3 Compare and contrast wireless security protocols and authentication methods.**

- Protocols and encryption
  - WEP
  - WPA
  - WPA2
  - TKIP
  - AES
- Authentication
  - Single-factor
  - Multifactor
  - RADIUS
  - TACACS

✓ **2.4 Given a scenario, detect, remove, and prevent malware using appropriate tools and methods.**

- Malware
  - Ransomware
  - Trojan
  - Keylogger
  - Rootkit
  - Virus
  - Botnet
  - Worm
  - Spyware
- Tools and methods
  - Antivirus
  - Anti-malware
  - Recovery Console
  - Backup/restore
  - End-user education
  - Software firewalls
  - DNS configuration

✓ **2.5 Compare and contrast social engineering, threats, and vulnerabilities.**

- Social engineering
  - Phishing
  - Spear phishing
  - Impersonation
  - Shoulder surfing
  - Tailgating
  - Dumpster diving
- DDoS
- DoS
- Zero-day

- Man-in-the-middle

- Brute force

- Dictionary

- Rainbow table

- Spoofing

- Non-compliant systems

- Zombie

✓ **2.6 Compare and contrast the differences of basic Microsoft Windows OS security settings.**

- User and groups

  - Administrator

  - Power user

  - Guest

  - Standard user

- NTFS vs. share permissions

  - Allow vs. deny

  - Moving vs. copying folders and files

  - File attributes

- Shared files and folders

  - Administrative shares vs. local shares

  - Permission propagation

  - Inheritance

- System files and folders

- User authentication

  - Single sign-on

- Run as administrator vs. standard user

- BitLocker

- BitLocker To Go

- EFS

✓ **2.7 Given a scenario, implement security best practices to secure a workstation.**

- Password best practices
  - Setting strong passwords
  - Password expiration
  - Screensaver required password
  - BIOS/UEFI passwords
  - Requiring passwords
- Account management
  - Restricting user permissions
  - Logon time restrictions
  - Disabling guest account
  - Failed attempts lockout
  - Timeout/screen lock
  - Change default admin user account/password
  - Basic Active Directory functions
    - Account creation
    - Account deletion
    - Password reset/unlock account
    - Disable account
- Disable autorun
- Data encryption
- Patch/update management

✓ **2.8 Given a scenario, implement methods for securing mobile devices.**

- Screen locks
  - Fingerprint lock
  - Face lock
  - Swipe lock
  - Passcode lock
- Remote wipes

- Locator applications
- Remote backup applications
- Failed login attempts restrictions
- Antivirus/Anti-malware
- Patching/OS updates
- Biometric authentication
- Full device encryption
- Multifactor authentication
- Authenticator applications
- Trusted sources vs. untrusted sources
- Firewalls
- Policies and procedures
  - BYOD vs. corporate-owned
  - Profile security requirements

✓ **2.9 Given a scenario, implement appropriate data destruction and disposal methods.**

- Physical destruction
  - Shredder
  - Drill/hammer
  - Electromagnetic (Degaussing)
  - Incineration
  - Certificate of destruction
- Recycling or repurposing best practices
  - Low-level format vs. standard format
  - Overwrite
  - Drive wipe

✓ **2.10 Given a scenario, configure security on SOHO wireless and wired networks.**

- Wireless-specific
  - Changing default SSID
  - Setting encryption

- Disabling SSID broadcast
- Antenna and access point placement
- Radio power levels
- WPS
- Change default usernames and passwords
- Enable MAC filtering
- Assign static IP addresses
- Firewall settings
- Port forwarding/mapping
- Disabling ports
- Content filtering/parental controls
- Update firmware
- Physical security

This chapter will focus on the exam topics related to security. It will follow the structure of the CompTIA A+ 220-1002 exam blueprint, objective 2, and it will explore the 10 subobjectives that you need to master before taking the exam. The Security domain represents 24 percent of the exam.

2.1 Summarize the importance of physical security measures.

Physical security is a grab bag of elements that can be added to an environment to aid in securing it. It ranges from key fobs to retinal scanners. In this section, you will examine the physical security components as listed by CompTIA. Topics covered in this section include the following:

- Mantrap
- Badge reader
- Smart card
- Security guard
- Door lock
- Biometric locks
- Hardware tokens
- Cable locks
- Server locks
- USB locks
- Privacy screen
- Key fobs
- Entry control roster

Mantrap

A mantrap is a series of two doors with a small room between them. The user is authenticated at the first door and then allowed into the room. At that point, additional verification will occur (such as a guard visually identifying the person), and then they are allowed through the second door. These doors are normally used only in high-security situations. Mantraps also typically require that the first door is closed, prior to enabling the second door to open. Figure 7.1 shows a mantrap design.

FIGURE 7.1 Aerial view of a mantrap

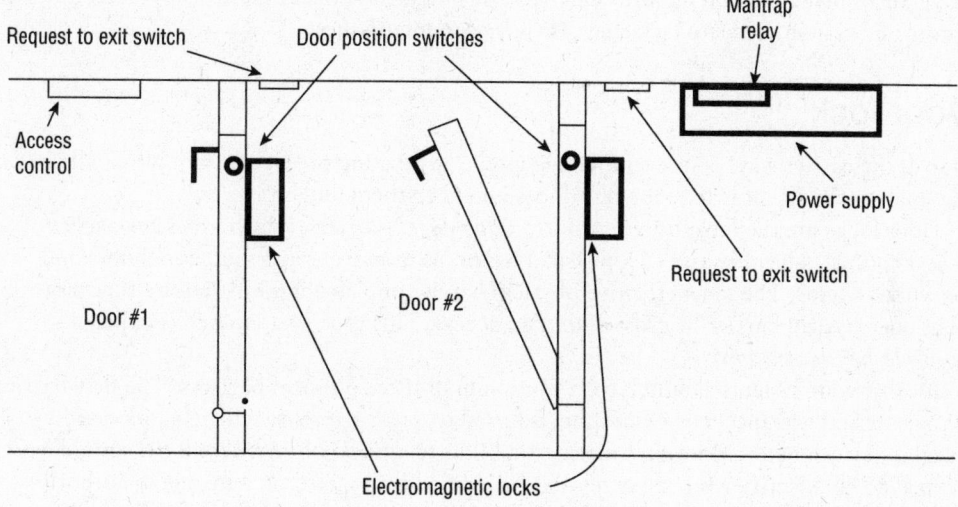

Badge reader

Radio frequency identification (RFID) is a wireless, no-contact technology used with badges or cards and their accompanying reader. The reader is connected to the workstation and validates against the security system. This increases the security of the authentication process because the user must be in physical possession of the smart card to use the resources. Of course, if the card is lost or stolen, the person who finds the card can access the resources it allows. Badge readers are used not only to provide access to devices but also to provide access to doors as well.

Smart card

A smart card is a type of badge or card that gives you access to resources, including buildings, parking lots, and computers. It contains information about your identity and access privileges. Each area or computer has a card scanner or a reader in which you insert your card.

Smart cards are difficult to counterfeit, but they're easy to steal. Once a thief has a smart card, that person has all the access the card allows. To prevent this, many organizations don't put any identifying marks on their smart cards, making it harder for someone to utilize them. Many modern smart cards require a password or PIN to activate the card, and they employ encryption to protect the card's contents.

Security guard

While many other less manual methods of monitoring are available, nothing takes the place of a human being. Security guards can exercise judgment and common sense (sometimes an automated system seems to lack that) as they encounter issues.

Door lock

One of the easiest ways to prevent people intent on creating problems from physically entering your environment is to lock your doors and keep them out.

Door locks are the most universal form of *physical barriers*, which are a key aspect of access control. The objective of a physical barrier is to prevent access to computers and network systems. The most effective physical barrier implementations require that more than one physical barrier be crossed to gain access. This type of approach is called a *multiple-barrier system.*

Ideally, your systems should have a minimum of three physical barriers. The first barrier is the external entrance to the building, referred to as a *perimeter*, which is protected by burglar alarms, external walls, *fencing*, surveillance, and so on. An *access list* should exist to specifically identify who can enter and be verified by a guard or someone in authority. The second barrier is the entrance into the building and could rely on such items as *ID badges* to gain access. The third barrier is the entrance to the computer room itself (and could require fobs, or keys). Each of these entrances can be individually secured, monitored, and protected with alarm systems.

Think of the three barriers this way: outer (the fence), middle (guards, locks, and mantraps), and inner (key fobs).

Although these three barriers won't always stop intruders, they will potentially slow them down enough that law enforcement can respond before an intrusion is fully developed. Once inside, a truly secure site should be dependent on a physical token for access to the actual network resources.

Biometric locks

Biometric devices use physical characteristics to identify the user. Such devices are becoming more common in the business environment. Biometric systems include hand scanners, retinal scanners, and, possibly soon, DNA scanners. To gain access to resources, you must pass a physical screening process. In the case of a hand scanner, this may include identifying fingerprints, scars, and markings on your hand. Retinal scanners compare your eye's retinal pattern to a stored retinal pattern to verify your identity. DNA scanners will examine a unique portion of your DNA structure to verify that you are who you say you are.

With the passing of time, the definition of *biometric* is expanding from simply identifying physical attributes about a person to being able to describe patterns in their behavior. Recent advances have been made in the ability to authenticate someone based on the key pattern they use when entering their password (how long they pause between each key, the amount of time each key is held down, and so forth). A company adopting biometric technologies needs to consider the controversy they may face (some authentication methods are considered more intrusive than others). It also needs to consider the error rate and that errors can include both false positives and false negatives.

Biometric systems, like most security tools, make mistakes. When the system improperly allows an individual in who should not be, it is called a *false acceptance* and the rate at which this occurs is called the *false acceptance rate*(FAR). When the system improperly rejects a legitimate user, it is called a *false rejection*, and the rate at which these occur is called the *false rejection rate*(FRR).

Hardware tokens

Physical tokens are anything that a user must have on them to access network resources and are often associated with devices that enable the user to generate a one-time password authenticating their identity. SecurID, from RSA, is one of the best-known examples of a physical token; learn more at www.rsa.com/node.aspx?id=1156.

Cable locks

While not all devices support this, larger mobile devices such as laptops come with a notch where you can attach a cable lock and lock the device to something solid, as you would lock a bicycle to a rack. This may even be advisable on some desktop systems if those systems are vulnerable to theft and contain sensitive data. Users who carry company devices that support cable locks should be instructed to never leave the device unattended and, if necessary, lock the device to an immovable object.

Server locks

Both rack and nonrack server systems can come with physical locks that prevent tampering with the server if physical access becomes possible. Having said that, all servers should be locked in a room, but the inclusion of physical server locks as well is an example of defense in depth.

USB locks

USB locks plug into the USB port. The lock prevents removal of the device, thus preventing use of the USB port.

Privacy screen

Privacy filters are either film or glass add-ons that are placed over a monitor and prevent the data on the screen from being readable when viewed from the sides. Only the user sitting directly in front of the screen is able to read the data. This is a good mitigation to shoulder surfing.

Key fobs

Key fobs are named after the chains used to hold pocket watches to clothes. They are security devices that you carry with you that display a randomly generated code that you can then use for authentication. This code usually changes quickly (every 60 seconds is probably the average), and you combine the code with your PIN for authentication.

Entry control roster

At any physical location where users are arriving and departing the facility, users should be authenticated through one of the mechanisms discussed in this section. There should be a recording of each user arriving and departing. This can be either a record of all successful and unsuccessful authentications on a log or, in the case of visitors who have no network account, a physical identification process of some sort. In any case, there should be an entry control roster in the form of a physical document that shows when each person entered and left the facility. This will serve as a backup in case the log is lost.

Exam essentials

Describe the purpose of a mantrap.   A mantrap is a series of two doors with a small room between them. The user is authenticated at the first door and then allowed into the room. At that point, additional verification will occur (such as a guard visually identifying the person), and then they are allowed through the second door.

2.2 Explain logical security concepts.

Whereas physical security focused on keeping individuals out, digital security focuses mostly on keeping harmful data/malware out. Topics covered in this section include the following:

- Active Directory
- Software tokens
- MDM policies
- Port security

- MAC address filtering
- Certificates
- Antivirus/Anti-malware
- Firewalls
- User authentication/strong passwords
- Multifactor authentication
- Directory permissions
- VPN
- DLP
- Access control lists
- Smart card
- Email filtering
- Trusted/untrusted software sources
- Principle of least privilege

Active Directory

Active Directory (AD) is the directory service used in Windows since Windows 2000. It is used to locate resources and is also the point of configuration for all things security in a Windows domain (a concept to be explained shortly). It has a hierarchical structure that can be leveraged when using one of the more powerful tools of AD, Group Policy. Let's survey some of the concepts of AD.

Login script

While not required, login scripts run as soon as a user completes successful authentication. These scripts can automate a wide variety of operations, like mapping drives for users and checking for updates.

Domain

When a new AD structure is created, a new forest containing one domain is created. By default, all objects residing in a domain share the same security policies. Domains can be subdivided into organizational units (OUs), which can be used as targets for additional policies that you would like to confine to the OU.

Group policy/updates

When group policies are created, they can be applied to both computers and users and can be applied at either the domain or the OU level in the hierarchy.

When policies are added or updated, these changes are refreshed at certain intervals on the computers. Outside of these intervals, devices also check when rebooting and starting up. Finally, administrators can force an update at any time using the gpudate command.

Organizational units

As noted, domains can be subdivided into OUs, and OUs can also have child OUs. You can build whatever structure suits the efficient application of policies. While policy inheritance can be prevented, doing so complicates things, and a well thought-out structure will result in allowing inheritance to operate.

Home folder

Home folders make it easier for an administrator to back up user files and manage user accounts by collecting the user's files in one location. If you assign a home folder to a user, you can store the user's data in a central location on a server and make backup and recovery of data easier and more reliable. If no home folder is assigned, the computer assigns the default local home folder to the user account. The home folder can use the same location as the My Documents folder.

Folder redirection

Along with creating a Home folder, folder redirection is an alternative method of automatically rerouting I/O to/from standard folders (directories) to use storage elsewhere on a network.

Software tokens

Software tokens are stored in software and can be duplicated. They are typically used in multifactor authentication mechanisms. Their purpose and use is the same as a hardware or physical token (described earlier in this chapter). Software tokens are cheaper than hardware tokens and do not have a battery that can run down as hardware tokens do.

MDM policies

Mobile Device Management (MDM) policies can be created in AD, or they can be implemented through MDM software. This software allows you to exert control over the mobile devices, even those you do not own if they have the software installed. These policies can force data encryption and data segregation, and they can be used to wipe a stolen device remotely.

Port security

One of the basic principles of security is to reduce the attack surface of all devices. This means shutting off all services and applications that are not required and closing all ports not being used. With respect to switches and hubs, it means disabling any ports that do not have devices connected to them. If this is not done, anyone could walk up to any unused wall outlet, plug in a device, get an IP address through DHCP, and be on your network.

But sometimes you want to prevent someone from unplugging a legitimate device and plugging in one that is not legitimate. That's where port security comes in. By configuring port security on the port, you can prevent the transmission of data by any device other than the legitimate one. You can even shut the port down if this occurs.

Port security can also refer to the limitation of access that allows only well-known TCP and UDP port numbers. Limiting access to allow only required ports reduces the attack surface.

MAC address filtering

Most APs and network switches offer the ability to turn on *MAC filtering*, but it is off by default. In the default state, any wireless client that knows the values looked for can join the network, and any device connected to a switch port can send traffic. When MAC filtering is used, the administrator compiles a list of the MAC addresses associated with the users' computers and enters those. When a client attempts to connect and other values have been correctly entered, an additional check of the MAC address is done. If the address appears in the allowed list, the client is allowed to join; otherwise, they are forbidden from doing so. On a number of wireless devices, the term *network lock* is used in place of MAC filtering, and the two are synonymous.

MAC address filtering at the wireless level is useless because it is quite simple to identify an allowed MAC address by sniffing the wireless frames. Then a hacker can simply change his MAC address to an allowed one.

 Adding port authentication to MAC filtering takes security for the network down to the switch port level and increases your security exponentially.

Certificates

A *certificate* is a text document that ties a user account to a public and private key pair created by a certificate server or certificate authority (CA). Certificates follow the X.509 standard, which requires them to include certain pieces of information.

- Certificate
- Version number
- Serial number
- Signature algorithm ID
- Issuer name
- Validity period
  - Not before
  - Not after

- Subject name
- Subject public key info
  - Public key algorithm
  - Subject public ley
- Issuer unique identifier (optional)
- Subject unique identifier (optional)
- Extensions (optional)
- Certificate signature algorithm
- Certificate Signature

Antivirus/Anti-malware

The primary method of preventing the propagation of malicious code involves the use of *antivirus software*, a type of application that is installed on a system to protect it and to scan for viruses as well as worms and Trojan horses. Most viruses have characteristics that are common to families of a virus or viruses. Antivirus software looks for these characteristics, or fingerprints, to identify and neutralize viruses before they impact you.

More than 200,000 known viruses, worms, bombs, and other malware have been defined. New ones are added all the time. Your antivirus software manufacturer will usually work hard to keep the definition database files current. The definition database file contains all the known viruses and countermeasures for a particular antivirus software product. You probably won't receive a virus that hasn't been seen by one of these companies. If you keep the virus definition database files in your software up-to-date, you probably won't be overly vulnerable to attacks.

> The best method of protection is to use a layered approach. Antivirus software should be at the gateways, at the servers, and at the desktop. If you want to go one step further, you can use software at each location from different vendors to make sure you're covered from all angles.

Firewalls

Firewalls are one of the first lines of defense in a network. There are different types of firewalls, and they can be either stand-alone systems or included in other devices such as routers or servers. You can find firewall solutions that are marketed as hardware only and others that are software only. Many firewalls, however, consist of add-in software that is available for servers or workstations.

> Although solutions are sold as "hardware only," the hardware still runs some sort of software. It may be hardened and in ROM to prevent tampering, and it may be customized—but software is present nonetheless.

The basic purpose of a firewall is to isolate one network from another. Firewalls are becoming available as appliances, meaning they're installed as the primary device separating two networks. *Appliances* are freestanding devices that operate in a largely self-contained manner, requiring less maintenance and support than a server-based product.

Firewalls function as one or more of the following:

- Packet filter
- Proxy firewall
- Stateful inspection firewall

 To understand the concept of a firewall, it helps to know where the term comes from. In days of old, dwellings used to be built so close together that if a fire broke out in one, it could easily destroy a block or more before it could be contained. To decrease the risk of this happening, firewalls were built between buildings. The firewalls were huge brick walls that separated the buildings and kept a fire confined to one side. The same concept of restricting and confining is true in network firewalls. Traffic from the outside world hits the firewall and isn't allowed to enter the network unless otherwise invited.

The firewall shown in Figure 7.2 effectively limits access from outside networks, while allowing inside network users to access outside resources. The firewall in this illustration is also performing proxy functions.

FIGURE 7.2   A proxy firewall blocking network access from external networks

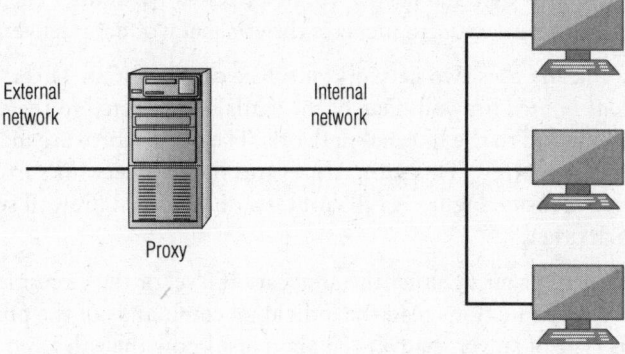

 Although firewalls are often associated with outside traffic, you can place a firewall anywhere. For example, if you want to isolate one portion of your internal network from others, you can place a firewall between them.

The following list discusses three of the most common functions that firewalls perform:

Packet Filter Firewalls   A firewall operating as a *packet filter* passes or blocks traffic to specific addresses based on the type of application. The packet filter doesn't analyze the data of a packet; it decides whether to pass it based on the packet's addressing information. For instance, a packet filter may allow web traffic on port 80 and block Telnet traffic on port 23. This type of filtering is included in many routers. If a received packet request asks for a port that isn't authorized, the filter may reject the request or simply ignore it. Many packet filters can also specify which IP addresses can request which ports and allow or deny them based on the security settings of the firewall.

Packet filters are growing in sophistication and capability. A packet filter firewall can allow any traffic that you specify as acceptable. For example, if you want web users to access your site, then you configure the packet filter firewall to allow data on port 80 to enter. If every network were exactly the same, firewalls would come with default port settings hard-coded, but networks vary, so the firewalls don't include such settings.

Proxy Firewalls   A *proxy firewall* can be thought of as an intermediary between your network and any other network. Proxy firewalls are used to process requests from an outside network; the proxy firewall examines the data and makes rule-based decisions about whether the request should be forwarded or refused. The proxy intercepts all the packages and reprocesses them for use internally. This process includes hiding internal IP addresses.

The proxy firewall provides better security than packet filtering because of the increased intelligence that a proxy firewall offers. Requests from internal network users are routed through the proxy. The proxy, in turn, repackages the request and sends it along, thereby isolating the user from the external network. The proxy can also offer caching, should the same request be made again, and can increase the efficiency of data delivery.

A proxy firewall typically uses two network interface cards (NICs). This type of firewall is referred to as a *dual-homed* firewall. One of the cards is connected to the outside network, and the other is connected to the internal network. The proxy software manages the connection between the two NICs. This setup segregates the two networks from each other and offers increased security. Figure 7.3 illustrates a dual-homed firewall segregating two networks from each other.

The proxy function can occur at either the application level or the circuit level. *Application-level proxy* functions read the individual commands of the protocols that are being served. This type of server is advanced and must know the rules and capabilities of the protocol used. An implementation of this type of proxy must know the difference between GET and PUT operations, for example, and have rules specifying how to execute them. A *circuit-level proxy* creates a circuit between the client and the server and doesn't deal with the contents of the packets that are being processed.

FIGURE 7.3   A dual-homed firewall segregating two networks from each other

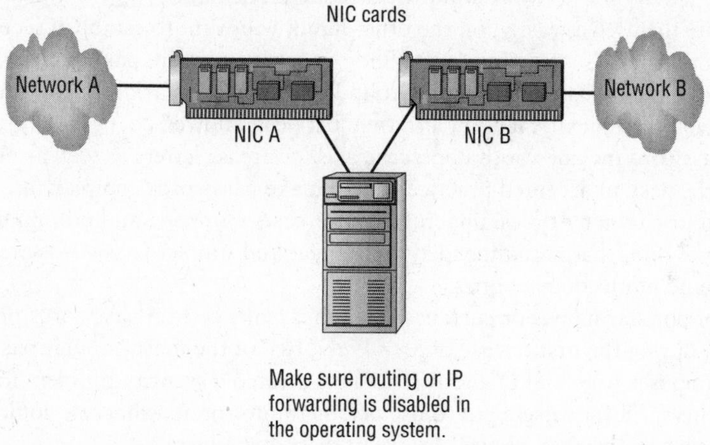

NIC cards

Network A   NIC A   NIC B   Network B

Make sure routing or IP
forwarding is disabled in
the operating system.

A unique application-level proxy server must exist for each protocol supported. Many proxy servers also provide full *auditing, accounting,* and other usage information that wouldn't normally be kept by a circuit-level proxy server.

Stateful Inspection Firewalls   The last section on firewalls focuses on the concept of stateful inspection. *Stateful inspection* is also referred to as *stateful packet filtering.* Most of the devices used in networks don't keep track of how information is routed or used. After a packet is passed, the packet and path are forgotten. In stateful inspection (or stateful packet filtering), records are kept using a state table that tracks every communications channel. Stateful inspections occur at all levels of the network and provide additional security, especially in connectionless protocols such as *User Datagram Protocol* (UDP) and *Internet Control Message Protocol* (ICMP). This adds complexity to the process. Denial-of-service (DoS) attacks present a challenge because flooding techniques are used to overload the state table and effectively cause the firewall to shut down or reboot.

User authentication/strong passwords

You can set up many different parameters and standards to force the people in your organization to conform with security practices. In establishing these parameters, it's important that you consider the capabilities of the people who will be working with these policies. If you're working in an environment where people aren't computer savvy, you may spend a lot of time helping them remember and recover passwords. Many organizations have had to reevaluate their security guidelines after they've invested great time and expense to implement high-security systems.

Setting authentication security, especially in supporting users, can become a high-maintenance activity for network administrators. On one hand, you want people to be able to authenticate themselves easily; on the other hand, you want to establish security that protects your company's resources. In a Windows server domain, password policies can be configured at the domain level using Group Policy objects. Variables you can configure include password complexity, length, and time between allowed changes.

A good password includes both uppercase and lowercase letters as well as numbers and symbols. In the past an accepted practice was to make passwords complex (using at least three of the four character types: uppercase, lowercase, numbers, and non-numeric figures), but recently the NIST has recommended that longer and simpler passwords are more secure than shorter and more complex ones.

Be wary of popular names or current trends that make certain passwords predictable. For example, during the first release of *Star Wars*, two of the most popular passwords used on college campuses were C3PO and R2D2. This created a security problem for campus computer centers. Educate users not to use personal information that one could easily guess about them, such as their pet names, anniversary, or birthdays.

Multifactor authentication

There are three factors of authentication: knowledge factors (something you know, such as a password), characteristic factors (some physical characteristic, such as a thumbprint), and behavioral factors (something you do, such as a voice analysis).

When more than one of these factors is required to authenticate, it is called *multifactor authentication*. It is *not* multifactor authentication if it uses two forms of the same factor of authentication such as a password and a PIN (both knowledge factors). An example of multifactor authentication is the requirement of a PIN and a retina scan.

Directory permissions

The protection of a directory service is based on the initial selection of network operating system and its deployment infrastructure. After these foundational decisions are made, you need to fully understand the technologies employed by your selected directory services system and learn how to make the most functional yet secure environment possible. This will usually require the addition of third-party security devices, applications, services, and solutions.

As for the permission on directories themselves, that is governed by NTFS, which was discussed in Chapter 6, "Operating Systems."

Security and Permission Tips for Users

Once you've made the choice of operating system and infrastructure, there is not much your users can do to improve or change the security of the directory services deployed. However, you can educate them to ensure that they don't become tools for an attacker bent on compromising your organization's security. Pass along the following dos and don'ts:

- Ensure that your client software is using the most secure form of authentication encryption supported by both the client and the authentication servers.

- Use encrypted software and protocols whenever possible, even for internal communications.

- Change your password according to the company's password policy.

- Use a company-established minimum character password that is unique for each account. While many companies set the minimum at 8 characters, it is not uncommon to see this set at 16.

- Never write your password down, or if you do, divide it up into several pieces and store each in a different secure location (such as a home safe, a gun cabinet, a chemical supply locker, or a safety deposit box).

- Never share your password or your logon session with another person; this includes your friends, spouse, and children.

- Verify that your client always interacts with an authentication server during the network logon process and does not use cached credentials.

- Allow all approved updates and patches to be installed onto your client.

- Ensure that all company data is copied back to a central file server before disconnecting from a logon session.

- Back up any personal data onto verified removable media.

- Never walk away from a logged-on workstation.

- Employ a password-protected screensaver.

- Don't use auto-logon features.

- Be aware of who is around you (and may be watching you) when you log on and when you work with valuable data.

- Never leave a company laptop, mobile phone, or PDA in a position where it can be stolen or compromised while you are away from the office. Cable locks should be used to keep notebooks securely in place whenever you are off-site.

VPN

Virtual private network (VPN) connections are remote access connections that allow users to securely connect to the enterprise network and work as if they were in the office. These connections use special tunneling protocols that encrypt the information being transferred between the user and the corporate network. Anywhere users, business partners, or vendors are allowed remote access to the network, VPN connections should be used. VPNs were discussed in Chapter 6.

DLP

Data loss prevention (DLP) solutions are designed to prevent sensitive material from purposefully or inadvertently escaping the organization. These solutions allow you to specify exactly what actions each user may take with respect to a document. For example, you may choose to allow the document to be read but neither printed nor forwarded to another user.

Access control lists

Access control lists (ACLs) are sets of rules that either control access to a resource or are configured on a router or firewall to control the type of traffic allowed to enter or leave an interface. These lists are what make packet filtering firewalls work. Using these lists, an administrator can at a granular level define who can send specific types of traffic to specific locations. For example, you could prevent a user from using Telnet to connect to the sales server, without preventing him from using Telnet to connect to any other devices and without impacting any of his other activities.

Smart card

Smart cards were discussed in detail in the section "Smart cards" later in this chapter. While the emphasis there was on using smart cards for physical access to facilities, these cards can also be used to log on to the network and thus to access resources.

Email filtering

While email filtering is typically discussed in the context of preventing spam, the organization must also be concerned about the contents and types of email sent by its users. Because the users are representing the organization in everything they do, you want them to follow certain guidelines. Email filtering allows for the recognition and the blocking of messages that contain content that is not compliant with these guidelines. Configuring the filtering solution in such a way that it recognizes and blocks non-compliant emails while also leaving compliant emails unaffected can be a tremendous challenge.

Trusted/untrusted software sources

Users frequently download and install software and not always from the safest sources. While policies should definitely reflect the desire of the organization to prevent unauthorized software downloads and installation, you may have to go beyond policies and implement a software restriction tool that prevents users from doing this. If you want to prevent all downloads and installations by users, you can use a Group Policy in Windows to require administrator privileges to do any downloading or installing. If your goal is to allow some installations but not others, you can use additional policies to define exactly which applications are allowed and which are not.

Principle of least privilege

The concept of least privilege is a simple one: When assigning permissions, give each user only the permissions they need to do their work and no more. This is especially true with administrators. Users who need administrative-level permissions should be assigned two accounts: one for performing nonadministrative, day-to-day tasks and the other to be used only when performing administrative tasks that specifically require an administrative-level user account. Those users should be educated on how each of the accounts should be used.

The biggest benefit to following this policy is the reduction of risk. The biggest headache is trying to deal with users who may not understand it. A manager, for example, may assert that he should have more permission than those who report to him, but giving those permissions to him also opens up all the possibilities for inadvertently deleting files, crippling accounts, and so forth.

A least-privilege policy should exist, and be enforced, throughout the enterprise. Users should have only the permissions and privileges needed to do their jobs and no more. ISO standard 27002 (which updates 17799) sums it up well: "Privileges should be allocated to individuals on a need-to-use basis and on an event-by-event basis, i.e., the minimum requirement for their functional role when needed." Adopting this as the policy for your organization is highly recommended.

Exam essentials

Be able to describe why antivirus software is needed.   Antivirus software looks at a virus and takes action to neutralize it based on a virus-definition database. Virus-definition database files are regularly made available on vendor sites.

Understand the need for user education.   Users are the first line of defense against most threats, whether physical or digital. They should be trained on the importance of security and how to help enforce it.

2.3 Compare and contrast wireless security protocols and authentication methods.

CompTIA wants administrators of SOHO networks to be able to secure those networks in ways that protect the data stored on them. This objective looks at the security protection that can be added to a wireless or wired SOHO network. The subobjectives covered in this chapter include the following:

- Protocols and encryption
- Authentication

Protocols and encryption

More and more, networks are using wireless as the medium of choice. It is much easier to implement, reconfigure, upgrade, and use than wired networks. Unfortunately, there can be downsides, and security is one of the largest.

The 802.11 standard applies to wireless networking, and there have been many versions of it released; the main ones are a, b, g, n, and ac. Encryption has gone from very weak (WEP) to much stronger with increments along the way, including WPA, WPA2, and implementations of TKIP and AES.

Wireless protocols are covered in detail in Chapter 2, "Networking".

WEP

Wired Equivalent Privacy (WEP) was the standard created as a first stab at security for wireless devices. It is now considered one of the most vulnerable protocols available for security; see Chapter 2 for details.

WPA

The *Wi-Fi Protected Access* (WPA) and *Wi-Fi Protected Access 2* (WPA2) technologies were designed to address the core problems with WEP. These technologies implement the 802.11i standard. WPA implements most—but not all—of 802.11i to communicate with older wireless cards (which might still need an update through their firmware to be compliant), while WPA2 implements the full standard and is not compatible with older cards.

WPA2

WPA2 implements the full 802.11i standard for security and is not compatible with older wireless cards.

TKIP

WPA was able to increase security by using a *Temporal Key Integrity Protocol* (TKIP) to scramble encryption keys using a hashing algorithm. The keys are issued an integrity check to verify they have not been modified or tampered with during transit. While a good solution, it was far from perfect. Corporate security today favors WPA2 since it replaces TKIP with Counter Mode with Cipher Block Chaining Message Authentication Code Protocol (CCMP).

AES

CCMP uses 128-bit Advanced Encryption Security (AES) with a 48-bit initialization vector, making it much more difficult to crack and minimizing the risk of a replay attack.

WPA and WPA2

While WPA and WPA2 are primarily covered in Chapter 2, we need to say a few words more about these protocols. There are four variants, as described in Table 7.1.

TABLE 7.1 WPA and WPA2

Protocol	Authentication	Encryption
WPA Personal	Passwords	TKIP
WPA Enterprise	RADIUS	TKIP
WPA2 Personal	Passwords	AES
WPA2 Enterprise	RADIUS	AES

WARNING

Never assume that a wireless connection is secure. The emissions from a wireless portal may be detectable through walls and for several blocks from the portal. Interception is easy to accomplish, given that RF is the medium used for communication. Newer wireless devices offer data security, and you should use it. You can set newer WAPs and wireless routers to nonbroadcast. This is also sometimes called *disabling the broadcast* of the SSID. Given the choice, you should choose to use WPA2, WPA, or WEP at its highest encryption level in that order.

Authentication

Authentication occurs when a user provides a username (identification) and then proper credentials (the authentication). In this section, we'll look at the types of authentication and then at authentication, accounting, and authorization (AAA) services.

Single-factor

As discussed under "Mutifactor authentication" earlier, there are three factors of authentication: knowledge factors (something you know, such as a password), characteristic factors (some physical characteristic, such as a thumbprint), and behavioral factors (something you do, such as a voice analysis). When only one type is used (for example, password only), it is called single-factor.

Multifactor

When two different types of factors are required (such as something you know and something you have), it is called *multifactor authentication*. It is important for you to understand that using two or more of the same type of factors (such as a password and a PIN, both something you know) is not multifactor authentication. However, when multifactor authentication is used for mobile devices, the level of security is significantly increased.

RADIUS/TACACS

When users are making connections to the network through a variety of mechanisms, they should be authenticated first. These users could be accessing the network through any of the following:

- Dial-up remote access servers
- VPN access servers
- Wireless access points
- Security-enabled switches

At one time each of these access devices would perform the authentication process locally on the device. The administrators would need to ensure that all remote access policies and settings were consistent across them all. When a password required changing, it had to be done on all devices.

To streamline this process, the Remote Authentication Dial-In User Service (RADIUS) and Terminal Access Controller Access-Control System Plus (TACACS+) networking protocols were developed to provide centralized authentication and authorization. These services can be run at a central location, and all the access devices, such as the access point (AP), remote access, virtual private network (VPN), and so on, can be made clients of the server. Whenever authentication occurs, the TACACS+ or RADIUS server performs the authentication and authorization. This provides one location to manage the remote access policies and passwords for the network.

Another advantage of using these systems is that the audit and access information (logs) are not kept on the access server.

TACACS and TACACS+ are Cisco proprietary services that operate in Cisco devices, whereas RADIUS is a standard defined in RFC 2138. Cisco has implemented several versions of TACACS over time. It went from TACACS to XTACACS to the latest version, TACACS+. The latest version provides authentication, accounting, and authorization, which is why it is sometimes referred to as an AAA service. TACACS+ employs tokens for two-factor, dynamic password authentication. It also allows users to change their passwords.

RADIUS is designed to provide a framework that includes three components. The *supplicant* is the device seeking authentication. The *authenticator* is the device to which they are attempting to connect (AP, switch, remote access server), and the *RADIUS server* is the authentication server. Note that the device seeking entry is not the RADIUS client. The authenticating server is the RADIUS server, and the authenticator (AP, switch, remote access server) is the RADIUS client.

In some cases, a RADIUS server can be the client of another RADIUS server. In that case, the RADIUS server acts as a proxy client for its RADIUS clients.

Exam essentials

Understand wireless connectivity.   Networks work in the same way whether there is a physical wire between the hosts or that wire has been replaced by a wireless signal. The same order of operations and steps are carried out regardless of the medium employed.

2.4 Given a scenario, detect, remove, and prevent malware using appropriate tools and methods.

Over time, best practices have been developed through trial and error that help minimize the chances of getting viruses and reduce the effort involved in getting rid of malware. Some of these practices are discussed in this section. The topics covered in this section include the following:

- Malware
- Tools and methods

Malware

Malware is a category of software that performs malicious activities on a device. It might wipe the hard drive or create a back door. In this section, we'll look at types of malware and attacks.

Ransomware

Ransomware is a type of malware that usually encrypts the entire system or an entire drive with an encryption key that only the hacker possesses. Once she encrypts the machine, she will hold the data residing on the device hostage until a ransom is paid.

The latest version of this attack arrives as an attachment that appears to be a resume. However, when the attachment is opened, the malware uses software called Cryptowall to encrypt the device. What usually follows is a demand for $500 to decrypt the device.

Trojan

Trojan horses are programs that enter a system or network under the guise of another program. A Trojan horse may be included as an attachment or as part of an installation program. The Trojan horse can create a back door or replace a valid program during installation. It then accomplishes its mission under the guise of another program. Trojan horses can be used to compromise the security of your system, and they can exist on a system for years before they're detected.

The best preventive measure for Trojan horses is not to allow them entry into your system. Immediately before and after you install a new software program or operating system, back it up! If you suspect a Trojan horse, you can reinstall the original programs, which should delete the Trojan horse. A port scan may also reveal a Trojan horse on your system. If an application opens a TCP or IP port that isn't supported in your network, you can track it down and determine which port is being used.

Keylogger

A keylogger records everything typed and sends a record of this to the attacker. It can be implemented as a malicious software package, maybe even as part of a rootkit; or it may be a hardware device inserted between the keyboard and the USB port.

Rootkit

Rootkits have become the software exploitation program du jour. They are software programs that have the ability to hide certain things from the operating system. With a rootkit, there may be a number of processes running on a system that don't show up in Task Manager, or connections may be established/available that don't appear in a Netstat display—the rootkit masks the presence of these items. The rootkit does this by manipulating function calls to the operating system and filtering out information that would normally appear.

Unfortunately, many rootkits are written to get around antivirus and antispyware programs that aren't kept up-to-date. The best defense you have is to monitor what your system is doing and catch the rootkit in the process of installation.

Virus

Viruses can be classified as polymorphic, stealth, retroviruses, multipartite, armored, companion, phage, and macro viruses. Each type of virus has a different attack strategy and different consequences.

Estimates for losses due to viruses are in the billions of dollars. These losses include financial loss as well as lost productivity.

The following sections will introduce the symptoms of a virus infection, explain how a virus works, and describe the types of viruses you can expect to encounter and how they generally behave. I'll also discuss how a virus is transmitted through a network.

Symptoms of a virus/malware infection

Many viruses will announce that you're infected as soon as they gain access to your system. They may take control of your system and flash annoying messages on your screen or destroy your hard disk. When this occurs, you'll know that you're a victim. Other viruses will cause your system to slow down, cause files to disappear from your computer, or take over your disk space.

 Because viruses are the most common malware, the term *virus* is used in this section.

You should look for some of the following symptoms when determining whether a virus infection has occurred:

- The programs on your system start to load more slowly. This happens because the virus is spreading to other files in your system or is taking over system resources.

- Unusual files appear on your hard drive, or files start to disappear from your system. Many viruses delete key files in your system to render it inoperable.

- Program sizes change from the installed versions. This occurs because the virus is attaching itself to these programs on your disk.

- Your browser, word-processing application, or other software begins to exhibit unusual operating characteristics. Screens or menus may change.

- The system mysteriously shuts itself down or starts itself up and does a great deal of unanticipated disk activity.

- You mysteriously lose access to a disk drive or other system resources. The virus has changed the settings on a device to make it unusable.

- Your system suddenly doesn't reboot or gives unexpected error messages during startup.

This list is by no means comprehensive. What is an absolute, however, is that you should immediately quarantine the infected system. It is imperative that you do all you can to contain the virus and keep it from spreading to other systems within your network or beyond.

How viruses work

A virus, in most cases, tries to accomplish one of two things: render your system inoperable or spread itself to other systems. Many viruses will spread to other systems given the chance and then render your system unusable. This is common with many of the newer viruses.

If your system is infected, the virus may try to attach itself to every file in your system and spread each time you send a file or document to other users. When you give removable media to another user or put it into another system, you then infect that system with the virus.

Most viruses today are spread using email. The infected system attaches a file to any email that you send to another user. The recipient opens this file, thinking it's something you legitimately sent them. When they open the file, the virus infects the target system. The virus might then attach itself to all the emails the newly infected system sends, which in turn infects the recipients of the emails. Figure 7.4 shows how a virus can spread from a single user to thousands of users in a short time using email.

FIGURE 7.4   An email virus spreading geometrically to other users

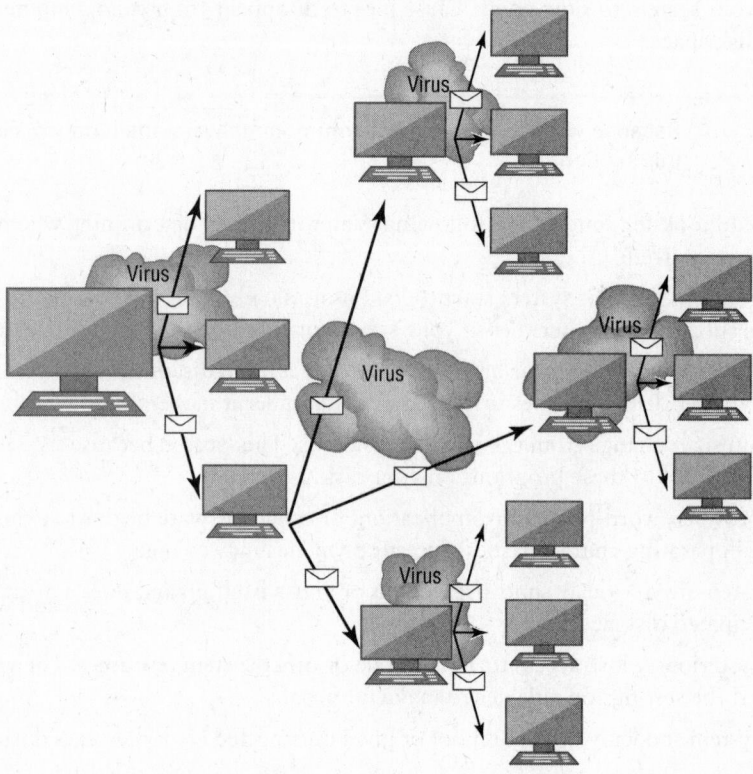

Types of viruses

Viruses take many different forms. The following sections briefly introduce these forms and explain how they work. These are the most common types, but this isn't a comprehensive list.

 The best defense against a virus attack is to install and run antivirus software. The software should be on all workstations as well as the server.

Armored Virus   An *armored virus* is designed to make itself difficult to detect or analyze. Armored viruses cover themselves with protective code that stops debuggers or disassemblers from examining critical elements of the virus. The virus may be written in such a way that some aspects of the programming act as a decoy to distract analysis while the actual code hides in other areas in the program.

From the perspective of the creator, the more time it takes to deconstruct the virus, the longer it can live. The longer it can live, the more time it has to replicate and spread to as many machines as possible. The key to stopping most viruses is to identify them quickly and educate administrators about them—the very things that the armor intensifies the difficulty of accomplishing.

Companion Virus   A *companion virus* attaches itself to legitimate programs and then creates a program with a different filename extension. This file may reside in your system's temporary directory. When a user types the name of the legitimate program, the companion virus executes instead of the real program. This effectively hides the virus from the user. Many of the viruses that are used to attack Windows systems make changes to program pointers in the Registry so that they point to the infected program. The infected program may perform its dirty deed and then start the real program.

Macro Virus   A *macro virus* exploits the enhancements made to many application programs. Programmers can expand the capability of applications such as Microsoft Word and Excel. Word, for example, supports a mini-BASIC programming language that allows files to be manipulated automatically. These programs in the document are called *macros*. For example, a macro can tell your word processor to spell-check your document automatically when it opens. Macro viruses can infect all the documents on your system and spread to other systems via email or other methods.

Multipartite Virus   A *multipartite virus* attacks your system in multiple ways. It may attempt to infect your boot sector, infect all your executable files, and destroy your application files. The hope here is that you won't be able to correct all the problems and will allow the infestation to continue. The multipartite virus in Figure 7.5 attacks your boot sector, infects application files, and attacks your Word documents.

FIGURE 7.5   A multipartite virus commencing an attack on a system

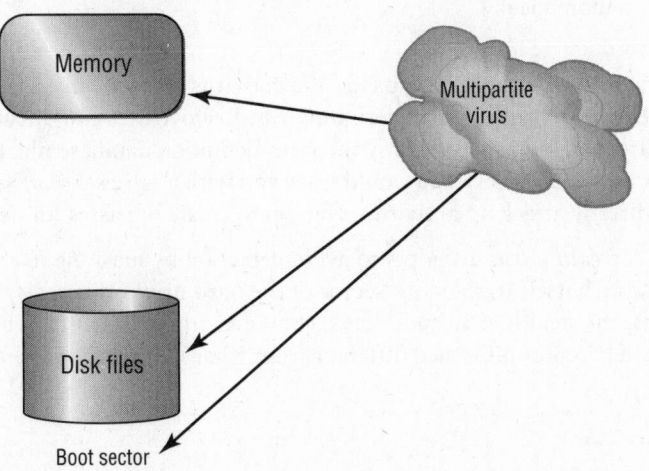

Phage Virus   A *phage virus* alters other programs and databases. The virus infects all these files. The only way to remove this virus is to reinstall the programs that are infected. If you miss even a single instance of this virus on the victim system, the process will start again and infect the system once more.

Polymorphic Virus   *Polymorphic viruses* change form in order to avoid detection. The virus will attempt to hide from your antivirus software. Frequently, the virus will encrypt parts of itself to avoid detection. When the virus does this, it's referred to as *mutation*. The mutation process makes it hard for antivirus software to detect common characteristics of the virus. Figure 7.6 shows a polymorphic virus changing its characteristics to avoid detection. In this example, the virus changes a signature to fool antivirus software.

FIGURE 7.6   The polymorphic virus changing its characteristics

A *signature* is an algorithm or other element of a virus that uniquely identifies it. Because some viruses have the ability to alter their signature, it is crucial that you keep signature files current, whether you choose to manually download them or configure the antivirus engine to do so automatically.

Retrovirus   A *retrovirus* attacks or bypasses the antivirus software installed on a computer. You can consider a retrovirus to be an anti-antivirus. Retroviruses can directly attack your antivirus software and potentially destroy the virus definition database file. Destroying this information without your knowledge would leave you with a false sense of security. The virus may also directly attack an antivirus program to create bypasses for itself.

Stealth Virus   A *stealth virus* attempts to avoid detection by masking itself from applications. It may attach itself to the boot sector of the hard drive. When a system utility or program runs, the stealth virus redirects commands around itself to avoid detection. An infected file may report a file size different from what is actually present to avoid detection. Figure 7.7 shows a stealth virus attaching itself to the boot sector to avoid detection. Stealth viruses may also move themselves from file A to file B during a virus scan for the same reason.

FIGURE 7.7 A stealth virus hiding in a disk boot sector

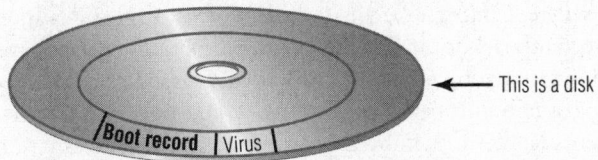

Boot record | Virus

← This is a disk

Present Virus Activity

New viruses and threats are released on a regular basis to join the cadre of those already in existence. From an exam perspective, you need to be familiar with the world only as it existed at the time the questions were written. From an administrative standpoint, however, you need to know what is happening today.

To find this information, visit the CERT/CC Current Activity web page at www.us-cert.gov/ current/current_activity.html. Here you'll find a detailed description of the most current viruses as well as links to pages on older threats.

Botnet

A bot is a type of malware that installs itself on large numbers of computers through infected email, downloads from websites, Trojan horses, and shared media. Once installed, the bot has the ability to connect back to the hacker's computer. After that, the hacker's server controls all the bots located on these machines. At a set time, the hacker may direct the bots to take some action, such as to direct all the machines to send out spam messages, mount a DoS attack, or perform phishing or any number of malicious acts. The collection of computers that act together is called a *botnet*, and the individual computers are called *zombies*. By recruiting many zombies to assist in the attack, the attacker greatly magnifies its effect.

Worm

A worm is different from a virus in that it can reproduce itself, it's self-contained, and it doesn't need a host application to be transported. Many of the so-called viruses that have made the news were actually worms. However, it's possible for a worm to contain or deliver a virus to a target system.

By their nature and origin, worms are supposed to propagate, and they use whatever services they're capable of to do that. Early worms filled up memory and bred inside the RAM of the target computer. Worms can use TCP/IP, email, Internet services, social media sites, or any number of possibilities to reach their target.

Spyware

Spyware differs from other malware in that it works—often actively—on behalf of a third party. Rather than self-replicating, like viruses and worms, spyware is spread to machines by users who inadvertently ask for it. The users often don't know they have asked for the spyware but have done so by downloading other programs, visiting infected sites, and so on.

The spyware program monitors the user's activity and responds by offering unsolicited pop-up advertisements (sometimes known as *adware*), gathers information about the user to pass on to marketers, or intercepts personal data such as credit card numbers.

Tools and methods

Whereas physical security focused on keeping individuals out, digital security focuses mostly on keeping harmful data/malware out. The areas of focus are antivirus software, anti-malware, Recovery Console, backup/restore, end-user education, software firewalls, and DNS configuration. Each of these is addressed in the sections that follow.

Antivirus/Anti-malware

The primary method of preventing the propagation of malicious code involves the use of *antivirus software*. Antivirus and anti-malware are discussed in Chapter 2.

Recovery Console

The Recovery Console isn't installed on a Windows system by default. To install it, follow these steps:

1. Place the Windows disc in the system.

2. From a command prompt, change to the i386 directory of the CD.

3. Type **winnt32 /cmdcons**.

4. A prompt appears, alerting you to the fact that 7 MB of hard drive space is required and asking whether you want to continue. Click Yes.

Upon successful completion of the installation, the Recovery Console is added as a menu choice at the bottom of the startup menu. To access it, you must choose it from the list at startup. If more than one installation of Windows exists on the system, another boot menu will appear, asking which you want to boot into, and you must make a selection to continue.

To perform this task, you must give the administrator password. You'll then arrive at a command prompt. You can give a number of commands from this prompt, two of which are worth special attention: exit restarts the computer, and help lists the commands you can give. Table 7.2 explains some options.

TABLE 7.2 Recovery Console options

Option	Explanation
Startup Repair	Fixes missing or damaged system files, which might prevent Windows from starting correctly
System Restore	Restores your computer's system files to an earlier point in time without affecting your files, such as e-mail, documents, or photos
System Image Recovery	Requires a system image, a personalized backup of the partition that contains Windows, and includes programs and user data, like documents, pictures, and music
Windows Memory Diagnostic Tool	Scans your computer's memory for errors

Backup/restore

Backups are duplicate copies of key information, ideally stored in a location other than the one where the information is currently stored. Backups include both paper and computer records. Computer records are usually backed up using a backup program, backup systems, and backup procedures.

The primary starting point for disaster recovery involves keeping current backup copies of key data files, databases, applications, and paper records available for use. Your organization must develop a solid set of procedures to manage this process and ensure that all key information is protected. A security professional can do several things in conjunction with systems administrators and business managers to protect this information. It's important to think of this problem as an issue that is larger than a single department.

The information you back up must be immediately available for use when needed. If a user loses a critical file, they won't want to wait several days while data files are sent from a remote storage facility. Several types of storage mechanisms are available for data storage.

Working Copies   *Working copy* backups—sometimes referred to as *shadow copies*—are partial or full backups that are kept on the premises for immediate recovery purposes. Working copies are frequently the most recent backups that have been made.

Typically, working copies are intended for immediate use. These copies are often updated on a frequent basis.

Many file systems used on servers include *journaling*. Journaled file systems (JFSs) include a log file of all changes and transactions that have occurred within a set period of time (such as the last few hours). If a crash occurs, the operating system can look at the log files to see which transactions have been committed and which ones haven't. This technology works well and allows unsaved data to be written after the recovery and the system (usually) to be successfully restored to its condition before the crash.

On-Site Storage   *On-site storage* usually refers to a location on the site of the computer center that is used to store information locally. On-site storage containers are available that allow computer cartridges, tapes, and other backup media to be stored in a reasonably protected environment in the building.

On-site storage containers are designed and rated for fire, moisture, and pressure resistance. These containers aren't *fireproof* in most situations, but they're *fire-rated*: A fireproof container should be guaranteed to withstand damage regardless of the type of fire or temperatures, whereas fire ratings specify that a container can protect the contents for a specific amount of time in a given situation.

If you choose to depend entirely on on-site storage, make sure the containers you acquire can withstand the worst-case environmental catastrophes that could happen at your location. Make sure as well that those containers are in locations where you can easily find them after the disaster and access them (near exterior walls, and so on).

Off-Site Storage   *Off-site storage* refers to a location away from the computer center where paper copies and backup media are kept. Off-site storage can involve something as simple as keeping a copy of backup media at a remote office, or it can be as complicated as a nuclear-hardened high-security storage facility. The storage facility should be bonded, insured, and inspected on a regular basis to ensure that all storage procedures are being followed.

Determining which storage mechanism to use should be based on the needs of the organization, the availability of storage facilities, and the budget available. Most off-site storage facilities charge based on the amount of space you require and the frequency of access you need to the stored information.

Three methods exist to back up information on most systems.

Full Backup   A *full backup* is a complete, comprehensive backup of all files on a disk or server. The full backup is current only at the time it's performed. Once a full backup is made, you have a complete archive of the system at that point in time. A system shouldn't be in use while it undergoes a full backup because some files may not get backed up. Once the system goes back into operation, the backup is no longer current. A full backup can be a time-consuming process on a large system.

Incremental Backup   An *incremental backup* is a partial backup that stores only the information that has been changed since the last full or incremental backup. If a full backup were performed on a Sunday night, an incremental backup done on Monday night would contain only the information that changed since Sunday night. Such a backup is typically considerably smaller than a full backup. This backup system requires that each incremental backup be retained until a full backup can be performed. Incremental backups are usually the fastest backups to perform on most systems, and each incremental tape is relatively small.

Differential Backup   A differential backup is similar in function to an incremental backup, but it backs up any files that have been altered since the last full backup; it makes duplicate copies of files that haven't changed since the last differential backup. If a full backup was performed on Sunday night, a differential backup performed on Monday night would capture the information that was changed on Monday. A differential backup completed on Tuesday night would record the changes in any files from Monday and any changes in files on Tuesday. As you can see, during the week each differential backup would become larger; by Friday or Saturday night, it might be nearly as large as a full backup. This means the backups in the earliest part of the weekly cycle will be very fast, and each successive one will be slower.

When these backup methods are used in conjunction with each other, the risk of loss can be greatly reduced. You should never combine an incremental backup with a differential backup. One of the major factors in determining which combination of these three methods to use is time—ideally, a full backup would be performed every day. Several commercial backup programs support these three backup methods. You must evaluate your organizational needs when choosing which tools to use to accomplish backups.

Almost every stable operating system contains a utility for creating a copy of configuration settings necessary to reach the present state after a disaster. As an administrator, you must know how to do backups and be familiar with all the options available to you.

End-user education

In many cases, users are partly responsible for a virus infection. After an infection occurs is a great time to impress on users the principles of secure computing. They should be reminded that antivirus software and firewalls can go only so far in protecting them and that they should exercise safe browsing habits and refrain from opening any attachments in email from unknown sources, regardless of how tempting.

Software firewalls

You can add a second layer of defense by utilizing personal or software firewalls on devices. This can be in addition to your network firewall and help prevent attacks locally on machines. The Windows Firewall is a good example of such a software firewall.

DNS configuration

Domain Name System Security Extensions (DNSSEC) is a new version of DNS that provides to DNS clients (resolvers) origin authentication of DNS data, authenticated denial of existence, and data integrity, but not availability or confidentiality. It helps to prevent the use of rogue DNS servers that lead users to malicious sites.

Exam essentials

Describe the options available in Windows System recovery.   These include Startup Repair, System Restore, System Image Recovery, and Windows Memory Diagnostic Tool.

2.5 Compare and contrast social engineering, threats, and vulnerabilities.

This objective explores security threats and vulnerabilities. A number of important topics are discussed in this section that fall into the realm of two broad categories: social engineering and malware. You'll look at malware and then several different types of attacks, as well as some of the reasons your network is vulnerable. This list is far from inclusive because new variants of each are being created by miscreants on a regular basis. The list does, however, include everything CompTIA expects you to know for the exam. Subobjectives covered in this section include the following:

- Social engineering
- DDoS
- DoS
- Zero-day
- Man-in-the-middle
- Brute force
- Dictionary
- Rainbow table
- Spoofing
- Non-compliant systems
- Zombie

Social engineering

Social engineering is a process in which an attacker attempts to acquire information about your network and system by social means, such as by talking to people in the organization. A social-engineering attack may occur over the phone, by email, or by a visit. The intent is to acquire access information, such as user IDs and passwords. When the attempt is made through email or instant messaging, it is known as *phishing* (discussed later) and often is made to look as if it is coming from sites where users are likely to have accounts (eBay and PayPal are popular).

These types of attacks are relatively low-tech and are more akin to con jobs. Take the following example. Your help desk gets a call at 4 a.m. from someone purporting to be the vice president of your company. She tells the help-desk personnel that she is out of town to attend a meeting, her computer just failed, and she is sitting in a hotel trying to get a file from her desktop computer back at the office. She can't seem to remember her password and user ID. She tells the help-desk representative that she needs access to the information right away or the company could lose millions of dollars. Your help-desk rep knows how important this meeting is and gives the vice president her user ID and password over the phone.

Another common approach is initiated by a phone call or email from your software vendor, telling you that they have a critical fix that must be installed on your computer system. If this patch isn't installed right away, your system will crash and you'll lose all your data. For some reason, you've changed your maintenance account password and they can't log on. Your system operator gives the password to the person. You've been hit again.

Phishing

Phishing is a form of social engineering in which you simply ask someone for a piece of information that you are missing by making it look as if it is a legitimate request. An email might look as if it is from a bank and contain some basic information, such as the user's name. In the email, it will often state that there is a problem with the person's account or access privileges. They will be told to click a link to correct the problem. After they click the link—which goes to a site other than the bank's—they are asked for their username, password, account information, and so on. The person instigating the phishing can then use the values entered there to access the legitimate account.

One of the best counters to phishing is to simply mouse over the Click Here link and read the URL. Almost every time it is pointing to an adaptation of the legitimate URL as opposed to a link to the real thing.

The only preventive measure in dealing with social-engineering attacks is to educate your users and staff to never give out passwords and user IDs over the phone or via email or to anyone who isn't positively verified as being who they say they are.

When you combine phishing with Voice over IP (VoIP), it becomes known as *vishing* and is just an elevated form of social engineering. While crank calls have been in existence since the invention of the telephone, the rise in VoIP now makes it possible for someone to call you from almost anywhere in the world, without the worry of tracing, caller ID, and other features of the land line, and pretend to be someone they are not in order to get data from you.

Spear phishing

Two other forms of phishing to be aware of are *spear phishing* and *whaling*, and they are similar in nature. With spear phishing, the person conducting it uses information that the target would be less likely to question because it appears to be coming from a trusted source. As an example, instead of Wells Fargo sending you a message telling you to click here to fix a problem with your account, the message that comes in appears to be from your spouse and it says to click here to see a video of your children from last Christmas. Because it appears far more likely to be a legitimate message, it cuts through the user's standard defenses like a spear and has a higher likelihood of being clicked. Generating the attack requires much more work on the part of the miscreant and often involves using information from contact lists, friend lists from social media sites, and so on.

Whaling is nothing more than phishing, or spear phishing, for big users. Instead of sending out a To Whom It May Concern message to thousands of users, the whaler identifies one person from whom they can gain all the data they want—usually a manager or owner—and targets the phishing campaign at them.

Impersonation

Impersonation occurs when an individual pretends to be an IT technician, heating and air repairman, or other personnel to get in the facility or to convince someone to disclose sensitive information.

Shoulder surfing

Shoulder surfing involves nothing more than watching someone when they enter their sensitive data. They can see you entering a password, typing in a credit card number, or entering any other pertinent information. The best defense against this type of attack is simply to survey your environment before entering personal data. Privacy filters can be used that make the screen difficult to read unless you are directly in front of it.

Tailgating

Tailgating is the term used for someone being so close to you when you enter a building that they are able to come in right behind you without needing to use a key, a card, or any other security device. Many social-engineering intruders who need physical access to a site will use this method of gaining entry. Educate users to beware of this and other social-engineering ploys and prevent them from happening.

Mantraps are a great way to stop tailgating. A mantrap is a series of two doors with a small room between them that helps prevent unauthorized people from entering a building. For more information, see the earlier section "Mantrap."

Dumpster diving

It is amazing the information that can be gleaned from physical documents even in the age when there is such a push to go paperless. *Dumpster diving* is a common physical access method. Companies normally generate a huge amount of paper, most of which eventually winds up in dumpsters or recycle bins. Dumpsters may contain information that is highly sensitive in nature (such as passwords after a change and before the user has the new one memorized). In high-security and government environments, sensitive papers should be either shredded or burned. Most businesses don't do this. In addition, the advent of "green" companies has created an increase in the amount of recycled paper, which can often contain all kinds of juicy information about a company and its individual employees.

DDoS

A distributed denial-of-service (DDoS) attack is one in which the attacker recruits additional devices (called *zombies*) to assist in the attack. This greatly magnifies the effect of the denial of service.

DoS

A denial-of-service (DoS) attack is one in which the attacker's goal is to make the device unavailable to do its job. It consumes all the resources of the device leaving none for its regular work.

Zero-day

Vulnerabilities are often discovered in live environments before a fix or patch exists. Such vulnerabilities are referred to as *zero-day* vulnerabilities. A zero-day attack is one that occurs when a security vulnerability in an application is discovered on the same day the application is released. Monitoring known hacking community websites can often provide an early alert because hackers often share zero-day exploit information.

New zero-day attacks are announced on a regular basis against a broad range of technology systems. You should create an inventory of applications and maintain a list of critical systems to manage the risks of these attack vectors.

Man-in-the-middle

A man-in-the-middle (MITM) attack is one in which the hacker uses one of several techniques to position himself in the middle of a current communication session between two devices. One way he might do this is by polluting the ARP cache (mappings of IP addresses to MAC addresses) such that the users on either end of the session think they are sending data to one another when in reality they are sending it to the hacker. This allows the hacker to monitor the entire conversation.

Brute force

A brute-force attack is a password attack that operates by attempting every possible combination of characters that could be in a password. These can be performed online or offline. Given enough time and processing power, any password can be cracked, so most enterprises use some sort of password policy that locks an account after a certain number of incorrect attempts. For this reason, online attacks are largely unsuccessful.

In contrast, the offline mode of the attack requires the attacker to steal the password file first but enables an unconstrained guessing of passwords, free of any application- or network-related rate limitations.

Dictionary

Dictionary attacks rely on the use of large files that contain words from the dictionary. These attacks are most often attempts to crack an encrypted password by encrypting each word in the dictionary file using the same algorithm used to encrypt the users' passwords and then comparing this value to the encrypted password for a match. These attacks are performed offline to eliminate the disabling of the account through password policies.

Rainbow table

Rainbow tables are used to speed the process of comparing captured password hashes to character combinations. In the absence of a rainbow table, the process is to take the character combination, hash it, and compare the hash. A *rainbow table* is a list of character combinations that have been pre-hashed. *Salting* the password, or adding a random character before hashing, can help defeat the use of rainbow tables.

Spoofing

Spoofing is the process of masquerading as another user or device. It is usually done for the purpose of accessing a resource to which the hacker should not have access or to get through a security device such as a firewall that may be filtering traffic based on a source IP address.

Spoofing can take various forms. The hacker may change her IP address to one that belongs to a trusted user or device to get through a firewall filtering at the IP layer. In other cases, she might spoof the MAC address of a trusted device to defeat layer 2 security applied on a switch or wireless access point (AP). It could also be the spoofing of a username and password to access a resource. Finally, it might be the spoofing of an email address to launch one of the email-based attacks.

Non-compliant systems

Upon infection, some viruses destroy the target system immediately. The saving grace is that the infection can be detected and corrected. Some viruses won't destroy or otherwise tamper with a system; they use the victim system as a carrier. The victim system then infects servers, file shares, and other resources with the virus. The carrier then infects the target system again. Until the carrier is identified and cleaned, the virus continues to harass systems in this network and spread.

You should use some type of enterprise-grade malware management system that scans the network for non-compliant devices. Most of these systems can automate the entire process of locating, isolating, and remediating non-compliant devices.

Zombie/botnet

Botnets and zombies were described in the earlier section "Botnet," under objective 2.4.

Exam essentials

Know the characteristics and types of viruses used to disrupt systems and networks. Several different types of viruses are floating around today. The most common ones are polymorphic viruses, stealth viruses, retroviruses, multipartite viruses, and macro viruses.

Know the various types of social engineering.   Social-engineering variants include shoulder surfing (watching someone work) and phishing (tricking someone into believing they are communicating with a party other than the one they are communicating with). Variations on phishing include vishing and whaling as well as spear phishing.

2.6 Compare and contrast the differences of basic Microsoft Windows OS security settings.

There is an entire domain dedicated to security for A+. Add to that, CompTIA also provides security certifications with Security+ and CompTIA Advanced Security Practitioner+ (CASP+), so you can see how important this topic is to those creating the exam. Because of that, make sure you have a good understanding of the topics covered here.

You want to make certain that your Windows systems, and the data within them, are kept as secure as possible. The security prevents others from changing the data, destroying it, or inadvertently harming it. This can be done by assigning users the least privileges possible and hardening as much of the environment as possible. The following are the subobjectives covered in this section:

- User and groups
- NTFS vs. share permissions
- Shared files and folders
- System files and folders
- User authentication
- Run as administrator vs. standard user
- BitLocker
- BitLocker-To-Go
- EFS

User and groups

There are a number of groups created on the operating system by default. The following sections look at the main ones of these.

Administrator

The Administrator account is the most powerful of all: It has the power to do everything from the smallest task all the way up to removing the operating system. Because of the great power it holds and the fact that it is always created, many who try to do harm will target this account as the one they try to break into. To increase security, during the installation of the Windows operating systems in question, you are prompted for a name of a user who will be designated as the Administrator. The power then comes not from being truly called Administrator (in my case it might now be tmcmillan, mcmillant, or something similar) but from being a member of the Administrators group (notice the plural for the group and singular for the user).

Because members of the Administrators group have such power, they can inadvertently do harm (such as accidentally deleting a file that a regular user could not). To protect against this, the practice of logging in with an Administrators account for daily interaction is strongly discouraged. Instead, system administrators should log in with a user account (lesser privileges) and change to the Administrators group account (elevated privileges) only when necessary for specific tasks.

Power user

The Power Users group is not as powerful as the Administrators group. Membership in this group gives read/write permission to the system, allowing members to install most software but keeping them from changing key operating system files. This is a good group for those who need to test software (such as programmers) and junior administrators. While the Power Users group exists in Windows Vista, 7, 8, 8.1, and 10, it is mostly there for legacy purposes and no longer has any more privileges than a standard user.

Guest

The Guest account is created by default (and should be disabled) and is a member of the Guests group. For the most part, members of Guests have the same rights as Users except they can't get to log files. The best reason to make users members of the Guests group is if they are accessing the system only for a limited time.

 As part of operating system security, you should rename the default Administrator and Guest accounts that are created at installation.

Standard user

This group is the default that regular users belong to. Members of this group have read/write permission to their own profile. They cannot modify system-wide Registry settings or do much harm outside of their own account. Under the principle of least privilege, users should be made a member of the Users group only unless qualifying circumstances force them to have higher privileges.

NTFS vs. share permissions

The New Technology File System (NTFS) was introduced with Windows NT to address security problems. Before Windows NT was released, it had become apparent to Microsoft that a new filesystem was needed to handle growing disk sizes, security concerns, and the need for more stability than FAT32 provided. NTFS was created to address those issues.

Although FAT was relatively stable, if the systems that were controlling it kept running, it didn't do well when the power went out or the system crashed unexpectedly. One of the benefits of NTFS was a transaction tracking system, which made it possible for Windows NT to back out of any disk operations that were in progress when Windows NT crashed or lost power.

With NTFS, files, directories, and volumes can each have their own security. NTFS's security is flexible and built in. Not only does NTFS track security in ACLs, which can hold permissions for local users and groups, but each entry in the ACL can specify what type of access is given—such as Read, Write, Modify, or Full Control. This allows a great deal of flexibility in setting up a network. In addition, special file-encryption programs were developed to encrypt data while it was stored on the hard disk.

Microsoft strongly recommends that all network shares be established using NTFS. Several current operating systems from Microsoft support both FAT32 and NTFS. It's possible to convert from FAT32 to NTFS without losing data, but you can't do the operation in reverse (you would need to reformat the drive and install the data again from a backup tape).

> If you're using FAT32 and want to change to NTFS, the convert utility will allow you to do so. For example, to change the E drive to NTFS, the command is convert e: /FS:NTFS.

Share permissions apply only when a user is accessing a file or folder through the network. Local permissions and attributes are used to protect the file when the user is local. With FAT and FAT32, you do not have the ability to assign "extended" or "extensible" permissions, and the user sitting at the console effectively is the owner of all resources on the system. As such, they can add, change, and delete any data or file that they want.

With NTFS as the filesystem, however, you are allowed to assign more comprehensive security to your computer system. NTFS permissions are able to protect you at the file level. Share permissions can be applied to the directory level only. NTFS permissions can affect users logged on locally or across the network to the system where the NTFS permissions are applied. Share permissions are in effect only when the user connects to the resource via the network.

> Share and NTFS permissions are not cumulative. Permission must be granted at both levels to allow access. Moreover, the effective permission that the user has will be the most restrictive of the combined NTFS permission and the combined share permissions.

Allow vs. deny

Within NTFS, permissions for objects fall into one of three categories: allow, not allow, and deny. When viewing the permissions for a file or folder, you can check the box for Allow, which effectively allows that group that action. You can also uncheck the box for Allow, which does not allow that group that action. Alternatively, you can check the box Deny, which prevents that group from using that action. There is a difference between not allowing (a cleared check box) and Deny (which specifically prohibits), and you tend not to see Deny used often. Deny, when used, trumps other permissions.

Permissions set at a folder are inherited down through subfolders, unless otherwise changed. Permissions are also cumulative: if a user is a member of a group that has read permission and a member of a group that has write permission, they effectively have both read and write permission.

Moving vs. copying folders and files

When you copy a file, you create a new entity. When you move a file, you simply relocate it and still have but one entity. This distinction is important for understanding permissions. A copy of a file will generally have the permissions assigned to it that are placed on newly created files in that folder—regardless of what permissions were on the original file.

A moved file, on the other hand, will attempt to keep the same permissions it had in the original location. Differences will occur if the same permissions cannot exist in the new location—for example, if you are moving a file from an NTFS volume to FAT32, the NTFS permissions will be lost. If, on the other hand, you are moving from a FAT32 volume to an NTFS volume, new permissions will be added that match those for newly created entities.

Folder copy and move operations follow similar guidelines to those with files.

File attributes

Permissions can be allowed or denied individually on a per-folder basis. You can assign any combination of the values shown in Table 7.3.

TABLE 7.3   NTFS directory permissions

NTFS Permission	Meaning
Full Control	This gives the user all the other choices and the ability to change permission. The user also can take ownership of the directory or any of its contents.
Modify	This combines the Read & Execute permission with the Write permission and further allows the user to delete everything, including the folder.
Read & Execute	This combines the permissions of Read with those of List Folder Contents and adds the ability to run executables.

NTFS Permission	Meaning
List Folder Contents	The List Folder Contents permission (known simply as List in previous versions) allows the user to view the contents of a directory and to navigate to its subdirectories. It does not grant the user access to the files in these directories unless that is specified in file permissions.
Read	This allows the user to navigate the entire directory structure, view the contents of the directory, view the contents of any files in the directory, and see ownership and attributes.
Write	This allows the user to create new entities within the folder, as well as to change attributes.

Clicking the Advanced button allows you to configure auditing and ownership properties. You can also apply NTFS permissions to individual files. This is done from the Security tab for the file. Table 7.4 lists the NTFS file permissions.

TABLE 7.4   NTFS file permissions

NTFS permission	Meaning
Full Control	This gives the user all the other permissions as well as permission to take ownership and change permission.
Modify	This combines the Read & Execute permission with the Write permission and further allows the user to delete the file.
Read	This allows the user to view the contents of the file and to see ownership and attributes.
Read & Execute	This combines the Read permission with the ability to execute.
Write	This allows the user to overwrite the file, as well as to change attributes and see ownership and permissions.

By default, the determination of NTFS permissions is based on the *cumulative* NTFS permissions for a user. Rights can be assigned to users based on group membership and individually; the only time permissions do not accumulate is when the Deny permission is invoked.

Shared files and folders

You can share folders, and the files within them, by right-clicking them and choosing Share With (Windows 7, Windows Vista, and Windows 8) from the context menu. In Windows 7, the context menu asks who you want to share the folder or file with (see Figure 7.8).

FIGURE 7.8   Sharing a folder in Windows 7

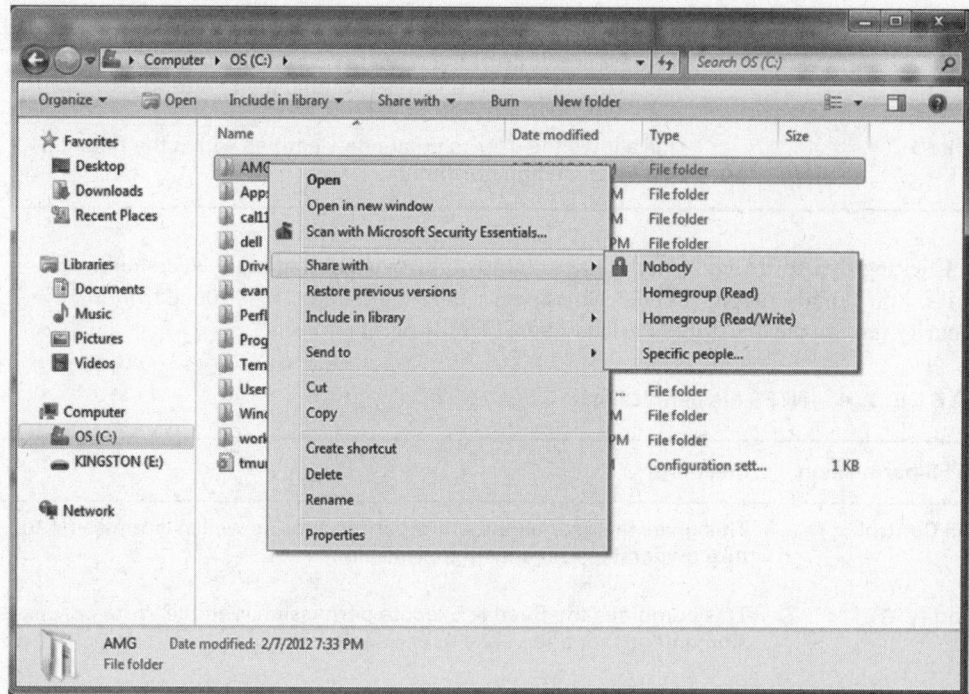

The options you see on the context menu will depend on the type of network you are connected to—a domain, a workgroup, or a Homegroup (the one shown in Figure 7.8). If you turn on password-protected sharing (the default), the person accessing the share has to give a username and password to access the shared entity.

The advanced sharing settings will come up if you try to share something in one of the Public folders or make other changes. This interface, shown in Figure 7.9, can also be accessed through the Network and Sharing Center applet in the Control Panel and is used to change network settings relevant to sharing.

FIGURE 7.9   Advanced sharing in Windows 7

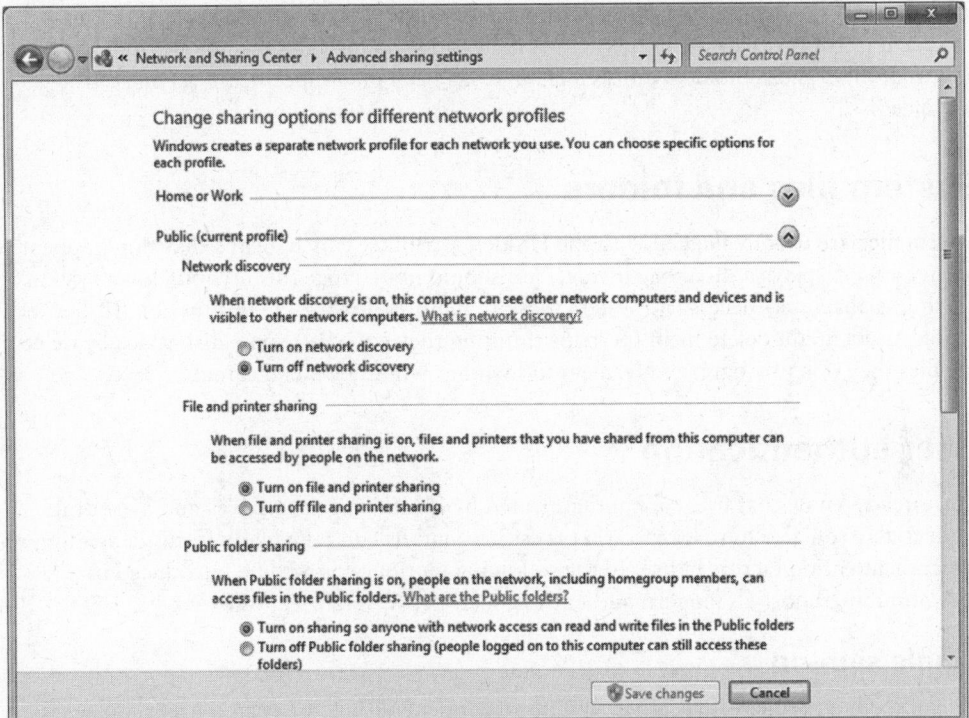

Administrative shares vs. local shares

Administrative shares are created on servers running Windows on the network for administrative purposes. These shares can differ slightly based on which OS is running but always end with a dollar sign ($) to make them hidden. There is one for each volume on a hard drive (c$, d$, and so on) as well as admin$ (the root folder, usually c:\windows), and print$ (where the print drivers are located). These are created for use by administrators and usually require administrator privileges to access.

Local shares, as the name implies, are those created locally and are visible with the icon of a group of two individuals.

Permission propagation

As mentioned earlier, permissions are cumulative. A user who is a member of two groups will effectively have the permissions of both groups combined. In cases where a user has a Deny permission from a group he is in, that overrules all other permissions he may have from other groups.

Inheritance

Inheritance is the default throughout the permission structure unless a specific setting is created to override this. A user who has read and write permissions in one folder will have that in all the subfolders unless a change has been made specifically to one of the subfolders.

System files and folders

System files are usually flagged with the Hidden attribute, which means they don't appear when a user displays a directory listing. You should not change this attribute on a system file unless absolutely necessary. System files are required for the OS to function. If they are visible, users might delete them (perhaps thinking they can clear some disk space by deleting files they don't recognize). Needless to say, that would be a bad thing!

User authentication

You already know that users are authenticated by identifying themselves and providing credentials. You also have learned that these credentials can take many forms depending on the authentication factors in use. In the following section, you will be introduced to a feature found in almost all modern authentication systems, single sign-on.

Single sign-on

One of the big problems that larger systems must deal with is the need for users to access multiple systems or applications. This may require a user to remember multiple accounts and passwords. The purpose of a single sign-on (SSO) is to give users access to all the applications and systems they need when they log on. This is becoming a reality in many environments, including Kerberos, Microsoft Active Directory, Novell eDirectory, and some certificate model implementations.

Single sign-on is both a blessing and a curse. It's a blessing in that once users are authenticated, they can access all the resources on the network and browse multiple directories. It's a curse in that it removes the doors that otherwise exist between the user and various resources.

Run as administrator vs. standard user

One of the security recommendations from Microsoft is to have administrative users log on with a standard user account and, when necessary, elevate the privileges of the account temporarily to perform a task and then remove that permission when the task is complete.

This is done by running the task, tool, or utility as an administrator. This can be done by right-clicking the tool and selecting Run as Administrator. Once the tool is closed, that security session ends, and the permissions are returned to those of a standard user. Having these highly privileged accounts logged in as infrequently as possible helps prevent hackers from gaining control of these accounts when they are live.

BitLocker/BitLocker To Go

BitLocker is the whole-drive encryption tool that can also seal a device such that it will not boot if any system files are altered. It can also lock the drive to a particular machine, preventing anyone from stealing the drive and connecting it to another device. BitLocker was covered in Chapter 6.

BitLocker To Go provides the same encryption technology to help prevent unauthorized access to the files stored on removable drives.

EFS

The Encrypting File System (EFS) is an encryption tool built into Windows Vista Business, Enterprise and Ultimate, Windows 7 (EFS is not fully supported on Windows 7 Starter, Home Basic, or Home Premium), Windows 8 or 8.1 Professional or Enterprise, and Windows 10. It allows a user to encrypt files that can be decrypted only by the user who encrypted the files. It can be used only on NTFS volumes but is simple to use.

To encrypt a file in Windows 8.1, simply right-click the file, access the file properties, and on the General tab click the Advanced button. That will open the Advanced Attributes dialog box, as shown in Figure 7.10. On this page, check the Encrypt Contents To Secure Data box.

FIGURE 7.10 Advanced attributes

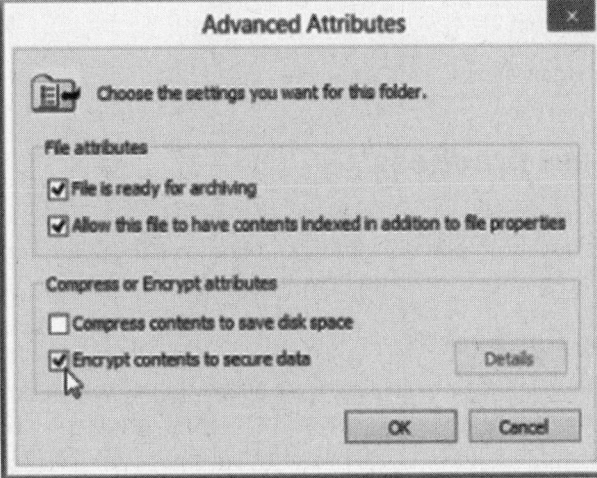

Exam essentials

Know the difference between single sign-on and multifactor authentication.   Single sign-on is the concept of having the user be authenticated on all services they access after logging in once. Multifactor authentication is not the opposite of single sign-on but merely requires more than one entity to be authenticated, for security purposes.

Know the NTFS permissions.   Permissions can be allowed or denied individually on a per-folder and per-file basis. Know the values shown in Tables 7.3 and 7.4.

2.7 Given a scenario, implement security best practices to secure a workstation.

In the previous objectives, the importance of user education has been mentioned. The user represents the weakest link in the security chain, whether the harm comes to them in the form of malware, social engineering, or simply avoidable mistakes. The workstation represents the digital arm of the user and must be properly and adequately secured to keep the user—and the network—protected.

A number of best practices are involved with securing a workstation. While a checklist could take many pages, depending on your environment, CompTIA has identified five that should appear on any roster. The following are the subobjectives covered in this section:

- Password best practices
- Account management
- Disable autorun
- Data encryption
- Patch/update management

Password best practices

One of the strongest ways to keep a system safe is to employ strong passwords and educate your users in the best security practices. In this section, you'll explore various techniques that can enhance the security of your user passwords.

Setting Strong Passwords

Passwords should be as long as possible. Most security experts believe a password of 10 characters is the minimum that should be used if security is a real concern. If you use only the lowercase letters of the alphabet, you have 26 characters with which to work. If you add the numeric values 0 through 9, you'll get another 10 characters. If you go one step further and add the uppercase letters, you'll then have an additional 26 characters, giving you a total of 62 characters with which to construct a password.

Most vendors recommend that you use nonalphabetical characters such as #, $, and % in your password, and some go so far as to require it.

If you used a 4-character password, this would be $62 \times 62 \times 62 \times 62$, or approximately 14 million password possibilities. If you used 5 characters in your password, this would give you 62 to the fifth power, or approximately 920 million password possibilities. If you used a 10-character password, this would give you 62 to the tenth power, or 8.4×10^{17} (a very big number) possibilities. As you can see, these numbers increase exponentially with each character added to the password. The 4-digit password could probably be broken in a fraction of a day, whereas the 10-digit password would take considerably longer and consume much more processing power.

If your password used only the 26 lowercase letters from the alphabet, the 4-digit password would have 26 to the fourth power, or 456,000 password combinations. A 5-character password would have 26 to the fifth power, or more than 11 million, and a 10-character password would have 26 to the tenth power, or 1.4×10^{14}. This is still a big number, but it would take considerably less time to break it. As noted earlier, NIST now considers password length more important than complexity.

 To see tables on how quickly passwords can be surmised, visit `www.lockdown.co.uk/?pg=combi&s=articles`.

Password expiration

The longer that a password is used, the more likely it is that it will be compromised in some way. It is for this reason that requiring users to change their passwords at certain intervals increases the security of their passwords. You should require users to set a new password every 30 days (more frequently for higher-security networks), and you must also prevent them from reusing old passwords. Most password management systems have the ability to track previously used passwords and to disallow users from recycling old passwords.

Screensaver required password

A screensaver should automatically start after a short period of idle time, and that screensaver should require a password before the user can begin the session again. This method of locking the workstation adds one more level of security.

BIOS/UEFI passwords

Passwords should be configured and required to access either the BIOS or UEFI settings on all devices. If this is not the case, it would be possible for someone to reboot a device, enter the settings, change the boot order, boot to an operating system residing on a USB or optical drive, and use that OS as a platform to access data located on the other drives. While this is a worst-case scenario, there is also less significant mayhem a malicious person could cause in the BIOS and UEFI.

Requiring passwords

Make absolutely certain you require passwords (such a simple thing to overlook in a small network) for all accounts, and change the default passwords on system accounts.

Account management

While I touched on one account management technique previously (preventing the reuse of passwords), there are a number of additional account management best practices that you should know and implement.

Restricting user permissions

When assigning user permissions, follow the principle of least privilege (discussed earlier) by giving users only the bare minimum they need to do their job. Assign permissions to groups, rather than users, and make users members of groups (or remove them from them) as they change roles or positions.

Logon time restrictions

Most users have a set work schedule, and it is only during these works hours that the user should access the network and its resources. Since an active account is an account vulnerable to misuse, any time in which you can disable an account while still allowing users to do their jobs enhances security, since a disabled account cannot be used for malicious purposes.

For this reason, many administrators allow users to log in only during certain hours. Typically, access is allowed from about an hour before their workday until about an hour after the day ends (to allow some flexibility). For certain users who tend to work throughout the day and night, this system may not work.

Disabling guest account

To secure the system, disable all accounts that are not needed (especially the guest account). Next, rename the accounts if you can (Microsoft won't allow you to rename an account to Administrator). Finally, change the passwords from the defaults and add them to the cycle of passwords that routinely get changed.

Failed attempts lockout

Earlier you learned that a brute-force attack is a password attack that attempts all character combinations until the password is discovered. You also learned that the attacks are typically performed offline and not in a live environment. Why is that? It's because almost all password systems are set up to allow only a set number of failed password attempts before the account is locked. While this policy may generate more password reset calls than you would like, that effect can be mitigated by implementing a complementary policy that allows the account to be automatically reenabled after a set amount of time (say five minutes). When this policy is communicated to the users, they know just to wait for five minutes and try again.

Timeout/screen lock

While the relative sensitivity of the data appearing on the screen of a user's computer can vary from time to time and from user to user, it is a good practice to protect that information when someone steps away from the device. Moreover, when the device is in an out-of-the-way location, it may even afford someone the chance to browse the device. For this reason, you should require on all devices a password-protected screensaver that kicks in after a short period of inactivity.

Change default admin user account/password

All Windows devices and all infrastructure devices such as routers, firewalls, switches, and wireless access points and controllers come with default administrator accounts and default passwords. The names of these accounts and the default passwords are well known to malicious individuals. They can be looked up in five minutes on the Internet. Always change the default names and passwords for these accounts; otherwise, you may find someone else "owning" the device at some point in time.

Basic Active Directory functions

As an A+ technician you are not expected to be an expert in Active Directory, but you are expected to be able to perform basic account management in AD. Let's go over the basic account operations.

Account creation

To create a new account in Active Directory Users And Computers, use the following steps:

1. Open Active Directory Users And Computers MMC.

2. Right-click the organizational unit where you would like the accounts to be located. Select New and then User from the context menu that appears.

3. Fill out the fields in the New Object – User window, including first name, last name, and logon name (the minimum). Then select Next.

4. Fill in the password and confirm it. As shown in Figure 7.11, select "User must change password at next logon" and select Next.

FIGURE 7.11   Creating a new account in the New Object window

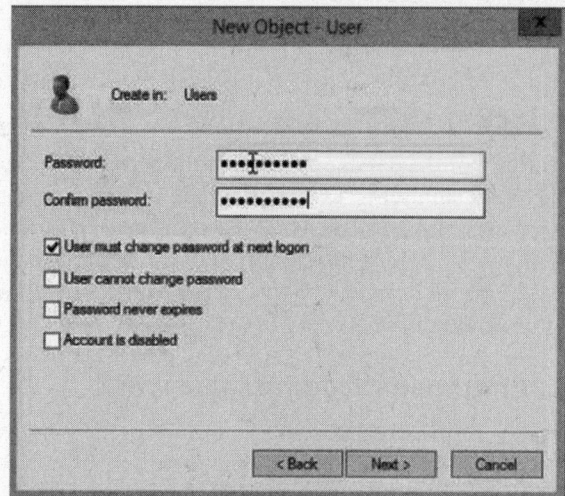

5.   This completes the creation of the new account.

Account deletion

To delete an account, follow these steps:

1.   Open Active Directory Users And Computers MMC.

2.   Right-click the organizational unit where the account is located.

3.   Right-click the account. Select Delete. Answer Yes to the dialog box confirming your section. The account is deleted.

Make sure first!

Prior to deleting an account, you should first disable it for a period and make sure that there is no resource (such as an encrypted file) that can be reached only through the account.

Password reset/unlock account

To reset a password, follow these steps:

1.   Open the Active Directory Users And Computers MMC.

2.   Right-click the organizational unit where the account is located.

3.   Right-click the account. Select Change Password. Enter the new password. Answer Yes to the dialog box confirming your section. The password is changed.

To unlock an account, follow these steps:

1. Open Active Directory Users And Computers MMC.
2. Right-click the organizational unit where the account is located.
3. Right-click the account. Clear the Account Is Disabled option. Answer Yes to the dialog box confirming your section. The account is enabled.

Disable account

To disable an account, follow these steps:

1. Open Active Directory Users And Computers MMC.
2. Right-click the organizational unit where the account is located.
3. Right-click the account. Select Disable. Answer Yes to the dialog box confirming your section. The account is disabled.

Disable autorun

It is never a good idea to put any media in a workstation if you do not know where it came from or what it is. The reason is that the media (CD, DVD, USB) could contain malware. Compounding matters, that malware could be referenced in the Autorun.inf file, causing it to be summoned when the media is inserted in the machine and requiring no other action. Autorun.inf can be used to start an executable, access a website, or do any of a large number of different tasks. The best way to prevent a user from falling victim to such a ploy is to disable the AutoRun feature on the workstation.

Microsoft has changed (by default, disabled) the AutoRun function on Windows Vista, Windows 7, Windows 8, and Widows 10, though running remains the default action for PCs using Windows XP through Service Pack 3. The reason Microsoft changed the default action can be summed up in a single word: security. That text-based Autorun.inf file not only can take your browser to a web page but also can call any executable file, pass along variable information about the user, or do just about anything else imaginable. Simply put, it is *never* a good idea to take any media whose source or contents you have no idea of and plug it into your system. Such an action opens up the user—and their network—to any number of possible tribulations. An entire business's data could be jeopardized by such a minuscule act if a harmful CD were placed in a computer at work by someone with elevated privileges.

Data encryption

While data encryption is possible both on a drive level (BitLocker) and on an individual file level (EFS), always keep in mind the cost of encryption and save this tool for instances where you really need it. By cost I mean that any encrypted file must be decrypted to be opened and encrypted again to be saved. This requires CPU cycles on the device. If you attempt to encrypt everything, the performance of the device may make it practically unusable. You must strike a balance between security and usability.

Patch/update management

While many patches and updates either repair something that doesn't work or add functionality, many others close a security hole. These are called *hotfixes* because they come out as soon as they are available, and you need to apply them as soon as possible (after testing them in a nonproduction environment).

For best results in patch management, you should deploy an automated system that can check for, download, and make available to the network all patches and updates for all systems. A good example of such a system is Microsoft Windows Server Update Services (WSUS), which can manage the updates for both servers and clients and for other operating systems as well.

> **WARNING** All patches should be deployed in a test environment prior to live deployment. This ensures that systems will not be adversely affected by an update that has issues.

Exam essentials

Understand the need for good passwords.   Passwords are the first line of defense for protecting an account. A password should be required for every account, and strong passwords should be enforced. Users need to understand the basics of password security and work to keep their accounts protected by following company policies regarding passwords.

List some techniques that enhance account management.   These techniques include but are not limited to disabling unused accounts, requiring frequent password changes, preventing the reuse of passwords, requiring complex passwords, and defining login hours for users.

2.8 Given a scenario, implement methods for securing mobile devices.

If laptops are easy to steal, smaller mobile devices are even more so. Because mobile devices are increasingly used to store valuable data and to perform functions once the domain of laptops and desktops, the need to secure these devices has grown. In this section, methods of securing mobile devices will be discussed. The topics addressed in objective 2.8 include the following:

- Screen locks
- Remote wipes
- Locator applications

- Remote backup applications
- Failed login attempts restrictions
- Antivirus/Anti-malware
- Patching/OS updates
- Biometric authentication
- Full device encryption
- Multifactor authentication
- Authenticator applications
- Trusted sources vs. untrusted sources
- Firewalls
- Policies and procedures

Screen locks

One of the most basic (but not necessarily the most utilized) security measures you can take is to implement a screen lock on the device. This is akin to implementing the password you use to log on to your desktop or laptop, but it's amazing how few people use this basic security measure. This can prevent someone from using the mobile device if it is stolen. There are several ways screen locks can be implemented, and in the following sections you'll examine each method.

Fingerprint lock

A fingerprint lock is one that uses the fingerprint of the user as credentials to authenticate the user and, when successful authentication completes, unlocks the screen. Because it relies on biometrics, it is for the most part more secure than using a passcode or a swipe.

Face lock

A face lock is one that uses a facial scan of the user to authenticate the user and, when successful authentication completes, unlocks the screen. It also is more secure than a passcode or swipe process.

Swipe lock

Swipe locks use a gesture or series of gestures, sometimes involving the movement of an icon to open the screen. In some cases, they require only knowledge of the mobile platform in use; they offer no security to the process because no authentication of the user is occurring. In other instances like Android, they require a pattern between nine dots to be swiped to unlock the device.

Passcode lock

Setting the password on an Android phone is done by navigating to Settings Location & Security ➤ Change Screen Lock. On the Change Screen Lock page, you can set the length of time the device remains idle until the screen locks as well as choose a method from None, Pattern, PIN, or Password. Select Password and then enter the desired password.

On an iOS-based device, navigate to Settings ➤ Settings ➤ Passcode Lock to set the password and Settings ➤ General ➤ Auto-Lock to set the amount of time before the iPhone locks.

Remote wipes

Remote wipes are instructions sent remotely to a mobile device that erase all the data when the device is stolen. In the case of the iPhone, this feature is closely connected to the locator application (discussed in the next section). To perform a remote wipe on an iPhone (which requires iOS 5), navigate to Settings ➤ iCloud. On this tab, ensure that Find My iPhone is enabled (set to On). Next, use the browser to go to iCloud.com and log in using the Apple ID you use on your phone.

Next, select the icon Find My iPhone. The location of the phone will appear on a map. Click the *i* icon next to the location. In the dialog box that opens, select Remote Wipe. You will be prompted again to verify that is what you want to do. Select Wipe Phone.

The Android phones do not come with an official remote wipe. You can, however, install an Android app that will do this. Once the app, Lost Android, is installed, it works in the same way the iPhone remote wipe does. In this case, you log into the Lost Android website using your Google login. From the site, you can locate and wipe the device.

Android Device Manager, which is loaded on newer versions of Android, is available for download to any version of Android from 2.3 onward providing almost identical functionality to that of the iPhone.

Locator applications

Locator applications like the Lost Android app for Android are available where apps are sold for Androids. These apps allow you to locate the device, to lock the device, and even to send a message to the device offering a reward for its return. Finally, you can remotely wipe the device. The iOS devices and the newer Android devices have this feature built in, and it performs all the same functions.

Remote backup applications

Backing up your data with the iPhone can be done by connecting the device to a Mac and using iTunes to manage the content. (The data can also be backed up to a PC that has iTunes.) As users start to use the mobile device as their main tool, this may not be an optimal way to manage backups. New apps like Mozy are available that perform an online backup, which is attractive because the laptop or desktop where you backed up your data is not always close at hand, but the Internet usually is.

Android has always taken a cloud approach to backups. There are many Android apps now that can be used to back up data to locations such as Dropbox or Box.net.

Failed login attempts restrictions

Most of us have become accustomed to the lockout feature on a laptop or desktop that locks out an account after a certain number of failed login attempts. This feature is available on a mobile device and can even be set to perform a remote wipe of the device after repeated failed login attempts.

On the iOS, the Erase Data function can be set to perform a remote wipe after 10 failed passcode attempts. After six failed attempts, the iPhone locks out users for a minute before another passcode can be entered. The device increases the lockout time following each additional failed attempt.

The Android does not have this feature built in but does provide APIs that allow enterprise developers to create applications that will do this.

Antivirus/Anti-malware

Mobile devices can suffer from viruses and malware just like laptops and desktops. Major antivirus vendors such as McAfee and Kaspersky make antivirus and anti-malware products for mobile devices that provide the same real-time protection that the products do for desktops. The same guidelines apply for these mobile devices: Keep them up-to-date by setting the device to check for updates whenever connected to the Internet.

Patching/OS updates

Security patches and operating system updates are available on an ongoing basis for both the iOS and the Android. For the iPhone, both operating system updates and security patches are available at the Apple support site. Automatic updates can be enabled for the device in iTunes. Use the Check For Updates button located in the middle of iTunes.

An auto-update feature is built into Android, and you can also manually check for patches and updates by navigating to Settings ➤ About Phone ➤ System Updates. Selecting these options will cause the phone to check for, download, and install patches or updates.

Biometric authentication

Most mobile devices now offer the option to incorporate biometrics as an authentication mechanism. The two most common implementations of this use fingerprint scans or facial scans or facial recognition technology. While there can be issues with both false negatives (the denial of a legitimate user) and false positives (the admission of an illegitimate user), they offer much better security than other authentication mechanisms.

Full device encryption

Full device encryption is available for smartphones and other mobile devices. Most companies choose to implement this through the use of an enterprise mobility management system, since it can also manage the installation of updates, the tracking of devices, and the deployment of remote wipes and GPS location services when needed. There are also third-party applications that can provide full device encryption.

Multifactor authentication

Authentication factors describe the method used to verify the user's identity. As described for other devices, there are three available authentication factors:

- Something you know (such as a password)
- Something you are (such as a fingerprint)
- Something you have (such as a smart card)

When two different types of factors are required (such as something you know and something you have), it is called *multifactor authentication*. It is important to understand that using two or more of the same type of factors (such as a password and a PIN, both something you know) is not multifactor authentication. However, when multifactor authentication is used for mobile devices, the level of security is significantly increased.

Authenticator applications

Authenticator applications, such as Google Authenticator, make it possible for a mobile device to use a time-based one-time password (TOTP) algorithm with a site or system that requires such authentication. In the setup operation, the site provides a shared secret key to the user over a secure channel to be stored in the authenticator app. This secret key will be used for all future logins to the site. The user will enter a username and password into a website or other server, generate a one-time password for the server using TOTP running locally, and type that password into the server as well. The server will then also run TOTP to verify the entered one-time password. While Google makes versions for multiple mobile platforms, there are also other third-party solutions.

Trusted sources vs. untrusted sources

Applications and utilities for mobile devices can come from both trusted and untrusted sources. An example of a trusted source is the official Google Play site or the Apple Store. That doesn't mean these are the only trusted sources, but users should treat this issue with the same approach they have been taught with regard to desktop and laptop computers.

Any piece of software, be it an application, tool, or utility, can come with malware attached. Users should be trained to regard any software downloads with suspicion. It may be advisable to use an enterprise mobility management system to prevent users from downloading any software to a company-owned mobile device. You also may want to deselect the setting shown in Figure 7.12, which is an Android device setting. Apple devices warn users with a pop-up message when they download from an unknown source.

FIGURE 7.12   Allowing applications from unknown sources

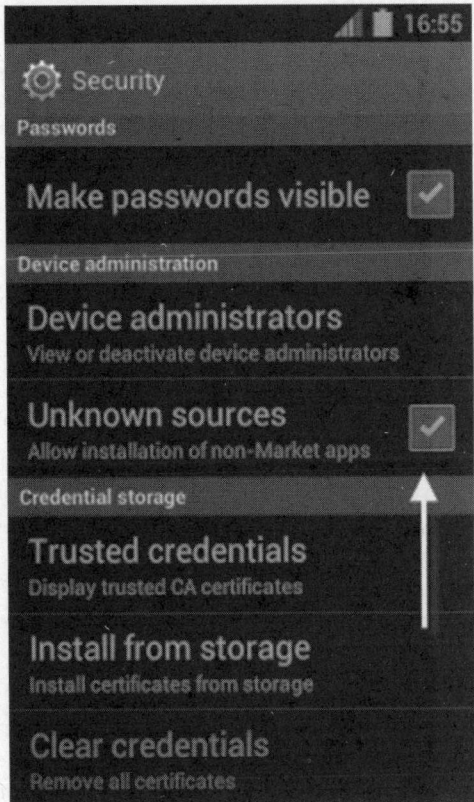

Firewalls

Because today's mobile devices function more like laptops and desktop systems, they need the same protection. Mobile device firewall products are those that install on the device and protect the device in the same way a personal firewall on a desktop system, such as the Windows Firewall, does.

The disadvantage to this approach is that the software runs continuously, thus placing an ongoing load on the battery. Likewise, intrusion prevention and intrusion detection software can be placed on mobile devices, again with the same effect on battery lifetime.

If you need another reason to invest in an enterprise mobility management system, this is it. Most solutions include a firewall product of some sort in the suite. One consideration when choosing a solution is to balance the features you need against the memory footprint of the solution, because memory is a scarce resource in mobile devices.

Policies and procedures

With the introduction of mobile devices to the network, changes and additions may be called for in the organizational security policy. As procedures are derived from broader policies, these changes will also impact the procedures that users are required to follow. In this section, you'll look at two issues that need to be considered with respect to policies and procedures.

BYOD vs. corporate-owned

One of the decisions that must be made is whether to allow only company-owned mobile devices on the network or to allow personal devices as well. Many organizations have launched bring-your-own-device (BYOD) initiatives. While this certainly makes the users happy, it brings with it new challenges in securing a wide range of user devices running on all sorts of platforms.

One of the ways enterprises have successfully implemented these initiatives without sacrificing the security of the network is by turning to enterprise mobility management systems. These systems can be used to control a wide variety of mobile devices and to manage the installation of updates, the tracking of devices, and the deployment of remote wipes and GPS location services when needed. Without one of these utilities, deploying BYOD can be a security nightmare.

Profile security requirements

The baseline or minimum security settings required on all mobile devices must be determined and standardized. This may require the creation of multiple security *profiles* based on different mobile device models and types, but the theory is the same. By defining a collection of security settings, implementing them on all devices, and constantly monitoring the settings for changes, you can ensure that these settings are maintained.

Exam essentials

Describe the options available to secure the data on a mobile device.   These options include passcode locks, remote wipes, locator applications, failed login attempt restrictions, and remote backup applications.

List other security guidelines for mobile devices.   Always keep antivirus definitions up-to-date and set the mobile device to automatically check for OS updates and patches.

2.9 Given a scenario, implement appropriate data destruction and disposal methods.

Think of all the sensitive data written to a hard drive. The drive can contain information about students, clients, users—anyone and anything. That hard drive can be in a desktop PC, a laptop, or even a printer (many laser printers above consumer grade offer the ability to add a hard drive to store print jobs). If it falls into the wrong hands, you can lose valuable data and also risk a lawsuit for not properly protecting privacy. An appropriate data destruction/disposal plan should be in place to avoid any potential problems.

Since data on media holds great value and liability, that media should never be simply tossed away for prying eyes to stumble upon. For the purposes of this objective, I'll talk about hard drives, and there are three key concepts to understand in regard to them: formatting, sanitation, and destruction. Formatting prepares the drive to hold new information (which can include copying over data already there). Sanitation involves wiping the data on the drive, whereas destruction renders the drive no longer usable. The subobjectives covered in this section include the following:

- Physical destruction
- Recycling or repurposing best practices

 While this objective is focused on hard drives, data can also be stored on portable flash drives, backup tapes, CDs, or DVDs. In the interest of security, I recommend that you destroy any of them before disposing of them as well.

Physical destruction

Physically destroying the drive involves rendering the component no longer usable. While the focus is on hard drives, you can also physically destroy other forms of media, such as flash drives and CD/DVDs.

Shredder

Many commercial paper shredders include the ability to destroy DVDs and CDs. Paper shredders, however, are not able to handle hard drives; and you need a shredder created for just such a purpose. Jackhammer makes a low-volume model that will destroy eight drives per minute and carries a suggested list price of just under $30,000.

Drill/hammer

If you don't have the budget for a hard drive shredder, you can accomplish similar results in a much more time-consuming way with a power drill. The goal is to physically destroy the platters in the drive. Start the process by removing the cover from the drive—this is normally done with a Torx driver (while #8 does not work with all, it is a good one to try first). You can remove the arm with a slotted screwdriver and then the cover over the platters using a Torx driver. Don't worry about damaging or scratching anything because nothing is intended to be saved. Everything but the platters can be tossed away.

As an optional step, you can completely remove the tracks using a belt sander, grinder, or palm sander. The goal is to turn the shiny surface into fine powder. This adds one more layer of assurance that nothing usable remains. Always be careful to wear eye protection and not breathe in any fine particles that you generate during the grinding/destruction process.

Following this, use the power drill to create the smallest particles possible. A drill press works much better for this task than trying to hold the drive and drill it with a handheld model. Finally you can use a hammer to destroy the platters as well; it provides a certain level of satisfaction if the drive died and you had to restore it from backup.

Even with practice, you will find that manually destroying a hard drive is time-consuming. There are companies that specialize in this and can do it efficiently. One such company is Shred-it, which will pick it up from you and provide a chain-of-custody assurance and a certificate of destruction upon completion. You can find out more about what it offers here:

www.shredit.com/shredding-service/What-to-shred/
Hard-drive-destruction.aspx

Electromagnetic/degaussing

Degaussing involves applying a strong magnetic field to initialize the media (this is also referred to as *disk wiping*). This process helps ensure that information doesn't fall into the wrong hands.

Since degaussing uses a specifically designed electromagnet to eliminate all data on the drive, that destruction also includes the factory prerecorded servo tracks. You can find wand model degaussers priced at just over $500 or desktop units that sell for up to $30,000.

Incineration

A final option that exists for some forms of storage is to burn the media. Regardless of whether the media is a hard drive, CD, DVD, solid-state drive, or floppy disk, the media must be reduced to ash, or in the case of hard drive platters, the internal platters must be physically deformed using heat.

Certificate of destruction

Certificates of destruction are documents that attest to either the physical destruction of the media on which sensitive data was located or a scientifically approved method of removing the data from a drive. Later in this chapter, you will be introduced to some methods of removal, both approved and unapproved.

These certificates are typically issued to the organization by a storage vendor or cloud provider to prove either that the data has been removed or that the media has been destroyed.

Recycling or repurposing best practices

Multiple levels of reformatting can be done to remove the contents of a drive. A standard format—accomplished using the operating system's format utility (or similar)—can mark space occupied by files as available for new files without truly deleting what was there. Such erasing—if you want to call it that—doesn't guarantee that the information isn't still on the disk and recoverable.

Low-level format vs. standard format

A low-level format (typically accomplished only in the factory) can be performed on the system, or a utility can be used to completely wipe the disk clean. This process helps ensure that information doesn't fall into the wrong hands.

IDE hard drives are low-level formatted by the manufacturer. Low-level formatting must be performed even before a drive can be partitioned. In low-level formatting, the drive controller chip and the drive meet for the first time and learn to work together. Because IDE drives have their controllers integrated into the drive, low-level formatting is a factory process with these drives and does not depend on the operating system.

 **WARNING** Never low-level format IDE or SCSI drives! They're low-level formatted from the factory, and you may cause problems by using low-level utilities on these types of drives.

The main thing to remember for the exams is that most forms of formatting included with the operating system do not actually completely erase the data. Formatting the drive and then disposing of it has caused many companies problems when the data has been retrieved by individuals who never should have seen it using applications that are commercially available.

Overwrite

Overwriting the drive entails copying over the data with new data. A common practice is to replace the data with 0s. A number of applications allow you to recover what was there prior to the last write operation, and for that reason, most overwrite software will write the same sequence and save it multiple times.

Drive wipe

If it's possible to verify beyond a reasonable doubt that a piece of hardware that's no longer being used doesn't contain any data of a sensitive or proprietary nature, that hardware can be recycled (sold to employees, sold to a third party, donated to a school, and so on). That level of assurance can come from wiping a hard drive or using specialized utilities.

Degaussing hard drives is difficult and may render the drive unusable.

If you can't be assured that the hardware in question doesn't contain important data, the hardware should be destroyed. You cannot, and should not, take a risk that the data your company depends on could fall into the wrong hands.

Exam essentials

Understand the difference between standard and low-level formatting.   Standard formatting uses operating system tools and makes the drive available for holding data without truly removing what was on the drive (thus the data can be recovered). A low-level format is operating system independent and destroys any data that was on the drive.

Understand how to physically destroy a drive.   A hard drive can be destroyed by tossing it into a shredder designed for such a purpose, or it can be destroyed with an electromagnet in a process known as degaussing. You can also disassemble the drive and destroy the platters with a drill or other tool that renders the data irretrievable.

2.10 Given a scenario, configure security on SOHO wireless and wired networks.

CompTIA wants administrators of SOHO networks to be able to secure those networks in ways that protect the data stored on them. This objective looks at the security protection that can be added to a wireless or wired SOHO network. First you'll look at issues specific to a WLAN, and then you'll take a look at security considerations for wired and wireless networks. The subobjectives covered in this chapter include the following:

- Wireless specific
- Change default usernames and passwords
- Enable MAC filtering
- Assign static IP addresses
- Firewall settings

- Port forwarding/mapping
- Disabling ports
- Content filtering/parental controls
- Update firmware
- Physical security

Wireless specific

Wireless networks present a unique set of challenges that wired networks do not. The communication methods are somewhat different, as are the attack methods. In this section, security issues that are relevant only to a WLAN are discussed.

Changing default SSID

Every wireless AP or wireless router on the market comes with a default SSID. Cisco models use the name *tsunami*, for example. You should change these defaults and create a new SSID to represent your WLAN. Typically, when hackers see a default SSID, they make the reasonable assumption that if the SSID was left at the default, the administrator password was as well. So if you also failed to change that, hackers can now log in, take over your AP, and lock you out.

Setting encryption

The available types of wireless encryption (WEP, WPA, WPA2, and so on) were discussed in Chapter 2, and summarized earlier in this chapter. Know that you should always enable encryption for any SOHO network you administer and that you should choose the strongest level of encryption you can work with. Keep in mind that WEP is no longer considered secure and WPA is considered weak, so avoid their use if possible.

Disabling SSID broadcast

One method of "protecting" the network that is often recommended is to turn off the SSID broadcast. The AP is still there and can be accessed by those who know about it, but it prevents those who are just scanning from finding it. This should be considered a weak form of security because there are still other ways, albeit a bit more complicated, to discover the presence of the AP besides the SSID broadcast.

Antenna and access point placement

Antenna placement can be crucial in allowing clients to reach the AP. There isn't any one universal solution to this issue, and it depends on the environment in which the AP is placed. As a general rule, the greater the distance the signal must travel, the more it will attenuate, but you can lose a signal quickly in a short space as well if the building materials reflect or absorb the signal. You should try to avoid placing APs near metal (including appliances) or near the ground. Placing them in the center of the area to be served, and high enough to get around most obstacles, is recommended.

On the other end of the spectrum, you have to contend with the problem of the signal traveling outside your intended network (known as *signal leakage*) and being picked up in public areas by outsiders. To lessen this problem, use RF-absorbent materials on external walls, essentially shielding the surroundings.

Radio power levels

On the chance that the signal is actually traveling too far, some APs include *power-level controls* that allow you to reduce the amount of output provided.

You can find a great source for information on RF power values and antennas on the Cisco site at www.cisco.com/c/en/us/support/docs/ wireless-mobility/wireless-lan-wlan/23231-powervalues-23231.html.

WPS

Wi-Fi protected setup (WPS) was a concept designed to make it easier for less knowledge-able users to add a new client to the WLAN without manually entering the security infor-mation on the client. One method involves pushing a button on the AP at the same time a client is attempting to join the network so that the settings are sent to the client. Other methods involve placing the client close to the AP, and near-field communication is used for the process.

Regardless of the details, as often happens when we try to make security simpler, we make it fail. It has been discovered that a hacker can identify the PIN used in a short period of time, and with it the network's WPA/WPA2 preshared key. For this reason, the Wi-Fi Alliance has recommended against using this feature.

Change default usernames and passwords

Default accounts include not only those created with the installation of the operating sys-tems but often also accounts associated with hardware. Wireless APs, routers, and similar devices often include accounts for interacting with, and administering, those devices. You should always change the passwords associated with those devices and, where possible, change the usernames.

If there are accounts that are not needed, disable them or delete them. Make certain you use strong password policies and protect the passwords with the same security you do for any users or administrators (in other words, don't write the router's password on an address label and stick it to the bottom of the router).

In Windows, the Guest account is automatically created with the intent that it is to be used when someone must access a system but lacks a user account on that system. Because it is so widely known to exist, I recommend that you not use this default account and instead create another one for the same purpose if you truly need one. The Guest account leaves a security risk at the workstation and should be disabled to prevent it from being accessed by those attempting to gain unauthorized access.

> Change *every* username and password that you can so they vary from their default settings.

Enable MAC filtering

The earlier section "MAC address filtering," under objective 2.2, explained the importance of enabling MAC filtering, which is turned off by default.

> Adding port authentication to MAC filtering takes security for the network down to the switch port level and increases your security exponentially.

Assign static IP addresses

While DHCP can be a godsend, a SOHO network is small enough that you can get by without it issuing IP addresses to each host. The advantage to assigning the IP addresses statically is that you can make certain which host is associated with which IP address and then utilize filtering to limit network access to only those hosts.

While static IP addressing may not be scalable in a wired network with many devices, in a small network, using static IP addressing will make it impossible for someone to just plug into your network without knowing your IP address scheme.

Firewall settings

All devices both wired and wireless should have personal firewalls enabled and configured to protect each system. In Windows, you can simply leverage the personal firewall that comes on all Windows Vista, 7, 8, 8.1, and 10 computers. For operating systems that don't come with a personal firewall, third-party software should be implemented for this purpose. These firewalls help to prevent other devices from connecting to each station without the approval of the users.

The presence of personal firewalls on all the devices does *not* mean you don't need a network firewall at the edge of the network and between sections of the network that may have varying security levels. You can find more information on firewalls under several objectives throughout this chapter.

Port forwarding/mapping

Another option to harden the entrance to the network is to deploy port forwarding or mapping. Port forwarding is a function typically performed on the same device that may be performing network address translation (NAT). One port number is set aside on the gateway for the exclusive use of communicating with a service in the private network, located on a specific host. External hosts must know this port number and the address of the gateway to communicate with the network-internal service. The purpose of this is to hide the real IP address of the destination device or server to protect it from connections outside the LAN.

Disabling ports

Disable all unneeded protocols/ports. If you don't need them, remove them or prevent them from loading. Ports not in use present an open door for an attacker to enter.

Many of the newer SOHO router solutions (and some of the personal firewall solutions on end-user workstations) close down the ICMP ports by default. Keep this in mind; it can drive you nuts when you are trying to see whether a new station, server, or router is up and running by using the ping command. This command depends on the use of ICMP.

Content filtering/parental controls

Content filtering software examines all web connections, and in some cases emails, for objectionable content or sites that have been identified as off-limits by the administrator. While this can be helpful in preventing the introduction of malware or in screening objectionable content, you should be aware that these filters are making educated guesses about what to deny and allow.

A filter will invariably deny content that should be allowed and allow content that should be denied. Try to be as specific as possible when defining keywords that are used to identify sites and content and set the expectation among users that the software is not perfect.

Parental controls operate on the same basic premise.

Update Firmware

In the past, updating firmware on devices such as APs, routers, and switches was considered to be desirable but optional. More and more security attacks are based on attacking the firmware, and for this reason firmware updates should be part of whatever automated update system you may be using (not to mention the additional functionality and bug elimination you may experience). It may be that you can get on a mailing list for each vendor so you can be notified when firmware updates are available. In any case, some systematic method must be developed to ensure these updates are maintained.

Physical security

Just as you would not park your car in a public garage and leave its doors wide open with the key in the ignition, you should educate users not to leave a workstation that they are logged into when they attend meetings, go to lunch, and so forth. They should log out of the workstation or lock it. "Lock when you leave" should be a mantra they become familiar with. Locking the workstation should require a password (usually the same as their user password) to resume working at the workstation.

Moreover, don't overlook the obvious need for physical security. Adding a cable to lock a laptop to a desk prevents someone from picking it up and walking away with a copy of your customer database. Laptop cases generally include a built-in security slot in which a cable lock can be added to prevent it from being carried away easily, like the one shown in Figure 7.13.

FIGURE 7.13   A cable in the security slot keeps the laptop from being carried away easily.

When it comes to desktop models, adding a lock to the back cover can prevent an intruder with physical access from grabbing the hard drive or damaging the internal components. You should also physically secure network devices—routers, APs, and the like. Place them in locked cabinets, if possible. If they are not physically secured, the opportunity exists for them to be stolen or manipulated in such a way to allow someone unauthorized to connect to the network.

Exam essentials

Know the names, purpose, and characteristics of wireless security.   Wireless networks can be encrypted through WEP and WPA technologies. Wireless controllers use special ID strings and must be configured in the network cards to allow communications. However, using ID string configurations doesn't necessarily prevent wireless networks from being monitored, and there are vulnerabilities specific to wireless devices.

Review Questions

You can find the answers in the Appendix.

1. Which of the following is a series of two doors with a small room between them?
   A. Mantrap
   B. Trapdoor
   C. Badgetrap
   D. Saferoom

2. Which of the following physical characteristics is used to identify the user?
   A. Hardware tokens
   B. Biometric locks
   C. Smart cards
   D. Badge readers

3. In which filtering is the physical address used?
   A. MAC address filtering
   B. Email filtering
   C. IP address filtering
   D. URL filtering

4. What firewall *only* passes or blocks traffic to specific addresses based on the type of application?
   A. Packet filter firewalls
   B. Proxy firewalls
   C. Stateful inspection firewalls
   D. NG firewall

5. Which of the following was created as a first stab at security for wireless devices?
   A. WPA
   B. WPA2
   C. TKIP
   D. WEP

6. Which of the following was used to increase security in WPA?
   A. TKIP
   B. AES
   C. IPSec
   D. SSL

7. Which type of virus covers itself with protective code that stops debuggers or disassemblers from examining critical elements of the virus?

    A. Companion

    B. Macro

    C. Armored

    D. Multipartite

8. What element of a virus uniquely identifies it?

    A. ID

    B. Signature

    C. Badge

    D. Marking

9. Which of the following is the term used for someone being so close to you when you enter a building that they are able to come in right behind you without needing to use a key, a card, or any other security device?

    A. Shadowing

    B. Spoofing

    C. Tailgating

    D. Keyriding

10. Which of the following is the process of masquerading as another user or device?

    A. Shadowing

    B. Spoofing

    C. Duplicating

    D. Masking

11. Which Windows group allows members to install most software but keeps them from changing key operating system files?

    A. Power user

    B. Guest

    C. Administrator

    D. User

12. Which NTFS permission is the least required to run a program?

    A. List folder contents

    B. Full Control

    C. Read

    D. Write

13. Which of the following passwords is the strongest?

     A. password

     B. pAssword

     C. Pa$$word

     D. P@ssw0rd

14. What principle should drive the granting of permissions?

     A. Separation of duties

     B. Least privilege

     C. Job rotation

     D. Open rights

15. Which type of screen lock uses gestures?

     A. Fingerprint

     B. Face

     C. Swipe

     D. Passcode

16. Which method is good for a lost mobile device?

     A. Remote wipe

     B. Geofencing

     C. Screen lock

     D. Segmentation of data

17. Which of the following involves applying a strong magnetic field to initialize the media?

     A. Degaussing

     B. Incineration

     C. Hammer

     D. Deleting

18. Which method of destroying the data on a hard drive is most effective?

     A. Degaussing

     B. Incineration

     C. Clearing

     D. Deleting

19. Which of the following was a concept that was designed to make it easier for less knowledgeable users to add a new client to the WLAN without manually entering the security information on the client?

    A. SSID

    B. WPS

    C. WEP

    D. WPA

20. Which of the following should always be changed from the default?

    A. SSID

    B. WPS

    C. WEP

    D. WPA

Chapter

8

Software Troubleshooting

COMPTIA A+ CERTIFICATION EXAM CORE 2 (220-1002) OBJECTIVES COVERED IN THIS CHAPTER:

✓ **3.1 Given a scenario, troubleshoot Microsoft Windows OS problems.**

- Common symptoms
  - Slow performance
  - Limited connectivity
  - Failure to boot
  - No OS found
  - Application crashes
  - Blue screens
  - Black screens
  - Printing issues
  - Services fail to start
  - Slow bootup
  - Slow profile load
- Common solutions
  - Defragment the hard drive
  - Reboot
  - Kill tasks
  - Restart services
  - Update network settings
  - Reimage/reload OS
  - Roll back updates

- Roll back devices drivers
- Apply updates
- Repair application
- Update boot order
- Disable Windows services/applications
- Disable application startup
- Safe boot
- Rebuild Windows profiles

✓ **3.2 Given a scenario, troubleshoot and resolve PC security issues.**

- Common symptoms
  - Pop-ups
  - Browser redirection
  - Security alerts
  - Slow performance
  - Internet connectivity issues
  - PC/OS lockup
  - Application crash
  - OS updates failures
  - Rogue antivirus
  - Spam
  - Renamed system files
  - Disappearing files
  - File permission changes
  - Hijacked email
    - Responses from users regarding email
    - Automated replies from unknown sent email
  - Access denied
  - Invalid certificate (trusted root CA)
  - System/application log errors

✓ **3.3 Given a scenario, use best practice procedures for malware removal.**

- 1. Identify and research malware symptoms.

- 2. Quarantine the infected systems.

- 3. Disable System Restore (in Windows).

- 4. Remediate the infected systems.

  - a. Update the anti-malware software.

  - b. Scan and use removal techniques (safe mode, pre-installation environment).

- 5. Schedule scans and run updates.

- 6. Enable System Restore and create a restore point (in Windows).

- 7. Educate the end user

✓ **3.4 Given a scenario, troubleshoot mobile OS and application issues.**

- Common symptoms

  - Dim display

  - Intermittent wireless

  - No wireless connectivity

  - No Bluetooth connectivity

  - Cannot broadcast to external monitor

  - Touchscreen non-responsive

  - Apps not loading

  - Slow performance

  - Unable to decrypt email

  - Extremely short battery life

  - Overheating

  - Frozen system

  - No sound from speakers

  - Inaccurate touch screen response

  - System lockout

  - App log errors

✓ 3.5 Given a scenario, troubleshoot mobile OS and application security issues.

- Common symptoms
  - Signal drop/weak signal
  - Power drain
  - Slow data speeds
  - Unintended WiFi connection
  - Unintended Bluetooth pairing
  - Leaked personal files/data
  - Data transmission over limit
  - Unauthorized account access
  - Unauthorized location tracking
  - Unauthorized camera/ microphone activation
  - High resource utilization

This chapter will focus on the exam topics related to software troubleshooting. It will follow the structure of the CompTIA A+ 220-1002 exam blueprint, objective 3, and it will explore the five subobjectives that you will need to master before taking the exam. The Software Troubleshooting domain represents 26 percent of the total exam.

3.1 Given a scenario, troubleshoot Microsoft Windows OS problems.

Because it's software and there are so many places where things can go wrong, the operating system can be one of the most confusing components to troubleshoot. Sometimes it seems a miracle that operating systems even work at all, considering the hundreds of files that work together to make the system function. In this section, common operating system issues and their solutions are covered. The topics addressed in objective 3.1 include the following:

- Slow performance
- Limited connectivity
- Failure to boot
- No OS found
- Application crashes
- Blue screens
- Black screens
- Printing issues
- Services fail to start
- Slow bootup
- Slow profile load
- Defragment the hard drive
- Reboot
- Kill tasks
- Restart services

- Update network settings
- Reimage/reload OS
- Roll back updates
- Roll back devices drivers
- Apply updates
- Repair application
- Update boot order
- Disable Windows services/applications
- Disable application startup
- Safe boot
- Rebuild Windows profiles

Common symptoms

What follows in this section can seem like a daunting list of symptoms the operating system can exhibit. But with a proper plan of action and good backup (always have a backup!), you can approach any of these problems with confidence. In many cases today, technicians have ceased to spend significant amounts of time chasing operating system issues, since the most important data is kept on servers, and computers can be reimaged so quickly that trouble-shooting doesn't warrant the effort. Nevertheless, you should know these basic symptoms and the approach to take when they present themselves.

Slow performance

Slow system performance can come from many issues. For the purposes of this discussion, I will focus on performance that deteriorates after being acceptable, as opposed to system performance that is poor from the outset (which could be a matter of insufficient resources such as RAM). Here is a list of possibilities:

- The first thing to check is the presence of a virus. If the system seems to have an over-abundance of disk activity, scan it for viruses using a virus program that resides externally on a CD/DVD or memory stick.
- Defragment the hard drive. The more fragmented it is, the slower the disk access will be.
- Check the space on the hard drive. When the partition or volume where the operating system is located becomes full, performance will suffer. This is why it is a good idea to store data and applications on a different partition from that holding the system files.
- Ensure that the latest updates are installed. In many cases, updates help to solve performance problems, so make sure they are current.
- Use Task Manager to determine whether a process is using too much memory or CPU or is simply locked up (not responding), and if necessary, end the process.

Limited connectivity

In some cases, the computer has connectivity to some but not all resources. When this is the case, issues that may reside on other layers of the OSI model should come under consideration. These include the following:

Authentication Issues   Does the user have permission to access the resource?

DNS Issues   You may be able to ping the entire network using IP addresses, but most access is done by name, not IP address. If you can't ping resources by name, DNS is not functional, meaning that either the DNS server is down or the local machine is not configured with the correct IP address of the DNS server. If recent changes have occurred in the DNS mappings or if your connection to the destination device has recently failed because of a temporary network issue that has been solved, you may need to clear the local DNS cache using the ipconfig/flushdns command.

Remote Problem   Don't forget that establishing a connection is a two-way street, and if the remote device has an issue, communication cannot occur. Always check the remote device as well. Any interconnecting device between the computer and resource, such as a switch or router, should also be checked for functionality.

Failure to boot

Booting problems can occur with corruption of the boot files or missing components. Common error messages include an invalid boot disk, inaccessible boot drive, missing NTLDR file, or missing BOOTMGR (some of which are discussed in more detail later in this section). Fortunately, during the installation of the operating system, log files are created in the %SystemRoot% and %SystemRoot%\Debug folders (C:\WINNT for older systems and C:\Windows for Windows 7, Windows 8, and Windows 10). If you have a puzzling problem, look at these logs and see whether you can find error entries there. With Windows 7, for example, the following are some of the log files created:

netsetup.log   This file differs from all the others in that it's in the Debug folder and not just %SystemRoot%. Entries in it detail the workgroup and domain options given during installation.

setupact.log   Known as the action log, this file is a chronological list of what took place during the setup. There is a tremendous amount of information here; of key importance is whether any errors occurred. The last lines of the file can show which operation was transpiring when the installation failed or whether the installation ended with errors. Like all the log files created during setup, this file is in ASCII text format and can be viewed with any viewer (WordPad, Word, and so on).

setuperr.log   The error log, as this file is commonly called, is written to at the time errors are noted in other log files. For example, an entry in setuperr.log may show that an error occurred, and you can find additional information about it in setuperr.log. Not only are the errors here, but the severity of each is also given.

You can configure problems with system failure to write dump files (debugging information) for later analysis when they occur by clicking Start ➤ Control Panel ➤ System and then clicking the Advanced System Settings option. The Advanced tab of the System Properties dialog box should open. Then click the Settings button in the Startup and Recovery section. Here, in addition to choosing the default operating system, you can configure whether events should be written to the system log, whether an alert should be sent to the administrator, and what type of memory dump should be written.

No OS found

The "no operating system found" message can result from a number of issues. Among them are the following:

- Nonsystem disk in the floppy drive
- Incorrect boot device order in the BIOS
- Corrupted or missing boot sector
- Corrupted boot files

In short, the operating system is not actually missing; the system is missing the file that can either locate it or load it. Follow the steps in this section with respect to the ntldr and boot.ini files.

In Windows 7, Windows 8, and Windows 10 if using Startup Repair does not work, you may need to create a bootable disc to boot the device. The directions for this vary between the systems but can be found on the Microsoft site. Then you have two approaches. For Windows 8, one approach is to follow these steps:

1. Insert the installation DVD or USB and boot Windows 8 from it.

2. On the Windows Setup page, select the language to install, the time and currency format, and the keyboard or input method; then click Next.

3. Click Repair Your Computer and select Troubleshoot.

4. Click Advanced Options, select Automatic Repair, and select the operating system.

The other approach is to try to rebuild the boot configuration data, booting from the Windows 8 installation media and following these instructions:

1. Insert the installation DVD or USB and boot Windows 8 from it.

2. On the Windows Setup page, select the language to install, the time and currency format, and the keyboard or input method; then click Next.

3. Click Repair Your Computer and select Troubleshoot.

4. Click Advanced Options, click the command prompt, type the following commands, and press Enter after each command:

```
Bootrec /fixmbr
Bootrec /fixboot
Bootrec /rebuildbcd
```

5. Restart the computer. Check whether you're able to boot now.

Application crashes

Another possible symptom of a malware infection is the crashing of applications. While this will occur from time to time for other reasons, when it is occurring repeatedly, you should suspect malware. When the application that is crashing is your antivirus software, this is an even stronger indication of malware because disabling or damaging your antivirus protection is the first thing that some types of malware attempt to do.

Blue screens

Once a regular occurrence when working with Windows, blue screens (also known as the blue screen of death, or BSOD) have become less common. Occasionally, systems will lock up; you can usually examine the log files to discover what was happening when this occurred and take steps to correct it. Remember, when dealing with a blue screen, always ask yourself, "What did I just install or change?" In many cases, the change is involved in the BSOD. Also keep in mind that (as the instructions on the blue screen will tell you) a simple reboot will often fix the problem. Retaining the contents of the BSOD can help troubleshoot the issue. In most instances, you can find the BSOD error in Microsoft's knowledge base to help with troubleshooting.

The Apple pinwheel is displayed automatically by WindowServer when an application cannot handle all the events it receives. (WindowServer is the background process that runs the mac OS X graphical user interface.) To find out whether the CPU is a bottleneck on performance, use Activity Monitor (/Applications/Utilities) to monitor CPU usage. The pinwheel or beach ball may also appear if you don't have enough RAM.

Software can also cause the pinwheel. Open Activity Monitor's CPU tab and sort by the % CPU column in descending order; the apps at the top are the ones using the most CPU cycles. If an application is frozen, it will appear in red. If it is *not* a process with root listed as the user, quit it.

Black screens

While a black screen may indicate a loss of connectivity to the display or loss of power to the display, when you rule that out, it can be a deeper issue. It could indicate that the basic input/output system (BIOS), which is the firmware on the motherboard that has the low-level instructions required by the board to load the OS, is corrupted. This means you won't even get the Dell or HP screen you normally see during bootup.

If you see it after seeing the firmware screen, then the system is having an issue locating the boot files. It could also be that the hard drive is dead, which means the files cannot be accessed.

Printing issues

Printing issues generally depend on the symptom. See objective 3.11 in Chapter 3, "Hardware."

Services fail to start

Sometimes when the system is started, you receive a message that tells you a service failed to start. When that occurs, use the event log to determine the service that failed. Then, to interact with the service, access the Administrative Tools section of Control Panel and choose Services. This starts the Services console. You can right-click any service and choose to start, stop, pause, resume, or restart it. You can also double-click the service to access its properties and configure such things as the startup type, dependencies, and other variables.

If the service refuses to start, it could be that a service on which it depends will not start. To determine what services must be running for the problem service to start, select the Dependencies tab of the service's Properties dialog box, as shown in Figure 8.1.

FIGURE 8.1   Service dependencies

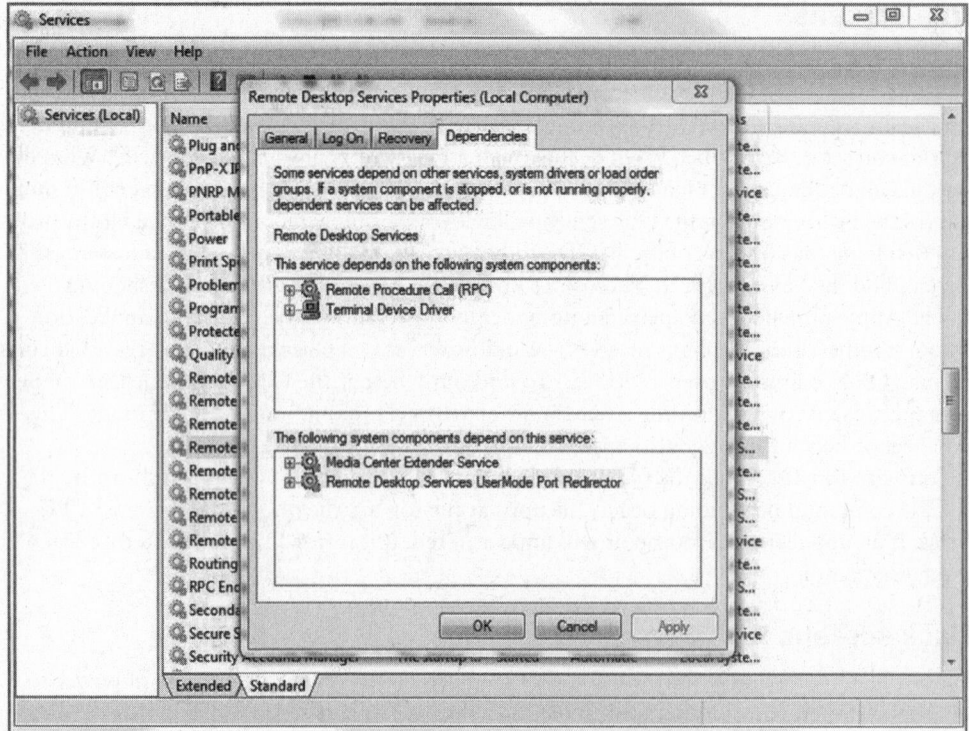

In the figure you can see that the Remote Desktop service depends on both the RPC and Terminal Device Driver services to function. Try starting these services first. In some cases, you may need to trace the dependencies up several levels to get things going.

Slow bootup

Slow bootups can be caused by a number of issues. First, it could be that the system is struggling for resources. This might indicate a memory or hard drive issue. It also can slow down the startup if many programs are set to start at bootup.

In cases where the computer belongs to a domain, it could also be having trouble locating the domain controller and perhaps performing policy updates.

Finally, it could be that the device is set to access a Distributed File System (DFS) share or other type of remote drive and locating it is the issue. (DFS is a system used to provide connections to shared folders without known their physical location.) The cause could also be the next issue in the list.

Slow profile load

Remote profiles are loaded from remote servers, and when location issues like the ones discussed in the previous section are present, this will hold up the startup process.

Common solutions

The following are some common approaches to addressing the issues described in the previous section.

Defragment the hard drive

Defragmentation tools are used to reorganize the physical location of the data on the hard drive so as to locate all pieces of a file together in the same place. When this is done, it improves the performance of the drive. All operating systems come with built-in defragmentation tools, and their operation can be scheduled for a time convenient to the user. This also frees the user (and the technician) from having to think about running the tool on a regular basis. Figure 8.2 shows the Drive Optimization tool in Windows 8.1. To arrive at this tool, swipe in from the right edge of the screen, tap Search (or if you're using a mouse, point to the upper-right corner of the screen, move the mouse pointer down, and click Search), enter **Defragment** in the search box, tap or click Defragment, and optimize your drives.

FIGURE 8.2   The Drive Optimization tool

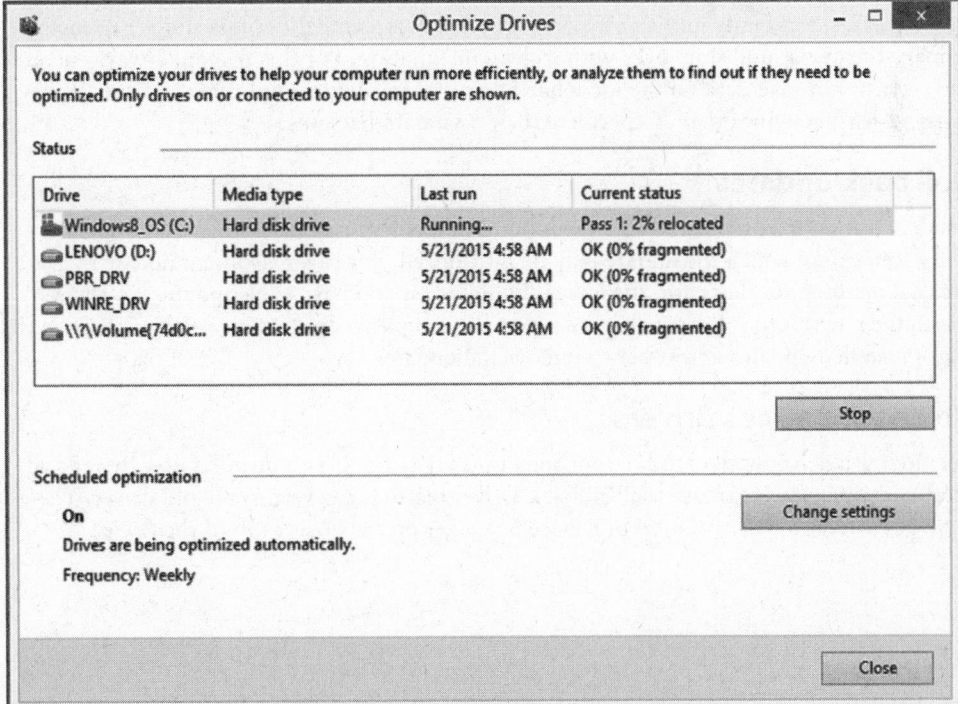

Reboot

You would be surprised how many system issues can be solved by a simple reboot. Therefore, the first step in many guides is a reboot. Always try this first.

Kill tasks

In some cases, slow performance comes from fluky applications or a frozen process. While a reboot will solve this, you can also go to Task Manager and kill the process there as well.

Restart services

In some cases, it may not be necessary to kill the service. It may be advisable to simply restart the service. See the earlier section "Services fail to start."

Update network settings

In many cases a simple update of the network settings can solve a connectivity issue. In most scenarios, devices are making use of a DHCP server; so, simply executing the `ipconfig/release` and `ipconfig /renew` commands will cause an update of the settings. If you find after this that the device has an address in the 169.254.0.1 through 169.254.255.254 range, the client is not finding the DHCP server. It could be that the server is not on the same segment as the device or that it is down or out of IP addresses.

Reimage/reload OS

In some cases, especially in the case of a serious malware infection, it is simpler to just reimage the device and start over with a clean installation. For this reason, always encourage users to *not* save data on the local hard drive, as this will complicate the issue. If they insist, at least convince them to perform their own data backups.

Roll back updates

Vendors test updates before rolling them out, but it is impossible for them to anticipate every scenario in which the update may be introduced. For this reason, an update might break something. In that case, the issues should occur soon after the update. It's always worth the attempt to roll back the update, as it is simple to do. Just locate the update in the list of installed updates and select to remove the update.

Roll back devices drivers

It's rare for a driver update to fail, but sometimes they do. If you install a new driver and there is an issue, you can use the Rollback Driver feature to revert to the old driver. The Rollback Driver button is found in Device Manager on the Driver tab of the device.

Apply updates

While updates sometime cause issues, in most cases they solve issues. When an issue involves possible driver problems, check to see whether any of the devices involved have new updates available. You can try this at Windows Update or by going to the vendor website. Sometimes they have tools that can scan your entire system for potential driver updates.

Repair application

To repair an application, consult the application vendor website. Most applications allow for a repair function if you attempt to reinstall the application when it is already installed.

Repair operating system

In some cases, the easiest way to repair an issue is to completely reinstall the operating system. This is one of the biggest reasons you should encourage users to store data on servers rather than the workstation. However, operating system vendors are beginning to offer some options that are less drastic. They have also made it easier to perform various recovery types with no media.

For example, in Windows 8, 8.1, and 10, there are several options presented when you choose to repair the computer. They are Refresh, Reset, and Restore. The effects of using the three options are as follows:

Refresh   This reinstalls Windows and keeps your personal files and settings. It also keeps the apps that came with your PC and the apps you installed from the Windows Store.

Reset   This reinstalls Windows but deletes your files, settings, and apps—except for the apps that came with your PC.

Restore   This is a way to undo recent system changes you've made by returning the system configuration to a previous point in time. It does not delete any files or applications, unless the application was installed after the restore point was taken.

To access these options, follow these steps:

1. Swipe in from the right edge of the screen, tap Settings, and then tap Change PC Settings. (If you're using a mouse, point to the upper-right corner of the screen, move the mouse pointer down, click Settings, and then click Change PC Settings.)

2. Tap or click Update And Recovery and then tap or click Recovery.

3. You will now see the three options shown in Figure 8.3.

FIGURE 8.3 Recovery

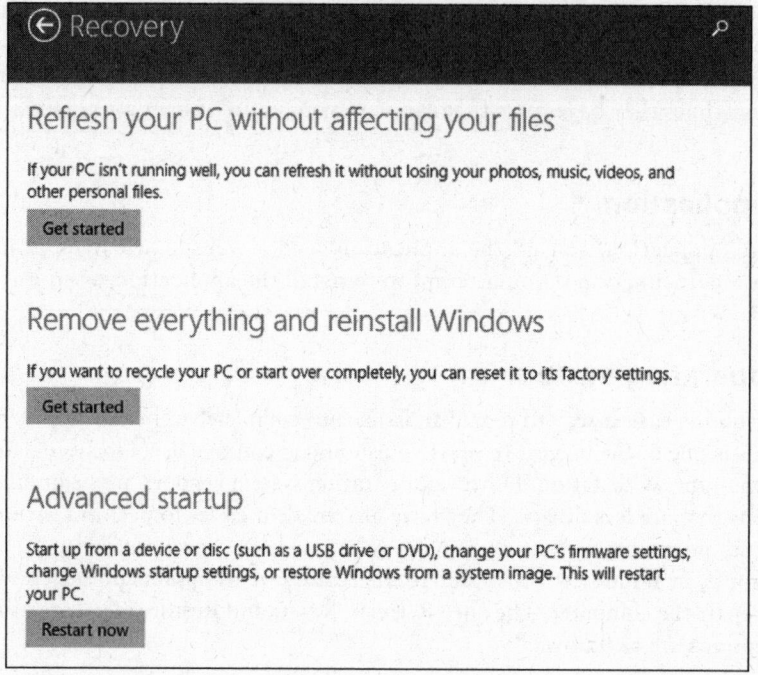

Update boot order

Bootrec.exe is a tool available on the installation DVD of Windows 7, 8, 8.1, and 10 that can be used to repair the following:

- Master boot record (MBR)
- Boot sector
- Boot configuration data (BCD) store

It is a command-line tool that becomes available when you reboot to the installation CD; to use it, choose Repair Your Computer, select the problematic operating system, and choose System Recovery Options. In the options presented, choose Command Prompt. The command and its options are shown here:

- Bootrec/fixmbr: Attempts to repair the master boot record
- Bootrec/fixboot: Writes a new boot sector to the system partition
- Bootrec/scanos: Scans the systems for supported installations and adds them to the list displayed at bootup
- Bootrec/rebuildbcd: Completely rebuilds the BCD store

Disable Windows services/applications

In some rare cases it can be a Windows service or a Windows application (those built into the operating system) that causes the issue. Disabling services is a matter of locating the service in the Services console, right-clicking it, and selecting Disable.

For Windows applications you must go to Programs and Features in Control Panel. Locate the application and disable it from there. On the left side of this dialog box select Turn Windows Features On and Off. From the next dialog box select the application and disable it.

Disable application startup

A slow start may be the result of too many services and applications starting at startup. The MSCONFIG utility helps you troubleshoot startup problems by allowing you to selectively disable individual items that normally are executed at startup. There is no menu command for this utility, so in Windows 10, for example, you use Start ➤ Run, type **msconfig**, and press Enter. It works in most versions of Windows, although the interface window is slightly different among versions. Figure 8.4 shows an example in Windows 10.

FIGURE 8.4   MSCONFIG

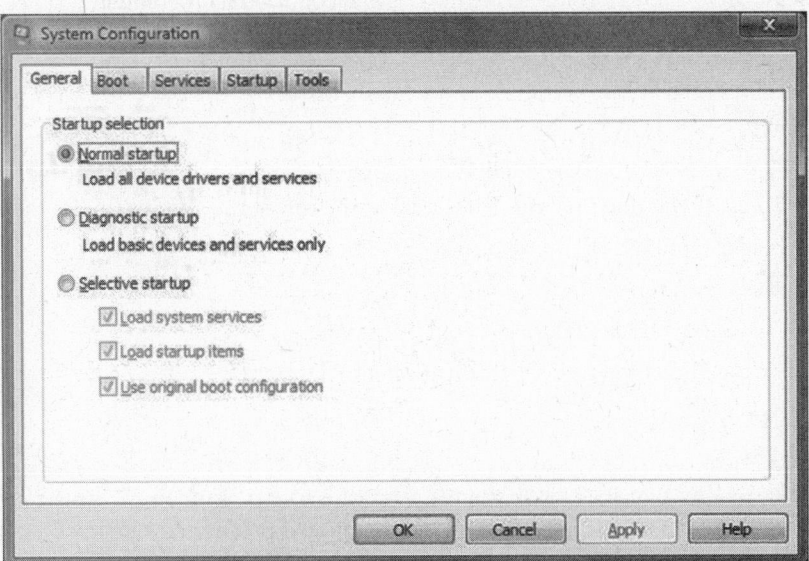

Safe boot

In many cases, a system will not boot in regular mode but will do so in safe mode. Safe mode loads the operating system but none of the drivers, with the exception of those absolutely essential to the system and those required for use of the keyboard, the mouse, and the basic display (VGA mode).

If the system will start in safe mode but not otherwise, it is most likely a bad driver that is causing the system to hang during the bootup. One option to try for a quick fix is to perform a System Restore procedure to a point in time before the driver problem occurred. You can also use the Rollback Driver feature to revert to the older but functional driver. The problem with this approach is that you have not identified the problem driver, so the issue may emerge again later.

If you go to Device Manager and check the status of all the devices, you should see a device that has a problem. Try updating the driver, which may be a better long-term solution. Another option is to look in the system log in Event Viewer; the problem driver may be specified in a message there as well.

Rebuild Windows profiles

To fix a corrupted user profile on a Windows 7, 8, or 10 computer, follow these steps:

1. Go to Control Panel.

2. Go to User Accounts (or Accounts And Family Safety ➢ User Accounts).

3. Click Manage Another Account.

4. Click Create A New Account to create a new account on your computer.

5. Type a name and choose an account type.

6. Click Create Account.

7. Choose Account Type For New User.

8. Open File Explorer or My Computer.

9. Click Tools. If you don't see the Tools item at the top of the window, press the Alt key.

10. Click Folder Options.

11. Go to the View tab.

12. Check the Show Hidden Files And Folders option.

13. Uncheck the Hide Protected Operating System Files option.

14. Click Apply.

15. Click OK.

16. Go to C:\Users\OLD_USERNAME, where C:\ is where your Windows 7 is installed and OLD_USERNAME is the username that has the corrupted profile error.

17. From this folder (OLD_USERNAME), select all files except Ntuser.data, Ntuser.data.log, and Ntuser.ini.

18. Right-click these files (except the files mentioned in the previous step) and click Copy.

19. Go to C:\User\NEW_USERNAME, where NEW_USERNAME is the username you created as new.

20. Paste all files in this folder, NEW_USERNAME.

21. Restart the computer and log in with the new username you've created.

Exam essentials

Identify the most common symptoms of operating system and system boot problems.
These include BSODs, boot failures, problems from improper shutdowns, spontaneous
shutdowns/restarts, devices that fail to start, missing DLL messages, services failures, compatibility errors, slow system performance, files that fail to open, missing items (NTLDR,
boot.ini, operating system, GUI), and invalid boot disk.

Identify the most common solutions to operating system issues.   These include but are
not limited to defragmenting the hard drive, rebooting, killing tasks, restarting services,
updating network settings, reimaging/reloading the OS, rolling back updates, rolling back
devices drivers. and applying updates.

3.2 Given a scenario, troubleshoot and resolve PC security issues.

System issues in many cases have security breaches at the root of the cause. It has become
almost a given that any problem that cannot be traced to any other cause should be
attacked by first scanning for viruses and malware. This section discusses common symptoms of security-related failures and tools that can be used to mitigate the damage. The
common symptoms addressed in objective 3.2 include the following:

- Pop-ups
- Browser redirection
- Security alerts
- Slow performance
- Internet connectivity issues
- PC/OS lockup
- Application crash
- OS updates failures
- Rogue antivirus
- Spam
- Renamed system files
- Disappearing files
- File permission changes
- Hijacked email

- Access denied
- Invalid certificate (trusted root CA)
- System/application log errors

Common symptoms

Systems can display many symptoms when something is amiss. Not all are malware related, but crazy things start to happen when malware is introduced to a computer. This section discusses some of the strange behaviors of computers that are infected as well as issues unrelated to malware.

Pop-ups

Although relatively benign when compared with malware in general, pop-ups are annoying to users. They also use system resources as they open and in some cases can introduce additional malware when they open.

Fortunately, most browsers now contain pop-up blockers that can prevent unwanted pop-ups. In some cases, users want pop-ups to be allowed—in fact, some website functions fail when a pop-up blocker is enabled. For that reason, users can use the Pop-Up Blocker Settings of Internet Explorer to allow pop-ups for certain websites, as shown in Figure 8.5. Other browsers usually have a similar setting.

FIGURE 8.5   The Pop-Up Blocker Settings dialog

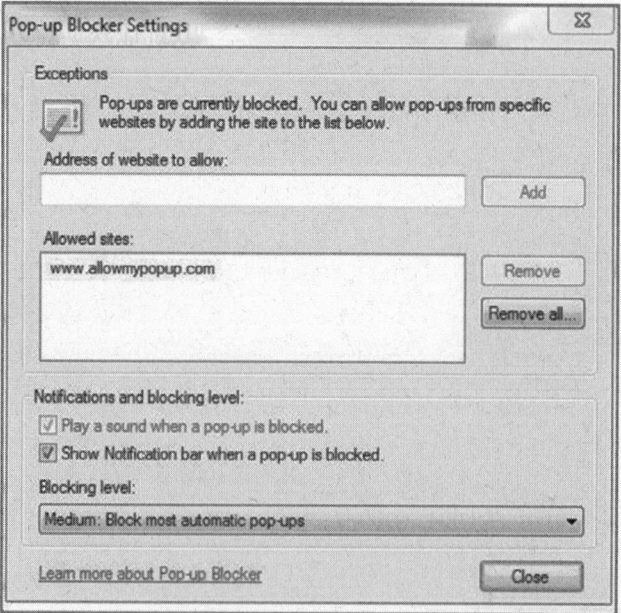

Browser redirection

A browser redirection is one of the most serious security problems. Browser hijacking software is external code that changes your Internet Explorer settings. It may include changing your home page or adding or removing items from your favorites. Some sites will be added that point to dubious content. In most cases, the home page will revert to the unwanted destination even if you change it manually because the hijacker made Registry changes to your system. To prevent this from occurring, remember these tips:

- Avoid suspect sites.
- Use and update an antivirus program regularly.
- Tighten your browser security settings.

Once you are a victim, you may have to apply antivirus software from an external source.

Security alerts

Sometimes you can tell by security warnings that the site you are on is attempting to attack your computer. This is true if you have a personal firewall such as Windows Firewall. It can also occur when you have the phishing filter enabled in Internet Explorer. You will know when the system asks you whether you want to allow access to your machine from the site. Unless you initiated a download, don't allow it.

Slow performance

A reduction in performance is one of the classic signs of malware infection. When no other reason can be isolated for the slowing of a system, scanning for malware is always recommended. All types of malware eat up significant system resources, starving the normal processes of the computer of the power they need.

Internet connectivity issues

Some malware will affect your Internet access. It may block you from accessing certain sites, or it may allow access to only a small number of sites. It has been reported that viral programs block access for certain programs and browsers while still allowing others to function. When access is denied, a message like the following is generated:

```
Unable to connect to HTTP Proxy. Your proxy may be misconfigured or
offline. -336
```

Moreover, this occurred even after the virus was supposedly cleaned from the system.

PC/OS lockup

It is quite common for the system to lock up when malware is attacking. You may notice when this occurs that the hard drive is very busy, although nothing appears to be going on. In some cases, you can use Task Manager to end the process that is locking everything up, and in other cases you simply must shut down the computer to break out of the lockup.

Application crash

Another possible symptom of a malware infection is the crashing of applications. While this will occur from time to time for other reasons, when it is occurring repeatedly, you should suspect malware. When the application that is crashing is your antivirus software, this is an even stronger indication of malware because disabling or damaging your antivirus protection is the first thing that some types of malware attempt to do.

OS updates failures

Malware may take certain measures to protect itself. One of these is to block you from accessing operating system update sites like Windows Update. You never notice this because these updates can be set to run automatically, so when they fail, it may not be obvious that they did.

Another action the malware can take along the same lines is to disable your antivirus software. For this reason, any time your antivirus program notifies you that it is not functional or cannot update itself, you should consider this possibility and get it back up and running (if you can) as soon as possible.

Rogue antivirus

If you receive messages (again usually at a suspect website) warning you that your system is infected, it will also usually offer to clean the system. At a minimum, they are trying to sell you anti-malware software through the bogus warning.

Worse, though, is that executing the "cleaning" sometimes results in the introduction of malware to the system—which was the whole point of the message to begin with. In general, pay no attention to these messages and try to close them and exit the website that generated them as quickly as possible.

Spam

A sudden increase in spam may indicate that adware has been installed on the machine. This type of malware monitors your activities so that it can more accurately target spam email. This is not particularly dangerous, but you have to wonder—if that malware got on your system, what *else* might lurk on your computer?

Renamed system files

Many viruses will rename system files and adopt the name of the system file. This can help the virus escape detection when scanning occurs since most virus definitions identify the virus by the name of the file that introduced the virus. This renaming of the system file can cause big problems when the file is required and the virus file is incapable of providing the required functionality.

Disappearing files

Another symptom of a viral infection is the deletion of files in the system. Many viruses delete key files in your system to render it inoperable. This could be one of the ways it renders any existing antivirus programs inoperable. It also can be part of disabling Internet access either completely or selectively.

File permission changes

If the malware is a rootkit or Trojan horse, it can change permissions to key files. The permissions would then allow access to remote systems. This can help to enhance the functionality of backdoors, which allow the computer to be controlled remotely.

Hijacked email

Viruses can also make changes to the email client that send a copy of all emails to another system. Depending on the content of email, this can make the user open to identity theft and can also be used in corporate espionage. It is especially harmful if the account is an IT administrator passing key enterprise security details through email.

The following are examples of evidence of email hijacking:

- Responses to email never sent by the user
- Automated replies from unknown people

Access denied

This can be a symptom of file permission changes. It can also be a message you get when you try to access the Internet in general or try to access specific sites such as those used for security updates and antivirus definitions.

Invalid certificate (trusted root CA)

When you are bombarded with certificate error messages at every website you visit, it's another sign of malware. Some types of malware interface with the certificate authentication process.

System/application log errors

If any of the symptoms mentioned here leave you with the suspicion you may have a malware infection, another place to look for clues is the operating system log or the application log (especially if you are having an issue with an application and you suspect malware).

Exam essentials

Identify the most common symptoms displayed from security issues.   These include but are not limited to pop-ups, browser redirection, security alerts, slow performance, Internet connectivity issues, PC/OS lockup, application crash, OS updates failures, rogue antivirus, spam, and renamed system files.

3.3 Given a scenario, use best practice procedures for malware removal.

Over time best practices have been developed through trial and error that help minimize the chances of getting viruses and reduce the effort involved in getting rid of malware. Some of these practices are discussed in this section. The topics addressed in objective 3.3 include the following:

- 1. Identify and research malware symptoms.
- 2. Quarantine the infected systems.
- 3. Disable System Restore (in Windows).
- 4. Remediate the infected systems.
- 5. Schedule scans and run updates.
- 6. Enable System Restore and create a restore point (in Windows).
- 7. Educate the end user.

1. Identify and research malware symptoms.

First identify the symptoms the malware is producing as clearly as you can. This can help identify the exact virus in some cases. In many scenarios, identifying the symptoms can help establish the severity of the infection, which is good to determine when IT resources are stretched thin and battles must be chosen.

2. Quarantine the infected systems.

The infected system should be quarantined—removed from the network to prevent a spread of the infection to other systems. This is why it is a good practice to keep data on servers so that when user systems need to be quarantined, a new machine can be quickly imaged for the user to reduce the impacts on productivity while the infected machine is cleaned.

3. Disable System Restore (in Windows).

System Restore is a useful tool in many cases, but when a virus infection occurs, it can be an ally of the virus. Virus scanners cannot clean infections from restore points, making reinfection possible. If a system restore is performed after running an antispyware utility, viral objects may reappear. Disable System Restore before attempting to clean a system. When you do this, you will delete all restore points in the system, including any that may have an infection.

4. Remediate the infected systems.

Once the infected system has been quarantined, you must take steps to clean it. This two-step process is discussed in this section.

a. Update the anti-malware software.

Before scanning the system with antivirus software, update the software and the engine if necessary. Definition files can change daily, and the virus may be so new that it is not contained in your current definitions file even if it is only a week old.

b. Scan and use removal techniques (safe mode, pre-installation environment).

Although you can run the scan and removal from the GUI, it is a best practice to do this either after booting to safe mode or from a pre-installation environment like Windows PE. Viruses that evade detection in the GUI cannot do so as easily in either of these environments.

5. Schedule scans and run updates.

The antivirus software can be scheduled to perform a scan of the system. You should set this up to occur when the system is not in use, like at night. The scanning process will go faster then and will not affect users. Also, set the software to automatically check for and install any updates to the definition files and to the engine when available.

6. Enable System Restore and create a restore point (in Windows).

Although it is recommended that you disable System Restore before cleaning an infection, it is a good idea to create a restore point after an infection is cleaned. This gives you a clean restore point going forward in case the system becomes infected again at some point. For non-Windows systems, a backup should be performed at this time.

7. Educate the end user.

In many cases, users are partly responsible for the virus infection. After an infection occurs is a great time to impress on users the principles of secure computing. They should be reminded that antivirus software and firewalls can go only so far in protecting them and that they should exercise safe browsing habits and refrain from opening any attachments in email from unknown sources, regardless of how tempting.

Exam essentials

Identify the steps to remove malware.   According to best practices, the steps to address malware removal are as follows:

1. Identify malware symptoms.
2. Quarantine infected system.

3. Disable System Restore.

4. Remediate infected systems, including updating antivirus software.

5. Scan and remove the malware.

6. Enable System Restore and create a restore point.

7. Educate end users.

3.4 Given a scenario, troubleshoot mobile OS and application issues.

Mobile devices have their own unique sets of issues that may not be encountered with desktop computers. In this section, I'll discuss common issues and their solutions. The common symptoms addressed in objective 3.4 include the following:

- Dim display
- Intermittent wireless
- No wireless connectivity
- No Bluetooth connectivity
- Cannot broadcast to external monitor
- Touchscreen non-responsive
- Apps not loading
- Slow performance
- Unable to decrypt email
- Extremely short battery life
- Overheating
- Frozen system
- No sound from speakers
- Inaccurate touch screen response
- System lockout
- App log errors

Common symptoms

Not all mobile device issues are unique to mobile devices. They suffer from many of the same issues as desktop machines. However, some problems are unique to mobile devices or at least more prone to occur with them, as you will learn in this section.

Dim display

With respect to laptops, the backlight and inverter can cause dimming problems, but in most cases the screen has been dimmed inadvertently with the function keys. It is also possible that the switch on the laptop that tells the system the lid is closed may be held down by some obstruction. Check that as well.

On smartphones you should first check the brightness settings to ensure that they have not been inadvertently changed. Many Android devices force you to choose between manual settings of brightness and auto-brightness; you may have changed that to use manual settings. Apple's iOS allows you to adjust brightness levels on an iPhone even when auto-brightness is turned on. To recalibrate the setting, turn auto-brightness off in the Brightness ➤ Wallpaper settings. Then go into an unlit room and drag the adjustment slider to make the screen as dim as possible.

Intermittent wireless

Almost all mobile devices today include an internal wireless card. This is convenient, but it can be susceptible to interference (resulting in low signal strength) between the device and the access point or cell tower. Do what you can to reduce the number of items blocking the signal between the two devices, and you'll increase the strength of the signal. It is also possible that the cable that connects the antenna to the laptop needs to be reseated. Smartphones can connect to a WLAN as well. These devices will suffer from blockage and interference issues the same as laptops.

No wireless connectivity

When there is no wireless connectivity, it is usually because of one of two things.

- The wireless capability is disabled (usually with a key combination or a function key); it is easy to disable inadvertently. There can also be a hardware switch on the side, front, or back of the case.
- The wireless antenna is bad or the cable needs to be reseated.

Try the following steps when troubleshooting a lack of wireless connectivity:

1. Power cycle the AP or wireless router.
2. Power cycle the device.
3. On a laptop, check the hardware wireless button (if the laptop has one).
4. On a smartphone or tablet, check your wireless settings to ensure that WiFi is on. Also make sure that Airplane mode is off.
5. Disconnect and reconnect.
6. Verify that the wireless device is using the correct password.

No Bluetooth connectivity

Bluetooth is also enabled and disabled with a key combination and can be disabled easily. The first thing to try is to reenable it. The second thing in a laptop to try is to reseat the antenna cable. If all else fails, try a new antenna. Like the WLAN NIC, this can also be a hardware switch on the side, front, or back of the case.

In smartphones and laptops, the problem also can occur after an upgrade or update of some sort. In these cases, it can be that the proper driver is missing from the upgrade or was somehow corrupted or overwritten during the upgrade process. Here are some additional things you might try on a smartphone:

1. Power cycle the device.

2. Remove the battery and put it back in.

3. Clear the Bluetooth cache. While each device is different, a common way to access this setting and clear the cache on Android is to open the phone's Settings, tap the More tab, tap Application Manager, select to view all, select Bluetooth Share, and tap Clear Cache.

4. Clear the Bluetooth data. While each device is different, a common way to access this setting and clear the data is to go to Settings, tap the More tab, tap Application Manager, select to view all, select Bluetooth Share, and select Clear Data.

5. Reboot the device in safe mode.

6. Make sure the device to which you are pairing has no issues.

7. As a last resort, perform a hard reset, which resets the device to factory defaults.

Cannot broadcast to external monitor

It's always possible that a hardware issue is causing an external monitor to not work when it's connected to a mobile device; but again, in most cases, the problem is an incomplete understanding of the key combination to use to send the output to the external monitor.

On some devices you need to use the Fn key in combination with the keys on the top row; on others you simply use the top-row keys. Before spending too much time troubleshooting, consult the documentation and ensure that you are using the correct procedure. In some models, an external monitor can also be controlled from the video control panel or from within PowerPoint or other presentation software.

Another issue with both smartphones and laptops is a mismatch in screen resolution between the source device and the destination. Finally, check the port used to connect the device and ensure that it is functional and enabled.

Touchscreen non-responsive

In some cases, a touchscreen is simply broken and must be replaced; in some cases the device must be replaced. In other cases, the issue is much less serious. If the screen still has the protective cover that comes on it, remove it. It can interfere with the operation of the screen. Make sure the screen is clean by cleaning it with a soft microfiber cloth. Ensure that the user's hands are dry because wet hands will cause an issue. Check these items first.

Then, before assuming the worst, try the following to solve the issue with laptops:

1. Perform a full shutdown of the device.
2. If it is a device that uses Windows, perform a Windows update. For other systems, check for an update at the vendor website.
3. Ensure that the system is set to consider your screen a touchscreen (laptop). This is a setting in Windows. Search for *tablet PC settings*.
4. Some devices support a touchscreen diagnostic test. Perform the test.
5. If the problem occurs after returning from sleep mode, check the power settings to see whether the screen is set to be functional while in sleep mode.

With smartphones, consider the following as well:

1. Reset the device. If your device does not have this function, remove the battery, memory card, or SIM card; then reinstall them.
2. Delete any applications you recently installed. Some third-party applications can cause your device to lock up or freeze.
3. Recalibrate the touchscreen. Look in the device's Settings menu for a calibration option.

Apps not loading

When an app will not load on a mobile device, the first item to check is that the app is the right version for the device. Not all apps work on all devices. When an app has been working and now won't open or load when you access it, try the following items:

- Check to see whether there is an update for the app.
- Force the app to quit. In Android, for example, in the multitask menu, swipe it away and then reopen it.
- If the issue involves downloading the app, check to make sure you have enough space for the app.
- If the app is resource intensive, ensure that your device has the resources to run the app.

Slow performance

The first thing to suspect when performance slows is insufficient internal storage space. This begins to occur over time and will only get worse until the issue is solved by removing something to free up some space.

Another issue is apps that run all the time. Close these apps and clear the app cache. While you can do this manually, third-party apps are available that can do this for you on a schedule. The following are some other items you may try:

- If an update is available, update your firmware.
- Reset the phone (back up the data first!).

Unable to decrypt email

While there are services that can encrypt your email messages for you, many users choose to do so themselves using third-party tools. This allows more control but also requires an understanding of how it works and what the recipient needs to decrypt your email messages.

When a user receives an email that cannot be decrypted, check these items:

- Ensure that the sender and the recipient are using the same encryption standard. If one user is using S/MIME and another PGP, there will be a problem.
- Both users need to be in possession of the public key of the other user.
- Both users need to have imported their respective private keys to their devices.

Considering the level of understanding that most users have of the way encryption works and its requirements, it is not surprising that services that handle all the keys are gaining in popularity.

Extremely short battery life

One of the biggest complaints users lodge against their mobile devices is short battery life. When a battery is nearing the end of its life cycle, it will begin to fail to hold a charge, so it could be you need a new battery. However, there are a number of other things you can do to mitigate the problem.

- Change the location and brightness settings, because these components really eat power.
- Turn off Bluetooth and WiFi when not needed. These also take power.
- Disable push notifications for nonessential apps.
- Close apps not in use.
- Prevent the device from overheating, which is bad for the battery.

Overheating

Mobile devices get hot from time to time. An inherent problem is a lack of ventilation. The following are some activities that will worsen this:

- Excessive gaming
- Continuous online browsing
- Old battery
- Using the device while charging the device

Some tactics that can help prevent overheating are as follows:

- Disable any unwanted functions.
- Turn it off when not in use.
- Don't leave the device in places like a hot car.
- Clean the battery contacts.

Frozen system

Dealing with a frozen device takes a similar approach to dealing with a slow device. Try the following items:

- Plug the phone into a charger and see whether it unlocks.
- Delete any unused apps or photos.
- Delete the data cache.

No sound from speakers

When a speaker on a mobile device is not functioning, in most cases it has simply been inadvertently turned off. After checking the settings described later in this section, you can assume that there is a hardware problem. In that case, with smartphones, it is typically advisable to send the device to the manufacturer, but with laptops, it is possible to replace the internal speakers.

To determine whether the settings are the issue, ensure that the speaker volume is up and the speaker is not disabled. On an Android, first test the loudspeaker by following these steps:

1. Go to the Home screen and tap the Phone icon.
2. Type *#7353# into the dialer as though you are dialing a phone number. A list of options will appear.
3. Tap Speaker, and music should start to play. You can tap Speaker again to silence the music.

To test the internal speaker, follow the same steps, but in step 3, tap Melody.

Music should start to play from the earpiece on the phone and allow you to see whether the speaker that you hold up to your ear to talk with people is working properly as well.

On an iPhone, follow these steps:

1. Go to Settings ➢ Sounds and drag the Ringer And Alerts slider to turn the volume up.
2. If you can hear sound from the speaker, then the speaker works.
3. If the device has a Ring/Silent switch, make sure it's set to ring. If you can see orange, it's set to silent.

Inaccurate touch screen response

In cases where the touchscreen is working but not responding correctly, the action you should take depends on the vendor. With Apple devices, try the following, and if there is no relief, contact Apple so the warranty is not voided:

1. If you have a case or screen protector on your device, try removing it.
2. Clean the screen with a soft, slightly damp, lint-free cloth.
3. Unplug your device.
4. Restart your device. If you can't restart, force your device to restart.

With Android devices, first restart the phone. If that doesn't work, perform a factory reset using these steps:

1. Make a backup of personal data, such as email and photos, because the process will erase all your files.
2. Open the Applications tab and tap Settings.
3. Tap Privacy and then Factory Data Reset.
4. Tap Reset Phone.

On a laptop, this issue may be solved by recalibrating the screen. While systems vary, the steps using Windows 7 are as follows:

1. Click Start, Control Panel, and Hardware And Sound.
2. Under Tablet PC Settings, tap Calibrate The Screen For Pen Or Touch Input.
3. On the Display tab, under Display options, tap Calibrate and then Yes to allow the program to make changes.
4. Follow the on-screen instructions to calibrate your touchscreen.

System lockout

When a user gets locked out of a device from typing too many incorrect passwords (or *patterns*) on an Android phone, there are several things you can try before resetting the device (which will delete all the data). First try this:

1. Enter your email address into the device.
2. In the password field, enter **null**.
3. If this works, you will then be prompted to enter a new pattern, and once again you have your phone back in action with all data intact.

If that fails, you will need to perform a factory reset, as described in the section "Inaccurate touch screen response."

On an iPhone, you can go to iForgot to unlock it with your existing password or reset your password. You can also click the Reset Password or Forgot Password button in the alert. Type your full email address when you're asked to enter your Apple ID.

App log errors

Just as in PCs, when you suspect an application is affected by malware, check the application log. This log may be hidden, so consult the documentation to determine how to show the file.

Exam essentials

Identify common mobile device issues. These include but are not limited to dim display, intermittent wireless, no wireless connectivity, no Bluetooth connectivity, cannot broadcast to external monitor, touchscreen not responding, and apps not loading.

3.5 Given a scenario, troubleshoot mobile OS and application security issues.

Mobile devices may use different operating systems than desktop systems, and their applications may be packaged a bit differently, but they still can suffer from security issues. It logically follows that they must be secured as well. In this final section of Chapter 8, I'll talk about the symptoms of security issues and describe some tools you can use in the struggle to protect these devices and their data. The following are the subobjective topics covered in this section:

- Signal drop/weak signal
- Power drain
- Slow data speeds
- Unintended WiFi connection
- Unintended Bluetooth pairing
- Leaked personal files/data
- Data transmission over limit
- Unauthorized account access
- Unauthorized location tracking
- Unauthorized camera/ microphone activation
- High resource utilization

Common symptoms

Just as desktop systems do, mobile devices will exhibit certain symptoms when security issues manifest themselves. This section surveys some of the more common symptoms of a security issue with a device.

Signal drop/weak signal

All mobile devices are going to experience some dropped calls and weak signals from time to time. However, a device that is fully charged and close to its cell tower or WiFi access point and still suffers these symptoms on a regular basis is probably infected with malware. You should scan the device using a malware product designed specifically for mobile devices.

Power drain

Another sign of a malware infection on a mobile device is rapid draining of the battery. This occurs because the malware is performing operations in the background. If the device is also suffering signal loss, this only increases this possibility. If the device is also rapidly eating all the data in your plan, it is almost certain the device has malware.

Slow data speeds

When malware is present and running in the background, it is using resources as well as running down your battery. That means when you are downloading or uploading data, the process is competing with the malware for resources. Therefore, slow data speeds may also be a sign of a malware infection.

Unintended WiFi connection

Some models of mobile devices such as smartphones will automatically connect to any available open WLAN (an open WLAN is one that does not require authentication). In most cases, users will be aware of this because they may be presented with a browser screen requiring the user to accept the terms of service. Not all networks do this, however, and if you have connected to a rogue access point managed by a malicious individual, you can be almost certain your connection will be so seamless you may not know you are connected.

The danger in this is that after the access point issues your device an IP address, you will find yourself residing in the same subnet as the malicious hacker, who can now launch a peer-to-peer attack on your device. To prevent this, set the mobile device to *not* automatically connect to any available wireless network. For example, on an iPhone, use these steps:

1. Launch the Settings app.
2. Tap Wi-Fi.
3. Tap the blue arrow to the right of a network.
4. Switch the Auto-Join tab to OFF.

Since you can perform this operation only for networks to which you have previously connected, an additional suggestion is to simply keep WiFi off and enable it only when you need to connect.

Unintended Bluetooth pairing

Unintended Bluetooth connections or pairings can also occur with mobile devices. This is also a security issue because several wireless attacks are made through a Bluetooth connection. Many users leave their Bluetooth settings in a state that makes connections to their peripheral devices easier to make. However, leaving them in a discoverable state also makes it easier for malicious individuals to create a Bluetooth pairing with your mobile device that makes wireless attacks through the Bluetooth connection possible.

Even though it adds a step to the process of pairing a new device to the mobile device, users should make their mobile devices undiscoverable as a default setting and enable this setting only when they need to create a new pairing with a trusted device. Many new devices (for example, iPhone 6) unfortunately don't have a setting to turn off discovery without disabling Bluetooth entirely. While the logic behind this is that the iPhone automatically prevents access to personal data through the Bluetooth connection, on any devices that make turning off discovery possible, it should be done.

Having said all this, if a device that is supposedly secured makes an unintended Bluetooth connection, it could be a clue that the device has been compromised through either malware or social engineering.

Leaked personal files/data

Obviously, if personal files located on a mobile device suddenly are gone or suddenly are found to be leaked, it is also a clue that the device has been compromised through either malware or social engineering.

Data transmission over limit

When certain types of malware begin to operate on a mobile device, they may transmit data from the device to the hacker, or vice versa. Since this uses your data plan without your knowledge, you may suddenly find yourself over your data limit. You may not find this out until you receive a data bill that exceeds your mortgage payment. In any cases such as this, the device should be immediately scanned for malware.

Unauthorized account access

Another sign that a mobile device has been compromised is when changes are made to your account that can be made only by the account holder, such as adding a feature or disabling a security function. In some cases, the carrier will notify you of changes of this nature, in case you weren't the one to make the change.

Unauthorized location tracking

Location tracking allows the device to determine your location for the purpose of tailoring search results. Location tracking can be disabled on a mobile device. In most cases, disabled location tracking is the default, and users will be asked by certain applications if they want to enable it. When a user has either never enabled this feature or has disabled this feature and it suddenly begins to track the location of the device, it is another indication that the device has been compromised.

Unauthorized camera/ microphone activation

Cameras and microphones can be either enabled or disabled on a mobile device. When a user either has never enabled these components or has disabled these components and the components begin to function, it is another indication that the device has been compromised.

High resource utilization

In any case where the device appears to be utilizing CPU and memory at a rate that is not consistent with the activities of the user, it is a sign that malware is possibly at work on the device. Malware will utilize resources in the process of performing whatever functions it has been deigned to perform. When there is unexplained excessive resource usage, it is another indication that the device has been compromised.

Exam essentials

Describe common mobile device issues.   Some of the symptoms include signal drop/weak signal, power drain, slow data speeds, unintended WiFi connections, and leaked personal files/data.

Review Questions

You can find the answers in the Appendix.

1. Which type of file *cannot* be copied from another machine if missing or corrupted?

   A. .dll

   B. boot.ini

   C. ntldr

   D. bootmgr

2. Which of the following is *not* a possible cause of a "no operating system found" message?

   A. Nonsystem disk in the floppy drive

   B. Incorrect boot device order in the BIOS

   C. Corrupted or missing boot sector

   D. System disk in the DVD drive

3. What is external code that changes your Internet Explorer settings?

   A. Man-in-the-middle attack

   B. Browser redirection

   C. SYN flood

   D. Fraggle

4. Which of the following is not a symptom of malware?

   A. Increase in performance

   B. Internet connectivity issues

   C. Browser redirection

   D. Pop-ups

5. Which of the following is the first step in malware removal?

   A. Remediate the infected systems.

   B. Quarantine the infected systems.

   C. Educate the end user.

   D. Identify and research malware symptoms.

6. What Windows service should be disabled before cleaning an infection?

   A. NAT

   B. System Restore

   C. Windows Firewall

   D. Antivirus

7. Which of the following does *not* negatively impact mobile battery life?

    A. Low brightness setting

    B. Location services

    C. Enabled Bluetooth

    D. Overheating device

8. Which of the following does not cause overheating of a mobile device?

    A. Excessive gaming

    B. Leaving phone on

    C. Old battery

    D. Continuous online browsing

9. Which of the following is *not* an indication of a security issue with a mobile device?

    A. Power drain

    B. Weak signal

    C. Slow speeds

    D. Low resource utilization

10. Which of the following is an indication of a security issue with a mobile device?

    A. Low resource utilization

    B. Disabled microphone

    C. Enabled camera

    D. Authorized account access

Chapter

9

Operational Procedures

COMPTIA A+ CERTIFICATION EXAM CORE 2 (220-1002) OBJECTIVES COVERED IN THIS CHAPTER:

✓ **4.1 Compare and contrast best practices associated with types of documentation.**

- Network topology diagrams
- Knowledge base/articles
- Incident documentation
- Regulatory and compliance policy
- Acceptable use policy
- Password policy
- Inventory management
  - Asset tags
  - Barcodes

✓ **4.2 Given a scenario, implement basic change management best practices.**

- Documented business processes
- Purpose of the change
- Scope the change
- Risk analysis
- Plan for change
- End-user acceptance
- Change board
  - Approvals
- Backout plan
- Document changes

✓ **4.3 Given a scenario, implement basic disaster prevention and recovery methods.**

- Backup and recovery
  - Image level
  - File level
  - Critical applications
- Backup testing
- UPS
  - Battery backup
- Surge protector
- Cloud storage vs. local storage backups
- Account recovery options

✓ **4.4 Explain common safety procedures.**

- Equipment grounding
- Proper component handling and storage
  - Antistatic bags
  - ESD straps
  - ESD mats
  - Self-grounding
- Toxic waste handling
  - Batteries
  - Toner
  - CRT
  - Cell phones
  - Tablets
- Personal safety
  - Disconnect power before repairing PC
  - Remove jewelry
  - Lifting techniques
  - Weight limitations
  - Electrical fire safety

- Cable management
- Safety goggles
- Air filter mask
- Compliance with government regulations

✓ **4.5 Explain environmental impacts and appropriate controls.**

- MSDS documentation for handling and disposal
- Temperature, humidity level awareness, and proper ventilation
- Power surges, brownouts, and blackouts
  - Battery backup
  - Surge suppressor
- Protection from airborne particles
  - Enclosures
  - Air filters/mask
- Dust and debris
  - Compressed air
  - Vacuums
- Compliance to government regulations

✓ **4.6 Explain the processes for addressing prohibited content/activity, and privacy, licensing, and policy concepts.**

- Incident response
  - First response
    - Identify
    - Report through proper channels
    - Data/device preservation
  - Use of documentation/documentation changes
  - Chain of custody
    - Tracking of evidence/documenting process
- Licensing/DRM/EULA
  - Open-source vs. commercial license
  - Personal license vs. enterprise licenses

- Regulated data
    - PII
    - PCI
    - GDPR
    - PHI
- Follow all policies and security best practices

✓ **4.7   Given a scenario, use proper communication techniques and professionalism.**

- Use proper language and avoid jargon, acronyms, and slang, when applicable
- Maintain a positive attitude/ project confidence
- Actively listen (taking notes) and avoid interrupting the customer
- Be culturally sensitive
    - Use appropriate professional titles, when applicable
- Be on time (if late, contact the customer)
- Avoid distractions
    - Personal calls
    - Texting/social media sites
    - Talking to coworkers while interacting with customers
    - Personal interruptions
- Dealing with difficult customers or situations
    - Do not argue with customers and/or be defensive
    - Avoid dismissing customer problems
    - Avoid being judgmental
    - Clarify customer statements (ask open-ended questions to narrow the scope of the problem, restate the issue, or question to verify understanding)
    - Do not disclose experiences via social media outlets
- Set and meet expectations/timeline and communicate status with the customer
    - Offer different repair/replacement options, if applicable
    - Provide proper documentation on the services provided
    - Follow up with customer/user at a later date to verify satisfaction

- Deal appropriately with customers' confidential and private materials
  - Located on a computer, desktop, printer, etc.

✓ **4.8 Identify the basics of scripting.**

- Script file types
  - .bat
  - .ps1
  - .vbs
  - .sh
  - .py
  - .js
- Environment variables
- Comment syntax
- Basic script constructs
  - Basic loops
  - Variables
- Basic data types
  - Integers
  - Strings

✓ **4.9 Given a scenario, use remote access technologies.**

- RDP
- Telnet
- SSH
- Third-party tools
  - Screen share feature
  - File share
- Security considerations of each access method

This chapter will focus on the exam topics related to security. It will follow the structure of the CompTIA A+ 220-1002 exam blueprint, objective 4, and it will explore the nine sub-objectives that you need to master before taking the exam. The Operational Procedures domain represents 23 percent of the total exam.

4.1 Compare and contrast best practices associated with types of documentation.

If you ever heard the adage "the job isn't done till the paperwork is done," then you may grasp the importance of documentation. In this section, we'll talk about some of documentation you should be generating and updating. Topics include the following:

- Network topology diagrams
- Knowledge base/articles
- Incident documentation
- Regulatory and compliance policy
- Acceptable use policy
- Password policy
- Inventory management

Network topology diagrams

All network diagrams should be kept in both hard copy and digital format. Moreover, this document must be closely integrated with the change management process. The change management policy should specifically call for the updating of this document at the conclusion of any change made to the network that impacts the network diagram and should emphasize that no change procedure is considered to be complete unless this update has occurred.

There are two types of network topologies, physical and logical. The physical diagram focuses on the cabling, connections, and locations of devices. The logical diagram illustrates data flows that may or may not follow the physical diagram.

Figure 9.1 shows a physical diagram, while Figure 9.2 illustrates a logical diagram.

FIGURE 9.1 A physical diagram

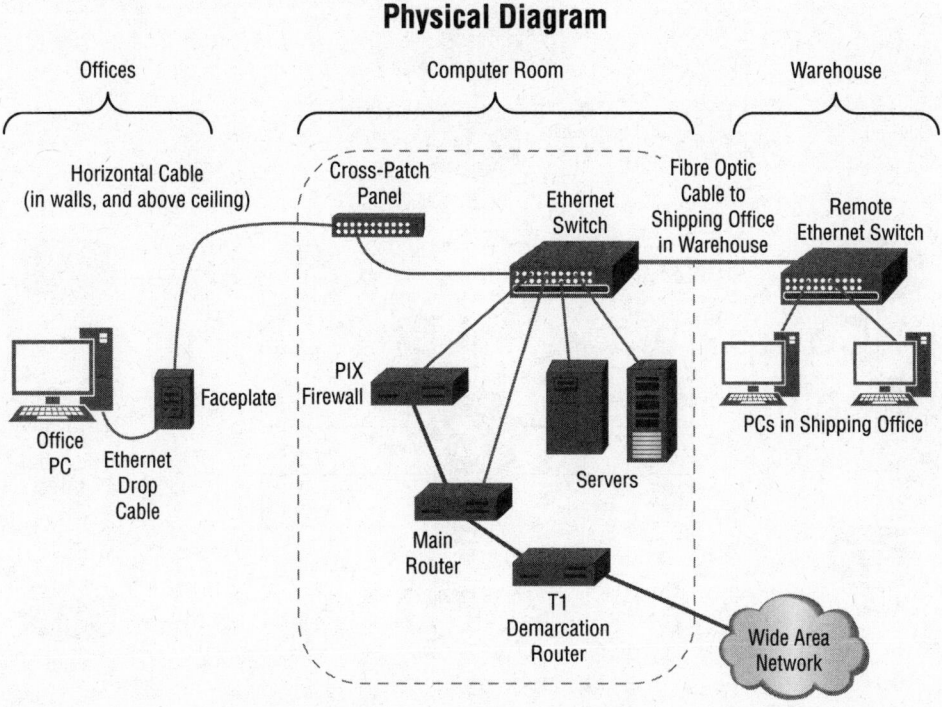

Knowledge base/articles

Often in the process of troubleshooting an issue, you may find useful information in a knowledge base article. Vendors share these documents to assist technicians. You should keep these articles and tie them to the issue they solved. This will help solve future instances of the same issue.

Incident documentation

Just as you should keep all technical articles that help to solve an issue, all incidents should be recorded in detail for future reference. This helps to identify recurring issues for which the root cause has yet to be determined. With regard to security incidents, your incident handling policy should support this effort.

FIGURE 9.2 A logical diagram

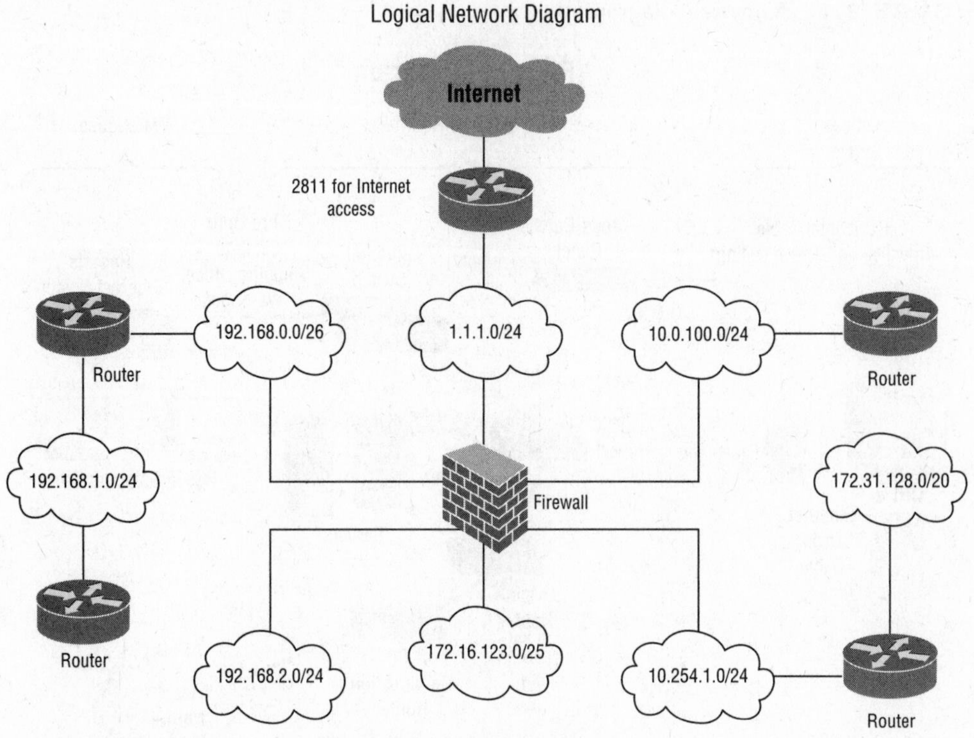

Logical Network Diagram

Regulatory and compliance policy

It is your responsibility, as an administrator and a professional, to know (or learn) the regulations that exist for dealing with safety. You should know them from the local level to the federal level and be familiar with the reporting procedures for incidents you are faced with.

If employees are injured, for example, you may need to contact the Occupational Safety and Health Administration (OSHA). On its website (www.osha.gov), you can find links to information about issues of compliance, laws and regulation, and enforcement.

When it comes to disposal of hardware, you can find a list of state laws here:

www.electronicsrecycling.org/public/ContentPage.aspx?pageid=14

The Environmental Protection Agency (EPA) offers basic information here:

www.epa.gov/osw/conserve/materials/ecycling/index.htm

Acceptable use policy

The most effective method of preventing viruses, spyware, and harm to data is education. Teach your users not to open suspicious files and to open only those files that they're reasonably sure are virus-free. They need to scan every disk, email, and document they receive before they open it. You should also have all workstations scheduled to be automatically scanned on a regular basis.

While education is important, in most cases you must also attempt to control what users do. An acceptable use policy (AUP) is a document that specifies what users can and cannot do, and it should be signed by all during the hiring process. This creates a contract that can be used later to form the basis for disciplinary measures. These measures or consequences for noncompliance should be spelled out ahead of time. The AUP should be reviewed at least annually, and if changes are made, personnel should have to re-sign the agreement.

Password policy

One of the strongest ways to keep a system safe is to employ strong password polices and educate your users in the best security practices. In this section, you'll explore various techniques that can enhance the security of your user passwords.

Setting strong passwords

Passwords should be as long as possible. Most security experts believe a password of 10 characters is the minimum that should be used if security is a real concern. If you use only the lowercase letters of the alphabet, you have 26 characters with which to work. If you add the numeric values 0 through 9, you'll get another 10 characters. If you go one step further and add the uppercase letters, you'll then have an additional 26 characters, giving you a total of 62 characters with which to construct a password.

Most vendors recommend that you use nonalphabetical characters such as #, $, and % in your password, and some go so far as to require it.

If you used a 4-character password, this would be $62 \times 62 \times 62 \times 62$, or approximately 14 million password possibilities. If you used 5 characters in your password, this would give you 62 to the fifth power, or approximately 920 million password possibilities. If you used a 10-character password, this would give you 62 to the tenth power, or 8.4×10^{17} (a very big number) possibilities. As you can see, these numbers increase exponentially with each position added to the password. The 4-digit password could probably be broken in a fraction of a day, whereas the 10-digit password would take considerably longer and consume much more processing power.

If your password used only the 26 lowercase letters from the alphabet, the 4-digit password would have 26 to the fourth power, or 456,000 password combinations. A 5-character password would have 26 to the fifth power, or more than 11 million, and a 10-character password would have 26 to the tenth power, or 1.4×10^{14}. This is still a big number, but it would take considerably less time to break it.

To see tables on how quickly passwords can be surmised, visit www.lockdown.co.uk/?pg=combi&s=articles.

Mathematical methods of encryption are primarily used in conjunction with other encryption methods as part of authenticity verification. The message and the hashed value of the message can be encrypted using other processes. In this way, you know that the message is secure and hasn't been altered.

Password expiration

The longer a password is used, the more likely it is that it will be compromised in some way. It is for this reason that requiring users to change their passwords at certain intervals increases the security of their passwords. You should require users to set a new password every 30 days (more frequently for higher security networks), and you must also prevent them from reusing old passwords. Most password management systems have the ability to track previously used passwords and to disallow users from recycling old passwords.

Changing default usernames/passwords

Default accounts represent a huge weakness in that every miscreant knows they exist. When an operating system is installed, whether on a workstation or a server, there are certain accounts created, and since the wrongdoer already knows the account name, it simplifies the process of getting into an account by requiring them to supply only the password. The first thing they will try, of course, is the default password if one exists.

Screensaver required password

A screensaver should automatically start after a short period of idle time, and that screensaver should require a password before the user can begin the session again. This method of locking the workstation adds one more level of security.

BIOS/UEFI

Passwords should be configured and required to access either the BIOS or UEFI settings on all devices. If this is not the case, it would be possible for someone to reboot a device, enter the settings, change the boot order, boot to an operating system residing on a USB or optical drive, and use that OS as a platform to access data located on the other drives. While this is a worst-case scenario, there is also much less mayhem a malicious person could cause in the BIOS and UEFI.

Requiring passwords

Make absolutely certain you require passwords (a simple thing to overlook in a small network) for all accounts, and change the default passwords on system accounts.

Inventory management

Inventory management includes knowing what you have. You can't know that something is missing until you take an inventory, so this should be done on a regular basis. What type of information is useful to record in these inventories? You may choose to record more, but three items should be included for sure.

Make

The manufacturer of the device should be recorded and the name they give the device should as well.

Model

The exact model number should be recorded in full, leaving nothing out. Sometimes those dangling letters at the end of the model number are there to indicate how this model differs from another or could indicate a feature, so record *all* of it.

Serial number

The serial number of the device should be recorded. This is a number that will be important to you with respect to the warranty and service support. You should be able to put your hands on this number quickly.

Asset tags

If your organization places asset tags on the devices, it probably means you have your own internal numbering or other identification system in place. Record that number and any other pertinent information that the organization deems important enough to place on the asset tag such as region, building, and so on.

Barcodes

One popular methods of tagging devices is with barcodes that can be read by scanners when performing an inventory. If these are RFID tags, they can even be read from a short distance.

Exam essentials

Explain the importance of asset management and documentation.   List what should be included when creating an asset inventory. Understand the importance of organizing and maintaining documentation. Describe some of the types of sensitive documents that require special treatment.

4.2 Given a scenario, implement basic change management best practices.

There is an old saying "too many cooks spoil the broth," and when it comes to managing networks, it certainly applies. When technicians make changes to the servers that are not centrally managed and planned, chaos reigns. In that environment, changes might be made that work at cross purposes to one another. All organizations need a change management process whereby all changes go through a formal evaluation process before they are implemented.

This process ensures that all changes support the goals of the organization and that the impact of each change is anticipated before the change is made. There should be a change management board (sometimes called a *change control board*) to which all changes are submitted for review. Only when the change has been approved should it be made. This section covers the following topics:

- Documented business processes
- Purpose of the change
- Scope the change
- Risk analysis
- Plan for change
- End-user acceptance
- Change board
- Backout plan
- Document changes

Documented business processes

As organizations grow and develop, they generate business processes they follow. Sometimes these processes become almost ingrained in users, but over time methods utilized may "drift" away from the original process. For this reason, all key business processes should be recorded and followed, and any change to such processes must undergo the change management examination to ensure that it is beneficial to the entire organization and supports all of its goals.

Purpose of the change

When any change is suggested, the proposed benefit derived from the change must be identified. Otherwise, there is no reason for the change. During the change management process, the relative costs and benefits to the overall organization will be weighed by a change management board or team.

Scope the change

In some cases, a change may be beneficial for some users or groups but not others. In that case, we may limit the change (called *scoping*) to only those it will benefit. While scoping is not possible with some changes (cases where all must share any changes), it can be utilized in some specific cases where a change can be segregated to only a set of users.

Risk analysis

Sometimes changes bring risk, and these risks must be identified. All changes should undergo a risk analysis process to identify such risks and any controls or countermeasures that can be implemented. The goal of such countermeasures may be either to reduce the risk to a level the organization is comfortable with or to eliminate it entirely.

Plan for change

Once a change has been approved, the timing of the change and its implementation must be carefully planned so as not to disrupt operations. Affected parties should be notified of the change and when it will occur. Any disruptions to service must be announced ahead of time so users can plan for doing without service for the planned period of downtime.

End-user acceptance

The change management board (discussed next) should include regular users so any proposed changes can be assessed for end-user acceptance. This can help to avoid widespread user dissatisfaction after the change.

Change board

The change management or change control board should contain a cross-section of representatives from the company. In this way each change can be assessed by each stakeholder group in the organization. The process should follow these steps:

1. All changes should be formally requested.
2. Each request should be analyzed to ensure that it supports all goals and polices.
3. Prior to formal approval, all costs and effects of the methods of implementation should be reviewed.

Approvals

After they're approved, the change steps should be developed.

Backout plan

During implementation, incremental testing should occur, relying on a predetermined fallback strategy if necessary.

Document changes

Complete documentation should be produced and submitted with a formal report to management.

Exam essentials

Describe the steps in change management.   These steps are as follows:

- All changes should be formally requested.
- Each request should be analyzed to ensure it supports all goals and polices.
- Prior to formal approval, all costs and effects of the methods of implementation should be reviewed.
- After they're approved, the change steps should be developed.
- During implementation, incremental testing should occur, relying on a predetermined fallback strategy if necessary.
- Complete documentation should be produced and submitted with a formal report to management.

4.3 Given a scenario, implement basic disaster prevention and recovery methods.

As an A+ technician you may be involved in planning and implementing measures that can reduce the likelihood or the impact of disasters both large and small. In this section, we'll cover disaster prevention and recovery. The topics include these:

- Backup and recovery
- Backup testing
- UPS
- Surge protector
- Cloud storage vs. local storage backups
- Account recovery options

Backup and recovery

Preventive maintenance is more than just manipulating hardware; it also encompasses running software utilities on a regular basis to keep the file system fit. These utilities can include scheduled backups, check disks, defragmentation, and updates.

Scheduled backups

Backups are duplicate copies of key information, ideally stored in a location other than the one where the information is currently stored. Backups include both paper and computer records. Computer records are usually backed up using a backup program, backup systems, and backup procedures.

The primary starting point for disaster recovery involves keeping current backup copies of key data files, databases, applications, and paper records available for use. Your organization must develop a solid set of procedures to manage this process and ensure that all key information is protected. A security professional can do several things in conjunction with systems administrators and business managers to protect this information. It's important to think of this problem as an issue that is larger than a single department.

The information you back up must be immediately available for use when needed. If a user loses a critical file, they won't want to wait several days while data files are sent from a remote storage facility. Several types of storage mechanisms are available for data storage.

Working Copies   *Working copy* backups—sometimes referred to as *shadow copies*—are partial or full backups that are kept on the premises for immediate recovery purposes. Working copies are frequently the most recent backups that have been made. Typically, working copies are intended for immediate use. These copies are often updated frequently.

Journaling   Many file systems used on servers include *journaling*. Journaled file systems (JFSs) include a log file of all changes and transactions that have occurred within a set period of time (such as the last few hours). If a crash occurs, the operating system can look at the log files to see which transactions have been committed and which ones haven't. This technology works well and allows unsaved data to be written after the recovery and the system (usually) to be successfully restored to its condition before the crash.

On-Site Storage   *On-site storage* usually refers to a location on the site of the computer center that is used to store information locally. On-site storage containers are available that allow computer cartridges, tapes, and other backup media to be stored in a reasonably protected environment in the building.

On-site storage containers are designed and rated for fire, moisture, and pressure resistance. These containers aren't *fireproof* in most situations, but they're *fire-rated*: A fireproof container should be guaranteed to withstand damage regardless of the type of fire or temperatures, whereas fire ratings specify that a container can protect the contents for a specific amount of time in a given situation.

If you choose to depend entirely on on-site storage, make sure the containers you acquire can withstand the worst-case environmental catastrophes that could happen at your location. Make sure as well that those containers are in locations where you can easily find them after the disaster and access them (near exterior walls, and so on).

Off-Site Storage   *Off-site storage* refers to a location away from the computer center where paper copies and backup media are kept. Off-site storage can involve something as simple as keeping a copy of backup media at a remote office, or it can be as complicated as a nuclear-hardened high-security storage facility. The storage facility should be bonded, insured, and inspected on a regular basis to ensure that all storage procedures are being followed.

Determining which storage mechanism to use should be based on the needs of the organization, the availability of storage facilities, and the budget available. Most off-site storage facilities charge based on the amount of space you require and the frequency of access you need to the stored information.

Image level

An image-level backup is also sometimes called a *bare-metal* backup. It is a backup in which the entire system is saved, including operating system, applications, configuration data, and files. It rapidly speeds up the recovery process because there is no need to reinstall the operating system and the applications or to configure the server again before restoring the data. It is called *bare metal* because this type of backup can be restored to a system with no operating system.

File level

Three methods exist to back up information on most systems.

Full Backup   A *full backup* is a complete, comprehensive backup of all files on a disk or server. The full backup is current only at the time it's performed. Once a full backup is made, you have a complete archive of the system at that point in time. A system shouldn't be in use while it undergoes a full backup, because some files may not get backed up. Once the system goes back into operation, the backup is no longer current. A full backup can be a time-consuming process on a large system.

Incremental Backup   An *incremental backup* is a partial backup that stores only the information that has been changed since the last full or incremental backup. If a full backup were performed on a Sunday night, an incremental backup done on Monday night would contain only the information that changed since Sunday night. Such a backup is typically considerably smaller than a full backup. This backup system requires that each incremental backup be retained until a full backup can be performed. Incremental backups are usually the fastest backups to perform on most systems, and each incremental tape is relatively small.

Differential Backup   A differential backup is similar in function to an incremental backup, but it backs up any files that have been altered since the last full backup. If a full backup was performed on Sunday night, a differential backup performed on Monday night would capture the information that was changed on Monday. A differential backup completed on Tuesday night would record the changes in any files from Monday and any changes in files on Tuesday. As you can see, during the week each differential backup would become larger; by Friday or Saturday night, it might be nearly as large as a full backup. This means the backups in the earliest part of the weekly cycle will be very fast, and each successive one will be slower.

When these backup methods are used in conjunction with each other, the risk of loss can be greatly reduced. You should never combine an incremental backup with a differential backup. One of the major factors in determining which combination of these three methods to use is time—ideally, a full backup would be performed every day. Several commercial backup programs support these three backup methods. You must evaluate your organizational needs when choosing which tools to use to accomplish backups.

Almost every stable operating system contains a utility for creating a copy of configuration settings necessary to reach the present state after a disaster. As an administrator, you must know how to do backups and be familiar with all the options available to you.

Critical applications

You can back up critical applications and their data either by utilizing an image backup (which would include operating system, applications, and application data) or by performing a file-level backup and ensuring that you have included the application data. The documentation that comes with the application should tell you the location of the data the application stores. Taking this approach will require reinstalling the application on a new machine to use the application data.

Backup testing

While many backup utilities offer a "verification process," nothing beats actually attempting to restore the data. While test restorations may not be appropriate after every backup, they should be done often to ensure that you have not been creating corrupt backups for days on end.

UPS

An *uninterruptible power supply* (UPS) is a solution to a number of power-related threats that can harm computers. Among them are the following:

Blackout   This is a complete failure of the power supplied.

Brownout   This is a drop in voltage lasting more than a few minutes.

Sag   This is a short-term voltage drop.

Spike   The opposite of a sag, this is a short (typically less than one second) increase in voltage that can do irreparable damage to equipment.

Surge   This is a long spike (sometimes lasting many seconds). Though a surge is typically a less intense increase in power, it can also damage equipment.

The two solutions to know for the power issues on the exam are battery backups and surge suppressors.

Battery backup

A battery backup, or UPS, keeps the system up and running when the normal power is removed (because of blackout, brownout, and so on). Even in installations that use generators to keep the systems running, battery backups are usually still used so they can keep the machines running while the generators come up to speed.

Most UPS units come with software that can be used to configure the actions to take when the battery backup is active. The software, for example, can be configured to shut down the connected devices when the battery begins to get low. Always ensure that the UPS provides the required voltage for all devices.

Surge protector

A surge suppressor keeps a spike from passing through it and onto the equipment that could be damaged. *Tripping* occurs when the breaker on a device such as a power supply, surge protector, or UPS turns off the device because it received a spike. If the device is a UPS, when the tripping happens, the components plugged in to the UPS should go to battery instead of pulling power through the line. Under most circumstances, the breaker is reset, and operations continue as normal. Figure 9.3 shows a surge-protector power strip, with the trip button to reset at the top.

FIGURE 9.3   The reset button on the top of a surge-protector power strip

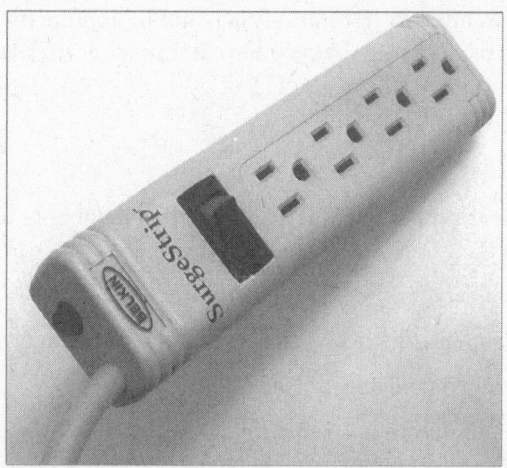

Nuisance tripping is the phrase used if tripping occurs often and isn't a result of a serious condition. If this continues, you should isolate the cause and correct it, even if it means replacing the device that continues to trip.

Surge suppressors (also known as *surge protectors)*, either stand-alone or built into the UPS, can help reduce the number of nuisance trips. If your UPS doesn't have a surge protector, you should add one to the outlet before the UPS to keep the UPS from being damaged if it receives a strong surge. Figure 9.4 shows an example of a simple surge protector for a home computer.

FIGURE 9.4   A simple surge protector

All units are rated by Underwriters Laboratories (UL) for performance. One thing you should never do is plug a UPS or computer equipment into a ground fault circuit interrupter (GFCI) receptacle. These receptacles are intended for use in wet areas, and they trip easily.

> **WARNING**   Don't confuse a GFCI receptacle with an isolated ground receptacle. Isolated ground receptacles are identifiable by orange outlets and should be used for computer equipment to avoid their picking up a surge passed to the ground by any other device.

Cloud storage vs. local storage backups

It is an option to store all backups in the cloud. The advantage is that you are protected against any disaster that destroys your local backup tapes. The disadvantage is that when you need the backups, if the cloud is your only option and you have no Internet access (a common occurrence during a natural disaster), you will be unable to access those backups until Internet access is restored. A more prudent approach may be a combination of both local and cloud storage.

Account recovery options

In rare cases users lose access to their accounts. If these accounts reside in your directory service such as Active Directory, you may be able to restore them using restoration procedures that are beyond the scope of this book. You can find more information here:

```
https://try.netwrix.com/active-directory-object-restore-bing?cID=7017
0000000lKo3&sID=5328154968&msclkid=5084e540b4e31609f880be847aba4cf2&
utm_source=bing&utm_medium=cpc&utm_campaign=US_EN_Paid_Search_Active_
Directory_Restore&utm_term=%2Brecover%20%2Bactive%20%2Bdirectory%20
%2Baccount&utm_content=Recover%20(deleted)%20ad%20account
```

If it is a Microsoft account, the recovery procedures can be found here:

https://support.microsoft.com/en-us/help/17875/microsoft-account-recover

Exam essentials

Describe power-related issues.   Among them are blackout (complete failure of the power supplied), brownout (a drop in voltage lasting more than a few minutes), sag (a short-term voltage drop), spike (the opposite of a sag, an increase in voltage typically less than second, which can do irreparable damage to equipment), and surge (a long spike, sometimes lasting many seconds, that although typically a less intense increase in power can also damage equipment).

List backup types.   Three methods exist to back up information on most systems: full, differential, and incremental. A full backup backs up everything. An incremental backup is a partial backup that stores only the information that has been changed since the last full or incremental backup. A differential backup is similar in function to an incremental backup, but it backs up any files that have been altered since the last full backup.

4.4 Explain common safety procedures.

This objective deals with potential hazards, both to you and to the computer system. It focuses on protecting humans from harm due to electricity and on protecting computer components from harm due to electrostatic discharge. The subobjectives included in this section are as follows:

- Equipment grounding
- Proper component handling and storage
- Toxic waste handling
- Personal safety
- Compliance with local government regulations

Equipment grounding

Electrostatic discharge (ESD) is one of the most dangerous risks associated with working with computers. Not only does ESD have the potential to damage components of the computer, but it can also injure you. Failing to understand the proper way to avoid it could cause you great harm.

The ESD that we are speaking about here does not have the capability to kill you since it doesn't have the amperage. What does represent a threat, though, is using a wrist strap of your own design that does not have the resistor protection built into it and then accidentally touching something with high voltage while wearing the wrist strap. Without the resistor in place, the high voltage would be grounded through you!

ESD is the technical term for what happens whenever two objects of dissimilar charge come in contact—think of rubbing your feet on a carpet and then touching a light switch. The two objects exchange electrons to equalize the electrostatic charge between them. If the device receiving the charge happens to be an electronic component, there is a good chance it can be damaged.

The likelihood that a component will be damaged increases with the use of complementary metal-oxide semiconductor (CMOS) chips because these chips contain a thin metal-oxide layer that is hypersensitive to ESD. The previous generation's transistor–transistor logic (TTL) chips are more robust than the CMOS chips because they don't contain this metal-oxide layer. Most of today's integrated circuits (ICs) are CMOS chips, so ESD is more of a concern lately.

The lowest static voltage transfer that you can feel is around 3,000 volts (it doesn't electrocute you because there is extremely little current). A static transfer that you can *see* is at least 10,000 volts! Just by sitting in a chair, you can generate around 100 volts of static electricity. Walking around wearing synthetic materials can generate around 1,000 volts. You can easily generate around 20,000 volts simply by dragging your smooth-soled shoes across a carpet in the winter. (Actually, it doesn't have to be winter to run this danger; it can occur in any room with very low humidity. It's just that heated rooms in wintertime generally have very low humidity.)

It would make sense that these thousands of volts would damage computer components. However, a component can be damaged with as little as 80 volts. That means if your body has a small charge built up in it, you could damage a component without even realizing it.

Just as you can ground yourself by using a grounding strap, you can ground equipment. This is most often accomplished by using a mat or a connection directly to a ground.

Proper component handling and storage

When handling computer components, such as motherboards, network cards, and such, it is easy to damage the delicate circuitry with the static electricity that builds up in your body in certain environments. In this section, we'll talk about how you can protect these components and how you should store them when not in use.

Antistatic bags

When working with components and when storing them, it is a good idea to store them in antistatic bags. Although you can buy these bags, replacement parts usually come in antistatic bags, and if you keep these bags, you can use them later. These bags also can serve as a safe place to lay a component temporarily while working on a device.

ESD straps

There are measures you can implement to help contain the effects of ESD. The easiest one to implement is the *antistatic wrist strap*, also referred to as an *ESD strap*. You attach one end of the ESD strap to an earth ground (typically the ground pin on an extension cord), or to the metal case, and wrap the other end around your wrist. This strap grounds your body and keeps it at a zero charge. Figure 9.5 shows the proper way to attach an antistatic strap.

FIGURE 9.5   Proper ESD strap connection

If you do not have a grounded outlet available, you can achieve partial benefit simply by attaching the strap to the metal frame of the PC case. Doing so keeps the charge equalized between your body and the case so that there is no electrostatic discharge when you touch components inside the case.

 An ESD strap is a specially designed device to bleed electrical charges away *safely*. It uses a 1 megaohm resistor to bleed the charge away slowly. A simple wire wrapped around your wrist will not work correctly and could electrocute you!

 Do not wear the antistatic wrist strap when there is the potential to encounter a high-voltage capacitor, such as when working on the inside of a monitor or power supply. The strap could channel that voltage through your body.

ESD mats

It is possible to damage a device simply by laying it on a bench top. For this reason, you should have an *ESD mat* (also known as an *antistatic mat*) in addition to an ESD strap. This mat drains excess charge away from any item coming in contact with it (see Figure 9.6). ESD mats are also sold as mouse/keyboard pads to prevent ESD charges from interfering with the operation of the computer.

FIGURE 9.6　Proper use of an ESD mat

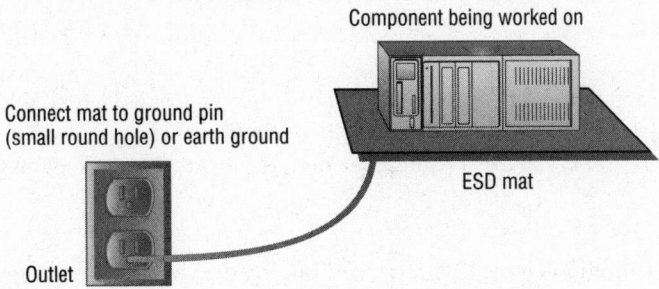

You can also purchase ESD floor mats for technicians to stand on while performing computer maintenance. These include a grounding cord, usually 6 to 10 feet in length.

Vendors have methods of protecting components in transit from manufacture to installation. They press the pins of ICs into antistatic foam to keep all the pins at the same potential, and circuit boards are shipped in antistatic bags, discussed earlier. However, keep in mind that unlike antistatic mats, antistatic bags do not drain the charges away—they should never be used in place of antistatic mats.

Self-grounding

Grounding is the electrical term for providing a path for an electrical charge to follow to return to earth. This term was mentioned earlier as it relates to ESD straps and mats, but it is the element of those that saves you from harm in the event of an electrical discharge—the charge passes to ground. The easiest way to ground yourself is to use a grounding strap.

Toxic waste handling

Many of the components in a computer should not simply be thrown in the trash because they contain toxic materials. In this section, you'll learn about proper handling and disposal of these components and materials.

Batteries

Batteries can contain a number of compounds and materials that should not make their way into landfills. The following are some examples:

- Rare earth metals
- Lead
- Cadmium
- Lithium
- Alkaline manganese
- Mercury

You should make battery recycling a standard procedure and follow local regulations for battery disposal when the time comes to dispose of the batteries.

Toner

Toner cartridges are another item that should not be thrown away. They should be recycled. Moreover, in any case where toner has been spilled you should clean up with a special vacuum made for that purpose. If you use a regular vacuum, the metal toner will damage the vacuum.

CRT

While most CRT monitors have been disposed of already, you may find yourself with a number of them that you need to get rid of. These cannot be thrown in the trash. The contents of the device are under pressure, and if something breaks the glass screen, there will be glass and other materials sprayed out with a force that could injure someone.

The monitor uses a lot of power as it directs electrons on the screen via a strong magnet. The electrons and magnet require a considerable amount of voltage to be able to do their task. Like power supplies, monitors have the ability to hold their charge a long time after the power has been disconnected.

You should never open a power supply or a monitor for the reasons discussed here. The risk of electrocution with these two devices is significant.

If you are not sure whether electricity is present, or its voltage, use a voltmeter. Figure 9.7 shows a simple voltmeter capable of working with both AC and DC currents.

FIGURE 9.7   A simple voltmeter

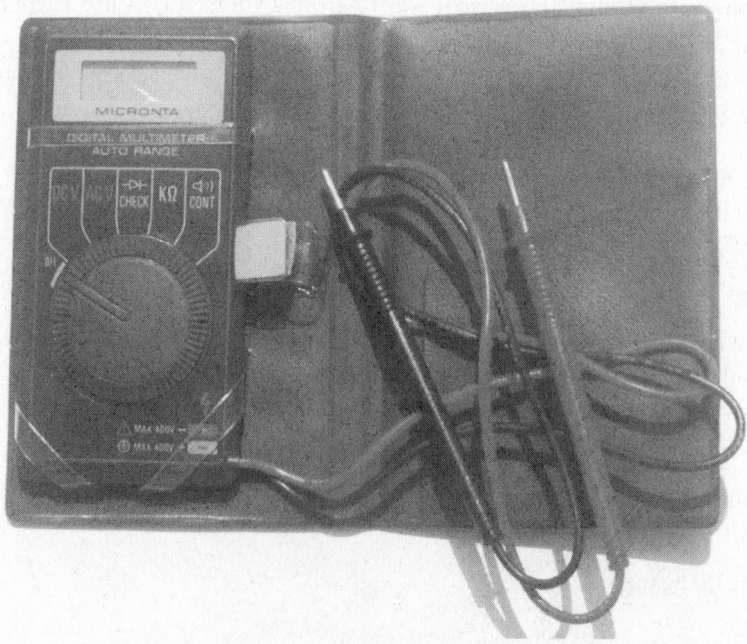

Many states have laws that govern the disposal of monitors since they are often classified as hazardous. CRT monitors contain high amounts of lead and other harmful materials such as arsenic, beryllium, cadmium, chromium, mercury, nickel, and zinc. To dispose of a monitor, contact a computer recycling firm and let them get rid of the monitor for you. CRT monitors must be disposed of according to the environmental regulations.

Cell phones

Cell phones should not be thrown away, as they contain many of the same compounds found in laptops and desktops. Since the majority of the time the device is still perfectly functional (the user simply wanted a new phone), it should be sold or donated so that someone else can make use of the phone.

Tablets

Treat tablets in the same way you would cell phones and either sell, recycle, or donate.

Personal safety

There is nothing on a computer, a server, a router, and so on, that cannot be replaced or repaired. The same, however, is not true for you. It is imperative that you protect yourself from harm and follow safety procedures when working with computers.

Disconnect power before repairing PC

You should never attempt to remove a case, open a case, or work on any element that is carrying electricity without first disconnecting it. If removing power to the device you are working on is more complicated than just unplugging it (requiring circuit breakers to be thrown, fuses to be removed, and so forth), then use a voltmeter to make sure the current is off at the device before proceeding.

Remove jewelry

Gold and other metals are great conductors of electrical current. The last thing you want while working on a problem is for the gold chain around your neck to fall against a capacitor. Take it off. While not all jewelry is metallic, all jewelry is a snagging hazard.

Lifting techniques

An easy way to get hurt is by moving equipment in an unsafe or improper way. Here are some safe lifting techniques to always keep in mind:

- Lift with your legs, not your back. When you have to pick something up, bend at the knees, not at the waist. You want to maintain the natural curve of the back and spine when lifting.
- Be careful to not twist when lifting. Keep the weight on your centerline.
- Keep objects as close to your body as possible and at waist level.
- Where possible, push instead of pull.

The goal in lifting should be to reduce the strain on lower back muscles as much as possible, since muscles in the lower back aren't nearly as strong as those in the legs or other parts of the body. Some people use a back belt or brace to help maintain the proper position while lifting.

Weight limitations

Closely related to lifting and moving equipment is the topic of weight limitations. If you believe the load is too much for you to carry, don't try to pick it up. Get help!

When possible, use a cart and always be aware of the environment. While you may be able to carry 80 pounds on a level surface without trouble, that amount will lessen if there are stairs, uneven floors, or narrow doorways. Map out the path you are going to take before you begin lifting and moving items.

Electrical fire safety

Repairing a computer is not often the cause of an electrical fire. However, you should know how to extinguish such a fire properly. Three major classes of fire extinguishers are available, one for each type of flammable substance: A for wood and paper fires, B for flammable liquids, and C for electrical fires. The most popular type of fire extinguisher today is the multipurpose, or ABC-rated, extinguisher. It contains a dry chemical powder that smothers the fire and cools it at the same time. For electrical fires (which may be related to a shorted-out wire in a power supply), make sure the fire extinguisher will work for class C fires. If you don't have an extinguisher that is specifically rated for electrical fires (type C), you can use an ABC-rated extinguisher.

Cable management

It can be time-consuming to tie up cables, run them in channels, and snake them through walls, but it is time well spent when it keeps one person from harm. It is all too easy to get tangled in a cable or trip over one that is run across the floor. Exposed cables should be routed properly and covered using cable-throughs and pass-throughs to reduce the likelihood of tripping as well as damage to the cables themselves.

Take the extra time to manage cables, and it will increase your safety as well as that of others who work in that environment.

Safety goggles

In any environment where you may get dust or harmful materials in your eyes, you should wear safety goggles. For example, when working in a dusty shop area where a computer is located, this might be advisable. Another example might be when you are cleaning up printer toner.

There are also safety glasses that can be used when spending long hours staring at a computer screen that will reduce the eye strain that comes with this type of activity.

Air filter mask

While safety goggles will protect your eyes from dust and other harmful particulates, they will do nothing to protect your lungs. Air filter masks should always be available, and technicians should be encouraged to wear them in any situation where safety goggles are called for or in any scenario where you have reason to believe that the surrounding air may contain harmful compounds.

Compliance with government regulations

It is your responsibility, as an administrator and a professional, to know (or learn) the regulations that exist for dealing with safety. You should know them from the local level to the federal level and be familiar with the reporting procedures for incidents you are faced with. For more information, see the section "Regulatory and compliance policy" earlier in this chapter.

Exam essentials

Understand ESD.   Electrostatic discharge occurs when two objects of unequal electrical potential meet. One object transfers some charge to the other one, just as water flows into an area that has a lower water level.

Understand the antistatic wrist strap.   The antistatic wrist strap is also referred to as an ESD strap. To use the ESD strap, you attach one end to an earth ground (typically the ground pin on an extension cord) and wrap the other end around your wrist. This strap grounds your body and keeps it at a zero charge, preventing discharges from damaging the components of a PC.

4.5 Explain environmental impacts and appropriate controls.

Environmental harm can come from many sources. Not only are temperature and humidity elements that must be controlled, but administrators also need to carefully monitor power, air, and particulates that can harm humans and computers. Not understanding environmental impact and controls can cause great harm. The following are the subobjectives covered in this section:

- MSDS documentation for handling and disposal
- Temperature, humidity-level awareness, and proper ventilation

- Power surges, brownouts, blackouts
- Protection from airborne particles
- Dust and debris
- Compliance with government regulations

MSDS documentation for handling and disposal

It is important that you know the potential safety hazards that exist when working with computer elements and how to address them. It is imperative that you understand such issues as *material safety data sheets* (MSDSs) and know how to reference them when needed. Any type of chemical, equipment, or supply that has the potential to harm the environment or people has to have an MSDS associated with it. These are traditionally created by the manufacturer, and you can obtain them from the manufacturer or from the Environmental Protection Agency at www.epa.gov.

These sheets are not intended for consumer use but are aimed at emergency workers and employees who are exposed to the risks of the particular product. Among the information they include are such things as boiling point, melting point, flash point, and potential health risks. They also cover storage and disposal recommendations and the procedures to follow in the case of a spill or leak.

Temperature, humidity level awareness, and proper ventilation

Three items closely related to an environmentally friendly computing environment are temperature, humidity, and ventilation. We will cover the most important elements with all three.

Temperature   Heat and computers don't mix well. Many computer systems require both temperature and humidity control for reliable service. The larger servers, communications equipment, and drive arrays generate considerable amounts of heat; this is especially true of mainframe and older minicomputers. An environmental system for this type of equipment is a significant expense beyond the actual computer system costs. Fortunately, newer systems operate in a wider temperature range. Most new systems are designed to operate in an office environment.

If the computer systems you're responsible for require special environmental considerations, you'll need to establish cooling and humidity control. Ideally, systems are located in the middle of the building, and they're ducted separately from the rest of the heating, ventilation, and air conditioning (HVAC) system. It's a common practice for modern buildings to use a zone-based air conditioning environment, which allows the environmental plant to be turned off when the building isn't occupied. A computer room will typically require full-time environmental control.

Humidity Level   Another preventive measure you can take is to maintain the relative humidity at around 50 percent. Be careful not to increase the humidity too far—to the point where moisture starts to condense on the equipment! It is a balancing act keeping humidity at the right level since low humidity causes ESD and high humidity causes moisture condensation. Both extremes are bad but have completely different effects.

Also, use antistatic spray, which is available commercially, to reduce static buildup on clothing and carpets. In a pinch, a solution of diluted fabric softener sprayed on these items will do the same thing.

At the least, you can be mindful of the dangers of ESD and take steps to reduce its effects. Beyond that, you should educate yourself about those effects so you know when ESD is becoming a major problem.

Ventilation   Rounding out temperature and humidity is ventilation. It is important that air—clean air—circulate around computer equipment to keep it cool and functioning properly. Server rooms require much more attention to ventilation than office spaces but are the subject of other exams (Server+, for example) and not test fodder for A+.

What is test fodder is the topic of ventilation within the computer itself—an inadequate flow of internal air within a computer is a common cause of overheating. To prevent this, know that all slot covers should remain in place and be replaced if a card is removed from the system. Know as well that internal fans should be periodically cleaned to ensure proper air flow. A missing slot cover or malfunctioning fan can lead to inadequate flow of internal air.

Power surges, brownouts, and blackouts

A number of power-related threats can harm computers. For more information, see the section "UPS" earlier in this chapter.

Battery backup

Battery backups were covered in the section "UPS" earlier in this chapter.

Surge suppressor

Surge suppressors were covered in the section "UPS" earlier in this chapter.

Protection from airborne particles

Computers don't do well with airborne particles. To protect them from such, you can use *enclosures* for your sensitive equipment and *air filters* to condition the air.

Enclosures

Enclosures can be considered the first line of defense against particulates. Enclosures are available that can filter the air, keep air out, and so on. Make certain that the enclosure you turn to for a solution still offers the necessary ventilation needed to prevent overheating.

Air filters

Most enclosures incorporate an air filter to clean the air before allowing it to enter. An analogy to think of is the air filter on a car, which keeps dirt, dust, bugs, and other things from the intake. When working with air filters, make certain they are kept clean and are changed per the manufacturer's requirements.

Dust and debris

One of the most harmful atmospheric hazards to a computer is dust. Dust, dirt, hair, and other airborne contaminants can get pulled into computers and build up inside. Because computer fans work by pulling air through the computer (usually sucking it in through the case and then pushing it out the power supply), it's easy for these items to enter and then become stuck. Every item in the computer builds up heat, and these particles are no exception. As they build up, they hinder the fan's ability to perform its function, and the components get hotter than they would otherwise. Figure 9.8 shows the inside of a system in use for only six months in an area with carpeting and other dusty surroundings.

FIGURE 9.8   Dust builds up inside the system.

Compressed air

You can remove dust and debris from inside computers with *compressed air* blown in short bursts. The short bursts are useful in preventing the dust from flying too far out and entering another machine, as well as in preventing the can from releasing the air in liquid form. Compressed air cans should be held 2–3 inches from the system and always used upright so the content is released as a gas. If the can becomes cold to the touch, discontinue using it until it heats back to room temperature.

 **WARNING** It's possible to use an air compressor instead of compressed-air cans when you need a lot of air. If you take this approach, make sure you keep the pounds per square inch (PSI) at or below 40, and include measures on the air compressor to remove moisture.

Vacuums

Dust can build up not just within the computer but also in crevices on the outside. Figure 9.9 shows USB ports on the back of a system that have become a haven for small dust particles. These ports need to be blown out with compressed air, or cleaned with an electronic *vacuum*, before being used, or degradation with the device connected to them could occur.

FIGURE 9.9   Dust collects in unused ports as well.

Compliance to government regulations

As careful as you try to be, there is always the possibility for accidents to occur. Accidents can be environment-related (for example, a flash flood no one could predict suddenly overtakes the server room and shorts out the wiring) or caused by humans (someone mixes the wrong cleaning chemicals together to try to make their own concoction). Regardless of the cause or circumstances, one thing is written in stone: You must fully and truthfully document the problem.

That documentation must be seen by internal parties (managers, human resources, and so on), and it may also need to be seen by external parties. The latter depends on the type of industry you are in and the type of incident that occurred. For example, if a large amount of battery acid is spilled on the ground, you should contact the Environmental Protection Agency (see reporting procedures at www.epa.gov). Always understand any hazards that come with the industry you work in and make sure that the proper reporting procedures are followed or OSHA, EPA, or other governmental entity may fine the company.

Exam essentials

Know what an MSDS is.   An MSDS is a material safety data sheet containing instructions for handling an item. It can be acquired from the manufacturer or from the EPA.

Know that you may need to report incidents.   When incidents happen, you must always document them, and every attempt should be made to do so both fully and truthfully. Depending on the type of incident, you may also need to report it to other authorities, such as the EPA.

Know what components are not suitable for a landfill.   Batteries, CRTs, and circuit boards are all examples of items that should not be thrown away normally because of the elements used in them. Batteries contain metals such as lead and nickel, circuit boards contain lead solder, and CRTs contain phosphors.

Know the safety procedures to follow when working with computers.   Be careful when moving computers or working around any electrical components. Know that liquids and computers don't mix, and keep the systems as clean and dust-free as possible to ensure optimal operation.

4.6 Explain the processes for addressing prohibited content/activity, and privacy, licensing, and policy concepts.

Working in the IT profession, it is entirely plausible that you will encounter a situation where you find proof of a user, or a number of users, engaging in activities that are prohibited. Those activities can include any number of things, and the prohibition may range from a company policy (you cannot use social media during working hours) all the way up to a federal law (you cannot traffic in child pornography). You have an obligation to respond appropriately and accordingly.

Regardless of whether you agree with a prohibition, when you encounter instances wherein activities are in violation of it, you must respond in a professional and legal manner. The following are the subobjectives covered in this section:

- Incident response
- Licensing/DRM/EULA
- Regulated data
- Follow all policies and security best practices

Incident response

The extent to which a security event causes harm to your network largely depends on the speed and quality of your response to the incident. By following a structured incident response policy, you greatly enhance the chances of minimizing the damage and the likelihood that you will be able to bring parties to justice in the case of illegal activity. The following sections cover some important guidelines regarding the incident response process.

First response

There are three crucial components to the first response: identifying the problem, reporting it through the proper channels, and preserving the data.

Identify

A part of identifying the problem involves identifying what policy or law prohibits such an action. Prohibited content generally falls within the following categories (this list should not be considered to represent everything prohibited, because many companies have other policies):

- Exploiting people (in any way, such as sexually, violently, and so on)
- Promoting harassment of any person or group
- Containing or promoting anything illegal or unauthorized
- Promoting racism, hatred, bigotry, or physical harm
- Containing adult content involving nudity or sexual acts
- Violating privacy rights, copyrights, contract rights, or defamation rights
- Viruses or malware of any sort
- Impersonation
- Soliciting information from anyone younger than 18
- Involving pyramid schemes, junk mail, chain letters, spamming, or the like

Report through proper channels

Once you have identified prohibited content or activity, you must report it through the proper channels. If the violation is one only of company policy, then usually the company's human resources department is the proper channel. If the violation is of a law, then often you must contact legal authorities—notifying the appropriate internal resources as well. If the violation is of a federal law and you tell only an internal resource (HR manager, for example), it does not absolve you of the responsibility if that person does not continue to report it up the appropriate chain.

 Law enforcement personnel are governed by the rules of evidence, and their response to an incident will be largely out of your control. You need to carefully consider involving law enforcement before you begin. There is no such thing as dropping charges. Once they begin, law enforcement professionals are required to pursue an investigation.

Data/device preservation

You have as well an obligation to preserve the content found until it is turned over to the appropriate authority. Doing so may require commandeering anything from a flash drive up to a network server. Until someone in a position of authority relieves you of the responsibility, you must preserve the data or device in the state in which you discovered it. If you are ever unsure of how to proceed, you should immediately contact your supervisor.

Because knowing what to do when something is discovered is something that may not come naturally, it is a good idea to include the procedures you'll generally follow in an *incident response plan* (IRP). The IRP outlines what steps are needed and who is responsible for deciding how to handle a situation.

 Your policies should clearly outline who needs to be informed in the company, what they need to be told, and how to respond to the situation.

Use of documentation/documentation changes

During the entire process, you should document the steps you take to identify, detect, and report the problem. This information is valuable and will often be used should the problem escalate to a court of law. Many help-desk software systems provide detailed methods you can use to record procedures and steps.

Chain of custody

An important concept to keep in mind when working with incidents is the *chain of custody*.

Tracking of evidence/documenting process

When you begin to collect evidence, you must keep track of that evidence at all times and show who has it, who has seen it, and where it has been, known as the *chain of custody*. The evidence must always be within your custody, or you're open to dispute about whether it has been tampered with.

Licensing/DRM/EULA

While many in the IT community would like to think that software, music files, and movie files should be free, that is not the case. Using any of these items without paying for them is *illegal*. Operating systems, application software, and many third-party utilities require a license to legally use the software. It also requires that you accept an end-user license agreement (EULA) whereby you agree to use the software as described in that agreement.

Music and movie files, on the other hand, are protected by digital rights management (DRM). This is a system that maintains control over these files and ensures that they are installed only on devices that belong to the person who purchased the file, with the end goal being to prevent users from sharing and giving these files away without paying for them.

Not all software requires a license. In the next sections, we'll talk about software that doesn't require a license and also discuss the differences between personal and enterprise licenses.

Open-source vs. commercial license

Open source software is software that is free and available to all. Commercial software, on the other hand, requires the purchase of a license to legally use the software. While there is the obvious monetary advantage to using open source software, the organization or user must typically have a deeper understanding of the software than may be required to use commercial software successfully. Another advantage of commercial software is the ongoing support the vendor can provide in using the software, while a user of open source software is pretty much on their own when issues arise. The good news is that open source software has large, active user communities, though it may be that their information can't be as authoritative as manufacturer support.

Personal license vs. enterprise licenses

While an individual software license entitles a single user to install and use a piece of commercial software, an enterprise license purchase is based on a number of seats or devices on which the software can be legally installed. Also, while each individual license will come with installation media, the purchase of an enterprise license comes with a single version of the installation media, which can be installed on the number of devices specified in the license agreement.

Regulated data

Some data types require special attention because they are regulated. This means their proper handling is specified by regulation. In this section we'll look at some of these types of data.

PII

Personally identifiable information (PII) is any piece of information about a user that can be used alone or in combination with other pieces of information to identify an individual user. While it is the responsibility of all organizations to protect PII that they may possess, it is especially important in certain regulated industries such as healthcare and finance.

The danger of leaking PII is that much of this information, such as address, Social Security number, and place of employment can be used to perform identity theft, a growing concern worldwide.

PCI

PCI-DSS v3.2, developed in April 2015, is the latest version of the PCI-DSS standard as of this writing. It encourages and enhances cardholder data security and facilitates the broad adoption of consistent data security measures globally.

GDPR

Beginning on May 25, 2018, the members of the EU began applying the General Data Protection Regulation (GDPR). The GDPR applies to EU-based organizations that collect or process the personal data of EU residents and to organizations outside the EU that monitor behavior or offer goods and services to EU residents. It gives a wider definition of personal and sensitive data to include online identifiers and genetic and biometrics data, such as cookies, IP address, health information, biometric data, and genetic information. The GDPR affects service providers that process personal data on behalf of an organization, including cloud services, call centers, and payroll services. It strengthens individual privacy rights.

PHI

Protected health information (PHI), also referred to as *electronic protected health information* (EPHI or ePHI), is any individually identifiable health information. NIST SP 800-66 provides guidelines for implementing the Health Insurance Portability and Accountability Act (HIPAA) Security Rule.

Follow all policies and security best practices

Every organization should have a security policy that drives all security-related activities and clearly spells out how sensitive data is handled and what specific operations the users are allowed to perform. The acceptable use policy is a document that each user should sign when hired and serves as a contract between the user and the company in detail. Moreover, this document, as well as the security guidelines that network technicians must follow, should be driven by well-established best practices. The following are some of the guidelines that should be included:

- Password policy
- Acceptable use policy
- Access control policy
- Remote access policy

   Part of your job is to educate users about the importance of these security policies and to monitor the environments for any violations of the policies.

Exam essentials

Report prohibited content and activities.   You have an obligation to report prohibited activities and content to the appropriate authorities when you uncover them. You must ascertain which authority is prohibiting the actions and notify them.

Document and preserve the evidence.   It is imperative that the evidence be documented and preserved until turned over to the appropriate authority. In some cases, this can include commandeering a removable drive, a computer, or even a server. Failure to do so can leave you facing fines and other punishments.

4.7 Given a scenario, use proper communication techniques and professionalism.

It's possible that you chose computers as your vocation instead of public speaking because you want to interact with people on a one-on-one basis. As unlikely as that possibility may be, it still exists.

Some have marveled at the fact that CompTIA includes questions about customer service on the A+ exam. A better wonder, however, is that there are those in the business who need to know these items and don't. Possessing a great deal of technology skill does not immediately endow one with great people skills. A bit more on appropriate behavior as it relates to the IT field follows. The following are the subobjectives covered in this section:

- Use proper language and avoid jargon, acronyms, and slang when applicable
- Maintain a positive attitude/project confidence
- Actively listen (taking notes) and avoid interrupting the customer
- Be culturally sensitive
- Be on time (if late, contact the customer)
- Avoid distractions
- Dealing with difficult customers or situations
- Set and meet expectations/timelines and communicate status with the customer
- Deal appropriately with customers' confidential and private materials

Use proper language and avoid jargon, acronyms, and slang, when applicable

Avoid using jargon, abbreviations, slang, and acronyms. Every field has its own language that can make those from outside the field feel lost. Put yourself in the position of someone not in the field, and explain what is going on using words they can relate to.

Be honest and fair with the customer, whoever that is, and try to establish a personal rapport. Tell them what the problem is, what you believe is the cause, and what can be done in the future to prevent it from recurring.

Alert your supervisor if there is a communication barrier with the customer (for example, the customer is deaf or does not speak the same language as you do). This is particularly important if the barrier will affect the problem resolution or the amount of time it will take.

If you're providing phone support, do the following:

- Always answer the telephone in a professional manner, announcing the name of the company and yourself.

- Make a concentrated effort to ascertain the customer's technical level, and communicate at that level, not above or below it.

Maintain a positive attitude/project confidence

Maintain a positive attitude. Your approach to the problem, and the customer, can be mirrored back. Moreover, project confidence in dealing with the issue because that engenders more cooperation and patience from the customer, both of which have a direct impact on the success of your troubleshooting efforts.

Actively listen (taking notes) and avoid interrupting the customer

Good communication includes listening to what the user, manager, or developer is telling you and making certain that you understand completely what they are trying to say. Just because a user or customer doesn't understand the terminology, syntax, or concepts that you do doesn't mean they don't have a real problem that needs addressing. You must, therefore, be skilled not only at listening but also at translating. Professional conduct encompasses politeness, guidance, punctuality, and accountability. Always treat the customer with the same respect and empathy you would expect if the situation were reversed. Likewise, guide the customer through the problem and the explanation. Tell them what has caused the problem they're currently experiencing and offer the best solution to prevent it from recurring.

Listen intently to what your customer is saying. Make it obvious to them that you're listening and respecting what they're telling you. If you have a problem understanding them, go to whatever lengths you need to in order to remedy the situation. Look for verbal and nonverbal cues that can help you isolate the problem. Avoid interrupting the customer because that telegraphs that what he has to say is not important enough to listen to.

Be culturally sensitive

It is important as well to be culturally sensitive—not everyone enjoys the same humor. Moreover, be mindful of the difference in the way business is conducted in different cultures and be flexible in your approach based on this. When you sense that the customer prefers a more formal relationship with you, try to reflect that in your approach.

Use appropriate professional titles, when applicable

While many folks are not put off at all when you address them by their first name, in many cultures it is considered rude to do so, and you should also address the customer using the appropriate title when applicable. Not all cultures are as informal as what you may have become accustomed to. Again, sensitivity to the customer's approach to you can be a valuable clue to how the customer would prefer to interact with you.

Be on time (if late, contact the customer)

Punctuality is important and should be part of your planning process before you ever arrive at the site. If you tell the customer you'll be there at 10:30, you need to make every attempt to be there at that time. If you arrive late, you have given them false hope that the problem would be solved by a set time. That false hope can lead to anger when you arrive late and appear to not be taking their problem as seriously as they are. Punctuality continues to be important throughout the service call and doesn't end with your arrival. If you need to leave to get parts, tell the customer when you'll be back, and then be there at that time. If for some reason you can't return at the expected time, alert the customer and inform them of your new return time.

In conjunction with time and punctuality, if a user asks how much longer the server will be down and you respond that it will up in five minutes only to have it remain down for five more hours, you're creating resentment and possibly anger. When estimating downtime, always allow for more time than you think you'll need, just in case other problems occur. If you greatly underestimate the time, always inform the affected parties and give them a new time estimate. Here's an analogy that will put it in perspective: If you take your car to get the oil changed and the counter clerk tells you it will be "about 15 minutes," the last thing you want is to be sitting there 4 hours later.

Avoid distractions

It is important that you avoid distractions while working on a customer's or user's problem. Those distractions can come in the form of personal calls, talking to co-workers, or personal interruptions.

If you arrive at the site to troubleshoot a problem and there are distractions there of the customer's making (children present, TV on, and so on), you should politely ask the customer to remove the distractions if possible. If the area you will be working in is cluttered with personal items (mementos from the state fair, stuffed animals, and so on), ask the customer to relocate the items as needed or ask them if it is OK to do so before you relocate the items.

Personal calls

Taking personal calls while working with a customer can make the customer feel as if their problem is being minimized. Spend time solving the problem and interacting with the customer and then attend to the personal calls when you leave.

If you are anticipating an important call that cannot be avoided, let the customer know beforehand so they will understand that this interruption is coming.

Texting/social media sites

Keep in mind that when you are supporting a customer, you are working on their time and not your own. You are also using their equipment, not your own. Consequently, avoid any use of the customer's equipment or time for personal texts or visits to social media sites. It is allowable to use the time and the equipment for legitimate research or other activities that are directly related to solving the customer's issues.

Talking to co-workers while interacting with customers

Just as taking personal calls can seem to minimize the importance of interacting with the customer, so too can talking to co-workers. The customer needs to be the focus of your attention until their problems have been addressed, and then you can attend to other matters.

If you must contact someone else while troubleshooting, always ask the customer's permission.

Personal interruptions

The broad category of personal interruptions includes anything that takes you away from focusing on the customer and is not job-related. Spend your time dealing with the customer first and solving their problems before attending to personal issues.

Dealing with difficult customers or situations

Handle complaints as professionally as possible. Accept responsibility for errors that may have occurred on your part, and never try to pass the blame. Remember, the goal is to keep them as a customer, not to win an argument.

Do not argue with customers and/or be defensive

Avoid arguing with a customer, because doing so serves no purpose; resolve their anger with as little conflict as possible. Moreover, don't be defensive when the customer questions your approach and thought process. While they may clueless about troubleshooting, they deserve to understand why you are doing what you are doing.

Avoid dismissing customer's problems

Just as personal calls and interruptions can make it seem as if you are not taking the customer seriously enough, so too can dismissing their problems as less important than they believe they are. It is important to put yourself in their shoes and see the issue from their perspective. What may seem trivial to you may be a vital issue for them.

Avoid being judgmental

It is important not to minimize their problem or appear to be judgmental.

Clarify customer statements (ask open-ended questions to narrow the scope of the problem, restate the issue, or question to verify understanding)

The most important skill you can have is the ability to listen. You have to rely on the customer to tell you the problem and describe it accurately. They can't do that if you're second-guessing them or jumping to conclusions before the whole story is told. Ask questions that are broad and open-ended at first and then narrow them down to help isolate the problem. This is particularly necessary when you are trying to solve the problem remotely. For example, start with questions like these:

- What were you doing before the problem occurred?
- What application were you using when the problem occurred?

It's also your job to help guide the user's description of the problem. Here are some examples:

- Is the printer plugged in?
- Is it online?
- Are any lights flashing on it?

Restate the issue to the customer to make sure that you correctly understand what they are telling you (for example, "There is only one green light lit, correct?"). Ask questions as needed that verify your understanding of the problem. The questions you ask should help guide you toward isolating the problem and identifying possible solutions.

Do not disclose experiences via social media outlets

Although it might make you feel better about a particularly trying experience with a customer to vent about it on social media, don't do that. Not only is it remotely possible that the post may somehow find its way to the attention of the customer, it reflects poorly on you as someone who shares his business dealings with the world.

Set and meet expectations/timeline and communicate status with the customer

Customer satisfaction goes a long way toward generating repeat business. If you can *meet* the customer's expectations, you'll almost assuredly hear from them again when another problem arises. If you can *exceed* the customer's expectations, you can almost guarantee that they will call you the next time a problem arises.

Customer satisfaction is important in all communication media—whether you're on-site, providing phone support, or communicating through email or other correspondence.

Share the customer's sense of urgency. What may seem like a small problem to you can appear to the customer as if the whole world is collapsing around them.

Offer different repair/replacement options if applicable

If there are multiple solutions to the problem the customer is encountering, offer options to them. Those options often include repairing what they already have or replacing it. If the repair could lead to a recurrence of the situation but the replacement will not, then that should be explained to them clearly.

The ramifications of each choice should be clearly explained along with costs (estimates, if necessary) so they can make the decision they deem in their best interest.

If you are unable to resolve the issue, explain to the customer what to do and make sure to follow up properly to forward the issue to appropriate personnel.

Provide proper documentation on the services provided

Document the services you provided so there is no misunderstanding on the part of the customer. Supply them with the documentation and keep a copy handy to refer to should any questions arise. Explain clearly the cause of the problem and how to avoid it in the future.

It is important that the documentation be complete so that if you do not refer to it for quite some time (years), you will still be able to understand and explain what was done.

Follow up with customer/user at a later date to verify satisfaction

When you finish a job, notify the user you're done. Make every attempt to find the user and inform them of the resolution. If it's difficult to find them, leave a note for them to find when they return, explaining the resolution. You should also leave a means by which they can contact you, should they have a question about the resolution or a related problem. In most cases, the number you leave should be that of your business during working hours and your pager, where applicable, after hours.

If you do not hear back from the customer, follow up with them at a later date to verify that the problem is resolved and they are satisfied with the outcome. One of the best ways to keep customers is to let them know that you care about their success and satisfaction.

Deal appropriately with customers' confidential and private materials

The goal of *confidentiality* is to prevent or minimize unauthorized access to files and folders and disclosure of data and information. In many instances, laws and regulations require specific information confidentiality. For example, Social Security records, payroll and employee records, medical records, and corporate information are high-value assets. This information could create liability issues or embarrassment if it fell into the wrong hands. Over the last few years, there have been several cases in which bank account and credit card numbers were published on the Internet. The costs of these types of breaches of confidentiality far exceed the actual losses from the misuse of this information.

Confidentiality entails ensuring that data expected to remain private is seen only by those who should see it. Confidentiality is implemented through authentication and access controls.

Just as confidentiality issues are addressed early in the design phase of a project, you as a computer professional are expected to uphold a high level of confidentiality. Should a user approach you with a sensitive issue—telling you their password, asking for assistance obtaining access to medical forms, and so on—it's your obligation as part of your job to make certain that information passes no further.

Located on a computer, desktop, printer, etc.

Technicians may come into contact with confidential information in the course of performing their job duties. That information could come in the form of data stored on a computer, information on a desktop, data (in any form) on a printer, and many other locations. When that possibility exists, ask users to remove such confidential information or close the application that displays it (saving their work before they close).

If the area where you will be working is cluttered with personal information (printed customer lists, and so on), ask the customer to relocate the items if possible. No confidential information should ever be disclosed to outside parties.

Exam essentials

Use good communication skills.   Listen to the customer. Let them tell you what they understand the problem to be and then interpret the problem and see whether you can get them to agree to what you're hearing them say. Treat the customer, whether an end user or a colleague, with respect, and take their issues and problems seriously.

Deal appropriately with confidential data.   You—as a computer professional—are expected to uphold a high level of confidentiality. No confidential information should ever be disclosed to outside parties.

4.8 Identify the basics of scripting.

Scripts are used to automate anything that can be accomplished at the command line. It prevents having to manually type in the commands and also allows you to schedule a script file to run at a certain time. Topics covered in this section include the following:

- Script file types
- Environment variables
- Comment syntax
- Basic script constructs
- Basic data types

Script file types

Script files can come in various file types. In this section we'll look at these file types.

.bat

Batch file or files with a .bat extension are used to automate a command or set of commands each time you execute the batch file.

.ps1

Files with this extension are used to script tasks in PowerShell, a powerful scripting language used by Microsoft.

.vbs

These are Visual Basic script files. The VBScript scripting language contains code that can be executed within Windows or Internet Explorer via the Windows-based script host.

.sh

Files that contain the .sh file extension are self-extracting files. The SH file contains selected files and a shell script along with instructions on how to extract the contents of the SH file archive.

.pyc

A .pyc file is one written in the Python language. Python runs on Windows, Mac OS X, and Linux/Unix.

.js

A JS file is a text file containing JavaScript code that is used to execute JavaScript instructions in web pages.

Environment variables

Environmental variables are default locations for various objects like the TEMP folder, for example. They are usually set during system startup by the system init script. They can be altered within a script or command from the default. In Microsoft Windows, each environment variable's default value is stored in the Windows Registry or set in the AUTOEXEC.BAT file. Some examples of environmental variables are as follows:

Linux/Unix

- $HOME contains the location of the user's home directory.
- $PWD points to the current directory.

Windows

- %CONFIG holds the symbolic name of the currently chosen boot configuration.
- %TEMP% (and %TMP%) contain the path to the directory where temporary files should be stored.

Comment syntax

Within a script you can include comments that are intended to be read by people but not to be processed. These might explain the rationale behind a script or give some historical perspective to the script. When including one, you indicate that the line is a comment (and not to be executed) by some sort of character set. For example, any text between // and the end of the line will be ignored by JavaScript (will not be executed). In PowerShell V2, <# #> can be used for block comments.

Basic script constructs

Within a script there are several tools or techniques you can use to make the script more efficient. Let's look at two of these tools.

Basic loops

Loops are used to get a script to go back to an earlier line and execute it again, perhaps with different data. Looping saves having to write the command over and over again within the script, once for each data piece. It is accomplished in many ways by different languages. For example, the following command in Linux/Unix displays the welcome message five times with a for loop:

```
#!/bin/bash
for i in 1 2 3 4 5
do
    echo "Welcome $i times"
done
```

This type of for loop is characterized by counting. The range is specified by a beginning (#1) and ending number (#5). The for loop executes a sequence of commands for each member in a list of items. This is a representative example in Bash, one of several shells or interfaces used to manage Linux.

Variables

Variables are characters that are placeholders for data. There are two actions you can perform for variables.

- Setting a value
- Reading the value

You can set the value of a variable with a command either outside of or within a script. To read the variable, place its name (preceded by a $ sign) anywhere in the script you want. Before the system (Bash in this case) interprets (or runs) every line, it first checks to see whether any variable names are present. For every variable it has identified, it replaces the variable name with its value. Then it runs that line of code and begins the process again on the next line.

Basic data types

When creating scripts, you use two data types.

Integers

An integer (from the Latin meaning "whole") is a number that can be written without a fractional component (1, 2, 3 but not 1.5, 1.6).

Strings

A string is a series of characters that often represents code that is executed and often implemented as an array data structure of bytes.

Exam essentials

Identify script file types.   These include .bat, .ps1, .vbs, .sh, .pyc, and .js.

Understand scripting terms.   These include strings, variables, integers, and basic loops.

4.9 Given a scenario, use remote access technologies.

As an A+ technician, there will be times when you need to make a remote connection to another device for the purpose of managing the device. In this section, we'll look at some of the options for this and the security issues with each.

RDP

Remote Desktop, which is not included in the Home editions of the Windows operating systems, allows members of the Administrators group to gain access to the workstation. (You can specifically allow other users as well.) By default, Remote Desktop is not enabled on Windows 7, but you can enable it from Remote Settings in the Control Panel applet System And Security. To enable Remote Desktop connections in Windows 7, follow these steps:

1. Right-click the Computer icon and choose Properties, or you can type system into the Start menu search box and then find the entry for System.

2. Click the Remote Settings link on the left side.

3. Select one of the two options allowing Remote Desktop connections, as shown in Figure 9.10.

FIGURE 9.10   Enabling Remote Desktop in Windows 7

To enable Remote Desktop connections in Windows 8, 8.1, and 10, follow these steps:

1. Open the desktop Control Panel and find the System panel there, or you can search for *Remote Access* in the Start menu or Start screen.

2. Click Allow Remote Access To Your Computer.

3. When the System Properties dialog box appears, select to allow Remote Desktop connections, as shown in Figure 9.11.

FIGURE 9.11   Enabling Remote Desktop in Windows 8

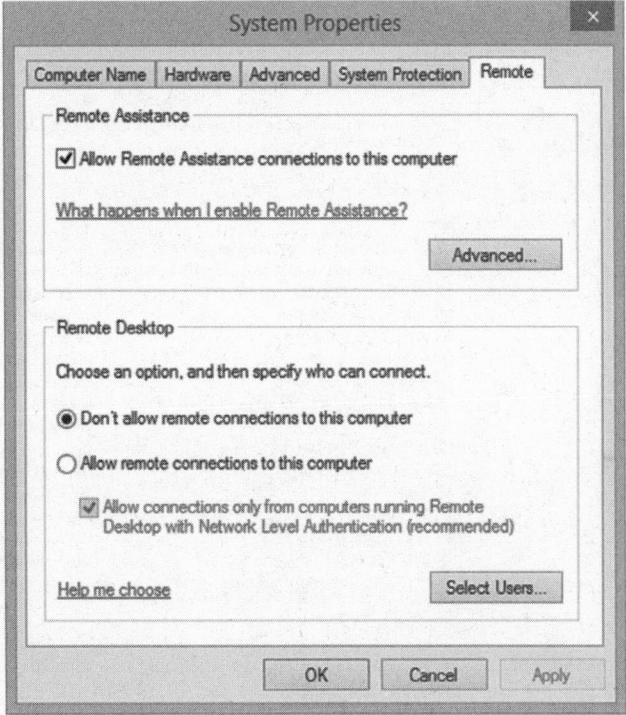

Telnet

Although a Telnet client comes on every Windows machine, the client is not installed by default. It is a handy tool to have, as it allows you to connect to a device at the command line and work at the command line. You should know, however, that Telnet transmits in clear text, so you would not want to use it to perform any sensitive operations (like changing a password). In Exercise 9.1, you will install the Telnet client on a Windows 10 computer.

EXERCISE 9.1

Installing the Telnet client

1. Right-click the Start menu and select Programs And Features.

2. In the page that is generated on the left side of the page, select Turn Windows Features On Or Off, as shown in Figure 9.12.

FIGURE 9.12 Programs And Features

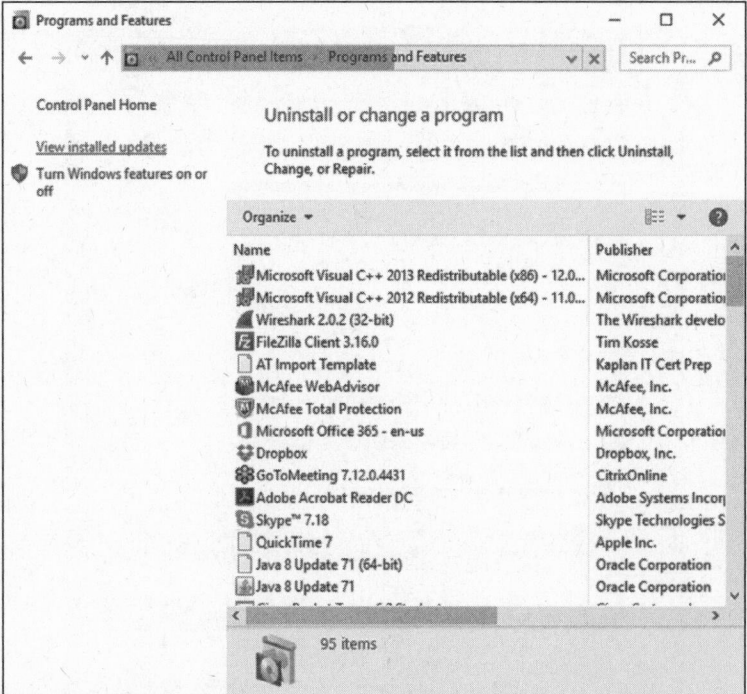

3. In the Turn Windows Features On Or Off page, scroll down until you see the Telnet client, as shown in Figure 9.13.

4. Check the box next to Telnet Client and then click OK. The client will be installed, and you will be notified when the installation is complete. You can now use it at the command line to connect to a remote machine by its IP address.

FIGURE 9.13   Turning Windows features on or off

SSH

If you don't need access to the graphical interface and you just want to operate at the command line, you have two options, Telnet and SSH. While Telnet works just fine, it transmits all of the data in clear text, which obviously would be a security issue. Therefore, the connection tool of choice has become Secure Shell (SSH). It's not as easy to set up, because it encrypts all of the transmissions, and that is not possible without an encryption key.

While the commands will be somewhat different based on the operating system, you must generate a key, which is generated using some unique information about the server as seed information so that the key will be unique to the server (the encryption algorithm will be well known). Once configured, the connection process will be similar to using Telnet, with the exception of course that the transmissions will be protected.

Third-party tools

There are also third-party tools that sometimes include screen and file sharing features. Let's briefly discuss these capabilities.

Screen share feature

Many of the collaboration or meeting software packages such Go to Meeting, WebEx, and Adobe Connect offer a screen sharing option. These are also possible in third-party remote access software such as Go To My PC, LogMeIn, and Remote PC.

File share

Many of the collaboration or meeting software packages such Go to Meeting, WebEx, and Adobe Connect also offer a file sharing option. In many collaboration solutions, multiple users can even edit a document at the same time. These are also possible in third-party remote access software such as Go To My PC, LogMeIn, and Remote PC.

Security considerations of each access method

Except for Telnet, which is completely insecure, RDP and third-party methods are generally secure and encrypted. However, you should ensure the following about the solution you select:

RDP   Ensure that all passwords are complex and that rights are restricted to the minimum to do the job.

SSH   Ensure that all passwords are complex and that rights are restricted to the minimum to do the job.

Third-Party Methods   Ensure that you understand the security capabilities and the shortcomings of the specific method under consideration.

Exam essentials

Describe common remote access tools.   These include Telnet, RDP, SSH, and third-party screen and file sharing tools such as LogMeIn and Go To My PC.

Review Questions

You can find the answers in the Appendix.

1. Which of the following is the least important piece of information to record about each device for proper asset inventory?

   A. Make

   B. Model

   C. Serial number

   D. Operating system

2. Which of the following is false with respect to change management?

   A. All changes should be formally requested.

   B. Each request should be analyzed to ensure it supports all goals and polices.

   C. After formal approval, all costs and effects of the methods of implementation should be reviewed.

   D. After they're approved, the change steps should be developed.

3. What is the process called that ensures all configuration changes are beneficial?

   A. Change management

   B. Acceptable use

   C. Separation of duties

   D. Risk analysis

4. Which of the following ensures an escape from changes that break something?

   A. Backout plan

   B. Phased deployment

   C. Communication process

   D. Request control

5. If you use incremental backups every day except Monday, when you do a full backup, how many backup tapes will be required if there is a drive failure on Wednesday after the backup has been made?

   A. 4

   B. 3

   C. 2

   D. 1

6. If you use differential backups every day except Monday when you do a full backup, how many backup tapes will be required if there is a drive failure on Wednesday after the backup has been made?

    A. 4

    B. 3

    C. 2

    D. 1

7. Which of the following is *not* a safe lifting technique to keep in mind?

    A. Lift with your back, not your legs

    B. Be careful to not twist when lifting

    C. Keep objects as close to your body as possible

    D. Where possible, push instead of pull

8. What class of fire extinguisher is used for paper fires?

    A. A

    B. B

    C. C

    D. D

9. Any type of chemical, equipment, or supply that has the potential to harm the environment or people has to have what document associated with it?

    A. SOW

    B. MSDS

    C. SLA

    D. MOU

10. What humidity level should be maintained for computing equipment?

    A. 50 percent

    B. 40 percent

    C. 60 percent

    D. 30 percent

11. Which of the following is the *not* part of the first response to an incident?

    A. Shut down the affected system

    B. Identify

    C. Report though proper channels

    D. Data/device preservation

12. Which of the following applies to EU-based organizations that collect or process the personal data of EU residents?

    A. PHI

    B. PII

    C. GDPR

    D. PCI-DSS

13. Which of the following is false regarding dealing with customers?

    A. Always answer the telephone in a professional manner, announcing the name of the company and yourself.

    B. Make a concentrated effort to ascertain the customer's technical level, and communicate above it.

    C. Use proper language (avoid jargon, acronyms, and slang when applicable).

    D. Maintain a positive attitude/project confidence.

14. Which of the following should the IT professional do when dealing with customers?

    A. Use appropriate professional titles, when applicable.

    B. Take personal calls.

    C. Use the customer's equipment for personal messages.

    D. Talk to co-workers while interacting with customers.

15. Which of the following is written in Python?

    A. .psi

    B. .vbs

    C. .sh

    D. .pyc

16. Which of the following is a number that can be written without a fractional component?

    A. Integer

    B. String

    C. Variable

    D. Loop

17. Which of the following is a command-line tool?

    A. RDP

    B. Screen sharing

    C. File sharing

    D. SSH

18. Which of the following is the least secure remote access technology?

    A. RDP

    B. Screen sharing

    C. Telnet

    D. SSH

Appendix

Answers to Review Questions

Chapter 1: Mobile Devices

1. D. The maximum transmission speeds are as follows:

    280 Mbps effective (USB 2 mode)

    1.6 Gbps effective (PCIe 1 mode)

    3.2 Gbps effective (PCIe 2 or USB 3 mode)

2. C. Thunderbolt ports are most likely to be found on Apple laptops, although they are now showing up on others as well. USB ports are typically found on all mobile devices, while Serial and PS/2 connecters are rarely found on mobile devices.

3. B. Some models of notebook PCs require a special T-8 Torx screwdriver. Most PC toolkits come with a T-8 bit for a screwdriver with interchangeable bits, but you may find that the T-8 screws are countersunk in deep holes so that you can't fit the screwdriver into them. In such cases, you need to buy a separate T-8 screwdriver, available at most hardware stores or auto parts stores. Phillips-head screwdrivers have a cross pattern on the tip and may be required. Hex heads are another type you may encounter, and metric drivers are those that are sized with the metric system.

4. B. When replacing the keyboard, one of the main things you want to keep in mind is to not damage the data cable connector to the system board.

5. C. If required, remove the connector attached to the old drive's signal pins and attach it to the new drive. Make sure it's right side up and do not force it. Damaging the signal pins may render the drive useless. The caddy, rails, and chassis are not easily damaged.

6. C. The 2.5-inch hard drives are smaller (which makes them attractive for a laptop where space is at a minimum); however, in comparison to 3.5-inch hard drives, they have less capacity and cache, and they operate at a lower speed.

7. A. The advantage of solid-state drives is that they are not as susceptible to damage if the device is dropped, and they are, generally speaking, faster as no moving parts are involved. They are, however, more expensive, and when they fail they don't generally give some advance symptoms like a magnetic drive will do.

8. A. A passive matrix screen uses a row of transistors across the top of the screen and a column of them down the side. It sends pulses to each pixel at the intersection of each row and column combination, telling it what to display. An active matrix screen uses a separate transistor for each individual pixel in the display, resulting in higher refresh rates and brighter display quality. Twisted nematic (TN) is the older of the two major technologies for flat-panel displays. While it provides the shortest response time, has high brightness, and draws less power than competing technologies, it suffers from poor quality when viewed from wide angles. In-Plane Switching (IPS) is a newer technology that solves the issue of poor quality at angles other than straight on.

9. D. In-Plane Switching (IPS) is a newer technology that solves the issue of poor quality at angles other than straight on. A passive matrix screen uses a row of transistors across the top of the screen and a column of them down the side. It sends pulses to each pixel at the intersection of each row and column combination, telling it what to display. An active matrix screen uses a separate transistor for each individual pixel in the display, resulting in higher refresh rates and brighter display quality. Twisted nematic (TN) is the older of the two major technologies for flat-panel displays. While it provides the shortest response time, has high brightness, and draws less power than competing technologies, it suffers from poor quality when viewed from wide angles.

10. D. With a hot dock, a laptop once put into suspended mode will recognize plug-and-play devices. A docking station essentially allows a laptop computer to be converted to a desktop computer. Laptop and table locks are used to secure mobile devices.

11. C. In cold docking, the laptop must be turned off and back on for the change to be recognized. In warm docking, the laptop must be put in and out of suspended mode for the change to be recognized. In hot docking, the change can be made and is recognized while running normal operations.

12. A. While many smart watches can also act as fitness monitors, there is a class of devices that specializes in tracking your movement. Fitness monitors read your body temperature, heart rate, and blood pressure. Extended reality is an exciting new field that includes both augmented reality and virtual reality. Today's smartphones are really computers that can make calls, and tablets have been in existence in some form or fashion since the early 1990s. Early on they were proprietary devices that didn't have a lot in common with desktop computers, but increasingly the two form factors have gravitated toward one another.

13. A. A global positioning system (GPS) uses satellite information to plot the global location of an object and uses that information to plot the route to a second location. Geofencing is the use of GPS to restrict communication to an area. Remote wipe is the cleaning of data from a lost or stolen device. There is no such thing as local wipe.

14. A. The two most common ports found on mobile devices are micro-USB and mini-USB. Both are small–form-factor implementations of the USB standard, the latest of which is USB 3.1. Thunderbolt ports are most likely to be found on Apple laptops, but they are now showing up on others as well. Serial and PS/2 connecters are rarely found on mobile devices.

15. A. Many external devices will ask for a PIN when you select the external device from the list of discovered devices. In many cases, the PIN is 0000, but you should check the manual of the external device.

16. A. The product release information (PRI) is the connection between the mobile device and the radio. From time to time this may need updating, which, when done, may add features or increase data speed. The preferred roaming list (PRL) is a list of radio frequencies residing in the memory of some kinds of digital phones. International Mobile Equipment Identification (IMEI) is used to identify a physical phone device, while International Mobile Subscriber Identification (IMSI) is used to identify a Subscriber Identification Module (SIM) card.

17. A. Mutual authentication is a process whereby not only does the server verify the credential of the client but the client also verifies the credential of the server. It adds additional security to the process. Single sign-on is a service that allows users to sign in once and have access to all resources. Multifactor authentication makes use of multiple factors of authentication to increase security. Biometrics is the use of physical factors of authentication.

18. D. Mutual authentication is a process whereby not only does the server verify the credential of the client but the client also verifies the credential of the server. It adds additional security to the process. Single sign-on is a service that allows users to sign in once and have access to all resources. Multifactor authentication makes use of multiple factors of authentication to increase security. Biometrics is the use of physical factors of authentication.

Chapter 2: Networking

1. D. POP3 uses port 110. SSH uses port 22, FTP uses ports 20 and 21, and Telnet uses port 23.

2. A. FTP uses ports 20 and 21. POP3 uses port 110, SSH uses port 22, and Telnet uses port 23.

3. B. SSH uses port 22, POP3 uses port 110, FTP uses ports 20 and 21, and Telnet uses port 23.

4. A. Switches operate at layer 2. Routers operate at layer 3. Repeaters and hubs operate at layer 1.

5. D. Hubs operate at layer 1. Switches and bridges operate at layer 2. Routers operate at layer 3.

6. B. Switches operate at layer 2. Routers operate at layer 3. Hubs and repeaters operate at layer 1.

7. B. The class B range is 172.16.0.0–172.31.255.255. The other ranges are correct.

8. A. Symmetric DSL (SDSL) offers an upload equal to the download speed. The other versions all have slower upload speed than download speed.

9. B. A demilitarized zone (DMZ) is an area where you can place a public server for access by people you might not trust otherwise. NAT is a service that maps private IP addresses to public IP addresses. The intranet is the internal network that should be protected. The Internet is the untrusted public network.

10. A. 802.11a operates in the 5.0 GHz range. The other standards all operate in the 2.4 GHz range.

11. D. 802.11a and 802.11g have a maximum rate of 54 MB, 802.11b has a maximum of 11 MB, and 802.11 has a maximum of 2 MB.

12. C. 802.11g has a distance that is the cell size of 125 ft. The others have a distance of 115 ft.

13. B. DNS servers resolve IP addresses to hostnames. HTTP servers are web servers. DHCP servers provide automatic IP configurations. SQL is a database server.

14. C. DHCP servers provide automatic IP configurations. DNS servers resolve IP addresses to hostnames. HTTP servers are web servers. SQL is a database server.

15. D. A SQL server is a database server. DNS servers resolve IP addresses to hostnames. HTTP servers are web servers. DHCP servers provide automatic IP configurations.

16. C. The Class B range is 128–191. The class A range is 1–126. The Class C range is 192–223.

17. B. The Class A range is 1–126. The class B range is 128–191. The Class C range is 192–223.

18. A. The Class C range is 192–223. The class A range is 1–126. The class B range is 128–191. The 224 range is for multicasting.

19. C. A personal area network (PAN) is a LAN created by personal devices. A wide area network (WAN) is a collection of two or more LANs, typically connected by routers and dedicated leased lines. Occasionally, a WAN will be referenced as a metropolitan area network (MAN) when it is confined to a certain geographic area, such as a university campus or city. Wireless mesh networks (WMN) are a form of an ad hoc WLAN that often consist of mesh clients, mesh routers, and gateways.

20. B. Metropolitan area network (MAN) is the term occasionally used for a WAN that is confined to a certain geographic area, such as a university campus or city. A personal area network (PAN) is a LAN created by personal devices. A wide area network (WAN) is a collection of two or more LANs, typically connected by routers and dedicated leased lines. Wireless mesh networks (WMN) are a form of an ad hoc WLAN that often consist of mesh clients, mesh routers, and gateways.

21. D. Wireless mesh networks (WMN) are a form of an ad hoc WLAN that often consist of mesh clients, mesh routers, and gateways. A personal area network (PAN) is a LAN created by personal devices. A wide area network (WAN) is a collection of two or more LANs, typically connected by routers and dedicated leased lines. Occasionally, a WAN will be referenced as a metropolitan area network (MAN) when it is confined to a certain geographic area, such as a university campus or city.

22. A. Wire crimpers look like pliers but are used to attach media connectors to the ends of cables. A cable stripper is used to remove the outer covering of the cable to get to the wire pairs within. A multimeter combines a number of tools into one. There can be slight variations, but a multimeter always includes a voltmeter, an ohmmeter, and an ammeter (and is sometimes called VOM as an acronym). A toner probe has two parts: the tone generator (called the *toner*) and the tone locator (called the *probe*). The toner sends the tone, and at the other end of the cable, the probe receives the toner's signal. This tool makes it easier to find the beginning and end of a cable.

23. C. A multimeter combines a number of tools into one. There can be slight variations, but a multimeter always includes a voltmeter, an ohmmeter, and an ammeter (and is sometimes called VOM as an acronym). Wire crimpers look like pliers but are used to attach media connectors to the ends of cables. A cable stripper is used to remove the outer covering of the cable to get to the wire pairs within. A toner probe has two parts: the tone generator (called the *toner*) and the tone locator (called the *probe*). The toner sends the tone, and at the other end of the cable, the probe receives the toner's signal. This tool makes it easier to find the beginning and end of a cable.

24. D. A toner probe has two parts: the tone generator (called the *toner*) and the tone locator (called the *probe*). The toner sends the tone, and at the other end of the cable, the probe receives the toner's signal. This tool makes it easier to find the beginning and end of a cable. Wire crimpers look like pliers but are used to attach media connectors to the ends of cables. A cable stripper is used to remove the outer covering of the cable to get to the wire pairs within. A multimeter combines a number of tools into one. There can be slight variations, but a multimeter always includes a voltmeter, an ohmmeter, and an ammeter (and is sometimes called VOM as an acronym).

Chapter 3: Hardware

1. C. Twisted pair is commonly used in office settings to connect workstations to hubs or switches. It comes in two varieties: unshielded (UTP) and shielded (STP). Fiber optic, serial, and coaxial do not come in shielded and unshielded versions.

2. B. Cat 5 transmits data at speeds up to 100 Mbps and was used with Fast Ethernet (operating at 100 Mbps) with a transmission range of 100 meters. It contains four twisted pairs of copper wire to give the most protection. Although it had its share of popularity (it's used primarily for 10/100 Ethernet networking), it is now an outdated standard. Newer implementations use the 5e standard. Cat 4 transmits at 16 Mbps, and Cat 6 transmits at 1 Gbps.

3. A. Fiber-optic cabling is the most expensive type of those discussed for this exam. Although it's an excellent medium, it's often not used because of the cost of implementing it. It has a glass core within a rubber outer coating and uses beams of light rather than electrical signals to relay data. None of the other options uses glass in its construction.

4. A. An RJ-11 is a standard connector for a telephone line and is used to connect a computer modem to a phone line. It looks much like an RJ-45 but is noticeably smaller. The RJ-45 is used for networking. RS 232 is a serial connector. BNC is a coaxial connector.

5. C. The RS-232 standard had been commonly used in computer serial ports. A serial cable (and port) uses only one wire to carry data in each direction; all the rest are wires for signaling and traffic control. An RJ-11 is a standard connector for a telephone line and is used to connect a computer modem to a phone line. It looks much like an RJ-45 but is noticeably smaller. The RJ-45 is used for networking.

6. D. Bayonet Neill–Concelman (BNC) connectors are sometimes used in the place of RCA connectors for video electronics, so you may encounter these connectors, especially when video equipment connects to a PC. In many cases, you may be required to purchase an adapter to convert this to another form of connection because it is rare to find one on the PC. An RJ-11 is a standard connector for a telephone line and is used to connect a computer modem to a phone line. It looks much like an RJ-45 but is noticeably smaller. The RJ45 is used for networking. RS-232 is a serial connector.

7. B. Portable computers (notebooks and subnotebooks) require smaller sticks of RAM because of their smaller size. One of the two types is small outline DIMM (SODIMM), which can have 72, 144, or 200 pins. DIMM is a full-size RAM type. Rambus is a type of RAM but not used in laptops, and BNC is a connector for coaxial cabling.

8. D. DDR SDRAM is Double Data Rate 2 (DDR2). This allows for two memory accesses for each rising and falling clock and effectively doubles the speed of DDR. DDR2-667 chips work with speeds at 667 MHz and are also referred to as PC2-5300 modules. DDR3 is the higher-speed successor to DDR and DDR2. Portable computers (notebooks and subnotebooks) require smaller sticks of RAM because of their smaller size. One of the two types is small outline DIMM (SODIMM), which can have 72, 144, or 200 pins.

9. B. DDR4 SDRAM is an abbreviation for double data rate fourth-generation synchronous dynamic random-access memory. DDR4 is not compatible with any earlier type of random-access memory (RAM). The DDR4 standard allows for DIMMs of up to 64 GB in capacity, compared to DDR3's maximum of 16 GB per DIMM. DDR3 and DDR2 are backward compatible, and there is no DDR5.

10. B. Compact Disc-ReWritable (CD-RW) media is a rewritable optical disc. A CD-RW drive requires more sensitive laser optics. It can write data to the disc but also has the ability to erase that data and write more data to the disc. CD, DVD, and CD-ROM are all read-only.

11. A. M.2, formerly known as the Next Generation Form Factor (NGFF), is a specification for internally mounted computer expansion cards and associated connectors. It replaces the mSATA standard. M.2 modules are rectangular, with an edge connector on one side, and a semicircular mounting hole at the center of the opposite edge. Non-Volatile Memory Host Controller Interface Specification (NVME) is an open logical device interface specification for accessing nonvolatile storage media attached via a PCI Express (PCIe) bus. Serial ATA and serial ATA 2.5 are computer bus interfaces that connects host bus adapters to mass storage devices such as hard disk drives, optical drives, and solid-state drives.

12. C. At 10,000 rpm, the latency will decrease to about 3 ms. Data transfer rates also generally go up with a higher rotational speed but are influenced by the density of the disk (the number of tracks and sectors present in a given area). Latency at 5400 rpm will be 5.56 ms. At 7200 it will be 4.17, and at 15000 it will drop to 2.

13. A. Laptops and other portable devices utilize an expansion card called the miniPCI. It has the same functionality as the PCI but has a much smaller form factor. PCI and PCIe are used in desktops. SATA is a drive connector.

14. A. Unified Extensible Firmware Interface (UEFI) is a standard firmware interface for PCs, designed to replace BIOS. NVRAM is RAM that retains its data during a reboot. CMOS is a battery type found on motherboards, and CHS is a drive geometry concept.

15. B. NVRAM is memory that does not lose its content when power is lost to the machine. Unified Extensible Firmware Interface (UEFI) is a standard firmware interface for PCs, designed to replace BIOS. CMOS is a battery type found on motherboards, and CHS is a drive geometry concept.

16. A. A keyboard, video, and mouse (KVM) device allows you to plug multiple PCs (usually servers) into the device and to switch easily back and forth from system to system using the same mouse, monitor, and keyboard. The KVM is actually a switch that all the systems plug into. There is usually no software to install. Just turn off all the systems, plug them all into the switch and turn them back on; then you can switch from one to another using the same keyboard, monitor, and mouse device connected to the KVM switch. CMOS is a battery type found on motherboards, and CHS is a drive geometry concept. NVRAM is memory that does not lose its content when power is lost to the machine.

17. B. When discussing bulbs for projectors, brightness is a description of light output, which is measured in lumens (not watts). Ensure that you are purchasing the correct bulb for the projector and maximize the life of the bulb by turning the projector off when not in use. A keyboard, video, and mouse (KVM) device allows you to plug multiple PCs (usually servers) into the device and to switch easily back and forth from system to system using the same mouse, monitor, and keyboard. Contrast is the relationship between dark and light. CHS is a drive geometry concept.

18. C. NFC components include an initiator and a target; the initiator actively generates an RF field that can power a passive target. This enables NFC targets to take simple form factors such as tags, stickers, key fobs, or cards that do not require batteries. When discussing bulbs for projectors, brightness is a description of light output, which is measured in lumens (not watts). Ensure that you are purchasing the correct bulb for the projector and maximize the life of the bulb by turning the projector off when not in use. A keyboard, video, and mouse (KVM) device allows you to plug multiple PCs (usually servers) into the device and to switch easily back and forth from system to system using the same mouse, monitor, and keyboard. CHS is a drive geometry concept.

19. C. In 2004, the ATX 12V 2.0 (now 2.03) standard was passed, changing the main connector from 20 pins to 24. The additional pins provide +3.3V, +5V, and +12V (the fourth pin is a ground) for use by PCIe cards. When a 24-pin connector is used, there is no need for the optional four- or six-pin auxiliary power connectors.

20. A. When using the AT power connector, the power cable coming from the power supply will have two separate connectors, labeled P8 and P9. When you are attaching the two parts to the motherboard, the black wires on one should be next to the black wires on the other for proper function.

21. C. The SATA power connector consists of 15 pins, with 3 pins designated for 3.3V, 5V, and 12V and with each pin carrying 1.5 amps. This results in a total draw of 4.95 watts + 7.5 watts + 18 watts, or about 30 watts.

22. C. A thick client has the applications installed locally and will need to have sufficient resources to support the applications. A thin client only sends commands and displays output with the application on the server. Network attached storage is a storage network that is IP based, while Storage Area Networks use a storage area protocol.

23. C. When discussing thin and thick clients, you should understand that a thick client is a PC that has all the capabilities of a standard PC. It runs all applications locally from its own hard drive. A thin client is one that has minimal capabilities and runs the applications (and perhaps even the operating system itself) from a remote server. There is no standard client or thin host.

24. C. The amount of RAM that is required depends on the number of VMs that you anticipate operating at the same time, not how many exist on the desktop. Total the memory requirements of each VM that will be open at the same time, in addition to the requirements of the host operating system. That should be the minimum. Then add more for overhead to ensure performance.

25. D. A proxy server address is optional.

26. B. A thick client is a standard PC. When discussing thin and thick clients, you should understand that a thick client is a PC that has all the capabilities of a standard PC. It runs all applications locally from its own hard drive. A thin client is one that has minimal capabilities and runs the applications (and perhaps even the operating system itself) from a remote server. There is no medium client or stationary client.

27. C. Ensure accountability by using no shared accounts. Each user should have a unique username/password combination. Audit trails should always be created.

28. A. When you install a printer driver for the printer you are using, it allows the computer to print to that printer correctly (assuming you have the correct interface configured between the computer and printer). Also, keep in mind that drivers are specific to the operating system, so you need to select the one that is both for the correct printer and for the correct operating system.

29. B. An optional component that can be added to printers (usually laser but also inkjet) is a duplexer. This can be an optional assembly added to the printer, or built into it, but the sole purpose of duplexing is to turn the printed sheet over so it can be run back through the printer and allow printing on both sides.

30 **C.** The orientation of a document refers to how the printed matter is laid out on the page. In the landscape orientation, the printing is written across the paper turned on its long side, while in portrait the paper is turned up vertically and printed top to bottom. The driver is the software that talks between the printer and the operating system. Duplexing makes it possible to print on both sides. To collate is to create multiple copies with all sets in correct page order.

31. A. Continuous-feed paper feeds through the printer using a system of sprockets and tractors. Sheet-fed printers accept plain paper in a paper tray. Dot matrix is continuous feed; everything else is sheet fed.

32. B. Never reuse paper in a laser printer that has been through the printer once. Although it may look blank, you're repeating the charging and fusing process on a piece of paper that most likely has something already on it.

33. A. This is a large circuit board that acts as the motherboard for the printer. It contains the processor and RAM to convert data coming in from the computer into a picture of a page to be printed. The imaging drum is the drum where the toner is placed on the correctly charged area. The toner cartridge is the container holding the toner. The maintenance kit contains items that should be changed periodically like rollers.

Chapter 4: Virtualization and Cloud Computing

1. B. Software as a service (SaaS) involves the vendor providing the entire solution. This includes the operating system, the infrastructure software, and the application. Infrastructure as a service (IaaS) provides only the hardware platform to the customer. Platform as a service (PaaS) provides a development environment. Security Information and Event Management (SIEM) is a system that aggregates all log files and analyzes them in real time for attacks.

2. A. When a company pays another company to host and manage a cloud environment, it is called a public cloud solution. If the company hosts this environment itself, it is a private cloud solution. A hybrid cloud solution is one in which both public and private clouds are part of the solution. A community cloud is one in which multiple entities use the cloud.

3. B. One of the advantages of a cloud environment is the ability to add resources as needed on the fly and release those resources when they are no longer required. This makes for more efficient use of resources, placing them where needed at any particular point in time. These include CPU and memory resources. This is called rapid elasticity because it occurs automatically according to the rules for resource sharing that have been deployed. On-demand refers to the ability of the customer to add resources as needed. Virtual sharing and stretched resources are not terms used when discussing the cloud.

4. A. There are three models for implementing VDI:

Centralized model: All desktop instances are stored in a single server, requiring significant processing power on the server.

Hosted model: Desktops are maintained by a service provider. This model eliminates capital cost and is instead subject to operation cost.

Remote virtual desktops model: An image is copied to the local machine, making a constant network connection unnecessary.

There is no local model.

5. C. Platform as a service (PaaS) involves the vendor providing the hardware platform or data center and the software running on the platform. This includes the operating systems and infrastructure software. The company is still involved in managing the system. Software as a service (SaaS) involves the vendor providing the entire solution. This includes the operating system, the infrastructure software, and the application. Infrastructure as a service (IaaS) provides only the hardware platform to the customer. Security Information and Event Management (SIEM) is a system that aggregates all log files and analyzes them in real time for attacks.

6. A. Some of the virtualization products, however (such as Microsoft's Hyper-V, Windows 7 Virtual PC, and Windows 8 Client Hyper-V), require that the motherboard support hardware-assisted virtualization. The benefit derived from using hardware-assisted virtualization is it reduces overhead and improves performance. It does not improve security, lower power consumption, or ease troubleshooting.

7. B. The hypervisor is the software that allows the VMs to exist. Dual inline memory module (DIMM) is a type of memory. There is no software called Azureware, and network address translation is a service that translates private IP addresses to public ones.

8. A. The hypervisor that manages the distribution of the physical server's resources can be either Type I or Type II. A Type I hypervisor (or native, bare metal) runs directly on the host's hardware to control the hardware and to manage guest operating systems. Type 2 runs on top of an operating system. There is no hybrid or core type.

9. A. A Type II hypervisor runs within a conventional operating system environment. With the hypervisor layer as a distinct second software level, guest operating systems run at the third level above the hardware. VMware Workstation Citrix Xen Server and VirtualBox exemplify Type II hypervisors.

10. B. A Type II hypervisor runs within a conventional operating system environment. With the hypervisor layer as a distinct second software level, guest operating systems run at the third level above the hardware. Container-based is a different approach to virtualization that holds instances in containers. There is no Type III.

Chapter 5: Hardware and Network Troubleshooting

1. B. The steps are as follows:

1. Identify the problem.
2. Establish a theory of probable cause (question the obvious).
3. Test the theory to determine cause.
4. Establish a plan of action to resolve the problem and implement the solution.
5. Verify full system functionality and, if applicable, implement preventive measures.
6. Document findings, actions, and outcomes.

2. D. The steps are as follows:

1. Identify the problem.
2. Establish a theory of probable cause (question the obvious).
3. Test the theory to determine cause.
4. Establish a plan of action to resolve the problem and implement the solution.
5. Verify full system functionality and, if applicable, implement preventive measures.
6. Document findings, actions, and outcomes.

3. A. One common reason for shutdowns is overheating. Often when that is the case, however, the system reboots itself rather than just shutting down.

4. D. A bad NIC driver would cause the NIC not to work but would not cause a system lockup.

5. B. Once a regular occurrence when working with Windows, blue screens (also known as the blue screen of death) have become much less frequent.

6. A. While Microsoft users have the BSOD to deal with, Apple users have also come to have the same negative feelings about the Pinwheel of Death. This is a multicolored pinwheel mouse pointer.

7. A. Pixels are the small dots on the screen that are filled with a color; as a group they present the image you see on the screen.

8. B. Artifacts are visual anomalies that appear on the screen. They might be pieces of images left over from a previous image or a "tear in the image" (it looks like the image is divided into two parts and the parts don't line up).

9. A. The backlight is the light in the device that powers the LCD screen. It can go bad over time and need to be replaced, and it can also be held captive by the inverter. The inverter takes the DC power the laptop is providing and boosts it up to AC to run the backlight. If the inverter goes bad, you can replace it on most models (it's cheaper than the backlight).

10. B. Touch flow, or TouchFLO, is a user interface feature designed by HTC. It is used by dragging your finger up and down or left and right to access common tasks on the screen. This movement is akin to scrolling the screen up and down or scrolling the screen left and right.

11. B. With laser printers, streaks usually indicate that the fuser is not fusing the toner properly on the paper. It could also be that the incorrect paper is being used. In laser printers, you can sometimes tell the printer that you are using a heavier paper. For dot-matrix, you can adjust the platen for thicker paper.

12. C. In laser printers, faded output usually indicates that the toner cartridge is just about empty. You can usually remove it, shake it, and replace it and then get a bit more life out of it before it is completely empty, but it is a signal that you are near the end.

13. B. You may be able to ping the entire network using IP addresses, but most access is done by name, not IP address. If you can't ping resources by name, DNS is not functional, meaning either the DNS server is down or the local machine is not configured with the correct IP address of the DNS server.

14. C. If the computer cannot connect to the default gateway, it will be confined to communicating with devices on the local network. This IP address should be that of the router interface connecting to the local network.

Chapter 6: Operating Systems

1. B. The Aero interface offers a glass design that includes translucent windows. It was new with Windows Vista. The Sidebar is an area of the desktop where gadgets can be placed. Metro is the name of an interface type, and the Start screen is the new opening interface to Windows.

2. A. Windows 7 renamed these Windows Desktop Gadgets. Metro apps are a type of application new in Windows, and widgets are an element of a graphical user interface (GUI) that displays information such as temperature. Shims are pieces of software that allow an application to be supported by a system that normally does not support it.

3. A. Rolled into the Action Center in Windows 7, this interface shows the status of, and allows you to configure, the firewall, Windows Update, virus protection, spyware and unwanted software protection, Internet security settings, UAC, and network access protection. Control Panel is a holding spot for many tools used in Windows. The Windows Firewall is a built in firewall for Windows systems. Defender is the Windows anti-malware solution.

4. B. In both Windows and Windows 8.1, the user interface is very different from earlier versions of Windows. The Start menu was removed, and the desktop replaced with a new look called Metro. The Aero interface offers a glass design that includes translucent windows. It was new with Windows Vista. Sidebar is an area of the desktop where gadgets can be placed. Start or the Start screen is a new opening interface to Windows.

5. D. Windows 7 requires 1 GB for 32-bit and 2 GB for 64-bit Windows 7 Professional.

6. D. Only Windows Home Starter can be upgraded to Windows 8.

7. B. The DIR command is simply used to view a listing of the files and folders that exist within a directory, subdirectory, or folder. The net use command allows for connecting to, removing, and configuring connections to shared resources. The cd command is used to change directories, and the ipconfig command is used to view and change network settings.

8. C. The change directory (cd) command is used to move to another folder or directory. It is used in both Unix and Windows. The dir command is simply used to view a listing of the files and folders that exist within a directory, subdirectory, or folder. The net use command allows for connecting to, removing, and configuring connections to shared resources. The ipconfig command is used to view and change network settings.

9. A. Device Manager shows a list of all installed hardware and lets you add items, remove items, update drivers, and more. Event Viewer allows for viewing various event logs. The Users And Groups tool is used to create and manage user and group accounts. The Sync Center is used to manage the synchronization of data between the local device and other locations.

10. B. Every program and process theoretically could have its own logging utility, but Microsoft has come up with a rather slick utility, Event Viewer, which, through log files, tracks all events on a particular Windows computer. Device Manager shows a list of all installed hardware and lets you add items, remove items, update drivers, and more. The Users And Groups tool is used to create and manage user and group accounts. The Sync Center is used to manage the synchronization of data between the local device and other locations.

11. C. Color depth is either the number of bits used to indicate the color of a single pixel, in a bitmapped image or video frame buffer, or the number of bits used for each color component of a single pixel. In Windows 7, this can be set on the Monitor tab of the properties of the adapter. Resolution has to do with the number of pixels (individual points of color) contained on a display monitor. Refresh rate describes how often the device "repaints" the display image. Pixel count is the same thing as resolution.

12. B. The refresh rate is the number of times in a second that a display updates its buffer and is expressed in Hertz. In Windows 7, the refresh rate is set using a drop-down box just above the setting for color depth. Color depth is either the number of bits used to indicate the color of a single pixel, in a bitmapped image or video frame buffer, or the number of bits used for each color component of a single pixel. In Windows 7, this can be set on the Monitor tab of the properties of the adapter. Resolution has to do with the number of pixels (individual points of color) contained on a display monitor. Pixel count is the same thing as resolution.

13. A. The minimum of RAM required should be viewed as just that, a minimum. Make sure you have more than required for satisfactory performance. You should not exceed the maximum resolution recommended for a device. Extra disk space will nor improve performance unless the disk is very full. As pixel count is the same as resolution you should not exceed the recommended count either.

14. C. Outside of the enterprise most installations occur by using the CD that came with the software or by placing these same files on a USB stick and accessing them from the USB drive. A network installation is when you load installation files over the network. A Remote Installation Service installation is a legacy method no longer supported. An unattended installation is one that uses an answer file to answer the prompts that appear during installation.

15. C. HomeGroup offers a simplified way to set up a home network. It allows you to share files (including libraries) and prevent changes from being made to those files by those sharing them (unless you give them permission to do so). A peer-to-peer network is the type of network created with a workgroup. A domain is a network with a directory service such as Active Directory. A workgroup is a small collection of computers grouped without a server.

16. A. net use can also be used to connect to a shared printer: net use lpt1: \\printername. The net user command is used to add, remove, and make changes to the user accounts on a computer. The robocopy command (Robust File Copy for Windows) is included with Windows 7, Windows 8, Windows 8.1, and Windows 10 and has the big advantage of being able to accept a plethora of specifications and keep NTFS permissions intact in its operations. If you are comfortable with the copy command, learning xcopy shouldn't pose too many problems. It's basically an extension of copy with one notable exception—it's designed to copy directories as well as files.

17. A. In Linux, a shell is a command-line interface, of which there are several types. A domain is a network type that includes a directory service. cmd is a command that when executed in the Run box opens the command prompt. A disk operating system (abbreviated DOS) is a computer operating system that can use a disk storage device, such as a floppy disk, hard disk drive, or optical disc.

18. B. In Apple, Mission Control provides a quick way to see everything that's currently open on your Mac. A shell is simply a command-line interface. A sandbox is an area where a process can be executed without impacting any other processes. Beeker is not a term used when discussing Apple.

Chapter 7: Security

1. A. A mantrap is a series of two doors with a small room between them. The user is authenticated at the first door and then allowed into the room. At that point, additional verification will occur (such as a guard visually identifying the person), and then the person is allowed through the second door. A trapdoor is a doorway that is usually hidden. A saferoom is a room that is impenetrable from outside, and badgetrap is not a term used when disusing doorway systems.

2. B. Biometric devices use physical characteristics to identify the user. Such devices are becoming more common in the business environment. Biometric systems include hand scanners, retinal scanners, and, possibly soon, DNA scanners. Hardware tokens are devices that contain security credentials. Smart cards are cards that contain a chip and credentials. Badge readers are devices that read the information on a card and allow or disallow entry.

3. A. As physical addresses are MAC addresses, MAC address filtering is the correct answer. Email filtering is the filtering of email addresses from which one is allowed to receive. IP address filtering is the type of filtering done on a router or firewall, based on IP addresses. URL filtering restricts the URLs that can be reached with the browser.

4. A. A firewall operating as a packet filter passes or blocks traffic to specific addresses based on the type of application. The packet filter doesn't analyze the data of a packet; it decides whether to pass it based on the packet's addressing information. A proxy firewall is one that makes the Internet connection on behalf of the user and can control where the user goes. Stateful firewalls monitor the state of every TCP connection, thus preventing network mapping. A new-generation firewall is one that operates on all levels of the OSI model.

5. D. Wired Equivalent Privacy (WEP) is a standard that was created as a first stab at security for wireless devices. Using WEP-encrypted data to provide data security has always been under scrutiny for not being as secure as initially intended. Wi-Fi Protected Access (WPA) and WPA2 are later methods that cane after WEP. Temporal Key Integrity Protocol is the encryption method used in WPA.

6. A. WPA was able to increase security by using a Temporal Key Integrity Protocol (TKIP) to scramble encryption keys using a hashing algorithm. Temporal Key Integrity Protocol is the encryption method used in WPA. Advanced Encryption Standard (AES) is the encryption used in WPA2. IPSec is an industry-standard encryption method, and Secure Sockets Layer (SSL) is an encryption method used in many VPNs.

7. C. An armored virus is designed to make itself difficult to detect or analyze. Armored viruses cover themselves with protective code that stops debuggers or disassemblers from examining critical elements of the virus. A companion virus is one that attaches to a file or adopts the name of a file. A macro virus is one that hides in macros, and a multipartite virus is one that has multiple propagation methods.

8. B. A signature is an algorithm or other element of a virus that uniquely identifies it. Because some viruses have the ability to alter their signature, it is crucial that you keep signature files current, whether you choose to manually download them or configure the antivirus engine to do so automatically. An ID is any types of identifying badge or marker. A badge is something worn to provide identification. Marking is not a word typically used when discussing algorithms or attacks.

9. C. Tailgating is the term used for someone being so close to you when you enter a building that they are able to come in right behind you without needing to use a key, a card, or any other security device. Many social-engineering intruders needing physical access to a site will use this method of gaining entry. Shadowing is when one user monitors another for training. Spoofing is the adoption of another's email address, IP address, or MAC address. Keyriding is not a word typically used when discussing social engineering.

10. B. Spoofing is the process of masquerading as another user or device. It is usually done for the purpose of accessing a resource to which the hacker should not have access or to get through a security device such as a firewall that may be filtering traffic based on source IP address. Shadowing is when one user monitors another for training. Duplication is the creation of a matching object. Masking is not a term used when discussing impersonation.

11. A. The Power Users group is not as powerful as the Administrators group. Membership in this group gives read/write permission to the system, allowing members to install most software but keeping them from changing key operating system files. This is a good group for those who need to test software (such as programmers) and junior administrators. The Guest group is used to allow restricted access to the device. The Administrators group allows full access to the device. The rights held by the Users group are a compromise between Admin and Guest.

12. D. This combines the permissions of Read with those of List Folder Contents and adds the ability to run executables. List Folder Contents allows viewing what items are in a folder. Full Control allows everything, and Read only allows reading documents.

13. D. Although length is now considered the most important password security factor, complexity is also a factor, and these examples are all the same length. The password P@ssw0rd contains four character types, the most of any of the options, which increases the strength of the password. Password and pAssword contains only two types of characters. Pa$$word contains three types.

14. B. When assigning user permissions, follow the principle of least privilege by giving users only the bare minimum they need to do their job. Separation of duties prescribes that any operation prone to fraud should be broken up into two operations with different users performing each. Job rotation has the same goal but accomplishes it by requiring users to move around from job to job. Open rights is not a term used when discussing permission and rights.

15. C. Swipe locks use a gesture or series of gestures, sometimes involving the movement of an icon to open the screen. In some cases, they require only knowledge of the mobile platform in use; they offer no security to the process because no authentication of the user is occurring. Fingerprint locks open when the correct fingerprint is presented. Facial locks require a matching face scan to open. Passcode locks require the configured passcode to unlock.

16. A. Remote wipe gives you the ability to delete all content when a device is stolen or lost. Geofencing allows you to restrict use of the device to a geographic area. Screen locks prevent access to the home screen on the device. Segmentation of data is the separation of personal data from enterprise data on a device.

17. A. Degaussing involves applying a strong magnetic field to initialize the media (this is also referred to as disk wiping). This process helps ensure that information doesn't fall into the wrong hands. Incineration is the burning of the storage device. Hammers can be used to destroy the device. Deleting is the least effective way of removing information.

18. B. Physically destroying the drive involves rendering the component no longer usable. Incineration is the burning of the storage device. Degaussing involves applying a strong magnetic field to initialize the media (this is also referred to as disk wiping). This process helps ensure that information doesn't fall into the wrong hands. Clearing is a method that still leaves the data recoverable with data forensics. Deleting is the least effective way of removing information.

19. B. Wi-Fi protected setup (WPS) was a concept that was designed to make it easier for less knowledgeable users to add a new client to the WLAN without manually entering the security information on the client. One method involves pushing a button on the AP at the same time a client is attempting to join the network so that the settings are sent to the client. Other methods involve placing the client close to the AP, and near-field communication is used for the process. Service Set identifier (SSID) is the name of the WLAN. Wired Equivalent Privacy (WEP) and Wi-Fi protected Access (WPA) are wireless security protocols.

20. A. Every wireless AP or wireless router on the market comes with a default SSID. Cisco models use the name tsunami, for example. You should change these defaults and create a new SSID to represent your WLAN. Wi-Fi protected setup (WPS) was a concept that was designed to make it easier for less knowledgeable users to add a new client to the WLAN without manually entering the security information on the client. One method involves pushing a button on the AP at the same time a client is attempting to join the network so that the settings are sent to the client. Other methods involve placing the client close to the AP, and near-field communication is used for the process. Wired Equivalent Privacy (WEP) and Wi-Fi protected Access (WPA) are wireless security protocols.

Chapter 8: Software Troubleshooting

1. B. The boot.ini file is specific to the machine. A .dll file is a file type and not a specific file. The ntldr is the file that loads the operating system. Bootmgr is a file in later systems that manages the boot process.

2. D. If there was a disk with system files in the DVD drive, the system would boot to it. A nonsystem disk, a corrupted or missing boot sector, and an incorrect boot order in the BIOS could all be possible causes.

3. B. A browser redirection is one of the most serious security problems. Browser hijacking software is external code that changes your Internet Explorer settings. It may include changing your home page or adding or removing items from your favorites. A man-in-the-middle attack is when the malicious individual positions himself between two communicating system, receiving all data. A SYN flood is a form of a DoS attack. Fraggle is an attack using UDP packets.

4. A. Malware decreases performance. It can cause Internet connectivity issues, browser redirection, and pop-ups.

5. D. The steps are as follows:
    1. Identify and research malware symptoms.
    2. Quarantine the infected systems.
    3. Disable System Restore (in Windows).
    4. Remediate the infected systems.
    5. Schedule scans and run updates.
    6. Enable System Restore and create a restore point (in Windows).
    7. Educate the end user.

6. B. Although it is recommended that you disable System Restore before cleaning an infection, it is a good idea to create a restore point after an infection is cleaned. This gives you a clean restore point going forward in case the system becomes infected again at some point. Network address translation, the Windows Firewall, and your antivirus should *not* be disabled.

7. A. A low brightness setting does not negatively impact battery life. A high setting, however, does. Location services, Bluetooth, and overheating do not negatively affect battery life.

8. B. While leaving the phone on will run down the battery, it will not alone cause it to overheat. Excessive gaming, using an old battery, and continuous online browsing will cause overheating.

9. D. On the contrary, evidence of malware or other issues is usually accompanied by very high resource utilization. Unusual loss of power, slow speeds, and a weak signal are all signs of security issues.

10. C. When cameras have been enabled when they weren't previously, it is an indication of compromise. Low resource utilization, a disabled microphone, and authorized use of the device are not symptoms of a security issue.

Chapter 9: Operational Procedures

1. D. While the OS may be important, for warranty issues these other pieces are more important. The make, model, and serial number are all important.

2. C. All costs and effects of the methods of implementation should be reviewed prior to formal approval. The other statements are true.

3. A. During the change management process, the relative costs and benefits to the overall organization will be weighed by a change management board or team. Acceptable use is a policy that defines what users can and cannot do. Separation of duties is a concept that says that any operation prone to fraud should be broken into two jobs and assigned to two people. Risk analysis is a process that identifies risk and mitigations.

4. A. During implementation, incremental testing should occur, relying on a predetermined fallback strategy if necessary. A phased deployment is one in which parts of the network are done at a time. While the communication process is important, it is not what allows for an escape. Request control is a process where change requests are managed and approved.

5. B. Since an incremental backup backs up everything that has changed since the last backup of any type, each day's tape is unique, so you will need the Monday full backup and the incremental tapes from Tuesday and Wednesday.

6. C. Since a differential backup backs up everything that has changed since the last full backup, each day's incremental tape contains what was on the previous day's tape. So, you only need the last differential and the last full backups.

7. A. Lift with your legs, not your back. When you have to pick something up, bend at the knees, not at the waist. The other options are all safety recommendation.

8. A. A is for wood and paper fires, B is for flammable liquids, C is for electrical fires, and D is for metal fires.

9. B. Any type of chemical, equipment, or supply that has the potential to harm the environment or people has to have a material safety data sheet (MSDS) associated with it. These are traditionally created by the manufacturer, and you can obtain them from the manufacturer or from the Environmental Protection Agency. A statement of work (SOW) is a document that indicates the work to be performed. A service level agreement is a document that indicates what is being paid and what the service consists of. A memorandum of understanding (MOU) is a document that indicates the intent of two parties to do something together.

10. A. Another preventive measure you can take is to maintain the relative humidity at around 50 percent. Be careful not to increase the humidity too far—to the point where moisture starts to condense on the equipment!

11. A. You never shut down the system until all volatile evidence has been collected. The other options are correct guidelines.

12. C. Beginning on May 25, 2018, the members of the EU began applying the General Data Protection Regulation (GDPR). The GDPR applies to EU-based organizations that collect or process the personal data of EU residents and to organizations outside the EU that monitor behavior or offer goods and services to EU residents. Personally identifiable information (PII) is data like an XSN number that is unique to the individual. Personal health information (PHI) is confidential medical records. Payment Card Industry/ Data Security Standards (PCI-DSS) is a standard for protecting credit card data.

13. B. If you're providing phone support, do the following:

Always answer the telephone in a professional manner, announcing the name of the company and yourself.

Make a concentrated effort to ascertain the customer's technical level, and communicate at that level, not above or below it.

The other options are all valid recommendations.

14. A. You should use appropriate professional titles, when applicable, and *never* take personal calls, use the customers equipment for personal messages, or talk to co-workers while interacting with customers.

15. D. A .pyc file is one written in the Python language. Python runs on Windows, Mac OS X, and Linux/Unix. A .vbs file is a Visual Basic file. An SH file is a script programmed for Bash, a type of Unix shell.

16. A. An integer (from the Latin integer meaning "whole") is a number that can be written without a fractional component (1, 2, 3 but not 1.5, 1.6). A string is a series of characters. Variables are used to store information to be referenced and manipulated in a computer program. A loop is a section of code that goes back to an earlier part of the script.

17. D. If you don't need access to the graphical interface and you just want to operate at the command line, you have two options, Telnet and SSH. While Telnet works just fine, it transmits all of the data in clear text, which obviously would be security issue. Remote Desktop and screen sharing are graphical concepts, while file sharing is not a command-line utility.

18. C. While Telnet works just fine, it transmits all of the data in clear text, which obviously would be a security issue. Remote Desktop and screen sharing are graphical concepts that's can be secured, while Secure Shell (SSH) is an encrypted technology.

Index

Note to the Reader: Throughout this index **boldfaced** page numbers indicate primary discussions of a topic. *Italicized* page numbers indicate illustrations.

A

Above Normal process priority, 385
acceptable use policies (AUPs), 584–585
access
    denied, 561
    printers, 294–295
    unauthorized, 573
access control lists (ACLs)
    description, 484
    VLANs, 97
access lists for entry, 472
access points (APs)
    description, 67
    SOHO networks, 72, 531–532
accessories for mobile devices, 36–39,
        37–38
accounts
    disabling, 519
    laptops, 201
    managing, 375, 408, 516–519, 518
    POP, 42–43
    recovery options, 595
    setup, 201
    unauthorized access, 573
ACLs (access control lists)
    description, 484
    VLANs, 97
acronyms, 613–614
action plans in problem solving, 257
Active Directory (AD)
    accounts, 517–519, 518
    concepts, 475–476
active heat sinks, 178
active hubs, 68
active listening, 614
active matrix screens, 16
active reader/active tags (ARATs), 84–85
active reader/passive tags (ARPTs), 84–85
AD (Active Directory)
    accounts, 517–519, 518
    concepts, 475–476
ad hoc printers, 204
adapters
    DVI to HDMI, 134, 135
    DVI to VGA, 136, 136
    USB to Ethernet, 135, 135
add-on video cards, 180, 180
Add/Remove Programs, 416
address bus, 171
ADF scanners, 184
ADMIN$ drive, 429
administrative shares
    vs. local, 511
    networking configuration, 429
administrative tools, 373–378

Administrator account
    passwords, 517
    security settings, 505–506
ADSL (asymmetric DSL), 76
Advanced Encryption Security (AES)
    description, 487
    SOHO networks, 81
Advanced Micro Devices (AMD) CPUs,
        174–176
Advanced Security tool, 375
Advanced tab
    Internet Options applet, 405–406, 406
    System utility, 412–413, 412
Advanced Technology Extended (ATX)
    form factor, 160, 160
    motherboard power supplies, 190, 190,
        193, 193
Aero interface, 328
AES (Advanced Encryption Security)
    description, 487
    SOHO networks, 81
AFP (Apple Filing Protocol), 64
AGP video cards, 180, 180
AIK (Automated Installation Kit), 344
air filters, 603, 606
airborne particles, 605–606
airplane mode
    configuring, 40
    settings, 23, 24
AirPrint technology, 207
alerts, security, 559
Allow permissions limitations, 508
Allow Remote Access To Your Computer
        option, 433
Allow Remote Assistance Connections To
        This Computer option, 435
Allow Remote Assistance Invitations To Be
        Sent From This Computer option, 434
alternative IP addresses, 437–438, 438
Always Show Icons, Never Thumbnails
        option, 410
Always Show Menus option, 411
AMD (Advanced Micro Devices) CPUs,
        174–176
answer files in OS upgrades, 341
antennas
    connectors and placement, 17–18
    SOHO networks, 531–532
antistatic bags, 597–598
antistatic mats, 598–599, 599
antistatic wrist straps, 597–598, 598
antivirus software, 496
    mobile devices, 523
    overview, 478
    rogue, 560
    SOHO networks, 75
    updates, 445

Anytime Upgrade, 341
APIPA (Automatic Private IP Addressing)
    overview, 92
    troubleshooting, 299–300
App History tab in Task Manager,
        384, 384
Apple Filing Protocol (AFP), 64
appliances
    firewalls, 479
    Internet, 88–90
application-level proxy functions, 480
application logs
    Event Viewer, 375
    malware clues in, 561
    mobile devices, 570
    problem solving, 256
applications
    cloud computing, 240–241, 241
    compatibility, 350
    configuring, 201
    crashes, 549, 560
    disabling, 555, 555
    installation, 424–426
    mobile devices, 567
    not loading problems, 284
    repairing, 553
    software requirements, 53
    SOHO networks, 75
    synchronizing, 51
    thick clients, 198
Applications tab in Task Manager,
        383, 383
approvals in change management, 589
apps in cloud computing, 240
APs (access points)
    description, 67
    SOHO networks, 72, 531–532
apt-get command, 458
ARATs (active reader/active tags), 84–85
archives, 445
armored viruses, 493
ARPTs (active reader/passive tags), 84–85
arrays, adding, 396
artifacts, video, 274
asset tags in inventory management, 587
assignments in port forwarding, 78
asymmetric DSL (ADSL), 76
AT Attachment (ATA) drives, 131–132,
        131–132
AT motherboards power supplies,
        190, 190
ATAPI (ATA Packet Interface), 133
attributes, file, 508–509
ATX (Advanced Technology Extended)
    form factor, 160, 160
    motherboard power supplies, 190, 190,
        193, 193

audio
  connectors, 166, *166*
  editing workstations, 195–196
  mobile devices, 287
  sound cards, 180, *181*, 197
augmented reality, 29–30, *29–30*
AUPs (acceptable use policies), 584–585
authentication
  limited connectivity, 547
  mobile devices, 53, 523–524
  multifactor, 482
  networks, 297
  passwords, 481–482
  servers, 88
  shared devices, 207
  single sign-on, 512
  wireless, 487–488
authenticators
  applications, 524
  RADIUS, 489
auto duplex settings in NICs, 439, *439*
autoconfigured IP addresses, 94
Automated Installation Kit (AIK), 344
Automatic Private IP Addressing (APIPA)
  overview, 92
  troubleshooting, 299–300
Automatically Type Into The Search Box
    option, 411
automobiles, synchronizing to, 50
AutoRun function, disabling, 519
autosensing NICs, 181
availability, print, 295

B

back-side bus (BSB), 171
backed-up print queues, 294
backlight, keyboard, 21
backout plans in change management, 589
backups and recovery
  disaster recovery, 497–499
  MacOS and Linux, 445, *446*
  remote, 522–523
  scheduled, 442, 590–593
  surge protectors, 594–595, *594–595*
  UPSs, 593–594
bad pixels, 274
badge readers, 471
barcodes
  in inventory management, 587
  scanners, 184
bare-metal backups, 592
barriers, 472
baseband updates, 47–48
Basic Input/Output System (BIOS)
  IDE drives, 155
  NICs, 440
  passwords, 168, 515
  settings, 167–171, *170–171*
  time and setting resets, 261
basic partitions, 345
.bat files, 619
batteries
  charging problems, 280
  CMOS, 171, *172*

mobile devices, 37, *38*, 286–288
  recycling, 599–600
  replacing, 13
  short life, 568
  simulated battery pulls, 284
  UPSs, 593–594
Bayonet Neill–Concelman (BNC)
    connectors, 121, 138, *138*
BD-R format, 149
BD-RE format, 149
beeps in POST, 259–260
Below Normal process priority, 385
belts in inkjet printers, 221
bias voltage in laser printers, 215
biometric authentication, 523
biometric locks, 473
BIOS. *See* Basic Input/Output System
    (BIOS)
BitLocker, 327, 513
BitLocker Drive Encryption, 423, *423*
BitLocker To Go, 513
black lines on printed page, 293–294
black screens, 549
blacklisting, 79
blackouts, 593
blank pages
  laser printers, 219
  printing, 296
blank screens on bootup, 260
Blu-ray standard, 148–149
Blue Screen of Death (BSOD), 263–264,
    271, 549
Bluetooth
  configuring, 40–42
  connectivity issues, 282, 565–566
  function keys, 21
  module replacement, 11–12
  pairing issues, 572
  printers, 204
  versions, 35
BNC (Bayonet Neill–Concelman)
    connectors, 121, 138, *138*
Bonjour technology, 207
bookmarks, synchronizing, 52
Boot Camp utility, 453, *454*
Boot tab in MSConfig tool, 379, *379*
BOOTP (Bootstrap Protocol), 94
Bootrec.exe tool, 554
bootup
  blank screens on, 260
  hard drive failures, 270
  to incorrect devices, 261
  methods, 339–340
  order, 554
  safe, 555–556
  settings, 167
  slow, 550
  troubleshooting, 547–548
botnets, 495
BranchCache, 327
bridges, 69
brightness
  projectors, 187
  screen, 20–21
bring-your-own-device (BYOD)
    initiatives, 526

brownouts, 593
browser redirection, 559
brute-force attacks, 503
BSB (back-side bus), 171
BSOD (Blue Screen of Death), 263–264,
    271, 549
burn-in, video, 276–277
burning smell, 263
bus speed setting, 171
business processes in change
    management, 588
BYOD (bring-your-own-device)
    initiatives, 526

C

cable locks
  laptops, 25, *25*
  using, 473
cable modems
  overview, 68–69
  SOHO networks, 76
Cable Select setting in IDE drives, 155, *156*
cable strippers, 103, *103*
cables
  hard drives, 131–134, *131–132*, *134*
  mobile devices, 288
  multipurpose, 127–130, *128–130*
  network, 120–124, *122–123*
  patch, 69, *69*
  peripherals, 130–136, *131–132*,
      134–136
  safety procedures, 602
  testers, 104
  troubleshooting, 300–301
  video, 124–127, *124–126*
caches
  buses, 171
  hard drives, 207
CAD (computer-aided design) workstations,
    194–195
calendars, synchronizing, 52
calibration
  inkjet printers, 222–223
  laser printers, 220
CAM (computer-aided manufacturing)
    workstations, 194–195
cameras
  description, 187
  security, 75–76
  unauthorized, 573
capacitors, distended, 267–268, *267*
carriages in inkjet printers, 221–222
cartridges for inkjet printers, 221
Cat 5 cable, 121
Cat 5e cable, 121
Cat 6 cable, 121
CCMP (Cipher Block Chaining Message
    Authentication Code Protocol), 81
cd command
  Linux, 455
  Windows, 353
CD-ROM
  booting from, 339
  overview, **148**

CD-ROM File System (CDFS), 347
CD-RW standard, 148
CDMA (Code Division Multiple Access), 100
cell phones
  applications, 240
  disposal, 601
  operating systems, 323
cellular cards, replacing, 12
cellular connections, 100
cellular data networks, configuring, 39–40
cellular mode, function keys for, 20
centralized VDI model, 241
certificates
  of destruction, 529
  elements, 477–478
  invalid, 561
  S/MIME, 44
CF (Compact Flash) cards, 153, *154*
chain of custody in incident response, 610
change boards, 589
change management, 587–590
changes in problem solving, 255
channels
  RAM, 144–145
  SOHO networks, 81
charge corona in laser printers, 211, 214
chargers, battery, 37, *38*
charging batteries, 280
charging step in laser printers, 214, *214*
Charms bar, 330, *331*
chip readers, 188
chkdsk command, 362–363
chmod command, 448, 456
chown command, 457
Chrome operating systems, 323
CHS values for hard drives, 150, *150*
CIFS (Common Internet File System)
  description, 64
  NFS, 347
Cipher Block Chaining Message
      Authentication Code Protocol
      (CCMP), 81
circuit-level proxies, 480
classes in IP addressing, 91–92
classful subnetting, 95
classless subnetting, 95
clean OS installations, 342
cleaning printers, 210
  inkjet, 222
  laser, 220
  thermal, 224
cleaning step in laser printers, 216, *217*
clicking noise in hard drives, 269
client-server network setup, 427–428, *428*
client-side virtualization, 242–245,
      244–245
clients, description, 101
clock settings, 171, *171*
clock speed in CPUs, 173
closed ports, 67
cloud computing
  measured services, 239
  metered services, 240
  models, 237–238
  network controllers, 67
  off-site email applications, 240
  on-demand, 239

overview, 237
printing, 205
rapid elasticity, 239
resource pooling, 239
review questions, 246–247
shared resources, 238–239
storage, 595
synchronization apps, 240
virtual application streaming,
      240–241, *241*
cmkdir command, 457
CMOS (complementary metal-oxide
      semiconductor)
  batteries, 171, *172*
  chips, 598
CMOS Setup program, 168–169
coaxial cable, 123–124, *123*
Code Division Multiple Access (CDMA),
      100
cold docking level, 24
collate settings for printers, 203
color
  printing problems, 295
  troubleshooting, 275
Color depth settings, 407, *407–408*
command line tools
  cd, 353
  chkdsk, 362–363
  copy, 366–367
  dir, 352–353
  diskpart, 363
  dism, 361
  format, 365–366
  gpresult, 364–365
  gpupdate, 364
  ipconfig, 354–355, *354–355*
  net use, 369–370, *369–370*
  net user, 370
  netstat, 358–359, *358*
  nslookup, 359–360
  overview, 351–352
  ping, 355–356, *356*
  question mark, 371
  robocopy, 368–369
  runas, 371–372
  sfc, 361–362
  shutdown, 361
  taskkill, 363–364
  tracert, 356–357, *357*
  xcopy, 367–368
COMMAND utility, 398
comments in scripts, 620
commercial software, 611
Common Internet File System (CIFS)
  description, 64
  NFS, 347
common ports, 62–65
common symptoms
  troubleshooting, 258–268, *265–267*
  video troubleshooting, 272–278,
      276–277
communication techniques and
      professionalism, 613
  active listening, 614
  cultural sensitivity, 614–615
  customer dealings, 617–619
  distractions, 615–617

proper language, 613–614
punctuality, 615
community clouds, 238
Compact Flash (CF) cards, 153, *154*
companion viruses, 493
compatibility
  applications, 425
  CPUs, 174–178, *177*
  operating systems, 322, 324, 338, 350
complementary metal-oxide semiconductor
      (CMOS)
  batteries, 171, *172*
  chips, 598
compliance
  documentation, 584
  environmental regulations, 607
  safety procedures, 603
component handling and storage, 597–599,
      598–599
Component Services tool, 374
compressed air, 606–607
computer-aided design (CAD) workstations,
      194–195
computer-aided manufacturing (CAM)
      workstations, 194–195
Computer Management tool, 373
concentrators in VPNs, 96
conditioning step in laser printers, 214, *214*
confidence, 614
confidential materials, 618–619
Connect To A Workplace option, 432
Connect To The Internet option, 431
connections
  mobile devices, 31–35, *32–33*
  networking, 99–101, 431–432
Connections tab in Internet Options applet,
      401, *401*
connectivity
  intermittent, 300
  Internet, 559
  laser printers, 219
  limited, 547
  networks, 297–300
  printing, 293
  thin clients, 199
  troubleshooting, 282
  wireless, 565–566
connectors
  common, 136–141, *137–138, 141*
  motherboards, 162–167, *162–166*
  power supplies, 191–194, *191–193*
constructs for scripts, 620–621
contacts, synchronizing, 51
content filtering in SOHO networks, 534
continuous feed printers, 209
continuous reboots, 261
Control Panel utilities
  BitLocker Drive Encryption, 423, *423*
  Credential Manager, 416, *416*
  Device Manager, 422, *423*
  Devices And Printers, 418, *419*
  Display, 406–408, *407–408*
  folder settings, 408–411, *409–410*
  HomeGroup, 417–418, *418*
  Internet Options, 400–406, *401–406*
  Network and Sharing Center, 421, *422*
  overview, 400

power options, 415–416
Programs and Features, 416, *417*
Sound, 419, *420*
Sync Center Control, 424, *424*
System, 411–413, *412–414*
Troubleshooting, 420–421, *421*
user accounts, 408
Windows Firewall, 414, *414*
controllers in laser printers, 210
cooling
CPUs, 178–179
gaming PCs, 197, *197*
copy command, 366–367
copying folders and files, 508
cores
CPUs, 172
virtualization workstations, 196
corporate email configuration, 42–47
cp command, 456
CPUs, 172
compatibility, 174–178, *177*
cooling, 178–179
cores, 172
gaming PCs, 196
GPUs, 174
hyperthreading, 173
replacing, 15
socket types, 174–178, *177*
speeds, 173–174
virtual technology, 173
workstations, 195–196
crash screens, 263–264, 271
crashes, application, 201, 549, 560
creased paper in printing, 291
Credential Manager, 416, *416*
credit card readers, 38, *38*
crimpers, 103
critical applications, backups for, 593
CRT monitor disposal, 600–601
cultural sensitivity, 614–615
cursors, ghost, 280
customers, dealing with, 616–619
cylinders
hard drives, 150, *150*
laser printers, 215

D

daisy chaining, 130
dark spots with laser printers, 219
Data_Bus_Error message, 264
data destruction and disposal
physical destruction, 527–529
recycling, 529–530
data loss prevention (DLP), 484
data preservation in incidents, 608–609
data privacy, 207–208
Data Sources tool, 374
data speeds for mobile devices, 572
data transmissions, over limit, 573
data types in scripts, 621
date settings, 349
DB-9 connectors, 139
DC jacks, replacing, 13

dd command, 459
DDoS (distributed denial-of-service)
attacks, 502
DDR (Double Data Rate) memory, 143–144
DDR2, 143
DDR3, 143
DDR4, 143
dead pixels, troubleshooting, 274
debris
removing, 606–607, *606–607*
thermal printers, 224
decryption problems in email, 285, 568
default SSIDs, 531
default subnet masks, 91–92, *95*
Defrag tool, 399
defragmenting drives, 551, *551*
degaussing for data destruction, 528
deleting AD accounts, 518
demilitarized zones (DMZs), 77–78
denial-of-service (DoS) attacks, 503
Deny permissions limitations, 508
dependencies in services, 550, *550*
desktop
cloud computing, 241, *241*
configuring, 200–201
MacOS and Linux, 450–451, *451*
synchronizing to, 50
thick client applications, 198
Windows operating systems, 328–332
destination network address translation
(DNAT), 98
Details tab in Task Manager, 389, *390*
developing step in laser printers, 215, *215*
Device Manager, 373, 422, *423*
Devices And Printers applet, 418, *419*
DHCP. *See* Dynamic Host Configuration
Protocol (DHCP)
dial-up connections
overview, 99
uses, 431
dictionary attacks, 503
differential backups, 499, 592
difficult customers, 616
digital rights management (DRM), 610
Digital Subscriber Line (DSL) modems,
68–69, 76–77
Digital Video Interface (DVI), 126, *126*
digitizers, 18–19
dim images, 275, 279, 565
DIMMs (dual inline memory modules)
circuit boards, 145
description, 141–142, *142*
dir command, 352–353
Direct Memory Access (DMA) channels,
156
directories. *See* folders
disabling
AD accounts, 519
airplane mode, 23
applications, 555, *555*
AutoRun function, 519
guest accounts, 516
Num Lock, 282
ports, 476–477, 534
services, 555
SSID broadcasts, 81, 302, 487, 531

touchpads, 21
Windows firewalls, 437
disappearing files, 560–561
disassembling mobile devices, 288
disaster prevention and recovery methods,
497–499, 590–593
Disk Management tool
adding drives, 396
arrays, 396
drive letters, 395, *395*
drive status, 391–392, *391*
extending partitions, 394
IDE drives, 156
initializing drives, 392–393, *393*
mounting drives, 392
overview, 390–391
shrinking partitions, 394–395,
394–395
splitting partitions, 394
storage spaces, 396–398, *396–397*
diskpart command, 363
disks. *See also* drives
imaging, 343
mirroring, 157, *157*
striping, 156–157, *157*
wiping, 528
dism command, 361
Display applet
Color depth settings, 407, *407–408*
refresh rate, 408, *408*
resolution settings, 406
Display File Icon On Thumbnails
option, 411
Display File Size Information In Folder Tips
option, 411
DisplayPort standard, 125–126, *126*
displays. *See also* screen
laptops, 15
dual, 20
types, 16–17
mobile devices, 565
distended capacitors, 267–268, *267*
distorted video geometry, 276, *276*
distorted video images, 276
distractions, 615–617
distributed denial-of-service (DDoS)
attacks, 502
Distributed mode in BranchCache, 327
DLP (data loss prevention), 484
DMA (Direct Memory Access) channels, 156
DMZs (demilitarized zones), 77–78
DNAT (destination network address
translation), 98
DNS. *See* Domain Name System (DNS)
DNSSEC (Domain Name System Security
Extensions), 499
Dock, 453, *453*
docking stations, 24–25
documentation, 582
acceptable use policies, 584–585
change management, 589
customer services, 618
incidents, 583, 610
inventory management, 586–587
knowledge base/articles, 583
mobile devices, 288

MSDSs, 604
network topology diagrams, 582–583, *583–584*
password policy, 585–586
problem solving, 257
regulatory and compliance policy, 584
documents, synchronizing, 52
Domain Name System (DNS)
alternative IP addresses, 438
configuring, 499
description, 63
IP addressing, 93
limited connectivity, 547
networks, 297
servers overview, 87
troubleshooting, 300
Domain Name System Security Extensions (DNSSEC), 499
domains
access in Windows, 327
Active Directory, 475
setup, 349, 427–428, *428*
Don't Show Hidden Files, Folders, And Drives option, 409
door locks
IoT-enabled, 76
overview, 472
DoS (denial-of-service) attacks, 503
dot-matrix printers, 224–226
Double Data Rate (DDR) memory, 143–144
DDR2, 143
DDR3, 143
DDR4, 143
drills for data destruction, 528
drive letters, assigning and changing, 395, *395*
drive not recognized problem, 270
Drive Optimization tool, 551, *551*
drivers
appropriate, 202–203
installing, 349–350
rolling back, 552
third-party, 348–349
updates, 443–444
drives
activity lights, 167
adding, 396
application space requirements, 425
encryption, 168–169
flash, 152–154, *152–154*, 339
formatting, 348, 529
fragmented, 551, *551*
hard. *See* hard drives
imaging, 343
MacOS and Linux, 447
mapping, 429
overwriting, 529
recycling, 529–530
scheduled maintenance, 442
SSDs, 10, 149, 339
wipes, 528, 530
DRM (digital rights management), 610
dropped signals, 571
drums in printers, 210
DSL (Digital Subscriber Line) modems, 68–69, 76–77

dual channel RAM, 144, *144*
dual-core CPUs, 172
dual displays for laptops, 20
dual-homed firewalls, 480, *481*
dual inline memory modules (DIMMs)
circuit boards, 145
description, 141–142, *142*
dual monitors for workstations, 196
duplex settings
NICs, 439, *439*
printers, 203
duplexing
inkjet printers, 221
laser printers, 218
dust
removing, 606–607, *606–607*
thermal printers, 224
DVD, booting from, 339
DVD-ROM standard, 148
DVI (Digital Video Interface), 126, *126*
DVI to HDMI adapters, 134, *135*
DVI to VGA adapters, 136, *136*
DXDIAG utility, 399
dye sublimation in thermal printers, 224
Dynamic Host Configuration Protocol (DHCP)
description, 64
IP addressing, 93–94
servers, 87
troubleshooting, 299–300
dynamic IP addresses, 92
dynamic partitions, 345

E

e-readers, 30–31
ebooks, synchronizing, 52
ECC (Error Correction Code) RAM, 145
EEPROM (electrically erasable programmable read-only memory) chips, 167
EFS (Encrypting File System), 327–328, *328*, 513, *513*
802.11a standard, 82–83, 204
802.11ac standard, 83
802.11b standard, 83
802.11g standard, 83
802.11n standard, 83
eight-pin 12V power supplies, **192**, *192*
electrical fire safety, 602
electrically erasable programmable read-only memory (EEPROM) chips, 167
electromagnets for data destruction, 528
electronic protected health information (EPHI), 612
electrophotographic (EP) printers. *See* laser printers
electrostatic discharge (ESD), 596–597
antistatic bags, 597–598
ESD mats, 598–599, *599*
ESD straps, 598, *598*
email
cloud computing applications, 240
configuring, 42

decryption problems, 285, 568
Exchange, 46–47
filtering, 484
Google, 46
hijacked, 561
iCloud, 45–46
IMAP, 43
mail servers, 88
POP accounts, 42–43
S/MIME, 44–45
synchronizing, 51
troubleshooting, 299
viruses, 492, *492*
Yahoo, 47
embedded systems, 90
emulator requirements for virtual machines, 243
enabling
airplane mode, 23
multimonitor taskbar, 330, *331*
Num Lock, 282
RDP, 433–435, *433–435*, 622–623, *622–623*
Windows firewalls, **437**
workspaces, 451, *451*
enclosures for airborne particles, 605
Encrypting File System (EFS), 327–328, *328*, 513, *513*
encryption
BitLocker, 513
BitLocker Drive Encryption, 423, *423*
data privacy, 208
drives, 168–169
mobile devices, 524
SOHO networks, 80–81, 531
Windows operating systems, 327–328, *328*, 513, *513*
wireless, 486–487
workstations, 519
end-of-life date for operating systems, 324
end-point management servers, 90
end-user acceptance in change management, 589
end-user device configuration in SOHO networks, 74–75
end-user education for malware, 499
end-user license agreements (EULAs), 610
enterprise licenses, 611
entry control roster, 474
environment variables in scripts, 620
environmental changes in problem solving, 255
environmental impacts, 603–604
airborne particles, 605–606
dust and debris, 606–607, *606–607*
government regulations, 607
MSDS documentation, 604
power-related threats, 605
printers, 209
temperature, humidity, and ventilation, 604–605
EP (electrophotographic) printers. *See* laser printers
EPHI (electronic protected health information), 612
equipment grounding, 596–597

error codes in printing, 219, 296
Error Correction Code (ECC) RAM, 145
eSATA
    cables, 132, *132*
    connectors, 140
    expansion cards, 182, *182*
ESD (electrostatic discharge), 596–597
    antistatic bags, 597–598
    ESD mats, 598–599, *599*
    ESD straps, 598, *598*
Ethernet
    cables, 121–122, *122*
    NICs, 181
    PoE, 70, *70*
    printers, 204
    USB to Ethernet adapters, 135, *135*
Ethernet over Power, 70, *71*
EULAs (end-user license agreements), 610
Event Viewer, 375–378, *376–377*
exceptions in firewalls, 436
Exchange email, 46–47
exFAT (Extended File Allocation Table), 346
exit rollers, troubleshooting, 292
expansion cards
    eSATA, 182, *182*
    NICs, 181
    sound, *180*
    USB, 181–182
    video, 179–180, *180*
expectations, customer, 617–619
expiration, passwords, 515, 586
EXPLORER utility, 399
exposing step in laser printers, 214, *214*
ExpressCard slots, 11
ext3 file system, 347
ext4 file system, 347
Extended File Allocation Table
    (exFAT), 346
extended reality, 29–30, *29–30*
extending partitions, 345, 394
extensions settings, 409, *409*
external caches, 171
external data bus, 171
external drives, booting from, 340
external monitors for mobile devices,
    282, 566
external shared resources in cloud
    computing, 239
external speed in CPUs, 173

F

F connectors, 121
faded printing, 291
failed attempts
    lockout, 516–517
    restrictions, 523
failed jobs in logs, 277
false acceptance rate (FAR) in biometric
    locks, 473
false rejection rate (FRR) in biometric
    locks, 473
fans for CPUs, 178
FAT (File Allocation Table)
    limitations, 507
    overview, 346–347

feeders
    inkjet printers, 221
    thermal printers, 223–224
fencing, 472
fiber-optic cabling
    characteristics, 122–123, *123*
    overview, 99
Fiber to the Home (FTTH), 99
fifth generation (5G) cellular
    technology, 86
File Allocation Table (FAT)
    limitations, 507
    overview, 346–347
file servers, 87
file systems, 346–348
File Transfer Protocol (FTP), 63
files
    attributes, 508–509
    backups, 592–593
    disappearing, 560–561
    moving and copying, 508
    permission changes, 561
    printing to, 226
    script, 619–620
    shared, 510–512, *510–511*
    sharing, 199, 626
    system, 512
filters
    air, 603, 606
    content, 534
    email, 484
    MAC addresses, 79, 477
Finder, 452, *452*
fingerprint locks, 521
fire-rated storage, 498
fire safety, 602
firewalls
    configuring, 437
    description, 67, 375
    enabling and disabling, 437
    exceptions, 436
    malware, 499
    managing, 414, *414*
    mobile devices, 525–526
    overview, 478–479, *479*
    packet-filter, 480
    proxy, 480–481, *481*
    SOHO networks, 75, 77–80, 533
    stateful inspection, 481
firmware
    radio, 48–49
    SOHO networks, 534
    updates, 167, 443–444, 534
first response in incidents, 609–610
fitness monitors, 28, *28*
568A/B cable, 122, *122*
flash drives
    booting from, 339
    overview, 152–154, *152–154*
flash memory for mobile devices, 39
flashing BIOS, 167
flatbed scanners, 184
flickering images, 275, 279
fluorescent backlighting, 16–17
Folder Options dialog box, 408
    General tab, 410, *410*
    View tab, 409–411, *409*

folders
    applications, 426
    description, 391
    extensions settings, 409, *409*
    moving and copying, 508
    permissions, 482–483
    redirection, 476
    shared, 510–512, *510–511*
    system, 512
Force Quit command, 449–450, *450*
form factors for motherboards, 160–162,
    160–161
format command, 365–366
formatting drives, 348, 529
Forwarded Events log, 375
forwarding, port, 78, 534
four-pin 12V power supplies, 192, *192*
four-pin Molex connectors, 140, *141*
fourth generation (4G) cellular
    technology, 85
FQDNs (fully qualified domain names), 93
fragmented drives, 551, *551*
frames, replacing, 14
frequencies in wireless protocols, 84
front panel connectors, 166
front-side bus (FSB), 171
frozen systems in mobile devices, 286, 569
FRR (false rejection rate) in biometric
    locks, 473
FSB (front-side bus), 171
Fsck tool, 447
FTP (File Transfer Protocol), 63
FTTH (Fiber to the Home), 99
full backups, 498, 592
Full Control permission, 508–509
full device encryption, 524
full duplex settings for NICs, 439, *439*
full formatting drives, 348
fully qualified domain names (FQDNs), 93
function keys in laptops, 19–23, *22–24*
fuser kits in printers, 210
fusing assemblies in laser printers,
    213, *213*
fusing step in laser printers, 216, *216*

G

Gadgets, 328
game controllers, 186, *186*
game pads, 36, *37*
gaming PCs, 196–197, *197*
garbled characters in printing, 219, 293
gateways
    alternative IP addresses, 438
    IP addressing, 91, 96
    troubleshooting, 298
General Data Protection Regulation
    (GDPR), 611–612
General tab
    Folder Options, 410, *410*
    Internet Options, 402–403, *403*
    MSConfig tool, 378, *378*
generalization process in operating system
    images, 343
geometric video distortion, 276, *276*
gestures, 452

GFCI (ground fault circuit interrupter) receptacles, *595*
ghosted images in printing, 219, **291**
Gigabit NIC, 199
global positioning system (GPS)
    mobile devices, 287
    overview, 31
    settings, 22–23, *23*
Global System for Mobile Communications (GSM), 100
goggles, 602
Google email, 46
Google Glass, 29, *29*
government regulations
    environmental impacts, 607
    safety procedures, 603
gpresult command, 364–365
GPS (global positioning system)
    mobile devices, 287
    overview, 31
    settings, 22–23, *23*
GPT (GUID Partition Table), 346
gpupdate command, 364
graphic workstations, 194–195
graphics processing units (GPUs)
    gaming PCs, 197
    integrated, 174
graylisting, 79
grep command, 454–455
ground fault circuit interrupter (GFCI) receptacles, *595*
grounding
    equipment, 596–597
    self-grounding, 599
group policies for Active Directory, 475–476
GSM (Global System for Mobile Communications), 100
guards, 472
guest accounts
    disabling, 516
    security settings, 506
guest operating systems in virtualization workstations, 196
GUID Partition Table (GPT), 346

H

half duplex settings in NICs, 439, *439*
hammers for data destruction, 528
hard drives
    cables, 131–134, *131–132*, *134*
    caches, 207
    configuring, 155–156, *156*
    magnetic, 149–151, *150*
    managing. *See* Disk Management tool
    partitioning. *See* partitions, hard drives
    replacing, 9–10
    troubleshooting, 268–272
    workstations, 195–196
hardware
    adapters, 134–136, *135–136*
    BIOS/UEFI settings, 167–171, *170–171*
    CMOS battery, 171, *172*
    compatibility, 350
    connectors, 136–141, *137–138*, *141*

CPU features, 172–179, *177*
desktop, 200–201
expansion cards, 179–183, *180–182*
gaming PCs, 196–197, *197*
hard drive cables, 131–134, *131–132*, *134*
laptops, 201–202
motherboards
    connectors types, 162–167, *162–166*
    form factors, 160–162, *160–161*
multipurpose cables, 127–130, *128–130*
network-attached storage devices, 199
network cables, 120–124, *122–123*
networking, 65–71, *68–71*
peripherals, 183–189, *185–186*, *189*
power supplies, 189–194, *190–193*
printers, 203–205
public devices, 205–208, *205–206*
RAM, 141–147, *144*, *146*
review questions, 228–233
storage devices, 147–159, *150*, *152–154*, *156–158*
thick clients, 198
thin clients, 198–199
video cables, 124–127, *124–126*
workstations, 194–196
hardware/device replacement in laptops.
    See laptops
hardware tokens, 473
HC1 headset computer, 30
HDMI (High-Definition Multimedia Interface)
    connectors, 125, *125*
    DVI to HDMI adapters, 134, *135*
HDSL (high bit-rate DSL), 76
heads
    hard drives, 150
    inkjet printers, 222
headsets
    description, 187
    mobile devices, 36
    virtual reality, 29–30, *29–30*, 184, *185*
Health Insurance Portability and Accountability Act (HIPAA) Security Rule, 612
healthy drive status, 391
heat sinks, 178–179
heating elements in thermal printers, 223–224
HFS (Hierarchical File System), 348
Hibernate power option, 415
hidden files settings, 409, *409*
Hide Empty Drives In The Computer Folder option, 411
Hide Extensions For Known File Types option, 409
Hide Protected Operating System Files option, 409, 411
Hierarchical File System (HFS), 348
high bit-rate DSL (HDSL), 76
High-Definition Multimedia Interface (HDMI)
    connectors, 125, *125*
    DVI to HDMI adapters, 134, *135*
high-end video workstations, 195

High process priority, 385
High-Voltage Power Supply (HVPS) in laser printers, 213
hijacked email, 561
HIPAA (Health Insurance Portability and Accountability Act) Security Rule, 612
home folders, 476
home network settings, 435
HomeGroup
    settings, 417–418, *418*
    vs. workgroups, 427
host cursors, 280
Hosted Cache mode, 327
hosted VDI model, 241
hostnames in IP addressing, 93
hosts
    services, 86–90
    virtualization workstations, 196
hot docking level, 24
hot-swappable drives
    booting from, 340
    description, 158
hotfixes for workstations, 520
hotspots
    configuring, 40
    mobile devices, 35, 100
HTTP (Hypertext Transfer Protocol), 63
HTTPS (Hypertext Transfer Protocol over Secure Sockets Layer), 64
hubs, 68
humidity control, 605
HVPS (High-Voltage Power Supply) in laser printers, 213
hybrid clouds, 238
hybrid drives, 10, 151, *152*
Hypertext Transfer Protocol (HTTP), 63
Hypertext Transfer Protocol over Secure Sockets Layer (HTTPS), 64
hyperthreading, 173
hypervisors, 173, **244–245**, *244–245*

I

IaaS (infrastructure as a service), 238
iCloud
    description, **452**
    email, 45–46
    synchronizing to, 50
ICMP (Internet Control Message Protocol), 481
icons, oversized, 277, *277*
ID badges, 472
IDE drives
    configuring, 155–156, *156*
    overview, 132–133, *132*
IDs in SCSI, 134
IDSs (intrusion detection systems), 89
ifconfig command, 457
image-level backups, 592
images
    operating systems, 343–344, 552
    printing to, 226
    recovery in MacOS and Linux, 447
ImageX utility, 343
imaging drum in laser printers, 211, *211*
imaging process in laser printers, 214–217, *214–217*

IMAP (Internet Message Access Protocol)
  description, 64
  email, 43
IMEI (International Mobile Equipment
    Identification), 49
impact printers, 209, 224–226
impersonation, 502
IMSI (International Mobile Subscriber
    Identification), 49
in-place OS upgrades, 333–334, 341–342
in-plane switching (IPS) displays, 16
incident response plans (IRPs), 610
incidents
  documentation, 583
  incident response, 608–610
incineration for data destruction, 528
incorrect color patterns, 275
incorrect devices, bootup to, 261
incremental backups, 498, 592
indicator lights, 263, 282
Information Technology eXtended (ITX)
    motherboards, 161, *161*
infrared (IR) connectors, 35
infrastructure
  changes, in problem solving, 255
  printers, 204
infrastructure as a service (IaaS), 238
inheriting permissions, 512
initializing drives, 392–393, *393*
injectors, PoE, 70, *70*
inkjet printers, 220–223, *220*
input voltages in power supplies,
    189–190
installation
  applications, 424–426
  drivers, 349–350
  operating systems, 340–344
  printers, 295
  RAM, 145–147, *146*
integers in scripts, 621
integrated commercial provider email
    configuration, 45–47
integrated print servers, 204–205
Integrated Services Digital Network
    (ISDN), 100
Intel CPUs, 176
interface
  configurations, 169–171, *170–171*
  Windows operating systems, 328–332,
    329, 331
interference, 300–301
intermittent connectivity, 300
intermittent device failure, 262
intermittent wireless, 280, 565
internal drives, booting from, 340
internal shared resources in cloud
    computing, 239
internal speed in CPUs, 173
internal USB connectors, 166, *166*
International Mobile Equipment
    Identification (IMEI), 49
International Mobile Subscriber
    Identification (IMSI), 49
Internet appliances, 88–90
Internet connections
  issues, 559
  networking, 99–101

Internet Control Message Protocol
    (ICMP), 481
Internet Message Access Protocol (IMAP)
  description, 64
  email, 43
Internet of Things (IoT) devices, 75–76
Internet Options applet, 400
  Advanced tab, 405–406, *406*
  Connections tab, 401, *401*
  General tab, 402–403, *403*
  Privacy tab, 403–404, *404*
  Programs tab, 404–405, *405*
  Security tab, 401–402, *402*
interruptions, 616
intranet servers, 87
intrusion detection systems (IDSs), 89
intrusion prevention systems (IPSs), 89
invalid certificates, 561
inventory management, 586–587
inverters in laptops, 18
iOS operating systems, 323
IoT (Internet of Things) devices,
    75–76
IP addressing
  alternative, 437–438, *438*
  APIPA, 92
  classes, 91–92
  conflicts, 301
  DHCP, 93–94
  DNS, 93
  gateways, 96
  IPv4 vs. IPv6, 94–95
  link local, 93
  NAT, 97–98
  overview, 90–91
  printers, 429, *430*
  SOHO networks, 73, 533
  subnet masks, 95–96
  VLANs, 97
  VPNs, 96–97
IPC$ drive, 429
ipconfig command, 354–355,
    354–355
IPS (in-plane switching) displays, 16
IPSs (intrusion prevention systems), 89
IR (infrared) connectors, 35
IRPs (incident response plans), 610
irq1_not_less_or_equal message, 264
ISDN (Integrated Services Digital
    Network), 100
ISP email configuration, 42–47
ITX (Information Technology eXtended)
    motherboards, 161, *161*
iwconfig command, 457

J

jams
  inkjet printers, 223
  laser printers, 218–219
  troubleshooting, 292
jargon, 613–614
jewelry, 601
journaled file systems (JFSs), 497–498,
    591
.js files, 620

K

Kensington locks, 25, *25*
key fobs, 474
keyboard, video, and mouse (KVM)
    devices, 188
keyboards
  backlight, 21
  description, 185
  replacing, 9
  sticking keys, 280
keychain drives, 152–153, *152*
keychain password system, 451–452
keyloggers, 490
kill command, 459
killing tasks, 552
Kindle devices, 30
knowledge base/articles, 583
KVM (keyboard, video, and mouse)
    devices, 188

L

land grid array (LGA) sockets, 177
language
  communication techniques, 613–614
  settings, 349
LANs (local area network), 101
laptop hardware and components
  digitizers, 18–19
  displays, 15–17
  hardware/device replacement, 8–9
    batteries, 13
    CPUs, 15
    DC jacks, 13
    hard drives, 9–10
    keyboards, 9
    memory, 10–11
    mini-PCIe cards, 12
    optical drives, 11
    plastics, 14
    screen, 12–13
    smart card readers, 11
    speakers, 14
    system boards, 14
    touchpads, 13
    video cards, 12
    wireless cards, 11–12
  inverters, 18
  microphones, 18
  webcams, 18
  WiFi antenna connectors, 17–18
laptops
  cloud computing, 241, *241*
  components, 201–202
  docking stations, 24–25
  dual displays, 20
  physical locks, *25*
  rotating and removable screens, 26
  special function keys, 19–23, *22–24*
laser printers, 210
  components, 210–213, *211–213*
  imaging process, 214–217, *214–217*
  maintenance, 218–220
  printing steps summary, 217–218, *218*

Launch Folder Windows In A Separate
   Process option, 411
LCD displays, 16
LDAP (Lightweight Directory Access
   Protocol), 65
leaked personal data, 573
least privilege concept, 485
LED backlighting, 16–17
LED displays, 17
legacy systems, 90
LGA (land grid array) sockets, 177
licensing, 610–611
lifting safety procedures, 601–602
light switches, IoT-enabled, 75
Lightning connectors, 139
   characteristics, 127, 128
   description, 33–34, 33
   limitations, 34
Lightweight Directory Access Protocol
   (LDAP), 65
limited connectivity, troubleshooting, 547
line-of-sight wireless, 101
line printers, 209
lines in laser printing, 219
link local addresses
   overview, 93
   troubleshooting, 299–300
Linux operating systems
   best practices, 441–445
   commands, 454–459
   description, 322–323
   features, 450–454
   overview, 440–441
   tools, 445–450, 446, 448, 450
liquid-based cooling cases, 178–179
List Folder Contents permission, 509
listening, active, 614
local area network (LANs), 101
local installations for applications, 425
local resources for networks, 298
Local Security Policy tool, 373
local shares, 511
local user permissions, 425
Local Users And Groups tool, 373
location data, synchronizing, 52
location tracking
   settings, 23, 23
   unauthorized, 573
locator applications, 522
lockout
   failed password attempts, 516–517
   system, 570
locks
   biometric, 472–473
   cable, 473
   door, 472
   IoT-enabled, 76
   laptops, 25
   network, 477
   screen, 517, 521–522
   server, 473
   USB, 473
lockups
   malware, 559
   system, 259
logical partitions, 346
logical unit numbers (LUNs) in SCSI, 134

login attempts restrictions, 523
login scripts for Active Directory, 475
logon time, restricting, 516
logs
   boot, 547–548
   Event Viewer, 375–377, 376–377
   failed jobs in, 277
   malware clues in, 561
   mobile devices, 570
   problem solving, 256
   system and application, 561
   troubleshooting, 268
LoJack product, 169
Long-Term Evolution (LTE) technologies,
   40, 85–86
loopback addresses, 94
loopback plugs, 104
loops in scripts, 621
loud noises
   hard drives, 269
   troubleshooting, 262
low-level drive format, 529
low memory errors in printing, 294
Low process priority, 385
low RF signals, 301–302
ls command, 454
LTE (Long-Term Evolution) technologies,
   40, 85–86
lumens for projectors, 187
LUNs (logical unit numbers) in SCSI, 134
lvcreate command, 446–447

M

M2 drives, 149
MAC address filters
   overview, 477
   SOHO networks, 79
MacOS operating systems
   best practices, 441–445
   description, 322
   features, 450–454, 451–454
   overview, 440–441
   tools, 445–450, 446, 448, 450
macro viruses, 493
magnetic hard drives
   overview, 149–151, 150
   vs. SSD, 10
magnetic readers, 188
mail servers, 88
maintenance
   drives, 442, 447
   printers, 209–210
      impact, 225–226
      inkjet, 222–223
      laser, 218–220
      thermal printers, 224
maintenance kits for laser printers, 220
malware
   keyloggers, 490
   lockups, 559
   log disclosure of, 561
   mobile devices, 523
   preventing, 496–499
   ransomware, 489–490
   removal best practices, 562–564

rootkits, 490
   slow performance, 559
   Trojan horses, 490
   unauthorized actions, 573
   viruses, 490–495, 492–495
man-in-the-middle (MITM) attacks, 503
managed switches, 66–67
MANs (metropolitan area networks), 102
mantraps, 470–471, 471
Manually Connect To A Wireless Network
   option, 431
mapping
   drives, 369, 370, 429
   ports, 78, 534
   printers, 429–430, 430
masks
   filter, 603
   subnet, 91–92, 95–96, 298, 438
master boot record (MBR), 346
master computers in operating system
   images, 343
Master setting in IDE drives, 155, 156
material safety data sheets (MSDSs), 604
mATX (mini-ATX) motherboards, 161
MBR (master boot record), 346
MDM (Mobile Device Management)
   policies, 476
measured services in cloud computing, 239
Media Center, 327
media options, 21, 22
media streaming with NAS devices, 199
media testers, 104
memory. See RAM
metered services in cloud computing, 240
meters, 103, 600, 600
Metro interface, 329–330, 329
metropolitan area networks (MANs), 102
mice, 185
Micro-SD cards, 153
Micro-SD slots, 39
Micro-USB
   connectors, 139
   ports, 32, 32
microphones
   description, 187
   laptops, 18
   unauthorized activation, 573
Microsoft Management Console (MMC),
   373–375, 398
Microsoft Windows. See Windows
   operating systems
MIMO (Multiple In/Multiple Out) feature,
   83
mini-ATX (mATX) motherboards, 161
Mini HDMI ports, 125
mini-ITX motherboards, 161–162
mini-PCIe cards, 12
Mini-SD cards, 154, 154
Mini-USB
   connectors, 139
   ports, 32, 32
miniPCI cards, 163, 164
mirroring, disk, 157, 157
Mission Control, 450–451
MITM (man-in-the-middle) attacks, 503
MMC (Microsoft Management Console),
   373–375, 398

Mobile Device Management (MDM)
  policies, 476
mobile devices
  accessories, 36–39, *37–38*
  characteristics, 26–31, *28–30*
  components, 201–202
  configuring, 39
    Bluetooth, 40–42
    email, 42–47
    PRI, 47–48
    radio firmware, 48–49
    VPN, 49
    wireless/cellular data network,
      39–40
  connections, 31–35, *32–33*
  disassembling, 288
  displays, 15–19
  laptop features, 19–26, *22–25*
  laptop hardware and components, 8–15
  mutual authentication, 53
  review questions, 54–56
  security, 520–521
    antivirus software, 523
    authentication, 524
    authenticator applications, 524
    biometric authentication, 523
    encryption, 524
    failed login attempts restrictions,
      523
    firewalls, 525–526
    locator applications, 522
    policies and procedures, 526
    remote backup applications,
      522–523
    remote wipes, 522
    screen locks, 521
    troubleshooting, 571–573
    trusted and untrusted sources,
      524–525, *525*
    updates, 523
  synchronizing, 50–53
  troubleshooting
    overview, 278–289, *281, 283*
    security, 571–573
    software, 564–570
models in inventory management, 587
modems, 68–69, 76–77
Modify permission, 508–509
Molex connectors
  examples, 140, *141*
  power connectors, 192
monitors. *See also* displays; screen
  connecting, 184
  mobile devices, 282, 566
  workstations, 196
motherboards
  connectors types, 162–167, *162–166*
  form factors, 160–162, *160–161*
  power supply adapters, 190, *190*
mounting drives, 392
moving folders and files, 508
MSConfig tool
  Boot tab, 379, *379*
  description, 398
  disabling application startup, *555, 555*
  General tab, 378, *378*
  Services tab, 379, *380*

  Startup tab, 380, *381*
  Tools tab, 382
MSDSs (material safety data sheets), 604
MSINFO32 utility, 399
MSTSC utility, 399
multiboot OS installations, 342
multicore processors
  gaming PCs, 196
  overview, 172
  workstations, 195
multifactor authentication
  description, 482
  mobile devices, 524
  security, 488
multimeters, 103
multimonitor taskbar, 330, *331*
multipartite viruses, 493, *493*
multiple-barrier systems, 472
multiple desktops in MacOS and Linux,
  450–451
Multiple In/Multiple Out (MIMO) feature,
  83
multipliers for CPU speed, 173
multipurpose cables, 127–130, *128–130*
multitouch, troubleshooting, 283–284, *283*
music, synchronizing, 51–52
mutation, virus, 494
mutual authentication in mobile devices, 53
mv command, 456

N

nano-ITX motherboards, 161
NAT (network address translation)
  IP addressing, 97–98
  SOHO networks, 79
navigation tools, 352–353
near field communications (NFC)
  description, 188
  overview, 34
  wireless protocols, 84
net use command, 369–370, *369–370*
net user command, 370
NetBIOS/NetBT, 64
NetBoot method, 340
netsetup.log file, 547
netstat command, 358–359, *358*
Network Access Control, 90
network address translation (NAT)
  IP addressing, 97–98
  SOHO networks, 79
Network and Sharing Center, 421, *422*
network-attached storage devices, 199
network-based IDS (NIDS), 89
network-based installations for
  applications, 425
Network File System (NFS), 347
network installations for operating systems,
  342–343
network interface cards (NICs)
  configuring, 73–74, *73–74*
  description, 67
  indicator lights, 263
  NAS devices, 199
  overview, 181
  power settings, 281, *281*

  properties, 439–440, *439*
  proxy firewalls, 480
  troubleshooting, 300–301
  virtual, 241–242
network time protocol (NTP) servers, 88
network topology diagrams, 582–583,
  583–584
networking, 62
  cables, 120–124, *122–123*
  hardware devices, 65–71, *68–71*
  host services, 86–90
  Internet connections, 99–101
  IP addressing, 90–98
  ports and protocols, 62–65
  review questions, 106–109
  settings updating, 552
  SOHO. *See* small office and home
    office (SOHO) networks
  thin clients, 199
  tools, 102–105, *103*
  troubleshooting, 297–304, *302–304*
  types, 101–102
  virtual machine requirements, 244
  wireless protocols, 82–86
networking configuration, 426–427
  alternative IP addresses, 437–438, *438*
  connections, 431–432
  domain setup, 427–428, *428*
  firewalls, 436–437
  HomeGroup vs. workgroups, 427
  network type, 435–436, *436*
  NIC properties, 439–440, *439*
  printers, 429–430, *430*
  proxy settings, 432, *432*
  Remote Assistance, 434–435, *435*
  Remote Desktop, 433–434, *433–434*
  shares, 429
Networking tab in Task Manager, 388, *388*
New Technology File System (NTFS)
  description, 347
  security settings, 506–509
Next Generation Form Factor (NGFF), 149
NFC (near field communications)
  description, 188
  overview, 34
  wireless protocols, 84
NFS (Network File System), 347
NGFF (Next Generation Form Factor), 149
NICs. *See* network interface cards (NICs)
NIDS (network-based IDS), 89
no image on screen, troubleshooting,
  273–274
no operating system found message, 548
noise
  hard drives, 269
  troubleshooting, 262
non-compliant systems, 504
Non-Volatile Memory Host Controller
  Interface Specification (NVMHCIS),
  149
nonimpact printers, 209
nonparity RAM, 145
nonvolatile random-access memory
  (NVRAM), 169, *170*
Nook devices, 30
Normal process priority, 385
NOTEPAD utility, 399

nslookup command, 359–360
NTFS (New Technology File System)
    description, 347
    security settings, 506–509
NTP (network time protocol) servers, 88
nuisance tripping, 594
Num Lock indicator lights, 282
NVM Express (NVMe), 149
NVMHCIS (Non-Volatile Memory Host
    Controller Interface Specification),
    149
NVRAM (nonvolatile random-access
    memory), 169, *170*

O

octets in IP addressing, 91
off-site email applications, 240
off-site storage, 498, 591–592
OLED (organic light-emitting diode)
    displays, 17
on-demand resource utilization in cloud
    computing, 239
on-site storage, 498, 591
onboard video cards, 179
1.8 inch hard drives, 10
open ports, 67
open source software, 611
operating system not found message, 270
operating systems, 321
    32-bit vs. 64-bit, 321–322
    boot methods, 339–340
    cell phones and tablets, 323
    compatibility, 324, 350
    driver installation, 349–350
    file systems, 346–348
    formatting, 348
    installation types, 340–344
    Linux. *See* Linux operating systems
    Mac. *See* MacOS operating systems
    partitioning, 344–346
    reloading, 552
    repairing, 553
    review questions, 460–462
    shared device settings, 206
    third-party drivers, 348–349
    time, date, region and language
        settings, 349
    updates, 560
    upgrade paths, 332–338
    vendor-specific limitations, 323–324
    virtualization workstations, 196
    Windows. *See* Windows operating
        systems
    workgroup vs. domain setup, 349
    workstations, 322–323
operational procedures, 582
    change management, 587–590
    communication techniques and
        professionalism, 613–619
    disaster prevention and recovery
        methods, 590–596, *594–595*
    documentation, 582–587, *583–584*
    environmental impacts, 603–608,
        606–607
    prohibited activities, 608–612

remote access technologies, 622–626,
    622–625
review questions, 627–630
safety, 596–603, *598–600*
scripts, 619–621
optical drives
    replacing, 11
    types, 147–149
organic light-emitting diode (OLED)
    displays, 17
organizational units (OUs), 476
orientation
    printers, 203
    screen, 21, *22*
OS X operating systems, 322
OUs (organizational units), 476
out-of-memory errors in laser printers, 219
output voltages in power supplies, 190
overclocking CPUs, 174
overheating
    mobile devices, 286, 568
    troubleshooting, 262
    video cards, 274
oversized images and icons, 277, *277*
overwriting drives, 208, 529

P

PaaS (platform as a service), 238
packet-filter firewalls, 480
page description language (PDL), 293
Page_Fault_in_nonpaged_area message,
    264
page printers, 209–210
pairing, Bluetooth, 41, 572
PANs (personal area networks), 102
paper
    feeding issues, 291–292
    impact printers, 225–226
    thermal printers, 224
paper jams
    inkjet printers, 223
    laser printers, 218–219
    troubleshooting, 292
paper transport assembly in laser printers,
    212, *212*
parental controls, 534
parity RAM, 145
partitions, hard drives
    extending, 394
    overview, 344–346
    shrinking, 394–395, *394–395*
    splitting, 394
passcode locks, 522
passive heat sinks, 178
passive hubs, 68
passive matrix screens, 16
password command, 455–456
passwords
    admin, 517
    BIOS, 168
    BIOS/UEFI, 515
    changing, 586
    expiration, 515, 586
    policies, 585–586
    rainbow tables, 504

requiring, 516, 586
resetting and unlocking, 518–519
screensavers, 515
SOHO networks, 532–533
strong, 481–482, 514–515, 585–586
synchronizing, 53
PAT (port address translation), 98
patch panels, 69, *69*
patches
    MacOS and Linux, 443
    mobile devices, 523
    workstations, 520
PCI-DSS standard, 611
PCI Express (PCIe)
    overview, 163, *163*
    power supply connectors, 192–193,
        193
    video cards, 180, *180*
PCI (Peripheral Component Interconnect)
    bus, 162–163, *162*
PCL (Printer Control Language), 293
PDF, printing to, 226
PDL (page description language), 293
performance
    hard drives, 269
    malware issues, 559
    mobile devices, 284–285, 567
    slow transfer speeds, 301
    System utility, 412–413, *412*
    troubleshooting, 546
Performance Monitor tool, 373
Performance tab in Task Manager, 387, *387*
perimeter barriers, 472
Peripheral Component Interconnect (PCI)
    bus, 162–163, *162*
peripherals
    cables for, 130–136, *131–132,*
        134–136
    purposes and uses, 183–189, *185–186,*
        189
permissions
    applications, 425
    changed, 561
    directory, 482–483
    inheriting, 512
    printers, 295
    propagation, 511
    restricting, 516
    security settings, 506–509
personal area networks (PANs), 102
personal calls, 615
personal data, leaked, 573
personal interruptions, 616
personal licenses, 611
personal package archives (PPAs), 443, *444*
personal safety, 601–603
personally identifiable information (PII), 611
PGA (pin grid array) sockets, 177, *177–178*
phage viruses, 494
PHI (protected health information), 612
phishing, 501
phones
    applications, 240
    disposal, 601
    operating systems, 323
    smartphones, 27
physical barriers, 472

physical data destruction, 527–529
physical locks for laptops, 25
physical security in SOHO networks, 535, 535
physical tokens, 473
pickup rollers in laser printers, 212
pico-ITX motherboards, 161
pictures, synchronizing, 51
PII (personally identifiable information), 611
pin codes for Bluetooth, 42
pin grid array (PGA) sockets, 177, 177–178
ping command, 355–356, 356
pinning to taskbar, 330
Pinwheel of Death (PWOD), 264–267, 265–266, 271, 549
PIO (Programmed Input/Output) setting, 156
pixels, troubleshooting, 274
Plain Old Telephone System (POTS), 99
plans
    change management, 589
    problem solving, 257
plastic filaments in 3D printers, 227, 227
plastics, replacing, 14
platform as a service (PaaS), 238
plenum cable, 121
PoE (Power over Ethernet), 70, 70
point-to-multipoint technology, 100
pointer drift, 280
policies and procedures for mobile devices, 526
polymorphic viruses, 494, 494
pools in cloud computing, 239
POP (Post Office Protocol), 63
Pop-Up Blocker Settings dialog box, 558, 558
pop-ups, 558, 558
port address translation (PAT), 98
port replicators, 24–25
ports
    disabling, 534
    email, 44
    forwarding, 78–79, 534
    mobile devices, 32–34, 32–33
    networking, 62–65
    open and closed, 67
    printer, 204, 206
    security, 476–477
positive attitudes, 614
Post Office Protocol (POP), 63
POST (power-on self-test), 259–260
POTS (Plain Old Telephone System), 99
power
    malware drains on, 571
    mobile devices, 281, 571
    options, 415–416
    power-related threats, 605
    safety procedures, 601
    troubleshooting, 263
    UPSs, 593–594
power button, 166
power-level controls in SOHO networks, 532
power light, 166
power line Ethernet bridges, 70, 71
power-on self-test (POST), 259–260

Power over Ethernet (PoE), 70, 70
power supplies, 189
    connectors, 191–194, 191–193
    input voltages, 189–190
    laser printers, 213
    motherboard adapters, 190, 190
    output voltages, 190
    wattage ratings, 191, 191
Power Users group, 506
PPAs (personal package archives), 443, 444
Preboot Execution Environment (PXE), booting from, 339
preferred roaming list (PRL), 47–48
PRI (product release information), 47–48
primary corona in laser printers, 211, 214
primary partitions, 345
principle of least privilege, 485
print heads
    impact printers, 225–226
    inkjet printers, 221
Print Management tool, 374
print servers, 87
print$ drive, 429
Printer Control Language (PCL), 293
printers
    3D, 227, 227
    configuring, 203
    impact, 224–226
    inkjet, 220–223, 220
    integrated print servers, 204–205
    laser. See laser printers
    overview, 208–210
    sharing, 203–208, 205–206
    sharing vs. mapping, 429–430, 430
    thermal, 223–224
    troubleshooting, 289–296
    virtual, 226
priorities
    print, 295
    processes, 385–386
privacy
    customer materials, 618–619
    shared devices, 207–208
privacy screens, 474
Privacy tab in Internet Options applet, 403–404, 404
private clouds, 238
private IP addresses, 92, 94
PRL (preferred roaming list), 47–48
Processes tab in Task Manager, 384–386, 385
product release information (PRI), 47–48
professional titles, 614–615
profiles
    rebuilding, 556
    security requirements, 526
    slow loads, 551
Programmed Input/Output (PIO) setting, 156
Programs and Features, 416, 417
Programs tab in Internet Options applet, 404–405, 405
prohibited activities
    incident response, 608–610
    licensing violations, 610–611
    overview, 608
    policies and best practices, 612
    regulated data, 611–612

projectors
    description, 187
    troubleshooting, 274–276, 276
propagation of permissions, 511
proper language in communication, 613–614
proprietary vendor-specific ports, 33
protected health information (PHI), 612
protective covers for mobile devices, 38
protocols
    networking, 62–65
    wireless, 486–487
proxy firewalls, 480–481, 481
proxy servers, 88
proxy settings in networking, 432, 432
ps command, 457–458
.ps1 files, 619
public clouds, 238
public devices, 205–208, 205–206
public network settings, 435, 436
punchdown tools, 104
punctuality, 615
purpose in change management, 588
pwd command, 455–456
PWOD (Pinwheel of Death), 264–267, 265–266, 271, 549
PXE (Preboot Execution Environment), booting from, 339
.pyc files, 620

Q

q command, 458
QR scanners, 184
Quality of Service (QoS)
    NICs, 440
    SOHO networks, 79–81
quality settings for printers, 203, 219
queries in DNS servers, 87
question mark (?) command, 371
questions in problem solving, 255
quick formatting drives, 348

R

radio firmware, configuring, 48–49
radio frequency identification (RFID)
    badge readers, 471
    NFC, 34
    wireless protocols, 84–85
radio power levels in SOHO networks, 532
RADIUS (Remote Authentication Dial-In User Service), 488–489
RADSL (rate-adaptive DSL), 76
RAID disks
    NAS devices, 199
    overview, 156–158, 157–158
    troubleshooting, 270–271
rainbow tables, 504
RAM
    application requirements, 425
    error correcting, 145
    operating systems, 322
    overview, 141–142, 141–142
    printers, 294

replacing, 10–11
slots, 145–147, *146*
system lockups, 259
types, 142–145, *144*
workstations, 195–196
Rambus dynamic RAM (RDRAM), 142, 145
Rambus inline memory modules (RIMMs), 142, 145
ransomware, 489–490
rapid elasticity in cloud computing, 239
rate-adaptive DSL (RADSL), 76
RDP (Remote Desktop Protocol)
connections, 433–434, *433–434*
description, 64
settings, 622–623, *623–624*
RDRAM (Rambus dynamic RAM), 142, 145
Read permission, 509
Read & Execute permission, 508–509
read/write failures in hard drives, 269
realms, 428
Realtime process priority, 386
reboots
continuous, 261
in troubleshooting, 552
rebuilding profiles, 556
recovery
account options, 595
image, 447
operating systems, 553, *554*
scheduled backups, 590–593
surge protectors, 594–595, *594–595*
UPSs, 593–594
Recovery Console, 496–497
recovery partitions, 344, 350
recycling drives, 529–530
redirection
browsers, 559
folders, 476
Redundant Array of Independent (or Inexpensive) Disks
NAS devices, 199
overview, 156–158, *157–158*
troubleshooting, 270–271
reference computers in operating systems images, 343
refresh rate for display, 408, *408*
refreshing operating systems, 344, 553
ReFS (Resilient File System), 348
REGEDIT utility, 398
region settings, 349
regulated data, 611–612
regulations
environmental impacts, 607
policy documentation, 584
safety procedures, 603
reimaging operating systems, 552
reloading operating systems, 552
remote access technologies
Remote Desktop, 622–623, *623–624*
security considerations, 626
SSH, 625
Telnet, 623–624, *624–625*
third-party tools, 625–626
Remote Assistance, 434–435, *435*
Remote Authentication Dial-In User Service (RADIUS), 488–489
remote backup applications, 522–523

Remote Desktop Protocol (RDP)
connections, 433–434, *433–434*
description, 64
settings, 622–623, *623–624*
Remote Disk icon, 453
remote installations of operating systems, 342–343
remote printing, 205
remote problems
limited connectivity, 547
networks, 298
Remote tab in System utility, 413, *413*
remote virtual desktops, 241
remote wipes, 522
removable laptop screens, 26
renamed system files, 560
repair OS installations, 342
repairing operating systems, 553
repeaters, 68, *68*
reporting incidents, 608
reservations in DHCP, 94
reset button, 167
resetting operating systems, 344, 553
Resilient File System (ReFS), 348
Resolution Enhancement Technology (RET), 219
resolution settings, display, 406
resources
cloud computing, 239
malware utilization of, 573
networks, 298–299
virtual machine requirements, 243
restarting services failures, 552
restore option for operating systems, 344
Restore Previous Folder Windows At Logon option, 411
restores
disaster recovery, 497–499
MacOS and Linux, 446
operating systems, 553
RET (Resolution Enhancement Technology), 219
retroviruses, 494
RF signals, troubleshooting, 301–302
RFID (radio frequency identification)
badge readers, 471
NFC, 34
wireless protocols, 84–85
RG-6 connectors, 139
RG-59 connectors, 139
RGB LEDs, 17
ribbons for impact printers, 225
RIMMs (Rambus inline memory modules), 142, 145
riser cards, 164, *165*
risk analysis in change management, 589
RJ-11 connectors, 137, *137*
RJ-45 connectors, 137, *137*
rm command, 456
robocopy command, 368–369
rogue antiviruses, 560
rollers
inkjet printers, 221
laser printers, 212, *212*, 215
troubleshooting, 292

rolling back
drivers, 552
updates, 552
rootkits, 490
rotating screens in laptops, 26
routers
description, 66
SOHO networks, 72
troubleshooting, 298, 301
RS-232 connectors, 138, *138*
rsync tool, 447
rules
firewalls, 436
port forwarding, 78
Run as Administrator, 512–513
runas command, 371–372

S

S.M.A.R.T. (Self-Monitoring, Analysis, and Reporting Technology) errors, 271–272
S/MIME configuration, 44–45
SaaS (software as a service), 238
safe boots, 555–556
safety goggles, 602
safety procedures, 596
component handling and storage, 597–599, *598–599*
equipment grounding, 596–597
government regulations, 603
personal, 601–603
toxic waste handling, 599–601, *600*
sags, 593
salting passwords, 504
SATA (Serial AT Attachment) drives
overview, 131–133, *131–132*
power connectors, 191, *191*
satellite connections, 100
scanners, 184
scanning assembly in laser printers, 211, *212*
scans, malware, 563
scheduled backups, 590–593
scheduling malware scans, 563
scope
change management, 588
IP addressing, 93
screen. *See also* displays
brightness, 20–21
locking, 517, 521–522
orientation, 21, *22*
privacy, 474
replacing, 12–13
rotating and removable, 26
sharing, 448–449, 625
screensavers, 515, 586
scripts
Active Directory, 475
basics, 619–621
SCSI (Small Computer System Interface)
connectors, 140
overview, 134, *134*
SD (Secure Digital) cards, 153, *153*
SDSL (symmetric DSL), 76
SECC (single-edge contact cartridge) sockets, 177–178, *177*

secondary caches, 171
sectors, hard drive, 150, *150*
Secure Boot standard, **169**
Secure Digital (SD) cards, 153, *153*
Secure Shell (SSH)
    description, 63
    overview, 625
Secure Sockets Layer (SSL) email settings,
    44
security
    ACLs, **484**
    Active Directory, 475–476
    antivirus software, 478
    applications, 426
    authentication. *See* authentication
    badge readers, 471
    BIOS, 168–169
    certificates, 477–478
    data destruction and disposal, 527–529
    directory permissions, 482–483
    DLP, **484**
    email filtering, 484
    entry control roster, 474
    firewalls, 478–481, *479, 481*
    hardware tokens, 473
    key fobs, 474
    locks, 472–473
    MAC address filtering, **477**
    malware
        preventing, 496–499
        types, 489–496, *492–495*
    mantraps, 470–471, *471*
    MDM policies, 476
    mobile devices, 520–526, *525*
    overview, 470
    port, 476–477
    principle of least privilege, **485**
    privacy screens, 474
    remote access technologies, 626
    review questions, 536–539
    security guards, 472
    smart cards, 471–472, 484
    software sources, **485**
    software tokens, 476
    SOHO networks, 530–535, *535*
    threats, **500**
        brute-force, **503**
        DDoS, **502**
        dictionary, **503**
        DoS, **503**
        MITM, **503**
        non-compliant systems, **504**
        rainbow tables, **504**
        social engineering, 500–502
        spoofing, **504**
        zero-day, **503**
    troubleshooting
        mobile devices, 571–573
        overview, 557–561, *558*
    virtual machines, 243
    VPNs, **484**
    Windows settings, 505–514, *510–511,
        513*
    wireless, 486–489
    workstations, 514–520, *518*
security cameras, IoT-enabled, 75–76

security guards, **472**
Security log in Event Viewer, 375
Security tab in Internet Options applet,
    401–402, *402*
Select The Type Item In The View option,
    411
self-grounding, **599**
Self-Monitoring, Analysis, and Reporting
    Technology (S.M.A.R.T.) errors,
    271–272
separate pads in laser printers, 212
Serial AT Attachment (SATA) drives
    overview, 131–133, *131–132*
    power connectors, 191, *191*
serial cables, 130, *131*
serial numbers in inventory management,
    587
serial ports, 204
Server Message Block (SMB), **64**
servers
    description, 101
    DHCP, 87, 299–300
    end-point management, 90
    integrated print, 204–205
    locks, 473
    RADIUS, 489
    roles, 86–88
Service Location Protocol (SLP), **64**
service set identifiers (SSIDs)
    changing, **531**
    disabling broadcasts of, 81, 531
    not found, 302–304, *302–304*
    SOHO networks, 72
services
    disabling, 555
    failures to start, 549–550, *550*
    restarting, 552
SERVICES.MSC utility, 398
Services tab
    MSConfig tool, 379, *380*
    Task Manager, 386, *386*
Set Up A Dial-Up Connection option, 432
Set Up A Wireless Ad Hoc (Computer-To-
    Computer) Network option, 431
Set Up A Wireless Router Or Access Point
    option, 431
Setup log in Event Viewer, 375
setupact.log file, *547*
setuperr.log file, *547*
sfc command, 361–362
.sh files, 620
shared devices, 205–208, *205–206*
shared files and folders, 510–512, *510–511*
shared resources in cloud computing,
    238–239
shares
    administrative, 511
    networking configuration, 429
    permissions, 506–509
    troubleshooting, 298
sharing
    files, 199, 626
    printers, 202–208, *205–206*, 429–430,
        430
    screen, 448–449, 625
sheet fed printers, 209

shell in Linux, 448
shielded twisted pair (STP) cable, **121**
shims, 338
short battery life, **286**
shoulder surfing, **502**
Show Drive Letters option, 411
Show Encrypted Or Compressed NTFS
    Files In Color option, 411
Show Hidden Files, Folders, And Drives
    option, 409
Show Pop-Up Description For Folder And
    Desktop Items option, 411
Show Preview Handlers In Preview Pane
    option, 411
shredders, 527
shrinking partitions, 394–395, *394–395*
shutdown command
    Linux, 455
    Windows, 361
shutdowns, unexpected, **259**
side-by-side apps in Windows, 329
signature pads, 186
signatures, virus, **494**
SIMMs (single inline memory modules)
    circuit boards, 145
    description, 141–142, *142*
Simple Mail Transfer Protocol (SMTP), **63**
Simple Network Management Protocol
    (SNMP), **65**
simulated battery pulls, 284
single channel RAM, **144**
single-core CPUs, 172
single-edge contact cartridge (SECC)
    sockets, 177–178, *177*
single-factor authentication, **488**
single inline memory modules (SIMMs)
    circuit boards, 145
    description, 141–142, *142*
single sign-on (SSO), 53, **512**
six-pin power-supply connectors, **192**
64-bit operating systems, 321–322
slang, 613–614
slave setting in IDE drives, 155, *156*
Sleep power option, 415
slots for RAM, 145–147, *146*
slow bootup, 550
slow performance
    hard drives, 269
    malware issues, 559
    mobile devices, 284–285, 567, 572
    transfer speeds, 301
    troubleshooting, 546
slow profile loads, 551
SLP (Service Location Protocol), **64**
Small Computer System Interface (SCSI)
    connectors, 140
    overview, 134, *134*
small office and home office (SOHO)
    networks
    access points, 72
    device sharing, 203–205
    drivers, 202–203
    end-user device configuration, 74–75
    firewall settings, 77–80
    Internet of Things devices, 75–76
    IP addressing, 73

modem configuration, 76–77
NIC configuration, 73–74, *73–74*
overview, 71–72
public devices, 205–208, *205–206*
routers and switches, 72
security, 530–531
    content filtering, 534
    firewalls, 533
    firmware updates, 534
    physical, 535, *535*
    port disabling, 534
    port forwarding, 534
    static IP addresses, 533
    usernames and passwords,
        532–533
    wireless, 531–532
    wireless settings, 80–81
small outline DIMMs (SODIMMs), 142,
    142, 146
smart card readers
    description, 188, *189*
    replacing, 11
smart cards, 471–472, 484
smart watches, 28
smartphones, 27
SMB (Server Message Block), 64
smearing in laser printers, 219
smell, burning, 263
smoke, 263
SMTP (Simple Mail Transfer Protocol), 63
snapshots, 446
SNMP (Simple Network Management
    Protocol), 65
social engineering, 500–502
social media data, synchronizing, 52
social media sites, 615–617
socket types
    CPUs, 174–178, *177*
    motherboards, 165–166
SODIMMs (small outline DIMMs), 142,
    142, 146
software
    antivirus. *See* antivirus software
    application requirements, 53
    compatibility, 322
    installing, 349–350
    licensing, 610–611
    troubleshooting
        malware removal, 562–564
        mobile devices, 564–570
        review questions, 574–575
        Windows. *See* Windows operating
            systems
    trusted and untrusted
        sources, 485
software as a service (SaaS), 238
software firewalls, 499
software tokens, 476
SOHO. *See* small office and home office
    (SOHO) networks
solid-state drives (SSDs)
    booting from, 339
    description, 149
    vs. other drive types, 10
sound. *See* audio
Sound applet, 419, *420*

sound cards
    description, 180, *181*
    gaming PCs, 197
spam, 560
spanned partitions, 345
speakers
    description, 187
    mobile devices, 36, 287
    replacing, 14
    troubleshooting, 569
spear phishing, 501
special function keys, 19–23, *22–24*
speed
    ATA standards, 133
    Bluetooth, 35
    bus, 171
    CPUs, 173–174
    DSL, 77
    eSATA, 140
    fiber-optic cabling, 124
    magnetic hard drives, 151
    mobile devices, 572
    NICs, 181, 440
    PCI cards, 164
    RAM, 144
    transfer, 301
    USB cables, 130
    wireless protocols, 84
spikes, 593
splitting partitions, 394
spoofing, 504
Spot Light tool, 452
spyware, 496
SSDs (solid-state drives)
    booting from, 339
    description, 149
    vs. other drive types, 10
SSH (Secure Shell)
    description, 63
    overview, 625
SSIDs. *See* service set identifiers (SSIDs)
SSL (Secure Sockets Layer) email settings, 44
SSO (single sign-on), 53, 512
Standby power option, 415
Start screen, 332
Startup Repair option, 497
Startup tab in MSConfig tool, 380, *381*
stateful inspection firewalls, 481
static eliminator strips in printing, 291–292
static IP addresses, 92, 533
status lights, 263
stealth viruses, 494–495
sticking keys, 280
storage devices, 147
    cloud, 595
    configuring, 155–159, *156–158*
    flash drives, 152–154, *152–154*
    hybrid drives, 151, *152*
    magnetic hard drives, 149–151, *150*
    network-attached, 199
    optical drives, 147–149
storage spaces, 396–398, *396–397*
STP (shielded twisted pair) cable, 121
streaks in printing, 290–291
strings in scripts, 621
striped partitions, 345

striping with parity, 157–158, *158*
strong passwords
    guidelines, 481–482
    overview, 514–515, 585–586
stuck pixels, 274
su command, 458
subnet masks
    alternative IP addresses, 438
    default, 91–92, 95
    IP addressing, 95–96
    troubleshooting, 298
sudo command, 458
supplicants in RADIUS, 489
surge protectors, 594–595, *594–595*
surges, 593
suspend power option, 415
swipe locks, 521
switches
    description, 66–67
    light, 75
    PoE, 70
    SOHO networks, 72
    troubleshooting, 301
swollen batteries, 287–288
symmetric DSL (SDSL), 76
symptoms
    troubleshooting, 258–268,
        265–267
    video issues, 272–278, *276–277*
    viruses, 491
Sync Center Control, 424, *424*
synchronizing
    cloud computing apps, 240
    laptops, 201
    mobile devices, 50–53
syslog servers, 88
Sysprep utility, 343–344
system boards
    form factors, 160–162,
        160–161
    replacing, 14
System Configuration tool, 374
System File Checker (SFC), 361–362
system files and folders
    overview, 512
    renamed, 560
System Image Recovery option, 497
system lockouts in mobile devices, 570
system lockups, 259
system logs
    Event Viewer, 375
    malware clues in, 561
    problem solving, 256
System Properties dialog box in Remote
    Desktop, 433–434, *433–434*
System Protection tab in System utility,
    413, *414*
system requirements for
    applications, 425
System Restore option, 497
System restore tool, 399
system utilities, 398–400
System utility, 411–412
    performance, 412–413, *412*
    Remote tab, 413, *413*
    System Protection tab, 413, *414*

T

T-8 Torx screwdrivers, 8
T568A and T568B cable, 122, *122*
tablets
    applications, 240
    disposal, 601
    features, 27
    operating systems, 323
TACACS+ (Terminal Access Controller
        Access-Control System Plus),
        488–489
tailgating, 502
tap pay devices, 188
tar utility, 445, 447
targets in SCSI, 134
Task Manager, 382–383
    App History tab, 384, *384*
    Applications tab, 383, *383*
    Details tab, 389, *390*
    Networking tab, 388, *388*
    Performance tab, 387, *387*
    Processes tab, 384–386, *385*
    Services tab, 386, *386*
    Users tab, 388, *389*
Task Scheduler tool, 374
taskbar, 330, *331*
taskkill command, 363–364
tasks, killing, 552
TCP (Transport Control Protocol)
    ports, 62–65
    printers, 206
    vs. UDP, 65
Telnet protocol, 63, 623–624, *624–625*
temperature control, 604
Temporal Key Integrity Protocol (TKIP)
    description, 487
    SOHO networks, 81
Terminal Access Controller Access-Control
        System Plus (TACACS+), 488–489
Terminal in Linux, 448, *448*
test pages, printing, 295
testing
    backups, 593
    problem solving theories, 256–257
tethering
    configuring, 40
    connections, 100
    mobile devices, 33
texting, 615–616
TFTs (thin-film transistors), 16
theories in troubleshooting, 256
thermal paste, 179
thermal printers, 223–224
thermostats, IoT-enabled, 75
thick clients
    description, 198
    desktop, 200
thin clients
    description, 198–199
    desktop, 200
thin-film transistors (TFTs), 16
third generation (3G) cellular technology,
        85

third-parties
    drivers, 348–349
    remote access technology tools,
        625–626
32-bit operating systems, 321–322
3D printers, 227, *227*
three-pin Molex connectors, 140, *141*
thumb drives, 152–153, *152*
Thunderbolt cables, 128, *128*
tiles, 329
time
    resets, 261
    settings, 349
Time Machine, 445–447, *446*
timeouts, 517
TKIP (Temporal Key Integrity Protocol)
    description, 487
    SOHO networks, 81
TN (twisted nematic) displays, 16
token ring connections, 181
tokens
    hardware, 473
    software, 476
tone generators and probes, 103–104
toner, 210–211, 220
toner cartridges, recycling, 600
Tools tab for MSConfig tool, 382
topology diagrams, 582–583, *583–584*
Touch flow interface, 282
touchpads
    description, 185–186, *186*
    disabling, 21
    replacing, 13–14
touchscreens
    configuring, 201
    digitizers, 18–19
    inaccurate, 569–570
    non-responsive, 566
    troubleshooting, 282
toxic waste handling, 599–601, *600*
TPM chips, 169
tracert command, 356–357, *357*
tracks, hard drive, 150, *150*
tractor feeds in impact printers, 225
transfer belts in laser printers, 212, *212*
transfer corona in laser printers, 213, *213*
transfer speeds, troubleshooting, 301
transferring step in laser printers, 215–216,
        216
transparent traffic forwarding, 98
Transport Control Protocol (TCP)
    ports, 62–65
    printers, 206
    vs. UDP, 65
triggering in port forwarding, 78
triple channel RAM, 145
tripping surge protectors, 594
Trojan horses, 490
troubleshooting
    common symptoms, 258–268, *265–267*
    hard drives, 268–272
    mobile devices, 278–289, *281, 283,*
        571–573
    networks, 297–304, *302–304*
    printers, 289–296

problem solving, 254–255
    action plans, 257
    documentation, 257
    problem identification, 255–256
    theories, 256
    verification, 257
review questions, 305–307
security
    mobile devices, 571–573
    Windows, 557–561, *558*
software. *See* software
video, 272–278, *276–277*
Troubleshooting applet, 420–421, *421*
trusted sources
    mobile devices, 524–525, *525*
    software, 485
TSP Dot mode, 283
TSP Grid mode, 283
20-pin power-supply connectors, 193, *193*
24-pin power-supply connectors, 193, *193*
twisted nematic (TN) displays, 16
2.5 inch hard drives, 10
Type I hypervisors, 244–245
Type II hypervisors, 245, *245*

U

UAC (User Account Control), 382
UDP (User Datagram Protocol)
    ports, 62–65
    stateful inspection firewalls, 481
    vs. TCP, 65
UEFI (Unified Extensible Firmware
        Interface)
    passwords, 515
    settings, 167–171, *170–171*
Ultra Direct Memory Access (UltraDMA),
        133, 156
unattended upgrade installations, 341
unauthorized access, 573
unavailable resources for networks,
        298–299
Unexpected_Kernel_Mode_Trap message,
        264
unexpected shutdowns, 259
unhealthy drive status, 391
Unified Extensible Firmware Interface
        (UEFI)
    passwords, 515
    settings, 167–171, *170–171*
unified threat management (UTM), 89
uninterruptible power supplies (UPSs),
        593–594
Universal Plug and Play (UPnP), 79
Universal Serial Bus (USB)
    adapters, 135, *135*
    booting from, 339
    cables, 129–130, *129–130*
    connectors, 139, 166, *166*
    expansion cards, 181–182
    flash drives, 152, *152*
    locks, 473
    ports, 32, *32*
    printers, 203–204

unmanaged switches, 67
unshielded twisted pair (UTP), 122
untrusted sources
    mobile devices, 524–525, *525*
    software, 485
updates
    antivirus/anti-malware, 445
    applying, 553
    boot order, 554
    drivers, 443–444
    failures, 560
    firmware, 167, 443–444, 534
    installing, 349–350
    limitations, 324
    Linux, 442–443, *442*
    MacOS, 443, *443*
    mobile devices, 47–48, 523
    network settings, 552
    rolling back, 552
    workstations, 520
Upgrade Advisor, 336, 338
upgrade paths for operating systems
    compatibility tools, 338
    overview, 332–335
    Upgrade Advisor, 338
    Windows 7, 335–337
    Windows 8, 337
    Windows 8.1, 337–338
    Windows 10, 338
UPnP (Universal Plug and Play), 79
UPSs (uninterruptible power supplies),
        593–594
USB. *See* Universal Serial Bus (USB)
USB 2.0/3.0, 130
USB-C
    connectors, **129**, *130*, 139
    ports, 32, *32*
USB to Ethernet adapters, **135**, *135*
Use Check Boxes To Select Items option,
        411
User Account Control (UAC), 382
User Account Management tool, 375
User Accounts dialog box, **408**
user and group security settings,
        505–506
User Datagram Protocol (UDP)
    ports, 62–65
    stateful inspection firewalls, 481
    vs. TCP, 65
user permissions for applications, 425
usernames
    changing, 586
    SOHO networks, 532–533
Users tab in Task Manager, 388, *389*
UTM (unified threat management), 89
UTP (unshielded twisted pair), 122

V

vacuums, 607
variables in scripts, 621
.vbs files, 619
VDIs (virtual desktop infrastructures),
        241–242

vendor-specific limitations for operating
        systems, 323–324
ventilation control, 605
verification in problem solving, 257
vertical lines on printed page, 293–294
very high bit-rate DSL (VHDSL), 76
VGA cables, 124, *124*
VGA mode, troubleshooting, 273
VHDSL (very high bit-rate DSL), 76
vi command, 459
video. *See also* displays; screen
    cables, 124–127, *124–126*
    expansion cards, 179–180, *180*
    troubleshooting, 272–278, *276–277*
    workstations, 195
video cards, replacing, 12
video drivers, system lockups for, 259
video editing workstations, 195–196
videos, synchronizing, 52
View tab
    Folder Options dialog box, 410–411
    folder settings, 409–411, *409*
virtual application streaming in cloud
        computing, 240–241, *241*
virtual desktop infrastructures (VDIs),
        241–242
virtual local area networks (VLANs), 97
virtual machines
    emulator requirements, 243
    hypervisors, 244–245, *244–245*
    network requirements, 244
    purpose, 242–243
    resource requirements, 243
    security requirements, 243
virtual memory performance, 412–413, *412*
virtual network interface cards (VNICs),
        241–242
virtual printers, 226
virtual private networks (VPNs)
    configuring, 49
    connections, 431
    IP addressing, 96–97
    security, 484
virtual reality (VR) headsets, 29–30,
        29–30, 184, *185*
virtual technology, 173
virtualization
    application streaming, 240–241, *241*
    client-side, 242–245, *244–245*
    desktop, 241–242
    review questions, 246–247
    workstations, 196
viruses
    antivirus software. *See* antivirus
            software
    infections, 491–492, *492*
    overview, 490–491
    symptoms, 491
    system lockups, 259
    types, 492–495, *493–495*
vishing, 501
VLANs (virtual local area networks), 97
VNICs (virtual network interface cards),
        241–242

voltages
    power supplies, 189–190
    settings, 170, *170*
voltmeters, 600, *600*
volume settings, 20
VPNs. *See* virtual private networks (VPNs)
VR (virtual reality) headsets, 29–30,
        29–30, 184, *185*

W

Wake-on-LAN (WoL) feature, 440
WANs (wide area networks), 101
warm docking level, 24
watches, 28
water-cooling for gaming PCs, 197, *197*
waterproofing mobile devices, 38
wattage ratings for power supplies, 191,
        191
wax transfer in thermal printers, 223
weak signals, 571
wearable technology devices, 27
web servers, 87
webcams
    description, 187
    laptops, 18
weight limitations, 602
WEP (Wired Equivalent Privacy)
    description, 486
    SOHO networks, 80
whaling, 501
white LEDs (WLEDs), 17
white lines on printed page, 294
whitelisting, 79
Wi-Fi Protected Access 2 (WPA2)
    description, 486
    SOHO networks, 80
Wi-Fi Protected Access (WPA)
    description, 486
    SOHO networks, 80
    variants, 487
Wi-Fi protected setup (WPS), 532
wide area networks (WANs), 101
WiFi
    antenna connectors, 17–18
    unintended connections, 572
WiFi analyzers, 104–105
Windows Compatibility Center, 338
Windows Firewall
    configuring, 437
    description, 375
    enabling and disabling, 437
    exceptions, 436
    managing, 414, *414*
    SOHO networks, 75
Windows Memory Diagnostic tool, 374,
        497
Windows operating systems
    application installation, 424–426
    command line tools. *See* command
            line tools
    Control Panel. *See* Control Panel
            utilities

corporate vs. personal needs, 327–328, 328
desktop styles and interfaces, 328–332, 329, 331
networking configuration. *See* networking configuration
overview, 322–325
security settings
authentication, 512
BitLocker, 513
EFS, 513, 513
NTFS vs. share permissions, 506–509
Run as Administrator, 512–513
shared files and folders, 510–512, 510–511
system files and folders, 512
user and groups, 505–506
tools, 372
administrative, 373–378, 376–377
Disk Management, 390–398, 391, 393–397
MSConfig, 378–382, 378–382
system utilities, 398–400
Task Manager, 382–389, 383–390
troubleshooting, 545–546
application crashes, 549
black screens, 549
blue screens, 549
booting, 547–548
connectivity, 547
fragmented drives, 551
missing OS, 548
performance, 546
service failures, 549–550, 550
slow bootup, 550
solutions, 551–557, 551, 554–555
upgrade paths, 332–338
Windows 7, 325
Windows 8, 325–326
Windows 8.1, 326
Windows 10, 326
Windows Server Update Services (WSUS), 520

Windows Setup program, 156
Windows Update tool, 399
wipes
drives, 528, 530
mobile devices, 522
wired connections, 431
Wired Equivalent Privacy (WEP)
description, 486
SOHO networks, 80
wired options for mobile devices, 32–34, 32–33
wired printers, 203
wireless
connections, 431
connectivity issues, 282
data network configuration, 39–40
function keys, 20
intermittent, 280, 565
mobile device options, 34–35
printers, 204
protocols, 82–86, 486–487
security, 486–489
settings, 201–202
SOHO network security, 531–532
SOHO network settings, 80–81
wireless cards
NICs, 181
replacing, 11–12
wireless mesh networks (WMNs), 102
wireless personal area networks (WPANs), 102
wireless wide area networks (WWANs), 431
WLEDs (white LEDs), 17
WMNs (wireless mesh networks), 102
WoL (Wake-on-LAN) feature, 440
work network settings, 435
workgroups
vs. HomeGroup, 427
setup, 349
working copy backups, 497–498, 591
workspace switchers, 451, 451
workstations
audio/video editing, 195–196
description, 101
graphic, 194–195
operating systems, 322–323

security, 514
account management, 516–519, 518
AutoRun function, 519
encryption, 519
passwords, 514–516
updates, 520
virtualization, 196
worms, 495–496
WPA (Wi-Fi Protected Access)
description, 486
SOHO networks, 80
variants, 487
WPA2 (Wi-Fi Protected Access 2)
description, 486
SOHO networks, 80
WPANs (wireless personal area networks), 102
WPS (Wi-Fi protected setup), 532
wrap plugs, 104
wrist straps, 597–598, 598
Write permission, 509
writing step in laser printers, 214, 214
WSUS (Windows Server Update Services), 520
WWANs (wireless wide area networks), 431

X

xcopy command, 367–368
xD-Picture cards, 154, 154
XP Mode in virtual machines, 243
XPS, printing to, 226

Y

Yahoo email, 47

Z

Z-Wave protocol, 85
zero-day vulnerabilities, 503
Zigbee technology, 85
zombies, 495